The Editor

EDWARD PECHTER'S books include *Dryden's Classical Theory of Literature, What Was Shakespeare?* and, most recently, *"Othello" and Interpretive Traditions.* He has taught at universities in the United States, England, and Canada and is Distinguished Professor Emeritus at Concordia University (Montreal) and Adjunct Professor of English at the University of Victoria, British Columbia.

A NORTON CRITICAL EDITION

William Shakespeare
OTHELLO

AUTHORITATIVE TEXT
SOURCES AND CONTEXTS
CRITICISM

Edited by

EDWARD PECHTER
CONCORDIA UNIVERSITY
AND
UNIVERSITY OF VICTORIA

W • W • NORTON & COMPANY • *New York* • *London*

For William S. Pechter, my big brother Billy.

W. W. Norton & Company has been independent since its founding in 1923, when William Warder and Mary D. Herter Norton first published lectures delivered at the People's Institute, the adult education division of New York City's Cooper Union. The Nortons soon expanded their program beyond the Institute, publishing books by celebrated academics from America and abroad. By mid-century, the two major pillars of Norton's publishing program—trade books and college texts—were firmly established. In the 1950s, the Norton family transferred control of the company to its employees, and today—with a staff of four hundred and a comparable number of trade, college, and professional titles published each year—W. W. Norton & Company stands as the largest and oldest publishing house owned wholly by its employees.

The text of this book is composed in Fairfield Medium
with the display set in Bernhard Modern.
Composition by Binghamton Valley Composition, Inc.
Manufacturing by the Maple-Vail Book Group.
Book design by Antonina Krass.
Production manager: Ben Reynolds.

Library of Congress Cataloging-in-Publication Data

Shakespeare, William, 1564–1616.
    Othello : authoritative text, sources and contexts, criticism / William
Shakespeare ; edited by Edward Pechter.
        p. cm.—(A Norton critical edition)
    Includes bibliographical references.

    ISBN 0-393-97615-7

    1. Othello (Fictitious character)—Drama. 2. Shakespeare, William, 1564–
1616. Othello. 3. Othello (Fictitious character) 4. Venice (Italy)—Drama. 5.
Jealousy—Drama. 6. Muslims—Drama. I. Pechter, Edward, 1941– II. Title.

PR2829.A2P43 2003
822.3'3—dc21   2003054117

W. W. Norton & Company, Inc., 500 Fifth Avenue, New York, N.Y. 10110
www.wwnorton.com

W. W. Norton & Company Ltd., Castle House,
75/76 Wells Street, London W1T 3QT

1 2 3 4 5 6 7 8 9 0

Contents

List of Illustrations

All illustrations courtesy of The Folger Shakespeare Library

Preface

Here are four things that happened during October 2001, the month that I began systematically putting together this book: 1) *O* was playing at my local cineplex, in Victoria, British Columbia. The film is set in a southern American high school where Odin (called "O"), a black basketball star, is driven to murder his girlfriend, Desi, by his teammate, Hugo ("white girls are snakes, bro"), himself motivated by jealousy (his father, the team coach, pays more attention to O than to his own son). 2) The Canadian Broadcasting Corporation aired a stylish made-for-television film in which, when John Othello becomes the first black commissioner of the London Metropolitan Police, his best friend and fellow officer, Ben Jago, is so furious at being bypassed for the job that he goads John into murdering his (of course white) girlfriend, Dessie. 3) The local bookstores were featuring the new Salman Rushdie novel. Focused on the India-born Malik "Solly" Solanka, *Fury* opens in New York, to which Solanka has fled from London after finding himself poised with a knife over the sleeping body of his English wife, Eleanor. The first chapter includes a reminiscence of their steamy first night together, during which Eleanor had talked out her honors-thesis interpretation of *Othello*. 4) The student newspaper at the University of Victoria, my home university, carried an opinion piece about the events of 9/11. In the accompanying photograph, the author, a Ugandan-born Indian Muslim in the Education Faculty, holds a clearly visible copy of *Othello*.

We might dismiss these events as accidents of time and place. *O* had been scheduled for release years earlier, but the Columbine shootings worried the distributors into a delay. British television audiences had seen the police drama months before Canadians, while U.S. audiences had to wait until 2002, when it was aired by PBS. Few people would have seen the 9/11 piece who weren't connected with my home university. Then too there is the subjective element: buy a Mazda and you're amazed to see how many Mazdas are on the road. As someone with a long professional career devoted to literary interpretation, I may be overly given to imposing coherent patterns on the blips that happen to coincide on my radar.

But with all allowances for coincidence and subjectivity, *Othello* seems to be in the air. It was certainly in the air during 1994 and 1995, when Americans (indeed, people all over the world) were obsessed with the O. J. Simpson murder trial: many people, academics and otherwise, were intrigued by the resonance they heard between *Othello* and the "crime of the century," as it was then breathlessly called. Moreover, *Othello* has generated powerful interest independently of—and earlier than—the Simpson story. During the past twenty-five years or so, *Othello* has become the Shakespearean tragedy of choice, replacing *King Lear* in the way *Lear* had earlier replaced *Hamlet* as the play that speaks most directly and powerfully to current interests. Robert Scholes, helping to design a new capstone English course for grade twelve, selects *Othello* as the one obligatory Shakespeare play because "the issues of cultural conflict are in the foreground" (136). Writing without direct pedagogical interests and for a different audience, Mitchell Greenberg sees much the same thing: *Othello* has a peculiar power "to haunt us as an uncanny projection, from the past, of our conflicted present" (1).

Conflict, though, is not unique to *Othello*; we need to be more specific. During the period of *Othello*'s ascendancy, literary and cultural analysis has been transformed by feminist, African American, and postcolonial critics, to whose central concerns the play seems directly to appeal. *Othello* focuses on marriage as a domestic relationship, where the most intimately private experience is nonetheless shaped by the pressures of society and political power. The play is preoccupied with questions of gender difference, the expectations of men and women for themselves and about each other, including those that underwrite and undermine marriage. It is preoccupied with racial difference as well. Its protagonist is an alien to white Christian Europe, what we would now call an immigrant, whose visible racial difference seems to be the defining aspect of his identity, the source of his charismatic power to excite interest and to generate horror. As a result, according to Thomas Cartelli, "*Othello* is well on the way to replacing *The Tempest* as a favored field of debate and contention both for scholars and critics of Shakespeare, and for the increasingly numerous workers in the field of postcolonial studies" (124). Or as Mythili Kaul puts it, introducing a collection of new essays by black writers on the play, "all the contributors" see *Othello* as "of utmost relevance today in terms of" a variety of "pressing contemporary issues," including "politics, colonial exploitation, cultural relativism, and, above all, race" (xii). These concentrations on gender and racial difference coincide with appalling intensity in the play's final image: Othello and Desdemona, the "old black ram" and "white ewe" Iago summoned to Brabantio's imagination at the beginning, locked in a perverse embrace on the marriage bed revealed finally as the place of murder.

This book inevitably reflects the intense current interest in *Othello*—in fact, enthusiastically embraces it—by including many critical commentaries that emphasize our concerns with race, sex, and gender. But this edition also includes a generous selection of earlier commentary and is designed to represent the continuities as well as significant ruptures between recent and traditional interpretations of the play. Earlier audiences of *Othello* would not have understood, let alone shared our kinds of interests in the play, and we have generated these interests in most cases without much conscious knowledge of critical or performance traditions. But these traditions matter, perhaps more than we think; they shape our desires and our understanding in ways of which we may be imperfectly aware. Current audiences and readers of *Othello* cannot exercise their interpretive freedom "just as they please," but "under circumstances directly encountered, given and transmitted from the past." Marx, whose remarks about history near the beginning of *The Eighteenth Brumaire of Louis Bonaparte* I have just quoted, concludes from this argument that the "tradition of all the dead generations weighs like a nightmare on the brain of the living" (15). This gloomy claim may be especially relevant to *Othello*, which is in large measure about the dead weight of inherited prejudice. But *Othello* furnishes glimmers of transcendence as well, and this edition provides readers with historical material that is not only grimly determining but also "edifying" in Richard Rorty's sense of the term—that is, useful for building new kinds of ideas.

The book follows the standard format of Norton Critical Editions. After the text of the play comes "Sources and Contexts," which prints the sixteenth-century narrative Shakespeare used for the plot of *Othello* and for many of its details. This section also includes a detailed discussion of various topics—Moors, Turks, blacks, Venetians, marriage and domesticity, fathers and daughters, female sexuality, and so on—through which the original audiences would presumably have engaged the play. Then comes "Criticism," including substantial excerpts from interpretive responses to *Othello* from its origins to the present. The book ends with a group of bibliographies for readers who want to go into greater detail about material included earlier in the book, or to expand their critical interests into related territories.

I am grateful to the Social Sciences and Humanities Research Council of Canada for a grant that facilitated the work for this book. A fellowship from the Folger Shakespeare Library, in Washington, D.C., allowed me to do much of the final research in the rich and friendly environment for which that institution and its staff are well known.

My thanks go to David Pechter for lending me his laptop, to Lesley
Pechter for line editing and proofreading, and to Alan Galey for
research assistance beyond my requests or expectations. Conversations with Farouk Mitha, in the Education Faculty of the University
of Victoria, helped make this book less parochial. My English
Department colleagues—especially Kim Blank, Evelyn Cobley, Arnie
Keller, Terry Sherwood, and David Thatcher—provided encouragement and useful suggestions. Andrew Hadfield kindly sent me
advance proofs for his *Literary Sourcebook*. Michael Neill let me see
draft discussions of *Othello*'s date and text for his forthcoming
Oxford edition of the play. Holly Carver, executive director of Iowa
University Press, gave me free access to material in my *"Othello" and
Interpretive Traditions*, where some of the discussion in this Norton
Critical Edition is developed at greater length. Finally, thanks to
everyone at Norton for their professionalism and helpfulness—especially to Carol Bemis, who was there with me from the beginning,
and to Kurt Wildermuth, whose intelligence and diligence are everywhere present in this book.

Works Cited

Cartelli, Thomas. *Repositioning Shakespeare: National Formations,
    Postcolonial Appropriations*. London and New York: Routledge,
    1999.
Greenberg, Mitchell. "Shakespeare's *Othello* and the 'Problem' of
    Anxiety." In *Canonical States, Canonical Stages: Oedipus, Other-
    ing, and Seventeenth-Century Drama*. Minneapolis and London:
    University of Minnesota Press, 1994, 1–32.
Kaul, Mythili. "Preface." In Kaul, ed. *"Othello": New Essays by Black
    Writers*. Washington D.C.: Howard University Press, 1997, ix–xii.
Marx, Karl. *The Eighteenth Brumaire of Louis Bonaparte*. New York:
    International Publishers, 1963.
Scholes, Robert. "Pacesetter English." In *The Rise and Fall of
    English: Reconstructing English as a Discipline*. New Haven: Yale
    University Press, 1998, 128–42.

A Note on the Text

This edition is based on the text printed in the First Folio (1623). Additions and emendations adopted from the First Quarto (1622) are not signaled in the text, but are specified in the Textual Notes printed after the Textual Commentary at the end of the play. All other interpolated material is placed within square brackets. The footnotes specify many of the earlier editors to whose learning and intelligence I am deeply indebted, keyed to the bibliography printed below—but perforce not all. Working on Shakespeare entails obligations beyond practical acknowledgment and (standing on the shoulders of sometimes anonymous giants) beyond even conscious knowledge.

Readers who want a sense of the complications involved in editing *Othello* and Shakespeare in general will want to look at the Textual Commentary (p. 119). A preliminary word is in order here, though, about two matters—stage directions and scene locations. In many cases where an action seems to be called for, the early texts include either no stage directions or imprecise generalities located indifferently somewhere in the vicinity of what appears to be the appropriate line. Beginning with Nicholas Rowe in 1709, editors have expanded upon these perfunctory practices, systematically repositioning, elaborating, and inventing stage directions to serve the needs of readers for whom the ability to think in terms of theatrical performance could not necessarily be taken for granted. I have continued in this tradition of editorial intervention, reproducing (and sometimes relocating) the stage directions added by earlier editors and inventing some of my own, as well as calling attention occasionally in the explanatory notes to stage actions that might seem to be suggested by the text. "Suggested" is the key word: "here are some things that might be done on stage at this point, among many other things—including nothing." Reading theatrically means acknowledging a long and continuing stage history in which Shakespearean texts have generously accommodated performers who have felt free to shape them to the exigencies of their particular situations.

Scene locators also begin with Rowe, again to accommodate readers; but the situation here is much more complicated because—as Peter Holland argues in a piece to which I am much indebted—Rowe was trying to accommodate his playgoing contemporaries as well. Theatrical performance had come to differ significantly from the kind Globe (or Blackfriars) audiences experienced when *Othello* was new, and scene location was one of the most significant of the changes. Where the eighteenth-century stage had developed a fairly sophisticated set of scenic properties and conventions in order to localize the action, distinguishing between inside and outside and between various external environments, Shakespeare's stage had effectively no scenery at all. The action took place in an unspecified place that could be inferred from the circumstances and that would (when required) be specified in the dialogue. The resulting flexibility allowed for "split scenes," where the action could shift back and forth between different places. In 3.4, for example, the "place is nowhere specified, only implied by character and action. Thus although much of the dialogue seems to assume an 'interior' and private setting, there is no discrepancy created when Cassio is told to 'walk here about' . . . and Bianca enters 'going to [Cassio's] lodging' " (Ross). In 4.2, similarly, the "scene starts indoors (cf. 28), and in some productions in Desdemona's bedroom. Later Roderigo wanders in [172], and it seems to be outdoors: one of the advantages of unlocalized staging" (Honigmann). "The truth is," as Edmond Malone puts it, after describing in detail the "great difficulties in ascertaining the place" of 4.2, that "our poet and his audience, in this instance as in many others, were content, from want of scenery, to consider the very same spot, at one and at the same time, as the outside and inside of a house."

A devoted and accomplished historian, Malone understood that scene locators were misleading. Nonetheless, following the practice of all his predecessors going back to Rowe, Malone included them in his 1790 edition (4.2 is said to take place in "A Room in the Castle"), as have most subsequent editors to this day (though often hedged about with square brackets or apologetic explanations, or relegated to the notes). This may be editorial inertia, against which many current editors, one following the other, like to inveigh; but inertia can be good as well as bad, and the reassuring familiarity provided by scene locators, especially in a text designed (as is this one) for a nonspecialist audience, might be argued to outweigh the disadvantages.

But this is by no means clear. Is it strictly true, as Lawrence Ross claims, that "no discrepancy" arises from Desdemona's "walk here about"? To be sure, since the earlier impression was not fixed or definite (we see no scenery, read no "A Room in the Castle"), the words are not experienced as a *contradiction*. Nonetheless, the exterior location does come on us as a new and surprising—discrepant—discovery. Shakespeare could have easily enough written his way out of this situation, but didn't, I believe, because he wants us to be emphatically aware of the exterior location: that Bianca emerges on her own into public space defies what we now call gender norms—a topic of paramount importance in the play. The play thus does more than take advantage of a convenient flexibility—it exploits the flexibility to achieve a significant dramatic effect.

There are many other instances in which Shakespeare has taken advantage of the unlocalized stage (perhaps better called the variously localized stage); here are three early on in the action. *One:* at the beginning of the play, we discover the location, a Venetian street at night, as part of a brutally sudden process that also locates the play's subject as bestial intercourse. The alarming effect is thrust upon us in the same way as it is on Brabantio, "with like timorous accent and dire yell / As when, *by night and negligence,* the fire / Is spied in populous cities" (1.1.72–74; emphasis mine). The emphasized locution bothered William Warburton in 1747 (see note to line 73), as well it might (eighteenth-century discomfort is frequently worth respecting): the phrase conjoins a sense of time and place with a sense of unpreparedness, as though merely to find oneself in a Venetian night scene entails anxiety and some inexplicable culpability—arguably the effects reinforced by the withheld and precipitously revealed location. *Two:* an audience at the beginning of act 2, not yet knowing it is in act 2, since the continuity of the action would create no decisive break between the simultaneously exiting Iago and the entering figures, would, before it can determine that it is located at (say) "A Seaport in Cyprus," be likely to hear the violent sound effects of the storm as produced by Iago's final words in act 1: "I have't! It is engendered! Hell and night / Must bring this monstrous birth to the world's light" (1.3.394–95). *Three:* Having failed (apparently) to tempt Cassio into salacious thoughts about Desdemona, Iago tries a new tactic: "Come, lieutenant, I have a stoup of wine, and here without are a brace of Cyprus gallants that would fain have a measure to the health of black Othello" (2.3.24–27). "Here without" must come as a bit of a surprise. There has been no reason to assume a change from the Herald's speech just earlier in 2.2, with its strong effect of exterior location. (In fact, 2.3 is, in all editions of the play prior to Theobald's in 1733, printed as a continuation of 2.2 rather than as a new scene.) To be sure, the fact goes by too quickly to have much significant consequence, but the play isn't done. "Where are they?" asks Cassio about the same gallants only a moment later (39). He can hardly have forgotten; apparently he is trying (desperately) to buy time before agreeing—against his better judgment, but he seems to have no choice—to what we know to be Iago's plot to destroy him. And now, in Iago's response, the play reminds us with renewed emphasis of the interior location: "Here at the door; I pray you call them in" (40). By abruptly revealing and then confirming an interior location, the play produces a notable discrepancy and (my main point) a functional one. Making us suddenly aware of Cassio's physical enclosure, it reinforces the sense that he is willy-nilly enmeshed inside the plot Iago is spinning to destroy him.

In all these cases, we are dealing with effects that (like gender norms) seem central to the play: entrapment, guilt, an irresistibly powerful Iago. In all these cases, scene locators would destroy or (minimally) diminish these effects. The point need not be exaggerated. The meanings reinforced by these effects are amply available without them. Nonetheless, I came in the course of producing this edition reluctantly to the conclusion that scene locators, no matter how qualified or inconspicuous, do more harm than good, so I have not written them into the text that follows.

The following works are cited in the footnotes and textual notes below:

Bible. Quotations are from *The Geneva Bible*. 1560. Rpt. Madison: University of Wisconsin Press, 1969.

Capell, Edward. *Mr. William Shakespeare: His Comedies, Histories, and Tragedies*. 10 vols. London, 1767–86.

———. *Notes and Various Readings to Shakespeare*. 3 vols. London, 1780. Rpt. New York: AMS Press, 1973.

Furness, Horace Howard. *A New Variorum Edition of Othello*. 7th ed. Philadelphia: Lippincott, 1886.

Hankey, Julie. *Othello*. Plays in Performance Series. Bristol: Bristol Classical Press, 1987.

Holland, Peter. Introduction. In Rowe, 1.vii–xxx.

Honigmann, E. A. J., ed. *Othello*. Arden 3 edition. Walton-on-Thames: Thomas Nelson, 1997.

Johnson, Samuel. *The Plays of William Shakespeare*. 8 vols. London, 1765. Notes rpt. in *The Works of Samuel Johnson*. Vols. 7 and 8, *Johnson on Shakespeare*. Ed. Arthur Sherbo. New Haven: Yale University Press, 1968.

Kernan, Alvin, ed. *Othello*. Signet Shakespeare. 2nd ed. New York: Penguin, 1998.

Kittredge, George Lyman, ed. *Othello*. 1941. 2nd ed. Rev. Irving Ribner. Waltham: Ginn, 1966.

Malone, Edmond. *The Plays and Poems of William Shakespeare*. 10 vols. London, 1790. Rpt. New York: AMS Press, 1966.

McDonald, Russ, ed. *Othello*. Pelican Shakespeare. New York: Penguin, 2001.

Mowat, Barbara A., and Paul Werstine, ed. *Othello*. The New Folger Library Shakespeare. New York: Washington Square Press, 1993.

OED. *Oxford English Dictionary*. 20 vols. 2nd ed. Prep. J. A. Simpson and E. S. C. Weiner. Oxford: Clarendon, 1989.

Pope, Alexander. *The Works of William Shakespear*. 6 vols. London, 1723–25.

Ridley, M. R., ed. *Othello*. New Arden edition. London: Methuen, 1962.

Ross, Lawrence J., ed. *Othello*. Indianapolis and New York: Bobbs-Merrill, 1974.

Rowe, Nicholas. *The Works of Mr. William Shakespear*. 6 vols. London, 1709. Rpt. London: Pickering & Chatto, 1999.

Sanders, Norman, ed. *Othello*. Cambridge: Cambridge University Press, 1984.

Schmidt, Alexander. *Shakespeare Lexicon and Quotation Dictionary*. 2 vols. 3rd ed. Rev. Gregor Sarrazin, 1902. Rpt. New York: Dover, 1971.

Shakespeare, William. All non-*Othello* references are to the Oxford edition as reprinted in *The Norton Shakespeare*. Ed. Stephen Greenblatt, et al. New York: Norton, 1997.

Steevens, George. *The Plays of William Shakespeare, With the Corrections and Illustrations of Various Commentators, To Which Are Added Notes by Samuel Johnson and George Steevens*. London, 1813.

Theobald, Lewis. *The Works of Shakespeare*. 7 vols. London, 1733. Rpt. New York: AMS Press, 1968.

Tynan, Kenneth, ed. *"Othello": The National Theatre Production*. New York: Stein and Day, 1967.

Warburton, William. *The Works of Shakespear*. 8 vols. London, 1747.

The Text of
THE TRAGEDY OF OTHELLO, THE MOOR OF VENICE

THE TRAGEDIE OF
Othello, the Moore of Venice.

Actus Primus. Scœna Prima.

Enter Rodorigo, and Iago.

Rodorigo.

Euer tell me, I take it much vnkindly
That thou (*Iago*) who haft had my purfe,
As if ý ftrings were thine,fhould'ft know of this.
    Ia. But you'l not heare me: If euer I did dream
Of fuch a matter, abhorre me.
    Rodo. Thou told'ft me,
Thou did'ft hold him in thy hate.
    Iago. Defpife me
If I do not. Three Great-ones of the Cittie,
(In perfonall fuite to make me his Lieutenant)
Off-capt to him: and by the faith of man
I know my price, I am worth no worffe a place.
But he (as louing his owne pride,and purpofes)
Euades them,with a bumbaft Circumftance,
Horribly ftufft with Epithites of warre,
Non-fuites my Mediators. For certes,faies he,
I haue already chofe my Officer. And what was he?
For-footh,a great Arithmatician,
One *Michaell Caffio,* a *Florentine,*
(A Fellow almoft damn'd in a faire Wife)
That neuer fet a Squadron in the Field,
Nor the deuifion of a Battaile knowes
More then a Spinfter. Vnleffe the Bookifh Theoricke:
Wherein the Tongued Confuls can propofe
As Mafterly as he. Meere pratle (without practife)
Is all his Souldierfhip. But he(Sir) had th'election;
And I (of whom his eies had feene the proofe
At Rhodes, at Ciprus,and on others grounds
Chriften'd,and Heathen)muft be be-leed,and calm'd
By Debitor,and Creditor. This Counter-cafter,
He (in good time) muft his Lieutenant be,
And I (bleffe the marke) his Moorefhips Auntient.
    Rod. By heauen,I rather would haue bin his hangman.
    Iago. Why,there's no remedie.
'Tis the curffe of Seruice;
Preferment goes by Letter,and affection,
And not by old gradation ,where each fecond
Stood Heire to'th'firft. Nov Sir, be iudge your felfe,
Whether I in any iuft terme am Affin'd
To loue the *Moore?*
    Rod. I would not follow him then.
    Iago. O Sir content you.
I follow him,to ferue my turne vpon him.
We cannot all be Mafters,nor all Mafters

Cannot be truely follow'd. You fhall marke
Many a durious and knee-crooking knaue;
That (doting on his owne obfequious bondage)
Weares out his time,much like his Mafters Affe,
For naught but Prouender, & when he's old Cafheer'd.
Whip me fuch honeft knaues. Others there are
Who trym'd in Formes,and vifages of Dutie,
Keepe yet their hearts attending on themfelues,
And throwing but fhowes of Seruice on their Lords
Doe well thriue by them.
And when they haue lin'd their Coates
Doe themfelues Homage.
Thefe Fellowes haue fome foule,
And fuch a one do I profeffe my felfe. For (Sir)
It is as fure as you are *Rodorigo,*
Were I the Moore,I would not be *Iago* :
In following him,I follow but my felfe.
Heauen is my Iudge,not I for loue and dutie,
But feeming fo, for my peculiar end:
For when my outward Action doth demonftrate
The natiue act, and figure of my heart
In Complement externe, 'tis not long after
But I will weare my heart vpon my fleeue
For Dawes to pecke at ; I am not what I am.
    Rod. What a full Fortune do's the Thicks-lips owe
If he can carry't thus?
    Iago. Call vp her Father :
Rowfe him,make after him,poyfon his delight,
Proclaime him in the Streets. Incenfe her kinfmen,
And though he in a fertile Clymate dwell,
Plague him with Flies:though that his Ioy be Ioy,
Yet throw fuch chances of vexation on't,
As it may loofe fome colour.
    Rodo. Heere is her Fathers houfe,Ile call aloud.
    Iago. Doe,with like timerous accent,and dire yell,
As when (by Night and Negligence) the Fire
Is fpied in populus Cities.
    Rodo. What hoa : *Brabantio,Siginor Brabantio,*hoa.
    Iago. Awake:what hoa, *Brabantio* : Theeues,Theeues.
Looke to your houfe,your daughter,and your Bags,
Theeues,Theeues.
    Bra. Aboue. What is the reafon of this terrible
Summons? What is the matter there?
    Rodo. Signior is all your Familie within?
    Iago. Are your Doores lock'd?
    Bra. Why? Wherefore ask you this?
    Iago. Sir,y'are rob'd,for fhame put on your Gowne,
                                                    Your

The Names of the Actors

Othello, the Moor [and General of the Venetian forces].
Brabantio, father to Desdemona [and a Venetian Senator].
Cassio, an honorable lieutenant [to Othello].
Iago, a villain [and Othello's standard bearer or ensign].
Roderigo, a gulled gentleman.   5
Duke of Venice.
Senators.
Montano, Governor of Cyprus.
Gentlemen of Cyprus.
Lodovico and Gratiano, two Noble Venetians [and kinsmen to
    Brabantio].   10
Sailors.
Clown.
Desdemona, wife to Othello.
Emilia, wife to Iago.
Bianca, a courtesan.   15

ACT I SCENE I

Enter RODERIGO *and* IAGO.

RODERIGO   Tush, never tell me! I take it much unkindly
    That thou, Iago, who hast had my purse

0. **The Names . . . Actors:** i.e., *Dramatis Personae* or, as we would say, "Characters"; reproduced in order from the list printed at the end of the folio text. Six other plays in the First Folio include similar lists under the same title, which continues to be used in later folios; in all cases, it specifies the names of the roles rather than the actors impersonating them.
   4. **villain:** The play repeatedly identifies Iago as a villain; at the beginning and end of the action, it emphatically associates him with "villainy," a "richer word than now, ranging from boorishness to discourtesy to extreme wickedness" (Honigmann). Commentators frequently connect him with "the Vice," a stock type in the old morality plays still sometimes performed in Shakespeare's day, whose dramatic function, to seduce the protagonist into evil, was performed with much boisterous comedy
   5. **gulled:** duped.
   12. **Clown:** Again, the play text provides authority for the designation (see the Speech Prefixes in 3.1 and 3.4). "*Clown* could = peasant" or "ignorant or rude fellow," but as "comic servant" (Honigmann), it looks like an updated version of the conventional "witty servant" in Roman comedy (the plays written in the third and second centuries B.C.E. by Plautus and Terence, whose plot complications and character types were much imitated on the Renaissance stage).
   15. **courtesan:** Something like "elegant lady of pleasure," this term also identifies a stock type of Roman comedy. Shakespeare uses the designation in other plays, but whoever compiled this list (probably not Shakespeare), though granted access by the text of *Othello* to an extraordinary abundance of descriptive terminology for Bianca, would not have been able to find this word.
   1. **Tush:** expression of irritation.

As if the strings were thine, shouldst know of this.
IAGO   'Sblood, but you'll not hear me! If ever I did dream
    Of such a matter, abhor me.
RODERIGO   Thou toldst me   5
    Thou didst hold him in thy hate.
IAGO   Despise me
    If I do not. Three great ones of the city,
    In personal suit to make me his lieutenant,
    Off-capped to him; and by the faith of man
    I know my price; I am worth no worse a place.   10
    But he, as loving his own pride and purposes,
    Evades them with a bombast circumstance,
    Horribly stuffed with epithets of war,
    Non-suits my mediators. For "Certes," says he,
    "I have already chose my officer." And what was he?   15
    Forsooth, a great arithmetician,
    One Michael Cassio, a Florentine,
    A fellow almost damned in a fair wife,
    That never set a squadron in the field,
    Nor the division of a battle knows   20
    More than a spinster; unless the bookish theorick,
    Wherein the tonguèd consuls can propose
    As masterly as he. Mere prattle without practice
    Is all his soldiership. But he, sir, had th' election;
    And I—of whom his eyes had seen the proof   25
    At Rhodes, at Cyprus, and on other grounds,
    Christened and heathen—must be beleed and calmed
    By debitor and creditor. This countercaster,
    He in good time must his lieutenant be,
    And I—God bless the mark!—his Moorship's ancient.   30

----

3. **of this:** As with "such a matter" and "him" following, the referent is unclear; we have to guess pending clarification within the scene.

4. **'Sblood:** by God's blood.

7. **great ones of the city:** politically influential Venetians.

9. **Off-capped:** removed their hats respectfully.

12–13. **bombast . . . of war:** intimidatingly high-sounding military jargon.

14. **Non-suits:** rejects. **Certes:** surely; the word may have sounded old-fashioned or bombastic to Shakespeare's audience.

16. **arithmetician:** theorist; six syllables: *-cian* and *-tion* normally pronounced "shee-UN."

18. **A fellow . . . wife:** Without explanation, the line plants an association between male desire in marriage and sin.

19–23. **That never . . . as he:** has no more experience in the deployment of troops than a woman has, except for the pedantic abstractions he shares with glib politicians.

27. **beleed:** like a stalled ship; "Cassio had got to the wind of him" (Malone).

28. **countercaster:** someone who tallies accounts with tokens.

30. **God . . . mark:** expresses disgust at an unjust situation. **ancient:** ensign or standard-bearer; a lower rank than lieutenant (= "place-holder" or substitute, who occupies the author-itative position in the commander's absence). **his Moorship:** a pun on the conventionally respectful "his worship" (as in the quarto).

RODERIGO   By heaven, I rather would have been his hangman.
IAGO   Why, there's no remedy. 'Tis the curse of service;
   Preferment goes by letter and affection,
   And not by old gradation, where each second
   Stood heir to th' first. Now, sir, be judge yourself   35
   Whether I in any just term am affined
   To love the Moor.
RODERIGO   I would not follow him then.
IAGO   O, sir, content you.
   I follow him to serve my turn upon him.
   We cannot all be masters, nor all masters   40
   Cannot be truly followed. You shall mark
   Many a duteous and knee-crooking knave
   That, doting on his own obsequious bondage,
   Wears out his time, much like his master's ass,
   For naught but provender; and when he's old—cashiered.   45
   Whip me such honest knaves! Others there are
   Who, trimmed in forms and visages of duty,
   Keep yet their hearts attending on themselves
   And, throwing but shows of service on their lords,
   Do well thrive by them; and when they have lined their coats, 50
   Do themselves homage. These fellows have some soul,
   And such a one do I profess myself. For, sir,
   It is as sure as you are Roderigo,
   Were I the Moor, I would not be Iago.
   In following him, I follow but myself.   55
   Heaven is my judge, not I for love and duty,
   But seeming so, for my peculiar end;
   For when my outward action doth demonstrate
   The native act and figure of my heart
   In complement extern, 'tis not long after   60

33. **letter and affection:** influence and bias.
34. **old gradation:** traditional promotion through seniority.
36. **affined:** obliged.
39. **serve my turn upon:** get my own back from.
42. **knee-crooking:** bowing.
45. **provender:** animal fodder.
46. **Whip me:** i.e., they deserve what they get as far as I'm concerned.
47. **trimmed . . . visages:** putting on shows.
51. **Do themselves homage:** defer to their own needs.
53–54. **It is . . . be Iago:** This sounds like a self-evident truism, but isn't; Iago's meaning "may be, 'Were I in the Moor's place, I should be quite another man than I am.' Or, 'if I had the Moor's nature, if I were such an honest dunce as he is, I should be just a fit subject for men that "have some soul" to practise upon' " (Furness, quoting Hudson).
56. **not I:** I do not serve (elliptical).
57. **peculiar:** personal.
58–60. **outward . . . complement extern:** visible behavior corresponds to private intention.

But I will wear my heart upon my sleeve
For daws to peck at. I am not what I am.
RODERIGO   What a full fortune does the thick-lips owe
If he can carry't thus!
IAGO   Call up her father,
Rouse him, make after him, poison his delight.   65
Proclaim him in the streets, incense her kinsmen,
And though he in a fertile climate dwell,
Plague him with flies. Though that his joy be joy,
Yet throw such chances of vexation on't,
As it may lose some color.   70
RODERIGO   Here is her father's house. I'll call aloud.
IAGO   Do, with like timorous accent and dire yell
As when, by night and negligence, the fire
Is spied in populous cities.
RODERIGO   What ho, Brabantio! Signior Brabantio, ho!   75
IAGO   Awake! what ho, Brabantio! Thieves, thieves!
Look to your house, your daughter, and your bags!
Thieves, thieves!

[*Enter*] BRABANTIO *above at a window.*

BRABANTIO   What is the reason of this terrible summons?
What is the matter there?   80
RODERIGO   Signior, is all your family within?
IAGO   Are your doors locked?
BRABANTIO   Why? Wherefore ask you this?
IAGO   Zounds, sir, you're robbed! For shame, put on your gown!
Your heart is burst, you have lost half your soul.
Even now, now, very now, an old black ram   85
Is tupping your white ewe. Arise, arise!

62. **daws:** birds reputed for stupidity. **I am not what I am:** The second "am" must be taken to mean "seem." In Exodus 3:1, God declares, "I am that I am."
63. **owe:** possess.
64. **carry't:** pull it off.
65. **him:** The "first and second" pronouns seem "to relate to different persons" (Capell), slipping from "her father" to "the thick-lips."
69. **chances:** possibilities.
70. **lose some color:** diminish in intensity.
72. **like timorous accent:** such frightening noise.
73. **by night and negligence:** i.e., "*by night*, and *thro' negligence*. Otherwise the particle *by* would be made to signify *time* applied to one word, and *cause* applied to the other" (Warburton, but see discussion on p. xv).
78. **STAGE DIRECTION** *above:* "on the small upper stage above and to the rear of the main platform stage, which resembled the projecting upper story of an Elizabethan house" (Kernan).
83. **Zounds:** by God's wounds. **gown:** either senator's robe or appropriate night attire (accusing Brabantio of shameful negligence).
85. **very:** right or truly (emphatic).
86. **tupping:** used to describe animal copulation.
87. **snorting:** snoring; but the modern sense of animal noises is available. **bell:** alarm to warn of fire or insurrection.

Awake the snorting citizens with the bell,
Or else the devil will make a grandsire of you.
Arise, I say!

BRABANTIO   What, have you lost your wits?

RODERIGO   Most reverend signior, do you know my voice?   90

BRABANTIO   Not I; what are you?

RODERIGO   My name is Roderigo.

BRABANTIO   The worser welcome!
I have charged thee not to haunt about my doors;
In honest plainness thou hast heard me say
My daughter is not for thee. And now in madness,   95
Being full of supper and distemp'ring draughts,
Upon malicious knavery, dost thou come
To start my quiet.

RODERIGO   Sir, sir, sir—

BRABANTIO   But thou must needs be sure,
My spirits and my place have in their power   100
To make this bitter to thee.

RODERIGO   Patience, good sir.

BRABANTIO   What tell'st thou me of robbing? This is Venice;
My house is not a grange.

RODERIGO   Most grave Brabantio,
In simple and pure soul, I come to you.

IAGO   Zounds, sir; you are one of those that will not serve God   105
if the devil bid you. Because we come to do you service,
and you think we are ruffians, you'll have your daughter
covered with a Barbary horse; you'll have your nephews
neigh to you; you'll have coursers for cousins and
jennets for germans.   110

BRABANTIO   What profane wretch art thou?

IAGO   I am one, sir, that comes to tell you your daughter
and the Moor are making the beast with two backs.

BRABANTIO   Thou art a villain.

IAGO   You are a senator.   115

BRABANTIO   This thou shalt answer. I know thee, Roderigo.

RODERIGO   Sir, I will answer anything. But I beseech you,
If't be your pleasure, and most wise consent,

96. **distemp'ring draughts:** alcohol.
98. **start:** startle.
100. **spirits and . . . place:** anger and influential position.
103. **grange:** isolated rural abode.
108–10. **covered . . . germans:** Iago shifts abruptly from one kind of horse to another (the Barbary steed having a particular association with the Moor) and from one example of human kinship to another, paying more attention to alliteration than to the specific familial connections (all are "germans" or close relatives). The common ground is bestial contamination; like "tupping" earlier, "covered" was used to describe animal copulation.
113. **making the beast with two backs:** a proverbial image representing human sexual intercourse as bestial.

As partly I find it is, that your fair daughter,
At this odd-even and dull watch o'th' night,   120
Transported with no worse nor better guard
But with a knave of common hire, a gondolier,
To the gross clasps of a lascivious Moor—
If this be known to you, and your allowance,
We then have done you bold and saucy wrongs.   125
But if you know not this, my manners tell me
We have your wrong rebuke. Do not believe
That from the sense of all civility
I thus would play and trifle with your reverence.
Your daughter, if you have not given her leave,   130
I say again, hath made a gross revolt,
Tying her duty, beauty, wit and fortunes
In an extravagant and wheeling stranger
Of here and everywhere. Straight satisfy yourself.
If she be in her chamber or your house,   135
Let loose on me the justice of the state
For thus deluding you.
BRABANTIO   Strike on the tinder, ho!
Give me a taper, call up all my people!
This accident is not unlike my dream;
Belief of it oppresses me already.   140
Light, I say, light!   *Exit [above].*
IAGO   Farewell, for I must leave you.
It seems not meet nor wholesome to my place
To be produced—as, if I stay, I shall—
Against the Moor. For I do know the state,
However this may gall him with some check,   145
Cannot with safety cast him; for he's embarked
With such loud reason to the Cyprus wars,
Which even now stands in act, that for their souls

120. **odd-even and dull watch:** neither night nor morning; indefinite.
122. **But:** than.
124. **your allowance:** done with your permission.
128. **from:** contrary to.
131. **gross:** great; also outrageous (as in Othello's "gross clasps" just earlier [123]).
132. **wit:** reason or understanding.
133. **extravagant and wheeling:** wandering without restraint outside established boundaries.
134. **Straight:** immediately.
137. **Strike on the tinder:** to make flame for a torch.
139. **accident:** unanticipated happening.
143. **produced:** summoned for testimony.
145. **gall him with some check:** irritate him with some restraint.
146. **cast:** dismiss.
147. **loud:** urgent.
148. **even now stands in act:** are being undertaken at this very moment (cf. "even now," 85); "wars" can be taken as a singular subject.

Another of his fathom they have none
To lead their business. In which regard,   150
Though I do hate him as I do hell pains,
Yet for necessity of present life
I must show out a flag and sign of love,
Which is indeed but sign. That you shall surely find him,
Lead to the Sagittary the raisèd search,   155
And there will I be with him. So farewell.   *Exit.*

Enter BRABANTIO [*below*] *in his nightgown*
with Servants and Torches.

BRABANTIO   It is too true an evil. Gone she is,
And what's to come of my despisèd time
Is naught but bitterness. Now, Roderigo,
Where didst thou see her?—O unhappy girl!—   160
With the Moor, say'st thou?—Who would be a father?—
How didst thou know 'twas she?—O, she deceives me
Past thought!—what said she to you?—Get more tapers,
Raise all my kindred! Are they married, think you?
RODERIGO   Truly I think they are.   165
BRABANTIO   O heaven! How got she out? O treason of the
blood!
Fathers, from hence trust not your daughters' minds
By what you see them act. Is there not charms
By which the property of youth and maidhood
May be abused? Have you not read, Roderigo,   170
Of some such thing?
RODERIGO   Yes, sir, I have indeed.
BRABANTIO   Call up my brother.—O, would you had had her!—
Some one way, some another.—Do you know
Where we may apprehend her and the Moor?
RODERIGO   I think I can discover him, if you please   175
To get good guard and go along with me.
BRABANTIO   Pray you lead on. At every house I'll call;
I may command at most.—Get weapons, ho!

149. **of his fathom:** with his abilities.
155. **Sagittary:** Centaur, a legendary creature with a man's head on a horse's body; its image would appear on the so-named inn, where Othello may be found.
156. **STAGE DIRECTION** *nightgown:* dressing gown (casual domestic attire, but not the current meaning).
158. **despisèd time:** miserable life, expressing grief at his loss and/or shame at the affront to his public image.
166. **treason of the blood:** rebellion against paternal authority and/or by passion against reason.
169. **property:** appropriate behavior.
170. **abused:** misled.
175. **discover:** uncover, reveal.

And raise some special officers of night.—
On, good Roderigo; I will deserve your pains.   *Exeunt.* 180

ACT I SCENE 2

Enter OTHELLO, IAGO [*and*] *Attendants, with Torches.*

IAGO   Though in the trade of war I have slain men,
    Yet do I hold it very stuff o'th' conscience
    To do no contrived murder. I lack iniquity
    Sometime to do me service. Nine or ten times
    I had thought t'have yerked him here under the ribs.   5
OTHELLO   'Tis better as it is.

IAGO   Nay, but he prated
    And spoke such scurvy and provoking terms
    Against your honor
    That with the little godliness I have
    I did full hard forbear him. But I pray you, sir,   10
    Are you fast married? Be assured of this,
    That the magnifico is much beloved,
    And hath in his effect a voice potential
    As double as the duke's. He will divorce you,
    Or put upon you what restraint or grievance   15
    The law, with all his might to enforce it on,
    Will give him cable.
OTHELLO   Let him do his spite;
    My services, which I have done the signiory,
    Shall out-tongue his complaints. 'Tis yet to know—
    Which, when I know that boasting is an honor,   20
    I shall promulgate—I fetch my life and being
    From men of royal siege; and my demerits
    May speak unbonneted to as proud a fortune
    As this that I have reached. For know, Iago,

    179. special officers of night: nocturnal patrols were a noted feature of the Venetian civic order (see p. 137, n. 8).
    180. deserve your pains: reward your efforts. **STAGE DIRECTION** *Exeunt:* "they leave the stage" (the Latin plural of *exit*—a distinction not subsequently maintained with rigor).
    2. very stuff: the essence.
    5. yerked: poked.
    10. did full hard forbear: could scarcely put up with.
    11. fast: securely (perhaps an implicit question about sexual consummation).
    12. magnifico: important person (Brabantio).
    14. double: powerful.
    17. cable: latitude.
    18. the signiory: the Venetian governors.
    19. to know: to be made known.
    22. siege: rank. **demerits:** merits; a secondary meaning even in Shakespeare's time.
    23. unbonneted: having "off-capped" (cf. 1.1.9); Othello claims he has earned his success, so should not need to remove his cap.

But that I love the gentle Desdemona,   25
I would not my unhousèd free condition
Put into circumscription and confine
For the sea's worth. But look, what lights come yond?

Enter CASSIO, *with Officers and Torches.*

IAGO   Those are the raisèd father and his friends.
You were best go in.
OTHELLO   Not I; I must be found.   30
My parts, my title, and my perfect soul
Shall manifest me rightly. Is it they?
IAGO   By Janus, I think no.
OTHELLO   The servants of the duke? And my lieutenant?
The goodness of the night upon you, friends.   35
What is the news?
CASSIO   The duke does greet you, general,
And he requires your haste-post-haste appearance
Even on the instant.
OTHELLO   What is the matter, think you?
CASSIO   Something from Cyprus, as I may divine.
It is a business of some heat. The galleys   40
Have sent a dozen sequent messengers
This very night at one another's heels,
And many of the consuls, raised and met,
Are at the duke's already. You have been hotly called for;
When, being not at your lodging to be found,   45
The Senate hath sent about three several quests
To search you out.
OTHELLO   'Tis well I am found by you.
I will but spend a word here in the house
And go with you.   [*Exit.*]
CASSIO   Ancient, what makes he here?
IAGO   Faith, he tonight hath boarded a land carrack.   50
If it prove lawful prize, he's made forever.

26. **unhousèd free condition:** undomesticated independence.
28. **the sea's worth:** immeasurable value.
29. **raisèd:** aroused.
31. **parts:** natural gifts (?). **title:** status or claim (?). **perfect soul:** clear conscience or guiltless spirit (?).
32. **manifest:** represent, reveal.
33. **Janus:** Roman deity with contradictory faces—one smiling, one frowning—on either side of his head.
39. **divine:** guess.
40. **heat:** urgency.
41. **sequent:** consecutive.
46. **sent about three several quests:** sent out three separate searches.
49. **makes he:** is he doing.
50. **boarded a land carrack:** got onto a treasure ship (sexual innuendo).

CASSIO   I do not understand.
IAGO   He's married.
CASSIO   To who?
IAGO   Marry, to—   [*Enter* OTHELLO.]
            Come, captain, will you go?
OTHELLO   Have with you.
CASSIO   Here comes another troop to seek for you.

                        Enter BRABANTIO [*and*] RODERIGO, *with*
                                Officers and Torches.

IAGO   It is Brabantio; general, be advised,   55
    He comes to bad intent.
OTHELLO   Holla, stand there!
RODERIGO   Signior, it is the Moor.
BRABANTIO   Down with him, thief!

                        [*They draw on both sides.*]

IAGO   You, Roderigo? Come, sir, I am for you.
OTHELLO   Keep up your bright swords, for the dew will rust
    them.
    Good signior, you shall more command with years   60
    Than with your weapons.
BRABANTIO   O thou foul thief, where hast thou stowed my
    daughter?
    Damned as thou art, thou hast enchanted her;
    For I'll refer me to all things of sense,
    If she in chains of magic were not bound,   65
    Whether a maid, so tender, fair, and happy,
    So opposite to marriage that she shunned
    The wealthy curlèd darlings of our nation,
    Would ever have, t' incur a general mock,
    Run from her guardage to the sooty bosom   70
    Of such a thing as thou—to fear, not to delight.
    Judge me the world if 'tis not gross in sense
    That thou hast practiced on her with foul charms,
    Abused her delicate youth with drugs or minerals
    That weakens motion. I'll have't disputed on;   75

---

53. **Marry:** by the Virgin Mary. **Have with you:** I'm ready.
59. **Keep up your bright swords:** Put away your unused weapons (the ironically dismissive command of an experienced soldier); perhaps an echo of "Put up thy sworde into the sheath" (John 18.11).
64. **refer me . . . sense:** appeal to all reasonable evidence.
68. **curlèd:** fashionably coifed.
69. **general mock:** widespread scorn.
70. **guardage:** parental custody.
72. **gross in sense:** self-evident; see 1.1.131 and note.
75. **motion:** natural inclination. **disputed on:** decided in court.

'Tis probable and palpable to thinking.
I therefore apprehend and do attach thee
For an abuser of the world, a practicer
Of arts inhibited and out of warrant.
Lay hold upon him; if he do resist   80
Subdue him at his peril!

OTHELLO   Hold your hands,
Both you of my inclining and the rest.
Were it my cue to fight, I should have known it
Without a prompter. Where will you that I go
To answer this your charge?

BRABANTIO   To prison, till fit time   85
Of law and course of direct session
Call thee to answer.

OTHELLO   What if I do obey?
How may the duke be therewith satisfied,
Whose messengers are here about my side
Upon some present business of the state   90
To bring me to him?

OFFICER   'Tis true, most worthy signior.
The duke's in council, and your noble self
I am sure is sent for.

BRABANTIO   How? The duke in council?
In this time of the night? Bring him away.
Mine's not an idle cause. The duke himself,   95
Or any of my brothers of the state,
Cannot but feel this wrong as 'twere their own;
For if such actions may have passage free,
Bondslaves and pagans shall our statesmen be.   *Exeunt.*

ACT I SCENE 3

Enter DUKE *and Senators, set at a table with lights and Attendants*

DUKE   There's no composition in this news
That gives them credit.

FIRST SENATOR   Indeed, they are disproportioned;
My letters say a hundred and seven galleys.

77. **attach:** arrest.
79. **inhibited:** prohibited.
82. **of my inclining:** on my side.
85–86. **till fit time . . . session:** two technically distinct ways of saying "till the law runs its course."
95. **an idle cause:** an unimportant case.
1. **composition:** coherence.
2. **gives them credit:** makes them believable.

DUKE   And mine a hundred forty.
SECOND SENATOR   And mine two hundred.
  But though they jump not on a just account—   5
  As in these cases where the aim reports
  'Tis oft with difference—yet do they all confirm
  A Turkish fleet, and bearing up to Cyprus.
DUKE   Nay, it is possible enough to judgment;
  I do not so secure me in the error,   10
  But the main article I do approve
  In fearful sense.
SAILOR *within*.   What ho! what ho! what ho!

Enter SAILOR.

OFFICER   A messenger from the galleys.
DUKE   Now, what's the
    business?
SAILOR   The Turkish preparation makes for Rhodes.
  So was I bid report here to the state   15
  By Signior Angelo.
DUKE   How say you by this change?
FIRST SENATOR   This cannot be
  By no assay of reason. 'Tis a pageant
  To keep us in false gaze. When we consider
  Th' importancy of Cyprus to the Turk,   20
  And let ourselves again but understand
  That, as it more concerns the Turk than Rhodes,
  So may he with more facile question bear it,
  For that it stands not in such warlike brace,
  But altogether lacks th' abilities   25
  That Rhodes is dressed in—if we make thought of this,
  We must not think the Turk is so unskillful
  To leave that latest which concerns him first,
  Neglecting an attempt of ease and gain
  To wake and wage a danger profitless.   30
DUKE   Nay, in all confidence, he's not for Rhodes.
OFFICER   Here is more news.

Enter a MESSENGER.

5. **jump not on a just account**: don't agree on an exact number.
6. **the aim reports**: estimates are given.
10–12. **so secure . . . fearful sense**: take advantage of the inconsistency to dismiss the basic threat.
18–19. **pageant . . . gaze**: show to divert us.
20. **the Turk**: the Turks—"he" for "they," here and following.
23. **with more facile question bear**: more easily conquer.
24. **stands not in such warlike brace**: is not in such a state of military alert.

MESSENGER   The Ottomites, reverend and gracious,
　　Steering with due course toward the isle of Rhodes,
　　Have there injointed them with an after fleet.   35
FIRST SENATOR   Ay, so I thought. How many, as you guess?
MESSENGER   Of thirty sail; and now they do re-stem
　　Their backward course, bearing with frank appearance
　　Their purposes toward Cyprus. Signior Montano,
　　Your trusty and most valiant servitor,   40
　　With his free duty recommends you thus,
　　And prays you to believe him.
DUKE   'Tis certain then for Cyprus.
　　Marcus Luccicos—is not he in town?
FIRST SENATOR   He's now in Florence.   45
DUKE   Write from us to him. Post-post-haste, dispatch!
FIRST SENATOR   Here comes Brabantio and the valiant Moor.

Enter BRABANTIO, OTHELLO, CASSIO,
IAGO, RODERIGO, and Officers.

DUKE   Valiant Othello, we must straight employ you
　　Against the general enemy Ottoman.

[To BRABANTIO.]

I did not see you; welcome, gentle signior.   50
We lacked your counsel and your help tonight.
BRABANTIO   So did I yours. Good your grace, pardon me.
　　Neither my place nor aught I heard of business
　　Hath raised me from my bed; nor doth the general care
　　Take hold on me. For my particular grief   55
　　Is of so floodgate and o'erbearing nature,
　　That it engluts and swallows other sorrows,
　　And it is still itself.
DUKE   Why? What's the matter?
BRABANTIO   My daughter, O my daughter!
SENATOR   Dead?
BRABANTIO   Ay, to me.
　　She is abused, stol'n from me and corrupted   60

　　33. **Ottomites:** Ottomans, Turks. **reverend and gracious:** respectful address to the senators ("sirs" understood).
　　35. **injointed:** combined. **after:** following; perhaps punning on "more aft."
　　37. **re-stem:** redirect.
　　38–39. **bearing ... purposes:** openly headed.
　　40–42. **Your trusty ... believe him:** conventionally deferential diplomatic formulas.
　　48. **straight:** immediately.
　　49. **general enemy Ottoman:** the Turks, hostile "to all Christians" (Mowat and Werstine; Honigmann).
　　53. **place:** senatorial position.
　　56. **floodgate and o'erbearing:** restraint-breaching.
　　60. **abused:** misled.

By spells and medicines bought of mountebanks;
For nature so preposterously to err,
Being not deficient, blind, or lame of sense,
Sans witchcraft could not.
DUKE   Whoe'er he be that in this foul proceeding   65
Hath thus beguiled your daughter of herself
And you of her, the bloody book of law
You shall yourself read in the bitter letter
After your own sense; yea, though our proper son
Stood in your action.
BRABANTIO   Humbly I thank your grace.   70
Here is the man. This Moor, whom now it seems
Your special mandate for the state affairs
Hath hither brought.
ALL   We are very sorry for't.
DUKE [To OTHELLO.]   What in your own part can you say to
this?
BRABANTIO   Nothing, but this is so.   75
OTHELLO   Most potent, grave, and reverend signiors,
My very noble and approved good masters:
That I have ta'en away this old man's daughter
It is most true; true I have married her.
The very head and front of my offending   80
Hath this extent, no more. Rude am I in my speech,
And little blessed with the soft phrase of peace;
For since these arms of mine had seven years' pith
Till now some nine moons wasted, they have used
Their dearest action in the tented field;   85
And little of this great world can I speak
More than pertains to feats of broils and battle,
And therefore little shall I grace my cause
In speaking for myself. Yet, by your gracious patience,
I will a round unvarnished tale deliver,   90
Of my whole course of love: what drugs, what charms,

61. **mountebanks:** con artists.
64. **sans:** without.
67–69. **the bloody book . . . own sense:** you can punish as severely as you think the law
allows.
69. **proper:** own.
70. **Stood in your action:** was vulnerable to your accusation.
77. **approved:** confirmed by experience.
80. **very head and front:** truly utmost extent (literally, true head and forehead).
81. **Rude:** inexperienced, unsophisticated.
83. **pith:** strength.
84. **nine moons wasted:** nine months ago.
84–85. **used . . . action:** been chiefly exercised.
87. **broils:** skirmishes.
90. **round:** direct.

What conjuration and what mighty magic—
For such proceeding I am charged withal—
I won his daughter.
BRABANTIO   A maiden never bold;
  Of spirit so still and quiet that her motion   95
  Blushed at herself; and she—in spite of nature,
  Of years, of country, credit, everything—
  To fall in love with what she feared to look on?
  It is a judgment maimed and most imperfect
  That will confess perfection so could err   100
  Against all rules of nature, and must be driven
  To find out practices of cunning hell
  Why this should be. I therefore vouch again
  That with some mixtures powerful o'er the blood,
  Or with some dram, conjured to this effect,   105
  He wrought upon her.
DUKE   To vouch this is no proof,
  Without more wider and more overt test
  Than these thin habits and poor likelihoods
  Of modern seeming do prefer against him.
SENATOR   But, Othello, speak;   110
  Did you by indirect and forced courses
  Subdue and poison this young maid's affections?
  Or came it by request and such fair question
  As soul to soul affordeth?
OTHELLO   I do beseech you
  Send for the lady to the Sagittary,   115
  And let her speak of me before her father.
  If you do find me foul in her report,
  The trust, the office I do hold of you,
  Not only take away, but let your sentence
  Even fall upon my life.
DUKE   Fetch Desdemona hither.   120
OTHELLO   Ancient, conduct them; you best know the place.

Exit [IAGO *and*] *two or three* [*Attendants*].

---

  95. motion: feeling or desire.
  96. Blushed at herself: embarrassed even her.
  97. years . . . credit: age, of Venetian convention, reputation.
  101. and must: The phrase is elliptical, implying a new and contrasting subject: "and *un*maimed judgment must. . . ."
  104. the blood: passion, desire.
  106. wrought: worked.
  107–09. more wider . . . seeming: The duke rejects fashionably superficial appearances ("modern seeming") for something more readily apparent ("overt") and dismisses shallow conventions and see-through garments ("habits" are clothes) for the implicitly naked truth.
  113. fair question: open and uncoerced conversation.
  117. foul: ugly; also "black," in implicit contrast to "fair" as white just earlier.

And till she come, as truly as to heaven
I do confess the vices of my blood,
So justly to your grave ears I'll present
How I did thrive in this fair lady's love   125
And she in mine.
DUKE   Say it, Othello.
✱ OTHELLO Her father loved me, oft invited me,
Still questioned me the story of my life
From year to year, the battles, sieges, fortunes
That I have past.   130
I ran it through, even from my boyish days
To th' very moment that he bade me tell it;
Wherein I spoke of most disastrous chances,
Of moving accidents by flood and field,
Of hair-breadth scapes i'th' imminent-deadly breach, 135
Of being taken by the insolent foe
And sold to slavery, of my redemption thence
And portance in my traveler's history;
Wherein of antars vast and deserts idle,
Rough quarries, rocks and hills whose heads touch heaven, 140
It was my hint to speak—such was my process—
And of the cannibals that each other eat,
The anthropophagi, and men whose heads
Do grow beneath their shoulders. These things to hear
Would Desdemona seriously incline,   145
But still the house affairs would draw her thence,
Which ever as she could with haste dispatch,
She'd come again and with a greedy ear
Devour up my discourse; which I, observing,
Took once a pliant hour and found good means 150
To draw from her a prayer of earnest heart
That I would all my pilgrimage dilate,
Whereof by parcels she had something heard,

123. **the vices of my blood:** my sinful desires.
128. **still:** constantly.
134. **moving accidents by flood and field:** affecting events on sea and land.
135. **imminent-deadly breach:** immediately life-threatening gap in fortifications.
137. **redemption:** liberation, ransom.
138. **portance:** bearing, deportment.
139. **antars vast and deserts idle:** huge caves and empty wildernesses.
141. **It was my hint:** it was my opportunity or occasion; I was called upon. **process:** a term from formal rhetoric meaning "narrative development"; refers at once to his life and to his account of it.
143. **anthropophagi:** Latinate version of cannibals ("man eaters").
150. **pliant:** convenient, perhaps implying a time when she was compliant.
151. **prayer of earnest heart:** a strongly felt request.
152. **dilate:** expand or elaborate on.
153. **by parcels:** in bits and pieces.

But not intentively. I did consent
And often did beguile her of her tears   155
When I did speak of some distressful stroke
That my youth suffered. My story being done,
She gave me for my pains a world of kisses; *Sighs*
She swore in faith 'twas strange, 'twas passing strange,
'Twas pitiful, 'twas wondrous pitiful.   160
She wished she had not heard it, yet she wished
(That heaven had made her such a man) She thanked me
And bade me, if I had a friend that loved her,
I should but teach him how to tell my story,
And that would woo her. Upon this hint I spake.   165
She loved me for the dangers I had past,
And I loved her that she did pity them.
This only is the witchcraft I have used.
Here comes the lady; let her witness it.

      Enter DESDEMONA, IAGO [*and*] *Attendants.*

DUKE I think this tale would win my daughter too.   170
 Good Brabantio, take up this mangled matter at the best.
 Men do their broken weapons rather use,
 Than their bare hands.
BRABANTIO   I pray you hear her speak.
 If she confess that she was half the wooer,
 Destruction on my head if my bad blame   175
 Light on the man. Come hither, gentle mistress.
 Do you perceive in all this noble company
 Where most you owe obedience?
DESDEMONA   My noble father,
 I do perceive here a divided duty.
 To you I am bound for life and education;   180
 My life and education both do learn me
 How to respect you; you are the lord of duty;
 I am hitherto your daughter. But here's my husband;
 And so much duty as my mother showed
 To you, preferring you before her father,   185

---

154. **intentively:** carefully, with sustained attention.
159. **passing:** surpassingly, beyond.
162. **made her:** made for her, made her into.
165. **hint:** opportunity or occasion; as in 142, the modern sense of "suggestion" should not be altogether eliminated.
171–73. **take up ... bare hands:** two versions of proverbial advice to make the best of a bad situation.
180. **education:** upbringing.
181. **learn:** teach.

So much I challenge that I may profess
Due to the Moor my lord.

BRABANTIO   God be with you; I have done.
Please it your grace, on to the state affairs;
I had rather to adopt a child than get it.
Come hither, Moor.   190
I here do give thee that with all my heart
Which, but thou hast already, with all my heart
I would keep from thee. For your sake, jewel,
I am glad at soul I have no other child,
For thy escape would teach me tyranny   195
To hang clogs on them. I have done, my lord.

DUKE   Let me speak like yourself and lay a sentence
Which, as a grise or step, may help these lovers
Into your favor.
When remedies are past, the griefs are ended   200
By seeing the worst, which late on hopes depended.
To mourn a mischief that is past and gone
Is the next way to draw new mischief on.
What cannot be preserved, when fortune takes,
Patience her injury a mockery makes.   205
The robbed that smiles steals something from the thief;
He robs himself that spends a bootless grief.

BRABANTIO   So let the Turk of Cyprus us beguile:
We lose it not so long as we can smile.
He bears the sentence well that nothing bears,   210
But the free comfort which from thence he hears.
But he bears both the sentence and the sorrow
That, to pay grief, must of poor patience borrow.
These sentences, to sugar or to gall,
Being strong on both sides, are equivocal.   215
But words are words; I never yet did hear
That the bruised heart was piercèd through the ear.
I humbly beseech you proceed to th' affairs of state.

DUKE   The Turk with a most mighty preparation

186. **challenge:** claim.
189. **get:** beget.
193. **For your sake, jewel:** because of you, my prized possession.
196. **hang clogs:** attach weights as on prisoners; impose stringent restraints.
197. **like yourself:** according to your own real interests or better nature. **lay a sentence:** put a proverb in place.
198. **grise:** stair.
200–07. **When remedies . . . grief:** Four aphorisms reiterate the idea that the patient acceptance of loss eliminates suffering.
208–17. **So let . . . of state:** Responding aphoristically, Brabantio claims that proverbs are contradictory ("equivocal") and anyway powerless to either cause or cure real grief; **piercèd** (217): either "wounded" or "lanced (for medicinal purposes)."

makes for Cyprus. Othello, the fortitude of the place is   220
best known to you; and though we have there a substitute
of most allowed sufficiency, yet opinion, a more
sovereign mistress of effects, throws a more safer
voice on you. You must therefore be content to slubber
the gloss of your new fortunes with this more stubborn   225
and boisterous expedition.

OTHELLO The tyrant custom, most grave senators,
  Hath made the flinty and steel [couch] of war
  My thrice-driven bed of down. I do agnize
  A natural and prompt alacrity   230
  I find in hardness and do undertake
  This present wars against the Ottomites.
  Most humbly, therefore, bending to your state,
  I crave fit disposition for my wife,
  Due reference of place, and exhibition,   235
  With such accommodation and besort
  As levels with her breeding.

DUKE Why, at her father's.

BRABANTIO   I will not have it so.

OTHELLO Nor I.

DESDEMONA   Nor would I there reside
  To put my father in impatient thoughts   240
  By being in his eye. Most gracious duke,
  To my unfolding lend your prosperous ear,
  And let me find a charter in your voice
  T' assist my simpleness.

DUKE What would you, Desdemona?   245

DESDEMONA That I love the Moor to live with him,
  My downright violence and storm of fortunes

220. **fortitude:** military strength.
221–22. **substitute . . . sufficiency:** a well-respected deputy.
222–24. **opinion . . . on you:** reputation, a better bet for results, makes you a more secure choice.
224. **slubber:** smear, sully.
225–26. **stubborn and boisterous:** unyielding and harsh.
229. **thrice-driven:** very soft (a fan drives away light feathers from heavy ones).
229–31. **agnize . . . hardness:** "acknowledge (that) I find a natural and ready eagerness (in myself) in (situations of) hardship" (Honigmann).
233. **bending to your state:** deferring to your authority.
234. **crave fit disposition:** seek appropriate arrangements.
235. **Due . . . exhibition:** "proper respect for her place (as my wife) and maintenance" (Honigmann).
236. **accommodation and besort:** adjustment (and probably the modern "housing") and company.
237. **levels with:** befits.
242. **prosperous:** favorable.
243. **charter:** authority.
244. **simpleness:** inexperience.

May trumpet to the world. My heart's subdued
Even to the very quality of my lord.
I saw Othello's visage in his mind,   250
And to his honors and his valiant parts
Did I my soul and fortunes consecrate,
So that, dear lords, if I be left behind,
A moth of peace, and he go to the war,
The rites for why I love him are bereft me,   255
And I a heavy interim shall support
By his dear absence. Let me go with him.
OTHELLO   Let her have your voice.
Vouch with me, heaven, I therefore beg it not
To please the palate of my appetite,   260
Nor to comply with heat (the young affects
In [me] defunct) and proper satisfaction;
But to be free and bounteous to her mind;
And heaven defend your good souls that you think
I will your serious and great business scant   265
When she is with me. No, when light-winged toys
Of feathered Cupid seel with wanton dullness
My speculative and officed instrument,
That my disports corrupt and taint my business,
Let housewives make a skillet of my helm,   270
And all indign and base adversities
Make head against my estimation.
DUKE   Be it as you shall privately determine,
Either for her stay or going. Th' affair cries haste,
And speed must answer it.   275
SENATOR   You must away tonight.
OTHELLO   With all my heart.

249. **Even . . . very:** For these intensifiers, cf. 1.1.85 and note.
250. **saw Othello . . . mind:** subsumed his foul face in his fair mind; saw Othello as he saw himself.
251. **honors and valiant parts:** distinctions and heroic qualities.
254. **moth:** inactive creature (deprived of Othello's attracting light?).
255. **rites:** military rituals; also marital rights (acknowledging sexual interest).
256. **heavy . . . support:** In Desdemona's metaphor, Othello's absence registers as a bodily weight on her.
260–62. **To please . . . satisfaction:** By adopting Capell's "me" for "my" (the emendation of choice among modern editors), we can gloss this very perplexing passage as: "to gratify sexual desire (youthful craving no longer being mine) and self-love"; **proper:** "often means little more than *own*" (Ridley) or "personal" (cf. line 69). In this reading, "the thing affirm'd by the speaker is only—that the violence of youthful passion was over with him; not all passions" (Capell). But few audiences come away from these words satisfied about Othello's or their own understanding: "what made the difficulty, will continue to make it" (Johnson).
266–68. **light-winged . . . instrument:** trivial love games blind my judgment; **seel:** cover a hawk's face with a hood.
270. **make a skillet of my helm:** transform my helmet to a cooking utensil.
271. **indign:** ignoble.
272. **Make head . . . estimation:** attack my reputation.

DUKE   At nine i'th' morning here we'll meet again.
   Othello, leave some officer behind,
   And he shall our commission bring to you,
   And such things else of quality and respect   280
   As doth import you.
OTHELLO   So please your grace, my ancient;
   A man he is of honesty and trust.
   To his conveyance I assign my wife,
   With what else needful your good grace shall think
   To be sent after me.
DUKE   Let it be so.   285
   Good night to every one. And, noble signior,
   If virtue no delighted beauty lack,
   Your son-in-law is far more fair than black.

                           [*Exit* DUKE.]

SENATOR   Adieu, brave Moor; use Desdemona well.

                [*Exeunt Senators and Officers.*]

BRABANTIO   Look to her, Moor, if thou hast eyes to see: 290
   She has deceived her father, and may thee. *Exit* [BRABANTIO].
OTHELLO   My life upon her faith!—Honest Iago,
   My Desdemona must I leave to thee.
   I prithee let thy wife attend on her,
   And bring them after in the best advantage.   295
   Come, Desdemona; I have but an hour
   Of love, of worldly matter and direction
   To spend with thee. We must obey the time.   *Exit Moor and*
                                     DESDEMONA.

RODERIGO   Iago?
IAGO   What say'st thou, noble heart?   300
RODERIGO   What will I do, think'st thou?
IAGO   Why, go to bed and sleep.
RODERIGO   I will incontinently drown my self.
IAGO   If thou dost, I shall never love thee after. Why,
   thou silly gentleman?   305
RODERIGO   It is silliness to live when to live is torment;
   and then have we a prescription to die when death is
   our physician.
IAGO   O villainous! I have looked upon the world

  280–81. such . . . import you: whatever else you require.
  283. conveyance: escort.
  287. delighted: an epithet transferred from "delightful" or "delighting"; "Shakspeare often uses the active and passive participles indiscriminately" (Malone).
  288. more fair than black: i.e., Othello's inner beauty makes him outwardly handsome.
  295. in the best advantage: at the most appropriate opportunity.
  297. worldly matter and direction: practical business and advice.
  303. incontinently: immediately, rashly.
  307–08. prescription . . . physician: authorization for suicide when death is a cure.

for four times seven years, and since I could distinguish   310
betwixt a benefit and an injury, I never found man that
knew how to love himself. Ere I would say I would
drown myself for the love of a guinea-hen, I would
change my humanity with a baboon.

RODERIGO   What should I do? I confess it is my shame   315
to be so fond, but it is not in my virtue to amend it.

IAGO   Virtue? a fig! 'Tis in ourselves that we are
thus or thus. Our bodies are our gardens, to the which
our wills are gardeners. So that if we will plant nettles
or sow lettuce, set hyssop and weed up thyme,   320
supply it with one gender of herbs or distract it with
many—either to have it sterile with idleness or manured
with industry—why, the power and corrigible authority
of this lies in our wills. If the balance of our lives
had not one scale of reason to poise another of sensuality,   325
the blood and baseness of our natures would
conduct us to most preposterous conclusions. But we
have reason to cool our raging motions, our carnal
stings or unbitted lusts; whereof I take this that you
call love to be a sect or scion.   330

RODERIGO   It cannot be.

IAGO   It is merely a lust of the blood and a permission
of the will. Come, be a man! Drown thyself? Drown
cats and blind puppies. I have professed me thy friend,
and I confess me knit to thy deserving with cables of   335

---

310. **four times seven:** A twenty-eight-year-old Iago coincides with the young (and hand-some) figure in Cinthio.

313. **guinea-hen:** woman (with contempt and sexual innuendo).

314. **change:** exchange.

316. **virtue:** either power or morality.

317. **Virtue? a fig!:** Iago presumably accompanies this contemptuous dismissal with an obscene gesture—either biting his thumb or thrusting it between two fingers.

319. **wills:** the modern "choice" or "volition," but associated with appetite or sexual drive.

319–20. **nettles . . . thyme:** plants with "complementary qualities of dryness and wetness and so believed to aid the growth of each other" (Sanders); Iago appears to advocate multi(horti)culturalism.

321–22. **supply . . . many:** sustain (our body) with one kind ("gender") or divide and confuse ("distract") it with variety; Iago now appears to advocate horticultural apartheid.

322–23. **either . . . industry:** If "manured" contrasts with "sterile," its primary meaning is "fertilized"; but Iago's rapid-fire speech makes unclear how the binaries in this phrase connect with the contradictory ones earlier.

323. **corrigible authority:** power to correct; perhaps also a power that may be corrected if we change our minds or wills.

326. **blood and baseness:** animal passion (literally, passion and animality).

328. **motions:** appetites.

329. **unbitted:** unreined, uncontrolled.

330. **sect or scion:** cutting or offshoot—i.e., subcategory.

332. **merely:** wholly.

335. **knit to thy deserving:** attached to your merit.

perdurable toughness. I could never better stead thee
than now. Put money in thy purse. Follow thou the
wars; defeat thy favor with an usurped beard. I say,
put money in thy purse. It cannot be long that Desdemona
should continue her love to the Moor—put money in   340
thy purse—nor he his to her. It was a violent commencement
in her, and thou shalt see an answerable sequestration—
put but money in thy purse. These Moors
are changeable in their wills—fill thy purse with money.
The food that to him now is as luscious as locusts   345
shall be to him shortly as bitter as coloquintida. She
must change for youth: when she is sated with his body,
she will find the errors of her choice. Therefore, put money
in thy purse. If thou wilt needs damn thyself, do
it a more delicate way than drowning—make all the money   350
thou canst. If sanctimony and a frail vow betwixt
an erring barbarian and super-subtle Venetian be
not too hard for my wits and all the tribe of hell, thou
shalt enjoy her. Therefore make money. A pox of drowning
thyself; it is clean out of the way. Seek thou rather   355
to be hanged in compassing thy joy than to be
drowned and go without her.

RODERIGO   Wilt thou be fast to my hopes, if I depend on
the issue?

IAGO   Thou art sure of me—go make money. I have   360
told thee often, and I retell thee again and again, I
hate the Moor. My cause is hearted; thine hath no less

336. **perdurable:** everlasting. **stead thee:** serve your needs.
337. **Put money in thy purse:** proverbially, "it's a sure thing," "you can count on it"; also
urging Roderigo to sell property for cash (to give Iago to help his cause).
338. **defeat . . . beard:** disguise your face with a false beard.
342. **answerable sequestration:** equally swift withdrawal of interest.
345. **locusts:** sweet carobs (fruits).
346. **coloquintida:** a sour apple.
347. **change for youth:** drop Othello for a younger lover.
349. **damn thyself:** suicide is a mortal sin.
350. **delicate:** pleasant.
351. **sanctimony . . . vow:** pretended righteousness and a weakly binding promise.
352. **erring barbarian . . . Venetian:** wandering foreigner—a "wheeling stranger / Of
here and everywhere" (1.1.133–34)—more specifically, a Berber, someone from Barbary;
"erring" also suggests straying, sinning, or just mistaking: as a naive outsider, Othello won't
be able to cope with Desdemona's duplicity as a "super-subtle Venetian."
353. **tribe of hell:** Iago frankly allies himself with the diabolical; "may be an aside" (Honigmann).
354. **A pox of:** "i.e., 'a curse on,' 'to hell with' (*pox* = venereal disease)" (McDonald).
355. **clean out of the way:** totally misdirected.
355–56. **Seek . . . hanged:** risk execution, but with innuendo: look for sexual satisfaction.
358. **fast:** securely allied, steadfast.
358–59. **depend . . . issue:** persevere in the outcome.
362. **hearted:** deeply motivated.

reason. Let us be conjunctive in our revenge against
him. If thou canst cuckold him, thou dost thyself a
pleasure, me a sport. There are many events in the   365
womb of time which will be delivered. Traverse, go,
provide thy money. We will have more of this tomorrow.
Adieu.

RODERIGO   Where shall we meet i'th' morning?

IAGO   At my lodging.   370

RODERIGO   I'll be with thee betimes.

IAGO   Go to, farewell. Do you hear, Roderigo?

RODERIGO   I'll sell all my land.   *Exit.*

IAGO   Thus do I ever make my fool my purse;
For I mine own gained knowledge should profane   375
If I would time expend with such a snipe
But for my sport and profit. I hate the Moor,
And it is thought abroad that 'twixt my sheets
H'as done my office. I know not if't be true,
But I for mere suspicion in that kind   380
Will do as if for surety. He holds me well;
The better shall my purpose work on him.
Cassio's a proper man. Let me see now . . .
To get his place and to plume up my will
In double knavery—how? how? Let's see . . .   385
After some time, to abuse Othello's ears
That he is too familiar with his wife.
He hath a person and a smooth dispose
To be suspected, framed to make women false.
The Moor is of a free and open nature   390
That thinks men honest that but seem to be so,
And will as tenderly be led by th' nose
As asses are. . . .
I have't! It is engendered! Hell and night
Must bring this monstrous birth to the world's light.   *Exit.* 395

(margin, rotated:) Silloquy

363. **be conjunctive:** join forces.
366. **Traverse:** get going, carry on.
371. **betimes:** early.
372. **Go to:** colloquial agreement: "okay."
374. **ever . . . purse:** always use fools for my advantage.
378. **thought abroad:** widely rumoured.
379. **done my office:** done my job, my business; had sex with Iago's wife.
380. **in that kind:** of that sort of thing.
381. **holds me well:** has a good opinion of me.
384. **plume up:** puff up my feathers, preen.
387–88. **he . . . his . . . He:** Many editors are at pains to identify these pronouns respectively as Cassio, Othello, and Cassio. Presumably, the references are uncertain. See 1.1.3 and 1.1.65 and notes.
388. **person . . . dispose:** Cassio is good-looking and charming.
390. **free and open:** generously trusting.

ACT 2 SCENE 1

Enter MONTANO *and two Gentlemen [one above].*

MONTANO   What from the cape can you discern at sea?

FIRST GENTLEMAN   Nothing at all; it is a high-wrought flood.
I cannot 'twixt the heaven and the main
Descry a sail.

MONTANO   Methinks the wind hath spoke aloud at land;   5
A fuller blast ne'er shook our battlements;
If it hath ruffianed so upon the sea,
What ribs of oak, when mountains melt on them,
Can hold the mortise? What shall we hear of this?

SECOND GENTLEMAN   A segregation of the Turkish fleet: 10
For do but stand upon the foaming shore,
The chidden billow seems to pelt the clouds;
The wind-shaked surge, with high and monstrous mane,
Seems to cast water on the burning Bear,
And quench the guards of th' ever-fixèd pole.   15
I never did like molestation view
On the enchafèd flood.

MONTANO   If that the Turkish fleet
Be not ensheltered and embayed, they are drowned;
It is impossible to bear it out.

Enter a Third Gentleman.

THIRD GENTLEMAN   News, lads! Our wars are done.   20
The desperate tempest hath so banged the Turks
That their designment halts. A noble ship of Venice
Hath seen a grievous wrack and sufferance
On most part of their fleet.

MONTANO   How? Is this true?

1. **What . . . sea:** addressed to the lookout position—presumably the same projecting upper stage where Brabantio appeared at 1.1.78.
2. **high-wrought flood:** stormy sea.
7. **ruffianed:** gusted fiercely (acted like a ruffian).
8–9. **What ribs . . . mortise:** what hull's curved timbers can avoid splitting under such huge waves' pressure?
10. **segregation:** dispersal.
12. **chidden:** rebuked by the wind or repelled from the shore; also "chiding" or "raging" (see "delighted," note to 1.3.287).
13. **high and monstrous mane:** i.e., like a huge animal's neck; punning on "main" (ocean).
14–15. **Bear . . . pole:** two brightly shining ("burning") stars in Ursa Minor, represented as guarding the polestar.
16. **like molestation:** such turmoil.
17. **enchafèd flood:** raging sea.
19. **bear it out:** endure the storm (without protection).
22. **designment halts:** project is crippled.
23. **grievous . . . sufferance:** experienced extensive damage.

THIRD GENTLEMAN   The ship is here put in,   25
  A Veronnesa. Michael Cassio,
  Lieutenant to the warlike Moor, Othello,
  Is come on shore; the Moor himself at sea,
  And is in full commission here for Cyprus.
MONTANO   I am glad on't—'tis a worthy governor.   30
THIRD GENTLEMAN   But this same Cassio, though he speak of
    comfort
  Touching the Turkish loss, yet he looks sadly
  And prays the Moor be safe; for they were parted
  With foul and violent tempest.
MONTANO   Pray heavens he be,
  For I have served him, and the man commands   35
  Like a full soldier. Let's to the seaside—ho!—
  As well to see the vessel that's come in
  As to throw out our eyes for brave Othello,
  Even till we make the main and th' aerial blue,
  An indistinct regard.
THIRD GENTLEMAN   Come, let's do so;   40
  For every minute is expectancy
  Of more arrivancy.

Enter CASSIO.

CASSIO   Thanks, you the valiant of the warlike isle,
  That so approve the Moor. O, let the heavens
  Give him defence against the elements,   45
  For I have lost him on a dangerous sea.
MONTANO   Is he well shipped?
CASSIO   His bark is stoutly timbered, and his pilot
  Of very expert and approved allowance;
  Therefore my hopes, not surfeited to death,   50
  Stand in bold cure.
[VOICES] *within.*   A sail! a sail! a sail!
CASSIO   What noise?
GENTLEMAN   The town is empty; on the brow o' th' sea
  Stand ranks of people, and they cry "A sail!"
CASSIO   My hopes do shape him for the governor.   *A shot.* 55

    26. Veronnesa: either a certain kind of vessel or a ship from Verona.
    29. is in . . . Cyprus: "is (heading) for Cyprus with full delegated authority here" (Hon-
igmann).
    31–32. speak . . . Touching: brings comforting news regarding.
    32. sadly: solemnly, worriedly.
    39–40. make . . . regard: become unable to distinguish sea from sky.
    44. approve: esteem.
    49. of very expert . . . allowance: acknowledged to be well experienced and competent.
    50–51. my hopes . . . cure: Cassio is hopeful but not overly optimistic.

SECOND GENTLEMAN They do discharge their shot of courtesy:
  Our friends at least.
CASSIO   I pray you, sir, go forth
  And give us truth who 'tis that is arrived.
SECOND GENTLEMAN I shall.   *Exit.*
MONTANO But, good lieutenant, is your general wived?   60
CASSIO Most fortunately: he hath achieved a maid
  That paragons description and wild fame,
  One that excels the quirks of blazoning pens,
  And in th' essential vesture of creation
  Does tire the ingener.

                      Enter Second Gentleman.

             How now? Who has put in?   65
SECOND GENTLEMAN 'Tis one Iago, ancient to the general.
CASSIO He's had most favorable and happy speed:
  Tempests themselves, high seas and howling winds,
  The guttered rocks and congregated sands,
  Traitors ensteeped to enclog the guiltless keel,   70
  As having sense of beauty, do omit
  Their mortal natures, letting go safely by
  The divine Desdemona.
MONTANO   What is she?
CASSIO She that I spake of, our great captain's captain,
  Left in the conduct of the bold Iago,   75
  Whose footing here anticipates our thoughts
  A se'night's speed. Great Jove, Othello guard,
  And swell his sail with thine own powerful breath,
  That he may bless this bay with his tall ship,
  Make love's quick pants in Desdemona's arms,   80
  Give renewed fire to our extinguished spirits,
  And bring all Cyprus comfort!

     Enter DESDEMONA, IAGO, RODERIGO, *and* EMILIA.

---

  57. at least: an allied ship, if not necessarily Othello's (as Cassio had hoped).
  62. paragons . . . fame: surpasses description and extravagant rumor.
  63. quirks of blazoning pens: ingenious poetic descriptions; *blasons* are conventional lyric poems that catalog the mistress's beautiful traits.
  64–65. th' essential vesture . . . ingener: her own natural excellence exhausts (and adorns—"tire" = attire) anyone contriving praise—an elaborately courtly renunciation of elaborate courtliness.
  69. guttered: furrowed, jagged.
  70. ensteeped . . . keel: submerged to obstruct the innocent (unknowing) ship.
  71. omit: renounce.
  72. mortal: deadly, lethal; more courtless: like Orpheus's music, Desdemona's divine beauty tames the natural world into suspending its threat to a higher (human) nature.
  74. captain's captain: As Othello rules the army, so Desdemona rules Othello.
  76–77. Whose . . . speed: whose arrival occurs a week earlier than we expected.
  80. quick: "rapid," but also "alive" and "imparting life" (renewing extinguished spirits).

                                    O, behold!
The riches of the ship is come on shore.
You men of Cyprus, let her have your knees.
Hail to thee, lady, and the grace of heaven,   85
Before, behind thee, and on every hand
Enwheel thee round.
DESDEMONA   I thank you, valiant Cassio.
  What tidings can you tell me of my lord?
CASSIO   He is not yet arrived, nor know I aught
  But that he's well and will be shortly here.   90
DESDEMONA   O, but I fear!—How lost you company?
CASSIO   The great contention of sea and skies
  Parted our fellowship.
[VOICES] *within.*   A sail! a sail!   [*A shot.*]
CASSIO   But hark—a sail.
GENTLEMAN   They give this greeting to the citadel;
  This likewise is a friend.
CASSIO   See for the news.   [*Exit Gentleman.*] 95
  Good ancient, you are welcome.
  [*To* EMILIA.]   Welcome, mistress.   [*Kisses
                                                          EMILIA.*]
  Let it not gall your patience, good Iago,
  That I extend my manners. 'Tis my breeding
  That gives me this bold show of courtesy.
IAGO   Sir, would she give you so much of her lips   100
  As of her tongue she oft bestows on me,
  You would have enough.
DESDEMONA   Alas, she has no speech.
IAGO   In faith, too much:
  I find it still when I have leave to sleep.
  Marry, before your ladyship, I grant,   105
  She puts her tongue a little in her heart
  And chides with thinking.
EMILIA   You have little cause to say so.
IAGO   Come on! come on! You are pictures out of door,
  Bells in your parlors, wildcats in your kitchens,   110

---

84. **have your knees:** receive your bows.
92. **contention:** four syllables (see note to 1.1.16).
97. **gall your patience:** vex your peace.
98. **extend . . . manners:** express or enlarge upon my greeting. **breeding:** upbringing, training, customary behavior.
100–01. **lips . . . tongue:** Iago's words slip glibly between the literal "kissing" and the metaphorical "speaking" and "scolding."
104. **leave:** permission (implicitly from her).
106–07. **She puts . . . thinking:** She berates me even when she is silent.
109. **You are pictures out of door:** You (women) are ideal images (pretty and silent) in public.
110. **bells . . . kitchens:** noisy and enraged in your house.

Saints in your injuries, devils being offended,
Players in your huswifery, and huswives in your beds.

DESDEMONA   O, fie upon thee, slanderer!

IAGO   Nay, it is true, or else I am a Turk:
You rise to play and go to bed to work.   115

EMILIA   You shall not write my praise.

IAGO   No, let me not.

DESDEMONA   What wouldst write of me, if thou shouldst praise
me?

IAGO   O, gentle lady, do not put me to't,
For I am nothing if not critical.

DESDEMONA   Come on, assay. There's one gone to the harbor?   120

IAGO   Ay, madam.

DESDEMONA   I am not merry, but I do beguile
The thing I am by seeming otherwise.—
Come, how wouldst thou praise me?

IAGO   I am about it, but indeed my invention   125
Comes from my pate as birdlime does from frieze:
It plucks out brains and all. But my muse labors,
And thus she is delivered:
If she be fair and wise, fairness and wit,
The one's for use, the other useth it.   130

DESDEMONA   Well praised! How if she be black and witty?

IAGO   *If she be black, and thereto have a wit,*
She'll find a white that shall her blackness fit.

DESDEMONA   Worse and worse!

EMILIA   How if fair and foolish?   135

IAGO   *She never yet was foolish that was fair,*
For even her folly helped her to an heir.

DESDEMONA   These are old fond paradoxes, to make fools
laugh i' th' alehouse. What miserable praise hast thou
for her that's foul and foolish?   140

111. **Saints . . . injuries:** looking innocent of the harms you inflict.
112. **Players . . . huswifery:** indifferent to (faking interest in) domestic responsibilities. **huswives:** pronounced "hussifs"; can slip from neutral ("housewives") to pejorative ("hussies").
114. **I am a Turk:** "I'm a monkey's uncle," but stronger: "turn Turk" (like "go native") evokes anxiety about reverting to the savagery of infidels.
115. **play:** "deceive" and "engage in sport" (sexual innuendo). **work:** i.e., sex is your real and serious interest.
120. **assay:** try.
122–23. **beguile . . . am:** distract myself from worrying about Othello (?); sometimes represented as an aside.
126. **pate:** head. **birdlime:** gummy stuff used to trap birds. **frieze:** coarse fabric.
129. *fair:* blonde and light-complexioned (conventional signs of female beauty at the time). *wit:* intelligence, cunning.
130. **The one . . . it:** attractiveness has value, cleverness cashes it in.
131. **black:** dark-complexioned or dark-haired—hence unattractive.
133. **white:** man (punning on "wight"), fair man (to complement her foul or black identity); center of a target or bull's eye (variously applicable sexual metaphors).
137. *folly:* foolishness, sexual indiscretion.
138–39. **old . . . alehouse:** i.e., trite barroom humor. The italics for Iago's misogynist

IAGO   *There's none so foul and foolish thereunto,*
But does foul pranks which fair and wise ones do.
DESDEMONA   O, heavy ignorance! Thou praisest the worst
best. But what praise couldst thou bestow on a deserving
woman indeed? One that in the authority of her   145
merit did justly put on the vouch of very malice itself.
IAGO   *She that was ever fair, and never proud,*
Had tongue at will, and yet was never loud,
Never lacked gold, and yet went never gay,
Fled from her wish, and yet said "now I may."   150
She that, being angered, her revenge being nigh,
Bade her wrong stay, and her displeasure fly.
She that in wisdom never was so frail
To change the cod's head for the salmon's tail.
She that could think, and ne'er disclose her mind,   155
See suitors following, and not look behind:
She was a wight (if ever such wights were) . . .
DESDEMONA   To do what?
IAGO   *To suckle fools and chronicle small beer.*
DESDEMONA   O, most lame and impotent conclusion! Do   160
not learn of him, Emilia, though he be thy husband.
How say you, Cassio? Is he not a most profane and liberal
counselor?
CASSIO   He speaks home, madam. You may relish
him more in the soldier than in the scholar.   165
IAGO [*Aside*.]   He takes her by the palm. Ay, well said, whisper!
With as little a web as this will I ensnare as great
a fly as Cassio. Ay, smile upon her, do! I will gyve thee
in thine own courtship.—You say true, 'tis so indeed.
—If such tricks as these strip you out of your   170
lieutenantry, it had been better you had not kissed your three

---

jokes, reproduced from the folio text, may signal a stylized delivery—as of familiar comic
routines.
    146. justly put on the vouch: deserve or encourage the approval; the reiterated emphases
("indeed . . . very . . . itself") urge Iago to give over the game for genuine belief.
    149. gay: elegantly dressed.
    150. Fled . . . I may: renounced desire, while knowing herself capable of acting on it.
    152. Bade . . . fly: commanded her (sense of) injury to restrain itself and her irritation to
disappear.
    154. cod's head . . . salmon's tail: unclear, but presumably another example of the self-
restraint exercised by "a deserving woman indeed" (144–45).
    159. To suckle . . . beer: for breeding and trivial domestic chores.
    162. profane and liberal: nasty and unrestrained.
    164. home: bluntly. **relish:** appreciate, take delight in.
    165. more . . . scholar: i.e., more for his directness than for his courtliness.
    166. said: done.
    168. gyve: shackle.
    170. tricks: ritualized gestures—i.e., the kisses Cassio blows to Desdemona.

fingers so oft, which now again you are most apt to play
the sir in. Very good! well kissed and excellent courtesy!
—'Tis so indeed.—Yet again, your fingers to your lips?
Would they were clyster pipes for your sake!   175
Trumpets within.   The Moor! I know his trumpet.
CASSIO   'Tis truly so.
DESDEMONA   Let's meet him and receive him.
CASSIO   Lo, where he comes.

Enter OTHELLO *and Attendants.*

OTHELLO   O, my fair warrior!
DESDEMONA   My dear Othello!   180
OTHELLO   It gives me wonder great as my content
  To see you here before me. O! my soul's joy,
  If after every tempest come such calms,
  May the winds blow till they have wakened death,
  And let the laboring bark climb hills of seas,   185
  Olympus-high, and duck again as low
  As hell's from heaven! If it were now to die,
  'Twere now to be most happy; for I fear
  My soul hath her content so absolute
  That not another comfort like to this   190
  Succeeds in unknown fate.
DESDEMONA   The heavens forbid
  But that our loves and comforts should increase
  Even as our days do grow.
OTHELLO   Amen to that, sweet powers!
  I cannot speak enough of this content;
  It stops me here; it is too much of joy.   195
  And this, and this—

172. **now again:** Either Cassio repeats his courtly gestures with Desdemona, or Iago is
thinking back to Cassio's earlier gentlemanly behavior ("play the sir") in kissing Emilia (98).
  173. **courtesy:** along with "courtship" (169), may echo the "manners" and "breeding" by
which Cassio earlier justified kissing Emilia (98).
  175. **clyster pipes:** used to administer rectal enemas or vaginal douches.
  176. **his trumpet:** the "recognizable call" or "tucket" associated with "distinguished people" (Ridley); also punning on "his strumpet" ("his whore").
  180. **warrior:** remembering her desire to share in "the rites" (1.3.255) of his military
occupation.
  187. **If it were now to die:** if death came to me now; "die" is a common pun for "have
sex."
  191. **succeeds:** follows.
  192. **comforts:** pluralizes Othello's term (190), variously glossed as "satisfaction,"
"delight," "gladness," and "relief (after distress)"; a word loaded with reiterated resonance (cf.
31, 82, and 205).
  194. **content:** another loaded and reiterated word (cf. 181, 189, and 292), with an erotic
charge hard to identify exactly.

They kiss.—

                the greatest discords be
That e'er our hearts shall make!
IAGO [*Aside.*]   O, you are well tuned now;
  But I'll set down the pegs that make this music,
  As honest as I am.
OTHELLO   Come, let us to the castle.
  News, friends; our wars are done. The Turks are drowned.   200
  How does my old acquaintance of this isle?—
  Honey, you shall be well desired in Cyprus;
  I have found great love amongst them. O, my sweet,
  I prattle out of fashion, and I dote
  In mine own comforts. I prithee, good Iago,   205
  Go to the bay and disembark my coffers.
  Bring thou the master to the citadel;
  He is a good one, and his worthiness
  Does challenge much respect. Come, Desdemona;
  Once more well met at Cyprus.   210

          Exit OTHELLO *and* DESDEMONA
          [*and all but* IAGO *and* RODERIGO].

IAGO   Do thou meet me presently at the harbor.
  Come thither. If thou be'st valiant—as they say base men,
  being in love, have then a nobility in their natures
  more than is native to them—list me. The lieutenant
  tonight watches on the court of guard. First I must tell   215
  thee this: Desdemona is directly in love with him.
RODERIGO   With him? Why, 'tis not possible.
IAGO   Lay thy finger thus, and let thy soul be instructed.
  Mark me with what violence she first loved
  the Moor, but for bragging and telling her fantastical   220
  lies. To love him still for prating, let not thy discreet

---

   198. set down the pegs: "slacken (the strings or pegs of a musical instrument)" (Honigmann); hence "untune" and perhaps implying "debase."
   199. As honest as I am: for all my supposed "honesty."
   201. my old acquaintance: addressed to Montano (cf. 35), or acknowledging a more generally communal acquaintanceship.
   202. well desired: sought after with much pleasure.
   204. out of fashion: in an inappropriate manner.
   206. disembark my coffers: unload my trunks.
   207. master: captain.
   209. challenge: command, merit.
   214. list: listen to.
   215. watches on the court of guard: "is on duty with the corps de garde, the patrol assigned to headquarters" (McDonald).
   218. thus: on your lips; i.e., be quiet.
   219. violence: intensity, compare Desdemona's "downright violence" (1.3.247).
   220. but: only, wholly.
   221. discreet: judicious.

heart think it. Her eye must be fed. And what delight
shall she have to look on the devil? When the blood
is made dull with the act of sport, there should be—
again to enflame it, and to give satiety a fresh appetite—   225
loveliness in favor, sympathy in years, manners
and beauties, all which the Moor is defective in. Now
for want of these required conveniences, her delicate
tenderness will find itself abused, begin to heave the
gorge, disrelish and abhor the Moor. Very nature will   230
instruct her in it and compel her to some second choice.
Now, sir, this granted—as it is a most pregnant and unforced
position—who stands so eminent in the degree of
this fortune as Cassio does? a knave very voluble, no
further conscionable than in putting on the mere form   235
of civil and humane seeming for the better compass
of his salt and most hidden loose affection. Why none!
why none! A slipper and subtle knave, a finder of occasion,
that has an eye can stamp and counterfeit advantages,
though true advantage never present itself.   240
A devilish knave! Besides, the knave is handsome, young
and hath all those requisites in him that folly and green
minds look after. A pestilent complete knave! And the
woman hath found him already.

RODERIGO   I cannot believe that in her; she's full of most   245
blessed condition.

IAGO   Blessed fig's-end! The wine she drinks is
made of grapes. If she had been blessed, she would

223. **the devil:** conventionally represented as foul and black.
223–24. **When . . . sport:** when (repeated or habitual) sexual activity jades desire.
226. **loveliness in favor:** good looks. **sympathy:** similarity.
228. **conveniences:** similarities.
228–29. **delicate tenderness:** exquisite sensibility, refined appetite.
229. **abused:** deceived; disappointed.
229–30 **heave the gorge:** vomit.
230. **Very nature:** nature itself, basic instinct.
232–33. **pregnant and unforced position:** self-evident and plausible claim.
233–34. **stands . . . as:** is better positioned to receive the benefits of this situation than.
234. **voluble:** glib, smooth-talking.
234–36. **no . . . seeming:** whose conscience extends only to outward appearances—the manners, not the morals.
236–37. **for . . . affection:** to improve the odds of satisfying his covert lust.
238. **slipper:** slippery. **finder of occasion:** opportunist.
239–40. **has . . . present itself:** can fraudulently manufacture advantages where no real or honest ones exist.
242. **green:** inexperienced.
243. **look after:** covet.
245–46. **full . . . condition:** most divinely virtuous.
247. **Blessed fig's-end:** See 1.3.317 and note.
247–48. **wine . . . grapes:** Continuing to disclaim ideas of religious transcendence, Iago insists that the wine is never transformed into the blood of Christ, as in the sacrament: Desdemona is only human—that is, libidinous.

never have loved the Moor. Blessed pudding! Didst thou
not see her paddle with the palm of his hand? Didst not   250
mark that?

RODERIGO Yes, that I did, but that was but courtesy.

IAGO Lechery, by this hand! an index and obscure
prologue to the history of lust and foul thoughts.
They met so near with their lips that their breaths   255
embraced together. Villainous thoughts, Roderigo: when
these mutualities so marshal the way, hard at hand
comes the master and main exercise, th' incorporate
conclusion. Pish! But, sir, be you ruled by me. I have
brought you from Venice. Watch you tonight. For   260
the command, I'll lay't upon you. Cassio knows you
not. I'll not be far from you. Do you find some occasion
to anger Cassio, either by speaking too loud or
tainting his discipline, or from what other course
you please, which the time shall more favorably minister.   265

RODERIGO Well.

IAGO Sir, he's rash and very sudden in choler and
haply may strike at you. Provoke him that he may; for
even out of that will I cause these of Cyprus to mutiny;
whose qualification shall come into no true taste again   270
but by the displanting of Cassio. So shall you
have a shorter journey to your desires by the means I
shall then have to prefer them, and the impediment
most profitably removed without the which there were
no expectation of our prosperity.   275

RODERIGO I will do this if you can bring it to any opportunity.

IAGO I warrant thee. Meet me by and by at the

---

249. pudding: sausage, blood pudding—continuing to sexualize the spiritual.
250. paddle with: caress. **his hand:** "i.e., Cassio's" (Mowat and Werstine). See 1.3.387–88 and note.
253. index: table of contents. **obscure:** concealed.
254. history: story, narrative.
257–59. mutualities . . . conclusion: reciprocally flirtatious gestures inaugurate a sequence leading irresistibly to full sexual intercourse. **incorporate:** bodily.
259. Pish: an expression of revulsion.
260. Watch you: Join the security patrol.
260–61. For . . . you: I'll arrange for you to have authority.
264. tainting his discipline: impugning his military professionalism; sullying his self-control.
266. Well: Okay.
267. sudden in choler: short-tempered.
268. haply: perhaps.
270–71. whose . . . Cassio: i.e., the only way to restore the populace to sober obedience is by eliminating ("displanting") Cassio. **qualification:** pacification or moderation (with "taste," a drinking metaphor: dilution).
273. prefer: advance.
277. I warrant thee: You have my word.

citadel. I must fetch his necessaries ashore. Farewell.

RODERIGO Adieu.   *Exit.*

IAGO That Cassio loves her, I do well believ't;   280
That she loves him, 'tis apt and of great credit.
The Moor, howbeit that I endure him not,
Is of a constant, loving, noble nature,
And I dare think he'll prove to Desdemona
A most dear husband. Now I do love her too,   285
Not out of absolute lust (though peradventure
I stand accountant for as great a sin),
But partly led to diet my revenge,
For that I do suspect the lusty Moor
Hath leaped into my seat—the thought whereof   290
Doth, like a poisonous mineral, gnaw my inwards,
And nothing can or shall content my soul
Till I am evened with him, wife for wife;
Or failing so, yet that I put the Moor
At least into a jealousy so strong   295
That judgment cannot cure; which thing to do,
If this poor trash of Venice, whom I trace
For his quick hunting, stand the putting on,
I'll have our Michael Cassio on the hip,
Abuse him to the Moor in the right garb   300
(For I fear Cassio with my nightcap too),
Make the Moor thank me, love me and reward me
For making him egregiously an ass,
And practicing upon his peace and quiet
Even to madness. 'Tis here, but yet confused;   305
Knavery's plain face is never seen till used.   *Exit.*

---

278. **his:** "i.e., Othello's" (Mowat and Werstine). See 1.3.387–88 and note.
281. **apt . . . credit:** likely and very plausible.
282. **howbeit that:** although.
287. **stand accountant for:** may be accused of.
288. **diet:** feed.
290. **leaped . . . seat:** i.e., "jumped" my wife.
291. **gnaw my inwards:** eat my guts.
297–98. **trace . . . hunting:** pursue in order to goad to an even faster (sexual) chase.
298. **stand the putting on:** is up to my incitement.
299. **on the hip:** in my power (a wrestling term).
300. **Abuse . . . garb:** slander him in an appropriate (effective) fashion.
301. **with my nightcap:** "wearing my pajamas"—i.e., doing my bedroom job.
303. **egregiously an ass:** extremely foolish.
304. **practicing upon:** plotting against.
305. **Even to madness:** i.e., not stopping until Othello is mad (elliptical; the literal sense may suggest that the madness belongs to Iago's intention rather than effect).
305–06. **'Tis here . . . till used:** i.e., I'm not sure how this will work, but villains never know what they're doing until they're actually doing it.

ACT 2 SCENE 2

Enter OTHELLO's HERALD *with a proclamation.*

HERALD [*Reads.*]   "It is Othello's pleasure, our noble and
    valiant
general, that upon certain tidings now arrived
importing the mere perdition of the Turkish fleet,
every man put himself into triumph—some to dance,
some to make bonfires, each man to what sport and   5
revels his addition leads him. For besides these beneficial
news, it is the celebration of his nuptial." So
much was his pleasure should be proclaimed. All offices
are open, and there is full liberty of feasting from this
present hour of five till the bell have told eleven. Heaven   10
bless the isle of Cyprus and our noble general Othello!   *Exit.*

[ACT 2 SCENE 3]

Enter OTHELLO, DESDEMONA, CASSIO, *and Attendants.*

OTHELLO   Good Michael, look you to the guard tonight.
    Let's teach ourselves that honorable stop,
    Not to outsport discretion.
CASSIO   Iago hath direction what to do;
    But notwithstanding, with my personal eye   5
    Will I look to't.
OTHELLO   Iago is most honest.
    Michael, goodnight. Tomorrow with your earliest
    Let me have speech with you.—Come, my dear love.
    The purchase made, the fruits are to ensue,
    That profit's yet to come 'tween me and you.   10
    Goodnight.   *Exit* [OTHELLO, DESDEMONA *and Attendants*].

                                          Enter IAGO.

CASSIO   Welcome, Iago; we must to the watch.
IAGO   Not this hour, lieutenant; 'tis not yet ten o'th' clock.
    Our general cast us thus early for the love of his Desdemona,

---

3. **mere perdition:** complete loss.
4. **put . . . triumph:** celebrate.
6. **his addition leads him:** is appropriate to his status.
8. **offices:** kitchens.
10. **told:** tolled.
1. **look you to:** supervise.
2. **honorable stop:** commendable restraint.
3. **outsport discretion:** celebrate beyond self-possession.
7. **with your earliest:** as early as possible.
13. **cast:** got rid of, dismissed.

who let us not therefore blame: he hath not yet made wanton 15
the night with her, and she is sport for Jove.

CASSIO She's a most exquisite lady.

IAGO And, I'll warrant her, full of game.

CASSIO Indeed, she's a most fresh and delicate creature.

IAGO What an eye she has! Methinks it sounds a parley to
provocation. 20

CASSIO An inviting eye; and yet, methinks, right modest.

IAGO And when she speaks, is it not an alarum to love?

CASSIO She is indeed perfection.

IAGO Well, happiness to their sheets! Come, lieutenant,
I have a stoup of wine, and here without are a 25
brace of Cyprus gallants that would fain have a measure
to the health of black Othello.

CASSIO Not tonight, good Iago. I have very poor
and unhappy brains for drinking. I could well wish
courtesy would invent some other custom of entertainment. 30

IAGO O, they are our friends; but one cup; I'll
drink for you.

CASSIO I have drunk but one cup tonight, and that
was craftily qualified too; and behold what innovation
it makes here. I am unfortunate in the infirmity and 35
dare not task my weakness with any more.

IAGO What, man! 'Tis a night of revels—the gallants
desire it.

CASSIO Where are they?

IAGO Here at the door; I pray you call them in. 40

CASSIO I'll do't, but it dislikes me.   *Exit.*

IAGO If I can fasten but one cup upon him
With that which he hath drunk tonight already,
He'll be as full of quarrel and offense
As my young mistress' dog. Now my sick fool, Roderigo, 45
Whom love hath turned almost the wrong side out,

manipulation (margin)

13–15. **thus early** and **not yet:** Iago's phrases put a different spin on Othello's "earliest"
(7) and "yet to come" (10).
18–19. **game:** can mean "spirit" but carries a nasty sexual innuendo, which Cassio's agreement ("Indeed") suggests he does not (or pretends not to) understand.
20–23. **parley** and **alarum:** military signals; i.e., Desdemona solicits sexual advances.
25. **stoup:** "tankard (of varying sizes)" (Honigmann); "large drinking vessel" (Mowat and
Werstine). **without:** outside.
26. **brace:** couple. **have a measure:** drink.
29. **unhappy:** unfortunate.
30. **courtesy . . . entertainment:** social convention determined some other form of celebration.
34. **craftily qualified:** carefully diluted.
34–35. **behold . . . here:** Cassio points to some sign of transformation ("innovation"),
perhaps his unsteady legs.
41. **it dislikes me:** I'd prefer not.
45. **my young mistress':** referring generically (= "milady's") to a girl's untrained dog.

To Desdemona hath tonight caroused
Potations pottle-deep; and he's to watch.
Three else of Cyprus (noble swelling spirits,
That hold their honors in a wary distance,   50
The very elements of this warlike isle)
Have I tonight flustered with flowing cups,
And they watch too. Now, 'mongst this flock of drunkards
Am I to put our Cassio in some action
That may offend the isle. But here they come.   55

        Enter CASSIO, MONTANO *and Gentlemen* [*with wine*].

If consequence do but approve my dream,
My boat sails freely, both with wind and stream.
CASSIO   'Fore God, they have given me a rouse already.
MONTANO   Good faith, a little one; not past a pint, as I am a
    soldier.   60
IAGO   Some wine, ho!

                                              [*Sings.*]

        And let me the cannikin clink, clink,
        And let me the cannikin clink.
        A soldier's a man,
        O man's life's but a span,   65
        Why then, let a soldier drink.

    Some wine, boys!
CASSIO   'Fore God, an excellent song!
IAGO   I learned it in England, where indeed they are
    most potent in potting. Your Dane, your Germans,   70
    and your swag-bellied Hollander—drink, ho!—are
    nothing to your English.
CASSIO   Is your Englishman so exquisite in his drinking?
IAGO   Why, he drinks you with facility your Dane
    dead drunk. He sweats not to overthrow your Almaine.   75

47–48. caroused . . . deep: drunk full glasses.
49. else: others. swelling: puffed up, ambitious.
50. hold . . . distance: i.e., are careful to protect—and thus aggressive in countering any threat to—reputation.
51. very elements . . . isle: i.e., they capture the essential edginess of the Cypriot situation.
56. consequence . . . dream: matters proceed as I hope.
58. rouse: drink.
62. cannikin: "small drinking can; -kin is diminutive" (Honigmann).
65. but a span: short.
70. most potent in potting: big drinkers.
71. swag-bellied: fat-gutted, beer-bellied.
70–71. Your . . . your . . . your: i.e., the typical Dane et al.
73. exquisite: refined. Cassio sees drinking as a courtly accomplishment.
75. your Almaine: i.e., the typical German.

He gives your Hollander a vomit ere the next
pottle can be filled.
CASSIO   To the health of our general!
MONTANO   I am for it, lieutenant, and I'll do you justice.
IAGO   O sweet England!   80

[*Sings.*]

    King Stephen was and-a worthy peer,
      His breeches cost him but a crown;
    He held them sixpence all too dear,
      With that he called the tailor lown.
    He was a wight of high renown,   85
      And thou art but of low degree;
    'Tis pride that pulls the country down,
      And take thy auld cloak about thee.

Some wine, ho!
CASSIO   'Fore God, this is a more exquisite song than the other.   90
IAGO   Will you hear't again?
CASSIO   No, for I hold him to be unworthy of his place
that does those things. Well, God's above all, and
there be souls must be saved, and there be souls must
not be saved.   95
IAGO   It's true, good lieutenant.
CASSIO   For mine own part—no offense to the general,
nor any man of quality—I hope to be saved.
IAGO   And so do I too, lieutenant.
CASSIO   Ay; but by your leave, not before me. The   100
lieutenant is to be saved before the ancient. Let's have
no more of this. Let's to our affairs. God forgive us our
sins. Gentlemen, let's look to our business. Do not
think, gentlemen, I am drunk. This is my ancient, this
is my right hand, and this is my left. I am not drunk   105
now. I can stand well enough, and I speak well enough.
GENTLEMAN   Excellent well.
CASSIO   Why, very well then. You must not think, then,
that I am drunk.   *Exit.*
MONTANO   To th' platform, masters; come, let's set the   110

---

79. **I am . . . justice:** I'll drink to that, and I'll match you glass for glass.
81–88. Adapted from an early ballad, "retaining the character of the original"—its "impatience with privilege" and " 'class' feeling. We may assume that Shakespeare's audience was
familiar with the ballad" (Honigmann).
84. **lown:** rogue.
88. **auld:** old.
92–93. **unworthy . . . things:** The referent for "those things" is unclear. Cassio's indefinite anxiety about self-betrayal resonates again in allusions, just following, to sin, forgiveness,
and salvation.

watch.   [*Exeunt some Gentlemen.*]

IAGO [*Detains* MONTANO.]   You see this fellow that is gone before:
  He's a soldier fit to stand by Caesar
  And give direction. And do but see his vice:
  'Tis to his virtue a just equinox,   115
  The one as long as th' other. 'Tis pity of him;
  I fear the trust Othello puts him in
  On some odd time of his infirmity
  Will shake this island.

MONTANO   But is he often thus?

IAGO   'Tis evermore his prologue to his sleep.   120
  He'll watch the horologe a double set
  If drink rock not his cradle.

MONTANO   It were well
  The general were put in mind of it.
  Perhaps he sees it not, or his good nature
  Prizes the virtue that appears in Cassio   125
  And looks not on his evils. Is not this true?

Enter RODERIGO.

IAGO [*Aside.*]   How now, Roderigo?
  I pray you after the lieutenant—go!   *Exit* RODERIGO.

MONTANO   And 'tis great pity that the noble Moor
  Should hazard such a place as his own second   130
  With one of an ingraft infirmity.
  It were an honest action to say so
  To the Moor.

IAGO   Not I, for this fair island.
  I do love Cassio well and would do much
  To cure him of this evil. But hark, what noise?   135

Enter CASSIO *pursuing* RODERIGO.

CASSIO   Zounds, you rogue! you rascal!

MONTANO   What's the matter, lieutenant?

CASSIO   A knave teach me my duty? I'll beat the knave into a
  twiggen bottle.

---

   115. **just equinox:** exact counterpart (like day and night at the equinox).
   117. **I fear . . . him in:** "The construction makes the pronoun *him* ambiguous in reference": if to Cassio, "trust" = position of authority; if to Othello, "trust" = "the state of
confidence Othello puts himself in" (Ross). See 1.3.387–88 and note.
   119. **shake this island:** produce general mayhem.
   121. **watch . . . double set:** stay up for two rounds of the clock—twenty-four hours.
   130. **second:** deputy, lieutenant.
   131. **ingraft:** "grown to be part of him" as "a shoot becomes part of the plant to which it
is grafted" (Mowat and Werstine).
   139. **twiggen:** wicker-covered; Cassio will leave a grid of welts on Roderigo.

RODERIGO   Beat me?   140
CASSIO   Dost thou prate, rogue?   [*Attacks* RODERIGO.]
MONTANO   Nay, good lieutenant! I pray you, sir, hold your hand.
CASSIO   Let me go, sir, or I'll knock you o'er the mazzard.
MONTANO   Come, come; you're drunk!
CASSIO   Drunk?   [CASSIO *and* MONTANO *fight.*] 145
IAGO [*Aside to* RODERIGO.]   Away, I say! Go out and cry a mutiny.
                                                    [*Exit* RODERIGO.]
    Nay, good lieutenant! God's will, gentlemen!
    Help ho! Lieutenant! Sir Montano!
    Help, masters! Here's a goodly watch indeed!   *A bell rung.*
    Who's that which rings the bell? Diablo, ho!   150
    The town will rise. God's will, lieutenant, hold!
    You'll be ashamed forever.

                          Enter OTHELLO *and Attendants.*

OTHELLO   What is the matter here?
MONTANO   Zounds, I bleed still; I am hurt to th' death.   [*Attacks*
                                                         CASSIO.]
    He dies.
OTHELLO   Hold, for your lives!   155
IAGO   Hold, ho! Lieutenant—sir—Montano—gentlemen!
    Have you forgot all place of sense and duty?
    Hold! The general speaks to you. Hold, for shame!
✱OTHELLO   Why, how now, ho? From whence ariseth this?
    Are we turned Turks? and to ourselves do that   160
    Which heaven hath forbid the Ottomites?
    For Christian shame, put by this barbarous brawl!
    He that stirs next, to carve for his own rage,
    Holds his soul light; he dies upon his motion.
    Silence that dreadful bell—it frights the isle   165
    From her propriety. What is the matter, masters?
    Honest Iago, that looks dead with grieving,
    Speak. Who began this? On thy love, I charge thee.

---

143. **mazzard:** head.
150. **the bell:** Roderigo has sounded the alarm, as Iago commanded. **Diablo:** devil.
160. **turned Turks:** the proverbial anxiety of reverting to the savagery of infidels (see 2.1.114 and note).
160–61. **to . . . Ottomites:** i.e., doing to ourselves what God prevented the Turks from doing to us; may allude to the widespread self-criticism of the time that Muslims were better unified than Christians.
163. **carve for his own rage:** feed his own anger.
164. **Holds . . . light:** is indifferent to the prospect of damnation.
166. **propriety:** true or appropriately peaceful condition.

IAGO   I do not know. Friends all, but now, even now.
　　In quarter and in terms like bride and groom   170
　　Divesting them for bed; and then, but now,
　　As if some planet had unwitted men,
　　Swords out and tilting one at other's breasts
　　In opposition bloody. I cannot speak
　　Any beginning to this peevish odds,   175
　　And would in action glorious I had lost
　　Those legs that brought me to a part of it.
OTHELLO   How comes it, Michael, you are thus forgot?
CASSIO   I pray you pardon me; I cannot speak.
OTHELLO   Worthy Montano, you were wont to be civil;   180
　　The gravity and stillness of your youth
　　The world hath noted, and your name is great
　　In mouths of wisest censure. What's the matter
　　That you unlace your reputation thus
　　And spend your rich opinion for the name   185
　　Of a night brawler? Give me answer to it.
MONTANO   Worthy Othello, I am hurt to danger.
　　Your officer, Iago, can inform you—
　　While I spare speech, which something now offends me—
　　Of all that I do know; nor know I aught   190
　　By me that's said or done amiss this night,
　　Unless self-charity be sometimes a vice,
　　And to defend ourselves it be a sin
　　When violence assails us.
OTHELLO   Now, by heaven,
　　My blood begins my safer guides to rule,   195
　　And passion, having my best judgment collied,
　　Assays to lead the way. Zounds, if I stir
　　Or do but lift this arm, the best of you

[margin note: Silence]

---

169.   **Friends . . . even now:** Honigmann detects a "cheeky" innuendo about what Othello and Desdemona were presumably doing "now, even now"; cf. "Even now, now, very now" (1.1.85).
170.   **In quarter and in terms:** i.e., acting and speaking.
172.   **some planet . . . men:** subject to some maddening supernatural force.
173.   **tilting . . . other's:** charging or thrusting at one another's; a (sexualized) metaphor from knightly combat.
174–75.   **I cannot . . . odds:** I don't know how this senseless quarrel began.
182–83.   **your name . . . censure:** your reputation is high among the most judicious.
184–85.   **unlace . . . opinion:** loosen the strings of (the purse containing the money of) your good name.
187.   **to danger:** seriously, critically.
189.   **something now offends:** i.e., is somewhat difficult.
192.   **self-charity:** looking to one's own needs.
195.   **blood:** anger. **safer guides:** more reliable (rational) faculties.
196.   **collied:** blackened (with coal); thus eclipsed or diminished.

Shall sink in my rebuke. Give me to know
How this foul rout began, who set it on;   200
And he that is approved in this offense,
Though he had twinned with me, both at a birth,
Shall lose me. What! in a town of war,
Yet wild, the people's hearts brimful of fear,
To manage private and domestic quarrel?   205
In night, and on the court and guard of safety?
'Tis monstrous. Iago, who began't?
MONTANO   If partially affined, or league[d] in office,
Thou dost deliver more or less than truth,
Thou art no soldier.
IAGO   Touch me not so near.   210
I had rather have this tongue cut from my mouth
Than it should do offense to Michael Cassio;
Yet I persuade myself to speak the truth
Shall nothing wrong him. This it is, general:
Montano and myself being in speech,   215
There comes a fellow crying out for help,
And Cassio following him with determined sword
To execute upon him. Sir, this gentleman
Steps in to Cassio and entreats his pause;
Myself the crying fellow did pursue,   220
Lest by his clamor—as it so fell out—
The town might fall in fright. He, swift of foot,
Outran my purpose; and I returned then rather
For that I heard the clink and fall of swords
And Cassio high in oath, which till tonight   225
I ne'er might say before. When I came back—
For this was brief—I found them close together
At blow and thrust, even as again they were
When you yourself did part them.

199. **sink in my rebuke:** fall in my chastisement.
200. **rout:** brawl. **set it on:** instigated it.
201. **approved:** proven to be guilty.
203. **lose me:** be deprived of my favor or regard. **of war:** in a state of military alert—cf. "this warlike isle" (51).
205. **manage:** engage in.
206. **night:** i.e., the most dangerous time. **court . . . safety:** the area where security is most necessary (see note to 2.1.215).
208. **partially . . . office:** biased as a result of personal or military connection (to Cassio).
210. **Touch . . . near:** Don't impugn my military discipline.
217. **determined:** "transferred epithet: Cassio was determined" (Honigmann; see note on "delighted," 1.3.287).
218. **execute upon:** act (perhaps lethally) against.
221. **so fell out:** in fact happened.
224. **fall:** downward stroke.
225. **high in oath:** raging profanely.

More of this matter cannot I report.   230
But men are men: the best sometimes forget.
Though Cassio did some little wrong to him,
As men in rage strike those that wish them best,
Yet surely Cassio, I believe, received
From him that fled some strange indignity   235
Which patience could not pass.

OTHELLO   I know, Iago,
Thy honesty and love doth mince this matter,
Making it light to Cassio. Cassio, I love thee,
But never more be officer of mine.—

Enter DESDEMONA *attended.*

Look if my gentle love be not raised up!—   240
I'll make thee an example.

DESDEMONA   What is the matter, dear?

OTHELLO   All's well, sweeting;
Come away to bed. [*To* MONTANO.]   Sir, for your hurts
Myself will be your surgeon. Lead him off.   [MONTANO *is led
off.*]

Iago, look with care about the town,   245
And silence those whom this vile brawl distracted.
Come, Desdemona; 'tis the soldier's life
To have their balmy slumbers waked with strife.

Exit MOOR, DESDEMONA *and Attendants.*

IAGO   What, are you hurt, lieutenant?

CASSIO   Ay, past all surgery.   250

IAGO   Marry, God forbid!

CASSIO   Reputation, reputation, reputation! O, I have
lost my reputation! I have lost the immortal part of
myself, and what remains is bestial. My reputation,
Iago, my reputation!   255

IAGO   As I am an honest man, I had thought you had
received some bodily wound; there is more sense in that
than in reputation. Reputation is an idle and most false
imposition, oft got without merit and lost without deserving.
You have lost no reputation at all, unless you   260

---

235. **strange indignity:** outlandish insult.
236. **pass:** ignore.
242. **sweeting:** sweetheart.
246. **distracted:** alarmed.
257. **sense:** "(1) feeling; (2) reason (for being concerned)" (Mowat and Werstine).
258. **idle:** useless, inconsequential.
259. **imposition:** extraneous addition.

repute yourself such a loser. What, man! there are
more ways to recover the general again. You are
but now cast in his mood, a punishment more in policy
than in malice, even so as one would beat his offenseless
dog to affright an imperious lion. Sue to   265
him again, and he's yours.

CASSIO   I will rather sue to be despised than to deceive
so good a commander with so slight, so drunken and so
indiscreet an officer. Drunk? And speak parrot? And
squabble? Swagger? Swear? And discourse fustian   270
with one's own shadow? O, thou invisible spirit of
wine! if thou hast no name to be known by, let us call
thee devil.

IAGO   What was he that you followed with your
sword? What had he done to you?   275

CASSIO   I know not.

IAGO   Is't possible?

CASSIO   I remember a mass of things, but nothing distinctly;
a quarrel, but nothing wherefore. O God! that
men should put an enemy in their mouths to steal away   280
their brains! that we should with joy, pleasance,
revel and applause transform ourselves into beasts!

IAGO   Why, but you are now well enough. How
came you thus recovered?

CASSIO   It hath pleased the devil drunkenness to give   285
place to the devil wrath; one unperfectness shows me
another, to make me frankly despise myself.

IAGO   Come, you are too severe a moraler. As the
time, the place and the condition of this country stands,
I could heartily wish this had not befallen; but since it is as   290
it is, mend it for your own good.

CASSIO   I will ask him for my place again, he shall tell
me I am a drunkard. Had I as many mouths as Hydra,

262. **recover the general:** get back into Othello's good graces.
263. **but now . . . mood:** dismissed in a mere fit of pique.
263–64. **more . . . malice:** motivated more by strategy than ill will.
264–65. **beat . . . lion:** i.e., making an example to establish authority (proverbial); "the 'lion' is either the Venetian army or the Cypriots" (Honigmann).
265. **Sue:** appeal.
269–70. **And speak . . . fustian:** Cassio twice charges himself with talking nonsense ("speak parrot" and "discourse fustian") and twice with picking fights ("squabble" and "swagger").
279. **wherefore:** about why it started.
281–82. **joy . . . applause:** presumably, the conventional social sanctions he worried about earlier (30).
286. **unperfectness:** imperfection.
287. **frankly:** unreservedly.
292. **I will ask:** if I were to ask.
293. **Hydra:** many-headed beast of ancient mythology.

such an answer would stop them all. To be now a sensible
man, by and by a fool, and presently a beast!—O,   295
strange! Every inordinate cup is unblessed, and the ingredient
is a devil.

IAGO   Come, come; good wine is a good familiar
creature if it be well used. Exclaim no more against it.
And, good lieutenant, I think you think I love you.   300

CASSIO   I have well approved it, sir: I drunk!

IAGO   You or any man living may be drunk at a
time, man. I tell you what you shall do. Our general's
wife is now the general. I may say so in this respect,
for that he hath devoted and given up himself to the   305
contemplation, mark and devotement of her parts
and graces. Confess yourself freely to her; importune
her help to put you in your place again. She is
of so free, so kind, so apt, so blessed a disposition,
she holds it a vice in her goodness not to do more   310
than she is requested. This broken joint between
you and her husband entreat her to splinter, and my
fortunes against any lay worth naming, this crack of
your love shall grow stronger than it was before.

CASSIO   You advise me well.   315

IAGO   I protest, in the sincerity of love and honest
kindness.

CASSIO   I think it freely; and betimes in the morning
I will beseech the virtuous Desdemona to undertake
for me. I am desperate of my fortunes if they check me.   320

IAGO   You are in the right. Good night, lieutenant; I
must to the watch.

CASSIO   Good night, honest Iago.   *Exit* CASSIO.

---

294. stop: put a plug (or stopper) on; silence.
295. presently: soon.
296. inordinate: excessive. **unblessed:** damned.
298. familiar: friendly or natural (disagreeing with Cassio's "strange"); also punning on a "familiar" as an evil spirit.
301. approved . . . drunk: demonstrated it by (taking your advice and) drinking.
303–04. Our . . . general: Desdemona commands Othello.
306. contemplation . . . devotement: three ways of describing rapt attention, suggesting that Othello has surrendered ("given up himself") to uxorious obsession. **parts:** natural gifts or qualities (cf. 1.2.31 and 1.3.251), but the sexual meaning is irresistible.
307. graces: charms, virtues.
309. apt: fit; likely to respond favorably (to your request).
312. splinter: set with a splint.
313. lay: bet. **crack of:** fracture in.
314. shall grow . . . before: based on proverbial lore about healed fractures; literally, Iago's words claim that the break will grow stronger.
316. protest: declare.
318. freely: without qualification. **betimes:** early.
319–20. undertake for me: take up my cause.
320. desperate of: in despair about. **check:** block.
321. in the right: correct; justified in your appeal.

IAGO   And what's he then that says I play the villain,
When this advice is free I give and honest,   325
Probal to thinking, and indeed the course
To win the Moor again? For 'tis most easy
Th' inclining Desdemona to subdue
In any honest suit: she's framed as fruitful
As the free elements; and then for her   330
To win the Moor, were't to renounce his baptism,
All seals and symbols of redeemèd sin,
His soul is so enfettered to her love
That she may make, unmake, do what she list,   *Silrloquy*
Even as her appetite shall play the god   335
With his weak function. How am I then a villain
To counsel Cassio to this parallel course
Directly to his good? Divinity of hell!
When devils will the blackest sins put on,
They do suggest at first with heavenly shows,   340
As I do now. For whiles this honest fool
Plies Desdemona to repair his fortune,
And she for him pleads strongly to the Moor,
I'll pour this pestilence into his ear:
That she repeals him for her body's lust,   345
And by how much she strives to do him good,
She shall undo her credit with the Moor.
So will I turn her virtue into pitch,
And out of her own goodness make the net,
That shall enmesh them all.
Enter RODERIGO.   How now, Roderigo?   350
RODERIGO   I do follow here in the chase, not
like a hound that hunts, but one that fills up the
cry. My money is almost spent; I have been tonight

326. **probal to thinking:** plausible when scrutinized.
328. **Th' inclining . . . subdue:** to get the compliant Desdemona to yield.
329–30. **framed . . . elements:** as generously disposed "as the unrestrained elements . . . to be used" (Honigmann).
331. **win:** convince.
332. **seals . . . sin:** guarantees and outward manifestations (like baptism and the other sacraments) of redemption from sin; another transferred epithet (see 217 and note).
333. **enfettered . . . love:** chained to his love for her or hers for him (or both).
334. **list:** pleases.
335–36. **her appetite . . . function:** either his desire for her or her lust for power (or both) will enjoy absolute control over his diminished judgment.
337. **parallel:** "*level* and *even with his design*" (Johnson).
338. **Divinity of hell!:** infernal theology—i.e., wicked goodness; Iago abruptly abandons his (now clearly hypocritical) denial of villainous designs.
342. **Plies:** repeatedly solicits.
344. **pestilence:** poison.
345. **repeals him:** seeks his reinstatement.
348. **pitch:** "black, malodorous, and extremely sticky" and "thus the perfect substance" to " 'enmesh' his victims" (Mowat and Werstine).
353. **cry:** trailing pack.

exceedingly well cudgelled; and I think the issue
will be I shall have so much experience for my pains,   355
and so, with no money at all, and a little more wit, return
again to Venice.

IAGO   How poor are they that have not patience!
What wound did ever heal but by degrees?
Thou know'st we work by wit and not by witchcraft,   360
And wit depends on dilatory time.
Does't not go well? Cassio hath beaten thee,
And thou by that small hurt hath cashiered Cassio.
Though other things grow fair against the sun,
Yet fruits that blossom first will first be ripe.   365
Content thyself awhile. By the mass, 'tis morning!
Pleasure and action make the hours seem short.
Retire thee; go where thou art billeted.
Away! I say; thou shalt know more hereafter.
Nay, get thee gone!   *Exit* RODERIGO.
                        Two things are to be done: 370
My wife must move for Cassio to her mistress—
I'll set her on—
Myself a while to draw the Moor apart
And bring him jump when he may Cassio find
Soliciting his wife. Ay, that's the way!   375
Dull not device by coldness and delay.   *Exit.*

Knows what to say

ACT 3 SCENE 1

Enter CASSIO, *Musicians and* CLOWN.

CASSIO   Masters, play here—I will content your pains—
Something that's brief; and bid, "Good morrow, general."

354. exceedingly well cudgelled: very badly beaten. issue: result.
355. so much: (only) this much. pains: efforts (with a pun).
361. dilatory: gradually unfolding; like his denial of witchcraft, an intriguing echo of Othello's speech to the senate (see 1.3.152 and 168).
363. cashiered: got dismissed.
364–65. Though . . . ripe: "sound like proverbs that ought to persuade Roderigo . . . but the lines themselves are obscure" (Mowat and Werstine).
367. Pleasure and action: can evoke sexual and/or military affairs, devising and/or implementing plots. make . . . short: i.e., "time flies when you're having fun."
368. billeted: lodged.
371. move: petition, plead.
373. a while: meanwhile.
374. jump: right at the very moment.
376. Dull not . . . delay: i.e., let's keep it quick and hot; device: "plot, stratagem; pleasure, desire" (Honigmann).
1. content your pains: reward your efforts.
2. Good morrow, general: "the traditional *aubade*: to wake bride and groom after the wedding night" (Honigmann).

CLOWN Why, masters, have your instruments been in Naples,
that they speak i'th' nose thus?

MUSICIAN How, sir? how?   5

CLOWN Are these, I pray you, wind instruments?

MUSICIAN Ay, marry, are they, sir.

CLOWN O, thereby hangs a tale!

MUSICIAN Whereby hangs a tale, sir?

CLOWN Marry, sir, by many a wind instrument that I   10
know. But, masters, here's money for you; and the general
so likes your music that he desires you for love's
sake to make no more noise with it.

MUSICIAN Well, sir, we will not.

CLOWN If you have any music that may not be heard,   15
to't again. But, as they say, to hear music the general
does not greatly care.

MUSICIAN We have none such, sir.

CLOWN Then put up your pipes in your bag, for I'll
away. Go! Vanish into air, away!   *Exit Musicians.*   20

CASSIO Dost thou hear, mine honest friend?

CLOWN No, I hear not your honest friend:
I hear you.

CASSIO Prithee keep up thy quillets. There's a poor
piece of gold for thee. If the gentlewoman that attends   25
the general be stirring, tell her there's one Cassio
entreats her a little favor of speech. Wilt thou do this?

CLOWN She is stirring, sir. If she will stir hither, I shall
seem to notify unto her.

CASSIO Do, good my friend.   *Exit CLOWN.*

  Enter IAGO.   In happy time, Iago.   30

IAGO You have not been abed then?

CASSIO Why, no; the day had broke before we parted.
I have made bold, Iago, to send in to your wife.

---

3. SPEECH PREFIX CLOWN: See note 12 to the Names of the Actors at the beginning
of the play.

3–10. **your instruments . . . wind instrument:** an explosion of sexual and scatological
puns. Men whose (sexual) instruments visit Naples contract syphilis, usually designated a
French or Italian disease ("the Neapolitan bone-ache," *Troilus and Cressida* 2.3.15–16), and
wind up losing their noses. "Wind" as flatulence introduces jokes about anality, sodomy, and
bestiality; "tale" puns on "tail," which suggests "penis."

18. **none such:** "perhaps a quibble: 'Nonesuch' was the name of a popular tune" (Honigmann).

24. **Prithee . . . quillets:** i.e., please, no more puns.

25–26. **the gentlewoman . . . general:** Emilia, who in serving Desdemona serves Othello
as well (see 4.2.103).

26. **stirring:** awake.

28. **stirring:** sexually appealing.

29. **seem to notify unto her:** inform her (mocking Cassio's elaborate courtliness).

30. **In happy time:** i.e., "just the man I want to see."

My suit to her is that she will to virtuous Desdemona
Procure me some access.

IAGO   I'll send her to you presently;   35
And I'll devise a mean to draw the Moor
Out of the way, that your converse and business
May be more free.

CASSIO   I humbly thank you for't.   *Exit* [IAGO].
                              I never knew
A Florentine more kind and honest.   40

                              Enter EMILIA.

EMILIA   Good morrow, good lieutenant. I am sorry
For your displeasure, but all will sure be well.
The general and his wife are talking of it,
And she speaks for you stoutly. The Moor replies
That he you hurt is of great fame in Cyprus   45
And great affinity, and that in wholesome wisdom
He might not but refuse you; but he protests he loves you
And needs no other suitor but his likings
To bring you in again.

CASSIO   Yet I beseech you,
If you think fit, or that it may be done,   50
Give me advantage of some brief discourse
With Desdemon alone.

EMILIA   Pray you come in.
I will bestow you where you shall have time
To speak your bosom freely.

CASSIO   I am much bound to you.   *Exit.*

ACT 3 SCENE 2

Enter OTHELLO, IAGO, *and Gentlemen.*

OTHELLO   These letters give, Iago, to the pilot,
And by him do my duties to the Senate.

---

35. **presently:** right away.
36. **a mean:** an occasion.
40. **A Florentine:** "even in one of my own countrymen" (Malone).
44. **stoutly:** "vigorously (stronger than today)" (Honigmann).
45–46. **of great . . . affinity:** well respected and well connected.
46. **wholesome wisdom:** healthy judgment; i.e., common sense or solicitude for the general good.
47. **might not but:** has to.
48. **And needs . . . likings:** "i.e., his own inclination would be sufficient by itself" (McDonald).
49. **bring you in again:** reinstate you.
54. **bosom:** inmost thoughts.
2. **by him . . . duties:** through him pay my respects.

That done, I will be walking on the works;
Repair there to me.
IAGO   Well, my good lord; I'll do't.
OTHELLO   This fortification, gentlemen, shall we see't?   5
GENTLEMAN   We'll wait upon your lordship.   *Exeunt.*

ACT 3 SCENE 3

Enter DESDEMONA, CASSIO, *and* EMILIA.

DESDEMONA   Be thou assured, good Cassio, I will do
All my abilities in thy behalf.
EMILIA   Good madam, do. I warrant it grieves my husband
As if the cause were his.
DESDEMONA   O, that's an honest fellow. Do not doubt, Cassio,   5
But I will have my lord and you again
As friendly as you were.
CASSIO   Bounteous madam,
Whatever shall become of Michael Cassio,
He's never anything but your true servant.
DESDEMONA   I know't; I thank you. You do love my lord;   10
You have known him long; and be you well assured
He shall in strangeness stand no farther off
Than in a politic distance.
CASSIO   Ay, but, lady,
That policy may either last so long,
Or feed upon such nice and waterish diet,   15
Or breed itself so out of circumstances,
That—I being absent, and my place supplied—
My general will forget my love and service.
DESDEMONA   Do not doubt that. Before Emilia here,
I give thee warrant of thy place. Assure thee,   20
If I do vow a friendship, I'll perform it
To the last article. My lord shall never rest:
I'll watch him tame and talk him out of patience;

---

3. works: fortifications.
4. Repair: come.
12–13. shall . . . politic distance: will keep only a strategic aloofness.
14. policy: i.e., tactical delay, intending eventual restoration of Cassio.
15. nice and waterish: finicky and thin.
16. breed: reproduce. **circumstances:** trivialities.
17. place supplied: position occupied.
19. doubt: fear.
20. give thee warrant of: guarantee.
23. watch him tame: "Hawks and other birds are tamed by keeping them from sleep"
(Steevens). **talk . . . patience:** keep talking to him about it until he loses patience.

His bed shall seem a school, his board a shrift;
I'll intermingle everything he does   25
With Cassio's suit. Therefore be merry, Cassio,
For thy solicitor shall rather die
Than give thy cause away.

                                        Enter OTHELLO *and* IAGO.

EMILIA   Madam, here comes my lord.
CASSIO   Madam, I'll take my leave.   30
DESDEMONA   Why, stay and hear me speak.
CASSIO   Madam, not now: I am very ill at ease,
    Unfit for mine own purposes.
DESDEMONA   Well, do your discretion.   *Exit Cassio.*
IAGO   Ha? I like not that.
OTHELLO   What dost thou say?   35
IAGO   Nothing, my lord; or if . . . I know not what.
OTHELLO   Was not that Cassio parted from my wife?
IAGO   Cassio, my lord? No, sure, I cannot think it
    That he would steal away so guilty-like,
    Seeing your coming.
OTHELLO   I do believe 'twas he.   40
DESDEMONA   How now, my lord?
    I have been talking with a suitor here,
    A man that languishes in your displeasure.
OTHELLO   Who is't you mean?
DESDEMONA   Why, your lieutenant, Cassio. Good my lord,   45
    If I have any grace or power to move you,
    His present reconciliation take;
    For if he be not one that truly loves you,
    That errs in ignorance and not in cunning,
    I have no judgment in an honest face.   50
    I prithee call him back.
OTHELLO   Went he hence now?
DESDEMONA   Yes, faith; so humbled
    That he hath left part of his grief with me
    To suffer with him. Good love, call him back.
OTHELLO   Not now, sweet Desdemon; some other time.   55
DESDEMONA   But shall't be shortly?
OTHELLO   The sooner, sweet, for you.

---

24. **school:** i.e., a place of rigorous instruction. **board a shrift:** dining table a confessional (where penance is prescribed).
28. **give . . . away:** abandon, renounce.
34. **your discretion:** what you judge appropriate.
42. **suitor:** supplicant; but not lacking the sense of romantic pursuit.
47. **His present . . . take:** effect an immediate reconciliation.
49. **in ignorance:** unintentionally.

DESDEMONA   Shall't be tonight, at supper?
OTHELLO   No, not tonight.
DESDEMONA   Tomorrow dinner then?
OTHELLO   I shall not dine at home;
    I meet the captains at the citadel.
DESDEMONA   Why then, tomorrow night, on Tuesday morn,   60
    On Tuesday noon or night, on Wednesday morn.
    I prithee name the time, but let it not
    Exceed three days. In faith, he's penitent;
    And yet his trespass, in our common reason—
    Save that they say the wars must make example   65
    Out of her best—is not almost a fault
    T' incur a private check. When shall he come?
    Tell me, Othello. I wonder in my soul
    What you would ask me that I should deny,
    Or stand so mamm'ring on? What? Michael Cassio,   70
    That came a-wooing with you? and so many a time,
    When I have spoke of you dispraisingly,
    Hath ta'en your part—to have so much to do
    To bring him in? By'r Lady, I could do much—
OTHELLO   Prithee no more. Let him come when he will: 75
    I will deny thee nothing.
DESDEMONA   Why, this is not a boon;
    'Tis as I should entreat you wear your gloves,
    Or feed on nourishing dishes, or keep you warm,
    Or sue to you to do a peculiar profit
    To your own person. Nay, when I have a suit   80
    Wherein I mean to touch your love indeed,
    It shall be full of poise and difficult weight
    And fearful to be granted.
OTHELLO   I will deny thee nothing.
    Whereon I do beseech thee grant me this,
    To leave me but a little to myself.   85
DESDEMONA   Shall I deny you? No. Farewell, my lord.
OTHELLO   Farewell, my Desdemona; I'll come to thee straight.
DESDEMONA   Emilia, come.—Be as your fancies teach you.

---

64. **in our common reason:** "i.e., looked at by ordinary standards" (McDonald).
65. **the wars:** the military profession (perhaps also alluding to the current warlike alert).
66–67. **is not . . . check:** hardly merits even a personal rebuke.
70. **so mamm'ring on:** in such hesitant uncertainty about; possibly, stammering so.
73. **ta'en your part:** argued on your behalf.
74. **bring him in:** reinstate him, as in 3.1.49; an unintended sexual suggestion—as earlier with "came a-wooing with you" and "ta'en your part."
76. **boon:** favor for herself.
79. **sue to:** beg. **peculiar:** particular.
81. **touch:** test.
82–83. **full of . . . granted:** serious and hard to decide and with risky consequences.

Whate'er you be, I am obedient. *Exit* DESDEMONA *and* EMILIA.
OTHELLO   Excellent wretch! Perdition catch my soul   90
But I do love thee! and when I love thee not,
Chaos is come again.
IAGO   My noble lord . . .
OTHELLO   What dost thou say, Iago?
IAGO   Did Michael Cassio, when you wooed my lady,
Know of your love?
OTHELLO   He did, from first to last.   95
Why dost thou ask?
IAGO   But for a satisfaction of my thought,
No further harm.
OTHELLO   Why of thy thought, Iago?
IAGO   I did not think he had been acquainted with her.
OTHELLO   O yes, and went between us very oft.   100
IAGO   Indeed!
OTHELLO   Indeed? Ay, indeed. Discern'st thou aught in that?
Is he not honest?
IAGO   Honest, my lord?
OTHELLO   Honest? Ay, honest.   105
IAGO   My lord, for aught I know.
OTHELLO   What dost thou think?
IAGO   Think, my lord?
OTHELLO   "Think, my lord?" By heaven, thou echo'st me
As if there were some monster in thy thought   110
Too hideous to be shown. Thou dost mean something:
I heard thee say even now thou lik'st not that,
When Cassio left my wife. What didst not like?
And when I told thee he was of my counsel,
Of my whole course of wooing, thou cried'st, "Indeed!"   115
And didst contract and purse thy brow together
As if thou then hadst shut up in thy brain
Some horrible conceit. If thou dost love me,
Show me thy thought.
IAGO   My lord, you know I love you.
OTHELLO   I think thou dost;   120
And for I know thou'rt full of love and honesty,
And weigh'st thy words before thou giv'st them breath,

90. **wretch:** can express endearment as well as distaste. **Perdition . . . soul:** I'll be damned (literally and idiomatically).
91. **when:** can mean "before" ("ere," according to Malone) or "if," as well as "as soon as."
100–01. **went between . . . Indeed:** i.e., carried messages between; but Iago's innuendo reinforces the subtextual impropriety of a "go-between."
112. **even now:** See 2.3.169 and note.
114–15. **of my . . . wooing:** my confidant; my participant throughout the courtship.
118. **conceit:** idea.
121. **for:** for that, because.

Therefore these stops of thine fright me the more:
For such things in a false disloyal knave
Are tricks of custom; but in a man that's just   125
They're close dilations, working from the heart
That passion cannot rule.

IAGO   For Michael Cassio,
I dare be sworn I think that he is honest.

OTHELLO   I think so too.

IAGO   Men should be what they seem,
Or those that be not, would they might seem none.   130

OTHELLO   Certain, men should be what they seem.

IAGO   Why then, I think Cassio's an honest man.

OTHELLO   Nay, yet there's more in this.
I prithee speak to me as to thy thinkings,
As thou dost ruminate, and give thy worst of thoughts   135
The worst of words.

IAGO   Good my lord, pardon me.
Though I am bound to every act of duty,
I am not bound to that all slaves are free to:
Utter my thoughts? Why, say they are vile and false—
As where's that palace whereinto foul things   140
Sometimes intrude not? Who has that breast so pure
But some uncleanly apprehensions
Keep leets and law-days, and in sessions sit
With meditations lawful?

OTHELLO   Thou dost conspire against thy friend, Iago,   145
If thou but think'st him wronged and mak'st his ear
A stranger to thy thoughts.

IAGO   I do beseech you,
Though I perchance am vicious in my guess
(As I confess it is my nature's plague
To spy into abuses, and oft my jealousy   150
Shapes faults that are not), that your wisdom
From one that so imperfectly conceits

---

123. **stops:** hesitations, pauses.
125. **of custom:** characteristic, habitual, to be expected.
126. **close:** secret, mysterious. **dilations:** effusions; delays; unfoldings, as of narratives
(see Iago's "dilatory time," 2.3.361, and note).
126–27. **working . . . rule:** i.e., proceeding from a reliably dispassionate source.
130. **Or those . . . none:** i.e., men who aren't (honest) shouldn't seem to be so.
134. **speak . . . thinkings:** say what's in your mind.
138. **that:** that which.
142. **uncleanly apprehensions:** dirty thoughts.
143. **Keep . . . sit:** appear in court together with; **leets, law-days,** and **sessions:** all refer
to legal proceedings.
146. **but:** merely.
150. **jealousy:** vigilance, suspicion, envy.
151. **Shapes:** constructs.

Would take no notice, nor build yourself a trouble
Out of his scattering and unsure observance.
It were not for your quiet, nor your good,   155
Nor for my manhood, honesty and wisdom,
To let you know my thoughts.

OTHELLO   What dost thou mean?

IAGO   Good name in man and woman, dear my lord,
Is the immediate jewel of their souls;
Who steals my purse steals trash: 'tis something, nothing;   160
'Twas mine, 'tis his, and has been slave to thousands.
But he that filches from me my good name
Robs me of that which not enriches him
And makes me poor indeed.

OTHELLO   By heaven, I'll know thy thoughts!

IAGO   You cannot, if my heart were in your hand,   165
Nor shall not, whilst 'tis in my custody.

OTHELLO   Ha?

IAGO   O, beware, my lord, of jealousy!
It is the green-eyed monster, which doth mock
The meat it feeds on. That cuckold lives in bliss
Who, certain of his fate, loves not his wronger;   170
But O, what damnèd minutes tells he o'er
Who dotes yet doubts, suspects yet strongly loves!

OTHELLO   O misery!

IAGO   Poor and content is rich, and rich enough,
But riches fineless is as poor as winter   175
To him that ever fears he shall be poor.
Good God, the souls of all my tribe defend
From jealousy!

OTHELLO   Why, why is this?
Think'st thou I'd make a life of jealousy,
To follow still the changes of the moon   180
With fresh suspicions? No! To be once in doubt

151–53. **your wisdom . . . notice:** your discretion would ignore someone given to such mistaken or inappropriate thoughts.
154. **scattering . . . observance:** "random and unfounded observations" (McDonald).
155. **were not for:** would not serve the interests of.
159. **immediate jewel:** most valuable possession or quality.
168–69. **mock . . . feeds on:** toys with its prey (the jealous lover); or (*as* the jealous lover) is repelled by his beloved or his own suspicions.
169–72. **That cuckold . . . strongly loves:** i.e., better to know and hate your betrayer than hang suspended in uncertainty about the fidelity of your beloved; **tells he o'er:** counts over and over again.
172. **dotes:** adores; with a hint of foolish infatuation or dotage.
175. **riches fineless:** infinite wealth.
177. **tribe:** Cf. 1.3.353 and note.
180. **follow . . . moon:** i.e., always ("still") wax and wane (like a lunatic).

Is once to be resolved. Exchange me for a goat
When I shall turn the business of my soul
To such exsufflicate and blowed surmises,
Matching thy inference. 'Tis not to make me jealous   185
To say my wife is fair, feeds well, loves company,
Is free of speech, sings, plays and dances:
Where virtue is, these are more virtuous.
Nor from mine own weak merits will I draw
The smallest fear or doubt of her revolt,   190
For she had eyes and chose me. No, Iago,
I'll see before I doubt; when I doubt, prove;
And on the proof there is no more but this:
Away at once with love or jealousy!
IAGO   I am glad of this; for now I shall have reason   195
To show the love and duty that I bear you
With franker spirit. Therefore, as I am bound,
Receive it from me. I speak not yet of proof.
Look to your wife; observe her well with Cassio;   *plants*
Wear your eyes thus: not jealous nor secure.   *'dcas in* 200
I would not have your free and noble nature   *head*
Out of self-bounty be abused. Look to't.
I know our country disposition well:
In Venice they do let God see the pranks
They dare not show their husbands; their best conscience   205
Is not to leave't undone, but [keep't] unknown.
OTHELLO   Dost thou say so?
IAGO   She did deceive her father, marrying you,
And when she seemed to shake, and fear your looks,
She loved them most.
OTHELLO   And so she did.
IAGO   Why, go to then.   210
She that, so young, could give out such a seeming
To seel her father's eyes up close as oak

182. **once:** at once; once and for all.
184. **exsufflicate and blowed surmises:** "(1) spat out and flyblown (i.e., disgusting) spec-
ulations, (2) inflated and blown abroad (rumored) notions" (McDonald).
185. **matching thy inference:** to correspond with your suggestion.
186. **feeds:** eats.
190. **revolt:** turning away (revulsion); infidelity.
192. **when:** See 91 and note.
200. **Wear your eyes:** either "observe" or "put on the appearance."
202. **self-bounty:** your own generosity; your inherent good nature.
203. **our country disposition:** how Venetian women act; with a nasty sexual pun (cf.
"country matters," *Hamlet* 3.2.105).
204. **they:** i.e., Venetian wives.
205. **best conscience:** utmost care; highest scruple.
211. **give out . . . seeming:** be so deceptive.
212. **seel:** See 1.3.267 and note. **close as oak:** i.e., the cloth hoodwinking Brabantio was
tight as (the grain of) oak.

He thought 'twas witchcraft . . . ; but I am much to blame.
I humbly do beseech you of your pardon
For too much loving you.

OTHELLO   I am bound to thee forever.   215

IAGO   I see this hath a little dashed your spirits.

OTHELLO   Not a jot, not a jot.

IAGO   I' faith, I fear it has.
I hope you will consider what is spoke
Comes from my love. But I do see you're moved.
I am to pray you not to strain my speech   220
To grosser issues nor to larger reach
Than to suspicion.

OTHELLO   I will not.

IAGO   Should you do so, my lord,
My speech should fall into such vile success
Which my thoughts aimed not. Cassio's my worthy friend—   225
My lord, I see you're moved.

OTHELLO   No, not much moved;
I do not think but Desdemona's honest.

IAGO   Long live she so! and long live you to think so!

OTHELLO   And yet how nature, erring from itself—

IAGO   Ay, there's the point! as to be bold with you,   230
Not to affect many proposed matches
Of her own clime, complexion and degree,
Whereto we see in all things nature tends—
Foh! one may smell in such a will most rank,
Foul disproportions, thoughts unnatural.   235
But, pardon me, I do not in position
Distinctly speak of her, though I may fear
Her will, recoiling to her better judgment,
May fall to match you with her country forms,
And happily repent.

220–22. **strain . . . suspicion:** push my words beyond misgiving into explicit imaginings ("grosser" and "larger" have sexual resonances; see 1.2.72 and note).
224–25. **vile success . . . aimed not:** nasty consequence I didn't intend; "*success* = outcome (good or bad)" (Honigmann).
229. **erring from itself:** straying from propriety; Othello echoes Brabantio's "nature so preposterously to err" (1.3.62). Iago had been echoing Brabantio earlier: with "Look to your wife" (199), cf. 1.3.290; with "She did deceive her father, marrying you" (208), cf. 1.3.291; with "fear your looks" (209), cf. 1.3.98.
230. **bold:** can refer to Iago's presumption or Desdemona's headstrong pursuit of Othello.
231. **affect:** like.
232. **clime, complexion and degree:** country, temperament, and social position.
234. **Foh:** calls upon the actor to express nausea. **such:** perversity like that. **will:** sexual appetite. **rank:** extreme, "(after smell) rancid, foul-smelling" (Honigmann).
236–37. **in position . . . her:** i.e., my claim is not about her in particular.
238. **recoiling:** reverting (with instinctive disgust).
239. **fall:** happen or descend. **match:** compare. **country forms:** typical Venetian appearances; but cf. 203 and note.
240. **happily:** perhaps.

OTHELLO   Farewell, farewell.   240
  If more thou dost perceive, let me know more.
  Set on thy wife to observe. Leave me, Iago.
IAGO [*Begins to depart.*]   My lord, I take my leave.
OTHELLO   Why did I marry? This honest creature, doubtless,
  Sees and knows more, much more, than he unfolds.   245
IAGO [*Returning.*]   My lord, I would I might entreat your honor
  To scan this thing no farther; leave it to time.
  Although 'tis fit that Cassio have his place
  (For sure he fills it up with great ability),
  Yet if you please to hold him off awhile,   250
  You shall by that perceive him and his means.
  Note if your lady strain his entertainment
  With any strong or vehement importunity;
  Much will be seen in that. In the meantime
  Let me be thought too busy in my fears   255
  (As worthy cause I have to fear I am),
  And hold her free, I do beseech your honor.
OTHELLO   Fear not my government.
IAGO   I once more take my leave.   *Exit.*
OTHELLO   This fellow's of exceeding honesty,   260
  And knows all qualities with a learned spirit
  Of human dealings. If I do prove her haggard,
  Though that her jesses were my dear heartstrings,
  I'd whistle her off and let her down the wind
  To prey at fortune. Haply for I am black,   265
  And have not those soft parts of conversation
  That chamberers have, or for I am declined
  Into the vale of years—yet that's not much—
  She's gone, I am abused, and my relief
  Must be to loathe her. O curse of marriage!   270
  That we can call these delicate creatures ours
  And not their appetites! I had rather be a toad

[Handwritten margin notes: "Siloquy", "repressed"]

248. **place:** military position.
249. **fills it up:** furnishes a sexual suggestion for "place."
251. **means:** procedures; also agents or go-betweens (i.e., Desdemona).
252. **strain his entertainment:** push for his reinstatement.
257. **free:** i.e., from any wrongdoing.
258. **Fear not my government:** Don't worry about my conduct.
262. **haggard:** untamed; "lit. a wild female hawk" (Honigmann).
263. **Though . . . heartstrings:** no matter how fondly I am attached to her; **jesses:** the straps tying the hawk to the falconer's wrist.
264–65. **whistle . . . fortune:** more hawking metaphors—"let her go to take her own chances."
265. **Haply for:** perhaps because.
266–67. **soft . . . have:** refined social skills of experienced courtiers.
268. **yet that's not much:** either "I'm not very old" or "age isn't very important."
269. **abused:** deceived.
271–72. **we:** men, husbands. **delicate creatures . . . appetites:** women, wives, who are legal possessions ("ours") while remaining sexually autonomous ("not their appetites").

And live upon the vapor of a dungeon
Than keep a corner in the thing I love
For others' uses. Yet 'tis the plague to great ones: 275
Prerogatived are they less than the base;
'Tis destiny unshunnable, like death;
Even then this forkèd plague is fated to us
When we do quicken.

Enter DESDEMONA *and* EMILIA.

Look where she comes!
If she be false, heaven mocked itself;   280
I'll not believe't.

DESDEMONA   How now, my dear Othello?
Your dinner, and the generous islanders
By you invited, do attend your presence.

OTHELLO   I am to blame.

DESDEMONA   Why do you speak so faintly?
Are you not well?   285

OTHELLO   I have a pain upon my forehead, here.

DESDEMONA   Faith, that's with watching; 'twill away again.
Let me but bind it hard, within this hour
It will be well.

OTHELLO   Your napkin is too little;

[*The handkerchief is dropped.*]

Let it alone. Come, I'll go in with you.   290

DESDEMONA   I am very sorry that you are not well.

Exit OTHELLO *and* DESDEMONA.

EMILIA   I am glad I have found this napkin;
This was her first remembrance from the Moor.
My wayward husband hath a hundred times
Wooed me to steal it. But she so loves the token   295

274–75. **keep . . . for others' uses:** another distinction between custody and possession;
corner: "small place . . . here with secondary sexual sense" (Honigmann); **thing:** Desdemona
or her "corner" (cf. "scan this thing no farther," 247).

275–76. **Yet . . . the base:** Othello claims it as a general rule (though without identifiable
authority) that men of high status ("great ones") are less well protected ("prerogatived")
against infidelity.

278. **this forkèd plague:** alluding to the cuckold's horns but also to the anatomical "corner" (cf. "poor, bare, forked animal," *King Lear* 3.4.91–92).

279. **do quicken:** are born; become sexually aroused (picking up on "death" as orgasm in
277; see note to 2.1.80).

280. **mocked itself:** counterfeited its own transcendent beauty (?).

282. **generous:** noble.

287. **watching:** sleeplessness; being on watch.

289. **napkin:** handkerchief.

290. **it:** either the handkerchief or the headache.

294. **wayward:** willful, perverse.

(For he conjured her she should ever keep it)
That she reserves it evermore about her
To kiss and talk to. I'll have the work ta'en out,
And giv't Iago; what he will do with it
Heaven knows, not I:
I nothing but to please his fantasy.   300

please
Iago/husband

Enter Iago.

IAGO   How now? What do you here alone?
EMILIA   Do not you chide; I have a thing for you.
IAGO   You have a thing for me? It is a common thing—
EMILIA   Ha?   305
IAGO   To have a foolish wife.
EMILIA   O, is that all? What will you give me now
   For that same handkerchief?
IAGO   What handkerchief?
EMILIA   What handkerchief?
   Why, that the Moor first gave to Desdemona,   310
   That which so often you did bid me steal.
IAGO   Hast stolen it from her?
EMILIA   No, faith; she let it drop by negligence,
   And to th' advantage I, being here, took't up.
   Look, here 'tis.
IAGO   A good wench, give it me.   315
EMILIA   What will you do with't, that you have been so earnest
   To have me filch it?
IAGO [*Taking it.*]   Why, what is that to you?
EMILIA   If it be not for some purpose of import,
   Giv't me again. Poor lady, she'll run mad
   When she shall lack it.
IAGO   Be not acknown on't;   320
   I have use for it. Go—leave me!   *Exit* EMILIA.
   I will in Cassio's lodging lose this napkin
   And let him find it. Trifles light as air
   Are to the jealous confirmations strong
   As proofs of holy writ. This may do something.   325

saicoate

---

296. **conjured:** strongly urged.
298. **work ta'en out:** design copied.
301. **I nothing:** elliptical—an implicit "do" or "know" or "am."
303–04. **thing . . . thing . . . common thing:** emphatically repeats Othello's "thing . . . for others' uses" (see 274–75 and note).
314. **to th'advantage:** fortunately, opportunely.
320. **lack:** miss. **Be . . . on't:** "in effect, don't acknowledge . . . a part in it, keep out of it" (Honigmann).
325. **holy writ:** the Bible.

The Moor already changes with my poison:
Dangerous conceits are in their natures poisons,
Which at the first are scarce found to distaste,
But with a little act upon the blood
Burn like the mines of sulphur.
Enter OTHELLO.   I did say so—   330
Look where he comes! Not poppy nor mandragora
Nor all the drowsy syrups of the world
Shall ever medicine thee to that sweet sleep
Which thou owedst yesterday.

OTHELLO   Ha! ha! false to me?

IAGO   Why, how now, general? No more of that!   335

OTHELLO   Avaunt! be gone! Thou hast set me on the rack.
I swear 'tis better to be much abused
Than but to know't a little.

IAGO   How now, my lord?

OTHELLO   What sense had I of her stol'n hours of lust?
I saw't not, thought it not; it harmed not me;   340
I slept the next night well, fed well, was free and merry;
I found not Cassio's kisses on her lips.
He that is robbed, not wanting what is stol'n,
Let him not know't, and he's not robbed at all.

IAGO   I am sorry to hear this.   345

OTHELLO   I had been happy if the general camp,
Pioneers and all, had tasted her sweet body,
So I had nothing known. O now, forever
Farewell the tranquil mind! farewell content!
Farewell the plumèd troops and the big wars   350
That makes ambition virtue! O, farewell!

327. **conceits:** ideas, thoughts.
328. **are scarce found to distaste:** hardly seem to repel appetite.
329. **act . . . blood:** effect on passion.
330. **mines of sulphur:** are hot and virtually inextinguishable.
331. **mandragora:** narcotic derived from the mandrake root.
332. **drowsy syrups:** sleep-inducing potions.
333. **medicine:** "restore by physic, cure" (Schmidt).
334. **owedst:** possessed. **Ha! ha!:** "a signal to the actor to make the appropriate noise" (Honigmann).
336. **Avaunt:** exclamation used to banish evil spirits. **the rack:** device that gradually stretched the limbs till they were pulled out of their sockets.
337. **abused:** deceived.
341. **fed:** ate.
343. **wanting:** missing.
346–47. **the general . . . and all:** the whole army, including even the most menial trench-diggers ("pioneers").
349. **content:** Cf. 2.1.194 and note.
350. **plumèd:** splendidly uniformed (literally, feathered; cf. 1.3.384 and note). **big:** mighty; violent; grand.
351. **makes ambition virtue:** endows personal motivation with a higher sanction (the public good?); for the singular verb after "wars," see 1.1.148 and note.

Farewell the neighing steed and the shrill trump,
The spirit-stirring drum, th' ear-piercing fife,
The royal banner and all quality,
Pride, pomp and circumstance of glorious war!   355
And O you mortal engines whose rude throats
Th' immortal Jove's dread clamors counterfeit,
Farewell! Othello's occupation's gone!

IAGO Is't possible, my lord?

OTHELLO [*grabs* IAGO *by the throat.*]   Villain, be sure thou prove
   my love a whore!   360
Be sure of it, give me the ocular proof,
Or by the worth of mine eternal soul,
Thou hadst been better have been born a dog
Than answer my waked wrath.

IAGO   Is't come to this?

OTHELLO   Make me to see't, or at the least so prove it   365
That the probation bear no hinge nor loop
To hang a doubt on, or woe upon thy life!

IAGO My noble lord—

OTHELLO   If thou dost slander her and torture me,
Never pray more; abandon all remorse;   370
On horror's head horrors accumulate;
Do deeds to make heaven weep, all earth amazed;
For nothing canst thou to damnation add
Greater than that.

IAGO   O grace! O heaven forgive me!
Are you a man? Have you a soul? or sense?   375
God buy you; take mine office. O wretched fool,
That lov'st to make thine honesty a vice!
O monstrous world! Take note, take note, O world:
To be direct and honest is not safe.

352. **trump:** trumpet.
354. **quality:** nature.
355. **Pride . . . circumstance:** elaborate pageantry.
356. **mortal engines:** deadly artillery. **rude throats:** harsh sounds.
357. **Th' immortal . . . clamors:** i.e., the thunderbolts hurled down by the chief Roman deity. **counterfeit:** reproduce, imitate (perhaps a hint of the modern "fake").
358. **occupation:** profession, (legitimating) position; "*occupy* could = cohabit with" (Honigmann).
360. **Villain, be sure:** Traditions extending back as far as to Rowe have Othello take Iago by the throat here in this "collaring scene."
361. **ocular:** visible.
366. **probation:** proof.
366–67. **bear . . . doubt on:** i.e., be absolutely certain (though the metaphors are obscure).
370. **remorse:** compassion; repentance.
371. **head:** "perhaps = summit" (Honigmann).
376. **God buy you:** "abbreviation for 'God be with you'—i.e., 'good-bye'" (McDonald).
377. **honesty a vice:** Iago claims to be "honest to a fault."

I thank you for this profit, and from hence   380
I'll love no friend, sith love breeds such offence.
OTHELLO   Nay, stay; thou shouldst be honest.
IAGO   I should be wise; for honesty's a fool
And loses that it works for.
OTHELLO   By the world,
I think my wife be honest, and think she is not;   385
I think that thou art just, and think thou art not.
I'll have some proof. My name, that was as fresh
As Dian's visage, is now begrimed and black
As mine own face. If there be cords or knives,
Poison, or fire, or suffocating streams,   390
I'll not endure it. Would I were satisfied!
IAGO   I see you are eaten up with passion;
I do repent me that I put it to you.
You would be satisfied?
OTHELLO   Would? Nay, and I will.
IAGO   And may . . . but how? how satisfied, my lord?   395
Would you, the supervisor, grossly gape on?
Behold her topped?
OTHELLO   Death and damnation! O!
IAGO   It were a tedious difficulty, I think,
To bring them to that prospect. Damn them then,
If ever mortal eyes do see them bolster   400
More than their own. What then? How then?
What shall I say? Where's satisfaction?
It is impossible you should see this,
Were they as prime as goats, as hot as monkeys,
As salt as wolves in pride, and fools as gross   405
As ignorance made drunk. But yet, I say,

380. profit: useful lesson. **from hence:** henceforth.
381. sith: since.
384. that it works for: "i.e. trust, and the rewards trust deserves" (Ross).
385. honest: chaste.
386. just: upright; right (i.e., accurate in your suggestion).
387. fresh: undefiled, clean.
388. Dian: Diana (Roman goddess of chastity).
389–90. cords . . . streams: means to commit suicide or murder.
391. satisfied: released from uncertainty.
393. put it: suggested Desdemona's possible infidelity; imparted this rage (?).
396. supervisor: observer (literally, someone who looks on from above); director. **grossly:** blatantly, lewdly (see 220–22 and note).
397. topped: Cf. "tupping" (1.1.86 and note).
400. bolster: a pillow or support (hence as a verb, metaphorically: to have sex).
401. more . . . own: illegitimately.
404. Were they: (even if) they were.
404–06. as prime . . . made drunk: three instances of animal lust, capped by drunkenness as bestial stupidity.

Reputation *Control* [handwritten]

If imputation and strong circumstances
Which lead directly to the door of truth
Will give you satisfaction, you might have't.
OTHELLO   Give me a living reason she's disloyal.   410
IAGO   I do not like the office.   *Silence* [handwritten]
But sith I am entered in this cause so far,
Pricked to't by foolish honesty and love,
I will go on. / I lay with Cassio lately,   *slower* [handwritten]
And being troubled with a raging tooth,   415
I could not sleep. There are a kind of men
So loose of soul that in their sleeps will mutter
Their affairs; one of this kind is Cassio.   *painting image / infecting* [handwritten]
In sleep I heard him say, "Sweet Desdemona,
Let us be wary, let us hide our loves!"
And then, sir, would he gripe and wring my hand,   420
Cry, "O sweet creature!" then kiss me hard,
As if he plucked up kisses by the roots
That grew upon my lips, laid his leg o'er my thigh,
And sigh, and kiss, and then cry "Cursèd fate   425
That gave thee to the Moor!"
OTHELLO   O monstrous! monstrous!
IAGO   Nay, this was but his
    dream.
OTHELLO   But this denoted a foregone conclusion;
'Tis a shrewd doubt, though it be but a dream.
IAGO   And this may help to thicken other proofs   430
    That do demonstrate thinly.
OTHELLO   I'll tear her all to pieces!
IAGO   Nay, yet be wise; yet we see nothing done;
    She may be honest yet. Tell me but this:
    Have you not sometimes seen a handkerchief

---

407. **imputation:** accusation; designation, assumption. **strong circumstances:** likely evidence.
408. **lead . . . truth:** "Othello is led in imagination to stand outside the closed bedroom door" (Ridley).
410. **living:** sustainable, valid.
411. **office:** task, duty.
412. **sith:** since. **cause:** matter, legal case.
413. **Pricked:** incited.
414. **I lay . . . lately:** That soldiers might share a bed is not by itself a noteworthy peculiarity.
415. **raging tooth:** toothache.
421. **gripe:** grip.
428. **denoted . . . conclusion:** indicated an already consummated experience.
429. **shrewd doubt:** acute fear.
431. **do demonstrate thinly:** i.e., are inadequately conclusive in themselves (cf. "thin habits," 1.3.108, and note).
432. **yet be wise:** continue to exercise self-control.

Spotted with strawberries in your wife's hand?   435
OTHELLO   I gave her such a one; 'twas my first gift.
IAGO   I know not that; but such a handkerchief—
   I am sure it was your wife's—did I today
   See Cassio wipe his beard with.
OTHELLO   If it be that—
IAGO   If it be that, or any, it was hers.   440
   It speaks against her with the other proofs.
OTHELLO   O that the slave had forty thousand lives!
   One is too poor, too weak for my revenge.
   Now do I see 'tis true. Look here, Iago:
   All my fond love thus do I blow to heaven.   445
   'Tis gone.
   Arise, black vengeance, from the hollow hell!
   Yield up, O love, thy crown and hearted throne
   To tyrannous hate! Swell, bosom, with thy fraught,
   For 'tis of aspics' tongues!
IAGO   Yet be content.   450
OTHELLO   O, blood! blood! blood!
IAGO   Patience, I say; your mind may change.
OTHELLO   Never, Iago. Like to the Pontic Sea,
   Whose icy current and compulsive course
   Ne'er keeps retiring ebb but keeps due on   455
   To the Propontic and the Hellespont,
   Even so my bloody thoughts with violent pace
   Shall ne'er look back, ne'er ebb to humble love,
   Till that a capable and wide revenge
   Swallow them up.   OTHELLO *kneels.*
                        Now, by yond marble heaven,   460
   In the due reverence of a sacred vow,
   I here engage my words.
IAGO   Do not rise yet.   IAGO *kneels.*
   Witness, you ever-burning lights above,
   You elements that clip us round about,

----

435. Spotted: decorated; stained. **strawberries:** to Shakespeare's audience, "might suggest a hidden evil, or the purity of the Virgin" (Honigmann).
440. or any . . . hers: wildly illogical (hence Malone's emendation—see Textual Notes), but Iago has never depended on logic.
448. hearted: ensconced in the heart.
449. fraught: load.
450. of aspics' tongues: i.e., venomous.
453. Pontic: Black.
454. compulsive: "compelled; or, compelling" (Honigmann); "irresistible and headlong" (Ross).
459. capable and wide: all-embracing and broad-ranging.
460. marble: obdurate; dispensing rigorous judgment.
463. ever-burning lights: stars; cf. the "ever-fixèd pole" of 2.1.15.
464. elements: either the heavenly bodies invoked again or the constituents of mutable nature. **clip:** embrace.

Witness that here Iago doth give up   465
The execution of his wit, hands, heart,
To wronged Othello's service. Let him command,
And to obey shall be in me remorse,
What bloody business ever.   [*They rise.*]
OTHELLO   I greet thy love,
Not with vain thanks but with acceptance bounteous,   470
And will upon the instant put thee to't.
Within these three days let me hear thee say
That Cassio's not alive.
IAGO   My friend is dead;
'Tis done at your request. But let her live.
OTHELLO   Damn her, lewd minx! O, damn her! damn her!   475
Come, go with me apart; I will withdraw
To furnish me with some swift means of death
For the fair devil. Now art thou my lieutenant.
IAGO   I am your own forever.   *Exeunt.* 480

ACT 3 SCENE 4

Enter DESDEMONA, EMILIA *and* CLOWN.

DESDEMONA   Do you know, sirrah, where lieutenant Cassio
lies?
CLOWN   I dare not say he lies anywhere.
DESDEMONA   Why, man?
CLOWN   He's a soldier, and for me to say a soldier lies,   5
'tis stabbing.
DESDEMONA   Go to; where lodges he?
CLOWN   To tell you where he lodges is to tell you where
I lie.
DESDEMONA   Can anything be made of this?   10
CLOWN   I know not where he lodges, and for me to devise
a lodging and say he lies here or he lies there were
to lie in mine own throat.
DESDEMONA   Can you inquire him out and be edified by report?

---

466. **wit, hands, heart:** mental, physical, and emotional capacities.
468–69. **to obey . . . ever:** See Johnson's gloss, p. 218. **remorse:** compassion (cf. 370).
471. **to't:** to the proof.
1. **sirrah:** fellow, boy; used to address a servant.
2. **lies:** resides.
5–6. **to say . . . stabbing:** a soldier accused of untruth would aggressively defend his honor.
7. **Go to:** expresses (perhaps amused) impatience: "no, really . . ."
11. **devise:** invent.
13. **in mine own throat:** i.e., blatantly, outrageously.
14. **edified:** instructed.

CLOWN   I will catechize the world for him—that is, make   15
    questions and by them answer.
DESDEMONA   Seek him, bid him come hither. Tell him I
    have moved my lord on his behalf and hope all will
    be well.
CLOWN   To do this is within the compass of man's wit,   20
    and therefore I will attempt the doing it.   *Exit* CLOWN.
DESDEMONA   Where should I lose the handkerchief, Emilia?
EMILIA   I know not, madam.
DESDEMONA   Believe me, I had rather have lost my purse
    Full of crusadoes; and but my noble Moor   25
    Is true of mind and made of no such baseness
    As jealous creatures are, it were enough
    To put him to ill-thinking.
EMILIA   Is he not jealous?
DESDEMONA   Who, he? I think the sun where he was born
    Drew all such humors from him.

                                    Enter OTHELLO.

EMILIA   Look where he comes.   30
DESDEMONA [*Aside.*]   I will not leave him now till Cassio be
    Called to him.—How is't with you, my lord?
OTHELLO   Well, my good lady. [*Aside.*]   O, hardness to
        dissemble!—
    How do you, Desdemona?
DESDEMONA   Well, my good lord.
OTHELLO   Give me your hand. This hand is moist, my lady.   35
DESDEMONA   It hath felt no age nor known no sorrow.
OTHELLO   This argues fruitfulness and liberal heart.
    Hot, hot, and moist. This hand of yours requires
    A sequester from liberty: fasting and prayer,
    Much castigation, exercise devout;   40
    For here's a young and sweating devil here
    That commonly rebels. 'Tis a good hand,

----

15. **catechize:** give religious instruction to.
16. **by:** by means of (as in the the catechism, the questions predetermine the answers).
18. **moved:** urged.
22. **should:** might.
25. **crusadoes:** gold coins (stamped with a cross). **but:** except that.
30. **Drew . . . him:** i.e., as though African heat evaporated those bodily fluids ("humors") that produced jealousy (Desdemona reverses conventional belief about Africans as hot-blooded).
31. **Cassio:** may be a disyllable (Cass-YO).
37. **argues:** suggests; a moist palm conventionally signified an abundantly affectionate and possibly lubricious nature. **liberal heart:** could imply virtue (cf. 3.3.188) or lasciviousness (cf. 2.1.162).
39. **sequester:** quarantine.
40. **castigation:** moral correction, discipline.
42. **commonly rebels:** frequently (promiscuously, lasciviously) disobeys.

A frank one.
DESDEMONA   You may indeed say so,
  For 'twas that hand that gave away my heart.
OTHELLO   A liberal hand. The hearts of old gave hands,   45
  But our new heraldry is hands, not hearts.
DESDEMONA   I cannot speak of this. Come now, your promise.
OTHELLO   What promise, chuck?
DESDEMONA   I have sent to bid Cassio come speak with you.
OTHELLO   I have a salt and sorry rheum offends me;   50
  Lend me thy handkerchief.
DESDEMONA   Here, my lord.
OTHELLO   That which I gave you.
DESDEMONA   I have it not about me.
OTHELLO   Not?
DESDEMONA   No, faith, my lord.
OTHELLO   That's a fault. That
    handkerchief
  Did an Egyptian to my mother give.
  She was a charmer and could almost read   55
  The thoughts of people. She told her, while she kept it,
  'T would make her amiable and subdue my father
  Entirely to her love; but if she lost it
  Or made a gift of it, my father's eye
  Should hold her loathèd, and his spirits should hunt   60
  After new fancies. She, dying, gave it me,
  And bid me, when my fate would have me wived,
  To give it her. I did so; and—take heed on't!—
  Make it a darling like your precious eye.
  To lose't or give't away were such perdition   65
  As nothing else could match.
DESDEMONA   Is't possible?
OTHELLO   'Tis true. There's magic in the web of it:
  A sibyl that had numbered in the world
  The sun to course two hundred compasses,
  In her prophetic fury sewed the work;   70

45–46. The hearts . . . not hearts: Unlike formerly, the current fashion is for marriage without sincere affection.
47. I . . . this: I don't know what you mean.
48. chuck: term of affection.
50. salt . . . me: irritating cold.
55. charmer: sorceress.
57. amiable: loveable, desirable.
61. fancies: objects of desire, sources of satisfaction.
64. darling: highly prized possession. eye: proverbially valuable body part, with sexual associations (the female "nether eye").
65. perdition: loss, catastrophe; cf. 3.3.90.
68–69. A sybil . . . compasses: "a 200-year-old prophetess" (Mowat and Werstine).
70. fury: rapture. work: design or pattern.

The worms were hallowed that did breed the silk,
And it was dyed in mummy, which the skillful
Conserved of maidens' hearts.

DESDEMONA   I'faith? Is't true?

OTHELLO   Most veritable; therefore look to't well.

DESDEMONA   Then would to God that I had never seen't!   75

OTHELLO   Ha? wherefore?

DESDEMONA   Why do you speak so startingly and rash?

OTHELLO   Is't lost? Is't gone? Speak, is't out o'th' way?

DESDEMONA   Heaven bless us!

OTHELLO   Say you?   80

DESDEMONA   It is not lost; but what an if it were?

OTHELLO   How?

DESDEMONA   I say it is not lost.

OTHELLO   Fetch't, let me see't!

DESDEMONA   Why, so I can; but I will not now.   85
   This is a trick to put me from my suit.
   Pray you let Cassio be received again.

OTHELLO   Fetch me the handkerchief, my mind misgives—

DESDEMONA   Come, come!
   You'll never meet a more sufficient man—   90

OTHELLO   The handkerchief!—

DESDEMONA   A man that all his time
   Hath founded his good fortunes on your love,
   Shared dangers with you—

OTHELLO   The handkerchief!

DESDEMONA   I'faith, you are to blame.

OTHELLO   Zounds!   *Exit* OTHELLO.   95

EMILIA   Is not this man jealous?

DESDEMONA   I ne'er saw this before.
   Sure, there's some wonder in this handkerchief;
   I am most unhappy in the loss of it.

EMILIA   'Tis not a year or two shows us a man.   100
   They are all but stomachs, and we all but food;
   They eat us hungerly, and when they are full
   They belch us.

---

72. **mummy:** medicine derived from dead bodies. **the skillful:** those adept in magic.
73. **Conserved of maidens':** distilled from virgins'.
77. **so startingly and rash:** with such fitful urgency.
78. **out o'th' way:** missing.
81. **an if:** if.
86. **put:** divert. **suit:** petition.
88. **misgives:** worries.
90. **sufficient:** capable (the word can have a sexual resonance).
100. **shows us a man:** "reveal[s] to us (women) what (a monster) a man is" (Honigmann).
101. **all but:** nothing but.
102. **hungerly:** hungrily, voraciously.
103. **belch:** puke.

Enter IAGO *and* CASSIO.

Look you, Cassio and my husband.

IAGO   There is no other way; 'tis she must do't;
And lo the happiness! go and importune her.   105

DESDEMONA   How now, good Cassio, what's the news with you?

CASSIO   Madam, my former suit. I do beseech you
That by your virtuous means I may again
Exist and be a member of his love,
Whom I, with all the office of my heart,   110
Entirely honor. I would not be delayed.
If my offense be of such mortal kind
That nor my service past nor present sorrows
Nor purposed merit in futurity
Can ransom me into his love again,   115
But to know so must be my benefit;
So shall I clothe me in a forced content
And shut myself up in some other course
To fortune's alms.

DESDEMONA   Alas, thrice-gentle Cassio,
My advocation is not now in tune.   120
My lord is not my lord, nor should I know him,
Were he in favor as in humor altered.
So help me every spirit sanctified
As I have spoken for you all my best
And stood within the blank of his displeasure   125
For my free speech. You must awhile be patient.
What I can do I will, and more I will
Than for myself I dare. Let that suffice you.

IAGO   Is my lord angry?

EMILIA   He went hence but now,

---

105. **happiness:** good luck; "look, here she is." **importune:** plead with.
109. **member:** the "bodies" of all Christians "are the members of Christ," which, when alienated through sin, become "the members of an harlot" (1 Corinthians 6.15).
110. **office:** duty, loyal service.
112. **mortal:** irredeemable; as distinct (in Roman Catholic theology) from a "venial" (minor, easily pardonable) sin.
113–15. **That . . . me:** That neither good works ("service") nor repentance ("sorrows") can earn ("merit") salvation ("ransom" = redeem from sin) is "Protestant doctrine" (Ross); but the mortal / venial allusion along with the general context of appealing to a feminine "virtuous means" (like the interceding Virgin Mary) suffuse the passage with an inclusive religious sentiment.
116. **to know . . . benefit:** Cassio would find satisfaction in at least being freed from doubt.
117. **clothe . . . content:** perforce take whatever protective advantage is available.
119. **fortune's alms:** as distinct from the charitable gifts of his lord.
120. **advocation:** advocacy. **in tune:** appropriate.
122. **favor:** appearance. **humor:** mood.
124. **As I have:** if I have not.
125. **blank:** center of a target (see "white," 2.1.133, and note).

And certainly in strange unquietness.   130
IAGO   Can he be angry? I have seen the cannon
When it hath blown his ranks into the air
And, like the devil, from his very arm
Puffed his own brother—and is he angry?
Something of moment then. I will go meet him;   135
There's matter in't indeed if he be angry.
DESDEMONA   I prithee do so.   *Exit* [IAGO].
                          Something sure of state—
Either from Venice, or some unhatched practice
Made demonstrable here in Cyprus to him—
Hath puddled his clear spirit; and in such cases   140
Men's natures wrangle with inferior things,
Though great ones are their object. 'Tis even so.
For let our finger ache, and it endues
Our other healthful members even to a sense
Of pain. Nay, we must think men are not gods,   145
Nor of them look for such observancy
As fits the bridal.—Beshrew me much, Emilia.
I was, unhandsome warrior as I am,
Arraigning his unkindness with my soul;
But now I find I had suborned the witness,   150
And he's indicted falsely.
EMILIA   Pray heaven it be
State matters, as you think, and no conception
Nor no jealous toy concerning you.
DESDEMONA   Alas the day! I never gave him cause.
EMILIA   But jealous souls will not be answered so;   155
They are not ever jealous for the cause,
But jealous for they're jealous. It is a monster
Begot upon itself, born on itself.
DESDEMONA   Heaven keep the monster from Othello's mind!

135. **of moment:** important.
137. **Something . . . of state:** some political matter.
138–39. **unhatched . . . demonstrable:** covert plot coming to his attention.
140. **puddled:** muddied; agitated.
141–42. **wrangle . . . object:** project their irritation onto trivialities.
142. **'Tis even so:** "Yes, that must be it."
144. **members:** bodily parts (see 107). **even to a:** to a similar or same.
146. **observancy:** attentiveness.
147. **As fits the bridal:** "expected on the wedding day" (McDonald). **Beshrew me:** mild oath—"shame on me."
148. **unhandsome warrior:** remembering Othello's "fair warrior" (2.1.180).
149. **Arraigning his unkindness:** accusing him of unnaturally cruel behavior.
150. **suborned:** corrupted. **the witness:** presumably "my soul," from whose earlier accusations she now experiences detachment ("I find").
152. **conception:** idea, invention.
153. **toy:** fantasy.
157. **for:** because of.
158. **begot:** conceived (sexually). **on:** from out of.

EMILIA   Lady, amen!   160
DESDEMONA   I will go seek him; Cassio, walk here about.
  If I do find him fit, I'll move your suit
  And seek to effect it to my uttermost.
CASSIO   I humbly thank your ladyship.   *Exeunt* DESDEMONA *and*
                                           EMILIA.

                          Enter BIANCA.

BIANCA   Save you, friend Cassio!
CASSIO   What make you from home?   165
  How is't with you, my most fair Bianca?
  I'faith, sweet love, I was coming to your house.
BIANCA   And I was going to your lodging, Cassio.
  What? keep a week away? seven days and nights?
  Eight score eight hours? And lovers' absent hours   170
  More tedious than the dial eight score times!
  O weary reckoning!
CASSIO   Pardon me, Bianca;
  I have this while with leaden thoughts been pressed,
  But I shall in a more continuate time
  Strike off this score of absence. Sweet Bianca,   175

             [*Gives her* DESDEMONA'S *handkerchief.*]

Take me this work out.
BIANCA   O, Cassio! whence came this?
  This is some token from a newer friend;
  To the felt absence now I feel a cause.
  Is't come to this? Well, well.
CASSIO   Go to, woman!
  Throw your vile guesses in the devil's teeth,   180

---

  162. fit: in a receptive mood.
  165. Save you: God save you. **make you:** are you doing away. Bianca is "out of door" (cf. 2.1.109) and "here alone" (cf. 3.3.302)—both conventionally improper.
  167. your house: Bianca is apparently a property owner—another unconventionality.
  170. eight score eight: 168 (7 times 24).
  170–72. And lovers' . . . reckoning: Bianca comically exaggerates a proverbial distinction between the clock ("dial") and the slow time of separated lovers, then pretends dismay at the computational complexity (160 times 168).
  173. I have . . . been pressed: "alluding to the torture known as 'pressing with weights' " (Ross).
  174. continuate: uninterrupted.
  175. Strike . . . score: cancel this obligation, pay this bill (punning on Bianca's "score").
  176. Take . . . out: copy this design for me (see 3.3.298).
  177. friend: variously glossed—"mistress" (Honigmann, Mowat and Werstine), "polite for 'paramour' " (Ross). The term is equivocal (it has to accommodate Bianca's own "friend Cassio," 165). See note 15 to the Names of the Actors at the beginning of the play. Iago's puzzling description of Cassio as "A fellow almost damned in a fair wife" (1.1.18) may in retrospect be relevant here. Bianca's costume might have clarified her identity on the Renaissance stage, but we cannot be sure.
  178. To . . . cause: i.e., now I understand why I haven't seen you.

From whence you have them. You are jealous now
That this is from some mistress some remembrance;
No, by my faith, Bianca.

BIANCA   Why, whose is it?

CASSIO   I know not neither; I found it in my chamber.
I like the work well; ere it be demanded,   185
As like enough it will, I would have it copied.
Take it and do't, and leave me for this time.

BIANCA   Leave you? Wherefore?

CASSIO   I do attend here on the general
And think it no addition, nor my wish,   190
To have him see me womaned.

BIANCA   Why, I pray you?

CASSIO   Not that I love you not.

BIANCA   But that you do not love me.
I pray you bring me on the way a little,
And say if I shall see you soon at night.

CASSIO   'Tis but a little way that I can bring you,   195
For I attend here; but I'll see you soon.

BIANCA   'Tis very good—I must be circumstanced.   *Exeunt*
                                                     omnes.

ACT 4 SCENE 1

Enter OTHELLO *and* IAGO.

IAGO   Will you think so?

OTHELLO   Think so, Iago?

IAGO   What,
To kiss in private?

OTHELLO   An unauthorized kiss!

IAGO   Or to be naked with her friend in bed
An hour or more, not meaning any harm?

OTHELLO   Naked in bed, Iago, and not mean harm?   5
It is hypocrisy against the devil.
They that mean virtuously, and yet do so,
The devil their virtue tempts, and they tempt heaven.

IAGO   If they do nothing, 'tis a venial slip;

---

190. **addition:** "mark of distinction" (Schmidt).
191. **womaned:** in female company.
197. **be circumstanced:** accept your conditions, accept things as they are; less patiently, "be put off with excuses" (?).
6. **hypocrisy . . . devil:** appearing to act sinfully while actually being good.
7. **do so:** i.e., be naked . . . in bed.
8. **tempts:** entices. **tempt:** dare or challenge to protect. "Thou shalt not tempt the Lord thy God" (Matthew 4.7).
9. **venial:** minor, easily pardoned; see note to 3.4.112.

But if I give my wife a handkerchief—   10
OTHELLO   What then?
IAGO   Why then, 'tis hers, my lord; and being hers,
  She may, I think, bestow't on any man.
OTHELLO   She is protectress of her honor too;
  May she give that?   15
IAGO   Her honor is an essence that's not seen;
  They have it very oft that have it not.
  But for the handkerchief—
OTHELLO   By heaven, I would most gladly have forgot it!
  Thou said'st—O, it comes o'er my memory   20
  As doth the raven o'er the infectious house,
  Boding to all!—he had my handkerchief.
IAGO   Ay, what of that?
OTHELLO   That's not so good now.
IAGO   What if I had said I had seen him do you wrong?
  Or heard him say—as knaves be such abroad   25
  Who (having by their own importunate suit
  Or voluntary dotage of some mistress
  Convincèd or supplied them) cannot choose
  But they must blab—
OTHELLO   Hath he said anything?
IAGO   He hath, my lord, but be you well assured,   30
  No more then he'll unswear.
OTHELLO   What hath he said?
IAGO   Faith, that he did . . . I know not what he did.
OTHELLO   What? What?
IAGO   Lie . . .
OTHELLO   With her?
IAGO   With her, on her; what you will.
OTHELLO   Lie with her? lie on her? We say lie on her   35
  when they belie her. Lie with her? Zounds, that's fulsome.—

---

  17. They have . . . have it not: One of these "haves" = "seems to have."
  21–22. the raven . . . all: a universally bad omen, here associated with spreading plague or sexual disease.
  25. knaves . . . abroad: scoundrels are around.
  26. importunate suit: perseverant wooing.
  27. voluntary dotage: willing infatuation.
  28. convincèd or supplied: seduced or sexually "serviced."
  34. With her, on her: Iago shifts emphasis from Othello's "her" to "with" and to a sequence of sexual positions, recapitulating the action of Cassio's dream ("lay with Cassio. . . . And then . . . laid his leg o'er my thigh," 3.3.414–24). **what you will:** "a conventional phrase—'as you like it'—ending with the sexually charged *will*" (McDonald); a "poisonous phrase: it implies 'anything you like to think (or do with her)' " (Honigmann).
  35–36. We say . . . belie her: For the plural pronouns ("we" and "they"), cf. 3.3.271 ff.; "belie" can = lie about or lie on top of (cf. the Clown's puns about Cassio's lodgings in 3.1.1 ff.).
  36. fulsome: disgusting; used of "rank" or in-heat sheep ("the fulsome ewes," *Merchant of Venice* 1.3.82).

Handkerchief! confessions! handkerchief!—To confess,
and be hanged for his labor. First to be hanged,
and then to confess: I tremble at it. Nature would not
invest herself in such shadowing passion without some   40
instruction. It is not words that shakes me thus. Pish!
Noses, ears and lips! is't possible? Confess? Handkerchief?
O devil!   *Falls in a trance.*
IAGO   Work on,
My medicine works! Thus credulous fools are caught,   45
And many worthy and chaste dames even thus,
All guiltless, meet reproach.—What ho! my lord!
My lord, I say! Othello?

                                        Enter CASSIO.

                        How now, Cassio?
CASSIO   What's the matter?
IAGO   My lord is fallen into an epilepsy.   50
This is his second fit; he had one yesterday.
CASSIO   Rub him about the temples.
IAGO   No, forbear.
The lethargy must have his quiet course;
If not, he foams at mouth and by and by
Breaks out to savage madness. Look, he stirs.   55
Do you withdraw yourself a little while;
He will recover straight. When he is gone,
I would on great occasion speak with you.

                                        [*Exit* CASSIO.]

How is it, general? Have you not hurt your head?
OTHELLO   Dost thou mock me?
IAGO   I mock you not, by heaven.   60
Would you would bear your fortune like a man!
OTHELLO   A hornèd man's a monster and a beast.
IAGO   There's many a beast then in a populous city,

39–41. I tremble . . . shakes me thus: Othello is usually taken to be referring to his own
fit: "(my) nature would not have been provoked to this paroxysm unless it had some motivation
more substantial than (mere) words"; but he may rather (or also) be referring to Desdemona.
"Nature" is conventionally gendered female, and Iago repeatedly associates it with Desdemona's sexual appetite: "very nature will instruct her" to "heave the gorge, disrelish and abhor"
Othello (2.1.229–31); "when she seemed to shake, and fear [Othello's] looks, / She loved
them most" (3.3.209–10).
40. shadowing: darkening, but color always registers literally in this play; also "imaging a
reality," as an actor would dress up ("invest") to shadow a substance: Othello or Desdemona
has been instructed to perform a passionate part.
45. My medicine: Cf. "my poison," 3.3.326.
53. lethargy: loss of consciousness. his: its. quiet: undisturbed.
58. great occasion: a matter of real importance.
60. mock me: i.e., by referring to the head-hurting cuckolds' horns.

And many a civil monster.
OTHELLO   Did he confess it?
IAGO   Good sir, be a man: 65
Think every bearded fellow that's but yoked
May draw with you. There's millions now alive
That nightly lie in those unproper beds
Which they dare swear peculiar. Your case is better.
O, 'tis the spite of hell, the fiend's arch-mock,   70
To lip a wanton in a secure couch,
And to suppose her chaste. No, let me know;
And knowing what I am, I know what she shall be.
OTHELLO   O, thou art wise, 'tis certain.
IAGO   Stand you a while
   apart,
Confine yourself but in a patient list.   75
Whilst you were here, o'er-whelmèd with your grief—
A passion most unsuiting such a man—
Cassio came hither. I shifted him away
And laid good 'scuses upon your ecstasy,
Bade him anon return and here speak with me,   80
The which he promised. Do but encave yourself,
And mark the fleers, the gibes and notable scorns
That dwell in every region of his face;
For I will make him tell the tale anew:
Where, how, how oft, how long ago and when   85
He hath and is again to cope your wife.
I say, but mark his gesture. Marry, patience!
Or I shall say you're all in all in spleen,
And nothing of a man.
OTHELLO   Dost thou hear, Iago?
I will be found most cunning in my patience;   90
But—dost thou hear?—most bloody.

64. **civil monster:** civilized beast.
65. **be a man:** take it patiently, keep your wits about you (but with more play on the natural man and the monstrous beast).
66. **bearded fellow:** mature man. **yoked:** joined in matrimony (like oxen or beasts of burden).
67. **draw:** compare; drag (as a cart).
68. **unproper:** indecent; "not (solely) his own" (Ridley).
69. **peculiar:** exclusively their own.
71. **lip . . . couch:** "kiss a whore in an apparently untainted bed" (McDonald).
73. **I am:** a cuckold (?); a real man (?). **shall be:** a whore (?); punished (?); dead (?).
75. **Confine . . . list:** i.e., keep your self-control.
79. **ecstasy:** fit (ex-stasis: the spirit stands outside the body, leaving it comatose).
80. **anon:** soon.
81. **encave:** conceal.
82. **fleers:** mockeries. **notable:** overt.
86. **cope:** encounter with.
88. **in spleen:** given over to bestial passion.

IAGO   That's not amiss,
  But yet keep time in all. Will you withdraw?

                                        [OTHELLO *withdraws.*]

  Now will I question Cassio of Bianca,
  A huswife that by selling her desires
  Buys herself bread and cloth. It is a creature   95
  That dotes on Cassio—as 'tis the strumpet's plague
  To beguile many and be beguiled by one.
  He, when he hears of her, cannot restrain
  From the excess of laughter. Here he comes.

                                        Enter CASSIO.

  As he shall smile, Othello shall go mad;   100
  And his unbookish jealousy must conster
  Poor Cassio's smiles, gestures and light behaviors
  Quite in the wrong. How do you, lieutenant?
CASSIO   The worser that you give me the addition
  Whose want even kills me.   105
IAGO   Ply Desdemona well, and you are sure on't.
  Now if this suit lay in Bianca's power,
  How quickly should you speed!
CASSIO   Alas, poor caitiff!
OTHELLO   Look how he laughs already!
IAGO   I never knew woman love man so.   110
CASSIO   Alas, poor rogue! I think, i'faith, she loves me.
OTHELLO   Now he denies it faintly and laughs it out.
IAGO   Do you hear, Cassio?
OTHELLO   Now he importunes him
  To tell it o'er. Go to! well said, well said!
IAGO   She gives it out that you shall marry her.   115
  Do you intend it?
CASSIO   Ha, ha, ha!

---

  92. **keep time:** maintain harmonious behavior; perhaps suggests "don't be premature in
revenge."
  94. **huswife:** "could mean 'prostitute', and clearly this is the sense in which Iago is using
it here. But Bianca appears not to be a professional courtesan exactly" (Sanders and see note
to 2.1.112). **desires:** "appetites" (Ross), but the word transfers feeling from Bianca's supposed
clients to herself; what she sells, presumably, is rather her desirability.
  96–97. **as 'tis . . . by one:** The "beguiler beguiled" was proverbial, but no authority is
available for Iago's application specifically to whores.
  101. **unbookish:** inexperienced. **conster:** construe.
  104. **addition:** title.
  105. **want:** lack.
  108. **speed:** prosper. **caitiff:** scoundrel.
  111. **rogue:** rascal; like "caitiff," available as a term of endearment.
  112. **denies it faintly:** pretends to protest.
  114. **Go to . . . well said:** carry on, well done.

OTHELLO   Do ye triumph, Roman? do you triumph?

CASSIO   I marry? What! a customer? Prithee bear some
charity to my wit; do not think it so unwholesome. Ha, ha,
ha!   120

OTHELLO   So, so, so, so! they laugh that wins.

IAGO   Faith, the cry goes that you marry her.

CASSIO   Prithee say true.

IAGO   I am a very villain else.

OTHELLO   Have you scored me? Well.   125

CASSIO   This is the monkey's own giving out. She is persuaded I
will marry her out of her own love and flattery, not out of my
promise.

OTHELLO   Iago beckons me; now he begins the story.

CASSIO   She was here even now; she haunts me in every
place. I was the other day talking on the sea bank   130
with certain Venetians, and thither comes the
bauble and falls me thus about my neck—

OTHELLO   Crying "O dear Cassio!" as it were: his gesture
imports it.

CASSIO   So hangs and lolls and weeps upon me, so shakes   135
and pulls me. Ha, ha, ha!

OTHELLO   Now he tells how she plucked him to my chamber.
O! I see that nose of yours, but not that dog I
shall throw it to.

CASSIO   Well, I must leave her company.   140

IAGO   Before me! look where she comes!

Enter BIANCA.

CASSIO   'Tis such another fitchew! marry, a perfumed
one! What do you mean by this haunting of me?

---

118. **triumph, Roman:** referring to the ceremonial celebrations of military conquest in ancient Rome.

119. **customer:** purveyor of custom, seller of goods—prostitute; Shakespeare more often uses "customer" in its modern sense, "consumer of goods," which may already be the primary meaning in the Renaissance. The same ambivalence in "desires" (see note to line 94).

119–20. **bear . . . wit:** give me credit for more sense.

120. **unwholesome:** diseased.

122. **cry:** noise; rumor.

125. **scored:** designated; branded; insulted (?).

126. **monkey:** associated with lust, though could suggest affection (cf. note to 111).

128. **beckons me:** signals me to approach or pay closer heed.

132. **bauble:** toy (dismissive contempt). **thus:** Cassio acts out a gesture, perhaps on Iago's body (cf. 3.3.414 ff.).

135. **So** and **so:** like "thus" (132), requires gestures. **shakes:** see 39–41 and note.

140. **I must leave her:** Cf. 3.4.187, 3.3.321, and 3.3.85; three relationships "are brought into focus" (Honigmann).

141. **look where she comes:** another significant reiteration—cf. 3.4.30, 3.3.331, 3.3.279, and 2.3.240.

142. **such another:** "like all the rest of them" (Ridley). **fitchew:** polecat, and emblem of lust, noted for its stench (hence "perfumed").

BIANCA   Let the devil and his dam haunt you! what
did you mean by that same handkerchief you gave   145
me even now? I was a fine fool to take it. I must take
out the work? A likely piece of work, that you should
find it in your chamber and know not who left it there!
This is some minx's token, and I must take out the work?
There, give it your hobby-horse! Wheresoever you had   150
it, I'll take out no work on't.
CASSIO   How now, my sweet Bianca?
How now? how now?
OTHELLO   By heaven, that should be my handkerchief!
BIANCA   If you'll come to supper tonight, you may; if   155
you will not, come when you are next prepared for.   *Exit.*
IAGO   After her, after her!
CASSIO   Faith, I must; she'll rail in the streets else.
IAGO   Will you sup there?
CASSIO   Faith, I intend so.   160
IAGO   Well, I may chance to see you, for I would very
fain speak with you.
CASSIO   Prithee come, will you?
IAGO   Go to; say no more.   *Exit* CASSIO.
OTHELLO [*Comes forward.*]   How shall I murder him, Iago?   165
IAGO   Did you perceive how he laughed at his vice?
OTHELLO   O Iago!
IAGO   And did you see the handkerchief?
OTHELLO   Was that mine?
IAGO   Yours, by this hand! and to see how he prizes   170
the foolish woman, your wife! She gave it him, and he
hath given it his whore.
OTHELLO   I would have him nine years a killing!—A
fine woman, a fair woman, a sweet woman!
IAGO   Nay, you must forget that.   175
OTHELLO   Ay, let her rot and perish and be damned tonight,
for she shall not live! No, my heart is turned to
stone; I strike it, and it hurts my hand.—O, the world
hath not a sweeter creature! She might lie by an emperor's
side and command him tasks.   180

147. **piece of work:** "a set phrase"; here = "a likely story!" (Honigmann).
149. **minx:** whore, as in Othello's description of Desdemona (3.3.475).
150. **hobby-horse:** "a man with a mock horse's body strapped round his waist . . . a figure
in May Day morris dances" (note to *Hamlet* 3.2.122); "mountable wench" (Ross).
154. **should:** must.
156. **you . . . prepared for:** I'm ready (and not before).
162. **fain:** much like to.
170. **by this hand:** I swear by my own hand. **prizes:** cherishes.
173. **nine . . . killing:** suffer prolonged torture.
180. **command him tasks:** like the lady in medieval romance, assigning quests to her
knight.

IAGO   Nay, that's not your way.

OTHELLO   Hang her!—I do but say what she is: so delicate
with her needle; an admirable musician (O, she will
sing the savageness out of a bear!); of so high and plenteous
wit and invention!   185

IAGO   She's the worse for all this.

OTHELLO   O, a thousand, a thousand times!—
And then of so gentle a condition!

IAGO   Ay, too gentle.

OTHELLO   Nay, that's certain.—But yet the pity of it, Iago! O   190
Iago, the pity of it, Iago!

IAGO   If you are so fond over her iniquity, give her patent
to offend, for if it touch not you it comes near nobody.

OTHELLO   I will chop her into messes! Cuckold me!

IAGO   O, 'tis foul in her.   195

OTHELLO   With mine officer!

IAGO   That's fouler.

OTHELLO   Get me some poison, Iago, this night. I'll not
expostulate with her, lest her body and beauty unprovide
my mind again. This night, Iago.   200

IAGO   Do it not with poison. Strangle her in her bed,
even the bed she hath contaminated.

OTHELLO   Good, good! The justice of it pleases. Very good!

IAGO   And for Cassio, let me be his undertaker.
You shall hear more by midnight.   205

OTHELLO   Excellent good!

    A trumpet [*within*].   What trumpet is that same?

IAGO   I warrant something from Venice.

            Enter LODOVICO, DESDEMONA, *and Attendants.*

'Tis Lodovico; this comes from the duke.
See, your wife's with him.

LODOVICO   God save you, worthy general.   210

---

184. **sing . . . bear:** like Orpheus's music in Greek mythology, taming wild nature.
184–85. **so high . . . invention:** such accomplished intelligence and abundant imagination.
188. **gentle a condition:** sweet disposition; noble birth.
189. **gentle:** Iago takes the word as meaning "pliant."
192. **fond . . . iniquity:** dote upon her wickedness. **patent:** licence, authority.
193. **touch:** concern; move.
194. **messes:** meal-sized gobbets; "bits" or "mincemeat."
199. **expostulate:** reason, argue, discourse. **body and beauty:** "bodily beauty—hendiadys" (Ross).
199–200. **unprovide my mind:** change my mind; disarm my mental faculty.
200. **again:** refers perhaps to the way her mere image has been repeatedly sapping his resolution throughout this exchange with Iago; perhaps to the actual experience of her bodily beauty at some unspecified earlier time (perhaps last night as distinct from "this night"?).
204. **be his undertaker:** undertake (take care of, dispose of) him.

OTHELLO   With all my heart, sir.

LODOVICO   The duke and the senators of Venice greet you.

[*Gives him a letter.*]

OTHELLO   I kiss the instrument of their pleasures.

[*Opens the letter and reads.*]

DESDEMONA   And what's the news, good cousin Lodovico?

IAGO   I am very glad to see you, signior.   215
Welcome to Cyprus.

LODOVICO   I thank you. How does Lieutenant Cassio?

IAGO   Lives, sir.

DESDEMONA   Cousin, there's fallen between him and my lord
An unkind breach; but you shall make all well.   220

OTHELLO   Are you sure of that?

DESDEMONA   My lord?

OTHELLO [*Reads.*]   "This fail you not to do, as you will . . ."

LODOVICO   He did not call: he's busy in the paper.
Is there division 'twixt my lord and Cassio?   225

DESDEMONA   A most unhappy one; I would do much
T' atone them, for the love I bear to Cassio.

OTHELLO   Fire and brimstone!

DESDEMONA   My lord?

OTHELLO   Are you wise?

DESDEMONA   What, is he angry?

LODOVICO   Maybe the letter moved him;
For, as I think, they do command him home,   230
Deputing Cassio in his government.

DESDEMONA   By my troth, I am glad on't.

OTHELLO   Indeed!

DESDEMONA   My lord?

OTHELLO   I am glad to see you mad.

DESDEMONA   Why, sweet Othello?

OTHELLO   Devil!   [*Strikes her.*]

DESDEMONA   I have not deserved this.   235

LODOVICO   My lord, this would not be believed in Venice,
Though I should swear I saw't. 'Tis very much;

---

213. **kiss:** i.e., defer to, though perhaps a literal action is called for. **instrument . . . pleas-ures:** means by which they convey their desires (with "kiss," possible sexual resonance).

227. **atone:** reconcile (make one). **love I bear:** i.e., affection I owe (carry as obligation or duty).

228. **wise:** discreet; sane.

231. **government:** position as governor.

233. **glad to see you mad:** happy ("satisfied") to see you have abandoned discretion and sanity (?).

237. **very much:** excessive, outrageous.

Make her amends—she weeps.
OTHELLO   O devil, devil!
  If that the earth could teem with woman's tears,
  Each drop she falls would prove a crocodile.   240
  Out of my sight!
DESDEMONA   I will not stay to offend you.
LODOVICO   Truly obedient lady!
  I do beseech your lordship call her back.
OTHELLO   Mistress!
DESDEMONA   My lord?   245
OTHELLO   What would you with her, sir?
LODOVICO   Who I, my lord?
OTHELLO   Ay, you did wish that I would make her turn.
  Sir, she can turn, and turn, and yet go on
  And turn again. And she can weep, sir, weep.
  And she's obedient; as you say, obedient,   250
  Very obedient.—Proceed you in your tears.—
  Concerning this, sir—O well-painted passion!—
  I am commanded home.—Get you away!
  I'll send for you anon.—Sir, I obey the mandate
  And will return to Venice.—Hence, avaunt!   255

                              [*Exit* DESDEMONA.]

  Cassio shall have my place. And, sir, tonight
  I do entreat that we may sup together.
  You are welcome, sir, to Cyprus.—Goats and monkeys!   *Exit.*
LODOVICO   Is this the noble Moor whom our full Senate
  Call all in all sufficient? Is this the nature   260
  Whom passion could not shake? whose solid virtue
  The shot of accident nor dart of chance
  Could neither graze nor pierce?
IAGO   He is much changed.
LODOVICO   Are his wits safe? Is he not light of brain?
IAGO   He's that he is; I may not breathe my censure.   265

---

  240. falls: lets fall. **prove a crocodile:** the proverbially misleading "crocodile tears."
  247. turn: return; but also change faith, as in "turn Turk" (2.3.160).
  248–49. can turn . . . turn again: is indefatigable in her capacity to shift allegiance; has an insatiable sexual appetite.
  250–51. obedient . . . Very obedient: The word comes to mean "compliant" in the sexual sense.
  255. avaunt: See 3.3.336 and note.
  256. my place: military command; sexual position.
  258. Goats and monkeys: Cf. 3.3.404.
  260. all in all sufficient: totally self-contained.
  260–61. nature . . . shake: Cf. lines 39–41.
  261–63. solid virtue . . . pierce: i.e., his inner strength was impervious to external assaults. **shot . . . chance:** Cf. "The slings and arrows of outrageous fortune," *Hamlet* 3.1.60.

What he might be—if what he might he is not—
I would to heaven he were.
LODOVICO   What! Strike his wife?
IAGO   'Faith, that was not so well; yet would I knew
    That stroke would prove the worst.
LODOVICO   Is it his use?
    Or did the letters work upon his blood   270
    And new create his fault?
IAGO   Alas, alas!
    It is not honesty in me to speak
    What I have seen and known. You shall observe him,
    And his own courses will denote him so
    That I may save my speech. Do but go after   275
    And mark how he continues.
LODOVICO   I am sorry that I am deceived in him.   *Exeunt.*

ACT 4 SCENE 2

Enter OTHELLO *and* EMILIA.

OTHELLO   You have seen nothing then?
EMILIA   Nor ever heard, nor ever did suspect.
OTHELLO   Yes, you have seen Cassio and she together.
EMILIA   But then I saw no harm, and then I heard
    Each syllable that breath made up between them.   5
OTHELLO   What, did they never whisper?
EMILIA   Never, my lord.
OTHELLO   Nor send you out o'th' way?
EMILIA   Never.
OTHELLO   To fetch her fan, her gloves, her mask, nor nothing?
EMILIA   Never, my lord.   10
OTHELLO   That's strange.
EMILIA   I durst, my lord, to wager she is honest,
    Lay down my soul at stake. If you think other,
    Remove your thought; it doth abuse your bosom.
    If any wretch have put this in your head,   15
    Let heaven requite it with the serpent's curse,
    For if she be not honest, chaste and true,

265–67. I may . . . he were:. Iago claims that his duty prevents him from criticism, then speaks obscurely in a way designed to reinforce suspicion about Othello's sanity.
    269. use: regular habit.
    274. courses: behavior.
    9. mask: "conventional public attire for women of the time" (Mowat and Werstine).
    12. durst: would dare.
    13. other: otherwise.
    16. the serpent's curse: "upon thy belly shalt thou go, and dust shalt thou eat all the dayes of thy life" (Genesis 3.14).

There's no man happy. The purest of their wives
Is foul as slander.

OTHELLO   Bid her come hither—go.   *Exit* EMILIA.

She says enough; yet she's a simple bawd   20
That cannot say as much. This is a subtle whore:
A closet lock and key of villainous secrets;
And yet she'll kneel and pray; I have seen her do't.

                              Enter DESDEMONA *and* EMILIA.

DESDEMONA   My lord, what is your will?

OTHELLO   Pray you, chuck, come
hither.

DESDEMONA   What is your pleasure?

OTHELLO   Let me see your eyes.   25
Look in my face.

DESDEMONA   What horrible fancy's this?

OTHELLO [*To* EMILIA.]   Some of your function, mistress:
Leave procreants alone and shut the door;
Cough or cry "hem" if anybody come.
Your mystery, your mystery! Nay, dispatch!   *Exit* EMILIA.   30

DESDEMONA   Upon my knee, what doth your speech import?
I understand a fury in your words,
But not the words.

OTHELLO   Why? What art thou?

DESDEMONA   Your wife, my lord, your true and loyal wife.

OTHELLO   Come, swear it! damn thyself!   35
Lest, being like one of heaven, the devils themselves
Should fear to seize thee. Therefore be double-damned:
Swear thou art honest!

DESDEMONA   Heaven doth truly know it.

OTHELLO   Heaven truly knows that thou art false as hell.

DESDEMONA   To whom, my lord? With whom? How am I false?   40

OTHELLO   Ah, Desdemon! away, away, away!

DESDEMONA   Alas the heavy day! Why do you weep?
Am I the motive of these tears, my lord?
If haply you my father do suspect

20–21. **she's . . . cannot:** i.e., any foolish procurer ("simple bawd") would maintain.
21. **This:** i.e., Emilia, but then slipping into Desdemona at some point in the speech.
22. **closet lock and key:** at once the space (a "closet" is a small often private, and female enclosure) as well as the means to protect and the tool to penetrate the space (cf. "thing," 3.3.274–75, and note).
27. **function:** office (as bawd).
28. **procreants:** breeders.
30. **mystery:** trade.
31. **Upon my knee:** "Kneeling in submission was not unusual" (Honigmann); in the absence of stage directions, actors / readers have to determine when she will rise.
36. **one of heaven:** i.e., beautifully angelic.
37. **double-damned:** adding perjury to adultery.

An instrument of this your calling back,   45
Lay not your blame on me. If you have lost him,
I have lost him too.
OTHELLO   Had it pleased heaven
To try me with affliction, had they rained
All kind of sores and shames on my bare head,
Steeped me in poverty to the very lips,   50
Given to captivity me and my utmost hopes,
I should have found in some place of my soul
A drop of patience. But, alas, to make me
The fixèd figure for the time of scorn
To point his slow and moving finger at!   55
Yet could I bear that too—well, very well;
But there where I have garnered up my heart,
Where either I must live or bear no life,
The fountain from the which my current runs
Or else dries up; to be discarded thence,   60
Or keep it as a cistern for foul toads
To knot and gender in!—Turn thy complexion there,
Patience, thou young and rose-lipped cherubin;
I here look grim as hell!
DESDEMONA   I hope my noble lord esteems me honest.   65
OTHELLO   O, ay, as summer flies are in the shambles,
That quicken even with blowing. O thou weed,
Who art so lovely fair and smell'st so sweet
That the sense aches at thee,
Would thou hadst never been born!   70
DESDEMONA   Alas, what ignorant sin have I committed?

45. **An instrument of:** instrumental in.
50. **Steeped:** immersed.
51. **utmost:** uttermost (i.e., fondest).
54–55. The stationery number at which the clock hand points accusatorily; i.e., the public mockery of the cuckold as an unbearably sustained embarrassment. **slow and moving:** slowly moving.
57. **garnered . . . heart:** stored my deepest feelings (most vital sustenance).
61. **keep it . . . toads:** Cf. "a toad" and "keep a corner" (3.3.272–74); **cistern:** cesspit.
62. **knot and gender:** fuck and breed. **Turn thy complexion there:** (1) direct your attention to that prospect; (2) transform your disposition—or (3) facial color—at that prospect.
64. **I . . . hell:** Many editors emend "I" in the quarto and the folio to "Ay" (which is in fact regularly represented as "I" in the early texts), often adding commas ("Ay, here look grim," "Ay, here look, grim"). The effect of this editorial intervention is to determine that Othello is addressing a command to the angelic boy (the personified "Patience"), rather than describing his own appearance. In the theater, "I" and "ay" would be indistinguishable.
66. **flies . . . shambles:** the "flesh-flies" that breed in ordure or rotting meat ("shambles" = slaughterhouse); cf. "exsufflicate," 3.3.184, and note.
67. **quicken:** are born; become aroused; cf. 3.3.279 and note. **even with blowing:** at the very moment—even now—when the eggs are deposited. For the association of flies, fertility, and contamination, cf. 1.1. 67–68. **weed:** perhaps suggested by "blowing" as "blooming."
71. **ignorant:** epithet transferred from Desdemona, who does not know what she is supposed to have done.

OTHELLO   Was this fair paper, this most goodly book,
Made to write "whore" upon? What committed?
Committed? O, thou public commoner!
I should make very forges of my cheeks   75
That would to cinders burn up modesty
Did I but speak thy deeds. What committed?
Heaven stops the nose at it, and the moon winks;
The bawdy wind that kisses all it meets
Is hushed within the hollow mine of earth   80
And will not hear't. What committed?
DESDEMONA   By heaven, you do me wrong!
OTHELLO   Are not you a strumpet?
DESDEMONA   No, as I am a Christian!
If to preserve this vessel for my lord
From any other foul unlawful touch   85
Be not to be a strumpet, I am none.
OTHELLO   What, not a whore?
DESDEMONA   No, as I shall be saved!
OTHELLO   Is't possible?
DESDEMONA   O, heaven forgive us!
OTHELLO   I cry you mercy then.
I took you for that cunning whore of Venice   90
That married with Othello.—You! Mistress!
That have the office opposite to Saint Peter
And keeps the gate of hell. You, you!

Enter EMILIA.

Ay, you.
We have done our course; there's money for your pains;
I pray you turn the key and keep our counsel.   *Exit.* 95

---

72. **this fair paper:** her white flesh.

73. **made to write "whore" upon:** Cf. Revelation 17.5: "And in her forhead was a name written, a Mysterie, great Babylon, the mother of whoredomes, and abominations of the earth."

73–74. **committed? / Committed?:** Othello's enraged repetitions here and in 77 and 81 depend on the word's Elizabethan application "particularly to unlawful acts of love" (Malone, who cites *King Lear* 3.4.77: "commit not with man's sworn spouse").

74. **public commoner:** "common whore" (Honigmann).

75–76. **forges . . . modesty:** "an image of blushing" (McDonald).

79. **The bawdy wind:** Even (understood) the promiscuous wind is embarrassed.

84. **this vessel:** my body (container of the spirit: a biblical metaphor).

88. **Is't possible:** "This question echoes through the play" (Honigmann, citing 2.3.277, 3.3.359, 3.4.66, and 4.1.42).

89. **cry you mercy:** beg your pardon.

92. **the office . . . Peter:** Christ gave St. Peter "the keyes of the kingdome of heaven," declaring that "upon this rocke I wil buylde my Church: and the gates of hel shal not overcome it" (Matthew 16.18–19).

93. **the gate of hell:** "term for the female genitalia" (McDonald).

94. **course:** business. **pains:** efforts.

EMILIA   Alas, what does this gentleman conceive?
  How do you, madam? how do you, my good lady?
DESDEMONA   Faith, half asleep.
EMILIA   Good madam,
  What's the matter with my lord?   100
DESDEMONA   With who?
EMILIA   Why, with my lord, madam.
DESDEMONA   Who is thy lord?
EMILIA   He that is yours, sweet lady.
DESDEMONA   I have none. Do not talk to me, Emilia;
  I cannot weep, nor answers have I none   105
  But what should go by water. Prithee tonight
  Lay on my bed my wedding sheets; remember,
  And call thy husband hither.
EMILIA   Here's a change indeed!   *Exit.*
DESDEMONA   'Tis meet I should be used so, very meet.
  How have I been behaved that he might stick   110
  The small'st opinion on my least misuse?

                                Enter IAGO *and* EMILIA.

IAGO   What is your pleasure, madam? How is't with you?
DESDEMONA   I cannot tell. Those that do teach young babes
  Do it with gentle means and easy tasks.
  He might have chid me so; for in good faith   115
  I am a child to chiding.
IAGO   What is the matter, lady?
EMILIA   Alas, Iago, my lord hath so bewhored her,
  Thrown such despite and heavy terms upon her,
  That true hearts cannot bear it.
DESDEMONA   Am I that name, Iago?
IAGO   What name, fair lady?   120
DESDEMONA   Such as she said my lord did say I was.
EMILIA   He called her whore. A beggar in his drink
  Could not have laid such terms upon his callet.

   96. **conceive:** think, imagine.
   106. **go by water:** be communicated through tears.
   107. **my wedding sheets:** "to remind Othello of their former love. . . . Also ominous, as wives were sometimes buried in their wedding sheets" (Honigmann).
   109. **meet:** appropriate; **used:** treated; either an appreciative reference to Emilia's kindness or a sarcastic reference to Othello's cruelty.
   110–11. **stick . . . misuse:** even casually reprimand any inconsequential lapse on my part.
   116. **a child:** responsive (because eager to please); inexperienced, unused.
   117. **bewhored:** (1) treated her like a whore (2) called her a whore (cf. "belie," 4.1.36); imposed whoredom on.
   118. **Thrown . . . her:** abused and berated her so; the metaphor, representing Othello's words as a painfully burdensome material weight, is reinforced by "bear" in the next line.
   123. **laid such terms upon:** sustains the metaphor of material weight. **callet:** "used by

IAGO   Why did he so?

DESDEMONA   I do not know; I am sure I am none such.   125

IAGO   Do not weep, do not weep. Alas the day!   *compassionate*

EMILIA   Hath she forsook so many noble matches,
Her father and her country and her friends,
To be called whore? Would it not make one weep?

DESDEMONA   It is my wretched fortune.

IAGO   Beshrew him for't!   130
How comes this trick upon him?

DESDEMONA   Nay, heaven doth know.

EMILIA   I will be hanged if some eternal villain,
Some busy and insinuating rogue,
Some cogging, cozening slave, to get some office,
Have not devised this slander. I will be hanged else.   135

IAGO   Fie! there is no such man; it is impossible.

DESDEMONA   If any such there be, heaven pardon him.

EMILIA   A halter pardon him, and hell gnaw his bones!
Why should he call her whore? who keeps her company?
What place? what time? what form? what likelihood?   140
The Moor's abused by some most villainous knave,
Some base notorious knave, some scurvy fellow.
O heaven, that such companions thou'dst unfold,
And put in every honest hand a whip
To lash the rascals naked through the world   145
Even from the east to th' west!

IAGO   Speak within door.

EMILIA   O, fie upon them! Some such squire he was
That turned your wit the seamy side without
And made you to suspect me with the Moor.

---

all our old writers for a strumpet of the basest kind" (cited in Furness); "like 'hussy,' 'strumpet,'
'minx,' 'harlot,' 'harlotry,' and 'whore,' . . . a term of abuse attached to women accused of
having sex outside of marriage" (Mowat and Werstine); see note to "friend" (3.4.177).
   127. **forsook:** turned down; abandoned. **matches:** husbands, marriages.
   130. **Beshrew:** shame on.
   131. **trick:** fantasy.
   132. **eternal:** metaphorically, "incorrigible, never-changing" (McDonald); literally,
"almost = a devil" (Honigmann).
   134. **cogging, cozening:** cheating, deceptive.
   138. **halter:** hangman's noose; like the "mercy" Graziano would "render" Shylock: "A halter, gratis. Nothing else, for God's sake" (*Merchant of Venice* 4.1.374).
   140. **form:** means, method.
   141. **abused:** deceived.
   142. **notorious:** outrageous (not "blatantly disreputable" because the villainy is hidden).
scurvy: disgusting (metaphorically, from the skin disease).
   143. **companions:** "fellow[s] in a bad sense" (Schmidt). **unfold:** reveal.
   146. **within door:** i.e., more quietly; transfers one measure of female propriety (enclosure
within domestic space) to another (silence). Cf. 3.4.165 and 2.1.109.
   147. **squire:** "gentleman" (with ironic contempt).
   148. **the seamy side without:** inside out.

IAGO   You are a fool; go to.

DESDEMONA   Alas, Iago,   150
  What shall I do to win my lord again?
  Good friend, go to him; for by this light of heaven,
  I know not how I lost him. Here I kneel:
  If e'er my will did trespass 'gainst his love,
  Either in discourse of thought or actual deed,   155
  Or that mine eyes, mine ears, or any sense
  Delighted them [in] any other form,
  Or that I do not yet, and ever did,
  And ever will (though he do shake me off
  To beggarly divorcement) love him dearly—   160
  Comfort forswear me! Unkindness may do much,
  And his unkindness may defeat my life,
  But never taint my love. I cannot say "whore."
  It does abhor me now I speak the word.
  To do the act that might the addition earn   165
  Not the world's mass of vanity could make me.

IAGO   I pray you be content; 'tis but his humor;
  The business of the state does him offence.

DESDEMONA   If 'twere no other—

IAGO   It is but so, I warrant.

                              [*Trumpets within.*]
  Hark how these instruments summon to supper.   170
  The messengers of Venice stays the meat;
  Go in, and weep not; all things shall be well.

Sensitivity
could save her?   *Exeunt* DESDEMONA *and* EMILIA.

                              ENTER RODERIGO.

  How now, Roderigo?

RODERIGO   I do not find that thou deal'st justly with me.

IAGO   What in the contrary?   175

RODERIGO   Every day thou doff'st me with some device,
  Iago, and rather, as it seems to me now, keep'st from

---

  153. **Here I kneel:** Cf. line 31 and note.
  154. **will:** desire. **did trespass 'gainst:** strayed from, performed an action that strayed
from.
  155. **discourse:** (verbal) process.
  157. **form:** appearance (but his).
  161. **forswear:** abandon.
  162. **defeat:** destroy.
  164. **abhor:** disgust; turn into a whore. Desdemona echoes "bewhored" (117) and "made
to write 'whore' upon" (73).
  165. **addition:** title, reputation.
  166. **the world's mass of vanity:** all earthly riches.
  171. **stays the meat:** wait for their meal.
  176. **doff'st me:** turn me away. **device:** subterfuge.

me all conveniency than suppliest me with the least
  advantage
of hope. I will indeed no longer endure it. Nor
am I yet persuaded to put up in peace what already I   180
have foolishly suffered.

IAGO Will you hear me, Roderigo?

RODERIGO Faith, I have heard too much; and your words and
  performances are no kin together.

IAGO You charge me most unjustly.   185

RODERIGO With naught but truth. I have wasted myself
  out of my means. The jewels you have had from
  me to deliver Desdemona would half have corrupted a
  votarist. You have told me she hath received them,
  and returned me expectations and comforts of sudden   190
  respect and acquaintance, but I find none.

IAGO Well, go to; very well.

RODERIGO Very well! go to! I cannot go to, man, nor
  'tis not very well. Nay, I think it is scurvy, and begin to
  find myself fopped in it.   195

IAGO Very well.

RODERIGO I tell you 'tis not very well. I will make myself
  known to Desdemona. If she will return me my
  jewels, I will give over my suit and repent my unlawful
  solicitation. If not, assure yourself I will seek   200
  satisfaction of you.

IAGO You have said now.

RODERIGO Ay, and said nothing but what I protest intendment
  of doing.

IAGO Why, now I see there's mettle in thee, and   205
  even from this instant do build on thee a better opinion
  than ever before. Give me thy hand, Roderigo.
  Thou hast taken against me a most just exception,
  but yet I protest I have dealt most directly in thy
  affair.   210

RODERIGO It hath not appeared.

178. **conveniency:** fit circumstances (for wooing Desdemona?).
180. **persuaded to put up in peace:** convinced to accept without a fight.
183–84. **your words . . . together:** you say one thing and do another.
186–87. **wasted . . . means:** pissed away my wealth.
189. **votarist:** nun.
190. **expectations and comforts:** comforting expectations.
190–91. **sudden respect:** prompt consideration.
195. **fopped:** duped.
201. **satisfaction:** the restoration of his money or of his honor (threatening a duel).
203–04. **but what . . . doing:** that I swear I won't act on.
205. **mettle:** "spirit, bravery (with pun on 'metal,' gold)" (McDonald).
208. **just exception:** legitimate complaint.
209. **directly:** forthrightly, honestly.

IAGO   I grant indeed it hath not appeared, and
your suspicion is not without wit and judgment.
But, Roderigo, if thou hast that in thee indeed which
I have greater reason to believe now than ever—I   215
mean purpose, courage and valor—this night
show it. If thou the next night following enjoy not
Desdemona, take me from this world with treachery
and devise engines for my life.
RODERIGO   Well, what is it? Is it within reason and compass?   220
IAGO   Sir, there is especial commission come from
Venice to depute Cassio in Othello's place.
RODERIGO   Is that true? Why, then Othello and Desdemona
return again to Venice.
IAGO   O no; he goes into Mauritania and taketh   225
away with him the fair Desdemona, unless his abode
be lingered here by some accident; wherein
none can be so determinate as the removing of
Cassio.
RODERIGO   How do you mean removing him?   230
IAGO   Why, by making him uncapable of Othello's
place—knocking out his brains.
RODERIGO   And that you would have me to do.
IAGO   Ay, if you dare do yourself a profit and a
right. He sups tonight with a harlotry, and thither   235
will I go to him. He knows not yet of his honorable
fortune. If you will watch his going thence, which
I will fashion to fall out between twelve and one,
you may take him at your pleasure. I will be near
to second your attempt, and he shall fall between   240
us. Come, stand not amazed at it, but go along with
me. I will show you such a necessity in his death that
you shall think yourself bound to put it on him. It
is now high suppertime, and the night grows to waste.
About it!   245

---

219. engines: instruments (of torture); plots.
220. within reason and compass: likely to succeed and practical to implement.
225. Mauritania: the North African home of Moors, probably registered less as geopolitical fact than as site of erotic fantasy ("taketh away . . . the fair Desdemona" sounds like a romance formula).
227. lingered: protracted.
228. determinate: decisive.
234–35. a profit and a right: something both beneficial and legitimate.
235. a harlotry: Bianca (see line 123 and note).
238. fashion to fall out: arrange to occur.
240–41. between us: as a result of our joint effort; perhaps suggesting the logistics of the assault.
244. suppertime: usually "at five or six o-clock" (Schmidt). grows to waste: i.e., time is passing, hurry up.

RODERIGO   I will hear further reason for this.
IAGO   And you shall be satisfied.   *Exeunt.*

ACT 4 SCENE 3

Enter OTHELLO, LODOVICO, DESDEMONA, EMILIA
and Attendants.

LODOVICO   I do beseech you, sir, trouble yourself no further.
OTHELLO   O, pardon me; 'twill do me good to walk.
LODOVICO   Madam, good night. I humbly thank your ladyship.
DESDEMONA   Your honor is most welcome.
OTHELLO   Will you walk, sir?
O, Desdemona—   5
DESDEMONA   My lord?
OTHELLO   Get you to bed on th' instant. I will be returned
    forthwith. Dismiss your attendant there. Look't
    be done.
DESDEMONA   I will, my lord.   10

    Exit [OTHELLO *with* LODOVICO *and Attendants.*]

EMILIA   How goes it now? He looks gentler than he did.
DESDEMONA   He says he will return incontinent,
    And hath commanded me to go to bed,
    And bid me to dismiss you.
EMILIA   Dismiss me?
DESDEMONA   It was his bidding; therefore, good Emilia,   15
    Give me my nightly wearing, and adieu.
    We must not now displease him.
EMILIA   I would you had never seen him.
DESDEMONA   So would not I: my love doth so approve him
    That even his stubbornness, his checks, his frowns—   20
    Prithee unpin me—have grace and favor.
EMILIA   I have laid those sheets you bade me on the bed.
DESDEMONA   All's one. Good faith, how foolish are our minds!
    If I do die before thee, prithee shroud me
    In one of these same sheets.
EMILIA   Come, come—you talk.   25

---

247. **And you shall be satisfied:** Cf. 3.3.394–95.
7–8. **returned forthwith:** back immediately.
12. **incontinent:** right away; but see 1.3.303 and note—the modern meaning, "without
control," is secondary but available.
20. **stubbornness:** harshness. **checks:** reprimands.
23. **All's one:** No matter.
25. **Come . . . talk:** i.e., stop talking nonsense, don't be silly.

DESDEMONA   My mother had a maid called Barbary;
    She was in love, and he she loved proved mad
    And did forsake her. She had a Song of "Willow"—
    An old thing 'twas, but it expressed her fortune—
    And she died singing it. That song tonight   30
    Will not go from my mind; I have much to do
    But to go hang my head all at one side
    And sing it like poor Barbary. Prithee dispatch.
EMILIA   Shall I go fetch your nightgown?
DESDEMONA   No, unpin me here.
    This Lodovico is a proper man.   35
EMILIA   A very handsome man.
DESDEMONA   He speaks well.
EMILIA   I know a lady in Venice would have walked
    barefoot to Palestine for a touch of his nether lip.
DESDEMONA [Sings.]

        The poor soul sat singing by a sycamore tree,   40
            Sing all a green willow;
        Her hand on her bosom, her head on her knee,
            Sing willow, willow, willow.
        The fresh streams ran by her and murmured her moans,
            Sing willow, willow, willow;   45
        Her salt tears fell from her and softened the stones,
            Sing willow, willow, willow.

    [To EMILIA.] Lay by these.
        [Sings.]
        Willow, willow.

    [To EMILIA.] Prithee hie thee—he'll come anon.   50
        [Sings.]
            Sing all a green willow must be my garland.
            Let nobody blame him, his scorn I approve.

---

26. **Barbary:** Barbara; "suggests the Barbary coast, home of the Moors" (Honigmann).
31–32. **I have much . . . But to:** "it is all I can do not to" (Ridley).
34. **unpin me here:** "presumably the fastenings of her dress or hair" (Sanders); cf. "unpin me" (21).
35. **proper:** true, good; Desdemona's apparently gratuitous comment has provoked much critical speculation.
39. **Palestine:** i.e., as a crusading lover; with Mauritania and Barbary, sustains the play's symbolic geography. **nether:** lower. **touch . . . lip:** a graphically sexual way of saying "kiss."
40–57. Like Iago's "King Stephen" (see note to 2.3.81–88), Desdemona's "Willow" is based on "a very old song" (Capell); its conventional treatment of lost or unrequited love would have been familiar to at least some of Shakespeare's audience. The sycamore is sometimes and the weeping willow is frequently evoked in this context.
48. **Lay by these:** Put these (sheets?) aside.
50. **Prithee . . . anon:** Cf. "Prithee dispatch" (33).
52. **approve:** Cf. 19.

Nay, that's not next. [*To* EMILIA.]   Hark, who is't that
    knocks?

EMILIA   It's the wind.

DESDEMONA [*Sings.*]

> I called my love false love, but what said he then?   55
>   Sing willow, willow, willow;
> If I court more women, you'll couch with more men.

[*To* EMILIA.] So, get thee gone, good night. Mine eyes do itch—
Doth that bode weeping?

EMILIA   'Tis neither here nor there.

DESDEMONA   I have heard it said so. O, these men, these men!   60
    Dost thou in conscience think—tell me, Emilia—
    That there be women do abuse their husbands
    In such gross kind?

EMILIA   There be some such, no question.

DESDEMONA   Wouldst thou do such a deed for all the world?

EMILIA   Why, would not you?

DESDEMONA   No, by this heavenly light!   65

EMILIA   Nor I, neither, by this heavenly light:
    I might do't as well i'th' dark.

DESDEMONA   Wouldst thou do such a deed for all the world?

EMILIA   The world's a huge thing:
    It is a great price for a small vice.   70

DESDEMONA   In troth, I think thou wouldst not.

EMILIA   In troth, I think I should—and undo't when
    I had done. Marry, I would not do such a thing for a
    joint ring, nor for measures of lawn, nor for gowns,
    petticoats, nor caps, nor any petty exhibition. But for   75
    all the whole world—'Uds pity! who would not make her
    husband
    a cuckold to make him a monarch? I should venture
    purgatory for't.

---

52. Nay, that's not next: i.e., no, that's wrong. Desdemona misremembers "Let nobody
blame me, her scornes I do prove" (the best-known version of the original; Honigmann, 340).

62. abuse: deceive.

63. gross kind: vile way.

70. price: prize, reward.

71–72. In troth: By my truth; a mild oath, presumably repeated by Emilia in affectionate
mockery.

74. joint ring: made of two or more pieces fitting together; a love or marriage token.
measures of lawn: "quantities of fine linen" (Honigmann).

75. petty exhibition: inconsequential offering.

76. Ud's pity: by the grace of God.

77. venture: risk.

78. purgatory: the realm in Roman Catholic (but not Protestant) depictions of the afterlife
where sins were expiated before souls entered heaven. For Emilia, adultery is only "a small
vice" (see "venial," 4.1.9, and note).

DESDEMONA   Beshrew me if I would do such a wrong
  For the whole world!   80
EMILIA   Why, the wrong is but a wrong i'th' world;
  and having the world for your labor, 'tis a wrong in
  your own world, and you might quickly make it right.
DESDEMONA   I do not think there is any such woman.
EMILIA   Yes, a dozen; and as many to'th' vantage as   85
  would store the world they played for.
  But I do think it is their husbands' faults
  If wives do fall. Say that they slack their duties
  And pour our treasures into foreign laps;
  Or else break out in peevish jealousies,   90
  Throwing restraint upon us; or say they strike us,
  Or scant our former having in despite.
  Why, we have galls; and though we have some grace,
  Yet have we some revenge. Let husbands know
  Their wives have sense like them. They see, and smell,   95
  And have their palates both for sweet and sour,
  As husbands have. What is it that they do
  When they change us for others? Is it sport?
  I think it is. And doth affection breed it?
  I think it doth. Is't frailty that thus errs?   100
  It is so too. And have not we affections,
  Desires for sport, and frailty, as men have?
  Then let them use us well; else let them know,
  The ills we do, their ills instruct us so.
DESDEMONA   Good night, good night. God me such uses send,   105
  Not to pick bad from bad, but by bad, mend!   *Exeunt.*

---

79. **Beshrew:** Shame on.
82. **for your labor:** (as a reward) for your efforts.
85. **a dozen:** "facetious understatement" (Honigmann). **as many . . . vantage:** another dozen.
86. **store:** "stock with people" (Schmidt), the products of their "labor." **played:** "gambled (with sexual undertone)" (McDonald).
88. **duties:** sexual responsibilities, the "debt" husbands and wives were enjoined to pay each other in order that both might "avoid fornication" (1 Corinthians 7.2).
89. **foreign:** outside the domain of marriage.
91. **Throwing restraint:** imposing restriction(s).
92. **scant:** diminish. **having:** allowance.
93. **galls . . . grace:** "capacities for resentment . . . goodness, forgiveness" (Mowat and Werstine).
99. **affection:** desire.
104. **instruct us so:** Cf. Shylock's "better the instruction" and the whole of his "Hath not a Jew" speech (*Merchant of Venice*, 3.1.49–61). "Such protests against 'double standards' were not uncommon" (Honigmann, citing *Comedy of Errors* 2.1.10 ff.).
105. **uses:** practices.
106. **Not . . . mend:** perplexing in the details, but clearly refusing Emilia's earthy and pragmatic relativism.

ACT 5 SCENE 1

Enter IAGO *and* RODERIGO.

IAGO Here, stand behind this bulk; straight will he come.
Wear thy good rapier bare, and put it home.
Quick, quick, fear nothing! I'll be at thy elbow.
It makes us or it mars us; think on that
And fix most firm thy resolution.   5
RODERIGO Be near at hand; I may miscarry in't.
IAGO Here, at thy hand. Be bold, and take thy stand.   [*Stands
                                                              aside.*]
RODERIGO I have no great devotion to the deed,
And yet he hath given me satisfying reasons;
'Tis but a man gone. Forth my sword: he dies!   10
IAGO I have rubbed this young quat almost to the sense,
And he grows angry. Now, whether he kill Cassio
Or Cassio him, or each do kill the other,
Every way makes my gain. Live Roderigo,
He calls me to a restitution large   15
Of gold and jewels that I bobbed from him
As gifts to Desdemona.
It must not be. If Cassio do remain,
He hath a daily beauty in his life
That makes me ugly; and besides, the Moor   20
May unfold me to him; there stand I in much peril.
No, he must die. But so—

                              Enter CASSIO.

                         I heard him coming.
RODERIGO I know his gate; 'tis he. Villain, thou diest!   [*Thrusts
                                                            at* CASSIO.]
CASSIO That thrust had been mine enemy indeed,
But that my coat is better than thou know'st.   25
I will make proof of thine.   [*Wounds* RODERIGO.]
RODERIGO   O, I am slain!

          [IAGO *wounds* CASSIO *in the leg and exits.*]

----

   1. **bulk:** small enclosure jutting out from the wall of the "tiring house" (where the actors attired themselves) at the rear of the stage.
   11. **quat:** pimple. **sense:** quick.
   14. **Live Roderigo:** should Roderigo live.
   16. **bobbed from him:** tricked him out of.
   21. **unfold:** reveal (cf. 4.2.143).
   25. **coat:** "hidden armor protecting the upper half of the body (like a bullet-proof vest)" (Ross).
   26. **STAGE DIRECTION** IAGO . . . *and exits:* Most editors, following eighteenth-century traditions, specify that Iago stabs Cassio from behind.

CASSIO   I am maimed forever! Help, ho! murder! murder!

Enter OTHELLO.

OTHELLO   The voice of Cassio. Iago keeps his word.
RODERIGO   O, villain that I am!
OTHELLO   It is even so.
CASSIO   O, help ho! light! a surgeon!   30
OTHELLO   'Tis he. O brave Iago, honest and just,
    That hast such noble sense of thy friend's wrong!
    Thou teachest me. Minion, your dear lies dead,
    And your unblest fate hies. Strumpet, I come.
    Forth of my heart those charms, thine eyes, are blotted.   35
    Thy bed, lust-stained, shall with lust's blood be spotted.

Exit OTHELLO.

Enter LODOVICO *and* GRATIANO.

CASSIO   What ho! no watch? no passage? Murder, murder!
GRATIANO   'Tis some mischance; the voice is very direful.
CASSIO   O help!
LODOVICO   Hark!   40
RODERIGO   O, wretched villain!
LODOVICO   Two or three groan. 'Tis heavy night;
    These may be counterfeits; let's think't unsafe
    To come into the cry without more help.
RODERIGO   Nobody come? Then shall I bleed to death.   45
LODOVICO   Hark.

Enter IAGO *with a light.*

GRATIANO   Here's one comes in his shirt, with light and
    weapons.
IAGO   Who's there? Whose noise is this that cries on murder?
LODOVICO   We do not know.
IAGO   Do not you hear a cry?
CASSIO   Here, here! for heaven sake, help me!
IAGO   What's the matter?   50

---

28. STAGE DIRECTION *Enter* OTHELLO: "usually enters 'above'" (Honigmann); cf.
note to 2.1.1.
    33. Minion: sweetheart (referring ironically to Desdemona).
    34. unblest: unholy, damned. **hies:** hastens.
    35. of: from. **blotted:** to blot is "to obliterate with ink; and hence to efface" (Schmidt; cf.
4.2.72–73).
    36. spotted: stained; cf. the handkerchief, "spotted with strawberries" (3.3.435).
    37. watch: night patrol. **passage:** passersby.
    38. direful: dreadful, dismal.
    42. heavy: bleak, dark.
    44. come into the cry: approach or enter the scene of clamor.
    47. shirt: night dress (as though roused from sleep).
    48. cries on: shouts of.

GRATIANO   This is Othello's ancient, as I take it.
LODOVICO   The same indeed, a very valiant fellow.
IAGO   What are you here that cry so grievously?
CASSIO   Iago? O, I am spoiled, undone by villains!
  Give me some help.   55
IAGO   O me, lieutenant! What villains have done this?
CASSIO   I think that one of them is hereabout
  And cannot make away.
IAGO   O treacherous villains!
  What are you there? Come in, and give some help.
RODERIGO   O, help me there!   60
CASSIO   That's one of them.
IAGO   O murd'rous slave! O villain! [*Stabs*
                                                  RODERIGO.]
RODERIGO   O damned Iago! O inhuman dog!
IAGO   Kill men i'th' dark?—Where be these bloody thieves?—
  How silent is this town!—Ho, murder, murder!—
  What may you be? Are you of good or evil?   65
LODOVICO   As you shall prove us, praise us.
IAGO   Signior Lodovico?
LODOVICO   He, sir.
IAGO   I cry you mercy. Here's Cassio hurt by villains.
GRATIANO   Cassio?   70
IAGO   How is't, brother?
CASSIO   My leg is cut in two.
IAGO   Marry, heaven forbid!
  Light, gentlemen. I'll bind it with my shirt.

Enter BIANCA.

BIANCA   What is the matter, ho? Who is't that cried?
IAGO   Who is't that cried?
BIANCA   O, my dear Cassio!   75
  My sweet Cassio! O Cassio, Cassio, Cassio!
IAGO   O notable strumpet! Cassio, may you suspect
  Who they should be that have thus mangled you?
CASSIO   No.
GRATIANO   I am sorry to find you thus; I have been to seek you.   80
IAGO   Lend me a garter. So . . . O for a chair
  To bear him easily hence!

---

54. **spoiled:** destroyed.
58. **make:** get.
66. **As you . . . praise us:** i.e., judge us by our actions.
69. **I cry you mercy:** Excuse me (for not recognizing you).
77. **notable:** flagrant.
81. **garter:** "band, worn as a sash or belt" (Honigmann), to use as tourniquet. **chair:**
"framework couch for carrying the wounded" (McDonald).

BIANCA   Alas, he faints! O Cassio, Cassio, Cassio!

IAGO   Gentlemen all, I do suspect this trash
To be a party in this injury.—   85
Patience awhile, good Cassio.—Come, come!
Lend me a light. Know we this face or no?
Alas! my friend and my dear countryman,
Roderigo! No—yes, sure! O heaven, Roderigo!

GRATIANO   What, of Venice?

IAGO   Even he, sir. Did you know him?   90

GRATIANO   Know him? Ay.

IAGO   Signior Gratiano? I cry your gentle pardon.
These bloody accidents must excuse my manners
That so neglected you.

GRATIANO   I am glad to see you.

IAGO   How do you, Cassio? O, a chair, a chair!   95

GRATIANO   Roderigo?

IAGO   He, he, 'tis he.   [A litter is brought in.]
                O, that's well said, the chair.
Some good man bear him carefully from hence;
I'll fetch the general's surgeon.—For you, mistress,
Save you your labor.—He that lies slain here, Cassio,   100
Was my dear friend. What malice was between you?

CASSIO   None in the world, nor do I know the man.

IAGO [To BIANCA.]   What, look you pale?—O, bear him out o'th'
air.
Stay you, good gentlemen.—Look you pale, mistress?—
Do you perceive the gastness of her eye?—   105
Nay, if you stare, we shall hear more anon.—
Behold her well; I pray you look upon her.
Do you see, gentlemen? Nay, guiltiness will speak
Though tongues were out of use.

                                        Enter EMILIA.

EMILIA   Alas, what is the matter? what is the matter, husband?   110

IAGO   Cassio hath here been set on in the dark
By Roderigo and fellows that are scaped.
He's almost slain, and Roderigo quite dead.

---

92. I cry . . . pardon: i.e., excuse me for not recognizing you; cf. "I cry you mercy" (69).
97. said: done.
100. Save . . . labor: don't trouble yourself.
103. out o'th' air: inside to a more secure and (it was assumed) less infectious environment.
105. gastness: terror.
106. stare . . . anon: you will soon confess the guilt betrayed by your appearance.
109. out of use: not used; her guilt is visible without verbal confirmation.

EMILIA Alas, good gentleman! alas, good Cassio!

IAGO This is the fruits of whoring. Prithee, Emilia,   115
Go know of Cassio where he supped tonight.—
What, do you shake at that?

BIANCA He supped at my house, but I therefore shake not.

IAGO O did he so? I charge you go with me.

EMILIA O fie upon thee, strumpet!   120

BIANCA I am no strumpet, but of life as honest
As you that thus abuse me.

EMILIA   As I? Fie upon thee!

IAGO Kind gentlemen, let's go see poor Cassio dressed.—
Come, mistress, you must tell's another tale.
Emilia, run you to the citadel,   125
And tell my lord and lady what hath happed.   [*Exit* EMILIA.]
Will you go on afore?   *Exeunt* [*all but* IAGO].
                    This is the night
That either makes me or foredoes me quite.   [*Exit.*]

ACT 5 SCENE 2

Enter OTHELLO *with a light,* DESDEMONA *in her bed* [*asleep*].

❋ OTHELLO It is the cause, it is the cause, my soul.
Let me not name it to you, you chaste stars.
It is the cause. Yet I'll not shed her blood,
Nor scar that whiter skin of hers than snow,
And smooth as monumental alabaster.   5
Yet she must die, else she'll betray more men.
Put out the ~~light~~, and then put out the light.
If I quench thee, thou flaming minister,
I can again thy former light restore,

117–18. **shake . . . shake:** Cf. 4.1.135 and note.
120. **fie:** shame.
128. **fordoes me quite:** totally breaks me.
0. **STAGE DIRECTION** *her bed:* may be thrust out from the tiring-house facade, or may be a stationary enclosure like the "bulk" located in front of it (see note to 5.1.1); in either case, curtained and uncurtained as required.
1–3. **the cause . . . the cause:** The phrase can mean "legal matter" and "principle . . . not merely a personal grievance" (McDonald). Both senses fit Othello's claim to be representing a disinterested and impersonal justice (hence his addresses to "the chaste stars" and "my soul"), but the "abruptness of this soliloquy makes it obscure" (Johnson; see p. 219 below).
3. **not shed her blood:** Cf. 4.1.201–02, but contrast the "oddly inconsistent" (Sanders) intention of 5.1.36: "Thy bed, lust-stained, shall with lust's blood be spotted." "Is it Shakespeare or Othello who cannot decide how she should be killed?" (Honigmann).
5. **monumental alabaster:** the white marble of funeral monuments.
7. **the light:** The second "light" must be metaphorical (= her life?).
8. **flaming minister:** the candle or torch, which ministers to his needs. "And of his Angels he saith, Hee maketh the spirits his messengers, and his ministers a flame of fire" (Hebrews 1.6).

Should I repent me. But once put out thy light,   10
Thou cunning'st pattern of excelling nature,
I know not where is that Promethean heat
That can thy light relume. When I have plucked thy rose,
I cannot give it vital growth again;
It needs must wither. I'll smell thee on the tree.   15

> [*He smells, then kisses her.*]

O balmy breath, that dost almost persuade
Justice to break her sword! One more; one more.

> [*He kisses her.*]

Be thus when thou art dead, and I will kill thee
And love thee after. One more, and that's the last.

> *He kisses her.*

So sweet was ne'er so fatal. I must weep,   20
But they are cruel tears. This sorrow's heavenly:
It strikes where it doth love. She wakes.
DESDEMONA   Who's there? Othello?
OTHELLO   Ay, Desdemona.
DESDEMONA   Will you come to bed, my lord?
OTHELLO   Have you prayed tonight, Desdemon?
DESDEMONA   Ay, my lord.   25
OTHELLO   If you bethink yourself of any crime
    Unreconciled as yet to heaven and grace,
    Solicit for it straight.
DESDEMONA   Alack, my lord, what may you mean by that?
OTHELLO   Well, do it, and be brief; I will walk by.   30
    I would not kill thy unprepared spirit.
    No, heavens forfend! I would not kill thy soul.
DESDEMONA   Talk you of killing?

---

11. **cunning'st pattern . . . nature:** (1) supreme achievement of natural excellence; (2) perverse surpassing of the natural (cf. "cunning," 4.2.90).
12. **Promethean heat:** "divine spark" (McDonald); "Prometheus stole fire from heaven with which he animated an image he had made of clay and was punished by Jupiter" (Ross).
13. **relume:** rekindle.
15. **I'll smell thee on the tree:** "Thee" compresses Desdemona's identity into what was, two lines earlier, only a part of that identity ("thy rose"); cf. 4.2.22 and note.
15. **STAGE DIRECTION *smells, then kisses:*** Othello's "smell thee" may be metaphorical for "kiss thee," but given that "the sense of smell is so important" throughout the play (Honigmann), this stage direction takes Othello's words literally.
17. **Justice:** conventionally represented as a woman with a sword in one hand, scales in the other. **One more; one more:** Cf. "And this, and this," 2.1.196.
20. **fatal:** lethal, inescapable.
22. **strikes . . . love:** Cf. Hebrews 12.6: "For whom the Lord loveth, he chasteneth: and he scourgeth every sonne that he receiveth."
28. **solicit:** seek forgiveness. **straight:** right now.
32. **forfend:** forbid.

OTHELLO   Ay, I do.
DESDEMONA   Then heaven
  Have mercy on me!
OTHELLO   Amen, with all my heart!
DESDEMONA   If you say so, I hope you will not kill me.   35
OTHELLO   Humh.
DESDEMONA   And yet I fear you, for you're fatal then
  When your eyes roll so. Why I should fear, I know not,
  Since guiltiness I know not; but yet I feel I fear.
OTHELLO   Think on thy sins.
DESDEMONA   They are loves I bear to you.   40
OTHELLO   Ay, and for that thou diest.
DESDEMONA   That death's unnatural that kills for loving.
  Alas, why gnaw you so your nether lip?
  Some bloody passion shakes your very frame.
  These are portents; but yet I hope, I hope,   45
  They do not point on me.
OTHELLO   Peace, and be still.
DESDEMONA   I will so. What's the matter?
OTHELLO   That handkerchief,
  Which I so loved and gave thee, thou gav'st to Cassio.
DESDEMONA   No, by my life and soul! Send for the man
  And ask him.   50
OTHELLO   Sweet soul, take heed; take heed of perjury;
  Thou art on thy deathbed.
DESDEMONA   Ay, but not yet to die.
OTHELLO   Presently.
  Therefore confess thee freely of thy sin;
  For to deny each article with oath   55
  Cannot remove nor choke the strong conception
  That I do groan withal. Thou art to die.
DESDEMONA   Then Lord have mercy on me!
OTHELLO   I say amen.
DESDEMONA   And have you mercy too! I never did

---

    37. fatal: Cf. line 20.
    40. loves I bear to you: i.e., the pure wifely affections that are no sins at all (?); she has just declared feeling guiltless.
    41. that: i.e., revealing your lust, with "bear" heard as "bare" = reveal (?); perhaps Othello hears an echo of "the love I bear to Cassio" (4.1.227).
    42. That death . . . loving: If "death" means "killing" (what he administers), she declares Othello's admixture of feelings—killing and loving after—to be perverse ("unnatural").
    44. passion shakes: Cf. 4.1.135 and 4.1.260–61 and notes.
    46. Peace . . . still: "And he rose up, and rebuked the winde, and said unto the sea, Peace, and be still" (Mark 4.39).
    52. thy deathbed: See note to 4.2.107.
    56–57. nor choke . . . withal: with "conception" and "groan" (as with labor pains), suggests that Othello thinks of himself as unabortably pregnant; cf. Iago's "monstrous birth" (1.3.395).

Offend you in my life; never loved Cassio   60
But with such general warranty of heaven
As I might love. I never gave him token.
OTHELLO   By heaven, I saw my handkerchief in's hand!
O perjured woman! thou dost stone my heart,
And makes me call what I intend to do   65
A murder, which I thought a sacrifice.
I saw the handkerchief.
DESDEMONA   He found it then.
I never gave it him. Send for him hither.
Let him confess a truth.
OTHELLO   He hath confessed.
DESDEMONA   What, my lord?   70
OTHELLO   That he hath used thee.
DESDEMONA   How? unlawfully?
OTHELLO   Ay.
DESDEMONA   He will not say so.
OTHELLO   No, his mouth is stopped.
Honest Iago hath ta'en order for't.
DESDEMONA   O, my fear interprets. What, is he dead?
OTHELLO   Had all his hairs been lives, my great revenge   75
Had stomach for them all.
DESDEMONA   Alas, he is betrayed and I undone!
OTHELLO   Out, strumpet! Weep'st thou for him to my face?
DESDEMONA   O banish me, my lord, but kill me not!
OTHELLO   Down, strumpet!   80
DESDEMONA   Kill me tomorrow, let me live tonight!
OTHELLO   Nay, if you strive—
DESDEMONA   But half an hour!
OTHELLO   Being done, there is no pause.
DESDEMONA   But while I say one prayer!
OTHELLO   It is too late.

                                    Smothers her.

DESDEMONA   O Lord, Lord, Lord!   85
EMILIA *Calls within.*   My lord, my lord! What ho! My lord, my
lord!
OTHELLO   What noise is this? Not dead? not yet quite dead?

____

60. offend: wrong.
64. stone my heart: Cf. 4.1.177–78.
66. murder . . . sacrifice: See Johnson's note, p. 219.
73. ta'en order: arranged.
74. interprets: guesses the worst.
76. had stomach for: would have been able to swallow.
82. strive: resist.
83. Being done . . . pause: Othello's relentlessness has been variously and unsatisfactorily explained.

I that am cruel am yet merciful;
I would not have thee linger in thy pain.
So, so.   90
EMILIA *Within.*   What ho? my lord, my lord?
OTHELLO   Who's there?
EMILIA [*Within.*]   O good my lord, I would speak a word with
   you.
OTHELLO   Yes.—'Tis Emilia.—By and by.—She's dead.
'Tis like she comes to speak of Cassio's death.
The noise was high. Ha, no more moving?   95
Still as the grave. Shall she come in? Were't good?
I think she stirs again. No. What's best to do?
If she come in, she'll sure speak to my wife.
My wife, my wife! what wife? I have no wife.
O insupportable! O heavy hour!   100
Methinks it should be now a huge eclipse
Of sun and moon, and that th' affrighted globe
Did yawn at alteration.
EMILIA [*Within.*]   I do beseech you
That I may speak with you. O good my lord!
OTHELLO   I had forgot thee. O, come in Emilia.   105
Soft, by and by; let me the curtains draw.   [*He closes the bed
                                                                    curtains.*]
Where art thou? What's the matter with thee now?

                    [*He unlocks the door.*] Enter EMILIA.

EMILIA   O my good lord, yonder's foul murders done!
OTHELLO   What? now?
EMILIA   But now, my lord.   110
OTHELLO   It is the very error of the moon;
She comes more nearer earth than she was wont
And makes men mad.
EMILIA   Cassio, my lord, hath killed
A young Venetian called Roderigo.

---

90. So, so: "In the eighteenth century it became the custom to finish Desdemona off"
here with a dagger. "Modern Othellos have tended to respect Othello's intention of not scarring her, and have strangled her at 'So, so' " (Hankey); cf. 5.2.3 and note.
93. By and by: (I'll be there) in a moment.
95. high: loud.
103. yawn: Earthquakes (producing yawning chasms) and eclipses were said to accompany the fall into original sin and Christ's crucifixion; Othello feels Desdemona's death as a
cosmic "alteration."
110. But now: Even now; cf. 2.3.169 ff. and note.
111. very: authentic, essential (emphatic; see "very now," 1.1.85, and note). **error:** lapse,
delusion; in the root sense, straying or wandering (see "erring barbarian," 1.3.352, and note).
112. She: the moon (Luna). **she was wont:** normally.
113. mad: An association between lunacy and the moon was taken seriously at the time.
Cf. 3.3.180 and note.

OTHELLO   Roderigo killed? and Cassio killed?   115
EMILIA   No, Cassio is not killed.
OTHELLO   Not Cassio killed? Then murder's out of tune,
   And sweet revenge grows harsh.
DESDEMONA   O falsely, falsely murdered!
EMILIA   O Lord! what cry is that?   120
OTHELLO   That? What?
EMILIA   Out and alas! that was my lady's voice.   [*She opens the
                                                   bed curtains.*]
   Help, help ho, help! O, lady, speak again!
   Sweet Desdemona, O sweet mistress, speak!
DESDEMONA   A guiltless death I die.   125
EMILIA   O, who hath done this deed?
DESDEMONA   Nobody. I myself. Farewell.
   Commend me to my kind lord. O, farewell!   [*She dies.*]
OTHELLO   Why, how should she be murdered?
EMILIA   Alas, who
      knows?
OTHELLO   You heard her say herself it was not I.   130
EMILIA   She said so; I must needs report the truth.
OTHELLO   She's like a liar gone to burning hell!
   'Twas I that killed her!
EMILIA   O, the more angel she,
   And you the blacker devil!
OTHELLO   She turned to folly, and she was a whore.   135
EMILIA   Thou dost belie her, and thou art a devil.
OTHELLO   She was false as water.
EMILIA   Thou art rash as fire to say
   That she was false. O, she was heavenly true!
OTHELLO   Cassio did top her. Ask thy husband else.
   O, I were damned beneath all depth in hell   140
   But that I did proceed upon just grounds
   To this extremity. Thy husband knew it all.
EMILIA   My husband?
OTHELLO   Thy husband.
EMILIA   That she was false to wedlock?   145
OTHELLO   Ay, with Cassio. Had she been true,
   If heaven would make me such another world
   Of one entire and perfect chrysolite,

---

129. **should she be:** does it come about that she is.
136. **belie:** slander; cf. 4.1.35–36 and note.
139. **top:** See note to "tupping," 1.1.86. **else:** "if you doubt me" (Mowat and Werstine).
140. **were:** would be.
141. **But:** except.
147. **me such another world:** for me a world like this one.
148. **chrysolite:** precious stone, perhaps jasper, perhaps green or translucent white; in

I'd not have sold her for it.

EMILIA   My husband?

OTHELLO   Ay, 'twas he that told me on her first.   150
  An honest man he is, and hates the slime
  That sticks on filthy deeds.

EMILIA   My husband?

OTHELLO   What needs this iterance, woman?
  I say, thy husband.

EMILIA   O mistress, villainy hath made mocks with love!   155
  My husband say she was false?

OTHELLO   He, woman;
  I say, thy husband; dost understand the word?
  My friend, thy husband; honest, honest Iago.

EMILIA   If he say so, may his pernicious soul
  Rot half a grain a day! he lies to th' heart.   160
  She was too fond of her most filthy bargain.

OTHELLO   Ha!

EMILIA   Do thy worst.
  This deed of thine is no more worthy heaven
  Than thou wast worthy her.

OTHELLO   Peace, you were best!   165

                [*Moves threateningly toward her.*]

EMILIA   Thou hast not half that power to do me harm
  As I have to be hurt. O gull, O dolt!
  As ignorant as dirt! thou hast done a deed—

                        [*He draws his sword.*]

  I care not for thy sword; I'll make thee known,
  Though I lost twenty lives. Help, help, ho, help!   170
  The Moor hath killed my mistress! Murder, murder!

            Enter MONTANO, GRATIANO, IAGO *and others.*

MONTANO   What is the matter? How now, general?

EMILIA   O, are you come, Iago? You have done well,

Pliny, the material used by an Egyptian king for a statue of his wife; in Revelation (21.20),
the seventh foundation of the New Jerusalem.
  149. not have sold: Cf. Desdemona's reiterated "not for all the world" (4.3.64 ff.).
  151–52. the slime . . . deeds: Cf. the "lust-stained" bed (5.1.36) and the "cistern for foul
toads" (4.2.61).
  153. iterance: repetition.
  155. made mocks with: made a mockery of.
  160. to th' heart: flagrantly, outrageously.
  161. filthy bargain: disgusting marriage.
  165. Peace . . . best: Best shut up.
  168. dirt: excrement.

That men must lay their murders on your neck.
GRATIANO   What is the matter?   175
EMILIA   Disprove this villain, if thou be'st a man.
  He says thou told'st him that his wife was false.
  I know thou didst not; thou'rt not such a villain.
  Speak, for my heart is full.
IAGO   I told him what I thought, and told no more   180
  Than what he found himself was apt and true.
EMILIA   But did you ever tell him she was false?
IAGO   I did.
EMILIA   You told a lie, an odious damnèd lie!
  Upon my soul, a lie! a wicked lie!   185
  She false with Cassio? Did you say with Cassio?
IAGO   With Cassio, mistress! Go to, charm your tongue!
EMILIA   I will not charm my tongue; I am bound to speak:
  My mistress here lies murdered in her bed—
ALL   O heavens forfend!—   190
EMILIA   And your reports have set the murder on.
OTHELLO   Nay, stare not, masters; it is true indeed.
GRATIANO   'Tis a strange truth.
MONTANO   O monstrous act!
EMILIA   Villainy, villainy, villainy!   195
  I think upon't, I think I smell't. O villainy!
  I thought so then.—I'll kill myself for grief!
  O villainy! villainy!
IAGO   What, are you mad? I charge you get you home!
EMILIA   Good gentlemen, let me have leave to speak.   200
  'Tis proper I obey him, but not now.
  Perchance, Iago, I will ne'er go home.
OTHELLO   O! O! O!   *Falls on the bed.*
EMILIA   Nay, lay thee down and roar,
  For thou hast killed the sweetest innocent   205
  That e'er did lift up eye.
OTHELLO   O, she was foul!   [*Rises.*]

174. **lay . . . neck:** burden you with the responsibility for.
179. **full:** replete with such anxiety that she (1) can no longer speak or (2) requires reassurance (?).
181. **apt:** plausible; fitting or appropriate.
187. **charm:** "cast a spell on (i.e., silence)" (McDonald).
188. **bound:** obliged (by ties of duty and affection to Desdemona).
196. **think upon't:** am reflecting on it; "it's coming to me."
197. **then:** compels us to think back on the action (presumably to 4.2.132 ff.), without giving us the leisure or the details to be precise.
200. **Good gentleman . . . leave to speak:** Cf. Desdemona's "let me find a charter in your voice" (1.3.243).
201. **'Tis proper . . . not now:** Cf. Desdemona's "Whate'er you be, I am obedient" (3.3.89).

I scarce did know you, uncle. There lies your niece,
Whose breath, indeed, these hands have newly stopped.
I know this act shows horrible and grim.
GRATIANO   Poor Desdemon, I am glad thy father's dead;   210
Thy match was mortal to him, and pure grief
Shore his old thread in twain. Did he live now,
This sight would make him do a desperate turn;
Yea, curse his better angel from his side
And fall to reprobance.   215
OTHELLO   'Tis pitiful; but yet Iago knows
That she with Cassio hath the act of shame
A thousand times committed. Cassio confessed it,
And she did gratify his amorous works
With that recognizance and pledge of love   220
Which I first gave her. I saw it in his hand;
It was a handkerchief, an antique token
My father gave my mother.
EMILIA   O God! O heavenly God!
IAGO   Zounds, hold your peace!
EMILIA   'Twill out, 'twill out! I peace?   225
No, I will speak as liberal as the north;
Let heaven and men and devils, let them all,
All, all cry shame against me, yet I'll speak!
IAGO   Be wise, and get you home.

[IAGO *threatens* EMILIA *with his sword.*]

EMILIA   I will not!
GRATIANO   Fie! Your sword upon a woman?   230
EMILIA   O thou dull Moor, that handkerchief thou speak'st of
I found by fortune and did give my husband;
For often with a solemn earnestness—

207. **uncle:** Gratiano is "presumably Brabantio's brother" (Honigmann).
209. **shows:** looks.
211. **mortal:** lethal. **pure:** unalloyed.
212. **Shore . . . twain:** severed the cord of his old life (like the Fate Atropos in ancient mythology).
213–15. **desperate turn . . . reprobance:** act of despair, suicide. Gratiano imagines a morality play (a residually vital tradition at the time), in which good and bad angels contend whether the protagonist's soul should receive salvation or "fall to reprobance"—that is, be consigned to damnation, "for which *reprobation* was the technical theological term" (Ridley); cf. note 4 to the Names of Actors at the beginning of the play.
219. **gratify his amorous works:** requite his erotic labors.
220. **recognizance:** token.
222. **antique:** old; but the word often implies "grotesque" or perhaps "uncanny."
223. **My father . . . mother:** in 3.4.53 ff., Othello describes a different origin for the handkerchief; maybe a rich ambivalence, a theatrically inconsequential oversight, or both.
226. **liberal as the north:** "freely (and bitingly) as the north wind blows" (Kernan).
231. **dull:** dense.
232. **fortune:** chance.

More than indeed belonged to such a trifle—
He begged of me to steal't.

IAGO   Villainous whore!   235

EMILIA She give it Cassio? No, alas, I found it,
And I did giv't my husband.

IAGO   Filth, thou liest!

EMILIA By heaven, I do not! I do not, gentlemen.—
O murderous coxcomb! what should such a fool
Do with so good a wife?

OTHELLO   Are there no stones in heaven   240
But what serves for the thunder? Precious villain!

               The Moor runs at IAGO. IAGO *stabs his wife.*

GRATIANO The woman falls; sure he hath killed his wife.   *Exit*
                                                        IAGO.

EMILIA Ay, ay. O lay me by my mistress' side.   [*They do so.*]

GRATIANO He's gone, but his wife's killed.

MONTANO 'Tis a notorious villain. Take you this weapon,   245
Which I have here recovered from the Moor.
Come, guard the door without; let him not pass,
But kill him rather. I'll after that same villain,
For 'tis a damnèd slave.

               Exit MONTANO, GRATIANO [*and all but* OTHELLO *and*
                                              EMILIA].

OTHELLO   I am not valiant neither,
But every puny whipster gets my sword.   250
But why should honor outlive honesty?
Let it go all.

EMILIA   What did thy song bode, lady?
Hark, canst thou hear me? I will play the swan,
And die in music. [*Sings*] "Willow, willow, willow."

---

    239. coxcomb: cap worn by the court jester; she is calling Othello (or Iago) a fool.
    239–40. what should . . . wife: i.e., how does someone like you wind up with someone like her (or me)?
    240. stones in heaven: thunderbolts (sometimes called thunderstones), associated with godlike power.
    241. But . . . thunder: i.e., none left to administer heavenly justice; cf. "immortal Jove's dread clamors," 3.3.357, and note. **precious:** outrageous.
    241. STAGE DIRECTION IAGO . . . *wife:* That Frank Finlay, playing Iago opposite Laurence Olivier's Othello, dispatched his Emilia with "a brisk and business-like stab in the back" (Tynan) may owe something to eighteenth-century traditions (see 5.1.26 and note).
    245. notorious: flagrant (see 4.2.142 and note).
    247. without: on the outside.
    250. puny whipster: "foolish, insignificant person (cf. whippersnapper)" (McDonald).
    251. honor outlive honesty: an obscure distinction: perhaps "why should military reputation survive authentic inner virtue?"; perhaps "why should I survive the chaste Desdemona?"
    253–54. swan . . . music: "Proverbially, swans were said to sing at their deaths" (Mowat and Werstine).

Moor, she was chaste. She loved thee, cruel Moor.   255
So come my soul to bliss as I speak true!
So speaking as I think, alas, I die.   [*She dies.*]
OTHELLO   I have another weapon in this chamber;
It was a sword of Spain, the ice-brook's temper.
O, here it is.—Uncle, I must come forth.   260
GRATIANO [*Within.*]   If thou attempt it, it will cost thee dear;
Thou hast no weapon and perforce must suffer.
OTHELLO   Look in upon me then and speak with me,
Or, naked as I am, I will assault thee.

[*Enter* GRATIANO.]

GRATIANO   What is the matter?
OTHELLO   Behold, I have a weapon;   265
A better never did itself sustain
Upon a soldier's thigh. I have seen the day
That with this little arm and this good sword
I have made my way through more impediments
Than twenty times your stop. But O, vain boast!   270
Who can control his fate? 'Tis not so now.
Be not afraid, though you do see me weaponed.
Here is my journey's end, here is my butt
And very seamark of my utmost sail.
Do you go back dismayed? 'Tis a lost fear.   275
Man but a rush against Othello's breast
And he retires. Where should Othello go?

[*He looks toward the bed.*]

Now, how dost thou look now? O ill-starred wench,
Pale as thy smock. When we shall meet at compt,
This look of thine will hurl my soul from heaven,   280
And fiends will snatch at it.

[*He touches her.*]

259. **of Spain . . . temper:** origin and manufacturing process testifying to quality.
264. **naked:** unarmed; a "typically Shakespearean device: to follow the tragic moment of Emilia's death by this semi-comic trick" (Granville-Barker, quoted in Ridley).
268. **this little arm:** i.e., merely this arm.
270. **stop:** obstacle.
273. **butt:** destination.
274. **very seamark . . . utmost sail:** absolute boundary of my farthest voyage.
275. **a lost:** an unnecessary.
276. **Man but a rush against:** attack with only a reed.
277. **retires:** withdraws, retreats (a military term).
278. **ill-starred:** ill-fated.
279. **compt:** the Last Judgment. The details following conform to biblical descriptions and pictorial representations familiar at the time.

Cold, cold, my girl?
Even like thy chastity. O cursèd, cursèd slave!
Whip me, ye devils,
From the possession of this heavenly sight!
Blow me about in winds, roast me in sulphur,   285
Wash me in steep-down gulfs of liquid fire!
O Desdemon! dead Desdemon; dead. O, O!

Enter LODOVICO, CASSIO *in a chair,* MONTANO, *and* IAGO
with Officers.

LODOVICO   Where is this rash and most unfortunate man?
OTHELLO   That's he that was Othello; here I am.
LODOVICO   Where is that viper? Bring the villain forth.   290
OTHELLO   I look down towards his feet; but that's a fable;
If that thou be'st a devil, I cannot kill thee.   [*Wounds* IAGO.]
LODOVICO   Wrench his sword from him.
IAGO   I bleed, sir, but not
     killed.
OTHELLO   I am not sorry neither; I'd have thee live,
For in my sense 'tis happiness to die.   295
LODOVICO   O thou Othello, that was once so good,
Fallen in the practice of a cursèd slave,
What shall be said to thee?
OTHELLO   Why, anything:
An honorable murderer, if you will;
For naught I did in hate, but all in honor.   300
LODOVICO   This wretch hath part confessed his villainy.
Did you and he consent in Cassio's death?
OTHELLO   Ay.
CASSIO   Dear general, I never gave you cause.
OTHELLO   I do believe it, and I ask your pardon.   305
Will you, I pray, demand that demi-devil
Why he hath thus ensnared my soul and body?
IAGO   Demand me nothing. What you know, you know.
From this time forth I never will speak word.

286. **steep-down**: precipitous.
287. **STAGE DIRECTION** *chair*: litter; cf. 5.1.81 and note.
291. **that's a fable**: i.e., that cloven feet reveal the devil.
293. **but not killed**: Cf. 4.2.132 and note.
295. **in my sense**: feeling as I do. **'tis happiness to die**: Cf. "If it were now to die, / 'Twere now to be most happy" (2.1.187–8).
297. **Fallen in the practice**: With the theological burden of "fallen," "in" can mean "into" or "as a result of" Iago's plot ("practice").
299. **an honorable murderer**: Othello seems to take Lodovico's "to thee" (i.e., "what encouragement can we offer?") as "of thee" (i.e., "how should we tell your story?").
302. **consent**: collaborate.
308. **What . . . you know**: Cf. Pontius Pilate after the crucifixion: "What I have written, I have written" (John 19.22).

LODOVICO   What, not to pray?
GRATIANO   Torments will ope your lips.   310
OTHELLO   Well, thou dost best.
LODOVICO   Sir, you shall understand what hath befall'n,
   Which, as I think, you know not. Here is a letter
   Found in the pocket of the slain Roderigo,
   And here another. The one of them imports   315
   The death of Cassio, to be undertook
   By Roderigo.
OTHELLO   O villain!
CASSIO   Most heathenish and most gross!
LODOVICO   Now here's another discontented paper
   Found in his pocket too; and this, it seems,   320
   Roderigo meant t'have sent this damnèd villain,
   But that, belike, Iago in the interim
   Came in and satisfied him.
OTHELLO   O thou pernicious caitiff!—
   How came you, Cassio, by that handkerchief
   That was my wife's?
CASSIO   I found it in my chamber;   325
   And he himself confessed it but even now
   That there he dropped it for a special purpose
   Which wrought to his desire.
OTHELLO   O fool, fool, fool!
CASSIO   There is besides in Roderigo's letter
   How he upbraids Iago that he made him   330
   Brave me upon the watch, whereon it came
   That I was cast; and even but now he spake,
   After long seeming dead, Iago hurt him,
   Iago set him on.
LODOVICO [To OTHELLO.]   You must forsake this room and go
      with us.   335
   Your power and your command is taken off,
   And Cassio rules in Cyprus. For this slave,
   If there be any cunning cruelty
   That can torment him much and hold him long,
   It shall be his. You shall close prisoner rest   340
   Till that the nature of your fault be known

310. **What, not to pray:** i.e., not even to avoid eternal damnation? **Torments:** torture.
318. **heathenish and . . . gross:** godless (immoral) and disgusting.
319. **discontented:** "filled with grievances" (Honigmann).
322. **belike:** presumably.
323. **caitiff:** villain.
331. **Brave:** challenge, provoke.
332. **cast:** dismissed. **even but now:** Cf. "but even now" (326) and notes to 110 and 111.
339. **hold:** sustain, keep alive.
340. **close prisoner rest:** "remain a closely guarded prisoner" (Mowat and Werstine).

To the Venetian state. Come, bring away.

OTHELLO   Soft you; a word or two before you go.
I have done the state some service, and they know't;
No more of that. I pray you in your letters,   345
When you shall these unlucky deeds relate,
Speak of me as I am. Nothing extenuate,
Nor set down aught in malice. Then must you speak
Of one that loved not wisely but too well;
Of one not easily jealous but, being wrought,   350
Perplexed in the extreme; of one whose hand,
Like the base Judean, threw a pearl away
Richer than all his tribe; of one whose subdued eyes,
Albeit unusèd to the melting mood,
Drops tears as fast as the Arabian trees   355
Their medicinable gum. Set you down this;
And say besides that in Aleppo once,
Where a malignant and a turbanned Turk
Beat a Venetian and traduced the state,
I took by th' throat the circumcisèd dog,   360
And smote him—thus!   *He stabs himself.*

LODOVICO   O bloody period!

GRATIANO   All that is spoke is marred.

OTHELLO   I kissed thee ere I killed thee. No way but this,
Killing myself, to die upon a kiss.   *He [kisses DESDEMONA and]*
dies.

CASSIO   This did I fear, but thought he had no weapon,   365
For he was great of heart.

LODOVICO   O Spartan dog,
More fell than anguish, hunger, or the sea,

343. **Soft you:** wait a moment.
346. **unlucky:** unfortunate.
347. **extenuate:** alleviate, mitigate.
350. **wrought:** worked up or on by passion (or by Iago?).
352. **the base Judean:** "perhaps Judas Iscariot, betrayer of Christ, or Herod, who impulsively killed his wife" (McDonald); "base Indian" in the quarto suggests lowly ignorance, rather than willful evil.
353. **richer:** worth more; may evoke Matthew 13.45–46: "the kingdome of heaven is like to a merchant man, that seeketh good pearles, Who having found a pearle of great price, went and sold all that he had and bought it." **tribe:** "could be the tribes of Israel or an Indian tribe" (Honigmann); cf. 1.3.353. **subdued:** vanquished; cf. 1.3.248.
355. **Drops tears:** the present tense; he is weeping.
356. **medicinable gum:** probably myrrh, deemed curative (as were repentant tears).
357. **Aleppo:** cosmopolitan "city in Turkey [modern Syria] where Venetians were allowed special trading privileges but where it was death for a Christian to strike a Turk" (Kittredge).
360. **circumcisèd:** "a term of opprobrium and abuse" (Ross); bodily circumcision is enjoined on Moslems (and Jews), but Christians claim "circumcision made without hands . . . through the circumcision of Christ" (Colossians 2.11).
362. **period:** conclusion.
366. **Spartan:** may evoke silence, cruelty, envy (by association, never fully explained, with the ancient Greek city of Sparta).
367. **fell:** relentlessly destructive.

Look on the tragic loading of this bed:
This is thy work. The object poisons sight;
Let it be hid. Gratiano, keep the house   370
And seize upon the fortunes of the Moor,
For they succeed on you. To you, lord governor,
Remains the censure of this hellish villain;
The time, the place, the torture—O, enforce it!
Myself will straight aboard, and to the state   375
This heavy act with heavy heart relate.   *Exeunt.*

370. **hid:** a cue to draw the bed curtains. **keep:** guard.
371. **seize upon the fortunes:** take possession of the estate.
372. **they succeed on you:** you inherit them.
373. **censure:** judgment, punishment.

Textual Commentary

Othello exists in two early editions: as a quarto, of 1622 (Q), and as part of the First Folio, of 1623 (F). They differ first of all in their size as objects. For a quarto, "the printer folded the sheet twice, making four leaves (hence the name *quarto*), or eight pages front and back; this book was thus about 7 × 9 inches." For a folio, "the printer folded the sheet once, making two leaves, or four pages front and back; the book was thus about 9 by 14 inches (McDonald, 199)." In addition, they diverge in some of their contents: F includes some substantial passages—about 160 lines in all—missing from Q, possibly added on or (more probably) cut for performance (or perhaps for a particular performance); Q offers more detailed stage directions; Q includes oaths absent from F, probably deleted as a result of a statute passed in 1606 requiring the suppression of profanity in theatrical performance. In addition to these general differences, the two texts differ in thousands of specific readings, probably for a variety of reasons—some resulting from the practice of the compositors and printers responsible for the editions, some from theatrical cutting and the practice of "the actors themselves" (McMillin, *First Quarto*, i), some from Shakespeare's own revisions.

Textual scholars have developed many more or less plausible stories (some of them suggested just above) to account for the features of each text on its own and in relation to the other. Given the present state of knowledge (which is unlikely to change), these stories are inevitably speculative explanations, and none has succeeded in gaining anything close to universal acceptance. Meanwhile, editors have to make judgments based not only on the textual variables but on the interests, themselves various and difficult to determine, of their readers. This edition is based on F, primarily because of the quality of its additional material. As McMillin remarks, "no one doubts" that the F-only lines "are Shakespearian," but this is not just because they "are rich in metaphor and verbal energy" (McMillin, *First Quarto*, 2); including Desdemona's Willow Song and Emilia's speech on the double standard (to focus on just one scene), they contribute powerfully to the play's theatrical impact. From Q, I have included the oaths (these too are generally accepted as Shakespearean and reflect the emotional intensity of the play) and some more detailed stage directions (whether Shakespeare himself was responsible for them or not, they seem to reflect theatrical practice and offer interesting possibilities for performance). Finally, I have added a few Q-only lines and Q variants that seemed to add to the play's power. (Many other variants I resisted, without firm conviction, and I have included a representative sampling of these unadopted possibilities in the notes below.)

These procedures may sound commonsensical, and they in fact correspond more or less to the choices producing most modern editions of the play. However, textual scholars and critics have moved beyond the effective consensus that sustained previous practice and now disagree about not only the details of their work but the basic values and goals. Some of them doubt that it is desirable (even if it were possible) to get underneath textual corruption to an original authorial intention and would question the legitimacy of an even modestly conflated text like the one printed here. This skepticism is connected to a transfer of interest away from the literary or esthetic effects of engaging with the text and over to the social and cultural factors influencing textual transmission and theatrical history.

Readers interested in these questions are invited to look at the works listed below. McDonald's chapter provides a clear and helpful introduction to the general problem of editing Shakespeare; Foakes, Honigmann's *Stability*, Jowett, Kastan, and Werstine's "Narratives" focus more specifically on current controversies; the other items are addressed to the problems of *Othello* in particular. Even those readers who prefer not to bother with such matters should know that the text they read of *Othello*—whether it's the one printed here or any other—has been perforce shaped in significant ways by editorial assumptions and values that are (to put it mildly) subject to dispute. Editors change the spelling and punctuation of almost every line they transmit, sometimes with indisputably significant impact. Capell's "me" for "my," for instance (see 1.3.260–62, note, and Textual Notes), has won widespread acceptance in explaining a passage that arguably affects our view of the play as a whole. The emendation depends for its revisionary clarification not just on "the single change of a letter," but on "the putting in parenthesis what the oldest copy puts between comma's" (Capell). And while the changed letter or word is often highlighted in the text, the emended punctuation generally isn't signaled in even the Textual Notes of even the most scrupulous editors (e.g., "No sources are given for emendations of punctuation," Mowat and Werstine, 267).

Punctuation rarely assumes the self-evidently major consequence it does in the case of this emendation by Capell (though see 3.3.93, 4.2.64, and 4.3.18 for other examples). Nonetheless, even when individual editorial decisions about punctuation are trivial, they cannot help, multiplied by thousands of times, but have some effect on the meaning and impact. (Take a closer look at the first page of F, reproduced p. 2, and compare it with the text printed on the facing page to see how many changes get made to even a relatively clean early text by a relatively unintrusive editor.) Facsimile reproductions of original texts might seem to represent an alternative to editorial intervention; but they would not be intelligible to most readers and would entail the dissemination of what in many cases we believe to be errors. And in any case, facsimiles are, no less than conflated or emended texts, the product of editorial value judgments—in this case, the judgment to do nothing. What has sometimes been called "unediting" is just another kind of editing (Marcus). Editorial practice is interpretive through and through, as much so as critical practice. Editorial decisions are as much subject to dispute as are the discussions and arguments on display in the "Criticism" section of this book.

Works Cited

Foakes, R. A. "Shakespeare Editing and Textual Theory: A Rough Guide." *Huntington Library Quarterly* 60 (1999): 425–42.

Hill, W. Speed. "Editing *Othello:* The Indefatigible in Pursuit of the Intractable." *Shakespeare Newsletter* 246:50 (2000): 67 ff.

Honigmann, E. A. J. Letter to the Editor. *Shakespeare Newsletter,* 246:50 (2000): 66.

———. Letter to the Editor. *Shakespeare Newsletter,* 248–49:51 (2001): 10.

———. *The Stability of Shakespeare's Text.* London: Edward Arnold, 1965.

———. *The Texts of "Othello" and Shakespearian Revision.* London and New York: Routledge, 1996.

Jackson, MacDonald P. Review of Honigmann's *Texts of "Othello."* *Shakespeare Studies* 26 (1998): 364–72.

Jowett, John. "After Oxford: Recent Developments in Textual Studies." In *The Shakespearean International Yearbook 1: Where Are We Now in Shakespearean Studies?* Aldershot and Brookfield, Vt.: Ashgate, 1999, 65–86.

Kastan, David Scott. "The Mechanics of Culture: Editing Shakespeare Today." In *Shakespeare after Theory.* London and New York: Routledge, 1999, 59–70.

Marcus, Leah S. *Unediting the Renaissance: Shakespeare, Marlowe, Milton.* London and New York: Routledge, 1996.

McDonald, Russ. "What Is Your Text?" In *The Bedford Companion to Shakespeare: An Introduction with Documents.* 2nd ed. Boston and New York: Bedford / St. Martin's, 2001, 194–218

McMillin, Scott. "The *Othello* Quarto and the 'Foul-Paper' Hypothesis." *Shakespeare Quarterly* 51 (2000): 67–85.

———, ed. *The First Quarto of "Othello."* Cambridge: Cambridge University Press, 2001.

Werstine, Paul. Letter to the Editor. *Shakespeare Newsletter* 247:50 (2000): 94.

———. "Narratives about Printed Shakespeare Texts: 'Foul Papers' and 'Bad' Quartos." *Shakespeare Quarterly* 41 (1990): 65–86.

———. Review of Honigmann's *Texts of "Othello." Shakespeare Quarterly* 51 (2000): 240–44.

Textual Notes

Most of the notes below indicate either (1) readings adopted from Q, or (2) nonadopted Q readings judged of interest for one reason or another (again, only a sampling; thousands of Q variants go unremarked). Each note begins with the reading of this edition to the left of the bracket; if no alternative source is specified, this reading derives from F. If no alternative is specified on the right side of the bracket, the variant there derives from Q. If the present reading derives from Q, this derivation is signaled with a "Q" immediately to the right of the bracket, and the rejected F reading follows the signal. Hence the two categories described above would take the following forms: (1) present reading] Q; rejected F reading, or (2) present reading] unadopted Q reading.

The names cited in the notes are keyed to the editions listed in the bibliography printed on pages xvi–xvii. Q2 refers to the Second Quarto, published in 1630 by an anonymous editor who evidently had access to both F and Q1. In many cases where stage directions added to this text derive from a long editorial tradition, usually going back to the eighteenth century, I have not bothered to specify origins. In some cases where I have adopted stage directions specific to recent editions, the source is identified in the notes below. Abbreviations are used as follows: *abs* = absent; NS = new scene, SD = stage direction, and SP = speech prefix.

1.1: 1. Tush] Q; *abs.* 4. 'Sblood] Q; *abs.* 13–14. of war, / Non-suits] of war, / And in conclusion / Non-suits. 22. tonguèd] togèd. 26. other] Q; others. 27. Christened] Christian. 30. God] Q; *abs.* 30. Moorship's] worship's. 63. full] Q; fall. 69. chances] changes. 78 SD. *at a window*] Q; *abs.* 105. Zounds] Q; *abs.* 118–134. If't be . . . satisfy yourself] *abs.* 120. odd-even] Malone; odd even. 143. producted] produced. 151. pains] Q; apines. 156 SD. *in his nightgown*] Q; *abs.* 179. night] Q; might.

1.2: 28 SD. *Officers and*] Q; *abs.* 34 duke] Q; dukes. 68. darlings] Q; darling. 84. Where] Q; Whether. 87. I] Q; *abs.*

1.3: 0 SD. *Enter* DUKE *and Senators, set at a Table with lights and Attendants*] Q; *Enter* DUKE, *Senators and Officers*. 59 SP. SENATOR] ALL; FIRST SENATOR (Mowat and Werstine); SENA-TORS (Kernan). 106 SP. DUKE] Q; *abs.* 121 SD. *Exit two or three*] Q; *abs.* 129. battles] Q; battle. 129. fortunes] Q; fortune. 140. rocks and hills whose heads] Q; rocks, hills, whose head. 142. other] Q; others. 143. anthropophagi] Q; antropophague. 144. Do grow] Grew. 146. thence] Q; hence. 154. intentively] Q; instinctively. 158. kisses] sighs. 165. hint] heat. 199. Into your favor] Q; *abs.* 217. ear] Q; ears. 228. couch] Pope; coach, F; cooch, Q. 239. Nor would I there reside] Nor I. I would not there reside. 246. That I love the Moor] That I did love the Moor. 247. storm] scorn. 249. very quality] utmost pleasure. 262. me] Capell (attributed to Upton); my, F and Q. 262. defunct] F and Q; distinct (Theobald). 268. instrument] instruments. 275–76. And speed . . . tonight] And speed must answer; you

must hence tonight. / DESDEMONA Tonight, my lord? / DUKE This night. 291 SD. *Exit*]
Exeunt. 297. worldly] Q; wordly. 298 SD. *Exit Moor and* DESDEMONA] Q; *Exit*. 324. balance]
Q; brain; beam (Theobald). 352. super-subtle] a super-subtle. 376. a snipe] Q; snpe. 379.
H'as] Q; She h'as. 395 SD. *Exit*] Q; *abs.*

2.1: 12. chidden] chiding. 19 SD. *Third*] Q; *abs.* 33. prays] Q; pray. 40 SP. THIRD] Q; *abs.*
42. arrivancy] arrivance. 51 SP. *within*] MESSENGER. 55 SD. *A shot*] Q; *abs.* 56 SP. SECOND]
Q; *abs.* 59 SP. SECOND] Q; *abs.* 65 SD. *Second*] Q; *abs.* 66 SP. SECOND] Q; *abs.* 80. Make
love's quick pants in] And swiftly come to. 82. And bring all Cyprus comfort] Q; *abs.* 88.
me] Q; *abs.* 94. this] their. 176 SD. *Trumpets within*] Q; *abs.* 196 SD. *They kiss*] Q; *abs.*
212. thither] hither. 225. again] Q; a game. 238. finder of] finder out of. 239. has] Q; he's.
257. mutualities] Q; mutabilities. 297. trash] trace. 300. right] rank.

2.2: 10. Heaven] Q; *abs.*

2.3: 0 NS. ACT 2 SCENE 3] Theobald, Capell, et seq. 35. unfortunate] Q; infortunate. 49.
else] lads. 54. to put] Q; put to. 58. God] Q; Heaven. 68. God] Q; Heaven. 73. Englishman]
Q; Englishmen. 88. And] Then. 90. 'Fore God] Q; Why. 93. God's] Q; Heaven's. 102. God]
abs. 128 SD. *Exit* RODERIGO] Q; *abs.* 136. Zounds] Q; *abs.* 147. God's will] Q; Alas. 149
SD. *A bell rung*] Q; *abs.* 151. God's will, lieutenant, hold] Q; Fie fie, lieutenant. 154.
Zounds] Q; *abs.* 197. Zounds, if I] Q; If I once. 208. leagued] Pope; league, F and Q. 223.
then rather] the rather. 248 SD. MOOR, DESDEMONA *and Attendants*] Q; *abs.* 251. God] Q;
heaven. 269–73. Drunk . . . devil] *abs.* 279. God] Q; *abs.* 283. Why, but] Q; Why? But
320. me] me here. 331. were't] Q; were. 363. hath] hast. 366. By the mass] Q; In troth.
372–73. I'll set her on— / Myself a while to draw the Moor apart] Q; I'll set her on myself
a while to draw the Moor apart.

3.1: 21. hear, mine] hear me, mine, F; hear mine, Q. 26. general] general's wife. 30. CASSIO
Do, good my friend] Q; *abs.* 48–49. his likings / To bring] his likings / To take the safest
occasion by the front / To bring. 54 SD *Exit*] Q; *abs.*

3.3: 52. Yes, faith] Q; I sooth. 60. on] or. 61. on Wednesday] or Wednesday. 74. By'r Lady]
Q; Trust me. 89 SD. DESDEMONA *and* EMILIA] Q; *abs.* 94. you] Q; he. 109. By heaven] Q;
Alas. 114. of] in. 138. that all slaves are free to] Q; that: All slaves are free. 142. But some]
Q; Wherein. 150. oft] Q; of. 157. What dost thou mean?] Zounds. 164. By heaven] Q; *abs.*
177. God] Q; heaven. 181. once] Q; *abs.* 187. dances] dances well. 204. God] Q; Heaven.
206. leave't] leave. 206. keep't] Q2; kept, F; keep, Q. 217. I'faith] Q; Trust me. 219. my]
Q; your. 225. Which my thoughts aimed not] As my thoughts aim not at. 250. hold] Q;
abs. 261. qualities] Q; quantities. 275. to] of. 280. heaven mocked] O then heaven mocks.
284. to] Q; too. 287. Faith] Q; Why. 291 SD. OTHELLO *and* DESDEMONA] Q; *abs.* 313. No,
faith] Q; No, but. 326. The Moor . . . poison] *abs.* 329. act] art. 339. of] Q; in. 362. mine]
man's. 384–91. By the world . . . satisfied] *abs.* 387. My] Her, Q2. 394. and] *abs.* 396.
supervisor] Q; supervision. 412. in] into. 420. wary] merry. 424. laid] then laid; lay, Rowe
and many subsequent editors. 425. sigh . . . kiss . . . cry] sighed . . . kissed . . . cried.429.
'Tis] IAGO 'Tis. 430 SP. IAGO] *abs.* 440. it] any, it, Q; any that, Malone and many subsequent
editors. 447. the hollow hell] thy hollow cell. 453–60. Iago . . . heaven] *abs.* 455. Ne'er
keeps] Ne'er feels, Q2. 460 SD. OTHELLO *kneels*] Q; *abs.* 462 SD. IAGO *kneels*] Q; *abs.*

3.4: 22. the] that. 31. now till] now; let. 53. faith] Q; indeed. 73. I'faith] Q; Indeed. 75. God]
Q; heaven. 79. Heaven] Q; *abs.* 85. can] can, sir. 94. I'faith] Q; In sooth. 94 to] this and
most editions; too, F and Q. 95. Zounds] Q; Away. 144. a] that. 159. the] that. 164 SD.
Exeunt DESDEMONA *and* EMILIA] Q; *abs.* 167. I'faith] Q; Indeed. 174. continuate] convenient. 183. by my faith] Q; in good troth.

4.1: 21. infectious] infected. 32. Faith] Q; Why. 36. Zounds] Q; *abs.* 45. works] work. 52.
No, faith] Q; *abs.* 77. unsuiting] Q; resulting. 101. conster] Q; conserve. 107. power]
Q; dower. 110. woman] a woman. 111. i'faith] Q; indeed. 122. Faith] Q; Why. 128. beck-
ons] Q; becomes. 158. Faith] Q; *abs.* 160. Faith] Q; Yes. 164 SD. CASSIO] Q; *abs.* 206 SD.
A trumpet] Q; *abs.* 210. God] Q; *abs.* 232. By my troth] Q; Trust me. 242 Truly obedient]
Truly, an obedient.

4.2: 18. their wives] her sex. 30. Nay] Q; May. 31. knee] knees. 33. But not the words] Q;
abs. 55. and moving finger at] unmoving fingers at—O O. 64. here, F and Q] there, Theobald, Capell, and many subsequent editors. 74–77. Committed . . . committed] *abs.* 81.
committed?] committed? Impudent strumpet! 103. Who . . . lady] *abs.* 111. least misuse]
greatest abuse. 116. to] at. 143. heaven] Q; heavens. 150. Alas] O Good, Q; O God,
Honigmann. 153–66. Here . . . me] *abs.* 157. them in] Q2; them or. 168. offence.] offence,
/ And he does chide with you. 183. Faith] Q; *abs.* 191. acquaintance] acquittance. 230.
removing] removing of. 235. harlotry] harlot.

4.3: 18. I would] Q; I, would; Ay—would, Honigmann and McDonald. 23. faith] Q; Father.
24. thee] Q; abs. 31–53. I have . . . not next] *abs.* 40. singing] sighing, Q2. 55–57. I called
. . . more men] *abs.* 60–63. I have . . . question] *abs.* 71. In troth] Good troth. 72. In troth]
By my troth. 76. 'Ud's pity] Q; Why. 87–104. But I . . . us so] *abs.* 105. God] Q; Heaven.
105. uses] usage.

5.1: 1. bulk] Q; bark. 22. But] Be't. 22. heard] hear. 26 SD. IAGO *wounds* CASSIO *in the leg and exits*] this edition; *abs*, F and Q; *Iago cuts Cassio behind in the Leg, and* Exit, Theobald; Iago rushes from his post, cuts Cassio behind in the Leg, and exit, Malone. 35. Forth] Q; For. 46 SD. *with a light*] Q; *abs*. 89. O heaven] Q; Yes, 'tis. 103. out] Q; *abs*. 104. gentlemen] gentlewoman. 109 SD. *Enter* EMILIA] Q; *abs*. 122. I? Fie] I: fough! fie.

5.2: 0 SD. *with a light*] Q; *abs*. 13. thy] the. 15. thee] it. 19 SD. *He kisses her*] *He smells, then kisses her*, Honigmann. 35. so] Q; *abs*. 58. Then Lord] Q; O heaven. 64. my] thy. 71. used] 'ud's death. 83. Being . . . pause] *abs*. 84 SD. *Smothers her*] *He stifles her*. 85. DESDEMONA O Lord, Lord, Lord] Q; *abs*. 86 SD. *Calls within*] Q; *At the door*. 87. noise] voice. 103. Did] Should. 120. O Lord] Q; Alas. 155–58. O mistress . . . honest Iago] *abs*. 171 SD. *and others*] Q; *abs*. 189–98. My mistress . . . villainy] *abs*. 203 SD. *Falls on the bed*] Q; *abs*. 224. O God! O heavenly God!] Q; O heaven! O heavenly powers! 224. Zounds] Q; Come. 225–26. 'Twill out . . . the north] 'Twill out, 'twill; I hold my peace, sir? no! / I'll be in speaking liberal as the air. 241 SD. *The Moor runs at* IAGO. IAGO *stabs his wife*] Q; *abs*. 242 SD. *Exit* IAGO] Q; *abs*. 243 SD. *They do so*] Ross; *abs*, F and Q. 246 here] Q; *abs*. 249 SD. MONTANO, GRATIANO] Q; *abs*. 272–77. Be not . . . Othello go] *abs*. 277 SD. *He looks toward the bed*] Mowat and Werstine; *abs*, F and Q. 281 SD. *He touches her*] Ross; *abs*, F and Q. 287 SD. *in a chair*] Q; *abs*. 297. cursèd] damnèd. 352. Judean] Indian. 361 SD. *He stabs himself*] Q; *abs*. 364 SD. *kisses* DESDEMONA *and*] Ross; Honigmann; *abs*, F and Q. 364 SD. *dies*] Q; *abs*. 368. loading] lodging.

SOURCES AND CONTEXTS

Othello in Its Own Time

The main textual source for *Othello* is Giraldi Cinthio's *Gli Heca-tommithi*. Concerned generally with love and marriage, Cinthio's collection of "A Hundred Tales" is divided into ten "Decades," the third of which focuses on marital infidelity. The seventh story of this Decade is printed below. Shakespeare, who read it in either the original Italian (1565) or a French translation (1584) or both, took this tale for the basic narrative of *Othello,* incorporating a great many of its details as well. At the same time, the play substantially reshapes the action, rhythm, and feeling; and while some of these changes may be attributed to the exigencies of adapting narrative to drama, others furnish a rich basis for speculation about the play's intended effects. In "Othello's Handkerchief: 'The Recognizance and Pledge of Love' " (p. 264 below), Lynda E. Boose discusses one example of meaningful alteration, in which the vague "Moorish design" of Cinthio's handkerchief becomes the specific "spotted with strawberries" of the play. Another example: out of almost nothing—two disconnected sentences in which Cinthio refers in passing to two apparently distinct women, neither of whom is named or speaks or contributes to the action, one designated as Cassio's wife, the other as a prostitute (*una meretrice;* Furness, 385)—Shakespeare creates the fascinating Bianca. Even unchanged details can be interesting—poison versus dagger as possible modes of dispatching Desdemona, for instance—illustrating the imaginative power by which the play transforms inert inconsequence into resonant significance.

In addition to Cinthio's tale, *Othello* seems indebted, less overtly and substantially, to a variety of other texts (see "Textual Sources" in the bibliography, p. 389). But in trying to account for the narrative bits and discursive topics that find their way into Shakespeare, recent commentators have sought to "expand [the] definition of *source*" beyond "less obviously influential books" (McDonald, 146, his emphasis), and even beyond writing altogether (in the strict sense) to cultural contexts—the ensemble of shared beliefs and assumptions within (and upon) which the play would have registered its impressions.[1] The pages below sketch out some of these contexts as

1. See Vaughan (3–5) for a succinct introduction to this topic and for intelligently inform-

they might have shaped original response to Othello and Desdemona: ideas about Moors, Turks, black Africans, and Venetians in
one case; about marriage and domesticity, fathers and daughters,
and female sexuality in the other.

"I think this tale would win my daughter too" (1.3.170): the Duke's
response to Othello's marvelous adventures seems designed to reinforce a sense of delight in Othello's romantic charisma. Renaissance
audiences must have been specially responsive to such exotic material. Geographical exploration of the Atlantic west and (more immediately relevant to *Othello*) extensive commerce with the
Mediterranean and African southeast nourished a popular travel literature, such as the collections put together by Richard Hakluyt and
Samuel Purchas, often reprinted and endlessly expanded between
the 1580s and 1620s.[2] Renaissance playwrights were eager to capitalize on this interest in remote settings and exotic strangers. During
roughly the same four-decade period, "there were dozens of plays
about Turks and Moors" (Matar, 4), with as many as seventeen productions in which "Turkish cruelty" and "Turkish villains" were
brought "to center stage"—a category excluding plays like *Othello*,
in which the Turkish menace is only marginal, "threatened and then
displaced" (Vitkus, *Three Turk Plays*, 2).

As Vitkus's comment suggests, affectionate admiration hardly
exhausts the range of response available to the original spectators.
As "an extravagant and wheeling stranger / Of here and everywhere"
(1.1.133–34), Othello is "a thing . . . to fear, not to delight" (1.2.71),
and thus likely to evoke anxiety as much as admiration. When Roderigo and Brabantio (along with Iago) express such xenophobic and
racist-sounding sentiments, original audiences likely would have
assented. Shakespeare evidently assumes such assent in his representation of Aaron the Moor in *Titus Andronicus* and of Portia, the
heroine of *The Merchant of Venice*, who contemptuously dismisses
her suitor, the Prince of Morocco, with "Let all of his complexion
choose me so" (2.7.79). In "*Othello* and Colour Prejudice" (p. 248
below), G. K. Hunter demonstrates that "a traditional view of what
Moors are like, i.e. gross, disgusting, inferior, carrying the symbol of
their damnation on their skin," was normal and overt in Shakespeare's time. This view seems to coincide even with official government policy, to judge from a Privy Council order in 1596 concerned
with "the great numbers of Negroes and blackamoors" in the realm

---

ative chapters on the global, military, racial, and marital discourses current when the play
was written.
2. Readers interested in Renaissance travel writing might start with Kamps and Singh, which
   includes sophisticated critical discussion, engaging excerpts from primary materials, and
   a wealth of bibliographical reference, or with Hadfield's fascinating anthology.

(McDonald, 302), reinforced in a royal proclamation of 1601 authorizing that "those kind of people" should be "sent out of the land" (Hughes and Larkin, 221–22).

According to Dr. Johnson (p. 217 below), Desdemona's affectionate interest in Othello should not be construed as particular to "any age or any nation." That the exotic details of Othello's speech come from a text of classical antiquity, Pliny's *Natural History,* more than from travel literature of the period may confirm Johnson: Othello's appeal transcends history. But if Desdemona's generous interest issues from a universal human "nature," so may the opposite response—an acute fear of and repulsion from the alien. According to John Gillies, "The need to constitute an identity by excluding the other is not just primal, but perennial" (6). These contradictory feelings of desire and aversion intensified during the nineteenth century, as summed up by A. C. Bradley (p. 235 below), for whom Othello's exotic appeal—"romantic," "strange," "mysterious," "not [of] our world [but] dark and grand, with a light upon him from the sun where he was born"—coexists uneasily with "the aversion of our blood, an aversion which comes as near to being merely physical as anything human can," at the prospect of Desdemona's sexual interest in a "coal-black" Othello.

Creaturely and geographical differences, then, seem to provoke deep and ambivalent fascination in all societies, from the ancient Greeks to the *Star Trek*s and *Alien*s spinning off endlessly on our TV and movie screens. Nonetheless, significant local variations remain to be explained. Nineteenth-century audiences observed Othello from within ideas of distinct and biologically determined identities. Given these scientific facts (as then construed), Bradley and his predecessors tried to manage contradictory feelings about Othello by imagining him as a tawny Moor rather than a black African. But this endeavor does not work for a play that lumps together the protagonist's black and Moorish attributes in an undiscriminating way. Such lumping, typical in the Renaissance, is evident in George Best's reference, written in 1578 and subsequently incorporated into Hakluyt's 1600 compendium, to "all these black Moores which are in Africa" (quoted in Newman, 147). Best's phrase conflates North African and sub-Saharan racial types within the then-standard term to describe someone like Othello—a "blackamoor." Hence also the Privy Council's designation of "those kind of people" as "Negroes and blackamoors," where the appositional phrase compounds the conflation. Richard Burbage, the original Othello, probably performed the part in blackface and Moorish costume—as a "blackamoor"; but Renaissance audiences probably wouldn't have registered the suggestions as contradictory, perhaps partly as a result of contemporary histrionic conventions, which did not coincide with realistic representation as we now understand it, but chiefly because they weren't used to thinking in terms of the scientific (or pseudo-scientific) categories of race and geography that were being contradicted.

At once a tawny Moor and a black African, Othello is also the "turbanned Turk" of his own description at the end (5.2.358). In the opening scene, Iago refers to "the Cyprus wars, / Which even now stands in act" (147–48), and the echo of his shocking sexual image just earlier, "Even now, now, very now, an old black ram / Is tupping your white ewe" (85–86), helps establish a structural analogy: as Othello invades the space of Brabantio's authority, so the Turks threaten Venice's political and economic interests. The Turkish peril seems to be playing on primal fears as well; according to the Duke, it is experienced "in fearful sense" (1.3.12), the word "fearful" echoing Brabantio's response to "such a thing" as Othello at the end of the preceding scene. The Turkish invasion raises the age-old specter of barbarian hordes assaulting Europe from the margins. Brabantio evokes the idea in order to dismiss it. "What tell'st thou me of robbing? This is Venice; / My house is not a grange" (1.1.102–03). By the next scene, however, Brabantio's confidence has been eroded: "if such actions may have passage free, / Bondslaves and pagans shall our statesmen be" (1.2.98–99).

"Pagans" may be the operative word here: the invading / supplanting barbarians are imagined as infidels. In a culture centered in religious belief, anxieties cluster around the specter of religious difference. This primacy of religious feeling helps explain the play's indifference to ethnic identity as such. The "word 'Moor' had no clear racial status," according to Hunter (below); it was used indiscriminately to describe any people "in that outer circuit of non-Christian lands where the saving grace of Jerusalem is weakest in its whitening power." Hence also the play's slippages among ethnic or racial and geographical categories. When Vitkus subsumes "Turks and Moors" within the "*anti-Islamic* tales told in the west," he fairly represents Renaissance habits of mind: Turks, Moors, blacks—these differences are inconsequential compared to their shared divergence from the one true faith.[3]

---

3. *Three Turk Plays*, 2, my emphasis. Similar slippages occur, despite substantial overlaps in the material considered, among the other books treating exotic aliens on the Renaissance English stage: "blacks" (Eldred Jones, Barthelemy, Tokson), "Africans" (Jones), "Moors" (D'Amico), and "Turks." Chew's chapter furnishes the dominant or umbrella concept— "Moslems"—even though, as a result of the "curious reluctance" throughout Renaissance Europe "to call Muslims by any name with a religious connotation," the term was significantly withheld from use. The preferred alternatives, "Saracens, Moors, Turks, or Tatars," had the "obvious purpose" to "reduce [Moslems] to something local or even tribal" (Bernard Lewis, quoted in Vitkus, *Three Turk Plays*, 9). Deprived of true religion (as Elizabethans understood it), Muslims were thus diminished to a racial or ethnic identity so inconsequential as to be no identity at all.

With the attenuating authority of religion in post-Renaissance culture, critical interest has taken possession of *Othello*—or been possessed by it—in surprisingly different ways. In the "Criticism"
section of this book, readers will encounter a thriving nineteenth-
century enterprise insisting that Othello is a tawny Moor rather than
a black African. The Moorish Othello allowed the Victorians to avert
disgust at the prospect of miscegenation, but as Julia Lupton argues,
to Renaissance audiences it probably worked the other way round:
the Muslim *refusal* of the New Law, like the Jewish, "might actually
challenge more deeply the integrity of the Christian paradigms set
up in the play as the measure of humanity" (74). The black Othello,
by contrast, unexposed as yet to the revelation of Christ, coincides
more closely with the sympathetic and unthreatening noble savage
implicit in Hunter's description of "Renaissance primitivism." The
contrast is reflected in the variant versions of Othello's final self-
description as either a "base Judean" or "base Indian."

At this point, some fine-tuning is in order. If the Renaissance is
(in Kwame Appiah's terminology) a "pre-racial" culture, it will exhibit
continuity as well as discontinuity with subsequent modes of belief.
To claim that " 'race' as we comprehend it now simply did not exist
until the nineteenth century" (Gilroy, 57) does not mean that the
Elizabethans lacked altogether a consciousness of distinct and biologically defined identities. In fact, "there is much evidence" to suggest "that the early modern English did differentiate North Africa
from the rest of the continent" (Bak, 200) and "recognized that Africans south of the Sahara were not at all the same people as the much
more familiar Moors" (Jordan, 5). Moreover, such recognitions had
increased during the period. Despite Hunter's claim that the Elizabethans "had little or no continuous contact with 'Moors,' " a dense
network of connections existed among Turks, Moors, and English
people in commercial, political, diplomatic, and military affairs. "To
numerous Britons, the Turks and Moors were men and women they
had known, not in fantasy and fiction, but with whom they had
worked and lived" (Matar, 6). So much *actual* interaction" (Matar,
7, his emphasis) could hardly have been without consequence for
the received ideas that lumped Turks, Moors, and sub-Saharan
blacks into one symbolic color. At the same time, the depth of this
impact remains difficult to determine with any confidence.

If we emphasize the extent to which "London theatergoers" saw
"the Turk" not as "an imaginary bogey" or a "fictional demon . . .
lurking at the edges of the civilized world," then the "exaggeration
and demonization" of Islam inherited from theological tradition is
"increasingly" subject to the influence of "real contact" (Vitkus,
Three Turk Plays, 3). The transformative power of such contact is
evident in Henry Blount's *Voyage Into the Levant* (1636): "couched

in secular logic" rather than "Christian supernaturalism," Blount's account "does not defend traveling on religious grounds, but in order to advance knowledge by means of rational inquiry" (MacLean, 90). Yet it would be misleading to imagine a rapidly decisive shift of attitude. As Vitkus acknowledges, citing Blount's admiration for the Turks as "the only modern people," the voices "in favor of toleration and openness toward Islam" did not achieve critical mass until "the second half of the seventeenth century" and "were rare" at the time when *Othello* was new (*Three Turk Plays*, 11). They may have been rarer still in the theatrical milieu in which it was first performed. The stage was probably less fully open to the enlightened beliefs finding their way into the working assumptions of trade and politics. "In the self-aware, created world of the English stage the blackness of Moorish characters made symbolic sense. But in the utilitarian writings of English diplomats the symbolic value of blackness was largely irrelevant" (Bak, 213). Matar suggests a similar compartmentalization: where the "facts and experience" of "actual meeting" produced "familiarity," the "cultural molds and imaginary portraits" derived from "literature and theology [and] ideology" consigned Muslims to "a place beneath the civilized European / Christian" (14). Given the theater's investment in inherited conventions and its appeal to imaginative interest, fictional symbols seem more likely to absorb the open-minded practicalities of "real contact" than to be absorbed within them.

Either interpretive trajectory seems plausible as a response to the economic and political situations of the time. Turkish power represented a real threat that might easily be subsumed within and reinforce primal fears. Between 1453, when they captured Constantinople, and 1571, when they seized Cyprus from the Venetians, the Ottoman Turks either conquered or laid siege to Athens, Otranto, Rhodes, Budapest, and Vienna. The victory of a Christian navy at the Battle of Lepanto (1571) proved only a temporary setback to the Turks, who "henceforth dominated the eastern Mediterranean" (Honigmann, 8). Perhaps *Othello*'s original audiences detected something of Lepanto's fragility in the unnamed victory that falls into the Venetians' laps at the beginning of the play. In any case, some of them retained this history as part of living memory, and their recollections would have been revitalized by the much-discussed presence of a Moorish retinue representing the king of Barbary at Elizabeth's court during 1600–01, and by the republication on King James's accession, in 1603, of his 1595 poem celebrating Lepanto.[4] Moreover, the Turkish domination in the Mediterranean was still consequential; it furnished an effective

---

4. For this material, see D'Amico, 7–40, Vaughan, 13–34, and Vitkus, *Three Turk Plays*, 7.

obstacle to the eastward expansion of European economic interests, providing a material reason why the English invested in the roundabout project of a western passage to the riches of the east.

But if economics helps reinforce the fear of a demonic other, it can also account for friendlier and more familiarized images. Queen Elizabeth was "the first English monarch to cooperate openly with the Muslims, and to allow her subjects to trade and interact with them without being liable to prosecution for dealing with 'infidels' " (Matar, 19). As a consequence, the Turks and the English became partners in the highly profitable enterprise of the "Levant trade"; in fact, the English were displacing the Venetians as the chief beneficiaries of this trade.[5] To complicate matters further, the Moors were sometimes political partners with the English as well. Jack D'Amico details the negotiations—undertaken throughout Elizabeth's reign (the embassy of 1600–01 was part of this) and sustained into James's—that sought to enlist Moorish support against the threats represented by continental European powers, especially France and Spain. "Relations between England and Morocco were extremely complex," D'Amico tells us, "and the opinions generated by those relations [varied] from the dangerously inscrutable alien to the exotically attractive ally" (39).

The context of religious feeling lets us most fully appreciate the intensity of contradictions during the period and their possible resonances for the play's first audiences. Although English-Moorish alliance may seem to imply a transcendence of credal difference, it is more likely evidence of the extreme complexity to which D'Amico refers. The threat of European invasion, which antedated the Spanish Armada of 1588 and lasted well into the seventeenth century, was consistently framed within religious beliefs: a Catholic assault against Protestant England. It was opposition to Catholic Spain that motivated the English to ally themselves with Ahmad bin Abdallah in his effort to regain the Moroccan throne.[6] The alliance went down to defeat at Alcazar (1578), but in his play *The Battle of Alcazar* commemorating the event (1591), George Peele celebrates the noble exploits of Tom Stukley as "a great Englishman who had gained honor while serving with Muslims, and who had met his death" fighting (in the play's words) "against the devill for Lord Mahamet." Since "Lord Mahamet" is himself routinely conceptualized as the devil during this period, the phrase is potentially puzzling. But the devil can take many forms. "Luther is quoted as saying in *Table Talk* that 'Antichrist is at the same time the Pope and the Turk,' " and "a link between pope and Turk . . . became a commonplace feature of Prot-

5. For the wealth of the Levant trade, which far exceeded trade in the Americas, see Davis.
6. All unattributed quotations in this and the following paragraph are from Matar (47–48), to whose detailed discussion I am much indebted.

estant historiography" (Vitkus, *Three Turk Plays,* 8). Some forms of
the diabolical, moreover, are more immediately threatening than
others, and anxieties about a Catholic invasion combined with convictions about a secret Catholic conspiracy operating inside England
produced what one Tudor historian characterizes as a national paranoia.[7]

From this angle, Peele's Stukley, fighting "against the devill for
Lord Mahamet," exhibits rational behavior. If Spain is England's
"supreme enemy" and the "Papists . . . the most nefarious of enemies," then the less urgently threatening Muslims are logical allies.
"Thou'dst shun a bear," as Lear says, "But if thy flight lay toward the
roaring sea, / Thou'dst meet the bear i'th'mouth" (3.4.10–12). It
seems unlikely, though, that such a neat cost-benefit analysis governed this anxiety-drenched situation. Some Protestants "expressed
a hope that the rival powers of Pope and Sultan would annihilate
each other, leaving a power vacuum that might be filled by an expansion of the Protestant Reformation" (Vitkus, "Early Modern Orientalism," 211). Even if "English Protestant animosity for Spanish or
Roman Catholic 'superstition' was usually stronger than feelings of
hostility toward the more distant Ottoman Muslims" (Vitkus, "Trafficking with the Turk," 39), the hierarchy implicit in any strategic
alliance was bound to be unstable, even reversible. Hence William
Lithgow, describing a visit to the Holy Sepulcher in Jerusalem in his
Totall Discourse of the Rare Adventures (1632), claims in one place
that the Turkish "Infidels" had "long agoe . . . beene converted to the
Christian Faith" were it not for the "abhominable Idolatries" of "the
Romaine Jesuites, Dominicans, and Franciscans there resident"
(33), but in another "that errors of Roman Catholic and Levantine
Christianity are a corruption brought on by contact with the Turks"
(Vitkus, "Trafficking with the Turk," 43). Despite the reassuring and
pragmatic biblical calculus, "my enemy's enemy" is never really "my
friend."

Such evidence doesn't lead to clear and univocal conclusions
about original responses to *Othello,* and the Venetian setting seems
to reinforce the interpretive instability. From one angle, of course,
stability is precisely what Venice represents in the play as the center
of civilized order; Brabantio again: "This is Venice; / My house is
not a grange." The implicit claim here must have seemed plausible
to many of the play's first audiences, for whom Venice mirrored

---

7. See Smith, and note Parker's reference below to "the context of this paranoid atmosphere"
(pp. 332–33) generated out of religious differences in late Elizabethan and early Jacobean
England. In their feelings about English Catholics, English Protestants may have experienced the same kind of (arguably pathological) disconnect as with Turks: lots of real,
familiar contact among neighbors and even friends on the one hand, intense anxiety and
fear of betrayal on the other—the latter intensified by a papal decree absolving English
Catholics of any obligations of loyalty to Queen Elizabeth.

English values: a politically independent and cosmopolitan commercial and maritime power, defending Christendom against the
infidels. But if Venetian virtue—its wealth, art, and social sophistication—could work powerfully to generate desire in English imaginations during the Renaissance (and later), Venice was also the
repellent image of Italianate greed and unrestrained sexuality—and
of course a decadent and threatening Catholicism.[8] This mythic Venice, something Shakespeare could count on his audiences including
with the baggage they carried into the theater, is at once where you
dream of being and where you fear you already are, a "dangerously
alien" and an "exotically attractive" image at the same time

D'Amico's words to describe Elizabethan feelings toward the
Moors seem to fit Venice as well, and the results are "extremely
complex" indeed. The conflict between Venetian and Turk defines
the play's foundation, but since each of the terms reproduces the
conflict in itself, the foundation tends to disintegrate. The effect is
to reinforce a fundamental ambivalence in the play's representation
of the protagonist. As with other Renaissance plays that, in Vitkus's
view, reflect "an anxious interest in Islamic power that is both complicated and overdetermined" (*Three Turk Plays*, 3), different spectators likely had different and contradictory reactions to different
performances of *Othello*. If Renaissance playwrights were, moreover,
"capable of simultaneously engaging and undermining the prejudices
of their audience" (Bak, 215), then some individuals, internalizing
contradictory responses, would have felt themselves positioned
between two forces of invading infidels, uneasily playing off one
against the other—like the Venetians in the play, enlisting Othello
to protect themselves against a danger that Othello symbolically represents.

Desdemona is evidently a secondary figure; rather than sustaining
her own interest, she supports the play's focus on the protagonist.
From another angle, though, she is the determining presence in the
play's action. At the end, she shares center stage with Othello (and
Emilia) in the "tragic loading of this bed" (5.2.368) and the one

---

8. The major advocate for the positive view of Venice as "represent[ing] the ideal of civilized
   European liberty" (Hadfield, *Literature, Travel, and Colonial Writing*, 232) is Contareno's
   Commonwealth and Government of Venice, in the 1599 translation by Lewis Lewkenor.
   The book was popular at the time, and Malone, in his 1790 edition of *Othello*, pointed
   out that the "officers of night" that Brabantio would raise (1.1.79) are several times
   referred to and highlighted in these terms by Lewkenor—something that led Malone (and
   most succeeding editors) to "have no doubt that Shakspeare, before he wrote this play,
   read" Contareno's book (1.236). Negative opinion about Venice was at least equally widespread during the period, though Coryat, perhaps the major popularizer of anti-Venetian
   sentiment, was published too late to be considered a textual source for *Othello*. For other
   discussions of the Renaissance context for Venice, see Hunter, Ann Jones, McPherson,
   Marrapodi, Greenberg (6 ff.), Vaughan (13–34), and Klein. For later, see Tanner. For
   bibliographical details, see Textual Sources in the bibliography, p. 389.

substantial report surviving from the play's early performances (discussed in the introduction to the "Criticism" section of this book) seems interested more in her than in Othello. At the beginning, when Othello calls upon her to verify his version of their courtship, the action stops pending her arrival and speech: the judgment of the duke and the senate hangs on her judgment. She guides not just characters' responses within the play but our response to it. For Bradley, Othello's color "concerns the character of Desdemona," as though her value depended on his, but the relation is fully reversible: the quality of Desdemona's desire for the protagonist determines his desirability—or not. In this sense, our feelings about Desdemona constitute the origin from which the interpretation of *Othello* proceeds. She is, like the ghost in Dover Wilson's reading of *Hamlet*, the "linchpin" of the play.

Unlike Othello, whose representation clearly assumes beliefs and feelings remote from any modern audience, Desdemona may seem not to need historical contextualization; but here too the impression is deceptive. We have become used to stories about the satisfactions and trials of marital and familial life. "All happy families are alike, each unhappy family is unhappy in its own special way": the well-known opening of *Anna Karenina* assumes domestic space as the default setting for fiction, and Tolstoy centers his novel on an adulterous wife, concluding with her violent death. The differences from *Othello* are real enough (Anna really is unfaithful, and she commits suicide), but the play's subject and genre are likely to seem familiar: a married couple whose feelings for one another, though largely without consequence for the public domain, produce a tragedy for themselves. To *Othello*'s first audiences, however, the play must have looked in some measure anomalous and even strange, one of the "new genres" Richard Helgerson describes in which "the nonaristocratic home . . . emerges not simply as an adjunct of state power but as an alternative to it, a space that by the late eighteenth century would be making its own claim to both representation and political value as the affective base for a new revolutionary order" (4). As heirs to this revolution, we take for granted certain values attached to "the family, sex and marriage" (to cite Lawrence Stone's seminal work in this area); but these institutions and practices were just emerging into a consciousness consistent with our own around the time *Othello* was first produced. To make matters more complicated, these new values existed with and were displacing more traditional ideas about women and the social order—ideas that, though much less familiar to modern audiences, must have contributed significantly to the responses of *Othello*'s first audiences, especially to Desdemona's central presence in the play.

To start with marriage: with the decline of the Catholic monastic ideal of celibacy and the rehabilitation of the natural domain, marriage came out from under the shadow of a necessary compromise (St. Paul's "better to marry than burn") into prominence as a justified and indeed sanctified condition. The Protestant investment in "holy matrimony" went beyond the traditional utilitarian sanctions (controlling lust, propagating and reinforcing the values of Christian community) to affirm the emotional bond between husband and wife. The values of "companionate marriage" were developed in a rich tradition of homiletic literature—sermons and practical manuals offering guidance about the choice of husband or wife (now less a matter of parental imposition) and about the kind of behavior likely to sustain affection between partners amid the inevitable complications and tribulations of a long shared life. The Protestant ideal achieves its most resonant poetic expression in *Paradise Lost* (1667), where Milton's panegyric, "Hail wedded Love" (4.750), celebrates Adam and Eve's marriage as the affectionate and spiritual center of individual and social experience.[9]

In Mary Beth Rose's pioneering study of this subject, the "transformation" by which marriage and the domestic domain acquire new "prestige and centrality" is first registered imaginatively on the Jacobean stage. In "striking contrast" to received tragic conventions in which a "heroism of public action," manifested in "political and military struggles," relegated "women, eros, and sexuality to the periphery," early seventeenth-century playwrights emphasize "a heroism of personal endurance, creating tragedies of private life" in which the "prominence of women as tragic heroes and / or of eros as a tragic subject increases remarkably" (95). The result is a new tragic mode centered in "the heroics of marriage" (93 ff.), for which *Othello* (along with Webster's *Duchess of Malfi*, 1613) serves Rose as prime exhibit.

The play, right from its opening movement, offers abundant evidence to support this claim. Nearly the whole of *Othello*'s first act is unnecessary for the action; it's not in Cinthio, eighteenth-century commentators found it an irritating transgression against "unity of place," and Arrigo Boito will eliminate it from the libretto of Verdi's opera *Otello* (1887). But the play goes out of its way to focus interest on the circumstances and feelings within which Othello and Desdemona choose each other. In describing this process, moreover, Desdemona's testimony may be the more powerfully interesting account. "That I love the Moor to live with him" (1.3.246): the bold insistence—more emphatically present than in the usually adopted and metrically more regular Q version, "That I did love the Moor . . ."—unequivocally avows her sexual desire for Othello before

9. For discussions of this material, see the Hallers, Schücking, Christopher Hill, and Ozment.

the full senate. Sex, of course, is not all she means in asserting her rights to the pleasure of Othello's company: "to live with him" entails sharing the exotic experiences his own speech earlier had described, as well as the heroic romance of military affairs to come, and the inner beauty she has intuited, "Othello's visage in his mind" (1.3.250), as the basis of a spiritual companionship between his "perfect soul" (1.2.31) and her own as "consecrate[d]" to him (1.3.252). Desdemona refuses the conventional distinctions—between body and spirit, private and public—and in so doing rejects the traditional supremacy of male to female value that seems to stand behind them. Equality inheres in her version of "holy matrimony" as a mutually elective affinity implicitly derived from the most profound depths of Protestant feeling—the equality of all individual souls before God. Othello's delighted "my fair warrior" on Cyprus strand (2.1.180) generously recognizes his wife's equal status. Desdemona's "unhandsome warrior" later in the play (3.4.148) acknowledges her struggle to maintain the integrity of her feeling faced with Othello's betrayal of faith. In this struggle, moreover, she is arguably more successful than he or anyone else in the play. If *Othello* is centered on "the heroics of marriage," then Desdemona, who most fully achieves and embodies these values, is the true protagonist.

But she isn't; the play's celebration of heroic marriage is deeply qualified. According to Valerie Wayne, "an antimatrimonial misogyny is the residual ideology articulated in this play through Iago and, eventually, Othello, and a general advocacy for marriage is projected as dominant through Desdemona" (168). Alternatively, however, *Othello* may be seen as dramatizing contradictions within "holy matrimony"—sentimental commitments to the old hierarchy, surviving amid newly emergent values. Renaissance discussions of companionate marriage seem to have served conservative as well as innovative interests. With the disestablishment of the Catholic hierarchy, a regulative institution deeply immersed in the day-to-day behavior of ordinary people disappeared, and the homiletic literature sought to fill this vacuum in authority. Whatever its implications for equality, the detailed descriptions of the thought, feeling, and behavior appropriate to marriage were sustained with incessant reminders about the authority of husbands over their wives—Stone's "reinforcement of the patriarchy." The "heroics of marriage" thus "collapses from within, dissolving inevitably from its own unresolved contradictions" (Rose, 131).[1]

In either case, a strong current of "antimatrimonial misogyny" runs through *Othello*, expressed in its most strikingly direct form as a violent aversion to the female body. Iago punningly refers to Des-

---

1. For some of the many skeptical reflections on the sort of claims made by the Hallers et al. cited just above, see Amussen, Davies, Jordan, and Underdown.

demona's "country disposition" and "country forms" in terms of a disgusting odor: "Foh! one may smell in such a will most rank" (3.3.203, 239, 234); and Othello becomes infected with the same revulsion, associating the "corner in the thing I love" with the "vapor of a dungeon," "a cistern for foul toads / To knot and gender in," and finally the hatred "honest" Iago feels for "the slime / That sticks on filthy deeds" (3.3.273–74, 4.2.61–62, 5.2.151–52). Such disturbing images have been explained in psychological or generic terms—an author's period of secret sorrow, tragedy's refusal of the life force in its maternal fertility. But in Gail Paster's work, an aversion to the female body emerges as neither pathological nor specific to any limited perspective, generic or otherwise, but rather the generally dispersed and normative view. According to the theory of bodily humors, accepted for centuries and still (in Paster's view) fully authoritative at the time of *Othello,* the female body (as the then-scientific understanding construed it) was inherently leakier than the male—more "effluent, overproductive, out of control"; and "it is precisely woman's literal saturation by the cold clamminess of the female complexion that philosophically undergirds the most virulent, most conservative forms of Renaissance misogyny" (*Body Embarrassed,* 21; "Unbearable Coldness," 430).

Renaissance misogyny is legitimated, moreover, by religious as well as scientific authority (a distinction less real for *Othello*'s audience than for us). As Boose argues below, Othello's "cause" at the end, his claim to administer punitive justice against female sexual transgression, derives not from some "alien" code attributable to "uncivilized notions of barbarian blackness," but "lies rather at the root of Western religious law" in the Hebrew Bible. Christianity thus inherits (and complicates) an anxiety about sex for which even the compromise of Pauline marriage affords inadequate relief. For spousal relations themselves are fraught with the risk of sin. Stephen Greenblatt cites a variety of Catholic commentators for whom, in St. Jerome's words, "an adulterer is he who is too ardent a lover of his wife" (248). According to Greenblatt, "the dark essence of Iago's whole enterprise" is "to play upon Othello's buried perception of his own sexual relations with Desdemona as adulterous" (233)—an argument that may illuminate Iago's much-discussed reference to Cassio as a "fellow almost damned in a fair wife" (1.1.18). Misogyny and sexual anxiety were never the totality of sanctioned Catholic belief, and the Reformers vigorously contested such views in their own claims for "holy matrimony"; Milton, indeed, goes out of his way to insist repeatedly on the inclusion of sexual pleasure in wedded love's "mysterious Law" (4.750). But given the longevity and depths of this tradition, "an underlying guilt and disgust about sexuality itself" (Snow, 388) must have been strongly enough present to

Renaissance audiences for *Othello*'s expressions of misogyny to receive at least a general form of conditional assent.

Compelling as they are, the play's sexual images should not be treated in isolation. As Patricia Parker argues in "*Othello* and *Hamlet*: Dilation, Spying and the 'Secret Place' of Woman" (p. 329 below), the anxieties about women expressed in *Othello* need to be located within the "networks of terms that shaped politics, institutions, and laws, as well as discourses of the body" at the time the play was written. In fact, the sociopolitical realm may be determining the psychosexual: so Ann Jennalie Cook argues, claiming that for "Shakespeare's audiences the fact of an unlikely alliance with a Moor might have been far less troubling than the elopement itself" as a rebellion against patriarchal authority (188). But it is hard to determine priority. Consider, for example, in *The Comedy of Errors*, Luciana's injunction to her sister, the shrewish wife Adriana, not to resist "the bridle" of husbandly authority:

> Why, headstrong liberty is lashed with woe.
> There's nothing situate under heaven's eye
> But hath his bound in earth, in sea, in sky.
> The beasts, the fishes, and the wingèd fowls
> Are their males' subjects and at their controls.
> Man, more divine, the master of all these,
> Lord of the wide world and wild wat'ry seas,
> Indued with intellectual sense and souls,
> Of more pre-eminence than fish and fowls,
> Are masters to their females, and their lords.
> Then let your will attend on their accords. (2.1.15–25)

The speech is predicated on an analogy among various hierarchies (man / beast, male / female, master / servant), all corresponding to divine ordinance ("heaven's eye"). Luciana's point is that aspiration beyond one's proper boundaries is futile and self-destructive: the cosmic order is irresistible. But reverse the affective trajectory and Luciana's words betray the fragility of that order, its vulnerability to assault by female self-assertion—a speech motivated less by confidence than by insecurity.

Adriana's speech may be understood within the context of "the woman question"—a literary debate begun around 1540 and sustained in a variety of texts for a century or more—arguing about matters such as the virtues inherent in or absent from female nature, the relation between nature and culture in defining female identity, the training appropriately given to or withheld from women, and the behavior legitimately expected or feared from them. The durability and wide dispersion of this debate suggests that it reflected deeply felt concerns; but according to Linda Woodbridge, who speaks with special authority on this material, the formal controversy about women was such a highly stylized and self-enclosed rhetorical game that its connections to social reality are hard to determine. In the popular culture of the period, on the other hand—and this includes the public theaters for which *The Comedy of Errors* and *Othello* were written—the obsessive focus on shrews, scolding wives and other insubordinate women may be more immediately revealing. In *Arden of Faversham* and *A Warning for Fair Women*, two domestic tragedies that held the stage during the 1590s, wives betray and then conspire with their lovers to kill their husbands. According to Frances E. Dolan, "husband-murder . . . captured the popular imagination and generated extensive representations," in pamphlets and ballads as well as plays, "despite the fact that it was never very common." Along with master-slaying, moreover, husband-murder was legally designated as petty treason—that is, as "a crime against civil authority" (13), even though "legal records suggest that women and servants were more often the victims than the perpetrators of domestic violence" (4).

In the face of such evidence, as Dolan remarks, "Many social historians agree that early modern England witnessed a crisis of order, focusing on gender relations" (17) and produced in significant measure by the increased importance attached to the domestic domain. The phenomenon of "women on top," in Natalie Zemon Davis's at once politically and sexually charged phrase, must have contributed as well, especially in England, where for so long Queen Elizabeth was the "one vital exception" to a social order in which "all forms of public and domestic authority . . . were vested in men" (Montrose, 64). Even here there are complications, however; as Amanda Shephard demonstrates, queenship could be the basis for protofeminism as well as for misogynist anxiety, even among conservative Catholic aristocrats, who might seem like the least hospitable constituency for such purportedly progressive ideas. Modern grids don't fit neatly over the Renaissance terrain, and the proliferation of variables— gender, social status, religious affiliation, etc.—make interpretive clarity very hard to achieve. The "woman question" was probably many different questions, clustered around a symbolic core that allowed for and encouraged multiple and contradictory sorts of engagement.

"If this be not barbarous," says the speaker/author of *Hic Mulier; or, The Man-Woman*, a 1620 contribution to the formal controversy about women, referring to the female arrogation of man's clothes and prerogatives, "make the rude Scythians, the untamed Moor, the naked Indian, or the wild Irish, Lords and Rulers of well-governed Cities" (Henderson, 269). The words sound uncannily like Brabantio's enraged anxiety cited earlier, "For if such actions may have passage free, / Bondslaves and pagans shall our statesmen be"; and the resonance allows us to consider an analogy implicit in the discussion so far. The unspecified "actions" Brabantio finds so alarming can refer equally to the assault on his authority as a Venetian senator by (in Roderigo's words) "an extravagant and wheeling stranger / Of here and everywhere" (1.1.133–34), and to the assault on his patriarchal authority from within his own family. The play's language supports the analogy. In describing Desdemona's "gross revolt," Roderigo echoes "the gross clasps of a lascivious Moor" just earlier (1.1.131, 123), thereby locating (just the wrong word) Othello and Desdemona in an unconfined space of erotic wandering, outside the constraints of stabilizing order. The functional vagueness of "thing" nourishes the analogy as well, identifying (again the wrong word) Othello's terrifyingly indefinite presence—"such a thing as thou" (1.2.71)—and Desdemona's "thing," the "appetite" that belongs to her, which Othello can never own, merely "keep" (3.3.272 and 274).

Cook furnishes yet another basis for this analogy, arguing that the play "seems deliberately to be setting up doubts about Desdemona in the spectator's mind" at the beginning, resolving them only gradually and not "permit[ting] the playgoer to trust fully" in her "until the concluding act" (189, 193). Similarly, Hunter (below) argues that the play "manipulates our sympathies" in its opening movements, "supposing that we will have brought to the theatre a set of careless assumptions about 'Moors,' " on to which it then, by evoking different traditions of belief, "complicating factors which had begun to affect thought in this day," requires us "to superimpose . . . new valuations" of Othello, diametrically opposed to the fear and loathing first generated by Iago. In focusing specifically on dramatic design and theatrical effect, Cook and Hunter articulate powerful interpretive structures to orchestrate the contradictory feelings and values generated by the action. In suggesting the superimposition of new or emergent ideologies over residual inheritances from the past, moreover, these structures allow us to connect with Raymond Williams's influential ideas about fiction as a "structure of feeling"—capable of foreshadowing values not yet available to conscious belief, and thus specially useful for negotiating social change.

We need to be cautious about these claims, however. For one thing, the analogous functions of Othello and Desdemona are not identical. As Ania Loomba argues, "the filtering of sexuality and race through each other's prism profoundly affects each of them," but it "does not *dissolve* the tensions between different forms of oppression" (41, her emphasis). Nineteenth-century critics made a similar point, though registering it in the very different vocabulary of an affective engagement with the characters: in the excerpts below, from Coleridge to Bradley, critics argue with each other and with themselves about whether Othello or Desdemona more deserves our sympathy. Although both share a difference from established authority, they differ from each other as well, generating sometimes contradictory responses from the audience. If the analogy should be questioned, so too should the relevance of the interpretive model itself. Hunter and Cook see a process of disconfirmation at work in the action of *Othello,* whereby the audience abandons its initial impressions for more enlightened views. But this is not the only or perhaps even the most plausible attempt to read the play's design. In much current critical representation, *Othello* works the other way around, as in Michael Neill's argument that the "play thinks abomination into being and then taunts the audience with the knowledge that it can never be *un*thought" (p. 315 below).

The play generously accommodates these contradictory claims, and others as well. *Othello*'s openness to a variety of interpretive desires helps explain its durability—the remarkable capacity it shares with other Shakespearean plays to excite the interests of readers and audiences in situations far removed from those of the early productions. Acknowledging this availability, moreover, is a way to respect the complexity of the original context as well. Given the multiplicity of beliefs and feelings and subject positions dispersed among Shakespeare's first audiences—the proliferation of variables and contradictions I have been emphasizing here—textual malleability seems like a strategic response: a pragmatic Shakespeare playing to the contingencies of a big room. Whatever values we place on authorial intention, an overdetermined text and an overdetermined historical context seem to reflect each other, and any attempt to arrest the flow of either textual or historical signification into a single structure of meaning seems wrongheaded.

In the same cautionary spirit, a final word about a related kind of overconfidence, in which, reviewing the institutionalized misogyny and apparently normative bigotry of Renaissance culture, we are tempted to congratulate ourselves on doing better than the past. The burden of my own "Too Much Violence" (p. 366 below) is that surprising continuities exist between current work on *Othello* and the misogynist critical traditions systematically repudiated by that work. Similar arguments can be made for racial politics as well. According to Robert J. C. Young, "If there is one constant characteristic of the history of the use of the word 'race', it is that however many new meanings may be constructed for it, the old meanings refuse to die. They rather accumulate in clusters of ever-increasing power, resonance and persuasion" (83). Even in the current "postracial" environment, when a new genetics has emptied the concept of "race" of scientific legitimacy, "racial thinking" persists in a form whose disguise may be augmenting its already pernicious effects. Walter Benn

Michaels and Paul Gilroy, though coming at the question with different national affiliations and from different political positions—not to mention different ethnic and (yes) racial identities—claim that contemporary critics arguing for multiculturalism and ethnicity in specific opposition to racial agendas radically depend on and therefore effectively sustain the idea of race they wish to eradicate.

According to Neil Taylor, "the removal of the blackface mask" in the 1995 Oliver Parker film version of *Othello* "seems like an act of liberation": it allows Laurence Fishburne "to operate almost literally as himself." In a similar spirit, Tony Howard claims that a 1991 cinematic spinoff of *Othello* called *True Identity* "confronted the black actor's right to play Othello and consigned an old myth to history" (306). For Hugh Quarshie, however, "the first Anglo-African actor to play major roles" in RSC productions of Shakespeare's histories (Taylor, i), "When a black actor plays Othello," he complies with the racial stereotype initiated by the play (in Quarshie's view) and sustained by its reception over time, so that "Othello is the one [Shakespearean part] which should most definitely not be played by a black actor" (19–20, 18, and 5). While Quarshie backs away from this conclusion, he first makes it plain why "liberation" from the prison of tradition is not such an easy matter: even as we consign our "old myths to history," historical continuity tends to revitalize them in different forms.

That the option to play Othello now exists for black actors—that black actors exist to exercise the option—is an unambiguous advance over the diminished possibilities available to black actors of earlier times: to Paul Robeson, for example, who performed the role three times in difficult circumstances in England and the United States in the mid-twentieth century; or to Ira Aldridge, who played the role regularly, mostly on East European and Russian stages during the nineteenth century.[2] We all need some sense of participating in a process, however long and gradual, of getting somewhere better than where we (or our ancestors) were. But some forms of reassurance are more sturdy than others;[3] and even the sturdy ones need to be

---

2. For Robeson, see Potter, who makes him the central figure in her recent account of *Othello* in performance. For Aldridge, see Cowhig, Errol Hill, Marshall and Stock, and Over, as well as the figure on p. 187.

3. Taylor, who commends the Parker film for breaking what "was once a taboo against the representation of the physical relationship between a black man and a white woman," adds that it "has now become possible, on stage and on film, to cut across racial and national stereotypes almost at will. In November 1997 Jude Kelly's stage production at the Lansburgh Theatre, Washington D.C.," starring Patrick Stewart, with an almost totally black supporting cast, permitted Othello to be "referred to as being black despite being patently white" (270, 271). This enthusiasm can be infectious, but it may suggest Fred Rogers, telling the American kids watching *Mr. Rogers' Neighborhood* that "you can grow up to be anything you want to," or *Blue Peter*, in Monty Python's takeoff: "Boys and girls, in today's program we'll learn how to build a tree house and how to eliminate racial prejudice from the world forever."

supplemented on occasion with less sunny prospects. *Othello* is one such occasion. Of all the many interpretive conclusions available to us in an attempt to understand *Othello* historically, a secure confidence in our power to escape the benighted errors of the past doesn't seem among the more plausible.

Works Cited

Amussen, Susan. "Gender, Family and the Social Order, 1560–1725." In Anthony Fletcher and John Stevenson, ed. *Order and Disorder in Early Modern England*. Cambridge and New York: Cambridge University Press, 1985, 196–217.

Appiah, Kwame Anthony. "Race." In Frank Lentricchia and Thomas McLaughlin, ed. *Critical Terms for Literary Study*. Chicago: University of Chicago Press, 1990, 274–87.

Bak, Greg. "Different Differences: Locating Moorishness in Early Modern Culture." *Dalhousie Review* 76 (1996): 197–221.

Barthelemy, Anthony Gerard. *Black Face, Maligned Race: The Representation of Blacks in English Drama from Shakespeare to Southerne*. Baton Rouge and London: Louisiana State University Press, 1987.

Chew, Samuel. "Moslems on the London Stage." In *The Crescent and the Rose: Islam and England during the Renaissance*. 1937. Rpt. New York: Octagon, 1965, 469–540.

Cook, Ann Jennalie. "The Design of Desdemona: Doubt Raised and Resolved." *Shakespeare Studies* 13 (1980): 187–96.

Coryat, Thomas. *Coryats Crudities*. 1611. Rpt. London: Scolar Press, 1978.

Cowhig, Ruth. "Actors Black and Tawny in the Role of Othello—and Their Critics." *Theatre Research International* 4 (1979): 133–46.

D'Amico, Jack. *The Moor in English Renaissance Drama*. Tampa: University of South Florida Press, 1991.

Davies, Kathleen M. "Continuity and Change in Literary Advice on Marriage." In Outhwaite, *Marriage and Society*, 58–80.

———. "The Sacred Condition of Equality—How Original Were Puritan Doctrines of Marriage?" *Social History* 2 (1977): 563–79.

Davis, Ralph. "England and the Mediterranean, 1570–1670." In F. J. Fisher, ed. *Essays in the Economic and Social History of Tudor and Stuart England, in Honour of R. H. Tawney*. Cambridge: Cambridge University Press, 1961, 274–87.

Davis, Natalie Zemon. "Women on Top." In *Society and Culture in Early Modern France*. Stanford: Stanford University Press, 1975, 124–51.

Dolan, Frances E. *Dangerous Familiars: Representations of Domestic*

Crime in England, 1550–1700. Ithaca and London: Cornell University Press, 1994.

Furness, Horace Howard, ed. *A New Variorum Edition of Othello*. 7th ed. Philadelphia: Lippincott, 1886.

Gillies, John. *Shakespeare and the Geography of Difference*. Cambridge Studies in Renaissance Literature and Culture 4. Cambridge: Cambridge University Press, 1994.

Gilroy, Paul. *Against Race: Imagining Political Culture behind the Color Line*. Cambridge, Ma.: Harvard University Press, 2000.

Greenberg, Mitchell. "Shakespeare's *Othello* and the 'Problem' of Anxiety." In *Canonical States, Canonical Stages: Oedipus, Othering, and Seventeenth-Century Drama*. Minneapolis and London: University of Minnesota Press, 1994, 1–32.

Greenblatt, Stephen. "The Improvisation of Power." In *Renaissance Self-Fashioning: From More to Shakespeare*. Chicago: University of Chicago Press, 1980, 222–54.

Hadfield, Andrew. *Literature, Travel, and Colonial Writing in the English Renaissance, 1545–1625*. Oxford: Clarendon, 1998.

———, ed. *Amazons, Savages, and Machiavels: Travel and Colonial Writing in English, 1550–1630: An Anthology*. Oxford and New York: Oxford University Press, 2001.

Haller, Mandeville and William. "The Puritan Art of Love." *Huntington Library Quarterly* 5 (1942): 235–72.

Helgerson, Richard. *Adulterous Alliances: Home, State, and History in Early Modern European Drama and Painting*. Chicago and London: University of Chicago Press, 2000.

Henderson, Katherine Usher, and Barbara F. McManus. *Half Humankind: Contexts and Texts of the Controversy about Women in England, 1540–1640*. Urbana and Chicago: University of Illinois Press, 1985.

Hill, Christopher. "The Spiritualization of the Household." In *Society and Puritanism in Pre-Revolutionary England*. New York: Schocken Books, 1964, 443–81.

Hill, Errol. *Shakespeare in Sable: A History of Black Shakespearean Actors*. Amherst: University of Massachusetts Press, 1986.

Honigmann, E. A. J. Introduction. In Honigmann, ed. *Othello*. Walton-on-Thames: Nelson, 1997, 1–111.

Howard, Tony. "Shakespeare's Cinematic Offshoots." In Russell Jackson, ed. *Cambridge Companion to Shakespeare on Film*. Cambridge: Cambridge University Press, 2000, 293–313.

Hughes, Paul L., and James F. Larkin, ed. *Tudor Royal Proclamations. Vol III: The Later Tudors (1588–1603)*. New Haven and London: Yale University Press, 1969.

Hunter, G. K. "English Folly and Italian Vice: The Moral Landscape of John Marston." In *Dramatic Identities and Cultural Tradition:*

Studies in Shakespeare and His Contemporaries. Liverpool: Liverpool University Press, 1978, 103–32

Jones, Ann Rosalind. "Italians and Others: Venice and the Irish in Coryat's *Crudities* and *The White Devil*." *Renaissance Drama* 18 (1987): 101–19.

Jones, Eldred. *Othello's Countrymen: The African in English Renaissance Drama*. London: Oxford University Press, 1965.

Jordan, Constance. *Renaissance Feminism: Literary Texts and Political Models*. Ithaca: Cornell University Press, 1990, 289–97.

Jordan, Winthrop. *White over Black: American Attitudes toward the Negro, 1550–1812*. Chapel Hill: University of North Carolina Press, 1968.

Kamps, Ivo, and Jyotsna G. Singh, ed. *Travel Knowledge: European "Discoveries" in the Early Modern Period*. New York: Palgrave, 2001.

Klein, Holger, and Michele Marrapodi, ed. *Shakespeare and Italy*. Lewiston, N.Y.: Edwin Mellen Press, 1999.

Lithgow, William. *Totall Discourse of the Rare Adventures, and painefull Peregrinations of a Long Nineteene Years Travayles, from Scotland, to the Most Famous Kingdomes in Europe, Asia and Affrica*. Excerpted by Vitkus in Kamps and Singh, *Travel Knowledge*, 29–34.

Loomba, Ania. *Gender, Race, Renaissance Drama*. Manchester: Manchester University Press, 1989.

Lupton, Julia Reinhard. "*Othello* Circumcised: Shakespeare and the Pauline Discourse of Nations." *Representations* 57 (1997): 73–89.

MacLean, Gerald. "Ottomanism before Orientalism? Bishop King Praises Henry Blount, Passenger in the Levant." In Kamps and Singh, *Travel Knowledge*, 85–96.

Malone, Edmond. *The Plays and Poems of William Shakespeare*. 10 vols. London, 1790. Rpt. New York: AMS Press, 1966.

Marrapodi, Michele, A. J. Hoenselaars, Marcello Cappuzzo, and L. Falzon Santucci, ed. *Shakespeare's Italy: Functions of Italian Locations in Renaissance Drama*. Manchester: Manchester University Press, 1993.

Marshall, Herbert, and Mildred Stock. *Ira Aldridge: the Negro Tragedian*. Carbondale: Southern Illinois University Press, 1968.

Matar, Nabil. *Turks, Moors and Englishmen in the Age of Discovery*. New York: Columbia University Press, 1999.

McDonald, Russ. " 'I Loved My Books': Shakespeare's Reading." In *The Bedford Companion to Shakespeare: An Introduction with Documents*. 2nd ed. Boston: Bedford St. Martins, 2001, 145–93.

McPherson, David C. *Shakespeare, Jonson, and the Myth of Venice*. Newark: University of Delaware Press, 1990.

Michaels, Walter Benn. *Our America: Nativism, Modernism, and Pluralism.* Durham: Duke University Press, 1995.

Montrose, Louis Adrian. " 'Shaping Fantasies': Figurations of Gender and Power in Elizabethan Culture." *Representations* 2 (1983): 61–94.

Newman, Karen. " 'And Wash the Ethiop White': Femininity and the Monstrous in *Othello*." In Jean E. Howard and Marion F. O'Connor, ed. *Shakespeare Reproduced: The Text in History and Ideology.* London: Methuen, 1987, 140–62.

Outhwaite, R. B., ed. *Marriage and Society: Studies in the Social History of Marriage.* New York: St. Martins, 1981.

Over, William. "New York's African Theatre: Shakespeare Reinterpreted." In Donald Hedrick and Bryan Reynolds, ed. *Shakespeare without Class: Misappropriations of Cultural Capital.* New York: Palgrave, 2000, 65–83.

Ozment, Stephen. *When Fathers Ruled: Family Life in Reformation Europe.* Cambridge, Ma.: Harvard University Press, 1983.

Paster, Gail Kern. *The Body Embarrassed: Drama and the Disciplines of Shame in Early Modern England.* Ithaca: Cornell University Press, 1993.

———. "The Unbearable Coldness of Female Being: Women's Imperfection and the Humoral Economy." *English Literary Renaissance,* 28 (1998): 416–40.

Potter, Lois. *Othello.* Shakespeare in Performance. Manchester: Manchester University Press, 2002.

Quarshie, Hugh. "Second Thoughts about *Othello*." ISA Occasional Paper No. 7. Chipping Camden: International Shakespeare Association, 1999.

Rose, Mary Beth. *The Expense of Spirit: Love and Sexuality in English Renaissance Drama.* Ithaca and London: Cornell University Press, 1988.

Schücking, Levin L. *The Puritan Family: A Social Study from the Literary Sources.* Trans. Brian Battershaw. New York: Schocken, 1969.

Shephard, Amanda. *Gender and Authority in Sixteenth-Century England: The Knox Debate.* Keele: Ryburn Publishing, 1994.

Smith, Lacey Baldwin. *Treason in Tudor England: Politics and Paranoia.* Princeton: Princeton University Press, 1986.

Snow, Edward. "Sexual Anxiety and the Male Order of Things in *Othello*." *English Literary Renaissance* 10 (1980): 384–412.

Stone, Lawrence. *The Family, Sex and Marriage in England, 1500–1800.* London: Weidenfeld and Nicolson, 1977.

Tanner, Tony. *Venice Desired.* Cambridge, Ma.: Harvard University Press, 1992.

Taylor, Gary. Preface to Quarshie, "Second Thoughts," i–ii.

Taylor, Neil. "National and Racial Stereotypes in Shakespeare Films." In Russell Jackson, ed. *Cambridge Companion to Shakespeare on Film*. Cambridge: Cambridge University Press 2000, 261–73.

Tokson, Elliot H. *The Popular Image of the Black Man in English Drama, 1550–1688*. Boston: G. K. Hall & Co., 1982.

Underdown, David. "The Taming of the Scold—the Enforcement of Patriarchal Authority in Early Modern England." In Outhwaite, *Marriage and Society*, 116–36.

Vaughan, Virginia Mason. *"Othello": A Contextual History*. Cambridge: Cambridge University Press, 1994.

Vitkus, Daniel J. "Early Modern Orientalism." In David R. Blanks and Michael Frassetto, ed. *Western Views of Islam in Medieval and Early Modern Europe: Perception of the Other*. New York: St. Martin's Press, 1999, 207–30.

————. "Trafficking with the Turk: English Travelers in the Ottoman Empire during the Early Seventeenth Century." In Kamps and Singh, *Travel Knowledge*, 35–52.

————, ed. *Three Turk Plays from Early Modern England*. New York: Columbia University Press, 2000.

Wayne, Valerie. "Historical Differences: Misogyny and *Othello*." In Wayne, ed. *The Matter of Difference: Materialist Feminist Criticism of Shakespeare*. Ithaca: Cornell University Press, 1991, 153–80.

Williams, Raymond. "Structures of Feeling." In *Marxism and Literature*. Oxford: Oxford University Press, 1977, 128–35.

Woodbridge, Linda. *Women and the English Renaissance: Literature and the Nature of Womankind, 1540–1620*. Urbana and Chicago: University of Illinois Press, 1984.

Young, Robert J. C. *Colonial Desire: Hybridity in Theory, Culture and Race*. London and New York: Routledge, 1995.

GIRALDI CINTHIO

[The Moor of Venice]†

There once lived in Venice a Moor, who was very valiant, and of a handsome person; and having given proofs in war of great skill and prudence, he was highly esteemed by the Signoria of the Republic, who in rewarding deeds of valour advanced the interests of the State.

† From Decade 3, story 7 of Cinthio's *Gli Hecatommithi* ("Hundred Tales"). The translator's notes have been omitted. For information about translations of Cinthio and other texts that may have influenced the composition of *Othello*, see "Textual Sources" in the bibliography, p. 389.

It happened that a virtuous lady, of marvellous beauty, named Disdemona, fell in love with the Moor, moved thereto by his valour; and he, vanquished by the beauty and the noble character of Disdemona, returned her love; and their affection was so mutual, that, although the parents of the lady strove all they could to induce her to take another husband, she consented to marry the Moor; and they lived in such harmony and peace in Venice, that no word ever passed between them that was not affectionate and kind.

Now it happened at this time that the Signoria of Venice made a change in the troops whom they used to maintain in Cyprus, and they appointed the Moor commander of the soldiers whom they despatched thither. Joyful as was the Moor at the honour proffered him,—such dignity being only conferred on men of noble rank and well-tried faith, and who had displayed bravery in arms,—yet his pleasure was lessened when he reflected on the length and dangers of the voyage, fearing that Disdemona would be pained at his absence. But Disdemona, who had no other happiness in the world than the Moor, and who rejoiced to witness the testimony of his valour her husband had received from so powerful and noble a Republic, was all impatient that he should embark with his troops, and longed to accompany him to so honourable a post. And all the more it vexed her to see the Moor so troubled; and not knowing what could be the reason, one day, when they were at dinner, she said to him, "How is it, O Moor, that when so honourable a post has been conferred on you by the Signoria, you are thus melancholy?"

The Moor answered Disdemona, "My pleasure at the honour I have received is disturbed by the love I bear you; for I see that of necessity one of two things must happen; either that I take you with me, to encounter the perils of the sea, or, to save you from this danger, I must leave you here in Venice. The first could not be otherwise than serious to me, for all the toil you would have to bear, and every danger that might befall you, would cause me extreme anxiety and pain. Yet, were I to leave you behind me, I should be hateful to myself, since in parting from you I should part from my own life."

Disdemona, on hearing this, replied, "My husband, what thoughts are these that wander through your mind? Why let such things disturb you? I will accompany you whithersoe'er you go, were it to pass through fire, as now to cross the water in a safe and well-provided ship: if indeed there are toils and perils to encounter, I will share them with you. And in truth I should think you loved me little, were you to leave me here in Venice, denying me to bear you company, or could believe that I would liefer bide in safety here, than share the dangers that await you. Prepare then for the voyage, with all the readiness which the dignity of the post you hold deserves."

The Moor, in the fulness of his joy, threw his arms around his wife's neck, and with an affectionate and tender kiss exclaimed, "God keep you long in such love, dear wife!" Then speedily donning his armour, and having prepared everything for his expedition, he embarked on board the galley, with his wife and all his troops; and setting sail, they pursued their voyage, and with a perfectly tranquil sea arrived safely at Cyprus.

Now amongst the soldiery there was an Ensign, a man of handsome figure, but of the most depraved nature in the world. This man was in great favour with the Moor, who had not the slightest idea of his wickedness; for despite the malice lurking in his heart, he cloaked with proud and valorous speech, and with a specious presence, the villainy of his soul, with such art, that he was to all outward show another Hector or Achilles.[1] This man had likewise taken with him his wife to Cyprus, a young, and fair, and virtuous lady; and being of Italian birth, she was much loved by Disdemona, who spent the greater part of every day with her.

In the same Company there was a certain Captain of a troop, to whom the Moor was much affectioned. And Disdemona, for this cause, knowing how much her husband valued him, showed him proofs of the greatest kindness, which was all very grateful to the Moor. Now the wicked Ensign, regardless of the faith that he had pledged his wife, no less than of the friendship, fidelity, and obligation which he owed the Moor, fell passionately in love with Disdemona, and bent all his thoughts to achieve his conquest; yet he dared not to declare his passion openly, fearing that, should the Moor perceive it, he would at once kill him. He therefore sought in various ways, and with secret guile, to betray his passion to the lady. But she, whose every wish was centred in the Moor, had no thought for this Ensign more than for any other man; and all the means he tried to gain her love, had no more effect than if he had not tried them. But the Ensign imagined that the cause of his ill success was that Disdemona loved the Captain of the troop; and he pondered how to remove him from her sight. The love which he had borne the lady now changed into the bitterest hate; and, having failed in his purposes, he devoted all his thoughts to plot the death of the Captain of the troop, and to divert the affection of the Moor from Disdemona. After revolving in his mind various schemes, all alike wicked, he at length resolved to accuse her of unfaithfulness to her husband, and to represent the Captain as her paramour. But knowing the singular love the Moor bore to Disdemona, and the friendship which he had for the Captain, he was well aware that, unless he practised an artful fraud upon the Moor, it were impossible to make him give ear to

1. In Homer's *Iliad*, Hector and Achilles are the leaders of the Trojan and Greek forces during the Trojan War, noted for their military valor or skill.

either accusation: wherefore he resolved to wait, until time and circumstance should open a path for him to engage in his foul project.

Not long afterwards, it happened that the Captain, having drawn
his sword upon a soldier of the guard, and struck him, the Moor
deprived him of his rank; whereat Disdemona was deeply grieved,
and endeavoured again and again to reconcile her husband to the
man. This the Moor told to the wicked Ensign, and how his wife
importuned him so much about the Captain, that he feared he
should be forced at last to receive him back to service. Upon this
hint the Ensign resolved to act, and began to work his web of
intrigue; "Perchance," said he, "the lady Disdemona may have good
reason to look kindly on him."

"And wherefore?" said the Moor.

"Nay, I would not step 'twixt man and wife," replied the Ensign;
"but let your eyes be witness to themselves."

In vain the Moor went on to question the officer,—he would proceed no further; nevertheless his words left a sharp stinging thorn
in the Moor's heart, who could think of nothing else, trying to guess
their meaning, and lost in melancholy. And one day, when his wife
had been endeavouring to pacify his anger toward the Captain, and
praying him not to be unmindful of ancient services and friendship,
for one small fault, especially since peace had been made between
the Captain and the soldier he had struck, the Moor was angered,
and exclaimed, "Great cause have you, Disdemona, to care so anxiously about this man! Is he a brother, or your kinsman, that he
should be so near your heart?"

The lady, with all gentleness and humility, replied, "Be not
angered, my dear lord; I have no other cause to bid me speak, than
sorrow that I see you lose so dear a friend as, by your own words,
this Captain has been to you: nor has he done so grave a fault, that
you should bear him so much enmity. Nay, but you Moors are of so
hot a nature, that every little trifle moves you to anger and revenge."

Still more enraged at these words, the Moor replied, "I could bring
proofs—by heaven it mocks belief! but for the wrongs I have
endured, revenge must satisfy my wrath."

Disdemona, in astonishment and fright, seeing her husband's
anger kindled against her, so contrary to his wont, said humbly and
with timidness, "None save a good intent has led me thus to speak
with you, my lord; but to give cause no longer for offence, I'll never
speak a word more on the subject."

The Moor, observing the earnestness with which his wife again
pleaded for the Captain, began to guess the meaning of the Ensign's
words; and in deep melancholy he went to seek that villain, and
induce him to speak more openly of what he knew. Then the Ensign,
who was bent upon injuring the unhappy lady, after feigning at first

great reluctance to say aught that might displease the Moor, at length pretended to yield to his entreaties, and said, "I can't deny, it pains me to the soul to be thus forced to say what needs must be more hard to hear than any other grief; but since you will it so, and that the regard I owe your honour compels me to confess the truth, I will no longer refuse to satisfy your questions and my duty. Know then, that for no other reason is your lady vext to see the Captain in disfavour, than for the pleasure that she has in his company whenever he comes to your house, and all the more since she has taken an aversion to your blackness."

These words went straight to the Moor's heart; but in order to hear more (now that he believed true all that the Ensign had told him), he replied, with a fierce glance, "By heavens, I scarce can hold this hand from plucking out that tongue of thine, so bold, which dares to speak such slander of my wife!"

"Captain," replied the Ensign, "I looked for such reward, for these my faithful offices,—none else; but since my duty, and the jealous care I bear your honour, have carried me thus far, I do repeat, so stands the truth, as you have heard it from these lips: and if the lady Disdemona hath, with a false show of love for you, blinded your eyes to what you should have seen, this is no argument but that I speak the truth. Nay, this same Captain told it me himself, like one whose happiness is incomplete until he can declare it to another: and, but that I feared your anger, I should have given him, when he told it me, his merited reward, and slain him. But since informing you, of what concerns more you than any other man, brings me so undeserved a recompense, would I had held my peace, since silence might have spared me your displeasure."

Then the Moor, burning with indignation and anguish, said, "Make thou these eyes self-witnesses of what thou tell'st, or on thy life I'll make thee wish thou hadst been born without a tongue."

"An easy task it would have been," replied the villain, "when he was used to visit at your house; but now, that you have banished him, not for just cause, but for more frivolous pretext, it will be hard to prove the truth. Still I do not forgo the hope, to make you witness of that which you will not credit from my lips."

Thus they parted. The wretched Moor, struck to the heart as by a barbed dart, returned to his home, and awaited the day when the Ensign should disclose to him the truth which was to make him miserable to the end of his days. But the evil-minded Ensign was, on his part, not less troubled by the chastity which he knew the lady Disdemona observed inviolate; and it seemed to him impossible to discover a means of making the Moor believe what he had falsely told him; and turning the matter over in his thoughts, in various ways, the villain resolved on a new deed of guilt.

Disdemona often used to go, as I have already said, to visit the
Ensign's wife, and remained with her a good part of the day. Now
the Ensign observed, that she carried about with her a handkerchief,
which he knew the Moor had given her, finely embroidered in the
Moorish fashion, and which was precious to Disdemona, nor less so
to the Moor. Then he conceived the plan, of taking this kerchief
from her secretly, and thus laying the snare for her final ruin. The
Ensign had a little daughter, a child three years of age, who was
much loved by Disdemona; and one day, when the unhappy lady had
gone to pay a visit at the house of this vile man, he took the little
child up in his arms, and carried her to Disdemona, who took her,
and pressed her to her bosom; whilst at the same instant this traitor,
who had extreme dexterity of hand, drew the kerchief from her sash
so cunningly, that she did not notice him, and overjoyed he took his
leave of her.

Disdemona, ignorant of what had happened, returned home, and,
busied with other thoughts, forgot the handkerchief. But a few days
afterwards looking for it, and not finding it, she was in alarm, lest
the Moor should ask her for it, as he oft was wont to do. Meanwhile
the wicked Ensign, seizing a fit opportunity, went to the Captain of
the troop, and with crafty malice left the handkerchief at the head
of his bed, without his discovering the trick; until the following
morning, when, on his getting out of bed, the handkerchief fell upon
the floor, and he set his foot upon it. And not being able to imagine
how it had come into his house, knowing that it belonged to Disdemona, he resolved to give it her; and waiting until the Moor had
gone from home, he went to the back door, and knocked. It seemed
as if fate conspired with the Ensign to work the death of the unhappy
Disdemona. Just at that time the Moor returned home, and hearing
a knocking at the back door, he went to the window, and in a rage
exclaimed, "Who knocks there?" The Captain, hearing the Moor's
voice, and fearing lest he should come downstairs and attack him,
took to flight without answering a word. The Moor went down, and
opening the door, hastened into the street, and looked about, but in
vain. Then returning into the house, in great anger, he demanded of
his wife who it was that had knocked at the door. Disdemona replied,
as was true, that she did not know: but the Moor said, "It seemed to
me the Captain."

"I know not," answered Disdemona, "whether it was he, or another
person."

The Moor restrained his fury, great as it was, wishing to do nothing
before consulting the Ensign, to whom he hastened instantly, and
told him all that had passed, praying him to gather from the Captain
all he could respecting the affair. The Ensign, overjoyed at the occur-
rence, promised the Moor to do as he requested; and one day he

took occasion to speak with the Captain, when the Moor was so placed that he could see and hear them as they conversed. And whilst talking to him of every other subject than of Disdemona, he kept laughing all the time aloud; and feigning astonishment, he made various movements with his head and hands, as if listening to some tale of marvel. As soon as the Moor saw the Captain depart, he went up to the Ensign, to hear what he had said to him. And the Ensign, after long entreaty, at length said, "He has hidden from me nothing, and has told me that he has been used to visit your wife whenever you went from home, and that on the last occasion she gave him this handkerchief, which you presented to her when you married her."

The Moor thanked the Ensign, and it seemed now clear to him that, should he find Disdemona not to have the handkerchief, it was all true that the Ensign had told to him. One day, therefore, after dinner, in conversation with his wife on various subjects, he asked her for the kerchief. The unhappy lady, who had been in great fear of this, grew red as fire at this demand; and to hide the scarlet of her cheeks, which was closely noted by the Moor, she ran to a chest, and pretended to seek the handkerchief: and after hunting for it a long time, she said, "I know not how it is—I cannot find it—can you perchance have taken it?"

"If I had taken it," said the Moor, "why should I ask it of you? but you will look better another time."

On leaving the room, the Moor fell to meditating how he should put his wife to death, and likewise the Captain of the troop, so that their death should not be laid to his charge. And as he ruminated over this day and night, he could not prevent his wife's observing that he was not the same toward her as he had been wont; and she said to him again and again, "What is the matter? what troubles you? how comes it that you, who were the most light-hearted man in the world, are now so melancholy?"

The Moor feigned various reasons in reply to his wife's questioning, but she was not satisfied; and, although conscious that she had given the Moor no cause, by act or deed, to be so troubled, yet she feared that he might have grown wearied of her; and she would say to the Ensign's wife, "I know not what to say of the Moor; he used to be all love toward me; but within these few days he has become another man; and much I fear, that I shall prove a warning to young girls not to marry against the wishes of their parents, and that the Italian ladies may learn from me not to wed a man whom nature and habitude of life estrange from us. But as I know the Moor is on such terms of friendship with your husband, and communicates to him all his affairs, I pray you, if you have heard from him aught that you may tell me of, fail not to befriend me." And as she said this, she wept bitterly.

The Ensign's wife, who knew the whole truth (her husband wishing to make use of her to compass the death of Disdemona), but could never consent to such a project, dared not, from fear of her husband, disclose a single circumstance: all she said was, "Beware lest you give any cause of suspicion to your husband, and show to him by every means your fidelity and love."

"Indeed I do so," replied Disdemona; "but it is all of no avail."

Meanwhile the Moor sought in every way to convince himself of what he fain would have found untrue; and he prayed the Ensign to contrive that he might see the handkerchief in the possession of the Captain. This was a difficult matter to the wicked Ensign, nevertheless he promised to use every means to satisfy the Moor of the truth of what he said.

Now the Captain had a wife at home, who worked the most marvellous embroidery upon lawn; and seeing the handkerchief, which belonged to the Moor's wife, she resolved, before it was returned to her, to work one like it. As she was engaged in this task, the Ensign observed her standing at a window, where she could be seen by all passers-by in the street; and he pointed her out to the Moor, who was now perfectly convinced of his wife's guilt. Then he arranged with the Ensign to slay Disdemona, and the Captain of the troop, treating them as it seemed they both deserved. And the Moor prayed the Ensign that he would kill the Captain, promising eternal gratitude to him. But the Ensign at first refused to undertake so dangerous a task, the Captain being a man of equal skill and courage; until at length, after much entreating, and being richly paid, the Moor prevailed on him to promise to attempt the deed.

Having formed this resolution, the Ensign, going out one dark night, sword in hand, met the Captain, on his way to visit a courtesan, and struck him a blow on his right thigh, which cut off his leg, and felled him to the earth. Then the Ensign was on the point of putting an end to his life, when the Captain, who was a courageous man, and used to the sight of blood and death, drew his sword, and, wounded as he was, kept on his defence, exclaiming with a loud voice, "I'm murdered!" Thereupon the Ensign, hearing the people come running up, with some of the soldiers who were lodged thereabouts, took to his heels, to escape being caught; then turning about again, he joined the crowd, pretending to have been attracted by the noise. And when he saw the Captain's leg cut off, he judged that, if not already dead, the blow must at all events end his life; and whilst in his heart he was rejoiced at this, he yet feigned to compassionate the Captain as he had been his brother.

The next morning the tidings of this affair spread through the whole city, and reached the ears of Disdemona; whereat she, who was kind-hearted and little dreamed that any ill would betide her, evinced the greatest grief at the calamity. This served but to confirm the Moor's suspicions, and he went to seek for the Ensign, and said to him, "Do you know, that ass my wife is in such grief at the Captain's accident, that she is well-nigh gone mad."

"And what could you expect, seeing he is her very soul?" replied the Ensign.

"Ay, soul forsooth!" exclaimed the Moor; "I'll draw the soul from out her body: call me no man, if that I fail to shut the world upon this wretch."

Then they consulted of one means and another—poison and daggers—to kill poor Disdemona, but could resolve on nothing. At length the Ensign said, "A plan comes to my mind, which will give you satisfaction, and raise cause for no suspicion,—it is this: the house in which you live is very old, and the ceiling of your chamber has many cracks; I propose we take a stocking, filled with sand, and beat Disdemona with it till she dies; thus will her body bear no signs of violence. When she is dead, we can pull down a portion of the ceiling, and thus make it seem as if a rafter falling on her head had killed the lady. Suspicion can not rest on you, since all men will impute her death to accident."

This cruel counsel pleased the Moor, and he only waited for a fitting time to execute the plot. One night, when he and Disdemona had retired to bed, the Ensign, whom the Moor had concealed in a closet which opened into the chamber, raised a noise in the closet, according to a concerted plan; whereat the Moor said to his wife, "Did you not hear that noise?"

"Indeed I heard it," she replied.

"Rise," said the Moor, "and see what 'tis."

The unhappy Disdemona rose from bed, and the instant she approached the closet, out rushed the Ensign, and being strong and of stout nerve, he beat her cruelly with the bag of sand across her back; upon which Disdemona fell to the ground, scarce able to draw her breath: but with the little voice she had left, she called upon the Moor for aid. But the Moor, leaping from bed, exclaimed, "Thou wickedest of women, thus has thy falseness found its just reward,— the recompense to wives, who counterfeiting love, place horns upon their husbands' brows."

The wretched lady, hearing these words, and feeling that she was near her end (for the Ensign had given her another blow), appealed to the justice of Heaven, since justice here had failed her, in proof of her fidelity and truth; and as she was thus calling Heaven to witness, the wicked Ensign inflicted a third blow, under which she sank lifeless on the floor.

Then the Ensign and the Moor, laying Disdemona on the bed, and wounding her head, pulled down part of the ceiling of the chamber,

as they had arranged; whereupon the Moor began to call aloud for
help, exclaiming that the house was falling. Hearing this uproar, the
neighbours all came running up, and there found Disdemona lying
dead beneath a rafter,—a sight which, from the good life of that poor
lady, did fill all hearts with sorrow.

On the following day Disdemona was buried, followed to the grave
by the universal grief of the people. But Heaven, the just regarder
of all hearts, willed not that so wicked a deed should go unpunished.
Ere long the Moor, whom Disdemona had loved more than her own
life, began to feel such sorrow at her loss, that he went wandering
about, as one bereft of reason, searching in every part of the house.
And reflecting in his thoughts that the Ensign had been the cause
that he had lost, with Disdemona, all joy in life, he conceived so deep
a hatred to that wicked man, he could not bear to set eyes on him;
and had it not been for his fear of the inviolable justice of the Signoria of Venice, he would have slain him openly. But being unable
to do this with safety, he deprived him of his rank, and would not
allow him to remain in his Company; whereat such an enmity arose
between the two, that no greater or more deadly can be imagined.

The Ensign, that wickedest of all bad men, now turned his
thoughts to injuring the Moor; and seeking out the Captain, whose
wound was by this time healed, and who went about with a wooden
leg, in place of the one that had been cut off, he said to him, " 'Tis
time you should be avenged for your lost limb; and if you will come
with me to Venice, I'll tell you who the malefactor is, whom I dare
not mention to you here, for many reasons, and I will bring you
proofs."

The Captain of the troop, whose anger returned fiercely, but without knowing why, thanked the Ensign, and went with him to Venice.
On arriving there, the Ensign told him that it was the Moor who had
cut off his leg, on account of the suspicion he had formed of Disdemona's conduct with him; and for that reason he had slain her,
and then spread the report that the ceiling had fallen and killed her.
Upon hearing which, the Captain accused the Moor to the Signoria,
both of having cut off his leg and killed his wife, and called the
Ensign to witness the truth of what he said. The Ensign declared
both charges to be true, for that the Moor had disclosed to him the
whole plot, and had tried to persuade him to perpetrate both crimes;
and that having afterwards killed his wife, out of jealousy he had
conceived, he had narrated to him the manner in which he had perpetrated her death.

The Signori of Venice, when they heard of the cruelty inflicted by
a barbarian upon a lady of their city, commanded that the Moor's
arms should be pinioned in Cyprus, and he be brought to Venice,
where with many tortures they sought to draw from him the truth.

But the Moor, bearing with unyielding courage all the torment, denied the whole charge so resolutely, that no confession could be drawn from him. But although, by his constancy and firmness, he escaped death, he was, after being confined for several days in prison, condemned to perpetual banishment, in which he was eventually slain by the kinsfolk of Disdemona, as he merited. The Ensign returned to his own country, and following up his wonted villainy, he accused one of his companions of having sought to persuade him to kill an enemy of his, who was a man of noble rank; whereupon this person was arrested, and put to the torture; but when he denied the truth of what his accuser had declared, the Ensign himself was likewise tortured, to make him prove the truth of his accusation; and he was tortured so that his body ruptured, upon which he was removed from prison and taken home, where he died a miserable death. Thus did Heaven avenge the innocence of Disdemona, and all these events were narrated by the Ensign's wife, who was privy to the whole, after his death, as I have told them here.

THE END.

CRITICISM

Othello in Critical History

Othello was evidently popular from its first performance (probably 1604), but only a few early comments have come down to us. Abraham Wright's diary entry of around 1637 refers to Othello and Iago as "two parts well penned" (Munro, 1.411). The 1640 edition of Shakespeare's *Poems* includes a poem by Leonard Digges in which "Honest *Iago,* or the jealous Moore" exemplify Shakespeare's theatrical power: "oh how the Audience, / Were ravish'd, with what wonder they went thence" (quoted in Evans, 1972). Both Wright and Digges assign equal power to the protagonist and antagonist, hero and villain of the piece—an unusual distribution of feeling for Shakespearean characters, registered in much subsequent interpretation. The most substantial early report records an Oxford performance witnessed by Henry Jackson in 1610:

> They also had tragedies, which they acted with propriety and fitness. In which (tragedies), not only through speaking but also through acting certain things, they moved (the audience) to tears. But truly the celebrated Desdemona, slain in our presence by her husband, although she pleaded her case very effectively throughout, yet moved (us) more after she was dead, when, lying on her bed, she entreated the pity of the spectators by her very countenance. (Quoted in Evans, 1978)

Jackson's focus on Desdemona, whose death seems to have left a stronger impression than Othello's, is extraordinary. A comparable interest in the female lead does not begin to appear until the nineteenth century and does not fully materialize until our own time. But in emphasizing the play's strongly direct appeal to an audience's emotions, Jackson's reaction is normative. It resonates with Digges's claim for Shakespeare's ravishing appeal, setting the tone for a tradition of response—theatrical audiences and critics testifying to the play's capacity to generate a deeply felt engagement—that continues to this day.

The thinness and conventionality of initial response, true for all Shakespeare's plays before the establishment of any critical tradition, does not allow for much confident speculation. With Thomas Rymer's *Short View of Tragedy* (1693), we move beyond sketchy and isolated comments into systematic analysis. Rymer's chapter on *Othello* submits Shakespeare's play to the neoclassical standards that would continue to dominate taste pretty much for the next century. The two quotations from Horace in the excerpt below give a sense of the values behind and effects sought by "the rules"—a mix of prescriptions and suggestions derived most immediately from recent French critics and going back through sixteenth-century Italian commentary to antiquity. With the first quotation, Rymer establishes the main idea of Horace's general introduction: make sure the parts fit together naturally so the poem will seem unified and avoid any shocking sense of discrepancy. In the second, Horace adds external consistency to internal, recommending that the poem correspond to conventional expectation and established tradition—again as a way to avoid jarring effects.

As Rymer saw it, *Othello* failed miserably to fulfil these requirements; instead of smoothly integrating its parts, the play violently conjoined contradictory kinds of material. Rymer makes his point with a memorably witty oxymoron: "The Tragedy of the Handkerchief." Handkerchiefs belong to the trivial world of domestic comedy, not to the noble and public dignity of tragedy. Crossing generic boundaries, the play breaks down social and professional distinctions as well, presenting characters against type in a way that assaults conventional expectation. Supreme military command has been conferred on a "blackamoor," who indulges in detailed description of the affection he feels for his new bride at times when the curt discourse of the barracks seems in order. His wife prattles on about love—fair enough; but she is a senator's daughter talking about a lover beneath her station and in circumstances above it, a formal senate deliberation about the threat of war. A senator is treated with a blatant disrespect inappropriate to his position. For the subaltern's part, instead of the honest soldier called for by tradition, we get a diabolical villain. In Rymer's summary judgment, *Othello* is "a bloody farce without salt or savor."

If Rymer looks narrow-minded and pedantic to us, he looked that way to most of his contemporaries as well. In *The Impartial Critick* (1693), John Dennis immediately rejected Rymer's general position as one "which instead of reforming" (as it claimed to do), "would ruine the English Drama" (quoted in Vickers, 2.60); and Charles Gildon followed a year later with his vindication of *Othello* excerpted below. The play's popularity, acknowledged grudgingly at the beginning of Rymer's chapter, sustained itself throughout the period when neoclassicism determined the critical agenda. Given the self-evident "beauties" Samuel Johnson describes in his summary assessment below—characters immediately engaging our deepest interest, an intensely thrilling plot—*Othello* proved as invulnerable to critical assault as it was (in Johnson's view) unneedful of "aid from critical illustration." From the beginning, neoclassical criticism recognized the transcendent prerogative of "genius" to "snatch a grace beyond the rules of art," and when Dr. Johnson in the preface to his 1765 edition of Shakespeare boldly rejected the unities of time and place, *Othello* was the example that naturally came to his mind. Addressing the more serious impropriety of Shakespeare's failure to maintain generic distinction, Johnson does not mention "The Tragedy of the Handkerchief," but he might as well have. He freely acknowledges that "contrary to the rules of criticism" Shakespeare's plays "are not in the rigorous and critical sense either tragedies or comedies" but insists that "there is always an appeal open from criticism to nature." The rules are just the means to an end, "to instruct by pleasing," and Shakespeare's "mingled drama" captivates our concern more deeply than the technically "regular" drama championed by people like Rymer: "whether to gladden or depress," Shakespeare "never fails to attain his purpose; as he commands us, we laugh or mourn, or sit silent with quiet expectation, in tranquillity without indifference" (Bronson, 15–17).

By this time, critics no longer felt obliged to engage with Rymer, and in the nineteenth century, Rymer was relegated to the status of an amusing curiosity. If we take him seriously these days, a lot of the impetus derives from the casual remarks T. S. Eliot dropped into two "tantalizing brief footnotes" (Zimansky, 260)—one declaring that Rymer "makes out a very good case" against *Othello,* the other that the case had never been submitted to "a cogent refutation" ("Four Elizabethan Dramatists," 97; and "*Hamlet,*" 121). For Rymer's immediate successors at least, Eliot's claim about nonrefutation seems abundantly justified. Eighteenth-century commentators dissent vigorously from Rymer's conclusions about *Othello,* but they seem unwilling or unable to reject the standards from which Rymer's conclusions were generated in the first place. In his 1733 edition of Shakespeare, Lewis Theobald, having defended Shakespeare against "Snarler and Buffoon-Criticks" like Rymer, nonetheless cannot resist quoting a full 130 words from Rymer's notorious (and funny) invective against "the *Tragedy of the Handkerchief*"— and then refuses to establish his own convictions: "Whether this be from the Spirit of a *true Critic,* or from the License of a *Railer,* I . . . leave it to every indifferent Judgment." The self-congratulatory open-mindedness barely conceals a troubled confession that "the coarse Pleasantries of Mr. *Rymer*" may constitute a legitimate response to *Othello* after all (Theobald, 7.447–48). In another instance, Theobald goes out of his way to point out one of *Othello*'s many temporal inconsistencies that Rymer himself had failed to include in his catalog. "Had Mr. *Rymer* intended, or known how, to make a serious and sensible Critic on this Play, methinks here is a fair Open given for Enquiry and Animadversion." As Zimansky remarks, in this comment Theobald, while seeming to distance himself from Rymer's apparently *non*-"serious and sensible" opinion about *Othello*, rather "shows how close he was to being Rymer's follower" (Zimansky, 264).

The excerpts from Charles Gildon reprinted below betray a similar ambivalence. In his *Miscellaneous Letters*, Gildon takes on Rymer's complaints about Iago's scurrility by claiming that "the clown and the valet jesting with their betters" was forced on Shakespeare by an audience demanding raucous clowning. Gildon evidently accepts Rymer's principles, and only a jingoistic cultural nationalism keeps him on Shakespeare's side. The most striking instance of hedging—or in fact flat contradiction—occurs when Gildon revisits the play in his *Critical Remarks*. Now it seems that Othello's military command and the transgressive marriage are indeed "shocking" violations of propriety after all. In effect, Rymer was basically right. Since the fable recounted in the *Remarks* is taken almost verbatim from the *Miscellaneous Letters*, Gildon must have had the earlier text in front of him, but he barely acknowledges, let alone explains, his radical change of belief.

Reversals and contradictions are not limited to relative lightweights like Theobald and Gildon. Dr. Johnson thunders that "Whoever ridicules" the process of Desdemona's falling in love "shows his ignorance, not only of history, but of nature and manners"; but commenting on Iago's "She did deceive her father, marrying you," Johnson feels moved to mount a strongly developed argument from the other side of the question, warning in Rymer's own vocabulary against the "irregularity" and "imprudent generosity of disproportionate marriages." The two comments are not exactly symmetrical (the latter proceeds generally, without specific reference to Desdemona), and they are sufficiently distant from one another to avoid any jarring discrepancy. Nonetheless, *Othello* seems to have generated contradictory feelings in Johnson, not unlike the monstrous incongruities of tone and subject matter, feeling and belief, that Rymer relentlessly deplores; and in the less formal or perhaps more jocular context of conversation, Johnson is not above echoing Rymer's witty description of the play's moral points: "In the first place, Sir, we learn from *Othello* this very useful moral, not to make an unequal match; in the second place, we learn not to yield too readily to suspicion. . . . No, Sir, I think *Othello* has more moral than almost any play" (Chapman, 745). Even the contrast between their final judgments—Johnson's admiration for, Rymer's rejection of the play—turns out not to be absolute. "I am glad that I have ended my revisal of this dreadful scene," he confesses about the play's catastrophe. "It is not to be endured."

Unconsciously echoing Rymer's language, Johnson goes back beyond him to the origin and chief spokesman for such views in the play itself—"honest" Iago. Iago is the chief irritant for Rymer—the embodiment of what is "most intolerable" in the play's "characters or manners" and the object of "by far the most famous of Rymer's accusations" (Zimansky, xxviii). Over and over he complains that Iago's malignity contradicts literary convention and reality: soldiers shouldn't be represented in such a way, and besides, they're not really like that. The point seems thick-headedly subjective even for Rymer, and Gildon's witty turning of the tables—if you can say Iago's not behaving like a real soldier, I can say you're not behaving like a real critic—might seem to have ended the matter. But Gildon couldn't leave it at that. He reversed himself on Iago as part of his general about-face in the 1710 *Remarks* excerpted below, but even earlier, his 1693 "Reflections" is tied up in knots with defenses of Shakespeare's Iago that seem as perversely misdirected as Rymer's attacks.[1] In this respect, Gildon anticipates William Warburton, who, in his 1747 edition of Shakespeare's works, is driven to similarly "cumbersome attempts" to justify the effect produced by Shakespeare's Iago.[2] We might say about eighteenth-century Iago commentary what Desdemona says to Othello in his crazy jealousy: "I understand a fury in your words, / But not the words" (4.2.33).

What was really bothering them? Gildon provides a clue in another one of his apparently shrewd responses that came to naught. Justifying the violence that irritated Rymer in Iago's "Even now, now, very now, an old black ram / Is tupping your white ewe" (1.1.85–86). Gildon observes that the brutal image succeeds in its design "to transport" Brabantio "from consideration to a violent passion." As a hasty afterthought tamped into the preface, this remark must have been peripheral to the main issues; hence Zimansky's comment that Gildon "merely evades Rymer's point that a *magnifico* must not be alarmed" (263). But the implicit concept of bad manners here—don't be rude to your betters—needs some historical clarification. When Gildon picks up on Rymer's phrase, referring the question of

1. In passages omitted from the excerpt below, Gildon piles up a smorgasbord plate of arguments against Rymer: we must pay attention to "national vices" as well as "respect the profession" of our characters, and Italians are selfish and vindictive in Iago's way. Horace did not mean to extend his dictum "to all degrees of soldiers," only Achilles, and in any case only to those previously represented and not to "some new person." Homer and Sophocles "have been guilty" of similar and worse improbabilities in their "extremely unproportionable" representations of deities and protagonists (110–12).

2. The phrase is Zimansky's, describing the ambivalent note Warburton appends to the description of Iago as "this hellish villain" at the end of the play. Beginning with an assault on Rymer as a "buffoon and caviller," Warburton nonetheless acknowledges that his objection to Iago "hath the appearance of sense," but then goes on at desperate length to argue that the Horatian norms apply only if a single example is represented, concluding that since Shakespeare offers a variety of soldiers, most of them "open, generous, and brave," as they are supposed to be, Iago's exceptionalism may be justified, and "thus Shakespeare stands clear" of Rymer's "impertinent criticism" (19:525–26).

"characters or manners" to the authority of "the same Rapin," both are working within the technical vocabulary of French neoclassicism. "Manners" here signifies within the context of *les bienséances externes* or "extrinsic proprieties"—the idea that characters should use speech and behavior in a way that coincides with the social beliefs and esthetic tastes of the audience. "If the subject doesn't conform to the spectators' feelings," as one authority put it, "it will never succeed."[3] In this context, Rymer's complaint is not so much that Iago offends Brabantio as that the play offends us.

And here Rymer seems right, not just for the "us" for whom he was writing, but for subsequent audiences as well.[4] If, as Joel Altman argues, Rymer's catalog of improbabilities and improprieties "turns out," by "setting the crucial question," to "have been the most influential" of *Othello* commentaries "after all" (131), this is because Rymer established, beyond the question itself, the tone of truculent rage, centered on the figure of Iago, with which the question is asked. Iago's capacity to generate irritation has survived the particular beliefs within which Rymer registered it. Later critics and spectators, though increasingly remote from the hierarchical social and political assumptions of Rymer's age, have nonetheless found themselves even more anxiously engaged with Iago's malevolence. This engagement is the starting point for Kenneth Burke's hugely influential piece excerpted below: "Iago has done this play some service" by propelling "the plot forward step by step for the audience's villainous entertainment and filthy purgation" (see pp. 245 and 248). The beliefs from which Burke's argument is generated—about private property, social organization, the anthropological function of drama, etc.—are ones Rymer would not have shared or perhaps even recognized, but Burke's self-disgusted fascination with Iago is nonetheless recognizably of a piece with the sentiments pulsating in Rymer's discussion of the play. In his complaint about *Othello*'s flouting of "extrinsic proprieties," Rymer seems to have stumbled onto what might seem like an intrinsic property of the play—its power, concentrated in the figure of Iago, to produce an angry and malign aversion; and we have found ourselves compelled to deal with a version of this disturbance ever since.

If Iago troubled Rymer and eighteenth-century audiences, the disturbance was much better contained than it was to become. Dr. Johnson unequivocally dismisses any possibility that Iago "should

---

3. I am translating from l'Abbé d'Aubignac's 1657 *Pratique du Théâtre* (Martino, 72). For a discussion of *les bienséances externes* see Bray, 224–30.
4. Later critics—Furness in the nineteenth century (167), Kirsch in the twentieth (11–15)—reenact the ambivalent performances of Gildon, Theobald, and Warburton—throwing up their hands in dismay at Rymer even while quoting him at length and thus disseminating the very opinions they declare so laughably stupid.

steal upon esteem." This assurance may be questioned (denial acknowledges the very feelings declared not to exist), but Johnson's detachment seems like a fair representation of the situation when he wrote. The substantial cuts in eighteenth-century performance texts indicate that Iago was not felt to be compelling. Gildon's "very good" authority for a clownish Iago on Shakespeare's stage may not be reliable, but Rymer's description of a mugging and buffoonish performance, with stereotypically villainous makeup and costume, evidently typified eighteenth-century production. In the early nineteenth century, however, "a new Iago emerged—an Iago with a light touch, a light step, a sprightly wit, who reveled in his own ingenuity and sometimes charmed the audience into reveling with him" (Carlisle, 225)—so much so that he quickly challenged Othello's prominence as the play's main attraction, a development signaled in the willingness among leading actors throughout the nineteenth century to take on either of the parts.

The "new Iago" was substantially created by Edmund Kean, the premier actor of the time, who inspired Hazlitt's pieces excerpted below. But if Kean's innovations found a receptive audience, this was in part owing to major shifts in the values and assumptions generating critical response. Nineteenth-century commentators start traditionally enough. They pick up (no doubt unconsciously) on Rymer's general sense of Iago as a jarring mixture of qualities and effects. They echo (perhaps deliberately) the specific phrase, "wickedness conjoined with abilities," by which Johnson identifies this mixture: "great intellectual activity, accompanied with a total lack of moral purpose" (Hazlitt); "what is admirable . . . in the mind and what is most detestable in the heart" (Coleridge); "absolute evil united with supreme intellectual power" (Bradley). But these echoes do not extend to Johnson's confidence that Shakespeare had avoided the "danger" of such a character's "steal[ing] upon esteem." The risk of "scandal" (Coleridge) and "of untruth or a desperate pessimism" (Bradley) is much more immediate now. Hazlitt claims that "nothing but the genius of Shakespeare" could have protected Desdemona's image against Iago's assault, but his subsequent discussion puts just this question in doubt.

Disagreeing with Johnson about the unities, Coleridge highlights the newly destabilized norms of nineteenth-century criticism. Johnson too had seen the rules as just a means to an end, but Coleridge throws "down the gloves with a full challenge" in a radically reimagined sense of the "great end . . . of poesy in general." For Coleridge, poetry needs to engage an esthetic "interest" independent of any specifically ethical content or purpose. This independence is just what Keats emphasizes in his description of "the poetical Character itself": it "has no self—it is every thing and nothing—It has no character—it enjoys light and shade; it lives in gusto, be it foul or fair, high or low, rich or poor, mean or elevated—It has as much delight in conceiving an Iago or an Imogen [the admirable heroine in *Cymbeline*]. What shocks the virtuous philosopher, delights the camelion Poet" (letter to Richard Woodhouse, October 27, 1818; Page, 172). This claim contrasts sharply with Dr. Johnson's view that "it is always a writer's duty to make the world better"; for Johnson, the fact that Shakespeare "carries his persons indifferently through right and wrong, and at the close dismisses them without further care, and leaves their examples to operate by chance" is not poetic virtue but a "fault" that "the barbarity of his age cannot extenuate" (Bronson, 19).

Whatever the Romantics lost relinquishing the stability of Johnson's ethical norms was compensated in a more fully developed capacity to acknowledge poetic effects. The Romantics located poetic value in the "power of exciting the sympathy of the reader";[5] and this intensely affective imaginative engagement accounts for nineteenth-century interest in Iago. In Hazlitt's description, Kean's Iago works on audiences through "the interest it excites, the sharper edge which it sets on their curiosity and imagination"; bad or good, "foul or fair" (in Keats's phrase), Iago resonates richly with "a natural tendency in the mind to strong excitement, a desire to have its faculties roused and stimulated to the utmost." Coleridge's Iago exemplifies the same intensity: "let the reader *feel*" the "disappointed vanity and envy" eating within Iago's mind, Coleridge enjoins us (Foakes, 112, Foakes's emphasis), so that we may experience the self-corrosive energy of his consciousness. For Bradley, Iago's "evil" nature may be more than we "can bear to contemplate," but "if we really imagine him, we feel admiration and some kind of sympathy."

Such responsiveness was in no way limited to the dark malignity of Iago. According to Coleridge, we should "feel Cassio's religious love of Desdemona's purity," and above all "we must perseveringly place ourselves in [Othello's] situation and under his circumstances" so that "we shall immediately feel the fundamental difference between the solemn agony of the noble Moor and the unnatural

5. This is the first "cardinal point" in Coleridge's chapter "Definitions of a Poem and Poetry" in the *Biographia Literaria* (1817), the effect of such power being "to transfer from our inward nature a human interest and a semblance of truth sufficient to procure for these shadows of imagination that willing suspension of disbelief for the moment, which constitutes poetic faith" (Engell, 7.2: 5–6). Hazlitt stresses the same points at the beginning of his lecture "On Poetry in General" (1818): "The best general notion which I can give of poetry is, that it is the natural impression of any object or event, by its vividness exciting an involuntary movement of imagination and passion, and producing, by sympathy, a certain modulation of the voice, or sounds, expressing it" (Howe, 5.1). In "Poetry for Poetry's Sake" (1901), Bradley defines poetry as "imaginative experience," the "succession of experiences—sounds, images, thoughts, emotions—through which we pass when we are reading as poetically as we can" (4).

fishing jealousies of Leontes" (the protagonist in Shakespeare's later play *The Winter's Tale*). That Othello is not jealous by nature is a point Coleridge never tires of repeating, and it became a basic premise throughout the nineteenth century.[6] At the end of this line, Bradley employs the same contrast with Leontes and echoes Coleridge's words: Othello "was not of a jealous temper" and "*any* man situated as Othello was would have been disturbed by Iago."[7] The terms with which Bradley registers feelings of jealousy and sexual anxiety suggest what is at stake in this denial: "ignoble . . . despicable . . . shrinking . . . ashamed . . . turn our eyes away . . . repulsive . . . repulsion . . . repulsiveness." Admit this range of feeling and the "noble Moor"—the "romantic figure" who "stirs . . . in most readers a passion of mingled love and pity which they feel for no other hero in Shakespeare"—might seem an unsustainable illusion.

Similar feelings of aversion motivate another reiterated denial in nineteenth-century commentary—Othello's blackness. For Charles Lamb, writing in 1811, "the courtship and wedded caresses" between "a young Venetian lady of the highest extraction" and "a *coal-black Moor*" would be "extremely revolting"—at least in the theater. Lamb's point was not altogether original,[8] but it resonated powerfully with innovations dating from the same decade: Kean's switch from the conventional blackface to a tawny makeup and Coleridge's insistence on a Moorish Othello to avoid the "monstrous" prospect of "this beautiful Venetian girl falling in love with a veritable negro." Denying Othello's blackness, like denying his jealousy, became a standard feature of nineteenth-century commentary on the play. Once again, the whole topic achieves summary discussion in Brad-

6. Coleridge frankly acknowledges his repetitions on this subject in an excerpt below, and in his *Table-Talk*, June 24, 1827, he repeats himself yet again: "I have often told you that I do not think there is any jealousy, properly so called, in the character of Othello" (Foakes,116). Henry N. Hudson quotes at length from Coleridge's "very bold and clear . . . defence of the Moor" against the charge of jealousy in his 1856 American edition of the play (397), complete with the Leontes contrast. The standard nature of the claim extends beyond Anglo-American traditions: "Jealousy! Othello is not jealous, he is trustful," observed Pushkin, and this remark alone testifies to the extraordinary profundity of our great poet's mind. Othello's soul is shattered and his whole outlook on life is confused because *his ideal has been destroyed.* But Othello would not start hiding, spying, peeping: he is trustful" (Dostoyevsky, 2:447).
7. Coleridge's notes for his Bristol lecture of November 9, 1813, centered on the Leontes contrast, prompt himself to furnish "Proofs of the contrary character in Othello": "Othello's *belief* not jealousy; forced upon him by Iago—and such any man would and must feel who had believed of Iago as Othello. His great mistake that WE know Iago for a villain from the first moment" (Foakes, 111). Terence Hawkes comments on this last claim that the "point presumably is that the audience is made more fully aware of Othello's mistake by their recognition of Iago as a villain from the first. Othello's tragedy is his *mistaken* belief, not his jealousy" (175).
8. Gildon's reversal below registers the same "shock" at the prospect of "admitting a Negro to commerce" with "a woman of virtue." In a lecture given February 16, 1774, William Kenrick argues that despite critical and theatrical consensus, Othello "was *not a black*, and at worst only of a *tawny* colour," primarily because "a young Lady of Desdemona's delicacy of sentiment could never have fallen in love with a Negro" (Vickers, 6.116).

ley, who notes that "American critics" especially express "horror" at the prospect of a "black Othello."[9] And although Bradley works hard to distance himself from Coleridge and those "very amusing" Americans, he winds up pretty much on their side of the issue, admitting that "the aversion of our blood" makes a black Othello effectively impossible, at least in the theater.

Nineteenth-century discussions of Othello's color oscillate uneasily between contradictory sentiments. Lamb frankly expresses racist feelings (Moors are "by many shades less unworthy of a white woman"), and Bradley can at least acknowledge participating in such feelings (the "aversion of *our* blood"). At the same time, however, Lamb argues that Desdemona's love for Othello registers on "the nobler parts of our nature" as "the perfect triumph of virtue over accidents," and Bradley dismisses racism as "filthy-minded cynic[ism]." These slippages make it hard to determine what Lamb and Bradley actually believe as individuals. Authentic Coleridgean belief is similarly elusive, hedged about with the qualifying phrase "as we are constituted," and complicated by other texts (such as the poem "Fears in Solitude"), which express an appalled guilt at belonging to (and thus participating in) a systematically racist society. But individual belief may not be the chief issue here; nineteenth-century discussion turns on rhetorical or esthetic as much as ethical questions. These critics are all committed to the idea of *Othello* as a heroic tragedy; in Hazlitt's description below, the play "substitutes imaginary sympathy for mere selfishness. It gives us a high and permanent interest, beyond ourselves, in humanity as such." According to Lamb and the others, however, nineteenth-century audiences would be unable to muster such a response to a black Othello on the stage; for them, the proper engagement was through the imagination—Othello as constructed in the mind's eye (see figs. 1–5, pp. 177–81).

Struggling almost a century after Lamb with the same "question whether, granted that Shakespeare's Othello was a black, he should be presented as a black in our theatres now," Bradley answers, "I dare say not. We do not like the real Shakespeare." Bradley's "real Shakespeare" is more truly an ideal Shakespeare. Like Coleridge's "poet for all ages" (an echo of Ben Jonson's tribute in the 1623 Folio, "He was not of an age, but for all time"), this is not a psychological or historical author but an interpretive assumption—the idea of

9. Hudson's introduction parades out in full the "veritable negro" paragraph (399–400) and uses Coleridge's arguments without acknowledgment (by then, twenty years later, they probably didn't need to be acknowledged) to reject the idea that Othello is imagined by Shakespeare "as a full-blooded Negro" (*Shakespeare: His Life*, 2.448). In a notorious instance, Mary Preston, writing in Maryland four years after the end of the American Civil War, acknowledges that "I have always *imagined* [*Othello*'s] hero as a white man" and then simply changes the facts to correspond with her desire. "Othello," she peremptorily declares, "*was a white* man!" (quoted in Furness, 395, Preston's emphases).

What Did (Does, Will) Othello Look Like?

Following are five images of Othello, dating from 1799 to the mid-1800s. Though keyed by their illustrators to particular scenes, they do not depict actual performances; setting the action in a stylized landscape (even the Venetian Campanile adds to this effect), they represent Othello as he might appear not to Kemble's or Kean's or Booth's audiences, but to an audience's collective imagination or mind's eye. The images are quite diverse—in terms of costume (Elizabethan armor, Moorish and Asian finery), physical posture, skin color and other racial markers (more or less woolly hair and thick lips). But in their own ways, all these Othellos are similarly exoticized, a process that, while it serves "to glamorize Othello's cultural background" (Potter, *Othello,* 187), tends at the same time to reduce the character to a kind of pretty object. Such representations may not strike a responsive chord with present-day audiences, but each makes sense, whether as "tawny Moor" or as "black African," as a product of its time. By the nineteenth century, militant Islam had dwindled to an unmenacing inconsequence, and institutionalized slavery in British colonial dependencies had diminished Africans to chattel. These orientalizing or abjectifying images may be understood as an attempt (perhaps somewhat desperate) at esthetic idealization—seeking to preserve some of the admiration appropriate to the protagonist of heroic tragedy.

Though evidence is not abundant, we have reason to believe that earlier Othellos registered differently on the mental or indeed material eye. Actors in the later seventeenth century performed the part not in the period costume of a remote place but "in the red coat of a British general" of the time (Potter, *Othello,* 187). This is of a piece with the naturalizing or normalizing arguments of eighteenth-century defenders of the play, who regularly rebutted Rymer's complaints by insisting that in historical fact Venice routinely employed foreigners to head its military. But perhaps the strongest evidence for an unexoticized Othello is on the front cover of this Norton Critical Edition. 'Abd al-Wahid bin Mas'ood bin Mohammad 'Annouri (I adopt Matar's transliteration, 33) arrived in London in August 1600, leading an embassy of sixteen Muslims. On and off for a period of six months, under the pretext of discussing trade, 'Abd al-Wahid explored with Elizabeth the possibility of a military alliance against Spain. Bernard Harris's detailed description includes some striking coincidences with *Othello.* One of the interpreters during negotiations was Lewis Lewkenor, whose translation of Contareno's book about Venice Shakespeare certainly used for the play. John Pory seems to have gained leverage from the embassy as publicity for his translation of Leo Africanus, which Shakespeare may well have used. Apparently as part of the attempt to disguise the military nature of the mission, negotiations included much emphasis on the route traveled by the ambassadors, which was to include Aleppo, the location central to Othello's memory in his final act.

We have no reason to believe that Shakespeare or many in his audience would have known such details, but considering the interest and discussion generated by 'Abd al-Wahid and his entourage during their sojourn so close to the play's first performances, this remarkable picture invites speculation about what Globe spectators saw in or around Richard Burbage's personation of Shakespeare's noble Moor. In one respect the "Portrait of a Moor" is similar to the nineteenth-century images. A good deal of attention is paid to exotic specifics—the flowing white robe, the turban, the sword (presumably like one of the "12 turkish swords" cataloged among the gifts "sent by the Great Turk in 1583"—Harris, 96). But while such details signify alterity, this image does not produce idealization or infantalization. On the contrary, the name, the date, the title, and the age of the subject combine to give the figure an immediate material presence, the effect secured chiefly by the image's most notable feature: 'Abd al-Wahid's compelling gaze—sinister if not threatening, confident, canny and sophisticated, directed unflinchingly at the observer's eye.

As for Othello's image now, no single or simple answer seems possible. When in 1984 the New Cambridge editor claimed that "only a Negroid Othello can produce the desired responses in the theatres of the Western world, at present and in the foreseeable future" (Sanders, 14), he was writing from within a specific place in the Western world (Tennessee) and a specific time (thirty years after Brown v. Board of Education). In addition, he was writing within the context of an emergent critical enterprise concerned with the residues of racist and colonialist exploitation. From this angle, Othello illustrated the "self-doubt of this displaced stranger," which "opens him so fatally to Iago's attack" (Neill, "Changing Places," 127), or the "precarious entry into the white world" of "a colonised subject existing on the terms of white Venetian society and trying to internalise its ideology" (Loomba, 48). This abject (though usually black) Othello is substantially continuous with the nineteenth-century images presented here, but has more recently been subjected to a skeptical historicist scrutiny: "by adopting the postcolonial template," Nabil Matar claims, critics "have projected the military and industrial decline of Muslim countries in the modern period" back onto the "attitude of a Renaissance Briton" who would view them rather with "fear, anxiety, and awe" (8). A more formidable and Moorish Othello seems to be emerging in current work; and in light of September 11, 2001, we might want to rewrite Sanders to claim that only a threateningly Moorish Othello "can produce the desired responses in the theatres of the Western world, at present and in the foreseeable future." We might even feel that this post-postcolonial image is closer to Othello as Shakespeare's audience saw him. But we are just doing what our nineteenth-century predecessors did—constructing Othello in the image of our own fears and desires. Given the consistently transformative history that has characterized Othello's image since the beginning, the only prediction we can confidently make is that if we are lucky enough to become the object of future historians' interests, the Othello imprinted on our mind's eye is bound to look strangely remote from the truth.

Fig. 1. Act 2, Scene 1: "O my fair warrior. . . ." Engraving by Thomas Stothard (1755–1834), R.A.; pub. Sept. 29, 1799.

Fig. 2. Act 1, Scene 3: "Here's my husband." Engraving by Richard Cook (1784–1857); pub. 1821.

Fig. 3. Act 2, Scene 1: Othello and Desdemona. Drawing by Henry Liverseege (1803–1832); no pub. date.

Fig. 4. Act 1, Scene 3: Othello Relating His Adventures. Engraving by Charles West Cope (1811–1890), R.A.; no pub. date.

Fig. 5. Act 3, Scene 4: "Fetch me that handkerchief." Engraving by Joseph Kenny Meadows (1790–1874); pub. 1845.

agency we might imagine to have produced the kind of *Othello* Hazlitt describes. Such idealization doesn't sit well with current taste; from our perspective, the denial of Othello's blackness seems like a refusal to deal with aspects of the play that ought to be acknowledged. Bradley understood that Shakespeare wasn't a cultural anthropologist and that any response to *Othello* working within the assumptions of nineteenth-century "racial science" was bound to be inadequate; Lamb and Coleridge register a similar sense of historical distance between "the imperfect state of knowledge respecting foreign countries in those days" and "our own" and between the ways seventeenth- and nineteenth-century audiences "are constituted." But to deny an explicitly racist repulsion is not to rule out equally violent forms of disgust and aversion associated with Othello's difference, especially when compounded with the sexual specificity of the play's language and action. Here too, in their denial of jealousy, nineteenth-century commentators are unwilling to acknowledge a range of emotional disturbance that the play seems designed to provoke. Othello is indeed no Leontes, but he does not altogether transcend the lunatic violence and coarse comedy associated with jealousy; and Bradley's claim that at the end Othello is an exalted figure whose "anger has passed" seems unconscionably resistant to a mass of contradictory evidence—from embedded stage directions, "your eyes roll so," "Some bloody passion shakes your very frame," to Othello's own acknowledgment of "my great revenge" and the perverse sexuality of "I will kill thee / And love thee after," about which Desdemona's "That death's unnatural that kills for loving" (see 5.2. 18–75) seems right.

When Bradley remarks that the issue of Othello's color "concerns the character of Desdemona," he makes a connection everywhere explicit in nineteenth-century commentary: if "black and white blood cannot be intermingled in marriage without a gross outrage upon the law of Nature," then Desdemona is an outrageous "wanton": "The blood must circulate briskly in the veins of a young woman, so fascinated, and so coming to the tale of a rude, unbleached African soldier." These words are from another one of those "amusing" Americans Bradley dismisses—namely John Quincy Adams, writing in 1835, six years after his term as president (65); but they are consistent with English critics, including Coleridge, who, faced with the "monstrous" prospect of Desdemona's sexual interest in a "veritable negro," insists not only on Othello's tawniness but on the absence of Desdemona's individuality: as a "sweet yet dignified" exemplar of the eternal feminine, Coleridge's Desdemona "has no character at all." Bradley at least acknowledges the early manifestations of Desdemona's powerful sexuality, but then insists that "this love and boldness" is superseded by "a love that knows not how to resist or resent," and that this "later impression . . . must be carried back and united with the earlier before we can see what Shakespeare imagined." The Shakespearean imagination at work here is of a piece with "the real Shakespeare"—an interpretive assumption that serves to ignore or at least discount contradictory evidence. Once again, its effect is to produce an image profoundly distasteful to current critical belief—the self-abnegating and domestically enclosed "angel in the house." Yet even as we dismiss this Desdemona as another construct of Victorian ideology, it retains a surprising residual power (so I argue in "Too Much Violence" below), even among critics invested in radically different beliefs about sexuality and gender.

The nineteenth-century denial of sexual and racial aversion may be summed up in a single phrase: resisting Iago. Throughout the play, Iago is the voice for such feelings. He thrusts them upon Brabantio (and us) at the beginning—"Even now, now, very now, an old black ram / Is tupping your white ewe" (1.1.85–86); his first words in the play, " 'Sblood, but you'll not hear me," are uncannily transferable to nineteenth-century commentary about *Othello*. But if this refusal makes for continuity with earlier critical response going back to Rymer, it also requires us to revise claims about an altogether "new Iago" in the nineteenth century, or about a new willingness to "feel" Iago's power from the inside. The will is there, surely enough, but enacted only in a limited capacity; Iago's contaminating point of view is after all quarantined—acknowledged, but then kept out of the purview of legitimate scrutiny. As Bradley puts it, we need to "turn our eyes away" from the visible actions of the stage to focus on the spiritual conflicts they represent: "if we fully imagine the inward tragedy in the souls of the persons as we read, the more obvious and almost physical sensations of pain or horror do not appear in their own likeness, and only serve to intensify the tragic feelings in which they are absorbed." Bradley's understanding of an authentically tragic response ("reconciliation" is his usual designation for it) aligns him with Lamb's rejection of theatrical performance in favor of a reading text—yet another form of denial and idealization reiterated consistently through nineteenth-century commentary.[1]

---

1. Bradley describes "reconciliation" at the end of lecture 1, on "The Substance of Shakespearean Tragedy": audiences, he claims, are occasionally granted an intuition that the final "agony counts as nothing against the heroism and love which appear in it and thrill our hearts. Sometimes we are driven to cry out that these mighty or heavenly spirits who perish are too great for the little space in which they move, and that they vanish not into nothingness but into freedom" (*Shakespearean Tragedy*, 29).

Like the other versions of nineteenth-century idealization, antitheatricalism was a European, not just an English phenomenon—common among German Romantics (Herder and Goethe, for examples). The idea became a kind of cliché, to judge from a reviewer's comment about Augustin Daly's 1888 New York production of *A Midsummer Night's Dream*: the "sophistical opinion" that "an essentially poetic work cannot be put upon the stage" has been "hammered into us year after year" to the point where "many of us accept it as

Theatrical production did not cease, of course, but as James R. Siemon and Michael Neill argue below, performance was idealized: elements of sexual and racial disgust—everything embodied in Iago's voice—were either played down or eliminated from the action so as not to interfere with the "tragic feelings" proper to "reconciliation." According to Neill, these efforts may have served to highlight the very improprieties they were designed to conceal. In any case, the repressed vulgarity quickly returned to claim its own space. In the early 1830s, Maurice Dowling's *Othello Travestie, An Operatic Burlesque Burletta* opened in London, probably the first importation of American minstrel style to England, where it achieved a popularity comparable to its American prominence (see MacDonald). According to Kenneth Gross's description of *Desdemonum*, an "Ethiopian burlesque" published in New York in 1874, "The minstrels translated Othello's proud, florid gesturing, his stagy exoticism, into more comic antics; his tragic nobility becomes, if anything, the risky dignity of the clown . . . parodying the more typically remote and noble Othello" of the high cultural tradition (102, 103). Hence even as Iago's voice was carefully constrained in one kind of production, another kind liberates it into tonal dominance.

This compartmentalizing process was not limited to *Othello*, with its specially problematic racial and sexual issues; it characterizes the institution of nineteenth-century Shakespearean production as a whole. While an idealized "real Shakespeare" was playing in the legitimate theater, other stages down the street were sending up the Bard in coarsely comic parodies—what Richard Schoch describes as the "not Shakespeare." In practical terms, the distinction could break down. According to Schoch, a good deal of audience crossover existed; frequently the same spectators (though "same" deserves some scrutiny) negotiated the space—back and forth, up and down—between high and low performances. Indeed, sometimes tragic nobility and "roars of mighty laughter" occupied the same stage in the sequence of a single performance (see fig. 6, p. 187). But whatever the experience, the conceptual segregation was always rigorously maintained to preserve the reconciliation deemed proper to the authentic tragic mode.

The notable exception to these processes of idealization and separation is Hazlitt. Hazlitt "feels" the manic excitement of Iago not just in the idealized space of readerly imagination. He lets the infectious brilliance of Kean's performance excite him, and the gusto with which he subsumes himself into Iago's malicious ingenuity propels him, like the character himself, "into the wildness and impetuosity

---

just and final" (Kennedy, 297). For the antitheatricalism in Bradley's version of the play, see Gauntlett.

of real enthusiasm." When he took Iago's "I am nothing if not critical" as his own motto for *A View of the English Stage* (1818), he was not just abstracting a witty phrase from its context. Coleridge's confession that he had "a smack of Hamlet my self, if I may say so" has been called "daring," but it seems tame compared to Hazlitt's acknowledgment that "For our part, we are a little of Iago's council in this matter."[2]

In the "matter" referred to, the long footnote on Desdemona reprinted below, Hazlitt goes as far as he can in acceding to the power of Iago's point of view. His contempt for any idealization of sexual desire is pure Iago—virtue, a fig! Even more striking, he locates the idea in an explicitly outrageous reading of Desdemona's sexuality, the "gross impropriety" of whose "personal connection" to an older black man reinforces precisely the "monstrous" prospect that Lamb, Coleridge, and Bradley labored hard to deny. The note shocked Hazlitt's readers. The *Examiner* editor, Leigh Hunt, though Hazlitt's friend and an entirely unsqueamish individual, wrote a lengthy response dissociating himself and the journal from such claims, and even the less sentimental (or more cynical) readers of our time explain it away as the quirky self-indulgence of some "private torment" or perhaps an "unhappy love-affair." Even Hazlitt may have thought he'd gone too far.[3]

But with all the pleasure he takes ventriloquizing Iago's manipulative aggression, Hazlitt does not abandon the balance of his critical intelligence. He never loses sight of the full perversity of Iago's not only destructive but self-destructive energy.[4] And on the other side, Hazlitt never undervalues the radiant beauty Iago wishes to destroy. His Othello is of a piece with the nineteenth-century tradition of the

---

2. For Coleridge's confession, see *Table Talk* for June 24, 1827 (Engell, 14.2:77). For "daring," see Levin (6). A peculiar affinity with Hamlet was not felt uniquely by Coleridge. It was something of a commonplace in the nineteenth century. Hazlitt remarks, "It is *we* who are Hamlet" (Howe, 4:232), but he is not thinking so much about himself as about the play's capacity to seem intimately relevant to an audience of variously different selves.

3. Hunt's response, "Note upon Note, Or a Word or Two on the Passion of Love, in Answer to Some Observations in our Last Week's *Examiner*," appeared in the August 14 issue, 525–26. Hunt shared Hazlitt's left-wing politics and wrote his response from prison, where he was serving a two-year sentence for a trumped-up charge of libeling the prince regent. For modern discussions, see Maclean (315–17) and Jones (152–53), from whom my quotations are taken. Hazlitt omitted the note when reprinting this material in two subsequent collections, and according to David Bromwich, he "later withdrew his allegation against her" (137). I don't know what evidence Bromwich has for this claim. Hazlitt's later omissions may have been as much abridgments as second thoughts or self-censorship. Howe reprints the note with some discussion in the final, *Miscellaneous Journalism* volume of his edition, 20:401–02.

4. Hazlitt's only substantial reservation about Kean's performance (mostly omitted from the discussion excerpted below) is its tendency to lighthearted charm, inappropriately imported (in Hazlitt's view) from Kean's Richard III. Hazlitt's acknowledgment of Iago's total psychopathy shows up a certain sentimentality in Bradley, whose Iago (again in passages not excerpted below) has at least some virtuous qualities and comes to ruin only by underestimating Emilia—this ruin being one of the elements supposedly producing a sense of "reconciliation" at the end.

Ira Aldridge as Othello

Ira Aldridge, shown here in a theatrical poster for his debut as Othello at Covent Garden, April 1833, was born in New York in 1807. He went to England in the 1820s and achieved considerable distinction in eastern Europe and Russia; he is only now, thanks chiefly to the pioneering work of Marshall and Stock and a few others (see p. 146, n. 2 above), beginning to be written back into the record from which the more restrictive interests of earlier historians effectively excluded him. Othello was Aldridge's signature role, and the actor's identification with Shakespeare's tragic Moor extended beyond the theater to color his life. The Senegalese origin advertised in this poster seems to be part of an autobiographical fiction he adopted and disseminated. According to his authorized (and perhaps even authored) *Memoir,* Aldridge's "forefathers were princes of the Fulah tribe, whose dominions were Senegal." As Marshall and Stock remark, recalling Othello's "fetch my life and being / From men of royal siege" (1.2.21–22), "The parallel" was "evidently too good to be missed by an actor with imagination" (15, 17).

Othello was only one of the roles contributing to Aldridge's "composite image"; equally important was the "pathetic ignorance of Mungo" (Potter, *Othello,* 117–18), the uppity slave in Isaac Bickerstaff's *The Padlock,* a comically song-filled melodrama that achieved great popularity throughout Aldridge's career. Mungo's part sounds intolerably racist to current ears, as does the depiction of the "cunning nigger" who outsmarts the possum and the raccoon in "Opossum Up a Gum Tree," the song Aldridge regularly performed, accompanying himself on guitar or banjo after performances of Othello and other more dignified roles. Yet Aldridge included both of these performances at the center of his repertoire, apparently with no reluctance; in fact, to judge from the *Memoir,* his ability to move between such different histrionic tonalities was a matter of professional pride:

> As both a tragic and a comic actor, Mr. Aldridge's talents are undeniably great. In tragedy he has a solemn intensity of style, bursting occasionally to a blaze of fierce invective or passionate declamation, while the dark shades of his face become doubly sombre in their thoughtful aspects; a nightlike gloom is spread over them, and an expression more terrible than paler lineaments can readily assume. In farce he is exceedingly amusing; the ebony becomes polished; the coal emits sparks. His face is the faithful index of his mind; and, as there is not a darker frown than his, there is not a broader grin. The ecstasy of his long, shrill note in "Opossum Up a Gum Tree" can only be equalled by the agony of his cry of despair over the body of Desdemona. (Quoted Marshall and Stock, 44)

The appreciation here requires compartmentalizations—of social values and esthetic effects—that may seem intolerable to us, but they were encouraged by the material arrangements of the theater at the time. Prior to the Theatres Act of 1843, only Drury Lane and Covent Garden had the

Fig. 6. Ira Aldridge's first appearance at Covent Garden in the role of Othello. A playbill of 1833.

right to present serious drama. If any other theaters wanted to do Shakespeare or other items from the legitimate repertoire, they had to include song-and-dance numbers—in effect turning them into a kind of burlesque. As this poster suggests, the distinction between the sites was not always carefully policed. It is hard to imagine what the Covent Garden audiences experienced or understood as they negotiated the distance between the grim catastrophe of *Othello* and the "roars of mighty laughter" of *The Elfin Sprite; and the Grim Grey Woman*. Perhaps an analogy exists with the Renaissance public stage, where the actors performed a brief dance at the end of their tragic performances, but the conceptual boundaries must have been more carefully guarded on the Victorian stage.

noble Moor, whose "frankness and generosity" demand "our sympathy" without reserve. His *Othello* "purifies the affections" in ways equal to anything claimed for it by Bradley's "reconciliation." Even his Desdemona rivals the self-denying sweetness of Coleridge and the others: "Bating the commencement of her passion, which is a little fantastical and headstrong (though even that may perhaps be consistently accounted for from her inability to resist a rising inclination), her whole character consists in having no will of her own, no prompter but her obedience."

These scrupulous qualifications refuse to ignore the strongly sexual Desdemona of the note or to discount this aspect of her in favor of some "later impression" of higher spirituality. Hazlitt would not disagree with Lamb's claim for "the nobler parts of our nature," but as a matter of principle, he will not declare the less nobler parts to be any less natural. The desires that bring us to witness heroic tragedy cannot be separated out, in his view, from the instincts that drive us to observe public executions. Hazlitt found his version of the "real Shakespeare" in the words of an effectively anonymous, prose-speaking lord, "The web of our life is of a mingled yarn" (*All's Well That Ends Well*, 4.3.69); and from this perspective Bradley's "reconciliation" is neither possible nor desirable. In the same way, Hazlitt should be distinguished "from Coleridge, with his demand for unity and the reconciliation of opposites. Temperamentally Hazlitt was better suited to diversity and the war of contraries; he no more wanted to be freed from conflict at the end of a work than at the beginning" (Bromwich, 191). Hazlitt values Shakespearean tragedy for the individualized complexity of its characters, but more for its capacity to generate conflict among the individuals, and most of all for "the effect of collision and contrast" by which it "raises the whole man within us."[5] The "whole man" here is like e. e. cummings's "manunkind": Hazlitt's humanity includes an inhuman element— again, as a matter of conscious principle. Whatever "personal torment" Hazlitt may have been experiencing at the time, the note on Desdemona is entirely consistent with Hazlitt's fundamental beliefs. Working out of these beliefs, he responds wholeheartedly to the contradictory voices of the "two parts well penned" in *Othello*, "Honest Iago, or the jealous Moore"—certainly better than other nineteenth-century critics, and arguably better than the versions we have produced in the Iagocentric twentieth century as well.

The modern *Othello* may be dated from T. S. Eliot's suggestion, excerpted below, that Othello's last speech represents a self-deluding "*bovarysme.*" Eliot's authority at this time is hard to overestimate; his

---

5. I am quoting from "On Shakespeare and Milton" and "On Poetry in General," both dating from 1818 (Howe, 5:50 and 5:6).

suggestive phrases ("objective correlative," "dissociation of sensibility") became the foundations for whole schools of critical thought. But "*bovarysme*" stuck because it coincided with contemporary feeling and belief as well. The huge spectacles framing *Othello*s on the nineteenth-century stage had become unsustainable esthetically as well as economically, either disappearing or removing themselves into the more capacious accommodations of grand opera. The moderns had no use for the idealized sentiments of their eminent Victorian forebears, and after the slaughter of World War I, they were frankly hostile to "the pride, pomp, and circumstance of glorious war" with which Bradley's Othello "comes before us." Eliot's transformation of the Noble Moor of nineteenth-century tradition into a feminized and bourgeois banality clearly struck a responsive chord. F. R. Leavis (whose charisma approximated Eliot's own) projected this image of Othello's last speech backward to reveal a protagonist who is self-deluding "from the beginning" of the play (139). After Leavis's full-scale assault on what he took to be Bradley's sentimentalization of Othello, the "romantic figure" eulogized in *Shakespearean Tragedy* quickly disappeared and a new generation of *Othello* critics keyed on the protagonist's "deficiency in adult self-awareness," "self-protectiveness," "pompousness" and "unredeemed egotism."[6]

This remarkable consensus around Othello's inadequacy seems odd to current taste, if not perverse. The social context for Shakespearean commentary has expanded and diversified greatly since Eliot's time, and when we look back from our own more inclusive institution, even a self-proclaimed outsider like Leavis comes across as the member of an exclusive club, denying Othello entry on the basis of ethical or psychological or maybe even racial criteria that seem narrowly censorious.[7] Small wonder current critics tend to ignore early twentieth-century criticism. Remarkable continuities exist however, between the modern *Othello* and our own version of

---

6. See Heilman, 171–74. For Leo Kirschbaum, "Eliot could have gone much further" in exposing the "self-deluded" and "romantic idealism" by which Othello refuses "to face the reality of his own nature." The excerpts in Scott (457 ff.) furnish a sense of the range and quantity of such discussion (including Eliot and Leavis and an Allardyce Nicoll piece antedating Eliot).

7. John Holloway attacks Leavis's claims about Othello's "voluptuous sensuality" as "grotesquely irrelevant" to "everyone's familiar knowledge about love, marriage and attraction between men and women" and inconsistent with "anyone in normal health" (164–65). For claims about Leavis's racist assumptions, see Neill, excerpted below (see n. 9, p. 311). Accusations of sexual pathology and racism do not seem edifying, but the "surprising . . . *personal* acrimony" and "peculiar viciousness" Peter Davison finds among recent critics has always characterized response to this play and "may stem from what in *Othello* subconsciously disturbs them" (10 and 13, Davison's emphasis). *Merchant of Venice* criticism seems to illustrate a similar animus for similar reasons, as in James Shapiro's ferocious attack on Hunter's supposed "efforts to protect Shakespeare and the Elizabethans from the taint of racism," designed (in Shapiro's view) to elevate Hunter's status as "a member of the academic establishment" (83–85).

the play. If G. K. Hunter's investment in Othello's "romanticism and epic grandeur" was exceptional when he wrote "*Othello* and Colour Prejudice" (excerpted below), it remains equally so these days.[8] Mark Rose's disenchanted view of *Othello* (in "Othello's Occupation," also excerpted below)—"the time came when the Elizabethan romances . . . no longer carry conviction"—is virtually indistinguishable from the antiheroic disillusion of Eliot and his followers. "Even without Iago's machinations," Rose claims, "the romantic image of the absolute worthiness of the lady is at best unstable." As an example of other critics who "have developed this aspect of Othello's vulnerability to Iago," Rose cites Stephen Greenblatt's 1980 account of the play, but he could as well have cited Leavis's central claim that "the essential traitor" of narcissism is, with Othello's initial appearance in the second scene of the play, already "within the gates" (139).[9]

At the same time, important differences remain between early twentieth-century versions of *Othello* and our own. Where Eliot and his followers emphasize some particular and presumably corrigible failure on the protagonist's part, Rose focuses not on Othello but on the outmoded system of chivalric values he is claimed to embody. In a similar way, Edward Snow identifies Othello's state of mind not with a particular pathology but with the normative system of belief operating in the play. "What erupts in Othello's jealousy is not primitive barbaric man but the voice of the father, not 'those elements in man that oppose civilized order' but the outraged voice *of* that order" (410, Snow's emphasis). This focus on the cultural system rather than on the individual subject helps generate many of the strongest current interpretations of the play.[1] Hence Michael D. Bristol's powerful reading of *Othello* (in "Charivari," printed below) as a "comedy of abjection" in which the "play's structure" should be "interpreted schematically as a carnivalesque derangement of marriage as a social institution and as an illustration of the contradictory role of heterosexual desire within that institution." Bristol does not deny Othello and Desdemona's charismatic presence, but insists that any potential transcendence we might infer from their individual appeal is contained within (and crushed by) the regulative (and punitive) force of systematic norms.

8. Hunter acknowledges his exceptional status with amused irony ("one has to be trained as a literary critic to find [Othello] unadmirable") and acknowledges the grandest of all exceptions, "The Noble Moor," the earlier British Academy lecture by Helen Gardner, an elegy for the values of heroic tragedy in which her own world had lost interest.
9. The idea that Iago represents something inherent in Othello is a recurrent feature in modern criticism. For explicit development of the idea, see the excerpts from Maud Bodkin and J. I. M. Stewart in Scott (468–70 and 500–03; Scott gives other examples introducing the Bodkin passage); the idea is still doing important business in Burke's analysis excerpted below.
1. For other examples, see the discussion of Paster, Cook, Boose, Greenblatt, and Parker in "*Othello* in Its Own Time," pp. 141–42 above.

Hunter acknowledged the power of cultural norms—those "unspoken assumptions" to which, because only "the hermit can stand outside them," we give the "multitude of our tiny and unnoticed assents." Nonetheless, he appealed to a variety of "complicating factors," both theological and sociological, by which he claimed audiences would find it "easy to abandon" the "careless assumptions" of their responses to the early action of the play in favor of "new valuations." For Michael Neill, though, writing from a position close to the center of current belief (in "Unproper Beds," excerpted below) the abandonment of the normative is not "easy"—or even possible. "The play thinks abomination into being and then taunts the audience with the knowledge that it can never be *un*thought."

These inescapable norms have been represented variously across the spectrum of current criticism in racial or ethnic, psychosexual, linguistic, and political terms. In perhaps the dominant version, we focus on the inherent vulnerability of Othello as a colonized or racialized subject (illustrated by the Neill and Loomba passages cited in connection with Othello's changing image, p. 176 above). From another angle, Othello's vulnerability inheres in his gender, "the impossible condition of male desire, the condition always already lost," that "inevitably soils that object" in which it invests itself and therefore "threatens to 'corrupt and taint' [Othello's] business from the start" (Adelman, 69, 63, and 65). In the linguistically oriented description developed out of post-Freudian psychoanalytic theory, Othello's fate is determined by desire itself, irrespective of gender. "If language is born of absence, so is desire, and at the same moment. This must be so. . . . Desire, which invests the self in another, necessarily precipitates a division in the subject" (Belsey, 86 and 95). Or again, Othello's transformation is simply the "clearest and most important" example of social and textual construction as a general condition: "In *Othello* the characters have always already experienced submission to narrativity" (Greenblatt, 273). Finally (though the examples could be multiplied pretty much indefinitely), Burke's analysis below of an anxiety in the private ownership of property has been developed into the claim that since "even to *be* at all, is to possess," individual identity is inherently insecure: "the barbarian has always been inside the gate of Venice, not in the person of Othello, but latent in the civil unconscious" (Calderwood, 10 and 8, Calderwood's emphasis). For critics writing after modernity, Leavis's "essential traitor" is now "always already" in the gates.

The play's name for this latent unconscious, Burke's "voice at the ear," is Iago, and this furnishes another way to chart the trajectory of post-Victorian *Othello*s: as response disengages from the extraordinary heroics of "an extravagant and wheeling stranger" (1.1.133), it invests in the sly insouciance of the canny insider, who "know[s]

our country disposition well" (3.3.203). Within theatrical production, this transfer of interest was accomplished during the nineteenth century. By the time Henry Irving and Edwin Booth traded
roles opposite each other in 1881, in performances that "revealed
two masterly Iagos and two unsatisfactory Othellos" (Odell, 2.376),
it was now "quite clear that Iago had emerged as the most interesting
role" (Hankey, 91). Subsequent stage practice has only reinforced
the effect. According to Martin Wine, the Othellos in four out of
five mid twentieth-century productions "were no match for the vividly realised Iagos who . . . developed their parts with such high spirits that they threw the emotional balance of [their] productions out
of kilter" (62).[2] To judge from response to the 1996 Branagh / Fishburne film, and to the 2001 New York Shakespeare Festival production, this "imbalance" in favor of Iago, whether lamented or
celebrated, has by now become something of a routine.[3]

  The origins of critical (as distinct from theatrical) Iagocentrism
may be harder to locate. From one angle, we can return to Eliot and
Leavis—or at least to Leavis: Eliot's disengagement from Othello's
romantic heroism found compensation not in Iago, in whom he
expresses no interest, but in the more private and theological virtue of humility. But when Leavis asserts the values of "a tough-
minded realist assessment" against "Bradley's 'idealizing' approach"
to *Othello*, the argument, as Christopher Norris observes, "becomes
oddly intertwined with the drama played out between Othello and
Iago" (59). In appropriating (or being appropriated by) Iago's voice,
Leavis established a disenchanted tone that has dominated critical
performance ever since. Consider the passages quoted earlier to
illustrate current belief: "always already," "inevitably," "necessarily,"

2. The exception, John Dexter's 1964 production at London's National Theatre, featured
   Laurence Olivier, probably the strongest stage presence of the time. Even he, though, was
   reluctant to take on Othello. He pointed out that the play "belonged to Iago, who could
   always make the Moor look a credulous idiot," speaking with authority, since he had played
   Iago to Ralph Richardson's Othello in 1938, in an "unrepentant scene-stealing spirit"
   (Hankey, 339). He agreed only on the condition that "If I take it on . . . I don't want a
   witty, Machiavellian Iago. I want a solid, honest-to-God N. C. O" (Tynan, 2).
3. Stanley Kauffmann complains that the protagonist in the movie "lacks size," "begins to
   dwindle," and so on (31). Terence Rafferty objects to a "thoroughly, helplessly Iagocentric"
   production: "Fishburne looks lost, and Branagh walks off with the movie. . . . Lacking a
   strong hero, the movie just drifts aimlessly from scene to scene; it's 'Othello' unmoored"
   (126 and 127). Much the same claims have been made about the New York Shakespeare
   Festival production at the Joseph Papp Public Theater (directed by Doug Hughes, with
   Liev Schreiber as Iago)—by Peter Chetta, Nina da Vinci Nichols, and Ben Brantley, who
   writes uncomplainingly that it exhibited "a definite imbalance. No one else in the cast, led
   by the gifted Keith David as Othello, comes close to matching Mr. Schreiber's playful
   interpretive intelligence." The 1999 production directed by Tony Taccone for the Oregon
   Shakespeare Festival (with Derrick Lee Weeden as Othello and Anthony Heald as Iago)
   was evidently an exception. According to Lois Potter (210, 211), "by contrast with most
   [recent] productions" of the play, "this one made Othello, not Iago, the focus of mystery
   and speculation," not only conveying " 'the play's true grandeur' " but making "one understand 'why the play is called *Othello* instead of *Iago*' " (quoting Robert Harwitt's *San
   Francisco Examiner* review).

"this must be so." In other words—Iago's words—"there's no remedy" (1.1.32). These critics know their "culture disposition" too well
to entertain any illusions about transcending social norms.[4]

From another angle, however, Iagocentrism considerably ante-
dates critical modernism; it derives from the formative influence at
the origins of *Othello* commentary, "The Ghost of Rymer."[5] Rymer
is just "a kind of critical Iago" (Newman, 152). In his malicious misconstruction of Desdemona, Rymer "becomes as subject to Iago's
inversions as Othello does" (Kirsch, 17). As Michael Neill develops
the idea below, "Rymer's appropriation of Iago's language" illustrates
an "odd ventriloquy," as though "the ensign's colonization of the
hero's mind were at work in the critic."

The ascendancy of Iago and the persistency of Rymer have added
immeasurable energy to modern versions of the play. The sexual
frankness of current response—our willingness, even eagerness, to
engage with the play's explicitly erotic feelings—may be owing indirectly to Rymer. In her influential essay reprinted here, Lynda E.
Boose's identification of the "spotted handkerchief" with "our final,
indelible vision of the blood-soaked bed" includes a nod to Rymer's
"infamous title," *The Tragedy of the Handkerchief,* as an "unwittingly
. . . ironic perception." But Rymer was hardly unwitting; he associated the handkerchief with Desdemona's garter and sexual smells,
imagining it as "rumpled up with [the] wedding sheets" and suddenly
"start[ing] up to disarm" Othello "whilst he was stifling her . . . to
stop his ungracious mouth." When Stanley Cavell, developing
Boose's innovative claims, argued that *Othello* makes us think "not
merely generally of marriage but specifically of the wedding night"
(131), he helped produce a thriving enterprise based on identifying
"a hidden scene of desire [as the] focus of compulsive fascination
for audience and characters alike" (Neill, " 'Hidden Malady,' " 98).[6]
But Rymer's reiterated acknowledgments of the same scene—"first
night no sooner warm in bed together," "no sooner in bed together,"
"bridegroom and bride in the first night of their coming together,"
"the very morning after her marriage," "go to the first time to bed,"
etc.—fully register the centrality of Othello and Desdemona's consummation to any account of the dramatic action.

---

4. For others who hear Iago's voice as dominating modern criticism, see Bayley, 129–30,
   Kirsch, 31, and Wine, 36.
5. "The Ghost of Rymer" is Nicholas Potter's rubric for discussing "The Moderns" (98–131)
   in his survey of *Othello* criticism, where the "invocation of [Rymer's] name is meant as a
   reminder that a new sternness entered criticism with the emergence of the 'modern' " (4).
6. For others among the many recent critical studies focused on the play's power to evoke
   startlingly intense sexual images and feelings, see (in alphabetical order): Adelman; Boose
   (" 'Let it be hid' "); Calderwood, 125 and 154; Greenberg, 27; Little; Maus ("Horns of
   Dilemma" and "Proof and Consequences"); Neill ("Changing Places"); Parker ("Fantasies"
   and "Shakespeare and Rhetoric"); Pechter; and Rudnytsky.

Rymer strikingly anticipates our concerns in formalist as well as thematic terms. Modern critics have been sharply attuned to *Othello*'s innovative generic mixtures. Rose sees it as more domestic than heroic tragedy, Hunter the other way round, but both recognize the risks *Othello* takes conjoining tonal effects usually kept distinct and apart. For Rose, indeed, the different kinds of emotions associated with the romantic and satiric modes embodied in Othello and Iago tend "to cancel each other out." Bristol's argument for the play as charivari seems to take us beyond tragedy of any kind, and in Peter Zadek's 1976 Hamburg production, the coarse brutality Bristol describes is pushed about as far as it can go: a demented Othello, having flung the dead Desdemona "over the curtain guide-line with her bottom towards the audience . . . like a 'slaughtered steer,' " throws "a kiss at her naked posterior" and then engages in a shouting match with the laughing spectators (Engle, 101). Othello has become his own Iago here, presiding over Bristol's "comedy of abjection" or (in Rymer's equally apt phrase) "Bloody Farce."

In both the sexual explicitness and the generic mixture, Rymer serves to highlight aspects of *Othello* that nineteenth-century audiences sought to diminish if not exclude. But if modern criticism in effect returns to Rymer, there is one notable difference. Rymer registered these matters as weaknesses in *Othello*. The generic slippage offended his sense of normative clarity. The sexual explicitness was offensive for the same reason. Rymer was not squeamish about the sex as such, but it belonged to the domestic and private, not the public and political realms within which tragic actions were supposed to unfold. Besides, the focus on the first night called attention to the play's temporal inconsistencies, the evidently irreconcilable contradictions between the impressions of an action compressed into a few days and one in which "the audience must suppose" a sustained extension of time "to make the plot operate" in a plausible manner.

This issue of temporal inconsistency provides a good way to clarify the differences between Rymer's version of the play and our own. Rymer's overkill dwells on every instance he can find where the play's extended time frame obtrudes on the main impression of a brief action. But he admits that "absurdities of this kind break no bones," and Gildon, even in his most Rymeresque mood, is similarly forgiving: "those little forgetfulnesses are not worth minding." But eighteenth-century commentators minded them nonetheless. Johnson, for whom the play was a triumph and for whom the unity of time was inconsequential, still cannot help but take cognizance of *Othello*'s temporal contradictions in passing, assuring us finally that only minor adjustments are required for the play to reach a "scrupulous regularity." By the late nineteenth century, so much commentary had accumulated around the issue that the New Variorum edition included an appendix of fifteen closely printed pages on the "Duration of the Action" (Furness, 358–72). In 1958, when M. R. Ridley devoted the last section of his New Arden introduction to the issue, it was designated "The 'Double-Time' Scheme" (lxvii–lxx). A *Scheme*: given the current understanding of *Othello* as intentionally focussing our perplexed attention on the lovemaking couple, what was once perceived as an improvisation to disguise a problem inherited from the source narrative is now interpreted as a deliberate effect. Much the same conclusion may be drawn about the generic indecorum: central to the play's rhetorical strategy, designed to disrupt conventional expectation, it's not a bug, it's a feature.

But then with what purpose or to what end are these features working? The early critics had a notorious problem determining the value of *Othello*. Gildon made fun of Rymer's attempts to identify the play's morals, but his own attempts were hardly more successful. It is not clear how serious Johnson was when he told Boswell that "*Othello* has more moral than almost any play"—and then wound up more or less reiterating Rymer's silly points as confirmation. Rymer deliberately mocks the effort to find a moral in *Othello*, though the anger and frustration he expresses when at "the end of the play we meet with nothing but blood and butchery, described much-what to the style of the last speeches and confessions of the persons executed at Tyburn" seem as heartfelt as Johnson's "I am glad that I have ended my revisal of this dreadful scene. It is not to be endured." Echoes of Johnson's confession resonate throughout the nineteenth century, and the detail from Rymer about public executions meanders through Hazlitt into William Winter, the American theater critic, who, writing about the "heartrending and terrible" qualities of *Othello*, claimed that the "mind cannot dwell upon it without an effort. . . . You feel as if you had seen a murder or attended an execution" (192–93).[7]

The moralizing tone and vocabulary of earlier criticism makes us uncomfortable, but they are not wholly discontinuous with current work. Important differences exist between Hazlitt's claim that the interpretation of *Othello* allows us to reach "a high and permanent interest, beyond ourselves, in humanity as such," and Karen Newman's that it enables us "to expose or demystify the ideological discourses which organize texts" (157); but both are committed to the idea that engaging with literary or theatrical fiction has consequences in the world and thus requires the exercise of value judgments. Such judgments are clearly at work when Ruth Cowhig

---

7. Furness quotes J. O. Halliwell-Phillipps's comments that "Many readers will probably sympathize with Dr Johnson's concluding observation" and that "a study of the drama of *Othello*" is "rather a painful duty than one of pleasure," adding his own view that, given "the unutterable agony of [its] closing Scene," he wishes "this Tragedy had never been written" (300).

affirms that "for myself, I only want to see black actors in the part" of Othello" (125), as they are equally in the opposite affirmation of Hugh Quarshie cited above (p. 146). Academic literary study purports to be witnessing the return of ethical criticism, but when was it ever really gone?

As the comments below suggest, response to *Othello* has changed radically over its long history. From Dr. Johnson's assurance that Iago does not steal upon esteem to the current view that Iago governs our experience of the play, it seems as if we have achieved a total reversal in our critical understanding of the play. Yet once again, as with the study of *Othello*'s sources, a self-congratulatory sense of critical progress seems like the wrong place to end. No good evidence suggests that we are doing any better than Dr. Johnson and his contemporaries in explaining why we attach such value to the play. In fact, the strongest Iagocentrists, like Neill and Bristol below, wind up repeating Dr. Johnson's claim that the play's final action is "not to be endured." Perhaps an acknowledgment that *Othello* is unendurable is as close as we can expect to get to the truth.

Works Cited

Adams, John Quincy. "Misconceptions of Shakspeare upon the Stage." In Peter Rawlings, ed. *Americans on Shakespeare, 1776–1914*. Aldershot, England, and Brookfield, Vermont: Ashgate, 1999, 61–66.

Adelman, Janet. *Suffocating Mothers: Fantasies of Maternal Origin in Shakespeare's Plays, "Hamlet" to "The Tempest."* New York and London: Routledge, 1992.

Altman, Joel B. " 'Preposterous Conclusions': Eros, *Enargeia*, and the Composition of *Othello*." *Representations* 18 (1987): 129–57.

Bayley, John. *The Characters of Love: A Study in the Literature of Personality*. London: Constable, 1960.

Belsey, Catherine. "Desire's Excess and the English Renaissance Theatre: *Edward II, Troilus and Cressida*, and *Othello*." In Susan Zimmerman, ed. *Erotic Politics: Desire on the Renaissance Stage*. London and New York: Routledge, 1992, 84–102.

Boose, Lynda E. " 'Let it be hid': Renaissance Pornography, Iago, and Audience Response." In Richard Marienstras and Dominique Guy-Blanquet, ed. *Autour d'"Othello."* Paris: C.E.R.L.A, à l'Institut Charles V, 1987, 135–43.

Bradley, A. C. "Poetry for Poetry's Sake." In *Oxford Lectures on Poetry*. Bloomington: Indiana University Press, 1961, 3–34.

———. *Shakespearean Tragedy: Lectures on "Hamlet", "Othello",*

"King Lear," "Macbeth." John Russell Brown, ed. 3rd ed. New York: St. Martin's, 1992.

Brantley, Ben. "A Revolt against God with No Apology," *New York Times* (December 10, 2001). http://www.nytimes.com/2001/12/10/arts/theater/10OTHE.html?ex=1009138490&ei=1&en=61ab73d6e4a3d645?

Bray, René. *La Formation de la Doctrine Classique en France.* Paris: Nizet, 1957.

Bromwich, David. *Hazlitt: The Mind of a Critic.* 2nd ed. New Haven and London: Yale University Press, 1999.

Bronson, Bertrand H., ed. *Selections from Johnson on Shakespeare.* New Haven and London: Yale University Press, 1986.

Calderwood, James. *The Properties of "Othello."* Amherst: University of Massachusetts Press, 1989.

Carlisle, Carol Jones. *Shakespeare from the Greenroom: Actors' Criticisms of Four Major Tragedies.* Chapel Hill: University of North Carolina Press, 1969.

Cavell, Stanley. *Disowning Knowledge in Six Plays of Shakespeare.* Cambridge: Cambridge University Press, 1987.

Chapman, R. W., ed. *Boswell's Life of Johnson.* London: Oxford University Press, 1953.

Chetta, Peter. "*Othello* at the Public Theater." *Shakespeare Newsletter* 51 (2001): 67.

Cowhig, Ruth. "Blacks in English Renaissance Drama and the Role of Shakespeare's *Othello*." In David Dabydeen, ed. *The Black Presence in English Literature.* Manchester: Manchester University Press, 1985, 1–25.

Davison, Peter. *Othello.* The Critics Debate Series. Atlantic Highlands, N.J.: Humanities Press International, 1988.

Dostoyevsky, Fyodor. *The Brothers Karamazov.* 2 vols. Trans. David Magarshack. Harmondsworth: Penguin, 1958.

Eliot, T. S. "Four Elizabethan Dramatists." In *Selected Essays.* New Edition, 1927. Rpt. New York: Harcourt Brace, 1950, 91–97.

———. "Hamlet." In *Selected Essays.* New Edition, 1927. Rpt. New York: Harcourt Brace, 1950, 121–26.

Engell, James, and W. Jackson Bate, ed. *The Collected Works of Samuel Taylor Coleridge.* London and Princeton: Routledge and Princeton University Press, 1983.

Engle, Ron. "Audience, Style, and Language in the Shakespeare of Peter Zadek." In Dennis Kennedy, ed. *Foreign Shakespeare; Contemporary Performance.* Cambridge: Cambridge University Press, 1993, 93–105.

Evans, G. B., et al, ed. *The Riverside Shakespeare.* Boston: Houghton Mifflin, 1997.

Foakes, R. A., ed. *Coleridge's Criticism of Shakespeare: A Selection.* London: Athlone, 1989.

Furness, Horace Howard, ed. *A New Variorum Edition of Othello.* 7th ed. Philadelphia: Lippincott, 1886.

Gardner, Helen. "The Noble Moor." *Proceedings of the British Academy* 41 (1955): 189–205.

Gauntlett, Mark. "The Perishable Body of the Unpoetic: A. C. Bradley Performs *Othello.*" *Shakespeare Survey* 47. Cambridge: Cambridge University Press, 1994, 71–80.

Greenberg, Mitchell. "Shakespeare's *Othello* and the 'Problem' of Anxiety." In *Canonical States, Canonical Stages: Oedipus, Othering, and Seventeenth-Century Drama.* Minneapolis and London: University of Minnesota Press, 1994, 1–32.

Greenblatt, Stephen. "The Improvisation of Power." In *Renaissance Self-Fashioning: From More to Shakespeare.* Chicago: University of Chicago Press, 1980, 222–54.

Gross, Kenneth. *Shakespeare's Noise.* Chicago: University of Chicago Press, 2001.

Hankey, Julie, ed. *Othello.* Plays in Performance Series. Bristol: Bristol Classical Press, 1987.

Harris, Bernard. "A Portrait of a Moor." *Shakespeare Survey 11.* Cambridge: Cambridge University Press, 1958, 89–97.

Hawkes, Terence, ed. *Coleridge's Writings on Shakespeare.* New York: G. P. Putnam's Sons, 1959.

Heilman, Robert. *Magic in the Web: Action and Language in "Othello."* Lexington: University of Kentucky Press, 1956.

Holloway, John. "Dr. Leavis and 'Diabolic Intellect.' " In *The Story of the Night: Studies in Shakespeare's Major Tragedies.* London: Routledge, 1961, 155–65.

Howe, P., ed. *The Complete Works of William Hazlitt.* 21 vols. London: Dent, 1930–34.

Hudson, Henry N. Introduction to the Tragedy of *Othello.* In *The Works of Shakespeare: The Text Carefully Restored According to the First Editions; with Introductions, Notes Original and Selected, and A Life of the Poet.* 11 vols. Boston and Cambridge: James Munroe and Co., 1856. 10:381–407.

———. *Shakespeare: His Life, Art, and Characters.* 2 vols. Boston: Ginn, 1872.

Jones, Stanley. *Hazlitt: A Life: From Winterslow to Frith Street.* Oxford: Clarendon, 1989.

Kauffmann, Stanley. "Shrinking Shakespeare." *New Republic* 214 (February 12, 1996): 30–31.

Kennedy, Judith M., and Richard F. Kennedy, ed. *Shakespeare: The Critical Tradition: "A Midsummer Night's Dream."* London and New Brunswick, N.J.: The Athlone Press, 1999.

Kirsch, Arthur. *Shakespeare and the Experience of Love*. Cambridge: Cambridge University Press, 1981.

Kirschbaum, Leo. "The Modern Othello." *English Literary History* 2 (1944): 283–96.

Leavis, F. R. "Diabolic Intellect and the Noble Hero." In *The Common Pursuit*. Rpt. Harmondsworth: Penguin, 1969, 136–59.

Levin, Harry. *The Question of "Hamlet."* New York: Viking, 1961.

Little, Arthur, Jr. " 'An essence that's not seen': The Primal Scene of Racism in *Othello*." *Shakespeare Quarterly* 44 (1993): 304–24.

Loomba, Ania. *Gender, Race, Renaissance Drama*. Manchester: Manchester University Press, 1989.

MacDonald, Joyce Green. "Acting Black: *Othello*, *Othello* Burlesques, and the Performance of Blackness." *Theatre Journal* 46 (1994): 231–49.

Maclean, Catherine Macdonald. *Born under Saturn: A Biography of William Hazlitt*. London: Collins, 1943.

Martino, Pierre, ed. *La Pratique du Théâtre* by François Hédelin, l'Abbé d'Aubignac. Algiers: Carbonel, 1927.

Matar, Nabil. *Turks, Moors and Englishmen in the Age of Discovery*. New York: Columbia University Press, 1999.

Maus, Katharine Eisaman. "Horns of Dilemma: Jealousy, Gender, and Spectatorship in English Renaissance Drama." *English Literary History* 54 (1987): 561–83.

———. "Proof and Consequences: Inwardness and Its Exposure in the English Renaissance." *Representations* 34 (1991): 29–52.

Munro, John, ed. *The Shakspere Allusion-Book: A Collection of Allusions to Shakspere from 1591 to 1700*. 2 vols. 1909. Rpt. London: Oxford University Press, 1932.

Neill, Michael. "Changing Places in *Othello*." *Shakespeare Survey* 37. Cambridge: Cambridge University Press, 1984, 115–31.

———. " 'Hidden Malady': Death, Discovery, and Indistinction in *The Changeling*." *Renaissance Drama* 22 (1991): 95–121.

Newman, Karen. " 'And Wash the Ethiop White': Femininity and the Monstrous in *Othello*." In Jean E. Howard and Marion F. O'Connor, ed. *Shakespeare Reproduced: The Text in History and Ideology*. London: Methuen, 1987, 140–62.

Nichols, Nina da Vinci. "No Magic in the Web." *Shakespeare Newsletter* 52 (2002): 21.

Norris, Christopher. "Post-Structuralist Shakespeare: Text and Ideology." In John Drakakis, ed. *Alternative Shakespeares*. London: Methuen, 1985, 47–66.

Odell, George C. D. *Shakespeare from Betterton to Irving*. New York: Scribner's, 1920.

Page, Frederick, ed. *Letters of John Keats*. Oxford: Oxford University Press, 1954.

Parker, Patricia. "Fantasies of 'Race' and 'Gender': Africa, *Othello*, and Bringing to Light." In Margo Hendricks and Parker, ed. *Women, 'Race,' and Writing in the Early Modern Period*. New York and London: Routledge, 1993, 84–100.

———. "Shakespeare and Rhetoric: 'Dilation' and 'Delation.' " In Parker and Geoffrey Hartman, ed. *Shakespeare and the Question of Theory*. London: Methuen, 1985, 57–74.

Pechter, Edward. " 'Have you not read of some such thing?': Sex and Sexual Stories in *Othello*." Shakespeare Survey 49. Cambridge: Cambridge University Press, 1996, 201–16.

Potter, Lois. *Othello*. Shakespeare in Performance. Manchester: Manchester University Press, 2002.

Potter, Nicholas. *William Shakespeare: Othello*. Columbia Critical Guides. New York: Columbia University Press, 2000.

Quarshie, Hugh. "Second Thoughts about *Othello*." ISA Occasional Paper No. 7. Chipping Camden: International Shakespeare Association, 1999.

Rafferty, Terence. "Fidelity and Infidelity." *New Yorker* 71 (December 18, 1995): 124–27.

Ridley, M. R., ed. *Othello*. London: Methuen, 1958.

Rudnytsky, Peter L. "The Purloined Handkerchief in *Othello*." In Joseph Reppen and Maurice Charney, ed. *The Psychoanalytic Study of Literature*. Hillsdale, N.J.: The Analytic Press, 1985, 57–74.

Sanders, Norman, ed. *Othello*. Cambridge: Cambridge University Press, 1984.

Schoch, Richard W. *Not Shakespeare: Bardolatry and Burlesque in the Nineteenth Century*. Cambridge: Cambridge University Press, 2001.

Scott, Mark W., ed. *Shakespearean Criticism: Excerpts from the Criticism of William Shakespeare's Plays and Poetry, from the First Published Appraisals to Current Evaluations*. Vol. 4. Detroit: Gale, 1987.

Shapiro, James. *Shakespeare and the Jews*. New York: Columbia University Press, 1996.

Snow, Edward. "Sexual Anxiety and the Male Order of Things in *Othello*." *English Literary Renaissance* 10 (1980): 384–412.

Theobald, Lewis. *The Works of Shakespeare*. 7 vols. London, 1733. Rpt. New York: AMS Press, 1968

Tynan, Kenneth, ed. *"Othello": The National Theatre Production*. New York: Stein and Day, 1967.

Vickers, Brian, ed. *Shakespeare: The Critical Heritage: Volume 2, 1693–1733*. London and Boston: Routledge & Kegan Paul, 1974.

————, ed. *Shakespeare: The Critical Heritage. Volume 6, 1774–1801.* London and Boston: Routledge and Kegan Paul, 1981.

Warburton, William, ed. *The Plays of William Shakespeare, With the Corrections and Illustrations of Various Commentators, To Which Are Added Notes by Samuel Johnson and George Steevens.* 21 vols. London, 1813.

Wine, Martin. *"Othello": Text and Performance.* London: Macmillan, 1984.

Winter, William. *Life and Art of Edwin Booth.* New York: Macmillan, 1893.

Zimansky, Curt A., ed. *The Critical Works of Thomas Rymer.* New Haven: Yale University Press, 1956.

THOMAS RYMER (1643?–1713)

["A Bloody Farce"]†

From all the tragedies acted on our English stage, *Othello* is said to bear the bell away. The subject is more of a piece, and there is indeed something like—there is, as it were, some phantom of—a fable. The fable is always accounted the soul of tragedy.[1] * * *

* * *

Shakespeare alters [the fable] from the original [Cinthio narrative] in several particulars but always, unfortunately, for the worse. He bestows a name on his Moor and styles him the Moor of Venice—a note of preeminence which neither history nor heraldry can allow him. Cinthio, who knew him best and whose creature he was, calls him simply a Moor * * * [and] we see no such cause for the Moor's preferment to that dignity. * * *

Then [there] is the Moor's wife, from a simple citizen in Cinthio dressed up with her top knots[2] and raised to be Desdemona, a senator's daughter. All this is very strange and therefore pleases such as reflect not on the improbability. This match might well be without the parents' consent. Old Horace long ago forbade the banns:

---

† From *A Short View of Tragedy* (1693). Spelling and punctuation have been modernized, and all quotations from *Othello* modified to conform with this Norton Critical Edition. All notes are the editor's. For information about Rymer, his criticism, and its textual sources, see section 4 of the bibliography, p. 393.

1. The fable (sometimes "argument") is roughly the action or plot. The term has technical suggestions deriving ultimately from Aristotle's *Poetics* and its many commentators.

2. Knots or bows of ribbon worn on the tops of their heads by fashionable women of Rymer's time.

> Sed non ut placidis Coeant immitia, non ut
> Serpentes avibus geminentur, tigribus agni.[3]

* * *

* * * [T]he moral, sure, of this fable is very instructive.

1. First, this may be a caution to all maidens of quality how, without their parents' consent, they run away with blackamoors.

* * *

2. Secondly, this may be a warning to all good wives that they look well to their linen.

3. Thirdly, this may be a lesson to husbands that before their jealousy be tragical the proofs be mathematical.

Cinthio affirms that "she [Desdemona] was not overcome by a womanish appetite, but by the virtue of the Moor." It must be a good-natured reader that takes Cinthio's word in this case, though in a novel. Shakespeare, who is accountable both to the eyes and to the ears, and to convince the very heart of an audience, shows that Desdemona was won by hearing Othello talk [quotes 1.3.133–44: "I spoke of most disastrous chances. . . . Do grow beneath their shoulders"].

This was the charm, this was the philter, the love powder that took the daughter of this noble Venetian. This was sufficient to make the blackamoor white and reconcile all, though there had been a cloven foot into the bargain.

A meaner woman might be as soon taken. * * *

* * * But it seems the noble Venetians have another sense of things. The duke himself tells us "I think this tale would win my daughter too" [1.3.170].

* * *

* * * [T]here is nothing in the noble Desdemona that is not below any country chambermaid with us.

* * *

The character of that state is to employ strangers in their wars; but shall a poet thence fancy that they will set a Negro to be their general, or trust a Moor to defend them against the Turk? With us a blackamoor might rise to be a trumpeter, but Shakespeare would not have less than a lieutenant-general. With us a Moor might marry

---

3. Rymer quotes lines 12–13 of Horace's popular *Ars Poetica* (*Art of Poetry*), written about 14 B.C.E. After acknowledging that poets are allowed license to invent "extravagant conceits" and unusual mixtures, Horace urges (in an eighteenth-century translation by George Colman), "But not the soft and savage to combine, / Serpents to doves, to tigers lambkins join."

some little drab or small-coal wench; Shakespeare would provide him the daughter and heir of some great lord or privy councillor, and all the town should reckon it a very suitable match. Yet the English are not bred up with that hatred and aversion to the Moors as are the Venetians, who suffer by a perpetual hostility from them. * * *

* * *

The characters or manners, which are the second part in a tragedy, are not less unnatural and improper than the fable was improbable and absurd.[4] Othello is made a Venetian general. We see nothing done by him nor related concerning him that comports with the condition of a general or, indeed, of a man, unless the killing himself to avoid a death the law was about to inflict upon him. When his jealousy had wrought him up to the resolution of his taking revenge for the supposed injury, he sets Iago to the fighting part to kill Cassio and chooses himself to murder the silly woman his wife, that was like to make no resistance.

His love and his jealousy are no part of a soldier's character, unless for comedy.

But what is most intolerable is Iago. He is no blackamoor soldier, so we may be sure he should be like other soldiers of our acquaintance; yet never in tragedy nor in comedy nor in nature was a soldier with his character. Take it in the author's own words: "some eternal villain / Some busy and insinuating rogue, / Some cogging, cozening slave, to get some office" [4.2.132–34]. Horace describes a soldier otherwise: "*Impiger, iracundus, inexorabilis, acer.*"[5] Shakespeare knew his character of Iago was inconsistent. In this very play he pronounces, "If . . . / Thou dost deliver more or less than truth, / Thou art no soldier" [2.3.208–10].

This he knew, but to entertain the audience with something new and surprising, against common sense and nature, he would pass upon us a close, dissembling, false, insinuating rascal instead of an open-hearted, frank, plain-dealing soldier, a character constantly worn by them for some thousands of years in the world.

* * *

Nor is our poet more discreet in his Desdemona. He had chosen a soldier for his knave and a Venetian lady to be the fool.

This senator's daughter runs away to a carrier's inn, the Sagittary, with a blackamoor; is no sooner wedded to him, but the very night

---

4. "Characters" and "manners" are (like "fable") technical terms—see "*Othello* in Critical History," pp. 169–70 above.

5. "Impatient, hot-tempered, ruthless, fierce" (*Ars Poetica*, 121). Horace's point is that if "you introduce yet again the 'far-famed Achilles,' " you should comply with the associations of the conventional epithets: "stick to tradition or see that your inventions be consistent" (in Edward Blakeney's 1928 translation).

she beds him is importuning and teasing him for a young smock-
faced Lieutenant Cassio. And though she perceives the Moor jealous
of Cassio, yet she will not forbear, but still rings "Cassio, Cassio" in
both his ears.

*   *   *

The first [characters] we see are Iago and Roderigo, by night in
the streets of Venice. After growling a long time together, they
resolve to tell Brabantio that his daughter is run away with the blackamoor. Iago and Roderigo were not of quality to be familiar with
Brabantio, nor had any provocation from him to deserve a rude thing
at their hands. Brabantio was a noble Venetian, one of the sovereign
lords and principal persons in the government, peer to the most
serene duke, one attended with more state, ceremony and punctilio
than any English duke or nobleman in the government will pretend
to. This misfortune in his daughter is so prodigious, so tender a point,
as might puzzle the finest wit of the most "supersubtle" Venetian to
touch upon it, or break the discovery to her father. See then how
delicately Shakespeare minces the matter: [quotes 1.1.75–89: "what
ho, Brabantio! . . . Arise, I say!"].

*   *   *

For the second act, our poet, having dispatched his affairs at Venice, shows the action next I know not how many leagues off in the
island of Cyprus. The audience must be there too, and yet our Bays[6]
had it never in his head to make any provision of transport ships for
them.

In the days that the Old Testament was acted in Clerkenwell by
the parish clerks of London, the Israelites might pass through the
Red Sea.[7] But alas, at this time we have no Moses to bid the waters
make way and to usher us along. Well, the absurdities of this kind
break no bones. They may make fools of us; but do not hurt our
morals.

*   *   *

But pass we to something of a more serious air and complexion.
Othello and his bride are the first night no sooner warm in bed
together, but a drunken quarrel happening in the garrison, two soldiers fight, and the general rises to part the fray. He swears: [quotes
2.3.194–207: "Now, by heaven . . . who began't?"].

6. Shakespeare, the Bard. In antiquity, the bay or laurel wreath was bestowed as a reward
   for poetic and other forms of achievement. Rymer is also alluding to Bays, the name of
   the playwright character in a popular contemporary spoof, Buckingham's *Rehearsal*.
7. Earlier in *A Short View*, Rymer had dismissed such "improbabilities" in the medieval dram-
   atizations of biblical history.

In the days of yore, soldiers did not swear in this fashion. What should a soldier say farther when he swears, unless he blaspheme? Action should speak the rest. What follows must be *ex ore gladii*;[8] he is to rap out an oath, not wire draw and spin it out. By the style one might judge that Shakespeare's soldiers were never bred in a camp, but rather had belonged to some affidavit office. Consider also throughout this whole scene how the Moorish general proceeds in examining into this rout; no Justice Clod-pate[9] could go on with more phlegm and deliberation. The very first night that he lies with the "Divine Desdemona" to be thus interrupted might provoke a man's Christian patience to swear in another style. But a Negro general is a man of strange mettle. Only his Venetian bride is a match for him. She understands that the soldiers in the garrison are by the ears together, and presently she at midnight is in amongst them.

> DESDEMONA   What is the matter, dear?
> OTHELLO   All's well now,
>   sweeting;
> Come away to bed. [2.3.242–43]

In the beginning of this second act, before they had lain together, Desdemona was said to be "our Captain's Captain"; now they are no sooner in bed together but Iago is advising Cassio in these words: [quotes 2.3.303–12: "Our general's wife . . . her to splinter"; and 327–36: " 'tis most easy . . . With his weak function"]. * * *

This kind of discourse implies an experience and long conversation, the honeymoon over, and a marriage of some standing. Would any man in his wits talk thus of a bridegroom and bride in the first night of their coming together?

Yet this is necessary for our poet; it would not otherwise serve his turn. This is the source, the foundation of his plot; hence is the spring and occasion for all the jealousy and bluster that ensues.

*   *   *

[Quotes Desdemona's supplication for Cassio, 3.3.54–61: "Good love, call him back. . . . on Wednesday morn."] After forty lines more at this rate, they part, and then comes the wonderful scene where Iago by shrugs, half words, and ambiguous reflections works Othello up to be jealous. One might think, after what we have seen, that there needs no great cunning, no great poetry and address, to make the Moor jealous. Such impatience, such a rout for a handsome young fellow the very morning after her marriage, must make him either to be jealous, or to take her for a changeling, below his jealousy. After this scene, it might strain the poet's skill to reconcile the

8. That is, "from the mouth of the sword"—barracks talk or, again, action rather than speech.
9. That is, blockhead.

couple and allay the jealousy. Iago can now only *actum agere* [play the part] and vex the audience with a nauseous repetition.

Whence comes it, then, that this is the top scene, the scene that raises *Othello* above all other tragedies in our theaters? It is purely from the action—from the mops and the mows, the grimace, the grins and gesticulation. Such scenes as this have made all the world run after Harlequin and Scaramuccio.[1]

* * *

"I have a pain upon my forehead, here" [3.3.286].

Michael Cassio came not from Venice in the ship with Desdemona, nor till this morning could be suspected of an opportunity with her. And 'tis now but dinner time, yet the Moor complains of his forehead. He might have set a guard on Cassio, or have locked up Desdemona, or have observed their carriage a day or two longer. He is on other occasions phlegmatic enough. This is very hasty. But after dinner we have a wonderful flight: [quotes 3.3.339–42: "What sense had I . . . on her lips"].

A little after this, says he: [quotes 3.3.410–26: "Give me a living reason . . . gave thee to the Moor!' "].

By the rapture of Othello, one might think that he raves, is not of sound memory, forgets that he has not yet been two nights in the matrimonial bed with Desdemona. But we find Iago, who should have a better memory, forging his lies after the very same mode. The very night of their marriage at Venice, the Moor and also Cassio were sent away to Cyprus. In the second act, Othello and his bride go the first time to bed. The third act opens the next morning. The parties have been in view to this moment. We saw the opportunity which was given for Cassio to speak his bosom to her; once, indeed, might go a great way with a Venetian. But once will not do the poet's business. The audience must suppose a great many bouts to make the plot operate. They must deny their senses, to reconcile it to common sense or make it any way consistent and hang together.

* * *

[Quotes 3.4.17–30: "Seek him . . . Drew all such humors from him."] By this manner of speech one would gather the couple had been yoked together a competent while. What might she say more had they cohabited and been man and wife seven years?

* * *

" 'Tis not a year or two shows us a man" [3.4.100].

As if for the first year or two Othello had not been jealous? This

1. Stock types of mime shows, derived from the Italian *commedia dell' arte.*

third act begins in the morning, at noon she drops the handkerchief, after dinner she misses it, and then follows all this outrage and horrible clutter about it. If we believe a small damsel in the last scene of this act, this day is effectually seven days. [Quotes 3.4.169–72: "What? keep a week away? . . . O weary reckoning!"]

Our poet is at this plunge, that whether this act contains the compass of one day, of seven days, or of seven years, or of all together, the repugnance and absurdity would be the same. * * *

* * *

Iago had some pretence to be discontent with Othello and Cassio, and what passed hitherto was the operation of revenge. Desdemona had never done him harm, always kind to him and to his wife, was his countrywoman, a dame of quality. For him to abet her murder shows nothing of a soldier, nothing of a man, nothing of nature in it. The ordinary of Newgate[2] never had the like monster to pass under his examination. Can it be any diversion to see a rogue beyond what the Devil ever finished? Or would it be any instruction to an audience? Iago could desire no better than to set Cassio and Othello, his two enemies, by the ears together, so he might have been revenged on them both at once; and choosing his own share the murder of Desdemona, he had the opportunity to play booty and save the poor harmless wretch. But the poet must do everything by contraries to surprise the audience still with something horrible and prodigious beyond any human imagination. At this rate he must out-do the Devil to be a poet in the rank with Shakespeare.

* * *

"Alas, Iago, / What shall I do to win my lord again?" [4.2.150–51].

No woman bred out of a pigsty could talk so meanly. After this she is called to supper with Othello, Lodovico, etc. After that comes a filthy sort of pastoral scene, where the "wedding sheets" and song of "willow" and her mother's maid, poor Barbary, are not the least moving things in this entertainment. * * *

* * *

* * * A noble Venetian lady is to be murdered by our poet in sober sadness, purely for being a fool. No pagan poet but would have found some machine for her deliverance. Pegasus would have strained hard to have brought old Perseus on his back, time enough, to rescue this Andromeda from so foul a monster. Has our Christian poetry no gen-

2. The chaplain of Newgate prison, whose duty it was to prepare prisoners for death.

erosity, nor bowels? Ha, Sir Lancelot! ha, St. George! will no ghost leave the shades for us in extremity, to save a distressed damsel?[3]

But for our comfort, however felonious is the heart, hear with what soft language he does approach her, with a candle in his hand: "Put out the light, and then put out the light. / If I quench thee, thou flaming minister, / I can again thy former light restore" [5.2.7–9].

Who would call him a barbarian, monster, savage? Is this a black-amoor? *Soles occidere & redire possunt*: the very soul and quintessence of Sir George Etherege.[4]

One might think the general should not glory much in this action, but make a hasty work on it and have turned his eyes away from so unsoldierly an execution. Yet is he all pause and deliberation, handles her as calmly and is as careful of her soul's health as it had been her father confessor. "Have you prayed to night, Desdemon?" [5.2.25]. But the suspense is necessary, that he might have a convenient while so to "roll his eyes" [5.2.39] and so to "gnaw his nether lip" [5.2.43] to the spectators. Besides the greater cruelty—*sub tam lentis maxillis.*[5]

But hark, a most tragical thing laid to her charge [quotes from 5.2.47–67: "That handkerchief . . . I saw the handkerchief"].

So much ado, so much stress, so much passion and repetition about a handkerchief. Why was not this called "The Tragedy of the Handkerchief?" What can be more absurd * * * ? * * * Had it been Desdemona's garter, the sagacious Moor might have smelled a rat; but the handkerchief is so remote a trifle no booby on this side Mauritania could make any consequence from it.

We may learn here that a woman never loses her tongue, even though after she is stifled. [Quotes 5.2.119–28: "O falsely, falsely murdered! . . . Commend me to my kind lord. O, farewell!"]

*   *   *

[M]ay we ask here what unnatural crime Desdemona or her parents had committed to bring this judgment down upon her, to wed a blackamoor and, innocent, to be thus cruelly murdered by him? What instruction can we make out of this catastrophe? Or whither must our reflection lead us? Is not this to envenom and sour our

---

3. Rymer refers to heroic rescues in Greek mythology (Perseus) and medieval romance (Sir Lancelot and St. George). His point is that Desdemona's undeserved death violates poetic justice—the complaint he returns to and sustains at the end.
4. Poet and playwright (1636?–1662?) much admired for his wittily satiric but affectionate treatment of love; sometimes referred to as "gentle George" or "easy Etherege." Rymer quotes a well-known line, "Suns can set and rise again," from a love lyric by Catullus that continues, "For us, once our brief light has set, / There's one unending night for sleeping" (Trans. Guy Lee, *The Poems of Catullus*. Oxford: Clarendon, 1990, 7).
5. "To be ground by jaws that crunch so slowly." Reportedly said by the Emperor Augustus, anticipating the fate of Rome under Tiberius's rule (Suetonius, *Tiberius* 21.2).

spirits, to make us repine and grumble at Providence and the government of the world? If this be our end, what boots it to be virtuous?

Desdemona dropped the handkerchief and missed it that very day after her marriage. It might have been rumpled up with her wedding sheets, and this night that she lay in her wedding sheets the fairy napkin (whilst Othello was stifling her) might have started up to disarm his fury and stop his ungracious mouth. Then might she (in a trance for fear) have lain as dead. Then might he, believing her dead, touched with remorse, have honestly cut his own throat by the good leave and with the applause of all the spectators, who might thereupon have gone home with a quiet mind, admiring the beauty of Providence, fairly and truly represented in the theater.

* * *

[At] the end of the play we meet with nothing but blood and butchery, described much-what to the style of the last speeches and confessions of the persons executed at Tyburn, with this difference—that there we have the fact and the due course of justice, whereas our poet, against all justice and reason, against all law, humanity and nature, in a barbarous arbitrary way, executes and makes havoc of his subjects, hab-nab [at random] as they come to hand. Desdemona dropped her handkerchief; therefore she must be stifled. Othello, by law to be broken on the wheel, by the foe's cunning escapes with cutting his own throat. Cassio, for I know not what, comes off with a broken shin. Iago is not yet killed, because there never yet was such a villain alive. The Devil, if once he brings a man to be dipped in a deadly sin, lets him alone to take his course, and now when the "Foul Fiend" has done with him, our wise authors take the sinner into their poetical service, there to accomplish him and do the Devil's drudgery.

Philosophy tells us it is a principle in the nature of man to be grateful.

History may tell us that John an Oaks, John a Stile,[6] or Iago were ungrateful. Poetry is to follow nature. Philosophy must be his guide. History and fact in particular cases of John an Oaks or John of Styles are of no warrant or direction for a poet. Therefore Aristotle is always telling us that poetry is * * * more general and abstracted, is led more by the philosophy, the reason and nature of things, than history, which only records things, higgledy-piggledy, right or wrong as they happen. History might without any preamble or difficulty say that Iago was ungrateful. Philosophy then calls him unnatural, but the poet is, not without huge labor and preparation, to expose the monster and after show the divine vengeance executed upon him. The

6. "John an Oaks" and "John a Stile" (or "John of Styles") are conventional designations of insignificant individuals: Mr. Smith, Mr. Jones, Joe Blow.

poet is not to add willful murder to his ingratitude: he has not anti-
dote enough for the poison. His Hell and Furies are not punishment
sufficient for one single crime of that bulk and aggravation.[7]

*   *   *

What can remain with the audience to carry home with them from
this sort of poetry for their use and edification? How can it work
unless (instead of settling the mind and purging our passions) to
delude our sense, disorder our thoughts, addle our brain, pervert our
affections, hair our imaginations, corrupt our appetite, and fill our
head with vanity, confusion, tintamarra, and jingle-jangle beyond
what all the parish clerks of London, with their Old Testament farces
and interludes in Richard II's time, could ever pretend to?[8] Our only
hopes for the good of their souls can be that these people go to the
playhouse as they do to church—to sit still, look on one another,
make no reflection, nor mind the play more than they would a sermon.

There is in this play some burlesque, some humor and ramble of
comical wit, some show and some mimicry to divert the spectators,
but the tragical part is plainly none other than a bloody farce without
salt or savor.

CHARLES GILDON (1665–1724)

[Comments on Rymer's *Othello*]†

From the Preface

In the hurry of writing, I forgot one very good defense of a passage
in the *Othello* of Shakespeare, which Mr. Rymer has loudly
exclaimed against, and which a very good friend of mine advised me
to insert in the preface; 'tis this: "Awake! what ho, Brabantio! . . . an
old black ram / Is tupping your white ewe" [1.1.76 and 85–86].

---

7. Rymer's insistence that tragedy transform historical fact into ethical or philosophical pre-
   cept was commonplace; the material elided from this passage includes a misquotation of
   Aristotle's *Poetics*, the effective origin of the claim.
8. Once again, Rymer returns to the medieval mystery plays ("Richard II's time" was the end
   of the fourteenth century) in objecting to *Othello*'s failure to achieve neoclassical clarity
   and control. *Hair*: to line with fur; presumably meant to suggest that the play is over
   provocative. *Tintamarra*: uproar.
† The first two passages are from the preface and the chapter "Some Reflections on Mr.
   Rymer's *Short View*" in Gildon's *Miscellaneous Letters* (1694); the third is from his *Remarks
   on . . . Shakespeare* (1710). Spelling and punctuation have been modernized, and all quotations from *Othello* modified to conform with this Norton Critical Edition. All notes are
   the editor's. For information about Gildon, his criticism, and its textual sources, see section
   5 of the bibliography, p. 394.

Mr. Rymer will have it that a rap at the door would better express Iago's meaning than all that noise; but if Mr. Rymer would consult the reason of the thing, he'll find that the noise Roderigo and Iago made contributed very much to their design of surprising and alarming Brabantio, by that to transport him from consideration to a violent passion.

*   *   *

From "Some Reflections"

As soon as Mr. Rymer's book came to my hands, I resolved to make some reflections upon it, though more to show my will than my abilities. But finding Mr. Dennis had almost promised the world a vindication of the incomparable Shakespeare, I quitted the design.[1]

*   *   *

But expecting thus long without hearing any farther of it, * * * [and] since I find some build an assurance on this general silence of all the friends of Shakespeare that Mr. Rymer's objections are unanswerable, I resolved to bestow two or three days on an essay to prove the contrary. * * *

*   *   *

Had our critic entertained but common justice for the heroes of his own country, he would have set Shakespeare's faults in their true light and distinguished betwixt his and the vices of the age. * * * This is the reason that most of his tragedies have a mixture of something comical: the Delilah of the age must be brought in, the clown and the valet jesting with their betters, if he resolved not to disoblige the auditors.[2] And I'm assured from very good hands that the person that acted Iago was in much esteem for a comedian, which made Shakespeare put several words and expressions into his part (perhaps not so agreeable to his character) to make the audience laugh, who had not yet learnt to endure to be serious a whole play. This was the occasion of that particular place so much hooted at by our historiographer royal: "Awake! what ho, Brabantio! . . . an old black ram / Is tupping your white ewe" [1.1.76–86]. * * *

1. John Dennis (1657–1734), probably the "very good friend" mentioned in Gildon's preface, published his *Impartial Critick* in 1693, taking on Rymer's *Short View* in general terms, but not dealing with the detailed attack on *Othello*.
2. The appeal of low comedy is associated with female temptation, like Delilah's of Samson (in Judges 16). Dr. Johnson, commenting on Shakespeare's inability to resist punning, said that a "quibble was to him the fatal Cleopatra for which he lost the world and was content to lose it."

*   *   *

To begin with the fable (as our critic has done), I must tell him he has as falsely, as ridiculously represented it, which I shall endeavor to put in a juster light.

*   *   *

The fable to be perfect must be admirable and probable. * * *
I suppose none will deny that it is admirable—that is, composed of incidents that happen not every day. Its antagonist concedes as much. There is therefore nothing but the probability of it attacked by him. * * *

*   *   *

All the reason he gives, or rather implies, for the first improbability is that 'tis not likely the state of Venice would employ a "Moor" (taking him for a Mohammedan) against the Turk, because of the mutual bond of religion. He indeed says not so, but takes it for granted that Othello must be rather for the Turkish interest than the Venetian, because a Moor. But I think (nor does he oppose it with any reason) the character of the Venetian state being to employ strangers in their wars, it gives sufficient ground to our poet to suppose a Moor employed by them as well as a German[3]—that is, a Christian Moor, as Othello is represented by our poet—for from such a Moor there could be no just fear of treachery in favor of the Mohammedans. * * * Why therefore an African Christian may not by the Venetians be supposed to be as zealous against the Turks as a European Christian I cannot imagine. * * *

*   *   *

'Tis granted a Negro here does seldom rise above a trumpeter, nor often perhaps higher at Venice. But then that proceeds from the vice of mankind, which is the poet's duty as he informs us to correct, and to represent things as they should be, not as they are. Now 'tis certain there is no reason in the nature of things why a Negro of equal birth and merit should not be on an equal bottom with a German, Hollander, Frenchman, etc. The poet, therefore, ought to do justice to nations as well as persons and set to rights, which the common course of things confounds. The same reason stands in force for this, as for punishing the wicked and making the virtuous fortunate,

---

3. A close relative, as in Iago's "jennets for germans" (1.1.110). Gildon's point is that Othello, though a Moor, is related by religious kinship and thus not altogether a "stranger" or foreigner.

which as Rapin[4] and all critics agree the poet ought to do, though it generally happens otherways. The poet has therefore well chosen a polite people to call off this customary barbarity of confining nations, without regard to their virtue and merits, to slavery and contempt for the mere accident of their complexion.

* * * I shall proceed to the probability of Desdemona's love for the Moor, which I think is something more evident against him. Whatever he aims at in his inconsistent ramble against this may be reduced to the person and the manner. Against the person he quotes you two verses out of Horace that have no * * * reference to this * * * unless he can prove that the color of a man alters his species and turns him into a beast or a devil. 'Tis such a vulgar error, so criminal a fondness of ourselves, to allow nothing of humanity to any but our own acquaintance of the fairer hew. * * * Any man that has conversed with the best travels or read anything of the history of those parts on the continent of Africa discovered by the Portuguese must be so far from robbing the Negroes of some countries there of humanity, that they must grant them not only greater heroes, nicer observers of honor, and all the moral virtues that distinguished the old Romans, but also much better Christians (where Christianity is professed) than we of Europe generally are. They move by a noble principle, more open, free, and generous, and not such slaves to sordid interest.

After all this, Othello being of "royal blood" and a Christian, where is the disparity of the match? If either side is advanced, 'tis Desdemona. And why must this Prince, though a Christian and of known and experienced virtue, courage, and conduct, be made such a monster that the Venetian lady can't love him without perverting nature? Experience tells us that there's nothing more common than matches of this kind, where the whites and blacks cohabit, as in both the Indies; and even here at home, ladies that have not wanted white adorers have indulged their amorous dalliances with their sable lovers without any of Othello's qualifications, which is proof enough that nature and custom have not put any such unpassable bar betwixt creatures of the same kind because of different colors, which I hope will remove the improbability of the person, especially when the powerful auxiliaries of extraordinary merit and virtues come to plead with a generous mind.

The probability of the person being thus confirmed, I shall now consider that of the manner of his obtaining her love. * * * [W]e may easily suppose the story of his fortunes and dangers would make an impression of pity and admiration at least on the bosom of a woman

---

4. René Rapin, an influential neoclassical critic of the seventeenth century, whose *Reflexions sur la poétique* (1674) Rymer had translated. Gildon is turning Rymer's authorities and ideas about "poetical justice" back against him.

of a noble and generous nature. No man of any generous principle but must be touched at suffering virtue and value the noble sufferer, whose courage and bravery bear him through uncommon trials and extraordinary dangers. Nor would it have less force on a woman of any principle of honor and tenderness; she must be moved and pleased with the narration, she must admire his constant virtue, and admiration is the first step to love, which will easily gain upon those who have entertained it.

* * *

[S]hould all I have said fail of clearing the probability of the fable from Mr. Rymer's objections, yet ought not that to rob Shakespeare of his due character of being a poet and a great genius, unless he will for the same reason deny those prerogatives to Homer and Sophocles. * * * [T]he latter, as Rapin justly observes, has not kept to probability even in his best performance, I mean in his *Oedipus Tyrannus;* for as Rapin has it, Oedipus "ought not to have been ignorant of the assassination of Laius. The ignorance he's in of the murder, which makes all the beauty of the intrigue, is not probable." And if a man would play the droll with this fable of *Oedipus,* it would furnish full as ridiculous a comment as witty Mr. Rymer has done from this of *Othello;* and sure, I can't err in imitating so great a critic.

First then, let all men before they defend themselves on the highway think well of what they do, lest not being mathematically sure he's at home he kill his own father. * * *

Next, let every younger brother that ventures to ride in another man's boots be very circumspect, lest he marries his own mother.

* * *

These are much more the consequence of this fable of *Oedipus* than those wondrous truths he draws from that of *Othello.* Nay, the moral Sophocles concludes his *Oedipus* with will serve as justly for *Othello,* viz. "That no man can be called happy before his death." But the whole fable of *Oedipus,* though much admired, is so very singular and improbable that 'tis scarce possible it ever could have happened; on the other hand, the fatal jealousy of Othello and the revenge of Iago are the natural consequences of our ungoverned passions, which by a prospect of such tragical effects of their being indulged may be the better regulated and governed by us. So that though *Othello* ends not so formally with a moral sentence, as *Oedipus* does, yet it sets out one of much greater value. * * *

* * *

But I have dwelled so long on the fable that I have not time enough to discuss the other parts, as the characters. * * * Nor can I proceed to a particular consideration of all the characters of the play at this time. Desdemona, I think, is the most faulty; but since our antagonist will have Iago the most "intolerable," I shall confine myself to that.

* * *

* * * The characters or manners, as the same Rapin observes, are to be drawn from experience, and that tells us that they differ in soldiers according to their nature and discipline; that also tells us that the camp is not free from designs, supplantings, and all the effects of the most criminal of passions. * * *

* * * But granting that Iago's character is defective something in the manners, * * * [and] though Mr. Rymer is so severe to deny that the character of Iago is that of a soldier, because so different from his military acquaintance, yet I'm confident he would take it extremely amiss if I should deny him to be a critic because so contrary to all the critics that I have met with, playing the merry droll instead of giving serious and solid reasons for what he advances.

From *Remarks on the Plays of Shakespeare*

* * *

I have drawn the fable with as much favor to the author as I possibly could, yet I must own that the faults found in it by Mr. Rymer are but too visible for the most part. That of making a Negro of the hero or chief character of the play would shock anyone; for it is not the rationale of the thing and the deductions that may thence be brought to diminish the opposition betwixt the different colors of mankind that would be sufficient to take away that which is shocking in this story, since this entirely depends on custom which makes it so. And on common women's admitting a Negro to a commerce with her everyone almost starts at the choice; much more in a woman of virtue; and indeed Iago, Brabantio, &c., have shown such reasons as make it monstrous. I wonder Shakespeare saw this in the persons of his play and not in his own judgment. If Othello had been made deformed and not over young but no black it had removed most of the absurdities, but now it pleases only by prescription. 'Tis possible that an innocent tender young woman who knew little of the world might be won by the brave actions of a gallant man not to regard his age or deformities; but nature, or (what is all one in this case) custom, having put such a bar as so opposite a color, it takes away our pity from her and only raises our indignation against him. * * *

Whether the motives of Othello's jealousy be strong enough to free him from the imputation of levity and folly I will not determine, since jealousy is born often of very slight occasions, especially in the breasts of men of those warmer climates. Yet this must be said:

Shakespeare has managed the scene [3.3] so well that it is that alone which supports his play and imposes on the audience so very successfully that, till a reformation of the stage comes, I believe it will always be kindly received.

Iago is a Character that can hardly be admitted into the tragic scene—though it is qualified by his being pushed on by revenge, ambition, and jealousy—because he seems to declare himself a settled villain. * * *

*   *   *

The Moor has not bedded his lady till he come to Cyprus, nay it was not done [cites "That profit's yet to come," 2.3.10], and yet it is before and after urged that she was or might be sated with him. But those little forgetfulnesses are not worth minding.

*   *   *

SAMUEL JOHNSON (1709–1784)

[Shakespeare, the Rules, and *Othello*]†

From the Preface

*   *   *

Whether Shakespeare knew the unities and rejected them by design or deviated from them by happy ignorance, it is, I think, impossible to decide, and useless to inquire. We may reasonably suppose that, when he rose to notice, he did not want[1] the counsels and admonitions of scholars and critics, and that he at last deliberately persisted in a practice which he might have begun by chance. As nothing is essential to the fable, but unity of action, and as the unities of time and place arise evidently from false assumptions and, by circumscribing the extent of the drama, lessen its variety, I cannot think it much to be lamented that they were not known by him or not observed. Nor if such another poet could arise should I very vehemently reproach him that his first act passed at Venice and his

† From Johnson's edition of Shakespeare (1765). Spelling and punctuation have been modernized, and all quotations from *Othello* modified to conform with this Norton Critical Edition. All notes are the editor's. For information about Johnson, his criticism, and its textual sources, see section 6 of the bibliography, p. 394.

1. Lack

next in Cyprus. Such violations of rules merely positive[2] become the comprehensive genius of Shakespeare, and such censures are suitable to the minute and slender criticism of Voltaire.[3]

* * *

Voltaire expresses his wonder that our author's extravagances are endured by a nation which has seen the tragedy of *Cato*. Let him be answered that Addison speaks the language of poets and Shakespeare of men.[4] We find in *Cato* innumerable beauties which enamor us of its author, but we see nothing that acquaints us with human sentiments or human actions; we place it with the fairest and the noblest progeny which judgment propagates by conjunction with learning, but *Othello* is the vigorous and vivacious offspring of observation impregnated by genius.

* * *

From Notes on *Othello*

Wherein of antres vast and deserts idle, / Rough quarries, rocks and hills whose heads touch heaven [1.3.139–40; Johnson quotes approvingly and expands on William Warburton, whose 1747 edition dismisses Rymer's ridicule of this passage as based on ignorance of "history"—that is, of the "fashion then," in Shakespeare's time, for exotic details about newly discovered lands].

Whoever ridicules this account of the progress of love shows his ignorance not only of history but of nature and manners. It is no wonder that in any age or in any nation a lady—recluse, timorous and delicate—should desire to hear of events and scenes which she could never see and should admire the man who had endured dangers and performed actions which, however great, were yet magnified by her timidity.

They're close dilations, working from the heart / That passion cannot rule [3.3.126–27].

The old copies give "dilations," except that the earlier quarto has "denotements," which was the author's first expression, afterwards changed by him, not to "dilations," but to "delations"; to *occult* and *secret accusations*, "working" involuntarily "from the heart," which,

---

2. *Merely positive:* conventional; "settled by arbitrary appointment" in Johnson's *Dictionary*.
3. The pen name of François-Marie Arouet (1694–1778), the eminent French philosopher who admired Shakespeare but believed him lacking in the classical artistry of the great French tragedians of the seventeenth century.
4. Joseph Addison (1672–1719) was a great influence on early eighteenth-century taste through his periodical *The Spectator. Cato,* his admired classical drama, was written for production in 1713.

though resolved to conceal the fault, "cannot rule" its "passion" of resentment.

She did deceive her father, marrying you, / And when she seemed to shake, and fear your looks, / She loved them most [3.3.208–10].

This and the following argument of Iago ought to be deeply impressed on every reader. Deceit and falsehood, whatever conveniences they may for a time promise or produce, are in the sum of life obstacles to happiness. Those who profit by the cheat distrust the deceiver, and the act by which kindness is sought puts an end to confidence.

The same objection may be made with a lower degree of strength against the imprudent generosity of disproportionate marriages. When the first heat of passion is over, it is easily succeeded by suspicion that the same violence of inclination which caused one irregularity may stimulate to another; and those who have shown that their passions are too powerful for their prudence will, with very slight appearances against them, be censured as not very likely to restrain them by virtue.

Let him command / And to obey shall be in me remorse, / What bloody business ever [3.3.468–70].

Iago devotes himself to "wrong'd Othello," and says, "Let him command whatever bloody business," and in me it shall be an act not of cruelty but "of tenderness to obey him"; not of malice to others, but of "tenderness" for him. If this sense be thought too violent, I see nothing better than to follow Mr. Pope's reading ["*Not* to obey"] as it is improved by Mr. Theobald ["*Nor* to obey"].

'Tis not a year or two shows us a man [3.4.100].

From this line it may be conjectured that the author intended the action of this play to be considered as longer than is marked by any note of time. Since their arrival at Cyprus, to which they were hurried on their wedding night, the fable seems to have been in one continual progress, nor can I see any vacuity into which a "year or two," or even a month or two, could be put. On the night of Othello's arrival a feast was proclaimed; at that feast Cassio was degraded and immediately applies to Desdemona to get him restored. Iago indeed advises Othello to hold him off a while, but there is no reason to think that he had been held off long. A little longer interval would increase the probability of the story, though it might violate the rules of the drama.

Nature would not / invest herself in such shadowing passion / without some instruction [4.1.39–41].

There has always prevailed in the world an opinion that when any great calamity happens at a distance notice is given of it to the suf-

ferer by some dejection or perturbation of mind, of which he discovers no external cause. This is ascribed to that general
communication of one part of the universe with another which is
called sympathy and antipathy; or to the secret monition, "instruction," and influence of a Superior Being, which superintends the
order of nature and of life. Othello says, "Nature could not invest
herself in such shadowing passion, without *instruction*. It is not
words that shake me thus." This passion, which spreads its clouds
over me, is the effect of some agency more than the operation of
words; it is one of those notices which men have of unseen calamities.

It is the cause, it is the cause, my soul. / Let me not name it to you,
you chaste stars. / It is the cause [5.2.1–3].

The abruptness of this soliloquy makes it obscure. The meaning,
I think, is this. "I am here," says Othello in his mind, "overwhelmed
with horror. What is the reason of this perturbation? Is it want of
resolution to do justice? Is it the dread of shedding blood? No; it is
not the action that shocks me, but it is the cause, *it is the cause, my
soul; let me not name it to you, ye chaste stars! it is the cause.*"

This sorrow's heavenly: / It strikes where it doth love [5.2.21–22].

This tenderness, with which I lament the punishment which justice compels me to inflict, is a holy passion.

I wish these two lines could be honestly ejected. It is the fate of
Shakespeare to counteract his own pathos.

O perjured woman! thou dost stone my heart, / And makes me call what
I intend to do / A murder, which I thought a sacrifice [5.2.64–66].

This line is difficult. "Thou hast hardened my heart and makest
me" kill thee with the rage of a "murderer," when "I thought to have
sacrificed thee" to justice with the calmness of a priest striking a
victim.

It must not be omitted that one of the elder quartos reads, "thou
dost stone *thy* heart," which I suspect to be genuine. The meaning
then will be, "thou forcest me" to dismiss thee from the world in the
state of the "murdered" without preparation for death, "when I
intended" that thy punishment should have been "a sacrifice" aton-
ing for thy crime.

I am glad that I have ended my revisal of this dreadful scene. It is
not to be endured.

That she with Cassio hath the act of shame / A thousand times
committed [5.2.217–18].

This is another passage which seems to suppose a longer space
comprised in the action of this play than the scenes include.

Final summary comment:

The beauties of this play impress themselves so strongly upon the attention of the reader that they can draw no aid from critical illustration. The fiery openness of Othello, magnanimous, artless, and credulous, boundless in his confidence, ardent in his affection, inflexible in his resolution, and obdurate in his revenge; the cool malignity of Iago, silent in his resentment, subtle in his designs, and studious at once of his interest and his vengeance; the soft simplicity of Desdemona, confident of merit and conscious of innocence, her artless perseverance in her suit, and her slowness to suspect that she can be suspected are such proofs of Shakespeare's skill in human nature as, I suppose, it is vain to seek in any modern writer. The gradual progress which Iago makes in the Moor's conviction and the circumstances which he employs to inflame him are so artfully natural that, though it will perhaps not be said of him as he says of himself that he is "a man not easily jealous," yet we cannot but pity him when at last we find him "perplexed in the extreme."

There is always danger lest wickedness conjoined with abilities should steal upon esteem, though it misses of approbation; but the character of Iago is so conducted that he is from the first scene to the last hated and despised.

Even the inferior characters of this play would be very conspicuous in any other piece, not only for their justness but their strength. Cassio is brave, benevolent, and honest, ruined only by his want of stubbornness to resist an insidious invitation. Roderigo's suspicious credulity and impatient submission to the cheats which he sees practiced upon him and which by persuasion he suffers to be repeated exhibit a strong picture of a weak mind betrayed by unlawful desires to a false friend; and the virtue of Emilia is such as we often find worn loosely but not cast off, easy to commit small crimes but quickened and alarmed at atrocious villainies.

The scenes from the beginning to the end are busy, varied by happy interchanges, and regularly promoting the progression of the story; and the narrative in the end, though it tells but what is known already, yet is necessary to produce the death of Othello.

Had the scene opened in Cyprus and the preceding incidents been occasionally related, there had been little wanting to a drama of the most exact and scrupulous regularity.

CHARLES LAMB (1775–1834)

[Othello's Color: Theatrical versus Literary Representation]†

* * *

Lear is essentially impossible to be represented on a stage. But how many dramatic personages are there in Shakespeare which, though more tractable and feasible (if I may so speak) than Lear, yet from some circumstance, some adjunct to their character, are improper to be shown to our bodily eye. Othello, for instance. Nothing can be more soothing, more flattering to the nobler parts of our nature, than to read of a young Venetian lady of highest extraction, through the force of love and from a sense of merit in him whom she loved, laying aside every consideration of kindred and country and color, and wedding with a *coal-black Moor* (for such he is represented, in the imperfect state of knowledge respecting foreign countries in those days, compared with our own, or in compliance with popular notions, though the Moors are now well enough known to be by many shades less unworthy of a white woman's fancy). It is the perfect triumph of virtue over accidents, of the imagination over the senses. She sees Othello's color in his mind. But upon the stage, when the imagination is no longer the ruling faculty, but we are left to our poor unassisted senses, I appeal to everyone that has seen Othello played whether he did not, on the contrary, sink Othello's mind in his color; and whether he did not find something extremely revolting in the courtship and wedded caresses of Othello and Desdemona; and whether the actual sight of the thing did not over-weigh all that beautiful compromise which we make in reading. And the reason it should do so is obvious, because there is just so much reality presented to our senses as to give a perception of disagreement, with not enough of belief in the internal motives—all that which is unseen—to overpower and reconcile the first and obvious prejudices.[1] What we see upon a stage is body and bodily action; what we

† From "On the Tragedies of Shakespeare, Considered with Reference to Their Fitness for Stage Representation" (1811). Spelling and puncutation have been modernized. For information about Lamb, his criticism, and its textual sources, see section 7 of the bibliography, p. 395.

1. The error of supposing that because Othello's color does not offend us in the reading it should also not offend us in the seeing is just such a fallacy as supposing that an Adam and Eve in a picture shall affect us just as they do in the poem. But in the poem we for a while have paradisiacal senses given us, which vanish when we see a man and his wife without clothes in the picture. The painters themselves feel this, as is apparent by the awkward shifts they have recourse to, to make them look not quite naked; by a sort of prophetic anachronism antedating the invention of fig leaves. So in the reading of the

are conscious of in reading is almost exclusively the mind and its movements; and this I think may sufficiently account for the very different sort of delight with which the same play so often affects us in the reading and the seeing.

*　*　*

WILLIAM HAZLITT (1778–1830)

[Iago, Heroic Tragedy, and Othello]†

From "On Mr. Kean's Iago" and "On Mr. Kean's Iago (Concluded)"

* * * The character of Iago, in fact, belongs to a class of characters common to Shakespeare, and at the same time peculiar to him, namely, that of great intellectual activity, accompanied with a total want of moral principle, and therefore displaying itself at the constant expense of others, making use of reason as a pander to will— employing its ingenuity and its resources to palliate its own crimes, and aggravate the faults of others, and seeking to confound the practical distinctions of right and wrong, by referring them to some overstrained standard of speculative refinement. Some persons, more nice than wise, have thought the whole of the character of Iago unnatural. Shakespeare, who was quite as good a philosopher as he was a poet, thought otherwise. He knew that the love of power, which is another name for the love of mischief, was natural to man. He would know this as well or better than if it had been demonstrated to him by a logical diagram, merely from seeing children paddle in the dirt, or kill flies for sport.[1] We might ask those who think the character of Iago not natural why they go to see it performed, but from the interest it excites, the sharper edge which it sets on their curiosity and imagination. Why do we go to see tragedies in general?

---

play, we see with Desdemona's eyes; in the seeing of it, we are forced to look with our own.

† The first excerpt is based on two theatrical reviews published in 1814; the second is from a book published in 1817. Spelling and punctuation have been modernized. Most of the quotations from *Othello* have been modified to conform with this Norton Critical Edition. Some of Hazlitt's quotations from memory are left uncorrected, but they include a reference to the act, scene, and line numbers printed above. All notes are the editor's, unless otherwise specified. For information about Hazlitt, his criticism, and its textual sources, see section 8 of the bibliography, p. 395.

1. An echo of Gloucester in *King Lear* 4.1.37–38: "As flies to wanton boys are we to the gods; / They kill us for their sport."

Why do we always read the accounts in the newspapers of dreadful fires and shocking murders, but for the same reason? Why do so many frequent executions and trials, or why do the lower classes almost universally take delight in barbarous sports and cruelty to animals, but because there is a natural tendency in the mind to strong excitement, a desire to have its faculties roused and stimulated to the utmost? Whenever this principle is not under the restraint of humanity or the sense of moral obligation, there are no excesses to which it will not of itself give rise, without the assistance of any other motive, either of passion or self-interest. Iago is only an extreme instance of the kind; that is, of diseased intellectual activity, with an almost perfect indifference to moral good or evil, or rather with a preference of the latter, because it falls more in with his favorite propensity, gives greater zest to his thoughts and scope to his actions. Be it observed, too (for the sake of those who are for squaring all human actions by the maxims of Rochefoucault[2]), that he is quite or nearly as indifferent to his own fate as to that of others; that he runs all risks for a trifling and doubtful advantage, and is himself the dupe and victim of his ruling passion—an incorrigible love of mischief, an insatiable craving after action of the most difficult and dangerous kind. Our ancient is a philosopher, who fancies that a lie that kills has more point in it than an alliteration or an antithesis; who thinks a fatal experiment on the peace of a family a better thing than watching the palpitations in the heart of a flea in an air-pump; who plots the ruin of his friends as an exercise for his understanding, and stabs men in the dark to prevent *ennui*. * * *

                    ☆   ☆   ☆

The general groundwork of the character of Iago as it appears to us is not absolute malignity but a want of moral principle, or an indifference to the real consequences of the actions which the meddling perversity of his disposition and love of immediate excitement lead him to commit. He is an amateur of tragedy in real life, and instead of exercising his ingenuity on imaginary characters or forgotten incidents, he takes the bolder and more desperate course of getting up his plot at home, casts the principal parts among his nearest friends and connections, and rehearses it in downright earnest, with steady nerves and unabated resolution. The character is a

2. La Rochefoucauld (1613–1680), the French writer and moralist, was known for his *Maximes et Réflexions Morales*, the unillusioned tone of which is fairly represented by the one Jonathan Swift used as the starting point for his "Verses on the Death of Dr. Swift": "In the misfortunes of our best friends, we find something not altogether displeasing." Hazlitt believed that the maxims "contain a good deal of truth" in acknowledging "the *mixed* nature of motives," but then falsely "argue as if they were *simple*, that is, had but one principle, and that principle the worst"; and that Shakespeare's "The web of our life is of a mingled yarn" offers a "better account of the matter." See "On Rochefoucault's Maxims" in Howe, 20: 36–41, 36–37.

complete abstraction of the intellectual from the moral being; or, in other words, consists in an absorption of every common feeling in the virulence of his understanding, the deliberate willfulness of his purposes, and in his restless untamable love of mischievous contrivance. * * *

*   *   *

* * * One of his most characteristic speeches is that immediately after the marriage of Othello: [quotes 1.1.63–70: "What a full fortune . . . lose some color"].

The pertinacious logical following up of his favorite principle in this passage is admirable. In the next, his imagination runs riot in the mischief he is plotting and breaks out into the wildness and impetuosity of real enthusiasm: [quotes 1.1.71–74: "Here is her father's house. . . . populous cities"].

* * * One of his most frequent topics, on which he is rich indeed and in descanting on which his spleen serves him for a muse, is the disproportionate match between Desdemona and the Moor. This is brought forward in the first scene and is never lost sight of afterwards [quotes 1.1.79–89: "What is the reason . . . Arise, I say!" and adds "And so on to the end of the passage"].

Now all this goes on springs well oiled. Mr. Kean's mode of giving the passage had the tightness of a drumhead and was muffled (perhaps purposely so) into the bargain.

This is a clue to the character of the lady which Iago is not at all ready to part with. He recurs to it again in the second act when, in answer to his insinuations against Desdemona, Roderigo says, "I cannot believe that in her; she's full of most blessed condition." IAGO: "Blessed fig's-end! The wine she drinks is made of grapes. If she had been blessed, she would never have loved the Moor" [2.1.245–49].

And again with still more effect and spirit afterwards, when he takes advantage of this very suggestion arising in Othello's own breast: [quotes 3.3.229–35: "And yet how nature . . . thoughts unnatural"]. This is probing to the quick. "Our Ancient" here turns the character of poor Desdemona, as it were, inside out. It is certain that nothing but the genius of Shakespeare could have preserved the entire interest and delicacy of the part and have even drawn an additional elegance and dignity from the peculiar circumstances in which she is placed. The character has always had the greatest charm for minds of the finest sensibility.

For our own part, we are a little of Iago's council in this matter; and all circumstances considered and Platonics out of the question, if we were to cast the complexion of Desdemona physiognomically, we should say that she had a very fair skin and very light auburn hair, inclining to yellow! We at the same time give her infinite credit for purity and delicacy of sentiment; but it so happens that purity and grossness "nearly are allied / And thin partitions do their bounds divide."[3] Yet the reverse does not hold; so uncertain and undefinable a thing is morality. It is no wonder that Iago had some contempt for it, "who knew all qualities of human dealings with a learned spirit" [cf. 3.3.261].[4] There is considerable gaiety and ease in his dialogue with Emilia and Desdemona on their landing. It is then holiday time with him, but yet the general satire will be acknowledged (at least by one half of our readers) to be biting enough, and his idea of his own character is finely expressed in what he says to Desdemona when she asks him how he would praise her—"O, gentle lady, do not put me to't, / For I am nothing if not critical" [2.1.118–19]. * * *

The habitual licentiousness of Iago's conversation is not to be traced to the pleasure he takes in gross or lascivious images, but to a desire of finding out the worst side of everything and of proving himself an overmatch for appearances. He has none of "the milk of human kindness" in his composition. His imagination refuses everything that has not a strong infusion of the most unpalatable ingredients, and his moral constitution digests only poisons. Virtue or goodness or whatever has the least "relish of salvation in it"[5] is, to his depraved appetite, sickly and insipid, and he even resents the good opinion entertained of his own integrity, as if it were an affront cast on the masculine sense and spirit of his character. Thus at the meeting between Othello and Desdemona he exclaims, "O, you are well tuned now; but I'll set down the pegs that make this music, / As honest as I am" [2.1.197–99]—deriving an indirect triumph over the want of penetration in others from the consciousness of his own villainy.

---

3. Hazlitt echoes John Dryden's *Absalom and Achitophel* (1681): "Great wits are sure to madness near allied, / And thin partitions do their bounds divide" (163–64).

4. If Desdemona really "saw her husband's visage in his mind," or fell in love with the abstract idea of "his virtues and his valiant parts" [cf. 1.3.250–51], she was the only woman on record, either before or since, who ever did so. Shakespeare's want of penetration in supposing that those are the sort of things that gain the affections might perhaps have drawn a smile from the ladies, if honest Iago had not checked it by suggesting a different explanation. It should seem by this as if the rankness and gross impropriety of the personal connection, the difference in age, features, color, constitution, instead of being the obstacle, had been the motive of the refinement of her choice and had, by beginning at the wrong end, subdued her to the amiable qualities of her lord. Iago is indeed a most learned and irrefragable doctor on the subject of love, which he defines to be "merely a lust of the blood and a permission of the will" [1.3.332–33]. The idea that love has its source in moral or intellectual excellence, in good nature or good sense, or has any connection with sentiment or refinement of any kind, is one of those preposterous and willful errors which ought to be extirpated for the sake of those few persons who alone are likely to suffer by it, whose romantic generosity and delicacy ought not to be sacrificed to the baseness of their nature, but who, treading secure in the flowery path marked out for them by poets and moralists, the licensed artificers of fraud and lies, are dashed in pieces down the precipice and perish without help. [Hazlitt's note]

5. Hamlet, discovering Claudius at prayer, decides to defer murdering him until a time when he is "about some act / That has no relish of salvation in't" (*Hamlet* 3.3.91–92).

*   *   *

If he is bad enough when he has business on his hands, he is still worse when his purposes are suspended, and he has only to reflect on the misery he has occasioned. His indifference when Othello falls in a trance is perfectly diabolical but perfectly in character.

> IAGO: How is it, general? Have you not hurt your head?
> OTHELLO: Dost thou mock me?
> IAGO: I mock you not, by heaven.
>   [4.1.59–60]

The callous levity which Mr. Kean seems to consider as belonging to the character in general is proper here, because Iago has no feelings connected with humanity; but he has other feelings and other passions of his own which are not to be trifled with.

We do not, however, approve of Mr. Kean's pointing to the dead bodies after the catastrophe. It is not in the character of the part, which consists in the love of mischief, not as an end but as a means, and when that end is attained, though he may feel no remorse, he would feel no triumph. Besides, it is not the text of Shakespeare. Iago does not point to the bed, but Lodovico bids him look at it: "Look on the tragic loading of this bed" &c [5.2.368].

From *The Characters of Shakespeare's Plays*

It has been said that tragedy purifies the affections by terror and pity. That is, it substitutes imaginary sympathy for mere selfishness. It gives us a high and permanent interest, beyond ourselves, in humanity as such. It raises the great, the remote, and the possible to an equality with the real, the little, and the near. It makes man a partaker with his kind. It subdues and softens the stubbornness of his will. It teaches him that there are and have been others like himself, by showing him as in a glass what they have felt, thought, and done. It opens the chambers of the human heart. It leaves nothing indifferent to us that can affect our common nature. It excites our sensibility by exhibiting the passions wound up to the utmost pitch by the power of imagination or the temptation of circumstances, and corrects their fatal excesses in ourselves by pointing to the greater extent of sufferings and of crimes to which they have led others. Tragedy creates a balance of the affections. It makes us thoughtful spectators in the lists of life. It is the refiner of the species, a discipline of humanity. * * * *Othello* furnishes an illustration of these remarks. It excites our sympathy in an extraordinary degree. The moral it conveys has a closer application to the concerns of human life than that of almost any other of Shakespeare's plays. "It comes directly home to the bosoms and business of men."[6] * * *

The picturesque contrasts of character in this play are almost as remarkable as the depth of the passion. The Moor Othello, the gentle Desdemona, the villain Iago, the good-natured Cassio, the fool Roderigo, present a range and variety of character as striking and palpable as that produced by the opposition of costume in a picture. Their distinguishing qualities stand out to the mind's eye, so that even when we are not thinking of their actions or sentiments, the idea of their persons is still as present to us as ever. These characters and the images they stamp upon the mind are the farthest asunder possible—the distance between them is immense; yet the compass of knowledge and invention which the poet has shown in embodying these extreme creations of his genius is only greater than the truth and felicity with which he has identified each character with itself, or blended their different qualities together in the same story. What a contrast the character of Othello forms to that of Iago! At the same time, the force of conception with which these two figures are opposed to each other is rendered still more intense by the complete consistency with which the traits of each character are brought out in a state of the highest finishing. The making one black and the other white, the one unprincipled, the other unfortunate in the extreme, would have answered the common purposes of effect and satisfied the ambition of an ordinary painter of character. Shakespeare has labored the finer shades of difference in both with as much care and skill as if he had to depend on the execution alone for the success of his design. * * *

* * * [I]n Othello, the doubtful conflict between contrary passions, though dreadful, continues only for a short time, and the chief interest is excited by the alternate ascendancy of different passions, by the entire and unforeseen change from the fondest love and most unbounded confidence to the tortures of jealousy and the madness of hatred. The revenge of Othello, after it has once taken thorough possession of his mind, never quits it, but grows stronger and stronger at every moment of its delay. The nature of the Moor is noble, confiding, tender, and generous; but his blood is of the most inflammable kind; and being once roused by a sense of his wrongs, he is stopped by no considerations of remorse or pity till he has given a loose to all the dictates of his rage and his despair. It is in working his noble nature up to this extremity through rapid but gradual transitions, in raising passion to its height from the smallest beginnings

6. An echo of Sir Francis Bacon, who, dedicating his *Essays* to Buckingham in 1625, reflects on their popularity in earlier editions: "it seems they came near to men's business and bosoms."

and in spite of all obstacles, in painting the expiring conflict between love and hatred, tenderness and resentment, jealousy and remorse, in unfolding the strength and the weakness of our nature, in uniting sublimity of thought with the anguish of the keenest woe, in putting in motion the various impulses that agitate this our mortal being, and at last blending them in that noble tide of deep and sustained passion, impetuous but majestic, that "flows on to the Propontic and knows no ebb" [cf. 3.3.453–56], that Shakespeare has shown the mastery of his genius and of his power over the human heart. The third act of *Othello* is his finest display, not of knowledge or passion separately, but of the two combined, of the knowledge of character with the expression of passion, of consummate art in the keeping up of appearances with the profound workings of nature and the convulsive movements of uncontrollable agony, of the power of inflicting torture and of suffering it. Not only is the tumult of passion in Othello's mind heaved up from the very bottom of the soul, but every the slightest undulation of feeling is seen on the surface as it arises from the impulses of imagination or the malicious suggestions of Iago. The progressive preparation for the catastrophe is wonderfully managed from the Moor's first gallant recital of the story of his love, of "the spells and witchcraft he has used" [cf. 1.3.61, 64, and 168], from his unlooked-for and romantic success, the fond satisfaction with which he dotes on his own happiness, the unreserved tenderness of Desdemona and her innocent importunities in favor of Cassio, irritating the suspicions instilled into her husband's mind by the perfidy of Iago and rankling there to poison, till he loses all command of himself, and his rage can only be appeased by blood. * * *

* * * In his conversations with Desdemona, the persuasion of her guilt and the immediate proofs of her duplicity seem to irritate his resentment and aversion to her; but in the scene immediately preceding her death, the recollection of his love returns upon him in all its tenderness and force; and after her death, he all at once forgets his wrongs in the sudden and irreparable sense of his loss: "My wife, my wife! what wife? I have no wife. / O insupportable! O heavy hour!" [5.2.99–100].

This happens before he is assured of her innocence; but afterwards his remorse is as dreadful as his revenge had been, and yields only to fixed and death-like despair. His farewell speech before he kills himself, in which he conveys his reasons to the senate for the murder of his wife, is equal to the first speech in which he gave them an account of his courtship of her and "his whole course of love" [cf. 1.3.91]. Such an ending was alone worthy of such a commencement.

If anything could add to the force of our sympathy with Othello or compassion for his fate, it would be the frankness and generosity of his nature, which so little deserve it. * * *

*   *   *

The character of Desdemona is inimitable both in itself and as it appears in contrast with Othello's groundless jealousy and with the foul conspiracy of which she is the innocent victim. Her beauty and external graces are only indirectly glanced at: we see "her visage in her mind" [cf. 1.3.250]; her character everywhere predominates over her person: "A maiden never bold; / Of spirit so still and quiet that her motion / Blushed at herself" [1.3.94–96]. * * *

In general, as is the case with most of Shakespeare's females, we lose sight of her personal charms in her attachment and devotedness to her husband.

> My heart's subdued
> Even to the very quality of my lord. . . .
> And to his honors and his valiant parts
> Did I my soul and fortunes consecrate. [1.3.248–49 and 251–52]

The lady protests so much herself, and she is as good as her word. The truth of conception, with which timidity and boldness are united in the same character, is marvelous. The extravagance of her resolutions, the pertinacity of her affections, may be said to arise out of the gentleness of her nature. They imply an unreserved reliance on the purity of her own intentions, an entire surrender of her fears to her love, a knitting of herself (heart and soul) to the fate of another. Bating the commencement of her passion, which is a little fantastical and headstrong (though even that may perhaps be consistently accounted for from her inability to resist a rising inclination[7]), her whole character consists in having no will of her own, no prompter but her obedience. Her romantic turn is only a consequence of the domestic and practical part of her disposition; and instead of following Othello to the wars, she would gladly have "remained at home a moth of peace" [cf. 1.3.253–54], if her husband could have stayed with her. Her resignation and angelic sweetness of temper do not desert her at the last. * * *

*   *   *

The character of Iago is one of the supererogations of Shakespeare's genius. * * * The part indeed would hardly be tolerated, even as a foil to the virtue and generosity of the other characters in the play, but for its indefatigable industry and inexhaustible resources, which divert the attention of the spectator (as well as his own) from the end he has in view to the means by which it must be accomplished. Edmund the bastard in *Lear* is something of the same char-

7. Iago. "Ay, too gentle." Othello. "Nay, that's certain." [4.1.189–90; Hazlitt's note]

acter placed in less prominent circumstances. Zanga is a vulgar caricature of it.[8]

SAMUEL TAYLOR COLERIDGE (1772–1834)

[Comments on *Othello*]†

On Iago

* * * [Shakespeare] had read nature too heedfully not to know that courage, intellect, and strength of character are the most impressive forms of power, and that to power in itself, without reference to any moral end, an inevitable admiration and complacency appertains * * * . But in the exhibition of such a character it was of the highest importance to prevent the guilt from passing into utter monstrosity * * * . For such are the appointed relations of intellectual power to truth and of truth to goodness that it becomes both morally and poetically unsafe to present what is admirable—what our nature compels us to admire—in the mind and what is most detestable in the heart as coexisting in the same individual without any apparent connection or any modification of the one by the other. That Shakespeare has in one instance, that of Iago, approached to this, and that he has done it successfully, is perhaps the most astonishing proof of his genius and the opulence of its resources. * * *

* * *

* * * In what follows [after Iago's description of Cassio as "A fellow almost damned in a fair wife" (1.1.18)], let the reader feel how—by and through the glass of two passions, disappointed vanity and envy—the very vices of which he is complaining are made to act upon him as if they were so many excellencies, and the more appropriately because cunning is always admired and wished for by minds conscious of inward weakness. But they act only by half, like music on an inattentive auditor, swelling the thoughts which prevent him from listening to it.

8. Zanga is the villain in *The Revenge,* a tragedy by Edward Young (1683–1765), first performed in 1721 and still popular in the early nineteenth century. Hazlitt describes it as "an obvious transposition of *Othello:* the two principal characters are the same, only their colors are reversed. The giving the dark, treacherous, fierce, and remorseless character to the Moor is an alteration which is more in conformity to our prejudices as well as to historical truth" (Howe, 5: 227).

† Most of the passages here come from the notes of a lecture Coleridge gave on *Othello* in 1819, regrouped under topics invented for this edition. Spelling and punctuation have been modernized, and the quotations from *Othello* modified to conform with this Norton Critical Edition. All notes are the editor's. For information about Coleridge, his criticism, and its textual sources, see section 9 of the bibliography, p. 396.

*   *   *

This speech ["Virtue? a fig!" etc. (1.3.317 ff.)] comprises the passionless character of Iago. It is all will in intellect, and therefore he is here a bold partisan of a truth, but yet of a truth converted into a falsehood by the absence of all the necessary modifications caused by the frail nature of man. * * * Iago's soliloquy [at the end of act 1]—the motive-hunting of a motiveless malignity—how awful it is! Yea, whilst he is still allowed to bear the divine image, it is too fiendish for his own steady view—for the lonely gaze of a being next to devil—and only not quite devil—and yet a character which Shakespeare has attempted and executed without disgust and without scandal!

On Othello

Roderigo turns off to Othello, and here [in 1.1.63–64: "What a full fortune does the thick-lips owe / If he can carry't thus!"] comes one, if not the only, seeming justification of our blackamoor or negro Othello. Even if we suppose this an uninterrupted tradition of the theater, and that Shakespeare himself—from want of scenes and the experience that nothing could be made too marked for the senses of his audience—had sanctioned it, would this prove aught concerning his intention as a poet for all ages?[1] Can we imagine him so utterly ignorant as to make a barbarous negro plead royal birth—at a time, too, when negroes were not known except as slaves? As for Iago's language to Brabantio, it implies merely that Othello was a Moor—that is, black. Though I think the rivalry of Roderigo sufficient to account for his willful confusion of Moor and Negro, yet even if compelled to give this up, I should think it only adapted for the acting of the day and should complain of an enormity built on a single word in direct contradiction to Iago's "Barbary horse" [1.1.108]. Besides, if we could in good earnest believe Shakespeare ignorant of the distinction, still why should we adopt one disagreeable possibility instead of a ten times greater and more pleasing probability? It is a common error to mistake the epithets applied by the *dramatis personae* to each other as truly descriptive of what the audiences ought to see or know. No doubt Desdemona saw Othello's visage in his mind, yet as we are constituted, and most surely as an English audience was disposed in the beginning of the seventeenth century, it would be something monstrous to conceive this beautiful Venetian girl falling in love with a veritable negro. It would argue a disproportionateness, a want of balance, in Desdemona, which Shakespeare does not appear to have in the least contemplated.

1. Coleridge is echoing Ben Jonson's commendatory verses at the beginning of the First Folio: "He was not of an age, but for all time!"

*   *   *

Observe in how many ways Othello is made first our acquaintance, then our friend, then the object of our anxiety [awaiting news during the storm in 2.1], before the deeper interest is to be approached.

*   *   *

Othello must not be conceived as a negro but a high and chivalrous Moorish chief. Shakespeare learned the spirit of the character from the Spanish poetry, which was prevalent in England in his time. Jealousy does not strike me as the point in his passion; I take it to be rather an agony that the creature, whom he had believed angelic, with whom he had garnered up his heart and whom he could not help still loving, should be proved impure and worthless. It was the struggle *not* to love her. It was a moral indignation and regret that virtue should so fall: "But yet the pity of it, Iago! O Iago, the pity of it, Iago!" [4.1.190–91]. In addition to this, his honor was concerned: Iago would not have succeeded but by hinting that his honor was compromised. There is no ferocity in Othello; his mind is majestic and composed. He deliberately determines to die, and speaks his last speech with a view of showing his attachment to the Venetian state, though it had superseded him.

*   *   *

Finally, let me repeat that Othello does not kill Desdemona in jealousy but in a conviction forced upon him by the almost super-human art of Iago—such a conviction as any man would and must have entertained who had believed Iago's honesty as Othello did. We, the audience, know that Iago is a villain from the beginning; but in considering the essence of the Shakespearean Othello, we must per-severingly place ourselves in his situation and under his circum-stances. Then we shall immediately feel the fundamental difference between the solemn agony of the noble Moor and the wretched fish-ing jealousies of Leontes and the morbid suspiciousness of Leonatus, who is in other respects a fine character.[2] Othello had no life but in Desdemona; the belief that she, his angel, had fallen from the heaven of her native innocence wrought a civil war in his heart. She is his counterpart, and like him is almost sanctified in our eyes by her absolute unsuspiciousness and holy entireness of love. As the curtain drops, which do we pity the most?

---

2. Leontes is the jealous husband in *The Winter's Tale* and Leonatus the jealous lover in *Cymbeline*.

On Desdemona

In Shakespeare's females the sweet yet dignified feeling of all that *continuates* society, as sense of ancestry, of sex, etc.—a purity unassailable by sophistry, because it does not rest on the analytic processes, but in feeling? Desdemona may be misinterpreted to the worst purposes—but in that same equipoise of the faculties during which the feelings *are* representative of all the past experience, not of the individual, but of all those by whom she has been educated, and of their predecessors *usque ad Evam* [as far back as Eve].

"Most women have no character at all," said Pope,[3] and meant it for satire. Shakespeare, who knew man and woman much better, saw that it, in fact, was the perfection of woman to be characterless. Everyone wishes a Desdemona or Ophelia for a wife—creatures who, though they may not always understand you, do always feel you, and feel with you.

On Textual Echoes and Interpretive Pleasure

[Quotes 1.3.290–92: "Look to her, Moor . . . My life upon / her faith!"] In real life, how do we look back to little speeches as presentimental of, or contrasted with, an affecting event! Even so Shakespeare, as secure of being read over and over, of becoming a family friend, provides this passage for his readers and leaves it to them.

On the Unities, Dr. Johnson, and Aesthetic Interest

Dr. Johnson has remarked that little or nothing is wanting to render *Othello* a regular tragedy but to have opened the play with the arrival of Othello in Cyprus and to have thrown the preceding act into the form of narration. Here then is the place to determine whether such a change would or would not be an improvement—nay (to throw down the gloves with a full challenge) whether the tragedy would or would not by such an arrangement become more regular—that is, more consonant with the rules dictated by universal reason on the true commonsense of mankind, in its application to the particular case. For in all acts of judgment it can never be too often recollected, and scarcely too often repeated, that rules are means to ends and, consequently, that the end must be determined

3. Alexander Pope's "Epistle II. To a Lady," published 1734, begins: "Nothing so true as what you once let fall, / 'Most Women have no Characters at all.' / Matter too soft a lasting stick to bear, / And best distinguish'd by black, brown, or fair."

and understood before it can be known what the rules are or ought to be. Now from a certain species of drama, proposing to itself the accomplishment of certain ends, * * * three rules have been abstracted. In other words, the means most conducive to the attainment of the proposed ends have been generalized and prescribed under the names of the three unities—the unity of time, the unity of place, and the unity of action—which last would, perhaps, have been as appropriately, as well as more intelligibly, entitled the unity of interest. With this last the present question has no immediate concern: in fact, its conjunction with the former two is a mere delusion of words. It is not properly a rule but in itself the great end not only of the drama but of the epic poem, the lyric ode, of all poetry—down to the candle-flame cone of an epigram—nay of poesy in general, as the proper generic term inclusive of all the fine arts as its species. But of the unities of time and place, which alone are entitled to the name of rules, the history of their origin will be their best criterion.

On Cassio, Unpossessive Affection, and Iago

[Quotes 2.1.60–65: "But, good lieutenant . . . tire the ingener."] Here is Cassio's warm-hearted yet perfectly disengaged praise of Desdemona and sympathy with the "most fortunately" wived Othello; and yet Cassio is an enthusiastic admirer, almost a worshipper, of Desdemona. O, that detestable code that excellence cannot be loved in any form that is female but it must needs be selfish! Observe Othello's "honest" and Cassio's "bold" Iago, and Cassio's full guileless-hearted wishes for the safety and love-raptures of Othello and "the divine Desdemona." And also note the exquisite circumstances of Cassio's kissing Iago's wife, as if it ought to be impossible that the dullest auditor should not feel Cassio's religious love of Desdemona's purity. Iago's answers are the sneers which a proud bad intellect feels towards woman and expresses to a wife. Surely it ought to be considered a very exalted compliment to women that all the sarcasms on them in Shakespeare are put in the mouths of villains.

A. C. BRADLEY (1851–1935)

["The Most Painfully Exciting and the Most Terrible" of Shakespeare's Tragedies]†

* * *

* * * Of all Shakespeare's tragedies * * * *Othello* is the most painfully exciting and the most terrible. From the moment when the temptation of the hero begins, the reader's heart and mind are held in a vice, experiencing the extremes of pity and fear, sympathy and repulsion, sickening hope and dreadful expectation. Evil is displayed before him, not indeed with the profusion found in *King Lear,* but forming, as it were, the soul of a single character, and united with an intellectual superiority so great that he watches its advance fascinated and appalled. He sees it, in itself almost irresistible, aided at every step by fortunate accidents and the innocent mistakes of its victims. He seems to breathe an atmosphere as fateful as that of *King Lear,* but more confined and oppressive, the darkness not of night but of a close-shut murderous room. His imagination is excited to intense activity, but it is the activity of concentration rather than dilation.

* * *

[Bradley offers four additional "distinguishing characteristics" to account for *Othello*'s uniquely "painful tension" beyond this "unusual" structure, "by which the conflict begins late, and advances without appreciable pause and with accelerating speed to the catastrophe."] In the second place, there is no subject more exciting than sexual jealousy rising to the pitch of passion; and there can hardly be any spectacle at once so engrossing and so painful as that of a great nature suffering the torment of this passion, and driven by it to a crime which is also a hideous blunder. Such a passion as ambition, however terrible its results, is not itself ignoble; if we separate it in thought from the conditions which make it guilty, it does not appear despicable; it is not a kind of suffering, its nature is active; and therefore we can watch its course without shrinking. But jealousy, and especially sexual jealousy, brings with it a sense of shame

† From *Shakespearean Tragedy: Lectures on "Hamlet," "Othello," "King Lear," "Macbeth,"* 1904 (3rd Ed.; New York: St. Martin's Press, 1992), 150–200. Reprinted with permission of Macmillan Publishers, Ltd. Bradley's quotations from *Othello* have been left unchanged but references to act, scene, and line numbers have been provided or altered to conform with this Norton Critical Edition. For information about Bradley and his criticism, see section 10 of the bibliography, p. 398.

and humiliation. For this reason it is generally hidden; if we perceive it we ourselves are ashamed and turn our eyes away; and when it is not hidden it commonly stirs contempt as well as pity. Nor is this all. Such jealousy as Othello's converts human nature into chaos, and liberates the beast in man; and it does this in relation to one of the most intense and also the most ideal of human feelings. What spectacle can be more painful than that of this feeling turned into a tortured mixture of longing and loathing, the 'golden purity' of passion split by poison into fragments, the animal in man forcing itself into his consciousness in naked grossness, and he writhing before it but powerless to deny it entrance, gasping inarticulate images of pollution, and finding relief only in a bestial thirst for blood? This is what we have to witness in one who was indeed 'great of heart' and no less pure and tender than he was great. And this, with what it leads to, the blow to Desdemona, and the scene where she is treated as the inmate of a brothel, a scene far more painful than the murder scene, is another cause of the special effect of this tragedy.[1]

(3) The mere mention of these scenes will remind us painfully of a third cause and perhaps it is the most potent of all. I mean the suffering of Desdemona. This is, unless I mistake, the most nearly intolerable spectacle that Shakespeare offers us. For one thing, it is *mere* suffering; and, *ceteris paribus* [everything else being equal], that is much worse to witness than suffering that issues in action. Desdemona is helplessly passive. She can do nothing whatever. She cannot retaliate even in speech; no, not even in silent feeling. And the chief reason of her helplessness only makes the sight of her suffering more exquisitely painful. She is helpless because her nature is infinitely sweet and her love absolute. I would not challenge Mr. Swinburne's statement that we *pity* Othello even more than Desdemona; but we watch Desdemona with more unmitigated distress.[2] We are never wholly uninfluenced by the feeling that Othello is a man contending with another man; but Desdemona's suffering is like that of the most loving of dumb creatures tortured without cause by the being he adores.

(4) Turning from the hero and heroine to the third principal character, we observe (what has often been pointed out) that the action and catastrophe of *Othello* depend largely on intrigue. * * * Iago's intrigue occupies a position in the drama for which no parallel can be found in the other tragedies * * * . Now in any novel or play, even

---

1. The whole force of the passages referred to can be felt only by a reader. The Othello of our stage can never be Shakespeare's Othello, any more than the Cleopatra of our stage can be his Cleopatra.
2. Algernon Charles Swinburne (1837–1901) wrote poetry, drama, and three books of Shakespeare criticism. Bradley cites him frequently, in this case *A Study of Shakespeare* (London: Chatto and Windus, 1880), 182: "when Coleridge asks 'which do we pity the most' at the fall of the curtain, we can surely answer, Othello." [Editor's note]

if the persons rouse little interest and are never in serious danger, a skilfully-worked intrigue will excite eager attention and suspense. And where, as in *Othello*, the persons inspire the keenest sympathy and antipathy, and life and death depend on the intrigue, it becomes the source of a tension in which pain almost overpowers pleasure. Nowhere else in Shakespeare do we hold our breath in such anxiety and for so long a time as in the later Acts of *Othello*.

(5) One result of the prominence of the element of intrigue is that *Othello* is less unlike a story of private life than any other of the great tragedies. And this impression is strengthened in further ways. In the other great tragedies the action is placed in a distant period, so that its general significance is perceived through a thin veil which separates the persons from ourselves and our own world. But *Othello* is a drama of modern life; when it first appeared it was a drama almost of contemporary life, for the date of the Turkish attack on Cyprus is 1570. The characters come close to us, and the application of the drama to ourselves (if the phrase may be pardoned) is more immediate than it can be in *Hamlet* or *Lear*. * * *

* * *

* * * [S]ome readers, while acknowledging, of course, the immense power of *Othello*, and even admitting that it is dramatically perhaps Shakespeare's greatest triumph, still regard it with a certain distaste * * * due chiefly to two causes. First, to many readers in our time, men as well as women, the subject of sexual jealousy, treated with Elizabethan fullness and frankness, is not merely painful but so repulsive that not even the intense tragic emotions which the story generates can overcome this repulsion. * * *

To some readers, again, parts of *Othello* appear shocking or even horrible. They think—if I may formulate their objection—that in those parts Shakespeare has sinned against the canons of art, by representing on the stage a violence or brutality the effect of which is unnecessarily painful and rather sensational than tragic. The passages which thus give offence are probably those already referred to,—that where Othello strikes Desdemona [4.1.234], that where he affects to treat her as an inmate of a house of ill-fame [4.2], and finally the scene of her death.

* * * The first, and least important, of the three passages—that of the blow—seems to me the most doubtful. I confess that, do what I will, I cannot reconcile myself with it. It seems certain that the blow is by no means a tap on the shoulder with a roll of paper, as some actors, feeling the repulsiveness of the passage, have made it. It must occur, too, on the open stage. And there is not, I think, a sufficiently overwhelming tragic feeling in the passage to make it bearable. But in the other two scenes the case is different. There, it

seems to me, if we fully imagine the inward tragedy in the souls of
the persons as we read, the more obvious and almost physical sensations of pain or horror do not appear in their own likeness, and
only serve to intensify the tragic feelings in which they are absorbed.
Whether this would be so in the murder-scene if Desdemona had to
be imagined as dragged about the open stage (as in some modern
performances) may be doubtful; but there is absolutely no warrant
in the text for imagining this, and it is also quite clear that the bed
where she is stifled was within the curtains,[3] and so, presumably, in
part, concealed.

* * *

* * * Othello's description of himself as

> one not easily jealous, but, being wrought,
> Perplexed in the extreme, [5.2.350–51]

is perfectly just. His tragedy lies in this—that his whole nature was
indisposed to jealousy, and yet was such that he was unusually open
to deception, and, if once wrought to passion, likely to act with little
reflection, with no delay, and in the most decisive manner conceiv-
able.

Let me first set aside a mistaken view. I do not mean the ridiculous
notion that Othello was jealous by temperament, but the idea, which
has some little plausibility, that the play is primarily a study of a
noble barbarian, who has become a Christian and has imbibed some
of the civilisation of his employers, but who retains beneath the surface the savage passions of his Moorish blood and also the suspiciousness regarding female chastity common among Oriental
peoples, and that the last three Acts depict the outburst of these
original feelings through the thin crust of Venetian culture. It would
take too long to discuss this idea,[4] and it would perhaps be useless
to do so, for all arguments against it must end in an appeal to the
reader's understanding of Shakespeare. If he thinks it is like Shakespeare to look at things in this manner; that he had a historical mind
and occupied himself with problems of 'Culturgeschichte' [cultural
history, anthropology]; that he laboured to make his Romans perfectly Roman, to give a correct view of the Britons in the days of
Lear or Cymbeline, to portray in Hamlet a stage of the moral consciousness not yet reached by the people around him, the reader will
also think this interpretation of *Othello* probable. To me it appears

---

3. The dead bodies are not carried out at the end, as they must have been if the bed had
   been on the main stage (for this had no front curtain). The curtains within which the bed
   stood were drawn together at the words, 'Let it be hid' [5.2.370].
4. The reader who is tempted by it should, however, first ask himself whether Othello does
   act like a barbarian, or like a man who, though wrought almost to madness, does 'all in
   honour' [5.2.300].

hopelessly un-Shakespearean. I could as easily believe that Chaucer meant the Wife of Bath for a study of the peculiarities of Somersetshire. I do not mean that Othello's race is a matter of no account. It has, as we shall presently see, its importance in the play. It makes a difference to our idea of him; it makes a difference to the action and catastrophe. But in regard to the essentials of his character it is not important; and if anyone had told Shakespeare that no Englishman would have acted like the Moor, and had congratulated him on the accuracy of his racial psychology, I am sure he would have laughed.

Othello is, in one sense of the word, by far the most romantic figure among Shakespeare's heroes; and he is so partly from the strange life of war and adventure which he has lived from childhood. He does not belong to our world, and he seems to enter it we know not whence—almost as if from wonderland. There is something mysterious in his descent from men of royal siege; in his wanderings in vast deserts and among marvellous peoples; in his tales of magic handkerchiefs and prophetic Sybils; in the sudden vague glimpses we get of numberless battles and sieges in which he has played the hero and has borne a charmed life; even in chance references to his baptism, his being sold to slavery, his sojourn in Aleppo.

And he is not merely a romantic figure; his own nature is romantic. * * * [Compared to Shakespeare's other tragic protagonists,] Othello is the greatest poet of them all. * * * And this imagination, we feel, has accompanied his whole life. He has watched with a poet's eye the Arabian trees dropping their med'cinable gum, and the Indian throwing away his chance-found pearl; and has gazed in a fascinated dream at the Pontic sea rushing, never to return, to the Propontic and the Hellespont; and has felt as no other man ever felt (for he speaks of it as none other ever did) the poetry of the pride, pomp, and circumstance of glorious war.

So he comes before us, dark and grand, with a light upon him from the sun where he was born. * * *

*   *   *

This character is so noble, Othello's feelings and actions follow so inevitably from it and from the forces brought to bear on it, and his sufferings are so heart-rending, that he stirs, I believe, in most readers a passion of mingled love and pity which they feel for no other hero in Shakespeare, and to which not even Swinburne can do more than justice. Yet there are some critics and not a few readers who cherish a grudge against him. * * * [E]ven when they admit that he was not of a jealous temper, they consider that he *was* 'easily jealous' * * * [—a "misconstruction of the text" derived from a "failure to realize certain essential facts," namely] that he is not Italian, nor even a European; that he is totally ignorant of the thoughts and the customary morality of Venetian women,[5] that he had himself seen in Desdemona's deception of her father how perfect an actress she could be. These suggestions are followed by a tentative but hideous and humiliating insinuation of what his honest and much-experienced friend fears may be the true explanation of Desdemona's rejection of acceptable suitors, and of her strange, and naturally temporary, preference for a black man. Here Iago goes too far. He sees something in Othello's face that frightens him, and he breaks off. Nor does this idea take any hold of Othello's mind. But it is not surprising that his utter powerlessness to repel it on the ground of knowledge of his wife, or even of that instinctive interpretation of character which is possible between persons of the same race,[6] should complete his misery, so that he feels he can bear no more, and abruptly dismisses his friend [3.3.242].

Now I repeat that *any* man situated as Othello was would have been disturbed by Iago's communication. * * *

The Othello of the Fourth Act is Othello in his fall. His fall is never complete, but he is much changed. * * *

But before the end there is again a change. The supposed death of Cassio [5.1] satiates the thirst for vengeance. The Othello who enters the bed-chamber with the words,

> It is the cause, it is the cause, my soul, [5.2.1]

is not the man of the Fourth Act. The deed he is bound to do is no murder, but a sacrifice. He is to save Desdemona from herself, not in hate but in honour; in honour, and also in love. His anger has passed; a boundless sorrow has taken its place; and

> this sorrow's heavenly:
> It strikes where it doth love. [5.2.21–22]

Even when, at the sight of her apparent obduracy, and at the hearing of words which by a crowning fatality can only reconvince him of her guilt, these feelings give way to others, it is to righteous indignation they give way, not to rage; and, terribly painful as this scene is, there is almost nothing here to diminish the admiration and love

5. To represent that Venetian women do not regard adultery so seriously as Othello does, and again that Othello would be wise to accept the situation like an Italian husband, is one of Iago's most artful and most maddening devices.

6. If the reader has ever chanced to see an African violently excited, he may have been startled to observe how completely at a loss he was to interpret those bodily expressions of passion which in a fellow-countryman he understands at once, and in a European foreigner with somewhat less certainty. The effect of difference in blood in increasing Othello's bewilderment regarding his wife is not sufficiently realised. The same effect has to be remembered in regard to Desdemona's mistakes in dealing with Othello in his anger.

which heighten pity.[7] And pity itself vanishes, and love and admiration alone remain, in the majestic dignity and sovereign ascendancy of the close. Chaos has come and gone; and the Othello of the Council-chamber and the quay of Cyprus has returned, or a greater and nobler Othello still. As he speaks those final words in which all the glory and agony of his life—long ago in India and Arabia and Aleppo, and afterwards in Venice, and now in Cyprus—seem to pass before us, like the pictures that flash before the eyes of a drowning man, a triumphant scorn for the fetters of the flesh and the littleness of all the lives that must survive him sweeps our grief away, and when he dies upon a kiss the most painful of all tragedies leaves us for the moment free from pain, and exulting in the power of 'love and man's unconquerable mind.'

* * *

The words just quoted come from Wordsworth's sonnet to Toussaint l'Ouverture.[8] Toussaint was a Negro; and there is a question, which, though of little consequence, is not without dramatic interest, whether Shakespeare imagined Othello as a Negro or a Moor. Now I will not say that Shakespeare imagined him as a Negro and not as a Moor, for that might imply that he distinguished Negroes and Moors precisely as we do, but what appears to me nearly certain is that he imagined Othello as a black man, and not as a light-brown one.

* * *

The horror of most American critics (Mr. Furness is a bright exception) at the idea of a black Othello is very amusing, and their arguments are highly instructive. But they were anticipated, I regret to say, by Coleridge, and we will hear him. [Quotes the last paragraph of the first Coleridge comment on Othello: "No doubt Desdemona . . . in the least contemplated," p. 231 above.] Could any argument be more self-destructive? It actually *did* appear to Brabantio 'something monstrous to conceive' his daughter falling in love with Othello,—so monstrous that he could account for her love only by drugs and foul charms. And the suggestion that such love would argue

7. See Note O. [In this note (402–03), Bradley accounts for his qualifying "almost," acknowledging that he is "shocked by the moral blindness or obliquity by which" Othello, in his response to Desdemona's dying words, "takes them only as a further sign of her worthlessness." Bradley's only argument to explain the effect away is, he admits, "unShakespearean." His final comment on the matter, in the last edition of *Shakespearean Tragedy*, is that "I wish to withdraw the whole Note."]
8. François Dominique Toussaint L'Ouverture (1744?–1803), a self-educated freed slave who organized Haitians to fight against European colonial power. [Editor's note]

'disproportionateness' is precisely the suggestion that Iago *did* make in Desdemona's case:

> Foh! one may smell in such a will most rank,
> Foul *disproportion*, thoughts unnatural. [3.3.234–35]

In fact he spoke of the marriage exactly as a filthy-minded cynic might now speak of the marriage of an English lady to a negro like Toussaint. Thus the argument of Coleridge and others points straight to the conclusion against which they argue.

But this is not all. The question whether to Shakespeare Othello was black or brown is not a mere question of isolated fact or historical curiosity; it concerns the character of Desdemona. Coleridge, and still more the American writers, regard her love, in effect, as Brabantio regarded it, and not as Shakespeare conceived it. They are simply blurring this glorious conception when they try to lessen the distance between her and Othello, and to smooth away the obstacle which his 'visage' offered to her romantic passion for a hero. Desdemona, the 'eternal womanly' in its most lovely and adorable form, simple and innocent as a child, ardent with the courage and idealism of a saint, radiant with that heavenly purity of heart which men worship the more because nature so rarely permits it to themselves, had no theories about universal brotherhood, and no phrases about 'one blood in all the nations of the earth' or 'barbarian, Scythian, bond and free'; but when her soul came in sight of the noblest soul on earth, she made nothing of the shrinking of her senses, but followed her soul until her senses took part with it, and 'loved with the love which was her doom'. It was not prudent. It even turned out tragically. She met in life with the reward of those who rise too far above our common level; and we continue to allot her the same reward when we consent to forgive her for loving a brown man, but find it monstrous that she should love a black one.[9]

9. I will not discuss the further question whether, granted that to Shakespeare Othello was a black, he should be represented as a black in our theatres now. I dare say not. We do not like the real Shakespeare. We like to have his language pruned and his conceptions flattened into something that suits our mouths and minds. And even if we were prepared to make an effort, still, as Lamb observes, to imagine is one thing and to see is another. Perhaps if we saw Othello coal-black with the bodily eye, the aversion of our blood, an aversion which comes as near to being merely physical as anything human can, would overpower our imagination and sink us below not Shakespeare only but the audiences of the seventeenth and eighteenth centuries.

As I have mentioned Lamb, I may observe that he differed from Coleridge as to Othello's colour, but, I am sorry to add, thought Desdemona to stand in need of excuse. 'This noble lady, with a singularity rather to be wondered at than imitated, had chosen for the object of her affections a Moor, a black. . . . Neither is Desdemona to be altogether condemned for the unsuitableness of the person whom she selected for her lover' (*Tales from Shakespeare*). Others, of course, have gone much further and have treated all the calamities of the tragedy as a sort of judgment on Desdemona's rashness, wilfulness and undutifulness. There is no arguing with opinions like this; but I cannot believe that even Lamb is true to Shakespeare in implying that Desdemona is in some degree to be condemned.

There is perhaps a certain excuse for our failure to rise to Shakespeare's meaning, and to realize how extraordinary and splendid a thing it was in a gentle Venetian girl to love Othello, and to assail fortune with such a 'downright violence and storm' [1.3.247] as is expected only in a hero. It is that when we first hear of her marriage we have not yet seen the Desdemona of the later Acts; and therefore we do not perceive how astonishing this love and boldness must have been in a maiden so quiet and submissive. And when we watch her in her suffering and death we are so penetrated by the sense of her heavenly sweetness and self-surrender that we almost forget that she had shown herself quite as exceptional in the active assertion of her own soul and will. She tends to become to us predominantly pathetic, the sweetest and most pathetic of Shakespeare's women, as innocent as Miranda and as loving as Viola, yet suffering more deeply than Cordelia or Imogen.[1] And she seems to lack that independence and strength of spirit which Cordelia and Imogen possess, and which in a manner raises them above suffering. She appears passive and defenceless, and can oppose to wrong nothing but the infinite endurance and forgiveness of a love that knows not how to resist or resent. * * *

Of course this later impression of Desdemona is perfectly right, but it must be carried back and united with the earlier before we can see what Shakespeare imagined. * * *

* * *

Iago stands supreme among Shakespeare's evil characters because the greatest intensity and subtlety of imagination have gone to his making, and because he illustrates in the most perfect combination the two facts concerning evil which seem to have impressed Shakespeare most. The first of these is the fact that perfectly sane people exist in whom fellow-feeling of any kind is so weak that an almost absolute egoism becomes possible to them, and with it those hard vices—such as ingratitude and cruelty—which to Shakespeare were far the worst. The second is that such evil is compatible, and even appears to ally itself easily, with exceptional powers of will and intellect. * * * How is it then that we can bear to contemplate him; nay, that, if we really imagine him, we feel admiration and some kind of sympathy? * * * [W]e are shown a thing absolutely evil, and—what is more dreadful still—this absolute evil united with supreme intellectual power. Why is the representation tolerable, and why do we not accuse its author either of untruth or of a desperate pessimism?

What is there to show that Shakespeare regarded her marriage differently from Imogen's [in *Cymbeline*]?
1. Heroines in *The Tempest, Twelfth Night, King Lear,* and *Cymbeline.* [Editor's note]

T. S. ELIOT

["The Last Great Speech of Othello"]†

* * *

* * * I have always felt that I have never read a more terrible exposure of human weakness—of universal human weakness—than the last great speech of Othello. I am ignorant whether any one else has ever adopted this view, and it may appear subjective and fantastic in the extreme. It is usually taken on its face value, as expressing the greatness in defeat of a noble but erring nature. [quotes 5.2.343–61: "Soft you . . . smote him—thus!"] What Othello seems to me to be doing in making this speech is *cheering himself up*. He is endeavouring to escape reality, he has ceased to think about Desdemona, and is thinking about himself. Humility is the most difficult of all virtues to achieve; nothing dies harder than the desire to think well of oneself. Othello succeeds in turning himself into a pathetic figure, by adopting an *aesthetic* rather than a moral attitude, dramatising himself against his environment. He takes in the spectator, but the human motive is primarily to take in himself. I do not believe that any writer has ever exposed this *bovarysme*,[1] the human will to see things as they are not, more clearly than Shakespeare.

KENNETH BURKE

Othello: An Essay to Illustrate a Method‡

OTHELLO.   Will you, I pray, demand that demi-devil
Why he hath thus ensnared my soul and body?
IAGO.   Demand me nothing: what you know, you know:
From this time forth I never will speak word.
LODOVICO.   What! not to pray?
GRATIANO.   Torments will ope your lips.
[5.2.306–10]

---

† From "Shakespeare and the Stoicism of Seneca" (1927), in *Selected Essays*, 3rd Ed. (London: Faber and Faber, 1951 [paperback, 1999], 130–31 (New York: Harcourt, Brace and Co., 1950), 110–11. Reprinted with the permission of Faber and Faber, Ltd. and Harcourt, Brace and Co.

1. Emma Bovary is the self-absorbed and self-deluding title character of Gustave Flaubert's novel *Madame Bovary*. [Editor's note]

‡ From *The Hudson Review* 4 (1951): 165–203. Reprinted with the permission of *The Hudson Review*. The author's quotations from *Othello* have been retained, but bracketed references are to this Norton Critical Edition. A footnote has been omitted.

I
Iago as Katharma

Othello: act v, scene ii. Desdemona, fated creature, marked for a tragic end by her very name (Desdemona: "moan-death") lies smothered. Othello, just after the words cited as our motto, has stabbed himself and fallen across her body. * * * Iago, "Spartan dog, / More fell than anguish, hunger, or the sea", is invited by Lodovico to "look on the tragic loading of this bed" [5.2.366–68]. *Exeunt omnes,* with Iago as prisoner, we being assured that they will see to "the censure of this hellish villain, / The time, the place, the torture" [5.2.373–74]. Thus like the tragic bed, himself bending beneath a load, he is universally hated for his ministrations. And in all fairness, as *advocatus diaboli* [devil's advocates] we would speak for him, in considering the cathartic nature of his role.

Reviewing, first, the definition of some Greek words central to the ritual of cure:

Katharma: that which is thrown away in cleansing; the offscourings, refuse, of a sacrifice; hence, worthless fellow. "It was the custom at Athens," lexicographers inform us, "to reserve certain worthless persons, who in case of plague, famine, or other visitations from heaven, were thrown into the sea," with an appropriate formula, "in the belief that they would cleanse away or wipe off the guilt of the nation." And these were *Katharmata.* Of the same root, of course, are our words *cathartic* and *catharsis,* terms originally related to both physical and ritual purgation.

A synonym for *katharma* was *pharmakos:* poisoner, sorcerer, magician; one who is sacrificed or executed as an atonement or purification for others; a scapegoat. It is related to *pharmakon:* drug, remedy, medicine, enchanted potion, philtre, charm, spell, incantation, enchantment, poison.

Hence, with these terms in mind, we note that Iago has done this play some service. Othello's suspicions, we shall aim to show, arise from within, in the sense that they are integral to the motive he stands for; but the playwright cuts through that tangle at one stroke, by making Iago a voice at Othello's ear.

What arises within, if it wells up strongly and presses for long, will seem imposed from without. One into whose mind melodies spontaneously pop, must eventually "hear voices". "Makers" become but "instruments", their acts a sufferance. Hence, "inspiration", "afflatus", "angels", and "the devil". Thus, the very extremity of inwardness in the motives of Iago can make it seem an outwardness. Hence we are readily disposed to accept the dramatist's dissociation. Yet villain and hero here are but essentially inseparable parts of the one fascination.

Add Desdemona to the inseparable integer. That is: add the privacy of Desdemona's treasure, as vicariously owned by Othello in manly miserliness (Iago represents the threat implicit in such cherishing), and you have a tragic trinity of ownership in the profoundest sense of ownership, the property in human affections, as fetishistically localized in the object of possession, while the possessor is himself possessed by his very engrossment (Iago being the result, the apprehension that attains its dramatic culmination in the thought of an agent acting to provoke the apprehension). The single mine-ownness is thus dramatically split into the three principles of possession, possessor, and estrangement (threat of loss). Hence, trust and distrust, though *living in* each other, can be shown *wrestling with* each other. *La propriété, c'est le vol.* Property fears theft because it is theft.

Sweet thievery, but thievery nonetheless. Appropriately, the first outcry in this play was of "Thieves, thieves, thieves!" when Iago stirred up Desdemona's father by shouting: "Look to your house, your daughter, and your bags! / Thieves! thieves!" [1.1.77–78]—first things in a play being as telltale as last things. Next the robbery was spiritualized: "You have lost your soul" [1.1.84]. And finally it was reduced to imagery both lewd and invidious: "An old black ram is tupping your white ewe" [1.1.85–86], invidious because of the social discrimination involved in the Moor's blackness. So we have the necessary ingredients, beginning from what Desdemona's father, Brabantio, called "the property of youth and maidenhood" [1.1.169]. (Nor are the connotations of *pharmakon,* as evil-working drug, absent from the total recipe, since Brabantio keeps circling about this theme, to explain how the lover robbed the father of his property in the daughter. So it is there, in the offing, as imagery, even though rationalistically disclaimed; and at one point, Othello does think of poisoning Desdemona.)

Desdemona's role, as one of the persons in this triune tension (or "psychosis"), might also be illuminated by antithesis. In the article on the Fine Arts (in the eleventh edition of the *Encyclopaedia Britannica*), the elements of pleasure "which are not disinterested" are said to be:

> the elements of personal exultation and self-congratulation, the pride of exclusive possession or acceptance, all these emotions, in short, which are summed up in the lover's triumphant monosyllable, "Mine."

Hence it follows that, for Othello, the beautiful Desdemona was not an aesthetic object. The thought gives us a radical glimpse into the complexity of her relation to the audience (her nature as a rhetorical "topic"). First, we note how, with the increased cultural and economic importance of private property, an aesthetic might arise antithetically to such norms, exemplifying them in reverse, by an idea of artistic enjoyment that would wholly transcend "mine-own-ness". The sharper the stress upon the *meum* [mine] in the practical realm, the greater the invitation to its denial in an aesthetic *nostrum* [ours].

We are here considering the primary paradox of dialectic, stated as a maxim in the formula beloved by dialectician Coleridge: "Extremes meet." Note how, in this instance, such meeting of the extremes adds to our engrossment in the drama. For us, Desdemona *is* an aesthetic object: we never forget that we have no legal rights in her, and we never forget that she is but an "imitation". But *what* is she imitating? She is "imitating" her third of the total tension (the disequilibrium of monogamistic love, considered as a topic). She is imitating a major perturbation of property, as so conceived. In this sense, however aloof from her the audience may be in discounting her nature as a mere playwright's invention, her role can have a full effect upon them only insofar as it draws upon firm beliefs and dark apprehensions that not only move the audience *within* the conditions of the play, but prevail as an unstable and disturbing cluster of motives *outside* the play, or "prior to" it. Here the "aesthetic," even in negating or transcending "mine-own-ness," would draw upon it for purposes of poetic persuasion. We have such appeal in mind when speaking of the "topical" element. You can get the point by asking yourself: "So far as catharsis and wonder are concerned, what is gained by the fact that the play imitates *this particular tension* rather than some other?"

In sum, Desdemona, Othello, and Iago are all partners of a single conspiracy. There were the enclosure acts, whereby the common lands were made private; here is the analogue, in the realm of human affinity, an act of spiritual enclosure. And might the final choking be also the ritually displaced effort to close a thoroughfare, as our hero fears lest this virgin soil that he had opened up become a settlement? Love, universal love, having been made private, must henceforth be shared vicariously, as all weep for Othello's loss, which is, roundabout, their own. And Iago is a function of the following embarrassment: Once such privacy has been made the norm, its denial can be but promiscuity. Hence his ruttish imagery, in which he signalizes one aspect of a total fascination.

So there is a whispering. There is something vaguely feared and hated. In itself it is hard to locate, being woven into the very nature of "consciousness"; but by the artifice of Iago it is made local. The tinge of malice vaguely diffused through the texture of events and relationships can here be condensed into a single principle, a devil, giving the audience as it were flesh to sink their claw-thoughts in. Where there is a gloom hanging over, a destiny, each man would conceive of the obstacle in terms of the instruments he already has for removing obstacles, so that a soldier would shoot the danger, a butcher thinks it could be chopped, and a merchant hopes to get rid of it by trading. But in Iago the menace is generalized. (As were you to see man-made law as destiny, and see destiny as a hag, cackling over a brew, causing you by a spell to wither.)

In sum, we have noted two major cathartic functions in Iago: (1) as regards the tension centering particularly in sexual love as property and ennoblement (monogamistic love), since in reviling Iago the audience can forget that his transgressions are theirs; (2) as regards the need of finding a viable localization for uneasiness (*Angst*) in general, whether shaped by superhuman forces or by human forces interpreted as super-human (the scapegoat here being but a highly generalized form of the overinvestment that men may make in specialization). Ideally, in childhood, hating and tearing-at are one; in a directness and simplicity of hatred there may be a ritual cure for the bewilderments of complexity; and Iago may thus serve to give a feeling of integrity.

These functions merge into another, purely technical. For had Iago been one bit less rotten and unsleeping in his proddings, how could this play have been kept going, and at such a pitch? Until very near the end, when things can seem to move "of themselves" as the author need but actualize the potentialities already massed, Iago has goaded (tortured) the plot forward step by step, for the audience's villainous entertainment and filthy purgation. * * *

* * *

G. K. HUNTER

Othello and Colour Prejudice†

It is generally admitted today that Shakespeare was a practical man of the theatre: however careless he may have been about maintaining consistency for the exact *reader* of his plays, he was not likely to introduce a theatrical novelty which would only puzzle his audience; it does not seem wise, therefore, to dismiss his theatrical innovations as if they were unintentional. The blackness of Othello is a case in

† From *Proceedings of the British Academy* 53 (1967): 139–63. Reprinted with the permission of the British Academy. The author's quotations from *Othello* have been retained, but bracketed references are to this Norton Critical Edition. For stunning visual and textual illustration as well as some footnote references omitted from this excerpt, readers should consult the original or the reprint in Hunter's *Dramatic Identities and Cultural Tradition: Studies in Shakespeare and His Contemporaries* (Liverpool: Liverpool University Press, 1978), 31–59.

point. Shakespeare largely modified the story he took over from Cinthio: he made a tragic hero out of Cinthio's passionate and bloody lover; he gave him a royal origin, a Christian baptism, a romantic *bravura* of manner and, most important of all, an orotund magnificence of diction. Yet, changing all this, he did not change his colour, and so produced a daring theatrical novelty—a black hero for a white community—a novelty which remains too daring for many recent theatrical audiences. Shakespeare cannot merely have carried over the colour of Othello by being too lazy or too uninterested to meddle with it; for no actor, spending the time in 'blacking-up', and hence no producer, could be indifferent to such an innovation, especially in that age, devoted to 'imitation' and hostile to 'originality'. In fact, the repeated references to Othello's colour in the play and the wider net of images of dark and light spread across the diction, show that Shakespeare was not only not unaware of the implication of his hero's colour, but was indeed intensely aware of it as one of the primary factors in his play.[1] I am therefore assuming in this lecture that the blackness of Othello has a theatrical purpose, and I intend to try to suggest what it was possible for that purpose to have been.

Shakespeare intended his hero to be a black man—that much I take for granted;[2] what is unknown is what the idea of a black man suggested to Shakespeare, and what reaction the appearance of a black man on the stage was calculated to produce. It is fairly certain, however, that some modern reactions are not likely to have been shared by the Elizabethans. The modern theatre-going European intellectual, with a background of cultivated superiority to 'colour problems' in other continents, would often choose to regard Othello as a fellow man and to watch the story—which could so easily be reduced to its headline level: 'sheltered white girl errs: said, "Colour does not matter" '—with a sense of freedom from such prejudices. But this lofty fair-mindedness may be too lofty for Shakespeare's play, and not take the European any nearer the Othello of Shakespeare than the lady from Maryland quoted in the Furness New Variorum edition: 'In studying the play of *Othello,* I have always *imagined* its hero a white man.' Both views, that the colour of Othello does not matter, and that it matters too much to be tolerable, err, I suggest, by over-simplifying. Shakespeare was clearly deliberate in keeping Othello's colour; and it is obvious that he counted on some positive audience reaction to this colour; but it is equally obvious that he did not wish the audience to dismiss Othello as a stereotype nigger.

1. See R. B. Heilman, 'More Fair than Black; Light and Dark in *Othello*', *Essays in Criticism*, i (1951), 313–35.
2. I ignore the many treatises devoted to proving that he was of tawny or sunburnt colour. These are, however, very worthy of study, as documents of prejudice.

Modern rationalizations about 'colour' tend to be different from those of the Middle Ages and Renaissance. We are powerfully aware of the relativism of viewpoints; we distinguish easily between different racial cultures; and explicit arguments about the mingling of the races usually begin at the economic and social level and only move to questions of God's providence at the lunatic fringe.

The Elizabethans also had a powerful sense of the economic threat posed by the foreign groups they had daily contact with—Flemings or Frenchmen—but they had little or no continuous contact with 'Moors', and no sense of economic threat from them.[3] This did not mean, however, that they had no racial or colour prejudice. They had, to start with, the basic common man's attitude that all foreigners are curious and inferior—the more curious the more inferior, in the sense of the proverb quoted by Purchas: 'Three Moors to a Portuguese; three Portuguese to an Englishman.'[4] They had also the basic and ancient sense that black is the colour of sin and death, 'the badge of hell, The hue of dungeons, and the Schoole of night' (as Shakespeare himself says).[5] This supposition is found all over the world (even in darkest Africa)[6] from the earliest to the latest times; and in the West there is a continuous and documented tradition of it. It may be worth while giving some account of this. In Greece and Rome black was the colour of ill luck, death, condemnation, malevolence. * * *

The coming of Christianity made no break in the tradition. Indeed, Christian eschatology seems to have taken over the black man from the underworld with great speed and enthusiasm. * * *

The linguistic change from Greek or Latin to English did not free the word *black* from the[se] associations. * * * This is a tradition that Shakespeare picks up in his description of Thomas Mowbray as a Crusader,

> Streaming the ensign of the Christian cross
> Against black pagans. Turks and Saracens.[7]

There was then, it appears, a powerful, widespread, and ancient tradition associating black-faced men with wickedness, and this tradition came right up to Shakespeare's own day. The habit of repre-

---

3. See G. K. Hunter, 'Elizabethans and Foreigners', *Shakespeare Survey*, xvii ('Shakespeare in His Own Age') (1964), 37–52. [Rpt. in Hunter's *Dramatic Identities* (see the daggered source note to this essay), 3–30.]
4. See M. P. Tilley, *A Dictionary of Proverbs* (1950), M. 1132.
5. *Love's Labour's Lost*, IV. iii. 254 f.
6. See V. W. Turner, 'Colour Classification in Ndembu Ritual', *Anthropological Approaches to the Study of Religion*, ed. M. Banton (1966); Arthur Leib, 'The Mystical Significance of Colours in . . . Madagascar', *Folk-lore*, lvii (1946), 128–33; Joan Westcott, 'The Sculpture and Myths of Eshu-Elegba, the Yoruba Trickster', *Africa*, xxxii (1962).
7. *Richard II*, iv. i. 94 f.

senting evil men as black-faced or negroid had also established itself in a pictorial tradition that persists from the Middle Ages through and beyond the sixteenth century. This appears especially in works showing the tormentors of Christ, in scenes of the Flagellation and the Mocking, though the tormentors of other saints are liable to have the same external characteristics used to show their evil natures. * * *

* * *

It is suggested by several of the authorities cited here that the pictorial tradition was associated with theatrical usage. Certainly the drama of the Middle Ages seems to have used black figures to represent the evil of this world and the next. Creizenach[8] describes the European diffusion of the black faces. The surviving accounts of the Coventry cycle[9] (which some think Shakespeare may have seen— and which he *could* have seen) retain the distinction between 'white (or saved) souls' and 'black (or damned) souls' * * * Even in a proverbial title like 'Like will to like quoth the Devil to the Collier' the widespread and universally accepted point is exposed as part of the air that Englishmen of Shakespeare's age breathed. Indeed, as late as Wycherley's *The Plain Dealer* (1676) stray reference to the Devil's blackness was supposed to be intelligible to a theatrical audience ('like a devil in a play . . . this darkness . . . conceals her angel's face').[1]

How mindlessly and how totally accepted in this period was the image of the black man as the devil may be seen from the use of 'Moors' or 'Morians' in civic pageants. 'Moors' were an accepted part of the world of pageantry.[2] There were Moors in London Lord Mayor's Pageants in 1519, 1521, 1524, 1536, 1541, 1551, 1589, 1609, 1611, 1624,[3] who seem to have acted as bogey-man figures to clear the way before the main procession. They were sometimes supplied with fireworks for this purpose, and in this function seem to have been fairly indifferent alternatives to green-men, wodewoses,[4] devils. As Withington has remarked,[5] 'it seems obvious that all these figures are connected'; they are connected as frightening marginal

8. *Geschichte des neuren Dramas*, i (1911), 201. * * *
9. Medieval townspeople performed plays representing events in biblical history, ranging from the fall into original sin to the resurrection of Christ. The cycle performed in Coventry (near where Shakespeare grew up) is one of the better known. [Editor's note]
1. *The Plain Dealer*, IV. ii.
2. Moors (like dwarfs and fools) were found also in the human menageries that the courts of the Renaissance liked to possess. The Moors at the court of James IV of Scotland appear often in the Treasurer's Accounts. * * *
3. See Malone Society Collections, iii (1945).
4. A wodewose or woodwose is "a wild man of the woods; a savage; a satyr, faun" (*O.E.D.*). [Editor's note]
5. R. Withington, *English Pageantry*, i (1918), 74.

comments on the human state—as inhabitants of those peripheral regions in the *mappae mundi* [world maps] where Moors, together with

> Anthropophagi and men whose heads
> Do grow beneath their shoulders, [1.3.144–45]

rubbed shoulders (such as these were) with Satyrs, Hermaphrodites, salvage [i.e., savage] men, and others of the species *semihoma*. * * *

Renaissance scepticism and the voyages of discovery might seem, at first sight, to have destroyed the ignorance on which such thoughtless equations of black men and devils depended. But this does not prove to have been so. The voyagers brought back some accurate reports of black and heathen; but they often saw, or said they saw, what they expected to see—the marvels of the East. In any case the vocabulary at their disposal frustrated any attempt at scientific discrimination. The world was still seen largely, in terms of vocabulary, as a network of religious names. The word 'Moor' had no clear racial status. The first meaning in the *O.E.D.* (with examples up to 1629) is 'Mahomedan'. And very often this means no more than 'infidel', 'non-Christian'. Like *Barbarian* and *Gentile* (or *Wog*) it was a word for 'people not like us', so signalled by colour. The word *Gentile* itself had still the religious sense of *Pagan,* and the combined phrase 'Moors and Gentiles' is used regularly to represent the religious gamut of non-Christian possibilities (see *O.E.D.* for examples). Similarly, *Barbary* was not simply a place in Africa, but also the unclearly located home of Barbarism, as in Chaucer (Franklin's Tale, 1451, Man of Law's Tale, 183).

I have suggested elsewhere that the discoveries of the voyagers had little opportunity of scientific or non-theological development.[6] And this was particularly true of the problems raised by the black-skinned races. No scientific explanation of black skins had ever been achieved, though doctors had long disputed it. * * * The theological explanation was left in possession of the field. Adam and Eve, it must be assumed, were white; it follows that the creation of the black races can only be ascribed to some subsequent *fiat.* The two favourite possibilities were the cursing of Cain and the cursing of Ham or Cham and his posterity[7]—and sometimes these two were assumed to be different expressions of the same event; at least one might allege, with Sir Walter Ralegh, that 'the sonnes of Cham did possesse the vices of the sonnes of Cain'.[8] The Cham explanation had the great advantage that 'the threefold world' of tradition could be described

---

6. G. K. Hunter, loc. cit.
7. See Genesis 4 and 9. [Editor's note]
8. *The History of the World*, 1.vi.2. [1614; Raleigh (1552–1618), was a courtier, explorer, poet, and moralist.]

in terms of the three sons of Noah—Japhet having produced the Europeans, Shem the Asiatics, while the posterity of Ham occupied Africa, or, in a more sophisticated version, 'the Meridionall or southern partes of the world both in Asia and Africa'—sophisticated, we should notice, without altering the basic theological assumption that Cham's posterity were banished to the most uncomfortable part of the globe, and a foretaste of the Hell to come. * * * When this is linked to the other point made in relation to the Cham story—that his posterity were cursed to be slaves—one can see how conveniently and plausibly such a view fitted the facts and desires found in the early navigators. Azurara, the chronicler of Prince Henry the Navigator's voyages,[9] tells us that it was natural to find blackamoors as the slaves of lighter skinned men:

> these blacks were Moors (i.e. Mahomedans) like the others, though their slaves, in accordance with ancient custom which I believe to have been because of the curse which, after the Deluge, Noah laid upon his son Cain [sic], cursing him in this way: that his race should be subject to all the other races in the world. And from his race these blacks are descended.[1]

The qualities of the 'Moors' who appear on the Elizabethan stage are hardly at all affected by Elizabethan knowledge of real Moors from real geographical locations, and, given the literary modes available, this is hardly surprising. It is true that the first important Moor-role—that of Muly Hamet in Peele's *The Battle of Alcazar* (c. 1589)—tells the story of a real man (with whom Queen Elizabeth had a treaty) in a real historical situation. But the dramatic focus that Peele manages to give to his Moorish character is largely dependent on the devil and underworld associations he can suggest for him—making him call up 'Fiends, Fairies, hags that fight in beds of steel' and causing him to show more acquaintance with the geography of hell than with that of Africa. Aaron in *Titus Andronicus* is liberated from even such slender ties as associate Muly Hamet with geography. Aaron is in the play as the representative of a world of generalized barbarism, which is Gothic in Tamora and Moorish in Aaron, and unfocused in both. The purpose of the play is served by a general opposition between Roman order and Barbarian disorder. Shakespeare has the doubtful distinction of making explicit here (perhaps for the first time in English literature) the projection of black wickedness in terms of negro sexuality. The relationship between Tamora and Aaron is meant, clearly enough, to shock our normal sensibilities and their black baby is present as an emblem of

9. Prince Henry the Navigator (1394–1460) helped sponsor many voyages of discovery from Europe to Africa, chiefly in search of a route to India. [Editor's note]
1. *Discovery and Conquest of Guinea* (Hakluyt Society, xcv [1896], 54).

disorder. In this respect, as in most others, Eleazer in *Lust's Domin-*
ion (c. 1600)—the third pre-*Othello* stage-Moor—is copied from
Aaron. The location of this play (Spain) gives a historically plausible
excuse to present the devil in his favourite human form—'that of a
Negro or Moor', as Reginald Scott[2] tells us—but does not really use
the locale to establish any racial points.

These characters provide the dominant images that must have
been present in the minds of Shakespeare's original audience when
they entered the Globe to see a play called *The Moor of Venice*—an
expectation of pagan deviltry set against white Christian civilization—
excessive civilization perhaps in Venice, but civilization at least 'like
us'. * * * It is in such terms that the play opens. We hear from men
like us of a man not like us, of 'his Moorship', 'the Moor', 'the thick-
lips', 'and old black ram', 'a Barbary horse', 'the devil', of 'the gross
clasps of a lascivious Moor'. The sexual fear and disgust that lies
behind so much racial prejudice are exposed for our derisive expectations to fasten upon them. And we are at this point bound to agree
with these valuations, for no alternative view is revealed. There is,
of course, a certain comic *brio* which helps to distance the whole
situation, and neither Brabantio, nor Iago nor Roderigo can wholly
command our identification. None the less we are drawn on to await
the entry of a traditional Moor figure, the kind of person we came
to the theatre expecting to find.

When the second scene begins, however, it is clear that Shakespeare is bent to ends other than the fulfilment of these expectations. The Iago / Roderigo relationship of I. i is repeated in the Iago
/ Othello relationship of the opening of I. ii; but Othello's response
to the real-seeming circumstance with which Iago lards his discourse
is very different from the hungrily self-absorbed questionings of Roderigo. Othello draws on an inward certainty about himself, a radiant
clarity about his own well-founded moral position. This is no 'lascivious Moor', but a great Christian gentleman, against whom Iago's
insinuations break like water against granite. Not only is Othello a
Christian, moreover, he is the leader of Christendom in the last and
highest sense in which Christendom existed as a viable entity, crusading against the 'black pagans'. He is to defend Cyprus against the
Turk, the 'general enemy Ottoman' [1.3.49]. It was the fall of Cyprus
which produced the alliance of Lepanto, and we should associate
Othello with the emotion that Europe continued to feel—till well
after the date of *Othello*—about that victory and about Don John of
Austria.[3]

2. Author (c. 1538–1599) of *Discovery of Witchcraft* (1584), which reflected skeptically on
   much current belief about demonic forces. [Editor's note]
3. See G. K. Hunter, loc. cit. [Don John of Austria (1545–1578) led the Venetian and Spanish forces that triumphed at Lepanto. See discussion in "*Othello* in Its Own Time," p. 134
   above.]

Shakespeare has presented to us a traditional view of what Moors are like, i.e. gross, disgusting, inferior, carrying the symbol of their damnation on their skin; and has caught our over-easy assent to such assumptions in the grip of a guilt which associates us and our assent with the white man representative of such views in the play—Iago. Othello acquires the glamour of an innocent man that *we* have wronged, and an admiration stronger than he could have achieved by virtue plainly represented. * * * Iago is a 'civilized' man; but where, for the 'inferior' Othello, appearance and reality, statement and truth are linked indissolubly, civilization for Iago consists largely of a capacity to manipulate appearances and probabilities:

> For when my outward action doth demonstrate
> The native act and figure of my heart
> In compliment extern, 'tis not long after
> But I will wear my heart upon my sleeve
> For daws to peck at: I am not what I am. [1.1.58–62]

Othello may be 'the devil' in appearance: but it is the 'fair' Iago who gives birth to the dark realities of sin and death in the play:

> It is engender'd. Hell and night
> Must bring this monstrous birth to the world's light
> [1.3.394–95]

The relationship between these two is developed in terms of appearance and reality. Othello controls the reality of action; Iago the 'appearance' of talk about action; Iago the Italian is isolated (even from his wife), envious, enigmatic (even to himself), self-centered; Othello the 'extravagant and wheeling stranger' is surrounded and protected by a network of duties, obligations, esteems, pious to his father-in-law, deferential to his superiors, kind to his subordinates, loving to his wife. To sum up, assuming that *soul* is reality and *body* is appearance, we may say that Iago is the white man with the black soul while Othello is the black man with the white soul. Long before Blake's little black boy had said

> I am black, but oh my soul is white.
> White as an angel is the English child,
> But I am black as if bereaved of light.

and before Kipling's Gunga Din:

> An' for all 'is dirty 'ide
> 'E was white, clear white inside . . .
> You're a better man than I am, Gunga Din![4]

---

4. William Blake (1757–1827), poet and artist, included "The Little Black Boy" in his *Songs of Innocence* (1789). Rudyard Kipling (1865–1936), poet and novelist, wrote extensively about Anglo-India. [Editor's note]

Othello had represented the guilty awareness of Europe that the 'foreigner type' is only the type we do not know, whose foreignness vanishes when we have better acquaintance. * * *

Othello is then a play which manipulates our sympathies, supposing that we will have brought to the theatre a set of careless assumptions about 'Moors'. It assumes also that we will find it easy to abandon these as the play brings them into focus and identifies them with Iago, draws its elaborate distinction between the external appearance of devilishness and the inner reality.

Shakespeare's playcraft, however, would hardly have been able to superimpose these new valuations on his audience (unique as they were in this form) if it had not been for complicating factors which had begun to affect thought in his day.

The first counter-current I should mention is theological in origin and is found dispersed in several parts of the Bible. It was a fairly important doctrine of the Evangelists that faith could wash away the stains of sin, and the inheritance of misbelief, that the breach between chosen and non-chosen peoples could be closed by faith. The apostle Philip baptised the Ethiopian eunuch and thereupon, says Bede,[5] the Ethiop changed his skin. * * *

Augustine[6] asks who are meant by the Ethiopians; and answers that all nations are Ethiopians, black in their natural sinfulness; but they may become white in the knowledge of the Lord. *Fuistis enim aliquando tenebrae; nunc autem lux in Domino* (Ephesians 5. 8 ["For ye were sometimes darkness, but now *are ye* light in the Lord," King James Version]). As late as Bishop Joseph Hall, writing one of his *Occasional Meditations* (1630) 'on the sight of a blackamoor', we find the same use of *nigra sum sed speciosa* [I am black only in appearance]:

> This is our colour spiritually; yet the eye of our gracious God and Saviour, can see that beauty in us wherewith he is delighted. The true Moses marries a Blackamoor; Christ, his church. It is not for us to regard the skin, but the soul. If that be innocent, pure, holy, the blots of an outside cannot set us off from the love of him who hath said, *Behold, thou art fair, my Sister, my Spouse*: if that be foul and black, it is not in the power of an angelical brightness of our hide, to make us other than a loathsome eye-sore to the Almighty.

The relevance of this passage to Othello need not be stressed.

*   *   *

5. Historian, theologian, and author (672?–735) of biblical commentaries. [Editor's note]
6. Saint Augustine (354–430), one of the most prominent of the early Church Fathers, is hugely influential for his autobiographical writing and ecclesiastical history, as well as for his biblical and theological commentaries. [Editor's note]

The sense that inferior and black-faced foreigners might in fact be figures from a more innocent world close to Christianity grew apace in the Renaissance as the voyagers gave their accounts, not of highly organized Mahomedan kingdoms, but of simple pagans, timid, naked as their mothers brought them forth, without laws and without arms (as Columbus first saw them and first described them) and perhaps having minds naturally prone to accept Christianity. The old ideals and dreams of travellers, the terrestial paradise, the fountain of youth, the kingdom of Prester John,[7] assumed a new immediacy. And so the old impulse to bring the Evangel to all nations acquired a new primitivist dynamic. * * * Alongside the view that such black pagans could only acquire Christian hope by enslavement grew an alternative vision of their innocence as bringing them near to God, by way of nature. Nowhere was the opposition between these two views more dramatically presented than in the famous debate at Valladolid between Sepulveda and Las Casas.[8] Sepulveda asserted that the American Indians were 'slaves by nature', since their natural inferiority made it impossible for them to achieve the light of the gospel without enslavement.[9] Las Casas, on the other hand, dwelt on the innocence of the Indians, living *secundum naturam,* on their natural capacity for devotion, and on the appalling contrast between the mild and timid Indians and the inhumanity of their 'civilized' or 'Christian' exploiters. Of these two it was of course Las Casas who made the greatest impact in Europe. We should not forget that the Valladolid debate was decided in his favour; but it was not in Spain, but in France and England that primitivism grew most rapidly. * * *

The crown of all such Renaissance primitivism is Montaigne's *Essays,*[1] and especially that on the Cannibals, where the criticism of Spanish Christianity has become a *libertin* critique of modern European civility. Shakespeare, in *The Tempest,* seems to show a knowledge of this essay, and certainly *The Tempest* reveals a searching interest in the status of Western civilization parallel to Montaigne's, and a concern to understand the point of reconciliation between innocence and sophistication, ignorance and knowledge.

Of course, we must not assume that Shakespeare, because he had

---

7. A mysterious king who, in a popular medieval legend, founded a perfect realm thought perhaps to exist somewhere in Africa or Asia. [Editor's note]
8. Described most fully in English in L. Hanke, *Aristotle and the American Indians* (1959).
9. See Eric Williams, *Documents of West Indian History* (1963), item 155, discussing the view that a 'negro cannot become a Christian without being a slave'. Cf. the summary of Sepulveda's position in Hanke, op. cit., pp. 44 f. The same views persist today, though with interesting modifications in the vocabulary: 'He (the Negro) requires the constant control of white people to keep him in check. Without the presence of the white police force negroes would turn upon themselves and destroy each other. The white man is the only authority he knows.' (Quoted in E. T. Thompson, *Race Relations* [1939], p. 174.)
1. The *Essays* of Michel de Montaigne (1533–1592), much admired for their skeptical detachment and (as we would now say) cultural relativism, are frequently echoed in Shakespeare. [Editor's note]

these concerns in *The Tempest*, must have had them also in *Othello*; but *The Tempest* at one end of his career, like *Titus Andronicus* at the other end, indicates that the polarities of thought on which *Othello* moves (if I am correct) were available to his mind.

I have spoken of 'polarities' in the plural because it is important to notice that Shakespeare does not present his *Othello* story in any simple primitivist terms. *Othello* is not adequately described as the exploitation of a noble savage by a corrupt European.[2] This is an element in the play, * * * but by giving too much importance to this it would be easy to underplay the extent to which Othello becomes what Iago and the society to which *we* belong assumes him to be.

There is considerable strength in the anti-primitivist side of the great Renaissance debate (as that is represented in *Othello*) and this lies in the extent to which the whole social organism pictured is one we recognize as our own, and recognize as necessarily geared to reject 'extravagant and wheeling strangers'. I speak of the social organism here, not in terms of its official existence—its commands, duties, performances; for in these terms Othello's life is well meshed into the state machine:

> My services which I have done the Signiory
> Shall out-tongue his complaints. [1.2.18–19]

I speak rather of the unspoken assumptions and careless prejudices by which we all conduct most of our lives. And it is in these respects that Iago is the master of us all, the snapper-up of every psychological trifle, every unnoticed dropped handkerchief. It is by virtue of such a multitude of our tiny and unnoticed assents that Iago is able to force Othello into the actions he expects of him. Only the hermit can stand outside such social assumptions; but, by marrying, Othello has become part of society in this sense, the natural victim of the man-in-the-know, the man universally thought well of. And Iago's knowingness finds little or no resistance. We all believe the Iagos in our midst; they are, as our vocabulary interestingly insists, the 'realists'.

The dramatic function of Iago is to reduce the white 'reality' of Othello to the black 'appearance' of his face, indeed induce in him the belief that all reality is 'black', that Desdemona in particular, 'where I have garnered up my heart'

> . . . that was fresh
> As Dian's visage, is now begrimed and black
> As mine own face. [3.3.387–89] * * *

---

2. But Iago's Spanish name (and his nautical imagery) may represent Shakespeare's awareness of this potentiality in his play at some level of his consciousness. The relevance of the figure of Sant' Iago Matamoros (Moor-slayer) has been suggested by G. N. Murphy, 'A Note on Iago's name', *Literature and Society*, ed. B. Slote (1964).

* * *

The dark reality originating in Iago's soul spreads across the play, blackening whatever it overcomes and making the deeds of Othello at last fit in with the prejudice that his face at first excited. Sometimes it is supposed that this proves the prejudice to have been justified. There is a powerful line of criticism on *Othello,* going back at least as far as A. W. Schlegel,[3] that paints the Moor as a savage at heart, one whose veneer of Christianity and civilization cracks as the play proceeds, to reveal and liberate his basic savagery: Othello turns out to be in fact what barbarians *have* to be.

This view, however comforting to our sense of society and our prejudices, does not find much support in the play itself. The fact that the darkness of 'Hell and night' spreads from Iago and then takes over Othello—this fact at least should prevent us from supposing that the blackness is inherent in Othello's barbarian nature. Othello himself, it is true, loses faith not only in Desdemona but in that fair quality of himself which Desdemona saw and worshipped: ('for she had eyes and chose me' [3.3.191]).

* * * The tragedy becomes, as Helen Gardner has described it, a tragedy of the loss of faith.[4] And, such is the nature of Othello's heroic temperament, the loss of faith means the loss of all meaning and all value, all sense of light:

> I have no wife,
> O insupportable! O heavy hour!
> Methinks it should be now a huge eclipse
> Of sun and moon, and that the affrighted globe
> Should yawn at alteration. [5.2.99–103]

Universal darkness has buried all.

But the end of the play is not simply a collapse of civilization into barbarism, nor a destruction of meaning. Desdemona *was* true, faith *was* justified, the appearance was not the key to the truth. To complete the circle we must accept, finally and above all, that Othello was not the credulous and passionate savage that Iago has tried to make him, but that he was justified in his second, as in his first, self-defence:

> For nought I did in hate, but all in honour. [5.2.300]

The imposition of Iago's vulgar prejudices on Othello ('These Moors are changeable in their wills' [1.3.344], etc.) is so successful that it takes over not only Othello but almost all the critics. But Iago's suppression of Othello into the vulgar prejudice about him can only be sustained as the truth if we ignore the end of the play. The wonderful

3. August Wilhelm Schlegel, *Lectures on Dramatic Art* (1815), ii. 189.
4. Helen Gardner, 'The Noble Moor', *Proceedings of the British Academy,* xli (1955).

recovery here of the sense of ethical meaning in the world, even in the ashes of all that embodied meaning—this requires that we see the final speech of Othello as more than that of a repentant black-amoor 'cheering himself up', as Mr. Eliot phrased it.[5] It is in fact a marvellous *stretto* of all the themes that have sounded throughout the play. I shall only dwell on Othello's self-judgement and self-execution, repeating and reversing the judgement and execution on Desdemona and so, in a sense, cancelling them. Othello is the 'base Indian' who threw away the white pearl Desdemona, but he is also the state servant and Christian who, when the Infidel or 'black Pagan' within him seemed to triumph,

> Took by the throat the circumcised dog
> And smote him—thus. [5.2.360–61]

With poetic justice, the Christian reality reasserts its superior position over the pagan appearance, not in terms that can be lived through, but at least in terms that can be understood. We may rejoice even as we sorrow, catharsis is achieved, for

> What may quiet us in a death so noble,[6]

as this in the Aleppo of the mind?

*   *   *

The domestic intensities of *King Lear* have been seen usefully and interestingly (by Theodore Spencer, for example) in relation to the intellectual history of the Renaissance.[7] The position of the king obviously calls on one set of traditional assumptions, while Edmund's doctrine of nature equally obviously draws on the views of the *libertins,* of Montaigne and Machiavelli.[8] The pressure of these larger formulations may be seen to add to the largeness of scope in the play. *Othello,* on the other hand, is thought not to be a play of this kind. 'The play itself is primarily concerned with the effect of one human being on another',[9] says Spencer. It is true that Iago operates in a less conceptualized situation than Edmund; but the contrast between his world view and that of Othello is closely related to the contrast between Edmund and Lear. On the one side we have the chivalrous world of the Crusader, the effortless superiority of the 'great man', the orotund public voice of the leader, the magnetism

---

5. T. S. Eliot, 'Shakespeare and the Stoicism of Seneca', reprinted in *Selected Essays* (1932), p. 130. [See above, p. 244.]
6. Hunter quotes John Milton's *Samson Agonistes* (published 1671), line 1724. [Editor's note]
7. Theodore Spencer, *Shakespeare and the Nature of Man* (1943).
8. Niccolò Machiavelli (1469–1527), political theorist, historian, and sometime playwright, fascinated (and often repelled) English Renaissance audiences for his supposedly amoral pragmatism. [Editor's note]
9. Spencer, op. cit. (1961 ed.), p. 126.

of the famous lover. The values of the world of late medieval and Renaissance magnificence seem compressed in Othello—crusader, stoic, traveller, believer, orator, commander, lover—Chaucer's parfit knight, Spenser's Red Cross, the Ruggiero of Ariosto.[1] In Iago we have the other face of the Renaissance (or Counter-Renaissance), rationalist, individual, empirical (or inductive), a master in the Machiavellian art of manipulating appearances, a Baconian or Hobbesian 'Realist'.[2]

In the conflict of Othello and Iago we have, as in that setting Edmund, Goneril and Regan against Lear and Gloucester, a collision of these two Renaissance views. Bradley points to a similarity between Lear and Othello, that they are both 'survivors of a heroic age living in a later and smaller world'. Both represent a golden age naïvety which was disappearing then (as now, and always). Lear's survival is across a temporal gap; his long life has carried him out of one age and stranded him in another. But Othello's travel is geographical rather than temporal, from the heroic simplicities of

> I fetch my life and being
> From men of royal siege [1.2.21]

into the supersubtle world of Venice, the most sophisticated and 'modern' city on earth, as it seemed to the Elizabethans.

Here, if anywhere, was the scene-setting for no merely domestic intrigue, but for an exercise in the quality of civilization, a contest between the capacities and ideals claimed by Christendom, and those that Christians were actually employing in that context where (as Marlowe says)

> . . . Indian Moors obey their Spanish lords.[3]

Othello's black skin makes the coexistence of his vulnerable romanticism and epic grandeur with the bleak or even pathological realism of Iago a believable fact. The lines that collide here started thousands of miles apart. But Shakespeare's choice of a black man for his Red Cross Knight, his Rinaldo,[4] has a further advantage. *Our* involvement in prejudice gives us a double focus on his reality. We admire him—I fear that one has to be trained as a literary critic to find him unadmirable—but we are aware of the difficulty of sustaining that vision of the golden world of poetry; and this is so because *we* feel the disproportion and the difficulty of his social life and of

1. Images of heroic chivalry in, respectively, *The Canterbury Tales* (late fourteenth century), *The Faerie Queene* (1590), and *Orlando Furioso* (1532). [Editor's note]
2. Hunter brings the philosophers Sir Francis Bacon (1561–1626) and Thomas Hobbes (1588–1679) into the same orbit of unillusioned free inquiry as Machiavelli and Montaigne earlier. [Editor's note]
3. Marlowe, *Doctor Faustus*, 1. i. 122.
4. Protagonist of an early poem by Torquato Tasso (1544–1595), subsequently appearing in Tasso's *Jerusalem Delivered*, translated into English in 1660. [Editor's note]

his marriage (as a social act). We are aware of the easy responses that Iago can command, not only of people on the stage but also in the audience. The perilous and temporary achievements of heroism are achieved most sharply in this play, because they have to be achieved in *our* minds, through *our* self-awareness.

LYNDA E. BOOSE

Othello's Handkerchief: "The Recognizance and Pledge of Love"†

> So much ado, so much stress, so much passion and repetition about an Handkerchief! Why was not this call'd the *Tragedy of the Hand-kerchief?* . . . Had it been *Desdemona's* Garter, the Sagacious Moor might have smelt a Rat: but the Handkerchief is so remote a trifle, no Booby, on this side *Mauritania*, cou'd make any consequence from it.
>
> —Thomas Rymer[1]

Although we recognize Rymer as an irresponsible detractor, we find it difficult to deny T. S. Eliot's contention that Rymer has never been adequately answered. The play forces us to recognize that for Othello and *Othello,* the whole tragedy revolves around a "trifle light as air." Unable to justify its enormous importance yet forced to concede that dramatic verisimilitude depends on exactly that, critics have often felt obliged to excuse Shakespeare for borrowing Cinthio's hankie or to insist that the point about the handkerchief is precisely the triviality of this object which the primitive invests with disproportionate significance.[2] Unfortunately, the first approach only evades the question as to why Shakespeare *did* adopt Cinthio's plot mechanism when he could so easily have eliminated it, changed it, or relegated it to minor dramatic importance. The alternative explanation, while relevant to Othello's actions, nonetheless strips the play of tragic gran-

---

† From *English Literary Renaissance* 5 (1975): 360–74. Reprinted with permission of *English Literary Renaissance.* The author's quotations from *Othello* have been retained, but bracketed references are to this Norton Critical Edition.

1. "A Short View of Tragedy" in *The Critical Works of Thomas Rymer,* ed. Curt A. Zimansky (New Haven, Conn., 1956), p. 164. [See above, p. 208.]

2. That the handkerchief's essence resides in its actual insignificance is the solution favored by the majority of scholars. For a sampling of this approach in recent *Othello* criticism see Leslie Fiedler, *The Stranger in Shakespeare* (New York, 1972), p. 149; Katherine S. Stockholder, "Egregiously an Ass: Chance and Accident in *Othello,*" *SEL,* 13 (1973), 265; and Nigel Alexander, "Thomas Rymer and *Othello,*" *ShS,* 21 (1968), 75. For related analyses that explain Othello's obsessive belief in the handkerchief by reference to his alien background, see Michael C. Andrews, "Honest Othello: The Handkerchief Once More," *SEL,* 13 (1973), 279; Abraham B. Feldman, "Othello's Obsessions," *American Imago,* 9 (1952), 159–62; and Peter G. Mudford, "*Othello* and the 'Tragedy of Situation,' " *English,* 20 (1971), 1–5.

deur and makes it a drama with no real issues except self-delusion of banal proportions. And we are here right back to Rymer and his Mauritanian Booby.

For an "intrinsic interpretation" of a literary work, Sigurd Burckhardt emphasizes that the "disturbing elements" within the piece must be regarded as "significant for the poem and crucial for interpretation. For the choice of a particular conceit, or perhaps the form in which the poet presents it, may be more decisive for the meaning of the whole than the fact that it was also used by other writers."[3] The disturbing handkerchief in *Othello* is just such a crux. Given the relative infrequency of stage props in Shakespeare's theater, where the characters and their speech alone usually direct the drama, the repetitive appearance of any stage prop must be considered as symbolically significant. Like the sword in *Hamlet,* the handkerchief is a "presentational image" which spans the entire drama and connects within its symbolic fabric the motive forces of the play.[4] The meaning of the handkerchief, however, may well lie hidden in rituals and customs which were accessible to Elizabethans but have since been lost.[5]

In searching out the symbolic value woven into the napkin and by extension into the play, we should take as our starting point the fact that *Othello* is, in one way or another, a play about a *marriage,* memorially the most ritualized and symbolized of all human acts. Shakespeare radically refocused his source material on just that fact. Whereas Cinthio's "Disdemona" and "The Moor" have apparently been married for some time, Shakespeare designed a whole first act emphatically concentrated on a bridal couple and the interruption of their wedding night and created a special scene [2.2] staged only to have "A Gentleman" proclaim the celebration of Othello's nuptials in language reminiscent of Theseus' proclamation in *A Midsummer Night's Dream* [5.1.346–53 in *The Norton Shakespeare*]. Although a tragedy, *Othello* is nonetheless embroidered with the symbolic motifs of marriage, motifs included in every Shakespearean play concerned with this ritual. Shakespeare altered Cinthio's plot in order to create a dual concentration on the issues of marriage and justice. These two central issues of the play are those which the handkerchief will ritually express.

In taking over Cinthio's handkerchief Shakespeare made a minor

---

3. See Appendix, "Notes on the Theory of Intrinsic Interpretation," in Burckhardt's *Shakespearean Meanings* (Princeton, N.J., 1968), pp. 302, 304–06.
4. See Maurice Charney, *Shakespeare's Roman Plays: The Function of Imagery in the Drama* (Cambridge, Mass., 1961), for "presentational image." See also Alan Dessen, "Hamlet's Poisoned Sword: A Study in Dramatic Imagery," *ShakS,* 5 (1969), 53–69, for a study of the relationship between sword as stage prop and the dramatic meaning of *Hamlet.*
5. C. L. Barber, *Shakespeare's Festive Comedy* (Princeton, N.J., 1959), provides perhaps the most informative study of partially forgotten ritual and festival customs and their implicit significance in various Shakespearean comedies.

but important change. Instead of leaving it a napkin embroidered simply and vaguely "alla moresca," he insistently created for his audience a highly visual picture of a square piece of white linen spotted with strawberry-red fruit. That the strawberries could be emblematic of virgin blood is logical both visually and metaphorically. The statement from *Venus and Adonis* (l. 460), "Or as the berry breaks before it staineth,"[6] is probably related; and as an appropriately red fruit they picture forth the desired dramatic idea. Additionally, strawberries had symbolical, received associations growing out of the long emblem tradition which the Renaissance inherited and utilized. According to Lawrence J. Ross, strawberries are among the most frequently found embroidery designs from the period. To the sixteenth century they had a time-honored association with the Virgin,[7] hence a logical connection with the concept of virginity itself. Considered by Elizabethan gardeners as the purest of fruits, the treble-leafed strawberry plant bore a red fruit from its initially white flower. Furthermore, the plant itself was a part of the generic rose family, the flower most frequently associated with love and desire.[8] These considerations make the details that Shakespeare added to Cinthio's handkerchief seem less arbitrary and the handkerchief itself far more articulate than before. What Shakespeare was representing was a visually recognizable reduction of Othello and Desdemona's wedding-bed sheets, the visual proof of their consummated marriage, the emblem of the symbolical act of generation so important to our understanding of the measure of this tragedy.

In his use of a sophisticated dramatic technique of visual reduction, Shakespeare depended on his audience to draw from an understanding of accepted custom and age-old cultural values. History unfortunately has a short memory when it comes to ritual significations. That stained wedding sheets might be communally displayed as evidence of the sanctified marital blood pact would be, no doubt, an idea offensive to modern sensibilities. The custom actually has,

6. All Shakespearean lines exclusive of *Othello* are quoted from *The Riverside Shakespeare*, ed. G. Blakemore Evans (Boston, 1974). Quotations from *Othello* are from the Arden edition, ed. M. R. Ridley (7th ed., 1958; rpt. London, 1962).

7. Lawrence J. Ross, "The Meaning of Strawberries in Shakespeare," *SRen*, 7 (1960), 225–40. Ross notes this association to the Virgin was a major motif of Catholic commentary and pre-Reformation art (p. 235). The strawberry was often pictured with a snake lurking menacingly under its leaves; perhaps because of the presence of the snake, it became an emblem commonly associated with the Garden of Eden. Other relevant points mentioned in this article are the connections with beautiful women and the ideas of love and seduction (p. 230); the citation from Wilhelm Franger, *The Millennium of Hieronymus Bosch*, which finds that the strawberry appearing as a prominent symbol in Bosch's painting "represents the essence of earthly voluptuous delight" (p. 231*n*.); and the mention of an early seventeenth-century embroidered cover for a Bible cushion where "the strawberry plant, prominently displayed in the foreground, is here associated (as frequently earlier) with the story of the falsely accused, chaste Susanna." At the bottom of the design the suggestive snake again appears (p. 238*n*.).

8. I am indebted to Professor Michael J. B. Allen for pointing out the botanical aspects which make the strawberry plant such a logical symbol for the Virgin and by extension virginity.

however, a long history—both recorded and implicit—in the ritual notions of marriage.[9] We can pick up recorded references to it in the fascinated documentaries of our nineteenth-century antiquarians, for whom the idea merits record only because it had by then become a historical curiosity. Although we cannot absolutely document its practice in Elizabethan England, we can infer from several important clues that the notion was at least apprehended within ritual consciousness at that time. In his 1621 compendium of proverbial information under the subsection "Symptomes of Iealosie," Robert Burton records customs demanding ocular proof of "the sheet stained from the first night" and "the bloody napkin":

> In some parts of *Greece* at this day, like those olde *Iewes,* they will not beleeue their wiues are honest, *nisi pannum menstruatum primâ nocte videant,*[1] our countriman *Sandes* in his perigrination, saith it is seuerely obserued, in *Zazinthus,* or *Zante,* and *Leo Afer* in his time at *Fez* in *Africke, non, credunt virginem esse nisi videant sanguineam mappam, si non, ad parentes pudore rejicitur.*[2] Those sheets are publikely shewed by their parents, and kept as a signe of incorupt virginity. (facsimile, *The Anatomy of Melancholy* 3.3.2.1)

Burton of course attributes the practice to Greeks, Jews, and Africans, but throughout *The Anatomy* he characteristically attributes any and all examples of extreme behavior to non-English, non-Protestant peoples. The 1529 divorce deliberations of Henry VIII and Catherine of Aragon provide a decidedly English example. At this famous inquiry the Queen's supporters attempted to collect just such evidence (dating back, as it would have, some thirty years!) as proof of Catherine's virginity at the time of her marriage to Henry, proof that her previous union with Arthur had never been consummated.[3] On the opposite side, Cardinal Wolsey maintained that the union with Arthur had been completed but that "the counsailers of

9. See William J. Fielding, *Strange Customs of Courtship and Marriage* (Garden City, N.Y., 1960), pp. 143–44. Noting that this ritual took place at the Charles V–Isabella of Braganza royal wedding in Spain, Fielding comments, "the fact that this formality prevailed in the exalted royal circles of Spain indicates the custom was implicit in the customs of the country."
   Walter Simpson, *A History of the Gipsies* (London, 1865), pp. 261–63, records the custom then current among Scottish gypsies. Edward J. Wood, *The Wedding Day in All Ages and Countries* (New York, 1869), p. 170, provides an interesting notation: "The early Spaniards had a custom, which they learned from the Moors," of hanging "evidences of the bride's purity" out of the wedding chamber window.
1. Unless they see the first night's bloody sheets. [Editor's note]
2. Without seeing the bloody sheets, they don't believe her virginal and send her back in shame to her parents. [Editor's note]
3. In his historical biography of Catherine, Garrett Mattingly writes that on June 25, 1529, "In an effort to establish that Catherine's marriage had been fully consummated, the government raked through enormous heaps of muck, most of it nearly thirty years old, and the ancient stenches steamed up unnoticed under the bored noses of the judges . . ." (*Catherine of Aragon* [Boston, 1941], p. 288).

Fardinando being resident here for that purposse, dyd send the sheets thei ley in, spotted with bloude into *Spaine*, in full testymonie & prouf thereof."[4]

This practice, which seems to have been a wide-spread folk custom throughout Europe, finds sanction in the most ancient source of Western law, the Book of Deuteronomy. Under the Geneva Bible subtitle "Of the wife not being founde a virgine," Deuteronomy enjoins that the "vesture" shall be spread before the city gate to be examined for "the tokens" of virginity: "If a man take a wife, and when he hathe lien with her, hate her, And lay slanderous things vnto her charge, and bring vp an euil name vpon her, and say, I toke this wife, and when I came to her I found her not a maid, Then shal the father of the maid and her mother take & bring the signes of the maides virginitie vnto the Elders of the citie to the gate. And the maides father shal say vnto the Elders, I gaue my daughter vnto this man to wife, and he hateth her: And lo, he laieth slanderous things vnto her charge, saying, I found not thy daughter a maid: lo, these *are the tokens* of my daughters virginitie: and they shal spreade the vesture before the Elders of the citie"[5] (Deut. 22.13–17). Significantly, the compilers of the 1560 Geneva Bible gloss the *vesture* as "the shete, wherein the signes of her virginitie were." This implies that the blood-stained sheet used as proof of virginity was an understood cultural assumption at this time. Whether or not bridal virginity was an Elizabethan reality, it was nonetheless an absolute value. Prospero's injunction to Ferdinand to break not "this virgin knot" [*Tempest* 4.1.15] or Claudio's rejection of Hero in *Much Ado* are only samplings of the overwhelming evidence. The age, in fact, seemed obsessed with the importance of it: the "virginity tests" administered to Beatrice Joanna in *The Changeling*[6] witness the relevance of the idea, and the subsequent "bed-switch trick" implies something important and something understood by the audience about proof of virginity that must be left in the bridal bed. The connections between lost virginity and blood stains are obvious in Deuteronomy, but they are obvious also in Talbot's metaphoric use of the image: "The ireful Bastard Orleance, that drew blood / From thee, my boy, and had the maidenhood / Of thy first fight" [*1H6* 4.6. 16–18.]

The handkerchief emerged imaginatively from the *Hecatommithi* narrative as a potent love token. The idea of "token" seems always to have carried overtones for Shakespeare of representative sexual exchange; he had already used it thus in *The Merchant of Venice*, *All's Well*, and *Troilus and Cressida*. Frequently, however, as if to

4. Richard Fiddes, *The Life of Cardinal Wolsey* (1724), II, 213.
5. The Geneva Bible (1560; facsimile rpt. Madison, Wisc., 1969). All citations are from this edition.
6. In Middleton and Rowley's play (1622), Beatrice Joanna substitutes her maid in the bridal bed to conceal her nonvirginity. [Editor's note]

underline the disparity between the important symbolic reality of the object and its trivial external appearance, he had specifically applied the term "trifle" to it. The napkin is called "a trifle" twice in *Othello*, but Bassanio has likewise said of Portia's token ring, "alas, it is a trifle" [*MV* 4.1.430]; Portia later reveals its valuable sexual identity when she describes it as "riveted with faith unto your flesh" [5.1.169] and quibbles that "For by this ring, the doctor lay with me" (l. 259). In *All's Well* the King calls for Bertram to "Send forth your amorous token for fair Maudlin" [5.3.68], and when Bertram produces Helen's ring the King demands:

> Confess 'twas hers, and by what rough enforcement
> You got it from her. She call'd the saints to surety
> That she would never put it from her finger,
> Unless she gave it to yourself in bed. [5.3.107–10]

When Pandarus tells Cressida he will come back to bring her "a token from Troilus," Cressida responds "By the same token, you are a bawd" [*Tro.* 1.2.280–81]. The token from Troilus again doubles as metaphor for the "gift" of sexual consummation. In a later play which has strong narrative parallels to *Othello*, Iachimo or "little Iago" steals the external symbol of marital consummation and brings the new husband to a murderous jealousy by producing false evidence. Posthumus earlier referred to the ring and bracelet he and Imogen exchanged as "our trifles" [*Cym*. 1.1.120]. But when Iachimo calls the diamond a "trifle" Imogen's new husband responds in a way which identifies the relationship of the external object to the invaluable act it represents: whereas the ring "may be sold or given, or if there were wealth enough for the purchase, or merit for the gift; the other is not a thing for sale, and only the gift of the gods" [1.4.82–85]. The point seems clear that the token, like the handkerchief in *Othello*, is never a trifle in the sense of something inconsequential. Objectively it is so only because it may be sold or given, stolen or misplaced; symbolically, however, the sexual act it represents is something absolute. It is a "gift of the gods" in *Cymbeline*, the "magic in the web" in *Othello*.

All this is evidence on the implicit level of the connections in Shakespeare's own mind between token and sexual consummation and those he could expect his audience to perceive between strawberry-spotted handkerchief and blood-spotted sheets. In *Othello* itself, however, Shakespeare also pointedly emphasized the identity.

One of the most significant ways in which he did so was by grafting a whole symbolic history onto the handkerchief, an addition not in Cinthio and one which makes no sense in terms of the play unless it implies a symbolic identity of this napkin. Interestingly, the "magic" which Othello relates as woven into this token is a history removed from the objective action of the drama and one which directs us back into the sphere of myth, custom, and symbolism, the precise level at which we are to identify the handkerchief. The apparent contradictions in Othello's two versions of the handkerchief legend make perfect sense on this level.

Othello says, "that handkerchief / Did an Egyptian to my mother give" [3.4.53–54], and by reference to Egypt the speech invokes an erotic aura for the context of the item:

> while she kept it
> 'Twould make her amiable, and subdue my father
> Entirely to her love: but if she lost it,
> Or made a gift of it, my father's eye
> Should hold her loathly. . . . [3.4.56–60]

Because it is the emblematic proof of the marital blood pledge, the mother's possession of it will guarantee her husband's love and fidelity. With perfect symbolic coherence the spotted handkerchief is then that which the mother gives her son for him to give to his bride. His bride is to "Make it a darling, like your precious eye"; and by inclusion of this double entendre referring to female genitalia, the legend of the handkerchief continues to focus our understanding on its sexual symbolism.[7] There is, Othello relates, "magic in the web" of this linen, the profoundly mythic magic of sexual union. Because the ritual origins of marital blood pledge stretch back into man's ancient consciousness, "A sibyl, that had number'd in the world / The sun to make two hundred compasses, / In her prophetic fury sew'd the work" [3.4.68–70]. The first handkerchief version concludes by creating a visual metaphor of the sacred human act and its promise of generation: "The worms were hallow'd that did breed the silk, / And it was dyed in mummy, with the skilful / Conserves of maidens' hearts"[8] [3.4.71–73]. This picture, which brings together the phallic allusion to "worms . . . that breed" and spots dyed from the conserved blood of virgins' hearts, actually *repeats* the picture of the handkerchief "spotted with strawberries." The repetition of the original visual image through a metaphor of consummation and maiden blood exactly identifies Othello's token to Desdemona and

---

7. Iago has earlier used this same double entendre in his obscene comment about Desdemona: "What an eye she has! methinks it sounds a parley of provocation" [2.3.20]. "Eye" is glossed by Eric Partridge as a reference to female genitalia in *Shakespeare's Bawdy* (1948; rpt. New York, 1969), p. 102.

8. I am here using Q1's reading "with . . . Conserves," where *Conserves* functions as a noun. Q2 reads "which . . . Conserve," and F, "Which . . . Conserve'd," both making a verb out of the word. The Arden edition (which here accepts Q2) comments: "the verb, meaning 'to make a preserve of,' is not the most appropriate word to describe the distillation of a liquor. . . ." I am convinced that the Q1 reading represents Shakespeare's intention of creating a second visual picture of the strawberry spots dyed or stained into the woven handkerchief.

tells us what indeed is the very "wonder in this handkerchief."[9] More-over, by his use of poetic legend to describe sexuality, Shakespeare elevates the act from the degradation of Iago's pornographic literal-ism into the realm of myth. It is important that we understand the act recorded on the handkerchief in terms of this mythic elevation in order that we understand what is ultimately destroyed.

Othello's second story, that it was "an antique token my father gave my mother," does not really contradict the first one but rather amplifies it.[1] Important here is our realization that the entire legend and almost every reference to the handkerchief must be read in terms of *symbolic logic*. In this context it is true that this token originates in antique myth and came to the mother from "Egypt." It is also true, however, that it was something the father gave the mother, that which every husband "gives" his bride, and that which Othello gave Desdemona as his "first token." Desdemona's stammering insistence that "it is not lost" may seem a troublesome deception in terms of literal fact, but it is perfectly true in terms of the handkerchief's mythic identity. She cannot actually lose it. Whereas Cinthio's "Bianca" is spied in the act of copying the patterned handkerchief, Shakespeare's Bianca comes on stage to emphasize her inability either to copy or "take out" the work. The "work" stained upon this symbolic token, the act between one husband and one wife, exists as a unique absolute and is therefore not subject to duplication or eradication.

The handkerchief enters the dramatic action only in [3.3]. Before that point it has never been mentioned, yet once injected into the drama it becomes the center around which the rest of the tragedy inexorably whirls. Appropriately, it first appears in Desdemona's pos-session in [3.3], receiving dramatic life only after the off-stage mar-ital consummation of the previous night. After the proclamation announcing their nuptial night, Othello has led Desdemona off to the bedroom with the comment, "The purchase made, the fruits are to ensue, / The profit's yet to come 'twixt me and you" [2.3.9–10].[2] When Desdemona enters in [3.3] she has with her Othello's token, the fruit-spotted emblem signifying the consummated value of their

9. Although her conclusions differ from mine, Katherine Stockholder likewise notes sexual suggestiveness in the image of "hallowed worms that bred the silk" and feels this whole image of the handkerchief "focuses the sense of sanctified physicality that pervades the play" (p. 266).

1. Andrews examines the critical polarity between those who accept Othello's first magical version as the "truth" and believe his second version to be a conscious deception and those who take the opposite stance. Andrews points out that no audience would ever notice "deception" in one version or the other (pp. 273–84).

2. The sense of Othello's words seems obvious. A comparable speech using the same meta-phor of "purchasing" is made when Juliet, newly married, awaits the arrival of Romeo: "O, I have bought the mansion of a love, / But not possess'd it, and though I am sold, / Not yet enjoy'd" [*Rom.* 3.2.26–28].

marriage, the value which—with terrible irony—Othello will destroy
over the loss of that same emblem of consummation. The tragic irony
always recognized as important to *Othello* is Promethean. Not only
does Othello murder Desdemona over her inability to produce the
very handkerchief he had himself seen in her hand just a short time
previously, but he also executes as a whore the very bride whose
virginal fidelity he physically experienced but hours earlier. By
designing the handkerchief as the ocular proof of Desdemona's fidelity, Shakespeare has constructed an avenue of audience insight into
a drama which is itself vitally concerned with concepts of vision.[3]
Because we have seen the proof positive of what a puzzled Othello
says to Iago, "I found not Cassio's kisses on her lips" [3.3.342],
Othello's ensuing demands for "ocular proof" of her lust ring across
the stage with ironic significance. The handkerchief that will become
to Othello evidence of her lust has always been evidence of exactly
the opposite nature.[4]

The embroidery on the handkerchief is most frequently referred
to in *Othello* as the "work." Through a patterned accretion of significance, Shakespeare forges a verbal echo by which he indicates the
symbolic meaning of the strawberry spots. George Rylands comments on the relevance of such iterative patterns: the "repetition of
a word in diverse contexts throughout the play, with its correlatives
and associates, often gives the clue to the poetic thought, the
dianoia, which informs the whole."[5] Iago first places the word in a
sexual context with his misogynistic comment, "You rise to play, and
go to bed to work" [2.1.115]. When the handkerchief is introduced
on stage, Emilia makes initial reference to its figuration as "work";
Othello [3.4.70] and Cassio [185] use the same term for the embroidery. The word next appears in the parodic marriage vows where it
metamorphoses in Iago's mouth to "bloody work" [3.3.469]. When
Othello succumbs to the powerful visual associations entangled in
"confess?—Handkerchief?—O devil," the word becomes an incantation Iago chants over the prostrate Othello, "Work on / My
medicine, work" [4.1.44–45]. Bianca reiterates the term with sliding
reference linking the embroidery to a sexual act when she says, "I
must take out the whole work, a likely piece of work, that you should

3. Maurianne S. Adams, " 'Ocular Proof' in *Othello*," *PMLA*, 79 (1964), 234–41, discusses
   how Shakespeare expanded Cinthio's casual references to sight into a thematic imagery
   of ocular proof. "Shakespeare seized what was potential in his source and translated it
   into a conflict among modes of vision and blindness" (p. 238).
4. See A. André Glaz, "Iago or Moral Sadism," *American Imago*, 19 (1962), 336, and Jean
   Jofen, "The Case of the Strawberry Handkerchief," *ShN*, 21 (1971), 14. The conclusions
   of both differ significantly from mine, but both do note some connection between the
   handkerchief and wedding sheet customs.
5. "Shakespeare's Poetic Energy," *Proceedings of the British Academy*, 37 (1951), 102. See
   also Robert B. Heilman, *Magic in the Web: Action and Language in "Othello"* (Lexington,
   Ky., 1956), esp. pp. 21–24.

find it in your chamber, and not know who left it there!" [4.1.146–48]. Again the word echoes in Othello's speech:

> And she did gratify his amorous works,
> With the recognizance and pledge of love,
> Which I first gave her; I saw it in his hand,
> It was a handkerchief; an antique token
> My father gave my mother. [5.2.219–23]

"Work" descriptively mutates here to something "amorous," and handkerchief is now described as the ancient *recognizance* or recorded evidence of the *pledge of love*. The final use of the word brings with it the tragic potential always inherent within this handkerchief and its work. When Lodovico says to Iago, "Look on the tragic lodging of this bed: / This is thy work, the object poisons sight, / Let it be hid . . ." [5.2.368–70], the "work" on the now blood-stained bed echoes back the handkerchief and the "work" woven into it. By the power of the reverberations that have collected around the term, Shakespeare has brought to tragic conclusion the central paradox of the play, the potent disequilibrium latent in the most loving act of humankind.

The power of the Shakespearean stage generates from what Inga-Stina Ewbank calls "a kind of purposeful dialectic between what is seen and what is said; between the power of words . . . [and] a visually presented reality."[6] The power is visual in such scenes as that where Coriolanus silently reaches for his mother's hand, where the sable-suited figure of Hamlet silently stalks the court, where Iago and Othello kneel in parodic pledge. The handkerchief image spanning *Othello* provides the same kind of visual / verbal bridge. When Emilia retrieves the dropped napkin, when Iago obtains it, and again when Bianca confronts Cassio with it, each character examines the "trifle" in a speech containing buried stage directions which suggest the handkerchief is held up for display to the audience. Mentioned no fewer than thirty-one times in the play, it is repeatedly before us either substantively or descriptively. The other great stage prop in this play is the bed—which, including references to "sheets," is mentioned twenty-five times. It is the off-stage object kept continually in focus by Iago's lewd references in [2.3]; it becomes the fixation of Othello's obsessive fantasies and the setting for "Cassio's dream"; and it is finally brought out on stage in the highly visual climax to receive its tragic lodging. The ocular picture of the spotted handkerchief and our final, indelible vision of the blood-soaked bed towards which the play relentlessly leads come together in the powerful verbal / visual echo, "Thy bed, lust stained, shall with lust's

6. " 'More Pregnantly Than Words': Some Uses and Limitations of Visual Symbolism," *ShS*, 24 (1971), 15.

blood be spotted" [5.1.36].[7] These are Othello's last words before he enters the bedroom to join Desdemona for the final bloody consummation, before he brings to fulfillment tragically both the literal and figurative "death"[8] which throughout has been signified in the very token that determines it.

The verbal and visual presence of the handkerchief reflects the image of the wedding sheets. This relationship between the two central stage props of *Othello* is a part of the broader structural tapestry of dramatic analogy, the Shakespearean use of mirrored reflection. Emilia's theft of the handkerchief, while on one hand serving the dramatic necessity of designing a character who knows how the napkin came into Cassio's possession, additionally serves to strengthen the handkerchief/sheets analogy. The effect of Emilia as thief (rather than Cinthio's Ensign) is to isolate her as both the agent whom Iago bids to steal the napkin and she whom Desdemona bids to lay out the fatal wedding sheets, the intermediary who never suspects the tragic implications of either action, she who finally must herself die on those same sheets because in fact she revealed her theft of the handkerchief.[9]

Few *Othello* commentators have failed to suspect that this vividly described object has some sort of implicit sexual association. Unfortunately, the majority of psychoanalytic interpretations—which run the gamut from "handkerchief as breast symbol and strawberries as nipples" to "handkerchief as penis, strawberries as glans"[1]—account only for dubious intuitions in Shakespeare's own subconscious and do not explain the napkin's significance as related to dramatic structure or audience apprehension. Kenneth Burke (and indeed Freud) did perceive the strawberry-spotted handkerchief was some sort of displaced genital symbol of Desdemona.[2] This connection is implied in Iago's initial comments about the handkerchief—that it will stir up dangerous conceits in Othello's mind which "with a little act upon the blood / Burn like the mines of sulphur" [3.3.329–30]. The words obviously refer to Hell, but they also anticipate the mad Lear's anatomization of women: "Beneath is all the fiends': there's hell, there's

---

7. Stockholder, p. 269, notes how these two images "ironically coalesce." Mudford, p. 5, also notices the verbal echo.

8. The fusion of the literal and figurative levels of meaning has often been noted. See especially Heilman, pp. 189–93.

9. For the idea of dramatic analogy see Kenneth Burke, "*Othello*: An Essay to illustrate a Method," *Hudson Review*, 4 (1951), 165–203. [See above, p. 244.] See also Francis Fergusson's *The Idea of a Theater* (Princeton, N.J., 1949), which discusses analogy as a central structural means of directing our attention to the relationship between concrete elements in a drama.

1. See, for example, Martin Wangh, "*Othello*, The Tragedy of Iago," *Psychoanalytic Quarterly*, 19 (1950), 202–12; M.D. Faber, "*Othello*: The Justice of it Pleases," *American Imago*, 28 (1971), 228–46; Robert Rogers, "Endopsychic Drama in *Othello*," *SQ*, 20 (1969), 213; and Gordon Ross Smith, "Igo [sic], the Paranoiac," *American Imago*, 16 (1959), 160–61.

2. Burke, p. 198. Burke concludes that it is an emblem of the private Desdemona "possessed by Othello," and relates the centrality of the object to his analysis of the ironies of property.

darkness, / There is the sulphurous pit, burning, scalding . . ." [*Lear*
4.6.126–27]. After conjuring up the erotically complex dream of
Cassio and Desdemona abed together, Iago immediately introduces
his most powerful gambit, the handkerchief associated with the
physical Desdemona. Exactly the same connective pattern is involved
at the opening of [act 4]. Again Iago shifts from talk of "naked with
her friend abed" to talk of a hypothetical handkerchief, and the mysterious power of the associational links between these subjects shat-
ters Othello's tenuous hold on rationality. As Burke notes,[3] the sense
of Othello's verbal fragmentation here is intelligible only through
the topics which find terrible association in his mind: "lie with her,
lie on her . . . belie her . . . handkerchief—confessions—handkerchief!" Unquestionably, the visualization of Cassio and Desdemona
in bed relates in Othello's mind to Cassio's possession of the symbolic token. Blinded to what this "evidence" actually proves, Othello
can now only believe that Cassio's ownership of the token must mean
that Cassio possessed the virginal Desdemona it symbolizes.

   The symbolic mystique of the handkerchief relates to the ancient
recognizance of the blood pledge. Within its fabric it also contains
the force which determines Othello's role in [act 5] as judicial priest.[4]
The final act stages a great deal more than an Othello victimized by
self-delusions, seizing upon an imagined role of justicer in order to
disguise murder as legal execution and rationalize the violence bred
from his military life. To see the tragic climax in this light is to leave
an Othello acting only out of a murderously personal motivation.
When he assumes the guise of judicial executioner, he is in some
senses adopting a role which gives him "positional assurance."[5] But
with paradoxical irony he is also truly executing his judicial role as
Governor by enacting the harsh dictates of a real and not self-
invented code of legality. The code from which Othello acts is not
an alien one which we can attribute to some uncivilized notions of
barbarian blackness; it lies, rather, at the root of Western religious
law. Deuteronomy 22 dictates the execution of a bride unable to
produce the necessary "ocular proof" of her marital fidelity, the
blood-stain "tokens" on her wedding sheets: "But if this thing be true,
that the maide be not found a virgin, Then they shal bring forthe the
maide to the dore of her fathers house, and the men of her citie shal
stone her with stones to death: for she hathe wroght follie in Israél,
by playing the whore in her fathers house: so thou shalt put euil

---

3. Burke, p. 198. Mudford also notes when Othello falls into his trance the handkerchief
   remains in the forefront of his mind (p. 5).
4. See particularly Winifred M. T. Nowottny, "Justice and Love in *Othello*," *UTQ*, 21 (1951–
   52), 330–44, on Othello's judicial role.
5. This is of course Heilman's phrase. See also Matthew N. Proser, *The Heroic Image in Five
   Shakespearean Tragedies* (Princeton, N.J., 1965), pp. 92–171, for a study of the effect
   which the military roles of Othello and Coriolanus play in their tragedies.

away from among you. If a man be found lying with a woman married to a man, then they shal dye euen bothe twaine: *to wit,* the man that lay with the wife, and the wife: so thou shalt put euil from Israél" (Deut. 22.20–22). Othello's rationale to kill Desdemona the whore "else she'll betray more men" [5.2.6] perfectly paraphrases the injunction in Deuteronomy to execute the bride who is a whore so as "to put euil away from among you"; that Cassio must die with her rephrases the law that "they shal dye euen bothe twaine."

Shakespeare did not conclude his play with an execution by stoning. Instead he focused his tragic climax squarely on the act of consummation, the *literal* act *symbolically* woven into the handkerchief and that which we finally see *symbolically* reenacted upon the now *literal* sheets. The power and meaning of the final scene greatly depend upon this dynamic fusion of handkerchief and wedding sheets, the sanctified union promising life and the tragic union culminating in death. Shakespeare threw out Cinthio's inartistic conclusion in order to create one tightly connected with this analogy. For the same structural considerations he did not use the biblical prescription from Deuteronomy. He retained its idea, however, through layered echoes in Othello's language as Othello moves into the role of judicial executioner. Obsessed still with thoughts of the handkerchief, Othello first uses the image in connection with the traditional idea, "heart of stone": "And let her rot, and perish, and be damned to-night for she shall not live; no, my heart is turn'd to stone; I strike it, and it hurts my hand . . ." [4.1.176–78]. The second use retains some sense of the traditional metaphor, but already the image has begun to move away and meld into an emerging picture of Desdemona being stoned. Here, verbally connected to the sacrificial punishment he is about to enact, Othello sees Desdemona's perjured words as the missiles which stone her:

> By heaven, I saw my handkerchief in his hand:
> O perjur'd woman, thou dost stone thy heart,
> And makest me call what I intend to do
> A murder, which I thought a sacrifice;
> I saw the handkerchief. [5.2.63–67]

When the truth about the handkerchief is revealed, Othello cries for condign punishment from the harsh God he envisions, seeking finally to be himself stoned by the heavens: "Are there no stones in heaven; / But what serves for the thunder?" [5.2.240–41].

When Iago first came into gleeful possession of the handkerchief, he had said that it would serve evidence like "confirmations strong / As proofs of holy writ" [3.3.324–25]. Within the "holy writ" of Deuteronomy 22.13–22 Shakespeare may well have found the suggestions that determined his reshaping of Cinthio's narrative:[6] the consummation of a new marriage, a new bride condemned without recourse or explanation and judicially executed because she lacks the single piece of necessary evidence to prove her innocence, and an adulterer condemned to die "bothe twaine" with the adulteress. Having several times already dramatized the idea of "token" as the stage symbol of sexual exchange, Shakespeare may well have noted the connection between "tokens of . . . virginitie" and the missing proof of fidelity within Deuteronomy 22. Within these passages also lay the visual image of the blood-spotted "shete," the solitary piece of legal evidence justifying execution.

By converting Cinthio's piece of linen into a symbolic reduction of the bridal sheets, Shakespeare seized upon a dynamic way of integrating his received plot mechanism into a central symbol around which the issues of marital consummation, judicial evidence, and murder perceived as legal execution could all cohere. As symbolic nexus, Othello's magical handkerchief not only spans the major issues of the play but also reaches into man's deepest cognitions about his sexuality, his myths, his religion, and his laws. In an appropriately Shakespearean way, Thomas Rymer unwittingly spoke with ironic perception when he added his infamous subtitle: *Othello: The Tragedy of the Handkerchief.*

MARK ROSE

Othello's Occupation: Shakespeare and the Romance of Chivalry†

> O now, for ever
> Farewell the tranquil mind! farewell content!
> Farewell the plumed troops, and the big wars
> That makes ambition virtue! O, farewell!
> Farewell the neighing steed and the shrill trump,
> The spirit-stirring drum, th' ear-piercing fife,
> The royal banner, and all quality,
> Pride, pomp, and circumstance of glorious war!
> And O you mortal engines, whose rude throats
> Th' immortal Jove's dread clamors counterfeit,
> Farewell! Othello's occupation's gone.[1]

---

6. Richmond Noble, *Shakespeare's Biblical Knowledge and Use of the Book of Common Prayer* (London, 1935), p. 220, cites this very passage, Deuteronomy 22.21, for Othello's identification of folly with whore: "She turn'd to folly, and she was a whore" [5.2.135].

† From *English Literary Renaissance* 15 (1985): 293–311. Reprinted with permission of *English Literary Renaissance*. The author's quotations from *Othello* have been retained, but bracketed references are to this Norton Critical Edition.

1. [3.3.348–58]. All citations of Shakespeare refer to *The Riverside Shakespeare*, ed. G. Blakemore Evans (Boston, Mass., 1974).

Othello's adieus to tranquility and content at the start of this speech
evoke something more like the pastoral than the military ideal. Even
when the imagery becomes explicitly military in the evocation of the
"plumed troops" and the "big wars" there is a subtle continuity with
the opening pastoralism. Here the lines suggest a transformation in
which "ambition," which is a vice in a world defined by pastoral
content, becomes a "virtue" in a martial context—that is, both a
positive good, and in the archaic sense of *virtu,* a source of strength.
Moreover, the static quality of "plumed troops" and "big wars" is
compatible with the feeling the lines convey that something like pastoral *otium* is being continued in a martial vein. Explicit activity
enters the picture when Othello imagines the world he has lost as a
parade of neighing horses and playing instruments—trumpet, drum,
and fife—an ascending procession of sound that climaxes in the god-
like roar of the cannon. "Farewell! Othello's occupation's gone." Six
times in eleven lines Othello says farewell. The repetition articulates
the speech, contributing to the sense of a procession passing with
Othello bidding adieu to each of the squadrons in the parade of his
life. It also unifies the speech, turning it into a nostalgic lament for
a paradoxically apprehended martial pastoral.

What has Othello lost? The contradictions in this speech, at once
static and active, pastoral and martial, convey the emotional urgency
with which an image of the perfected world of absolute being is here
fashioned. It is a world in which everything, including the neighing
of horses and the booming of cannon, takes on the aspect of music;
a world without stress, one in which even ambitious striving for glory
has been reconceived as a form of tranquility. To participate in the
harmonious clamor of this grand march in which mortal engines
counterfeit the huge sounds of immortal Jove is to live at the farthest
verge of human possibility. It is to be nearly as absolute as a god.
Plainly such a state of being, one in which there is no gap between
desire and satisfaction, between, as Macbeth puts it, the firstlings of
the heart and the firstlings of the hand, is a condition radically
incompatible with self-reflection, thought, or uncertainty of any
kind. To banish Othello from such an Eden, proof of Desdemona's
infidelity is unnecessary; mere suspicion will do as well as certainty.

Why should suspicion of Desdemona's infidelity end Othello's
occupation as a soldier? It helps to observe that Othello conceives
himself in this speech as a type of the knight validated by the absolute worthiness of the mistress he serves. Call the mistress into question and not only the knight's activity but his very identity collapses.
Of course in this case the mistress, the necessarily unattainable lady
of romance, has become the wife: sexual availability—as opposed to
the intensity of mere fantasizing—has entered the picture. Even

without Iago's machinations, then, the romantic image of the absolute worthiness of the lady is at best unstable. Others have developed this aspect of Othello's vulnerability to Iago.[2] Here let us note simply that this speech is a clue to Othello's romanticizing imagination. It is of a piece with his address to the Senate in which he retells the story of his adventures among cannibals and monsters, his speech to Desdemona about the magic in the web of the handkerchief in which he invokes witches and charms as a way of explaining its overwhelming significance, or his final speech in which he recalls the exotic turbaned Turk in order to explain why he is about to slay himself. One might interpret *Othello* as a kind of tragic *Don Quixote*, a play in which Shakespeare explores the ways in which a romanticizing imagination can lead to devastating error. Yet despite the appeal of such an approach—and certainly it would be illuminating up to a point—we should note that Othello's romanticism is neither so explicit as Don Quixote's nor so firmly demarcated from the general world of the narrative.

There are no giants or dragons in *Othello*. The play's military world consists of generals, lieutenants, and ancients rather than knights, squires, evil magicians, and faithless Saracens. It is a world in which career advancement can be presented as a plausible motive for action; it is a comparatively workaday place of fleets, intelligence reports, and expeditionary forces. But the proximate realism should not blind us to the play's romantic aspects. There are Christian soldiers and threatening infidels here. Othello, a black warrior of royal lineage who turns out to be capable of astonishing violence, has something of a Savage Knight about him, and Desdemona may well in the constancy of her affection recall a Princess of Love and Chastity. Iago is no magician—indeed, he explicitly denies that he works by witchcraft—and yet his ensnarement of Othello's soul together with his manipulation of his perceptions may recall Spenser's Archimago, who similarly provides Redcross with ocular proof of his lady's infidelity.[3] Moreover, all these elements reminiscent of chivalric romance—Othello's royal blood and adventurous past, the somewhat miraculous quality of Desdemona's innocence, the air of diabolical mystery that clings to Iago, the background of war with the infidel—are Shakespeare's additions to the Othello story as he found it in Cinthio's novella. Not just Othello's imagination but, I would suggest, Shakespeare's own is informed by the patterns of chivalric romance.

2. See in particular Stephen Greenblatt's exciting discussion in *Renaissance Self-Fashioning* (Chicago, Ill., 1980), pp. 222–57.
3. Redcross and Archimago are, respectively, the hero and the villain in book 1 of Edmund Spenser's romantic epic *The Faerie Queene* (1590). [Editor's note]

II

A few words about the Elizabethan chivalric revival are in order
here. As Roy Strong says, "It is one of the great paradoxes of the
Elizabethan world, one of its touchstones, that an age of social, political and religious revolution should cling to and deliberately erect a
façade of the trappings of feudalism."[4] Elizabethan culture was saturated with feudal idealism. In life and in art chivalric themes were
pervasive. By the 1580s the spectacular Accession Day Tilts had
reached their fully developed form. In this period, too, Robert
Smythson was designing such fantasy castles as Wollaton Hall, Sidney was writing the *Arcadia*, Spenser was writing *The Faerie Queene*,
and the London stages were populated by damsels in distress, knights
in armor, and wicked enchanters in dozens of plays—most now
lost—with names like *Herpetulus the Blue Knight and Perobia*, *The
History of the Solitary Knight*, and *Sir Clyomon and Sir Clamydes*.[5]
Chivalric fantasies of service to the Virgin Queen shaped Elizabethan court style and also affected foreign policy. One product of the
chivalric revival was Sidney's *Arcadia*, another was his death in 1586
in a campaign in which romantic notions continually obscured for
Eliza's knights the complex facts of a situation in which Dutch
burghers were attempting to throw off Spanish rule.[6]

Northrop Frye's conception of romance as "the search of the libido
or desiring self for a fulfillment that will deliver it from the anxieties
of reality but will still contain that reality"[7] might well be a gloss on
the Elizabethan effort to turn reality into a romance. The late sixteenth century was a time of dramatic social changes and probably
also a period of considerable social anxiety. London was burgeoning,
commerce was developing rapidly, old bonds of service and obligation were yielding to new relationships based on the marketplace,
and the religious unity of Europe was gone forever. Chivalric games
and ceremonies helped to obscure the relative newness of so many
of the noble families as well as the fact that, despite the continuing
prestige of war, the aristocracy had ceased to be a warrior class and
was becoming an administrative elite. By this period, as Lawrence
Stone has shown, there was little that was particularly feudal about
the English nobility, who from an early time had been deeply

---

4. *The Cult of Elizabeth: Elizabethan Portraiture and Pageantry* (London, 1977), pp. 161–
   62. See also Frances A. Yates, "Elizabethan Chivalry: The Romance of the Accession Day
   Tilts," in *Astraea: The Imperial Theme in the Sixteenth Century* (London, 1975), pp. 88–
   111.
5. On chivalric themes in architecture see Mark Girouard, *Robert Smythson and the Elizabethan Country House* (New Haven, Conn., 1983), esp. pp. 205–32. Betty J. Littleton
   discusses the romance dramas of the 1570s and 1580s and provides a list of titles in her
   critical edition of *Clyomon and Clamydes* (The Hague, 1968).
6. See Jan Albert Dop, *Eliza's Knights: Soldiers, Poets, and Puritans in the Netherlands* (Lei-
   den, 1981).
7. *The Anatomy of Criticism* (Princeton, NJ., 1957), p. 193.

engaged in entrepreneurial activity.[8] On the other hand, there was little that was clearly bourgeois—in the modern sense—about the sensibility of the Elizabethan middle class. Interestingly, the bourgeois hero tales of the 1590s and early 1600s—Deloney's *Jack of Newbury*, Dekker's *Shoemaker's Holiday* and other stories and plays celebrating the virtues of the new men of commerce—show middle-class figures in feudal postures, fighting and feasting like knights.[9] The usual aspiration of the successful businessman was not to oppose the interests of the landed aristocracy and gentry but to join them as soon as possible, one notable case in point being Shakespeare himself.

The chivalric revival assimilated the complexities of the present to a mythical world of the past, but at its center was the living Queen. In her own person Elizabeth held the contradictions of her culture together, and she did this in part by turning herself into a character, Gloriana, and her life and that of her country into a story. But the moment of magical balance was necessarily brief. By the late 1590s the fervor of the previous decade was gone. Corruption at court was more marked and commented on, and it had become increasingly more difficult for the Queen, who was now a full generation older than her principal courtiers, to play the role of the virginal beauty.[1] Nor should the traumatic effect of the Earl of Essex's rebellion and execution be underestimated.[2] Essex, who is one of the very few contemporary figures to whom Shakespeare directly alludes, was the inheritor of Philip Sidney's sword and of his position in the national imagination as the embodiment of chivalry. According to his biographer, his rise and sudden fall in 1601 probably effected the nation more deeply than any event since the defeat of the Spanish Armada.[3] In any case, the time came when the Elizabethan romances—both the romance enacted by the Queen and those composed by her poets and dramatists—could no longer carry conviction. Despite a brief revival of some of its themes in 1610–1612 at the court of Prince Henry, nothing like the special quality of Elizabethan chivalry could occur again.

8. See *The Crisis of the Aristocracy 1558–1641* (Oxford, 1965), esp. pp. 335–84. Diane Bornstein, *Mirrors of Courtesy* (Hamden, Conn., 1975), studies English chivalric manuals and makes a number of suggestive comments on the social functions of Renaissance chivalry.
9. See Laura Stevenson O'Connell's important "The Elizabethan Bourgeois Hero-Tale: Aspects of an Adolescent Social Consciousness," in *After the Reformation: Essays in Honor of J. H. Hexter*, ed. Barbara C. Malament (Philadelphia, Pa., 1980), pp. 267–90.
1. See J. E. Neale, "The Elizabethan Political Scene," in *Essays in Elizabethan History* (London, 1958), pp. 59–84, on the tenor of late Elizabethan court life. Stephen Orgel, "Making Greatness Familiar," *Genre*, 15 (1982), 41–48, has suggestive comments about late Elizabethan chivalry.
2. In February 1601, the earl of Essex staged an abortive coup against Queen Elizabeth, or (more precisely) against the Elizabethan courtiers who, he believed, were influencing the queen against him. He was promptly condemned for treason and beheaded. [Editor's note]
3. G. B. Harrison, *The Life and Death of Robert Devereux Earl of Essex* (London, 1937), pp. 274–75.

III

I know of no general study of Shakespeare's relation to the romance dramas of the 1570s and 1580s and to the Elizabethan chivalric revival.[4] Nevertheless, * * * the theme of both historical tetralogies is the disintegration of an absolute world of chivalry, and in this theme the histories might be said to look forward to Othello's farewell to arms.[5] * * *

The tone of Shakespeare's treatment of chivalric themes, like so much else, changes in the early seventeenth century. *Troilus and Cressida,* probably written the year after the Essex rebellion, is biting in its exposure of the putrefied core that seems to hide within the goodly armor of chivalric pretentions, and in *King Lear* not even the spectacular romance-like triumph of the unknown knight Edgar over his evil brother Edmund can prevent the ugly hanging of Cordelia and the play's tragic end. Particularly relevant to *Othello,* however, is the tragedy that immediately precedes it chronologically. It would be hard, I think, to overemphasize the importance of chivalry to *Hamlet.* The play takes its point of departure, and finds its image of the lost chivalric world, in Horatio's evocation of King Hamlet and King Fortinbras locked in a valiant single combat ratified by law and chivalry. It is this evocation of heroic combat in a past time when things were absolutely what they seemed to be that gives meaning to the great falling off that constitutes the play's present world. In creeping into the garden to poison his brother, Claudius has in effect poisoned chivalry. * * *

IV

"I'll pour this pestilence into his ear" [2.3.344]: the language with which Iago introduces his plan for undoing Othello strikingly recalls Claudius' poison poured into the porches of King Hamlet's ears. We can note, too, that Othello's farewell to arms figures in the play's structure in a manner analogous to the image of the kings in combat, providing in its martial pastoral a point of reference against which the present situation, Othello in the agonies of Iago's poison, is to be measured. But the fact that in *Othello* the nostalgic reference point comes in the middle rather than at the start of the tragedy is important; whereas in *Hamlet* chivalry is dead before the play begins,

4. There have been a number of interesting particular studies, among them Paul N. Siegel's "Shakespeare and the Neo-Chivalric Cult of Honor," *The Centennial Review of Arts and Sciences,* 8 (1964), 39–70, which focuses on the code of the duello; Sheldon Zitner's "Hamlet, Duellist," *University of Toronto Quarterly,* 34 (1969), 1–18, which discusses *Hamlet* and the duello; and Frances A. Yates' controversial *Shakespeare's Last Plays* (London, 1978), which discusses the late plays in the context of the chivalric revival at the court of Prince Henry.

5. Shakespeare's histories are often discussed as two groups of four plays, all written before 1600. [Editor's note]

in *Othello* we observe the process of the poisonous transformation. In fact we do more than observe, we participate. In *Hamlet* the audience's representative, the figure who draws us into dramatic engagement with his purposes, is the prince, and Claudius, as his antagonist, becomes in consequence a relatively opaque figure. In *Othello*, as in *Richard III* and *Macbeth*, Shakespeare plays the dynamics of theatrical engagement against moral judgment, and this is one reason that *Othello* does not lapse into melodrama. From the opening in which Iago manipulates Roderigo and Brabantio the play is structured so that we enter the action from Iago's point of view, and his many strategically placed soliloquies and asides confirm our dramatic engagement with him through at least the first half of the play. Othello himself is magnificent, a commanding and dominating figure, but until the temptation scene and the start of his falling off he is also, like Claudius, apprehended at a certain distance, observed as one might observe a public figure and a stranger.

Othello, the exotic black man from Africa, is a stranger in another, more literal, sense as well. In *Hamlet* and in the history plays the representatives of chivalric perfection—King Hamlet, Henry V in the first tetralogy, Edward the Black Prince as he is evoked at the start of the second tetralogy—are generally ancestral figures. Even the Earl of Richmond and Henry V in the second tetralogy are ancestral figures to the audience if not to the characters in the plays. In *Othello*, however, the knightly defender of Christian civilization is projected as an alien. Othello's blackness is the index of a different orientation toward the chivalric figure. Moreover, as many critics since Bradley have remarked, Iago is a kind of playwright, an artist carefully maneuvering his characters into position to bring his tragedy to fulfillment.[6] Perhaps, then, we can think of *Othello* as a play in which Shakespeare is recapitulating his own earlier representations of an absolute world of chivalry, alienating them, and through Iago representing something like his own role in plotting the disintegration of the absolute world.

V

> Put money in thy purse . . . I say put money in thy purse . . . put money in thy purse . . . put money in thy purse . . . fill thy purse with money . . . put money in thy purse . . . Make all the money thou canst . . . therefore make money . . . go make money . . . go, provide thy money . . . put money enough in your purse. [1.3.337–67]

It is more than a little tempting to think of Iago as an embodiment of the prodigious energies of the new commercialism of the Renais-

6. A. C. Bradley, *Shakespearean Tragedy* (London, 1904), pp. 230–31.

sance, and thus to turn *Othello* into an allegory in which bourgeois man destroys the representative of the older feudal values. Thus, whereas Othello speaks of the plumed troop and the royal banner in terms that evoke an activity of transcendent worth, Iago can talk casually of "the trade of war" [1.2.1]. Iago's speech is shot through with the language of commerce. "I know my price," he says when he describes being passed over for promotion, "I am worth no worse a place" [1.1.10], and, contrasting himself with Cassio, he dismissed the lieutenant as a mere accountant, a "debitor and creditor," and a "counter-caster" [1.1.28]. Yet even though he has money and purses on his mind, Iago's motive for bringing down Othello is certainly not profit. Moreover, Othello too can speak in commercial terms, as when he invites Desdemona to bed after their arrival in Cyprus: "Come, my dear love, / The purchase made, the fruits are to ensue; / The profit's yet to come 'tween me and you" [2.3.8–10].

To reduce *Othello* to historical allegory would plainly be to distort the play. Such a reduction would also be anachronistic. As Lawrence Stone and other social historians have taught us, we must beware of imagining anything like a clear-cut opposition in this period between a declining feudal class and a rising bourgeoisie.[7] The late sixteenth and early seventeenth centuries were a time of transition and contradiction, a period in which fundamentally incompatible social forms and structures of thought sat uneasily side by side in a manner that may make us think of those sixteenth-century account books kept partly in Arabic, partly in Roman numerals.[8] An old world of traditional forms and values was largely gone, but a new one had not yet clearly taken shape.

Particularly apparent were the tensions between the traditional feudal values of honor, loyalty, and service, and the less absolute imperatives of the marketplace. On the one hand honor might be regarded as a kind of religion, something worth dying for, as for instance when Cassio equates his good name with his soul: "Reputation, reputation, reputation! O, I have lost my reputation! I have lost the immortal part of myself, and what remains is bestial" [2.3.252–54]. On the other, it was often treated as merchandise. "I would to God thou and I knew where a commodity of good names were to be bought," Falstaff says mockingly to Hal (*1 Henry IV*, 1.2.82–83), and a few years later in the Jacobean debasement of honors, good names were openly traded like stocks and bonds. Thus Stone reports that in 1606 Lionel Cranfield bought the making of

---

7. The literature on this subject is vast, but besides Stone's *Crisis of the Aristocracy* see J. H. Hexter's seminal essays printed in revised versions in *Reappraisals in History* (London, 1961), esp. "The Myth of the Middle Class in Tudor England," pp. 71–116, and "Storm Over the Gentry," pp. 117–62.
8. I owe this apt image to O'Connell, "The Bourgeois Hero-Tale," p. 272.

six knights from his friend Arthur Ingram for £373.1s.8d.[9] In this transitional moment, no simple antithesis between the values of the marketplace and those of the field of honor is possible. Despite his skepticism about honor, Sir John Falstaff is not a bourgeois figure. Likewise, Antonio, the paragon of lordly generosity who is contrasted with Shylock in *The Merchant of Venice,* is not, as we might suppose given the values that he embodies, a feudal figure.[1] Perhaps, then, we should imagine the tension between feudal and commercial codes at this time as less like a modern class struggle than like a medieval psychomachia—that is, as a still internalized struggle in which members of the same group, or even at times a single individual, can be found operating inconsistently, now according to one set of values, now according to another.

The mediation of contradiction can be understood as one of the functions of drama or even of narrative generally. With this in mind let us briefly note that Shakespeare often plays romantic and absolute attitudes against contingent and commercial ones, building drama out of the tension. * * *

No practical resolution of the cultural contradiction may be possible but at least there can be the satisfactions of the achievement of narrative closure. In any case, *Othello,* too, incorporates the tension between romantic absolutism and the antithetical values of the marketplace, but here instead of being held in triumphant balance in the style of the 1590s, the brutal power latent in the contradiction is used to drive a tragedy.

VI

Let us begin by observing a major change that Shakespeare makes in the structure of Cinthio's narrative. In the novella the wicked ensign's revenge is not directed at the Moor so much as at the lady. Cinthio's ensign is a rebuffed suitor whose passion for Desdemona turns to hate. Shakespeare, however, pits Iago directly against Othello. One effect of this change is to obscure the villain's motive. Another is to alter the lady's position in the narrative structure, demoting her from one of the two ultimate figures in the story to an intermediary. Like the handkerchief with which she is associated, Desdemona becomes a kind of object, an instrument of Iago's revenge against Othello. Passed first from Brabantio's hands into the Moor's and then ignorantly thrown away, Shakespeare's Desdemona

9. *Crisis of the Aristocracy,* p. 77.

1. Giorgio Melchiori makes this point in his suggestive "Shakespeare and the New Economics of His Time," *Review of National Literatures,* 3 (1972), 123–37. Melchiori's general argument is that Shakespeare's ambiguity reveals his full awareness of the social changes taking place in his time, but his discussion is grounded in a misleading conception of clear class distinctions in the period.

figures in the narrative as property. Iago's revenge looks forward to the bourgeois style of a later age; he achieves satisfaction by depriving his enemy of his most valued possession.

At the same time that Shakespeare's narrative demotes Desdemona from a person to property, it also elevates her to an angel. Cinthio's lady is a rather matter of fact heroine, but Shakespeare's is a transcendent figure who refracts the long series of divine ladies that reaches back through the sonnet and romance heroines of the sixteenth century to, among others, Petrarch's Laura and Dante's Beatrice. Her conversation with Emilia about women who betray their husbands evokes the realm of the marketplace precisely in order to separate her from it absolutely. "Wouldst thou do such a deed for all the world?" she asks Emilia, who replies less romantically that while she would not do it for anything trivial such as a ring or a dress, she certainly would do it for the world: "The world's a huge thing; it is a great price / For a small vice" [4.3.69–70]. Later, guiltlessly dying, Desdemona refuses to blame Othello for anything: "Commend me to my kind lord. O, farewell!" [5.2.128]. At once property and an angel of selflessness, Desdemona, too, looks forward to the bourgeois age and to its conception of woman.

Behind the contradictions implicit in Shakespeare's Desdemona may be glimpsed the tensions of a moment of cultural transformation. In a penetrating observation, Kenneth Burke suggests that *Othello* incorporates an analogue in the realm of human affinity to the enclosure acts whereby common lands were made private. Shakespeare's play inscribes an act of spiritual enclosure, love transformed into private property. Whatever is owned may be seized. The fear of loss is integral to the principle of property and thus the threat that Iago represents comes as much from within Othello as from without; Shakespeare externalizes the already implicit fear in the figure of Iago, making the villain, in Burke's phrase, into a voice at Othello's ear. Othello and Iago, possessor and the threat of loss, are dialectically related parts of the one "fascination." Add Desdemona to the integral, Burke says, "and you have a tragic trinity of ownership in the profoundest sense of ownership, the property in human affections, as fetishistically localized in the object of possession."[2]

Property implies theft: therein lies the play's premise. Opening in Venice, the city of fabled commercial wealth, *Othello* is structured as a series of thefts. The first is a variant of the stock comic action of the stolen daughter that Shakespeare uses also in his other play set in Venice when Jessica escapes from Shylock's house laden with ducats and jewels. Here, in an episode that foreshadows his later and

2. "Othello: An Essay to illustrate a Method," *The Hudson Review*, 4 (1951), 165–203. In a few brilliant pages (pp. 165–69) Burke anticipates many of the points made here in a different context. [See above, pp. 244–48.]

more subtle arousing of Othello, Iago wakes Brabantio: "Awake! what ho, Brabantio! thieves, thieves! / Look to your house, your daughter, and your bags! / Thieves, thieves!" [1.1.76–78]. And a moment after: "Zounds, sir, y'are robb'd! For shame, put on your gown; / Your heart is burst, you have lost half your soul" [1.1.83–84].

Let us note the fusion of spiritual and proprietary ideas: Desdemona is both half her father's soul and a possession equivalent to his money. Let us note, too, that so far as the play is concerned Desdemona might have no mother. She is represented as wholly her father's possession, and the principal question concerning her at the opening is whether the transfer from father to husband has been rightfully made, whether she has in fact been stolen from Brabantio or properly won. Again, the play fuses spiritual and proprietary themes when in the Senate scene the Duke decides the case on romantic principles. "I think this tale would win my daughter too" [1.3.170], he comments on Othello's speech, and when Desdemona acknowledges that she freely loves the Moor, Brabantio must yield.

The play's first movement is "The Abduction of Desdemona"; the second is "The Theft of Cassio's Name." Cassio supposes that he is wholly responsible for the loss of his reputation, but we know that Iago, plying his victim with wine, has robbed him. The presentation of Cassio as a decent man changed into a drunken madman foreshadows the action with Othello to come, specifically, the theme of diabolic possession: "O thou invisible spirit of wine, if thou hast no name to be known by, let us call thee devil! . . . To be now a sensible man, by and by a fool, and presently a beast! O strange! Every inordinate cup is unbless'd, and the ingredient is a devil" [2.3.270–97]. To which Iago replies in language that plays upon the theme: "Come, come; good wine is a good familiar creature, if it be well us'd" [2.3.298–99].

In the transitional culture of the early modern period the concept of the soul is also affected by the hegemonic principle of property. Now a soul is something a person *has* as well as something a person *is*. We think, of course, of Marlowe's Faustus[3] selling his soul by contract like an aristocrat turning his land into cash; and it may be, too, that the interest in cases of possession and exorcism at the end of the sixteenth century reveals the influence of proprietary modes of thought.[4] In *Othello*, at any rate, the theme of diabolic possession

3. *Doctor Faustus* by Christopher Marlowe (1563–1592) was an immediate theatrical success in 1588–89 and frequently revived into the early seventeenth century. [Editor's note]

4. On possession and dispossession in Elizabethan England see Keith Thomas, *Religion and the Decline of Magic* (London, 1971), pp. 477–92, and D. P. Walker, *Unclean Spirits: Possession and Exorcism in France and England in the Late Sixteenth and Early Seventeenth Centuries* (London, 1981). On *Othello* see David Kaula's excellent "Othello Possessed: Notes on Shakespeare's Use of Magic and Witchcraft," *Shakespeare Studies*, 2 (1966),

is related to the play's concern with property. Here the ideas of soul, property, and honor join together in a complex dance of equivalences and ironies, as when Iago tells Brabantio that he has been robbed of half his soul or when Cassio speaks of his reputation as his immortal part.

The play's main action, which begins in the temptation scene when Iago at last turns to work directly upon Othello, depends upon this system of unstable equivalences. Speaking to Cassio, Iago has dismissed the loss of reputation as insignificant, but now he echoes Cassio when he proclaims the opposite to Othello:

> Good name in man and woman, dear my lord,
> Is the immediate jewel of their souls.
> Who steals my purse steals trash; 'tis something, nothing;
> 'Twas mine, 'tis his, and has been slave to thousands;
> But he that filches from me my good name
> Robs me of that which not enriches him,
> And makes me poor indeed. [3.3.158–164]

With the idea of theft thus implanted in his thoughts, Othello himself is soon speaking of robbery—"What sense had I in her stol'n hours of lust?" [3.3.339]—accusing Desdemona of filching her honor, which as her husband belongs ultimately to him, and thus of stealing also his own good name.

"I am your own for ever" [3.3.479]. When at the end of the temptation scene Iago says that he belongs to Othello forever we understand that he means the opposite of what he speaks: Othello is now his. Othello believes that Desdemona has been stolen from him but the truth is that he has been stolen from himself. The demi-devil Iago has taken possession of his soul. Soon, like a classic case of demonic possession, Othello will be thrashing on the ground, foaming and raving in a fit. Soon, too, diabolic powers will in effect speak through Othello's mouth as the smooth and authoritative cadences of what Wilson Knight calls the "Othello music" yield to the staccato fragments and ugly images associated with Iago. In this way the unitary world of absolute self-possession that is recapitulated in "Farewell the tranquil mind" is split open and Othello becomes estranged not only from Desdemona but from himself. Like Spenser's Redcross knight, who is also launched into a world of doubleness, Othello is propelled into a nightmare of duplicity in which his love and his doubt are at war with each other. This process of self-alienation climaxes in Othello's suicide, the one half of his divided self execut-

---

112–32. See also Stephen Greenblatt's extremely suggestive "*King Lear* and Harsnett's 'Devil-Fiction,' " *Genre,* 15 (1982), 239–42.

ing justice upon the other as once he administered justice to the Turk in Aleppo. Thus the narrative—although not of course the contradictions that drive the narrative—is resolved.

VII

Iago's diabolism is of course only metaphorical. Shakespeare is exploring a secular equivalent to demonic possession, showing how a terrible misapprehension can take control of a normally rational mind. *Othello,* in which there are neither ghosts, soothsayers, witches, nor supernatural prodigies, is one of the most secular of Shakespeare's tragedies. Nevertheless, it is significant that the word "devil" occurs in its various forms more often here than in any other Shakespeare play. The word "faith," too, is prominent whether it is used casually as in Iago and Cassio's discussion of Bianca where it occurs repeatedly as a mild expletive (4.1) or whether it is used portentously as in Othello's tremendous oath, "My life upon her faith" [1.3.292]. What Shakespeare is doing in this play is appropriating spiritual conceptions, turning them into metaphors for secular experiences. But metaphors work two ways. If *Othello* incorporates a process of demystification, the assimilation of the supernatural to the natural world, it also incorporates the antithetical movement. The story may not literally be the temptation and fall of man from faith, but the play is not purely domestic tragedy either. An interpretation may legitimately stress either the process of naturalization or the way the domestic drama suggests events of cosmic significance. Like all of Shakespeare's work, *Othello* is implicated in the Renaissance system of analogical thought in which the realms of matter and spirit are not yet wholly divided and distinguished. Thus the play can be at once domestic and cosmic, secular and supernatural.

Othello is fascinating as a historical document because of the way it inscribes a transitional moment in Western culture. In it we can almost see the supernatural realm receding. The feudal world of honor, fidelity, and service is becoming the bourgeois world of property and contractual relations. Heroic tragedy is turning into domestic tragedy. It was Shakespeare's fortune to partake of two worlds without belonging completely to either. Shakespeare's myriad-mindedness—the quality that Norman Rabkin speaks of as complementarity—has much to do with this particular historical situation, as does his endless self-consciousness, the metadramatic aspect of his plays that has been emphasized by Sigurd Burckhardt and James Calderwood.

* * *

VIII

* * * Shakespeare, who came to maturity in the 1580s at the height of the Elizabethan revival of chivalry, was not ready to write anti-romances like *Don Quixote* or *The Knight of the Burning Pestle*.[5] He was, I think, still too deeply possessed by the absolute world of fidelity. He could write about the death of chivalry or the corruption of chivalry but he could not distance himself sufficiently from its imaginative claims to burlesque it. As a principal shareholder in London's most successful theatrical company and an energetic accumulator of wealth in Stratford and London, Shakespeare evidently participated in the new ethos of the marketplace. But he was also still something of a romantic, even if an unillusioned one.

I suggested earlier that we might think of *Othello* as a play in which Shakespeare recapitulates his own earlier representations of the absolute world of chivalry and that we might regard Iago, the cunning artist of tragedy, as at least in part a representation of Shakespeare himself. Iago is not bourgeois man—that creature had not, so to speak, been thought in 1604. Nevertheless, he is a figure in which the age could find something like the bourgeois cast of mind, together with the multitude of fears and desires that it aroused, made manifest. But Iago is not simply the pragmatist and materialist that he seems to take himself to be. Why should he want to destroy Othello? Iago and Othello are reciprocal figures, part of the same— to use Burke's word—fascination. Just as Othello is possessed by Iago, so Iago is from the beginning of the play possessed by Othello. But though Iago succeeds in destroying the Moor and Desdemona as well, he does not, we might say, succeed in exorcising the spirit they embody. Desdemona remains a miracle of fidelity to the end, and Othello, released from the demi-devil's snares, dies reasserting his allegiance to his heroic self.

True enough; yet to conclude our discussion on this romantic note of sustained fidelity and reasserted heroism misrepresents the tenor of Shakespeare's play. Othello may be an honorable murderer but he is a murderer nonetheless, and at the story's end both Desdemona and the Moor are dead. The world of *Othello* is not that of the novel, the characteristic genre of bourgeois civilization, but neither is it that of Elizabethan romance. *Othello* represents an intermediate moment in cultural development and an intermediate form, tragedy. Romance incorporates certainties, absolute opposites of good and evil. Tragedy subverts, deconstructs, certainties and absolutes, or, as Fredric Jameson puts it, tragedy rebukes romance.[6] What Shake-

---

5. Cervantes's novel was published in 1605. Francis Beaumont's play was first performed probably in 1607. [Editor's note]

6. *The Political Unconscious: Narrative as a Socially Symbolic Act* (Ithaca, N.Y., 1981), pp. 115–16.

speare has done in *Othello* is to convert the material of Elizabethan romance into tragedy.

Tragedy involves *katharsis:* purging, cleansing, exorcising. The scapegoats of this particular tragic sacrifice are Desdemona and Othello, figures of an exquisite and dangerous romantic beauty. The high priest is Iago, who draws us as audience into dynamic engagement with his purposes, mobilizing destructive emotions that we may not wish to acknowledge. We participate with Iago in splitting open the absolutes of Othello's martial pastoral. We assist in his project of driving the romance hero and his lady out of the world, of torturing Othello and Desdemona to death. Like Othello, we too are in a sense possessed. But because this is theater we are simultaneously dispossessed. Iago engages our rapaciousness, jealousy, and fear, but he also allows us to alienate ourselves from those ungentle emotions, projecting them onto him. Thus he too becomes a scapegoat. Protagonist and antagonist cancel each other out.[7] We are left at the end with neither a reassertion of an old world nor a prefiguration of a new one, but a mere vacancy, or, rather, a tableau of corpses and a disconcerting promise that Iago too will be tortured.

JAMES R. SIEMON

"Nay, That's Not Next": *Othello,* [5.2] in Performance, 1760–1900†

Shakespeare's directing hand offers guidance to readers and performers, but individuals as well as eras have not merely ignored that direction but have, on occasion, firmly rejected it. When taken as a group, the evasions, embellishments, and outright contradictions of Shakespeare's text that win acceptance in the late eighteenth- and nineteenth-century performances of the final scene of *Othello* suggest a coherence of interpretation based on particular notions of both tragedy and femininity. Understanding the strains that the era put upon the scene, makes us more aware of those notions, and, at the same time, directs our attention to notable features of the Shakespearean text itself.[1]

7. Cf. Franco Moretti: Shakespeare "may announce the dawn of bourgeois civilization, but not by prefiguring it. On the contrary, he demonstrates inexorably how, obeying the old rules, which are the only ones he knows, the world can only fall apart," *Signs Taken For Wonders: Essays in the Sociology of Literary Forms* (London, 1983), p. 68. Moretti's exciting discussion of Elizabethan and Jacobean tragedy also appears in abridged form as " 'A Huge Eclipse': Tragic Form and the Deconsecration of Sovereignty," *Genre,* 15 (1982), 7–40.
† From *Shakespeare Quarterly* 37 (1986): 38–51. © Folger Shakespeare Library. Reprinted with permission of The Johns Hopkins University Press. The author's quotations from *Othello* have been retained, but bracketed references are to this Norton Critical Edition.
1. This essay is so heavily indebted to the influence of the late Bernard Beckerman that I

I

If, as William Winter maintains while looking back over nine-teenth-century productions, performances of *Othello* can be classi-fied according to their treatment of the final scene, it is not only because the scene demands crucial decisions about themes and characters.[2] The scene tests productions by its extremity, an emo-tional violence that elicited intensely negative reactions throughout the later eighteenth and the nineteenth centuries, from Dr. John-son's plaint—"I am glad that I have ended my revisal of this dreadful scene. It is not to be endured"—to the remarks of Halliwell as recorded in the Variorum edition:

> Without disputing the masterly power displayed in the compo-sition of the present tragedy, there is something to my mind so revolting, both in the present scene and in the detestable char-acter of Iago, which renders a study of the drama of *Othello* rather a painful duty than one of pleasure.

To which H. H. Furness adds:

> I do not shrink from saying that I wish this Tragedy had never been written. The pleasure, however keen or elevated, which the inexhaustible poetry of the preceding Acts can bestow, can-

---

wish to record here my immense gratitude to him. The essay is primarily based upon performance records in the Folger Shakespeare Library and the Harvard Theatre Collec-tion, especially the annotated promptbooks, which number 58 items (in a field defined by approximately 110 entries dating to 1900 in Charles H. Shattuck's *The Shakespeare Promptbooks* [Urbana: Univ.of Illinois Press, 1965]), and which document performances by leading actors in England and America. I am indebted to the Folger Shakespeare Library and the Harvard Theatre Collection for assistance and for permission to cite manuscript sources, to the Graduate School of Boston University for research funding and to Professor Lynda E. Boose, whose work on *Othello* has furnished ideas and insights too numerous to mention. Professor Shattuck offered trenchant criticism at an important phase of writ-ing.

I refer throughout to the final scene of *Othello* as *Othello*, [5.2], though it was variously labeled in the promptbooks and acting editions of the period under investigation. Quo-tations from the play itself, unless otherwise noted, are taken from the Arden edition of *Othello*, ed. M. R. Ridley (1958; rpt. New York: Random House, 1967).

Among invaluable critical sources for this study are: H. H. Furness's Variorum *Othello* (1886; rpt. New York: American Scholar Publications, 1965) with its notes on perfor-mance; Marvin Rosenberg's classic study, *The Masks of Othello* (Berkeley: Univ. of Cali-fornia Press, 1961), and his "The 'Refinement' of *Othello* in the Eighteenth Century British Theatre," *Studies in Philology*, 51 (1954), 75–94; Gino J. Matteo's *Shakespeare's "Othello": The Study and the Stage* (Salzburg: Institut für Englische Sprache und Literatur, 1974) treats the relation between criticism and performance. On this relation, *see* also C. J. Carlisle, "The Nineteenth-Century Actors Versus the Closet Critics," *Studies in Philology*, 51 (1954), 599–615. I have made abundant use of data and insights from Matteo and from Arthur Colby Sprague's *Shakespeare and the Actors* (Cambridge, Mass.: Harvard Univ. Press, 1948). Also very helpful is Carlisle's *Shakespeare from the Greenroom* (Chapel Hill: Univ. of North Carolina Press, 1969), which has a section on *Othello*, [5.2] in per-formance. Students of *Othello* in performance should see also William P. Halstead, *Shake-speare as Spoken: A Collation of 5000 Acting Editions and Promptbooks of Shakespeare*, 11 (Ann Arbor: Univ. Microfilms International, 1977–80).

2. William Winter, *Shakespeare on the Stage* (New York: Moffatt, 1911), p. 292.

not possibly to my temperament, countervail, it does but increase, the unutterable agony of this closing scene.[3]

Surely it is not the amount of violence that makes this scene "not to be endured," "revolting," and a source of "unutterable agony." Two murders, one wounding, and a suicide hardly qualify the scene as exceptionally bloody for Shakespeare. Nor in the case of Dr. Johnson does the objection seemingly arise from a belief that domestic violence is unsuitable for tragedy. Johnson's own *Irene* demands the murder of a wife at her husband's instigation, a murder, moreover, that evidently was enacted on stage during part of the play's brief life.[4] The objections stem, I suspect, rather from the particular manner of the violence implied in the Shakespearean text—a matter of concern among the actors of the period as well. "This last scene," Fanny Kemble writes in 1884, "presents technical difficulties in its adequate representation which have never yet been even partially overcome."[5]

Viewed in the context of the critics' repugnance and the performer's scepticism, performance records from the later eighteenth and the nineteenth centuries—roughly the period bracketed by the remarks of Johnson and Furness—constitute a fascinating body of evidence, for in them one can see a culture trying to control a text that it desires to experience in the theatre but that it also strongly disapproves. Unlike *King Lear, Othello* was not rewritten for the English stage with a more acceptable ending; audiences demanded the final scene with its mixture of violence and eroticism despite the horrors it evoked in critics and the technical worries it created for performers.[6] As a result, the theatre became a place where limits were tested, technical matters becoming the loci of contests between desire and permissibility.

---

3. Citation of Johnson's note from *Johnson on Shakespeare,* ed. Walter Raleigh (1908; rpt. London: Oxford Univ. Press, 1925), p. 200. Halliwell and Furness are cited in Furness's Variorum *Othello,* p. 300. See also Winter, p. 270.

4. See *The Poems of Samuel Johnson,* eds. David Nichol Smith and Edward L. McAdam (Oxford: Clarendon Press, 1974), pp. 274–75.

5. Fanny Kemble, "Salvini's *Othello,*" *Temple Bar,* 71 (1884), 368–78; 376.

6. A modified version was attempted for the French stage, but once having seen the final
  . scene in its English form, French audiences demanded it be played that way—despite professed shock and outbreaks of fainting. See *Blackwood's Magazine,* 18 (1825), 299–300. The play offers a contrast to *King Lear,* which held the stage in Nahum Tate's adapted version during the same period. It should be emphasized that evidence of actors working upon reasonably accurate Shakespearean texts is abundant and early. Restoration playbooks seem to have been full Shakespearean texts (see Matteo, pp. 59–60). The Folger Library possesses a copy of a 1747 duodecimo (London: C. Hitch) thought to be marked in Garrick's hand, which collates Quarto and Folio versions. Extensive cutting, however, is the usual theatrical practice from early on, as remarks by an early eighteenth-century observer reveal; see *Original and Genuine Letters sent to the Tatler and Spectator,* ed. Charles Lille (London, 1725), I, 256–57.

II

Decisions about the technical features of [5.2] are already important before a line of the scene has been spoken. As the text demands, Desdemona is always portrayed, when the scene opens, in bed asleep, her surroundings varying predictably enough with the particular period of the production. The surprising thing is the consistency with which the period keeps the bed approximately centered and as far upstage as possible, a position that Fanny Kemble found to create serious practical problems of visibility and audibility for Othello, whose first lines are most appropriately delivered while bending over Desdemona.[7] Not till the middle of the nineteenth century do performers like Fechter and Booth move the bed downstage and to one side, to a position, that is, from which Othello's facial expressions might be clearly observed as he kisses (and later kills) Desdemona and from which Desdemona's struggles might be easily concealed from the audience.[8] Perhaps the violence that takes place on that bed was made more tolerable, more "sacrificial" in the terminology of the period's commentators, through distance and symmetrical setting. " 'Tradition' was right in placing Desdemona's couch at a remote part of the stage," observes Sir Theodore Martin, who condemned Fechter's relocation of the bed for "bringing it so far forward that every detail is thrust painfully on our senses."[9] Similarly complex interactions between the desire to see and the need to be protected from unmediated vision reveal themselves through other decisions about technical features and stage business.

Othello's entry in [5.2] also entails a significant technical decision as it becomes, in the early eighteenth century, an entrance not only "with light" (as in Quarto directions) but also with "a sword." The armed entry can be documented on the stage as early as 1761, and it persists in acting editions as well as in actors' promptbooks into the twentieth century.[1] An 1822 acting edition criticizes the armed

---

7. Kemble, p. 378.
8. See Booth's note in Furness's Variorum, p. 292. Booth's relocation of the bed was thought to be so serious that when in 1881 he and Henry Irving alternated in the roles of Othello and Iago, Irving had the bed moved back to center stage on the nights he played the Moor. Alan Hughes, *Henry Irving, Shakespearean* (Cambridge: Cambridge Univ. Press, 1981), p. 149.
9. "Shakespeare and his Latest Stage Interpreters," *Fraser's Magazine,* 64 (1861), 772–86; 783. Demands that the murder be treated as a sacrifice span the period; see Samuel Foote, *A Treatise on the Passions, So Far as They Regard the Stage* (London: 1747), pp. 33–34; and Winter, p. 296. Mrs. James calls Desdemona a "victim consecrated from the first," *Shakespeare's Heroines* (London: 1897), p. 182. James Boaden praises Mrs. Siddons's skill "in the performance of this gentle sacrifice," *Memoirs of the Life of John Philip Kemble* (London: 1825), p. 258. See also *The Theatrical Journal,* 6 June 1855, p. 184; and Bell's acting edition (London: 1777), p. 84; *Punch,* 14 December 1861, p. 241.
1. Acting editions with the armed entry include: Garland, 1765; Butters, 1787–89; Barker, ca. 1800; Oxberry, 1819; Charpentier, 1882. Among the promptbooks are John Palmer, 1766; anonymous, 1783 (Folger PR 1241 C95); Richard Power, 1803; John Howard Payne, ca. 1810. More modern instances of such entry can be found in Henry Jewett's

entry as "incorrect and unnecessary," but includes it as "according to modern practice"; and, in fact, the evidence indicates that, during the late eighteenth and nineteenth centuries, the scene was felt to go better if—in spite of the decision for strangulation in [4.1] and the refusal to mar her perfect skin in [5.2] itself—Othello entered conspicuously carrying and sometimes even brandishing a sword. This initial entry with the sword leads, furthermore, to subsequent business in the middle of Othello's third line. The "yet" in "It is the cause. Yet I'll not shed her blood" is interpreted to suggest Othello in debate with himself, as if questions about using the knife were just being resolved; and whether or not Othello flourished a naked weapon, it became tradition for him to lay down a sword during his initial speech. Even Edwin Booth, although he did not follow his father, Junius Brutus Booth, in entering with lamp and naked scimitar, felt compelled to half-draw and then relinquish a dagger while speaking his line.[2]

The implications of syntax are not the only factors which possibly led actors to favor such questionable embellishments. After all, an entry with light and sword in this scene would precisely repeat the entry of Iago on his own murderous errand in the previous scene. The visual point made by the similar entries of villain and hero would be strong, and the potential similarity between the two figures may have been further reinforced by the staging of Iago's earlier entry "in his shirt" [5.1.47], a nocturnal attire appropriate to Othello in [5.2]. Thus their kinship in murder could be emphasized, even though the period cuts Othello's appearance in [5.1], thereby deleting his lines about modeling himself after Iago.[3] But would not a suggestion of similarity between Othello and Iago run counter to the age's nearly universal insistence on Othello's nobility?[4] Perhaps not, if the impression of outward similarity were rapidly to give way to a rep-

---

promptbook of 1895–96 (Folger *Othello* promptbook 35) and Lewis Waller's promptbook of 1906 (Folger *Othello* promptbook Folio 1). Editions that do not claim to be "as performed" also include the armed entrance from early in the eighteenth century: see, for example, Lewis Theobald's 1733 edition. The lines about lust's blood in [5.1] that might suggest a wavering in Othello's resolve are, as far as I have been able to verify, never included in acting editions or promptbooks during the period.

2. See Folger *Othello* promptbooks 27, 17, 9, and Harvard Theatre Collection Ms. 219; on Booth's father, see Winter, p. 257. An observer in 1791 suggests that the second "yet" of the passage ("yet she must die") was "generally" accompanied by a threatening gesture toward Desdemona and complains that Kemble's choice to make this gesture with a dagger was inconsistent with the lines about not scarring Desdemona's skin (*The Theatrical Guardian*, 2 April 1791, p. 35).

3. Some very slight evidence suggests that Booth employed similarly striped cloaks for hero and villain in the two scenes. Compare the photograph of Booth as Iago in [5.1] in Winter (p. 270)—presumably the same sort of cloak referred to in Folger *Othello* promptbook 3 as Iago's "striped black and white cloak"—with the references to a trailing, striped cloak in Harvard Theatre Collection Ms. 219.

4. For this insistence, see Matteo, chap. 5, and Carlisle, *Shakespeare from the Greenroom*, p. 207.

resentation of the internal differences that set them apart. And here Othello's candle has a possible part to play.

Since Desdemona is asleep when Othello enters, it would seem verisimilar by period standards that the stage be darkened, but if the scene were darkened, the full visual impact of the emotional agonies that differentiate Othello from Iago might be obscured by his Moorish makeup. Thus, there is a quite practical aspect to Othello's entry "with light," although entry with a candle (or, as in some cases, discovery with lamp) by no means solved the lighting problems of the scene as a whole. Even if performers did not universally follow the literalism of those eighteenth-century commentators who argued that a light must be extinguished during Othello's "put out the light" lines, the difficulty of lighting Othello's darkened face remained.[5] With the advent of more sophisticated lighting in the nineteenth century, it became popular to add a light source to the scene in the form of a window. The light from such a window—a "Green Medium, or Calcium Light, to strike on Othello's face through Window C from R" in Kean's touring performances; simulated moonlight in Booth's performances of the 1880s; or lightning flashes according to the records of Salvini (1875), R. B. Mantell (1888) and Charles B. Hanford (1895)—provided this important illumination.[6] Technical solutions to problems of lighting achieved perhaps the most melodramatic embodiment with Mantell, who used the din of thunder and flash of lightning in counterpoint with music that played until Desdemona awakened:

THUNDER AND LIGHTNING It is the cause, it is the cause, my soul,
Let me not name it to you, you chaste stars:
It is the cause THUNDER AND LIGHTNING yet I'll not shed her blood
Nor scar that whiter skin of hers than snow,
And smooth, as monumental alabaster; THUNDER AND LIGHTNING
Yet she must die, else she'll betray more men.
Put out the light, and then put out the light?
THUNDER AND LIGHTNING[7]

5. Samuel Foote, in comparing Garrick, Quin, and Barry as Othello, complains of the black makeup as hindering perceptions of the character (*Treatise*, p. 25). The failings of black makeup are discussed "as being destructive of the face, and preventing the possibility of the expression being noted" by Leman Thomas Rede in his consideration of Edmund Kean's innovative change to a brown preparation (*The Road to the Stage* [London: 1827], pp. 38–39); see also Carlisle, *Shakespeare from the Greenroom*, p. 190. See Theobald's remarks stressing the role of the candle on the darkened stage in *The Works of Shakespeare* (London: 1733), VII, 481.
6. Folger *Othello* promptbooks Tb 15 (Kean), 9 (Hanford), and 25 (Mantell). Salvini's standing by a window "with the lightning playing upon his face" in an 1875 performance is recorded in Joseph Knight's *Theatrical Notes* (London: 1893), pp. 23–24; see also Furness, p. 293. For Booth, see Harvard Theatre Collection Ms. 219. Forrest's use of moonlight and candle is described in Gabriel Harrison's *Edwin Forrest* (Brooklyn: 1889), pp. 92–93.
7. Folger *Othello* promptbook 25.

Such sublime effects run counter to implications of the text, of course, for (even leaving aside the reference to "chaste stars") when Othello later laments Desdemona's death—

> O heavy hour!
> Methinks it should be now a huge eclipse
> Of sun and moon, and that the affrighted globe
> Should yawn at alteration.
>
> [5.2.100–03]

—the pathos arises from the fact that no world-altering tempest lends universal resonance to his action. The death of Desdemona is a smaller, more human matter, something to be hidden, as Othello promptly hides it, and as the command to "let it be hid" (issued in the Shakespearean text, if not in the period's acting texts) would keep it. Might not some of the appeal of the simulated storm have arisen from the way such pyrotechnics counter the very domesticity potential in the scene's violence? A titanic, Byronic Othello sundering the universal order was perhaps more acceptable as a subject of high tragedy than the strangler of a defenseless wife.[8]

Yet defenseless she remains. Despite the inflation of Othello to sublime proportions, the agreement among performers concerning Desdemona's passivity is striking. A few productions in the mid-nineteenth century, most notably Charles Fechter's and Ira Aldridge's, have Desdemona attempt escape or resistance, it is true. While Fechter's performances apparently did not enact the full violence depicted by his stage directions, in Fechter's 1861 acting edition Desdemona "rushes to the door," and as Othello bars escape, "in mad fury, he whirls round his sword"; he "carries her to the bed on which he throws her; then stifles her cries with the pillow which he presses with both hands."[9] Aldridge, according to his Desdemona, Madge Kendal, "used to take Desdemona out of the bed by her hair and drag her around the stage before he smothered her"—a sequence "loudly hissed."[1] But such highly exciting action never really caught on in the theatre of the period, and, as we shall see, voiced objections have as much to do with notions of femininity as with standards of tragic decorum.

8. In reviewing an 1837 *Othello*, Charles Rice firmly rejects the domestic potential in Desdemona: "in the domestic the character is not to be reckoned." *The London Theatre in the Eighteen-Thirties*, eds. Arthur Colby Sprague and Bertram Shuttleworth (London: Society for Theatre Research, 1950), p. 57.

9. *Charles Fechter's Acting Edition of "Othello"* (London: 1861), p. 104. Commentary in *The Athenaeum*, 2 November 1861, p. 587, approves Fechter's decision not to follow these directions to the letter; see also *Fraser's Magazine*, 64 (December 1861), 783. Contrast Booth's rejection of such lively antics as practiced by Salvini; see Carlisle, *Shakespeare from the Greenroom*, p. 207.

1. Cited in Herbert Marshall and Mildred Stock, *Ira Aldridge: The Negro Tragedian* (Carbondale: Southern Illinois Univ. Press, 1968), p. 312.

Rejecting Salvini's practice, according to which Desdemona rises from bed to confront Othello in her initial lines, Fanny Kemble berates Salvini for failure to follow stage tradition and the manifest "intention of Shakespeare . . . who makes Othello tell his wife that she is on her death-bed, and in reply to this furious command, 'Peace, be still,' receives the answer, 'I will. . . . ' "[2] While leaving open the possibility that an actress "equal to the situation" might subsequently rise to throw herself in supplication at Othello's feet, Kemble asserts that as of 1884 no one had to her knowledge proven successful in such an active interpretation of Desdemona and she makes her own preference for a passive Desdemona clear:

> The terrified woman cowers down upon her pillow like a poor frightened child. Indeed the whole scene loses its most pitiful elements by allowing Desdemona to confront Othello standing, instead of uttering the piteous pleadings for mercy in the help-less prostration of her half recumbent position.[3]

In this preference, Kemble takes her place in a cultural tradition that spans the eighteenth and nineteenth centuries and is by no means limited to the theatre.

Three years before Dr. Johnson's 1765 edition of Shakespeare, Lord Kames's influential *Elements of Criticism* articulates the sentimentalist tradition into which the period's Desdemona will be made to fit.[4] Given the sentimentalist location of virtue in responsiveness, what could be a greater incitement to virtuous sentiment than the experience of innocent beauty in helpless distress? "Female beauty accordingly," Kames writes, "shows best in distress; being more apt to inspire love, than upon an ordinary occasion."[5] Would Desdemona

---

2. Kemble, p. 378.
3. Kemble, p. 378. Compare the outraged response to Brooke's Desdemona having "strug-gled, in almost an erect position" as "out of character, even in the presence of an extreme so desperate," and citing Brabantio's lines about the never bold Desdemona as definitive. *The Athenaeum*, 10 September 1853, p. 1074. For an early, contrasting view, at odds with majority opinion, see Carlisle's account of actor-manager George Swan's notes on *Othello*, sent to David Garrick in 1773 and recommending, among other innovations, physical skirmishes between Othello and Desdemona (Carlisle, *Shakespeare from the Greenroom*, pp. 254–57). Booth suggests Desdemona come from the bed briefly but she "rests trem-bling against it" before "sinking to her knees" and "half reclining on the steps and dais of the bed"; her subsequent brief struggle with Othello should be hidden from the audience by Othello (Furness Variorum, p. 301).
4. The tradition is amply documented in Joseph W. Donohue, Jr., *Dramatic Character in the English Romantic Age* (Princeton: Princeton Univ. Press, 1970), pp. 50–52 and chap. 5.
5. *Elements of Criticism* (1762; rpt. New York: 1823), 1, 76. For an account of the relations between sexual passion and sensibility in the eighteenth century, see Jean H. Hagstrum, *Sex and Sensibility* (Chicago: Univ. of Chicago Press, 1980); on the nineteenth century, see Peter Gay, *Education of the Senses* (New York: Oxford Univ. Press, 1984). Steven Marcus claims that the "cult of sensibility was at its origins connected with sexuality, with sexual claims and influences," and relates the impulses of sensibility to the language of Victorian pornography (*The Other Victorians* [New York: Basic Books, 1964], esp. p. 208). On woman as victim during the period, see note [2, p. 298] below."

be as appealing "in distress" if she made a show of physical resistance? The commentators of the period, both popular and learned, certainly insist on her passivity. So Hazlitt finds Desdemona's "whole character consists in having no will of her own."[6] Mrs. Jameson discovers that "gentleness gives the prevailing tone to the character— gentleness in its excess—gentleness verging on passiveness—gentleness, which not only cannot resent—but cannot resist." Furthermore, "in Desdemona we cannot but feel that the slightest manifestation of intellectual power or active will would have injured the dramatic effect."[7] Campbell's *Remarks on the Life and Writings of Shakespeare* (1838) gives the question its most explicit response:

> The terrors of the storm are also made striking to our imagination by the gentleness of the victim on which they fall,— Desdemona. Had one symptom of an angry spirit appeared in that lovely martyr, our sympathy with her would have been endangered; but Shakespeare knew better.[8]

And the tradition remains strong even in Bradley, for whom Desdemona

> is helplessly passive. She can do nothing whatever. She cannot retaliate even in speech; no, not even in silent feeling. And the chief reason of her helplessness only makes the sight of her suffering more exquisitely painful. She is helpless because her nature is infinitely sweet and her love absolute.[9]

This insistence on Desdemona as passive victim in the critic's meditation and the performer's representation, an insistence characteristic as well of the visual art derived from the play, which takes the juxtaposition of the armed Othello to the recumbent Desdemona as one of its most popular subjects, supports Nina Auerbach's thesis that the image of "prone womanhood" has a special attraction for the nineteenth century.[1] And the language evoked by the scene bolsters her argument that "Victorian womanhood is most delectable as a victim," as it mimics the language and strategies of pornography:

6. *Characters of Shakespeare's Plays* (London: 1817), p. 53. [See above, p. 299.]
7. *Shakespeare's Heroines*, pp. 175, 182.
8. Cited in Matteo, p. 239.
9. A. C. Bradley, *Shakespearean Tragedy* (1905; rpt. London: Macmillan, 1915), p. 179. [See above, p. 236.] Compare Ellen Terry on the role: "My appearance was right—I was such a poor wraith of a thing. But it took strength to act this weakness and passiveness of Desdemona's. I soon found that like Cordelia, she has plenty of character." These remarks appear in the preface to the Booth edition of *Othello,* ed. William Winter (New York: 1881).
1. The Folger Library is rich in illustrations of the scene; for convenient viewing, see Delacroix's *Othello and Desdemona* (1847–49) in Peter Raby, *"Fair Ophelia": A Life of Harriet Smithson Berlioz* (Cambridge: Cambridge Univ. Press, 1982), p. 180; and Winifred H. Friedman, *Boydell's Shakespeare Gallery* (New York: Garland, 1976), pls. 194–96.

> It is an unalloyed delight . . . to see her sad, fearful, yet gentle
> as a bruised dove bend meekly to the implacable jealousy of the
> swart Othello, and receive her death, while kissing the hand
> which gives it.[2]

Furthermore, the related phenomenon of inflating Emilia's reactions
to Othello's abuse of her lady into major, show-stopping expressions
of grand outrage, seems a particularly telling displacement of energy
from the idealized feminine victim onto a domestic "virago" double.[3]

The cultural anxieties that might give rise to such commonly
agreed upon decisions about the text (and commonly agreed upon
images of woman) seem clear in H. N. Hudson's championing of
Desdemona as an alternative to the emergent threat of "a new edition
of woman"—the "mannish" woman.[4] Rhapsodic in his praise of Desdemona as unspeakably divine, Hudson defines her essence as submission, a quality all-the-more awe inspiring for its absence among
contemporary women:

> Meek, uncomplaining, submissive even unto death where she
> owes allegiance, her character is not of the sort to take with a
> self-teaching, self-obeying generation; and I know not whether
> there be more of sacrilege in presuming to scrutinize her for
> myself or in holding her up for the scrutiny of others. The beauty
> of the woman is so hid in the obedience and affection of the
> wife, that it almost seems a profanation to praise it.
>
> (*Lectures on Shakespeare*, p. 336)

Hudson goes on to say that the "savans of the age" may sneer because
she "does not approve herself a champion of women's rights"
(p. 337), but Desdemona, in her reliance even unto death on the
"awful prerogative of defenselessness" (p. 338) stands as a reproach
to those "gone sick with a kind of atheistic philanthropy," and especially to those who champion a "heartless system of domestic equality and independence" that would reverse

> the doctrine and practice of our fathers, that married people
> 'must be complicated in affections and interest, that there be

---

2. For an account of the importance of such images and of the cultural forces making the
image of woman "most delectable as a victim" compelling for the period, see Auerbach's
Woman and the Demon (Cambridge, Mass.: Harvard Univ. Press, 1982), esp. the chapter
"The Myth of Womanhood: Victims." The cited passage is from *Tallis's Dramatic Magazine*
(April 1851), 168. Compare Francis Gentleman who claims "pity never received a more
powerful call than to see sleeping innocence at the brink of destruction" and describes
audience reaction as "every soft sensation is put into a tremulative state, and the susceptible spectator must feel an exquisite share of painful pleasure, to see a determined murderer, who moves us more to compassion than detestation" (*The Dramatic Censor*
[London: 1770], I, 147).
3. See James Boaden's *Memoirs of Mrs. Siddons* (London: 1893), p. 43; Matteo, pp. 181–82.
The term "virago" for Emilia is Francis Gentleman's.
4. H. N. Hudson, *Lectures on Shakespeare* (New York: 1848), II, 339.

no distinction among them of mine and thine;' and that 'their goods should be as their children, not to be divided, but of one possession and provision.'

(p. 340)

Whatever the psychological needs that might render feminine passivity attractive, Hudson's testimony reminds us of the social and economic dimension of that same appeal: Desdemona embodies allegiance to the spirit of the matrimonial property laws.

If critics and performers alike render Desdemona scarcely capable of her own defense, they also manage to reach a semblance of agreement concerning the manner of her death. In most eighteenth- and nineteenth-century productions, the Othello, who according to the Shakespearean text rolls his eyes and gnaws his lip in paroxysms of agitation, becomes too refined to strangle Desdemona with his bare hands. Descriptions from as early as 1725 indicate that a "stifling pillow" was the favored mode of murder, and using the pillow remains standard practice until the time of Charles Kemble and Macready, persisting, in fact, into the twentieth century.[5] A few mavericks—notably Italians like Salvini and Rossi—use bare hands. So, for example, Rossi kills Desdemona in an 1881 performance

> in full view of the audience . . . by strangling her with his hands after twisting her long hair about her neck, as he shook her violently and then dragged her about the bed and finally tossed her down upon the pillows. . . . Murmurs of dissatisfaction were audible in the house.[6]

Audiences may have demanded Desdemona's death, but they did not want to see it like this. So productions generally find means that at once reveal and conceal her dying agonies: either the pillow over her head or—another device running counter to implications of the text—closed curtains covering the bed.[7]

But the deed itself is prolonged in the text by being less than fully successful on the first attempt. Interestingly, although the second attack on Desdemona might seem to provide a promising opportunity for cutting, performances of the period keep both of Othello's acts of violence against her, and so are compelled, given the absence of Quarto or Folio stage directions, to find something to do on the lines:

5. Folger *Othello* promptbooks Folio 2 and Folio 3; early reference to the "stifling pillow" occurs in *Original and Genuine Letters*, I, 257. Twentieth-century examples include Paul Robeson's *Othello* of 1930 and Arthur Lithgow's Antioch Area Theatre production of 1954.
6. Sprague, p. 212.
7. The curtains are closed by Othello *after* the deed [5.2.106] in Quarto and Folio texts.

>   not yet quite dead?
> I that am cruel, am yet merciful,
> I would not have thee linger in they pain.
> So, so.
>
>   [87–90]

Until about 1770 Othello simply repeats his stifling actions on "So, so." In the 1770s, however, critics reiterate an argument that had been around since Rymer: stifled wives do not revive to speak again. And so, in spite of the text, in which Othello expressly tells Gratiano, "there lies your niece, / Whose breath these hands have newly stopp'd" [207–08], the dagger is chosen as the appropriate way to finish off Desdemona, a decision that meets with remarkable agreement for nearly a century thereafter. As the 1869 Booth / Hinton edition puts it, the stabbing, although not specified in original texts, is "according to the practice of the modern stage," and as far as I can tell, it is not until Salvini's performances of the 1880s that this collective agreement to circumvent the text is broken, Salvini putting his knees on Desdemona's breast on "So, so" in order to accelerate her end. Audience reaction to this violation of cultural unanimity was extremely negative.[8]

But would not the use of a dagger create potential problems of its own for a theatre concerned with verisimilitude? What about the resulting blood, for instance? Location of the bed far upstage could help solve such problems, and the advantages of death by dagger would seem attractive. Instead of an athletic struggle to enact a clumsy parody of a lover's embrace, the deed might become a less physical, more decorous procedure. Furthermore, use of the dagger facilitates the fixing of audience attention on Othello and his agonized sensibilities. So Booth is described in 1883:

> As he stabs her there is an expression of agonized loathing at his own deed & its necessity so vividly portrayed in his face, as he hangs his head & does not look at his own dagger nor at her, that it seems as if he could hardly do it![9]

Couple the use of the dagger with a pillow over Desdemona's face and the deed itself might need no further veiling. Thus decisions such as Booth's to enact the murder downstage or Macready's to hide the strangling behind curtains but allow the stabbing in full view of the audience might be understood as exploiting possibilities opened by new definitions of allowable liberty to be taken with the text,[1] yet the appeal of such new techniques in handling the murder

---

8. Sprague, p. 216.
9. Harvard Theatre Ms. 219. Compare Booth: "Hide your face in trembling hand while you stab and groan, 'so, so'; the steel is piercing your own heart" (Furness Variorum, p. 303).
1. For Macready, see Folger *Othello* promptbook 13.

deserves further consideration. Performers are encouraged to bring the murder up close to the audience, not merely because they have discovered technical means to get away with such proximity without offending audience sensibilities, but because, as the description of Booth's performance suggests, the age was prepared to appreciate the play, indeed to appreciate tragedy generally, primarily for its glimpses into the sensibilities of the tragic hero and his own self-destructive agonies. Manipulation of stage conditions—even against apparent directives of the text—enables performers to direct audience attention firmly toward Othello and his tragic self-destruction, making him, in our eyewitness's account, the suffering victim of necessity and his own noble nature. If, in the process, the brutality of the murder is obscured, the loss is, one suspects, not such as would trouble either Dr. Johnson or the predominant aesthetic of the period.

That aesthetic, as recently analyzed by Joseph Donohue, affects both critical perceptions and actors' representations of tragedy in three related ways. First of all, events in the overall plot are relegated to secondary status, becoming important only insofar as they manage to reveal character.[2] Second, concentration is further focused on a particular central character's reactions at highly charged moments.[3] Third, an emphasis on the need to feel sympathy for these central characters leads to reinterpretations of them.[4] These assumptions—that character is the essence of drama and that the momentary experiences of a particular character should be the center of attention and sympathy—neatly match sentimentalist preoccupations.[5] Lord Kames, for example, writes with obvious fascination about the "fluctuation of passion" that Othello manifests in the opening soliloquy of [5.2]:

> love and jealousy represented, each exerting its whole force, but without any struggle; Othello was naturally inflexible: and the tenderest love could not divert him from a purpose he approved as right, not even for a moment: but every thing consistent with such a character is done to reconcile the two opposite passions; he is resolved to put her to death, but he will not shed her blood, nor so much as ruffle her skin.[6]

2. Donohue, p. 197. On the general nineteenth-century interest in character rather than action in Shakespeare, see Robert W. Langbaum's chapter "Character versus Action in Shakespeare" in *The Poetry of Experience* (New York: Random House, 1957); and Aron Y. Stavisky, *Shakespeare and the Victorians* (Norman: Univ. of Oklahoma Press, 1969). Compare James Boaden's lament on the "rage of the English for action" which "throws away a thousand delicate and essential touches of character"—particularly by omitting the willow song scene from *Othello* (*Memoirs of Mrs. Siddons*, p. 322).
3. Donohue, pp. 193, 212.
4. Donohue, p. 205.
5. Donohue, p. 280.
6. Kames, I, 129.

And later critics will share Kames's sympathetic fascination with characters caught in the throes of the passionate moment. Concerning the great Edmund Kean, much praised for his Shakespearean roles by Coleridge, Byron, and Leigh Hunt, John Keats finds chiefly worthy of praise the actor's ability to deliver "himself up to the instant feeling, without a shadow of a thought about anything else."[7] Hazlitt praises Shakespeare above all else for providing ample opportunities for the display of fluctuating emotions instead of forcing his characters to "hurry on to action":

> It was in raising passion to its height, from the lowest beginnings and in spite of all obstacles, in showing the conflict of the soul, the tug and war between love and hatred, rage, tenderness, jealousy, remorse, in laying open the strength and weakness of human nature, in uniting sublimity of thought with the anguish of the keenest woe, in putting in motion all the springs and impulses which make up this our mortal being, and at last blending them in that noble tide of deep and sustained passion, impetuous but majestic, 'that flows on to the Propontic and knows no ebb,' that the great excellence of Shakespeare lay.[8]

Such intense concentration on the emotional state of the central character lends itself quite understandably to sympathy for him as one, in the case of Othello, "perplexed in the extreme," and that sympathy constitutes the dominant response from the time of Johnson to that of Bradley.[9]

III

Between Desdemona's fatal stabbing and Othello's own death, eighteenth- and nineteenth-century performers found two particularly interesting occasions for deviation from Shakespeare's text. First, Emilia is never granted her wish to be laid by Desdemona,

---

7. *Poetical Works and Other Writings of John Keats,* ed. H. B. Forman (New York: Scribner's Sons, 1938–39), V, 232.

8. *Hazlitt on Theater,* eds. William Archer and Robert Lowe (New York: Hill and Wang, 1957), pp. 69–70.

9. See Matteo, pp. 181, 252 and Carlisle, *Shakespeare from the Greenroom,* p. 207. Compare the writer who rejoices "with a secret satisfaction" upon seeing his female wards "betrayed into tears" as the "distress of the play was heightened" (p. 241) and who goes on to characterize the "torments which the Moor suffers" as "so exquisitely drawn, as to render him as much an object of compassion, even in the barbarous action of murdering Desdemona, as the innocent person herself who falls under his hand" (*Guardian,* 37 [23 April 1713], 241–43). In Foote's *Treatise on the Passions,* the actor is admonished that "the Strugglings and Convulsions that torture and distract [Othello's] Mind, upon his resolving to murder her, cannot be too strongly painted, nor can the Act itself be accomplished with too much Grief and Tenderness" (pp. 33–35). Benjamin Victor praises the role of Othello for calling forth "all the various Passions of the Soul" and maintains that "In the distressful passages, at the heart breaking Anguish of his Jealousy, I have seen all the Men, susceptible of the tender Passions, in Tears" (*The History of the Theatres of London and Dublin* [London: 1761], II, 9–13).

although some productions provide a "couch" for her repose.¹ Thus the bloody corpses do not end up in a pile on the bed. Second, the lines reporting Brabantio's death from grief at Desdemona's betrayal of him are regularly omitted. One can imagine the relief accorded the sensibilities of the audience by these minor but strategic narrowings of focus in both plot and action.

The most intriguing variations on the scene, however, occur in the final moments surrounding Othello's death. Here the frequency of modification is striking, with virtually every promptbook recording changes in wording or action. Actors like Booth and Forrest, who published their own acting versions of the play, not only change the ending from one edition to the next, but also revise the acting editions further in production promptbooks.² Thus, agreement about anything in this portion of the play is remarkable, yet the promptbooks do agree on some things.

From the earliest surviving eighteenth-century promptbook (1766) until the 1870s, virtually all performers cut the moments that follow Othello's death; performances, with very few exceptions, cut the lines which give Lodovico and Gratiano's judgment on Othello's suicide: "O bloody period! / All that's spoke is marr'd" [362]. And, in fact, of the 52 promptbooks that I have examined for performances between 1766 and 1900 which relate theatrical practice for Othello's death, 23 end the play on some version of his suicide lines—"I took by the throat the circumcised dog, / And smote him thus"—adding sometimes an invented exclamation—"O Desdemona"—to his rather abrupt end. Perhaps the impulse at work here is the desire to ennoble Othello by letting his agony, rather than Venetian concerns with the aftermath, conclude the play, but one may wonder why from the 1770s until the 1870s, even in the promptbooks that do suggest action after his self-slaughter, Othello appears almost never to have been allowed to die upon a kiss (in 45 of the 52 promptbooks, marked for Othello's final moments, the lines about having kissed Desdemona before he killed her are missing, either through cutting or omission).

There are copious descriptions of stage Othellos in their death throes struggling to reach Desdemona: Macready dragging himself, supported by furniture, from the footlights toward the distant bed; Kean falling backwards dead just before he can kiss his Desdemona; Phelps, Wallack, and Edwin Booth dying in similar attempts; Gus-

1. See, for example, Charles Kean's early promptbook, Folger *Othello* promptbook 11; Edmund Kean's 1831 promptbook, Folger *Othello* promptbook 17. Kemble's 1816 promptbook adds to the text the direction that Emilia "falls on the ground" (Folger *Othello* promptbook 19).
2. For instances of such revision, see Edwin Forrest's 1861 promptbook (Harvard Theatre Collection 13486.75.6), and Edwin Booth's preparation copy (Folger *Othello* promptbook 3).

tavus Brooke pulling down the bed curtains over himself and revealing in the process the unkissed Desdemona; Salvini staggering backward while keeping "his full front to the audience" and dying just before he can reach the bed.[3] And when actors do finally reach the bed for a kiss in the late nineteenth century, they are condemned to slide or roll back off. So Edwin Forrest kisses Desdemona while "upon one knee" and then falls to the floor, and in an 1895 Henry Jewett promptbook, Othello "kisses Desdemona falls from bed and rolls down steps onto stage."[4] Whatever the specific details of execution, the audience is spared the effects of Othello's "Falling upon Desdemona" as one 1802 acting edition printed in Manchester by R. W. Dean suggests, or, even more graphically, "He [falls across Desdemona and] dies," according to the Folger edition used for one twentieth-century performance.[5] The end result in the modified versions is the same: Desdemona's corpse is left in lovely, lonely isolation. Leaving her chaste bed thus unviolated by Othello's own bleeding corpse would, obviously, rid the scene of some of the more grossly physical elements in its mixture of eroticism and violence, but no such clear justification suggests itself for the last variation that the theatre of the period sometimes worked into the scene in the text's despite.

In the 1766 promptbook, Iago is removed from the stage before Othello's final apologia.[6] This change, while neither lessening the violence and eroticism nor materially reducing running time, robs the play of powerful theatrical possibilities. Edwin Booth's Iago, for example, stood over Othello's corpse, pointing at the body while "gazing up at the gallery with a malignant smile of satisfied hate."[7] Why then do such major figures as Kean, Kemble, the elder Booth, Phelps, Cooke, Young, Salvini, Forrest and others of less note move Iago's exit up, and in the process abandon such rich opportunities? Macready offers a clue when he dismisses Fechter's bizarre practice of having Othello begin his suicide blow as a violent gesture apparently directed toward Iago. Macready professes himself unconvinced that Othello's "lofty nature" could possibly "bestow a thought upon that miserable thing, Iago, when his great mind had made itself up to die! To me it was in the worst taste of a small melodramatic theatre."[8]

Here are terms aptly fitted to a particular view of tragedy: a lofty

3. Sprague, p. 221. For Salvini, see Edward Tuckerman Mason, *The Othello of Tommasso Salvini* (New York: 1890), p. 107.
4. Gabriel Harrison, *Edwin Forrest*, p. 96; Folger *Othello* promptbook, Folio 1.
5. Folger *Othello* promptbook, Folio 4.
6. Folger *Othello* promptbook 27.
7. Sprague, p. 223.
8. Sprague, p. 221.

nature, a great mind, that had made itself up—notice the absence of both body and other in Macready's phrasing—to self-destruction. In many of the period's stage versions, the role of Iago in the scene's second half, like that of Desdemona in its first half, has been reduced in order to keep attention where Dr. Johnson and his descendants probably would have preferred it—on the noble Moor and his own sad self-destruction.

To sum up. In the period's predominant mode of staging the final scene of *Othello,* audience gaze is first and last directed toward Othello. His face illuminated by candle, lamp, or simulated celestial light, he often enters in a threatening posture suggesting Iago's evil influence, and he virtually always is shown resisting an impulse to use his weapon on the sleeping Desdemona. The murder itself becomes the sacrifice of a largely passive victim by a protagonist whose own emotional conflicts are the center of attention. After smothering her with a pillow, or using bed curtains to block the view of his victim during the act, Othello's noble concern for her and the press of necessity force him to use a dagger to finish the deed. When the time comes for Othello's own final agony and death, audience attention is frequently directed away from Iago's important role in bringing about that death, its admiration for Othello's final gesture often uncompromised by the criticism of onlookers, and its vision unpoisoned by the sight of Othello topping the dead Desdemona in a potentially grotesque fulfillment of the promise to kill her and love her after.

If the performance records of this period may be said to cast a light backward to reveal anything about the Quarto and Folio texts themselves, they show, I believe, how much of the Shakespearean scene has to be adjusted, how many implicit and explicit directions have to be countermanded, before it will conform to the particular tragic mold favored by the majority of audiences, commentators, and performers of the eighteenth and nineteenth centuries. When change would come to the performance of Shakespeare on the twentieth-century stage, it would come gradually and piecemeal, as performers turned away from the traditional acting editions and the inherited business in response to increased demands for close study of relatively reliable Shakespearean texts. This performance "revolution" as it has been called is, of course, the product of many factors, but few would deny that one of its leading figures was one who, like Fanny Kemble, saw Salvini strangle his resistant Desdemona with bare hands—William Poel. And what Poel took away from his Salvini experiences was not Kemble's sense of having witnessed a violation of the manifest "intention" of Shakespeare but a belief that he had been granted a revelation, showing how every effect in a great per-

formance ought to be tested by reference to authoritative texts.[9]
More than half a century after Poel and the Elizabeth revival movement, after having experienced the further innovations to be wrought
by those from Harley Granville-Barker to Peter Brook who learned
from Poel and his followers, we might have less interest (or faith) in
an imagined capacity to get back to the play as the playwright might
have intended it, but the pressure to make the attempt is a real factor
in the theatre's eventual breaking with the traditional emphases that
this paper has traced.[1]

MICHAEL NEILL

Unproper Beds: Race, Adultery, and the Hideous in *Othello*†

There is a glass of ink wherein you see
How to make ready black-faced tragedy.
George Chapman,
Bussy D'Ambois, 4.2.89–90

I

The ending of *Othello* is perhaps the most shocking in Shakespearean tragedy. "I am glad that I have ended my revisal of this
dreadful scene," wrote Dr. Johnson; "it is not to be endured."[1] His
disturbed response is one that the play conspicuously courts: indeed
Johnson does no more than paraphrase the reaction of the scandalized Venetians, whose sense of the unendurable nature of what is
before them produces the most violently abrupted of all Shakespear-

9. On Poel's reaction to Salvini's *Othello*, see Robert Speaight, *William Poel and the Elizabethan Revival* (Cambridge, Mass.: Harvard Univ. Press, 1954), p. 28. J. L. Styan emphasizes Poel's effect in *The Shakespeare Revolution* (Cambridge: Cambridge Univ. Press,
1977). Styan cites Tyrone Guthrie, who calls Poel "the founder of modern Shakespearean
production," p. 64.

1. Styan traces Poel's lineage, p. 64ff. The various forces working to change Shakespearean
production in the period following the 1890s are delineated in Cary M. Mazer's *Shakespeare Refashioned* (Ann Arbor: UMI Research Press, 1981).

† From *Shakespeare Quarterly* 40 (1989): 383–412. © Folger Shakespeare Library.
Reprinted with the permission of The Johns Hopkins University Press. The author's quotations from *Othello* have been retained, but bracketed references are to this Norton
Critical Edition. This excerpt omits some of Neill's footnotes, some fascinating visuals,
and a sustained analysis of the play's action as "concentrating the audience's imagination"
on "the erotic act in the bedroom" (399). For this material, readers should consult the
original or the reprint in Neill's *Putting History to the Question: Power, Politics and Society
in English Renaissance Drama* (New York: Columbia University Press, 2000), 237–68.

1. Quoted in James R. Siemon, " 'Nay, that's not next': *Othello*, V.ii in performance, 1760–
1900," *Shakespeare Quarterly*, 37 (1986), 38–51, esp. p. 39. [See above, p. 290.]

ean endings. Though its catastrophe is marked by a conventional welter of stabbing and slaughter, *Othello* is conspicuously shorn of the funeral dignities that usually serve to put a form of order upon such spectacles of ruin: in the absence of any witness sympathetic enough to tell the hero's story, the disgraced Othello has to speak what amounts to his own funeral oration—and it is one whose lofty rhetoric is arrested in mid-line by the "bloody period" of his own suicide [5.2.362]. "All that's spoke is marred," observes Gratiano, but no memorializing tributes ensue. Even Cassio's "he was great of heart" [366] may amount to nothing more than a faint plea in mitigation for one whose heart was swollen to bursting with intolerable emotion;[2] and in place of the reassuring processional exeunt announced by the usual command to take up the tragic bodies, we get only Lodovico's curt order to close up the scene of butchery: "The object poisons sight: / Let it be hid" [369–70].[3] The tableau on the bed announces a kind of plague, one that taints the sight as the deadly effluvia of pestilence poison the nostrils.

The congruence between Dr. Johnson's desperately averted gaze and Lodovico's fear of contamination is striking; but it is only Johnson's agitated frankness that makes it seem exceptional. It makes articulate the anxiety evident almost everywhere in the play's history—a sense of scandal that informs the textual strategies of editors and theatrical producers as much as it does the disturbed reactions of audiences and critics. Contemplating the "unutterable agony" of the conclusion, the Variorum editor, Furness, came to wish that the tragedy had never been written;[4] and his choice of the word "unutterable" is a telling one, for this ending, as its stern gestures of erasure demonstrate, has everything to do with what cannot be uttered and must not be seen.

The sensational effect of the scene upon its earliest audiences is apparent from the imitations it spawned[5] and from the mesmerized

2. See Balz Engler, "Othello's Great Heart," *English Studies*, 68 (1987), 129–36. All *Othello* quotations are from the New Penguin edition, ed. Kenneth Muir (Harmondsworth: Penguin Books, 1968). All other Shakespeare quotations are from *The Riverside Shakespeare*, ed. G. Blakemore Evans (Boston: Houghton Mifflin, 1974).

3. The exceptional nature of this ending is also noted by Helen Gardner, "The Noble Moor," in Anne Ridler, ed., *Shakespeare Criticism 1935–1960* (Oxford: Oxford Univ. Press, 1963), pp. 348–70, esp. p. 366.

4. The Variorum *Othello*, ed. H. H. Furness (Philadelphia: J. B. Lippincott, 1886), p. 300; quoted in Siemon, p. 39. [See above, p. 290.]

5. Sensationalized bedchamber scenes that seem indebted to *Othello* include Lussurioso's murderous irruption into his father's bedchamber in *The Revenger's Tragedy* (c. 1606), Evadne's heavily eroticized murder of the king in *The Maid's Tragedy* (c. 1610), and the climatic bedroom scene that forms part of Ford's extensive reworking of *Othello* in *Love's Sacrifice* (c. 1632). Shakespeare himself appears to play on recollections of his own coup de theatre in the bedroom scene of *Cymbeline* (c. 1609); and it is treated to a parodic reversal in Fletcher's *Monsieur Thomas* (c. 1615), where the humiliation of the comic protagonist is accomplished by means of "*A bed discovered with a* [female] *black More in it*" (5.5.2, s.d.), provoking his Emilia-like cry, "Rore againe, devil, rore againe" (1. 41).

gaze of Henry Jackson, who left the first surviving account of *Othello* in performance. He saw *Othello* acted by the King's Men at Oxford in 1610 and wrote how

> the celebrated Desdemona, *slain in our presence by her husband,* although she pleaded her case very effectively throughout, yet moved us more after she was dead, when, *lying in her bed,* she entreated the pity of the spectators by her very countenance.[6]

More than any other scene, it was this show of a wife murdered by her husband that gripped Jackson's imagination; but even more disturbing than the killing itself seems to have been the sight of the dead woman "lying in her bed"—a phrase that echoes Emilia's outrage: "My mistress here lies murdered in her bed" [5.2.189]. For Jackson, the *place* seems to matter almost as much as the fact of wife-murder—just as it did to the nineteenth-century Desdemona, Fanny Kemble, when she confessed to "feel[ing] horribly at the idea of being murdered *in my bed.*"[7]

The same anxious fascination is reflected in the first attempts to represent the play pictorially: it was the spectacle of the violated marriage bed that Nicholas Rowe selected to epitomize the tragedy in the engraving for his 1709 edition; and his choice was followed by the actors David Garrick and Sarah Siddons, wanting memorials of their own performances.[8] In the great period of Shakespeare illustration from the 1780s to the 1920s, the bedchamber scene was overwhelmingly preferred by publishers and artists, whose images combined to grant it the same representative significance as the graveyard in *Hamlet* or the monument in *Antony and Cleopatra*—as if announcing in this display of death-in-marriage a gestic account of the play's key meanings. * * * Both graveyard and monument, however, in their different ways help to clothe the tragic ending in traditional forms of rhetoric and ceremony that mitigate its terrors, shackling death within a frame of decorum. What makes the ending of *Othello* so unaccountably disturbing and so threatening to its spectators is precisely the brutal violation of decorum that is registered in the quasi-pornographic explicitness of the graphic tradition. The illustrators' voyeuristic manipulation of the parted curtains and their invariable focus upon the unconscious invitation of Desdemona's gracefully exposed body serve to foreground not merely the perverse eroticism of the scene but its aspect of forbidden disclosure.

Even more striking is the fact that these images were often designed to draw readers into texts whose bowdlerizing maneuvers

---

6. Quoted in Julie Hankey, ed., *Othello,* Plays in Performance Series (Bristol: Bristol Classical Press, 1987), p. 18, italics added.
7. Quoted in Hankey, p. 315, italics added.
8. See Norman Sanders, ed., *Othello,* New Cambridge edition (Cambridge: Cambridge Univ. Press, 1984), p. 48.

aimed, as far as possible, to conceal everything that their frontis-pieces offer to reveal. While they could scarcely contrive to remove the scandalous property itself, late eighteenth- and nineteenth-century editors sought to restrict the curiosity that the final scene gratifies and to obscure its most threatening meanings by progres-sively excising from the text every explicit reference to the bed.[9]

Predictably enough, an even more anxious censorship operated in the theatre itself, where, however, its consequences were much more difficult to predict. In the most striking of many effacements, it became the practice for nineteenth-century Othellos to screen the murder from the audience by closing the curtains upon the bed. This move was ostensibly consistent with a general attempt at de-sensationalizing the tragedy, an attempt whose most obvious mani-festation was the restrained "Oriental" Moor developed by Macready and others.[1] But the actual effect of the practice was apparently quite opposite, raising to a sometimes unbearable intensity the audience's scandalized fascination with the now-invisible scene. Years later Westland Marston could still recall the "thrilling" sensation as Macready thrust "his dark despairing face, through the curtains," its "contrast with the drapery" producing "a marvellous piece of col-our";[2] and so shocking was this moment, according to John Forster, that in his presence a woman "hysterically fainted" at it.[3]

The reasons for so extreme a reaction can be glimpsed in the offended tone of the Melbourne *Argus* critic, attacking an 1855 pro-duction that had flouted this well-established convention: "[The] consummation," he indignantly insisted, "should take place behind the curtain and out of sight."[4] The revealing word "consummation," when set beside the "hysterical" reaction to Macready's "marvellous piece of colour,"[5] suggests that the bed was so intensely identified with the anxieties about race and sex stirred up by the play that it needed, as far as possible, to be removed from the public gaze. Yet the effect of such erasure was only to give freer play to the fantasy it was designed to check, so that the violent chiaroscuro of Mac-ready's blackened face thrust between the virgin-white curtains was

---

9. The process of cutting can be traced in Hankey.
1. For an account of the Orientalizing process that culminated in Beerbohm Tree's confident pronouncement that "Othello was an Oriental, not a negro: a stately Arab of the best caste," see Hankey, pp. 65–67, esp. p. 67.
2. Westland Marston, *Our Recent Actors,* quoted in Hankey, pp. 64, 317.
3. William Archer and Robert Lowe, eds., *Dramatic Essays by John Forster and George Henry Lewes,* quoted in Hankey, p. 64.
4. Quoted in Hankey, p. 317. This critic's reaction was echoed in the murmurs of dissatis-faction with which the audience greeted Rossi's 1881 London performance, when the Italian actor strangled his Desdemona in full view of the audience (see Siemon, p. 47). [See above, p. 299.]
5. To some observers Macready's restrained, gentlemanly, and dignified Moor seemed "almost English" (Hankey, p. 66); but the startling color contrast of this scene seems to have acted as a disturbing reminder of Othello's blackness and therefore (to the Victorian mind) of his savage sexuality.

experienced as a shocking sado-erotic climax. It was, of course, a stage picture that significantly repeated an off-stage action twice imagined in the first half of the play, when Othello, first in Venice (1.2) and then in Cyprus (2.3), is unceremoniously roused from his nuptial bed. The unconscious repetition must have had the effect of underlining the perverse eroticism of the murder just at the point where the parting of the bed-curtains and the display of Desdemona's corpse was about to grant final satisfaction to the audience's terrible curiosity about the absent scene that dominates so much of the play's action.

For all their ostentatious pudency, then, the Victorian attempts at containing the danger of the play's ending reveal a reading unsettlingly consistent with the most sensational recent productions, like Bernard Miles's 1971 Mermaid *Othello* or Ronald Eyre's at the National in 1979, with their extraordinary emphasis on the significance and visibility of a bed.[6] It is a reading in which the stage direction opening 5.2, *"Enter . . . Desdemona in her bed,"* announces ocular proof of all that the audience have most desired and feared to look upon, exposing to cruel light the obscure erotic fantasies that the play both explores and disturbingly excites in its audience. Forster's story of the woman who fainted at the sight of Macready's "dark despairing face" records a moment when (despite more than half a century of bleaching, "civilizing," and bowdlerizing) a subterranean image erupted to confirm the deep fears of racial / sexual otherness on which the play trades—fears that are made quite embarrassingly explicit in the feverish self-betrayals of a nineteenth-century Russian literary lady reacting to Ira Aldridge's performance of the part. In her account the play exhibits nothing less than the symbolic rape of the European "spirit" by the "savage, wild flesh" of black otherness:

> A full-blooded Negro, incarnating the profoundest creations of Shakespearean art, giving *flesh and blood* for the aesthetic judgment of educated European society. . . . How much nearer can one get to truth, to the very source of the highest aesthetic satisfaction? But *what is truth* . . . ? As the spirit is not the body, so the truth of art is not this profoundly raw flesh which we can take hold of, and call by name and, if you please, feel, pinch with our unbelieving, all-feeling hand . . . Not the Moscow Maly Theatre, but the African jungle should have been filled and

6. Both directors introduced the bed early, making it into the centerpiece of the brothel scene; and Miles, whose production notoriously highlighted the sexual suggestiveness of the murder with a naked Desdemona, emphasized the perverse excitements of the earlier scene by leaving Iago and Roderigo at the end "to argue amongst the discarded bedclothes and around the bed itself . . . [while Roderigo handled] the sheets in rapture." Eyre transposed this piece of stage business to his Othello at the beginning of the scene: Donald Sinden was directed to pull the sheets from Desdemona's laundry basket, throw them about the stage, and then at the line "This is a subtle whore" [4.2.21], press the soiled linen to his face—"sniffing [at it] like a hound," according to one reviewer. See Hankey, pp. 291, 281.

resounded with . . . the cries of this black, powerful, howling flesh. But by the very fact that that flesh is so powerful—that it is genuinely black, so naturally *un-white* does it howl—that savage flesh did its fleshly work. It murdered and crushed the spirit . . . one's spirit cannot accept it—and in place of the highest enjoyment, this blatant flesh introduced into art, this *natural* black Othello, pardon me, causes only . . . revulsion.[7]

It is as if in Macready's coup the strange mixture of thrilled agitation, horror, and shame voiced here became focused with an unbearable intensity upon the occupation of the bed, where the transgression of racial boundaries was displayed as an offence punishable by death.

II

The racial fear and revulsion lurking beneath the ambiguous excitements of the theatrical and pictorial traditions is made crudely explicit in an early nineteenth-century caricature, apparently of Ira Aldridge's Othello, published as Number 9 in the series *Tregear's Black Jokes* * * *. The caricaturist sublimates his anxiety at the scene's sexual threat through the burlesque device of transforming Desdemona into an obese black woman, her snoring mouth grotesquely agape. The racialism paraded here for the amusement of early nineteenth-century Londoners is rarely so openly exhibited, but it has tainted even the most respectable *Othello* criticism until well into the present century. A sense of racial scandal is a consistent thread in commentary on the play from Rymer's notorious effusions against the indecorum of a "Blackamoor" hero,[8] to Coleridge's assertion that Othello was never intended to be black and F. R. Leavis's triumphant demonstration that Othello was never intended for a hero.[9] It is as apparent in A. C. Bradley's nervously footnoted anxiety about how "the aversion of our blood" might respond to the sight of a black Othello[1] as it is in Charles Lamb's frank discovery of "something extremely revolting in the courtship and wedded caresses of Othello and Desdemona."[2] "To imagine is one thing," Bradley pro-

7. N. S. Sokhanskaya ("N. Kokhanovskaya") in a letter to the Slavophile newspaper *Dyen* (1863), quoted in Herbert Marshall and Mildred Stock, *Ira Aldridge: The Negro Tragedian* (London: Rockliff, 1958), pp. 265–66. See also Siemon, p. 45, for English reactions to the scene "that [mimic] the language and strategies of pornography." [See above, p. 297.]

8. Thomas Rymer, *A Short View of Tragedy* (1693), quoted in Brian Vickers, ed., *Shakespeare: The Critical Heritage*, 6 vols. (London and Boston: Routledge & Kegan Paul, 1974), Vol. 2, 27. [See above, pp. 202–03.]

9. F. R. Leavis, "Diabolic Intellect and the Noble Hero," in *The Common Pursuit* (London: Chatto and Windus, 1952), pp. 136–59. For acute analyses of the racial assumptions underlying Leavis's approach, see Hankey, pp. 109–16, and Martin Orkin, "Othello and the 'plain face' of Racism," *SQ*, 38 (1987), 166–88, esp. pp. 183–86, now incorporated in his *Shakespeare Against Apartheid* (Craighall, South Africa: Ad. Donker, 1987). Both show how much Leavis's interpretation contributed to Oliver's version of the tragedy.

1. *Shakespearean Tragedy* (1904; rpt. New York: St. Martin's Press, 1985), p. 165 n. [See above, p. 242.]

2. Quoted in Hankey, pp. 65–66. [See above, p. 221.]

tests, "and to see is another," making painfully explicit his reaction against what Edward Snow describes as the play's insistence upon "bringing to consciousness things known in the flesh but 'too hideous to be shown.'"[3] For the neo-Freudian Snow, however, these forbidden things are the male psyche's repressed fears of female otherness, which the accident of Othello's race "merely forces him to live out with psychotic intensity."[4] It is clear, however, that for Bradley it was precisely Othello's blackness that made the play's sexual preoccupations so upsetting.

For Coleridge the idea of a black hero was unacceptable because blackness was equivalent to savagery and the notion of savage heroism an intolerable oxymoron. His application of critical skin-lightener began a tradition of sterile and seemingly endless debate about the exact degree and significance of Othello's racial difference, on which critics dissipated their energies until well into the present century—M. R. Ridley's * * * Arden edition (1958), with its ludicrous attempt to substitute "contour" for "colour" as the principle of discrimination, being only the most disgraceful recent example.[5] Since Coleridge, arguments about race in *Othello* have almost invariably been entangled, more or less explicitly, with arguments about culture in which gradations of color stand for gradations of "barbarity," "animality," and "primitive emotion." If the dominant nineteenth-century tradition sought to domesticate the play by removing the embarrassment of savagery, the most common twentieth-century strategy has been to anthropologize it as the study of an assimilated savage who relapses into primitivism under stress. This was essentially Leavis's solution, and one can still hear it echoed in the New Cambridge editor's admiration for the weird mimicry of Laurence Olivier's "West African"/"West-Indian" Othello,[6] which he describes as a "virtuoso . . . portrait of a *primitive* man, at odds with the sophisticated society into which he has forced himself, *relapsing into barbarism* as a result of hideous misjudgement."[7]

---

3. "Sexual Anxiety and the Male Order of Things in *Othello*," *English Literary Renaissance*, 10 (1980), 384–412, esp. p. 387.
4. p. 400.
5. See M. R. Ridley, ed., *Othello,* Arden edition (London: Methuen, 1958), p. li.
6. The geographical referent of Olivier's mimicry significantly varies in different accounts of the production: Hankey, for example, refers to his "extraordinary transformation into a black African" (p. 111); Sanders praises "his careful imitation of West Indian gait and gesture" (p. 47); while Richard David speaks of "Olivier's . . . 'modern' negro, out of Harlem rather than Barbary" (*Shakespeare in the Theatre* [Cambridge: Cambridge Univ. Press, 1978], p. 46). The embarrassing conclusion must be that Olivier's much-praised fidelity to detail was simply fidelity to a generalized stereotype of "blackness."
7. Norman Sanders, p. 47, italics added. Sanders almost exactly paraphrases Laurence Lerner's account of the way in which "the primitive breaks out again in Othello," which Orkin uses to exemplify the way in which even liberal South African critics of the play find themselves reacting to it in terms of the paradigms of apartheid (pp. 184–85). Olivier himself declared that Othello "is a savage man," adding hurriedly, "not on account of his

At the other extreme stand revisionist readings like Martin Orkin's, which have sought to rehabilitate the tragedy by co-opting it to the anti-racist cause, insisting that "in its rejection of human pigmentation as a means of identifying worth, the play, as it always has done, continues to oppose racism."[8] Orkin's is an admirably motivated attempt to expose the racialist ideology underlying various critical and theatrical interpretations of the tragedy, but Shakespeare would surely have been puzzled to understand the claim that his play "opposes racism," cast as it is in a language peculiar to the politics of our own century.[9] It would no more have been possible for Shakespeare to "oppose racism" in 1604, one might argue, than for Marlowe to "oppose anti-semitism" in 1590: the argument simply could not be constituted in those terms. Julie Hankey, indeed, contemplating the pitfalls presented by Shakespeare's treatment of racial matters, concludes that his construction of racial difference is virtually beyond recovery, having become after four hundred years hopelessly obscured by a "patina of apparent topicality."[1] Hankey's position has at least the merit of historicist scruple but seems in the end evasive, not unlike those liberal critiques that rob the play of its danger by treating Othello's color simply as a convenient badge of his estrangement from Venetian society[2]—in effect a distraction to be cleared out of the way in order to expose the real core of the drama, its tragedy of jealousy.[3] But the history that Hankey herself traces is a testimony to the stubborn fact that *Othello* is a play full of racial feeling—perhaps the first work in English to explore the roots of such feeling; and it can hardly be accidental that it belongs to the very period in English history in which something we can now

---

colour; I don't mean that" (Hankey, p. 109); but it is a little difficult to know quite what else he could have meant—especially in the light of reviewers' reactions to his mimicry of negritude, which concluded "that Othello's brutality was either of the jungle and essentially his own, or that, as one of Nature's innocents, he had taken the infection from a trivial and mean white society" (p. 111). Whatever the case, the choice is simply between noble and ignoble savagery. For a good account of the ideas behind the Olivier production and critical reactions to it, see Hankey, pp. 109–13.

8. p. 188.
9. The word "racism" itself dates from only 1936, and "racialism" from 1907 (*OED*).
1. p. 15.
2. Here I include my own essay "Changing Places in *Othello*," *Shakespeare Survey*, 37 (1984), 115–31; I ought to have noticed more clearly the way in which racial identity is constructed as one of the most fiercely contested "places" in the play.
3. Honorable exceptions included Eldred Jones, *Othello's Countrymen: The African in English Renaissance Drama* (London: Oxford Univ. Press, 1965); G. K. Hunter's celebrated lecture on "Othello and Colour Prejudice," *Proceedings of the British Academy*, 53 (1967), 139–57. [See above, p. 248.]; Doris Adler, "The Rhetoric of *Black and White* in *Othello*," *SQ*, 25 (1974), 248–57; G. M. Matthews, "*Othello* and the Dignity of Man," in Arnold Kettle, ed., *Shakespeare in a Changing World* (London: Lawrence & Wishart, 1964), pp. 123–45; and Karen Newman, " 'And wash the Ethiop white': femininity and the monstrous in *Othello*," in Jean E. Howard and Marion F. O'Connor, eds., *Shakespeare Reproduced: The text in history and ideology* (New York and London: Methuen, 1987), pp. 141–62.

identify as a racialist ideology was beginning to evolve under the
pressures of nascent imperialism.[4] In this context it is all the more
curious, as Hankey notices, that Henry Jackson in 1610 seemed
utterly to ignore this aspect of the tragedy, presenting it simply as a
drama of wife-murder whose culprit is described in the most neutral
language as "her husband." We cannot now tell whether Jackson was
blind to the racial dimension of the action, or thought it of no interest
or merely too obvious to require mention. But I want to argue that
his attention to the bed suggests a way round the dilemma posed by
this odd silence: to explain why the bed should have caught his eye
is to begin to understand theatrical strategies for thinking about
racial otherness that are specific to the work's own cultural context.
If Jackson elected to say nothing about these matters, it may have
been because there was for him no real way of voicing them, in that
they were still in some deep sense *unutterable*. But they were there
on the bed for all to see.

What is displayed on the bed is something, in Othello's own profoundly resonant phrase, "too hideous to be shown" [3.3.111]. The
wordplay here (unusually, in this drama of treacherously conflicting
meanings) amounts to a kind of desperate iteration: what is *hideous*
is what should be kept *hidden*, out of sight.[5] "Hideous" in this sense
is virtually an Anglo-Saxon equivalent for the Latinate "obscene"—
referring to that which is profoundly improper, not merely indecent
but tainted (in the original sense) or unclean; and that which should
also, according to Shakespeare's own folk-etymology, be kept
unseen, *off-stage*, hidden.[6] The play begins with Iago's evocation of
just such an obscenity; it ends by seeking to return it to its proper
darkness, closing the curtains that Iago first metaphorically plucked
aside. In his frequently perceptive study of *Othello*, Edward Snow,
observing that the play's "final gesture is on the side of repression,"
goes on to stress how necessarily that gesture is directed at the bed:
"it is not just any object that is to be hidden but the 'tragic lodging'
of the wedding-bed—the place of sexuality itself."[7] But Snow's own

4. For more recent theoretical accounts of the evolution of a discourse of "Englishness" and
   "otherness" as an enabling adjunct of colonial conquest, see Stephen Greenblatt, *Renaissance Self-Fashioning: From More to Shakespeare* (Chicago and London: Univ. of Chicago
   Press, 1980), pp. 179–92; David Cairns and Shaun Richards, *Writing Ireland: colonialism,
   nationalism and culture* (Manchester: Manchester Univ. Press, 1988), chap. 1, "What ish
   my Nation?" pp. 1–21; and Anne Laurence, "The Cradle to the Grave: English Observation
   of Irish Social Customs in the Seventeenth Century," *The Seventeenth Century*, 3 (1988),
   63–84.
5. The wordplay, which may well reflect a folk-etymology, occurs elsewhere in Shakespeare:
   see, for example, *Twelfth Night*, 4.2.31 ("hideous darkness"), and *King John*, 5.4.22.
6. The proper derivation is from *caenum* = dirt; but the imagery of Carlisle's speech in
   Richard II clearly seems to imply the folk-etymology from *scaenum* = stage: "*show* so
   heinous, *black, obscene* a deed" (4.2.122); see also *Love's Labor's Lost*, 1.1.235–39.
7. p. 385.

strategy expressly requires that he himself suppress the anxiety that attaches to the bed as the site of racial transgression—the anxiety on which depends so much of the play's continuing power to disturb.

III

One of the terrifying things about *Othello* is that its racial poisons seem so casually concocted, as if racism were just something that Iago, drawing in his improvisational way on a gallimaufry [hetero-geneous mixture] of quite unsystematic prejudices and superstitions, made up as he went along. The characteristic pleasure he takes in his own felicitous invention only makes the effect more shocking. Iago lets horrible things loose and delights in watching them run; and the play seems to share that narcissistic fascination—or perhaps, better, Iago is the voice of its own fascinated self-regard. The play thinks abomination into being and then taunts the audience with the knowledge that it can never be *un*thought: "What you know, you know." It is a technique that works close to the unstable ground of consciousness itself; for it would be almost as difficult to say whether its racial anxieties are ones that the play discovers or implants in an audience as to say whether jealousy is something that Iago discovers or implants in Othello. Yet discovery, in the most literal theatrical sense, is what the last scene cruelly insists on. Like no other drama, *Othello* establishes an equivalency between psychological event (what happens "inside") and off-stage action (what happens "within"); thus it can flourish its disclosure of the horror on the bed like a psychoanalytic revelation.

The power of the offstage scene over the audience's prying imag-ination is immediately suggested by the irritable speculation of Tho-mas Rymer, the play's first systematic critic. Rymer spends several pages of his critique exposing what he regards as ludicrous inconsis-tencies between what the play tells the audience and what verisi-militude requires them to believe about the occupation of "the Matrimonial Bed." The time scheme, he insists, permits Othello and his bride to sleep together only once, on the first night in Cyprus, but "*once* will not do the Poets business: the *Audience* must suppose a great many bouts, to make the plot operate. They must deny their senses, to reconcile it to common sense."[8]

Rymer's method is taken to extraordinary extremes in a recent article by T.G.A. Nelson and Charles Haines, who set out to dem-onstrate, with a mass of circumstantial detail, that the marriage of Othello and Desdemona was never consummated at all. In this pre-viously unsuspected embarrassment is to be found an explanation

8. Rymer, quoted in Vickers, Vol. 2, p. 43. [See above, p. 206.]

for the extreme suggestibility of the hero, and thus the hidden spring of the entire tragic action.[9] Their essay is remarkable not for the ingenuity of its finally unsustainable argument about the sequential "facts" of a plot whose time-scheme is so notoriously undependable, but for what it unconsciously reveals about the effect of *Othello* upon its audiences. Their entire procedure mirrors with disturbing fidelity the habit of obsessive speculation about concealed offstage action, into which the play entraps the viewer as it entraps its characters. Nelson and Haines become victims, like the hero himself, of the scopophile economy of this tragedy and prey to its voyeuristic excitements.

Recently, Norman Nathan has attempted a point-by-point rebuttal of Nelson and Haines, the ironic effect of which is to entrap him in the very speculation he wishes to cut short. "If a lack of consummation is so important to this play, why isn't the audience so informed?" he somewhat testily enquires.[1] An answer might be—to make them ask the question. *Othello* persistently goads its audience into speculation about what is happening behind the scenes. This preoccupation with offstage action is unique in Shakespeare. Elsewhere, whenever offstage action is of any importance, it is almost always carefully described, usually by an eyewitness whose account is not open to question, so that nothing of critical importance is left to the audience's imagination. But in *Othello* the real imaginative focus of the action is always the hidden marriage-bed, an inalienably private location, shielded, until the very last scene, from every gaze.[2] This disquietingly absent presence creates the margin within which Iago can operate as a uniquely deceitful version of the *nuntius*,[3] whose vivid imaginary descriptions taint the vision of the audience even as they colonize the minds of Brabantio and Othello:

> IAGO: Even now, now, very now, an old black ram
> Is tupping your white ewe .,. . [1.1.85–86] * * *

9. T.G.A. Nelson and Charles Haines, "Othello's Unconsummated Marriage," *Essays in Criticism*, 33 (1983), 1–18. Their arguments were partially anticipated in a little-noticed article by Pierre Janton, "Othello's Weak Function," *Cahiers Élisabéthains*, 7 (1975), 43–50, and are paralleled in William Whallon, *Inconsistencies* (Cambridge: D. S. Brewer; Totowa, N.J.: Biblio, 1983). I regard my own willingness to take these arguments seriously ("Changing Places in *Othello*," p. 116, n. 1) as further evidence for the point I am making.

1. "Othello's Marriage is Consummated," *Cahiers Élisabéthains*, 34 (1988), 79–82, esp. p. 81.

2. This aspect of the play is recognized by Stanley Cavell in *Disowning Knowledge In Six Plays of Shakespeare* (Cambridge: Cambridge Univ. Press, 1987): "My guiding hypothesis about the structure of the play is that the thing *denied our sight* throughout the opening scene—the thing, the scene, that Iago takes Othello back to again and again, retouching it for Othello's enchafed imagination—is what we are shown in the final scene, the scene of murder" (p. 132). See also James L. Calderwood, *The Properties of* Othello (Amherst: Univ. of Massachusetts Press, 1989), p. 125.

3. The conventional dramatic messenger who brings reliable information and news. [Editor's note]

* * *

It would be laboring the point to demonstrate in detail the centrality of the bed in the play's denouement. The pattern of alternating revelations and concealments in the final scene is enacted through and largely organized around the opening and closing of those bed-curtains which, like theatrical inverted commas, figure so conspicuously in representations of the final scene [1, 106, 122, 370]. In the murder on the bed, with its shocking literalization of Desdemona's conceit of wedding-sheets-as-shroud ("thou art on thy deathbed" [53]), the nuptial consummation that the play has kept as remorselessly in view as tormentingly out of sight achieves its perverse (adulterate) performance. It is on the bed, moreover, that Othello (in the quarto stage direction) throws himself, as though in a symbolic reassertion of the husband's place, when he first begins to glimpse the depths of Iago's treachery [203]. His place is symbolically usurped in Emilia's request to "lay me by my mistress' side" [243], and its loss is cruelly brought home in the despair of "Where should Othello go?" [277]. He can reclaim it finally only through a suicide that symmetrically repeats Desdemona's eroticized murder:

> I kissed thee, ere I killed thee: no way but this,
> Killing myself, to die upon a kiss.
>
> [363–64]

The action of the play has rescued Othello and Desdemona from the calculated anonymity of Iago's pornographic fantasies, only for the ending to strip them of their identities once more: for most of the final scene, Othello is once again named only as "the Moor," and it is as if killing Desdemona had annihilated his sense of self to the point where he must repudiate even his own name ("That's he that was Othello: here I am" [1. 289]). Lodovico's speech reduces the corpses to the condition of a single nameless "object"—"the tragic loading of this bed" [368], "it"—something scarcely removed from the obscene impersonality of the image in which they were first displayed, "the beast with two backs" [1.1.113].[4] Like a man rubbing a dog's nose in its own excrement, Lodovico, as the voice of Venetian authority, forces Iago (and the audience with him) to look on what his fantasy has made ("This is thy work" [5.2.369]). But Iago's gaze is one that confirms the abolition of the lovers' humanity, and it thereby helps to license Lodovico's revulsion: "let it be hid." In that gesture of concealment, we may discern the official equivalent of Iago's retreat into obdurate silence: "Demand me nothing. What you know, you know: / From this time forth I never will speak word"

4. The relation between names and identity in the play is sensitively analyzed by Calderwood, pp. 40–45, 50–52.

[5.2.308–09]. Iago will no more utter his "cause" than Othello can nominate his; what they choose not to speak, we might say, Lodovico elects not to see.

IV

In so far as Lodovico voices the reaction of the audience, he articulates a scandal that is as much generic as it is social. It was precisely their sense of the play's ostentatious violation of the laws of kind that led Victorian producers to mutilate its ending. From the late eighteenth century it became usual to finish the play on the heroic note of Othello's suicide speech, tactfully removing the Venetians' choric expressions of outrage and dismay, as if recognizing how intolerably Lodovico's "Let it be hid" serves to focus attention on what it insists must not be attended to. By diverting the audience's gaze from this radical impropriety, the cut was meant to restore a semblance of tragic decorum to the catastrophe.[5] Other cuts sought to disguise as far as possible the erotic suggestiveness of the scene: in particular Othello's "To die upon a kiss" was almost invariably removed so as to ensure that at the curtain Desdemona's body would remain in chaste isolation upon a bed "unviolated by Othello's own bleeding corpse."[6] In this way the significance of the bed might be restricted to the proper monumental symbolism so solemnly emphasized in Fechter's mid-century production, where it was made to appear "as portentous as a catafalque prepared for a great funeral pomp."[7]

Of course Shakespeare's ending does play on such iconic suggestions but much more ambiguously. When Othello's imagination transforms the sleeping Desdemona to "monumental alabaster" [5.2.5], his figure draws theatrical power from the resemblance between Elizabethan tester tombs and the beds of state on which they were modelled.[8] But his vain rhetorical effort to clothe the violence of murder in the stony proprieties of ritual is thoroughly subverted by other conventional meanings that reveal the bed as a site

---

5. For a suggestive discussion of ideas of propriety and property in the play, see Calderwood, pp. 9–15.

6. Siemon, p. 50. [See above, p. 304.]

7. Henry Morley, *The Journal of a London Playgoer*, quoted in Hankey, p. 307. Fechter was the first to remove the bed from its traditional central position to the side of the stage, where he placed it with its back to the audience. If this was intended to diminish the threat of the scene, it apparently had the reverse effect, as Sir Theodore Martin complained, "bringing it so far forward that every detail is thrust painfully on our senses" (quoted in Siemon, p. 40). [See above, p. 292.]

8. The sense of this connection clearly persisted into the Restoration theatre: Rowe's illustration for *Antony and Cleopatra* (1709) shows the dead Cleopatra in her monument lying on what is evidently a bed, but in a posture recalling tomb-sculpture. It was not for nothing that the marriage-bed became a favorite model for so many Elizabethan and Jacobean dynastic tombs, where the figures of man and wife, frequently surrounded on the base of the tomb by their numerous offspring, signify the power of biological continuance, the authority of lineage. [*Elizabethan tester tombs*: the canopied beds of wealthy households, represented in funeral monuments.]

of forbidden mixture, a place of literary as well as social and racial adulteration.

If the first act of *Othello,* as Susan Snyder has shown, is structured as a miniature romantic comedy,[9] then the last act returns to comic convention in the form of cruel travesty. For the tragedy ends as it began with a bedding—the first clandestine and offstage, the second appallingly public; one callously interrupted, the other murderously consummated. A bedding, after all, is the desired end of every romantic plot; and Desdemona's "Will you come to bed, my lord" [5.2.24] sounds as a poignant echo of the erotic invitations which close up comedies like *A Midsummer Night's Dream*: "Lovers to bed" (5.1.364). But where comic decorum kept the bed itself offstage, consigning love's consummation to the illimitable end beyond the stage-ending, the bed in *Othello* is shamelessly displayed as the site of a blood-wedding which improperly appropriates the rites of comedy to a tragic conclusion.

The result, from the point of view of seventeenth-century orthodoxy, is a generic monster. Indeed, just such a sense of the monstrosity of the play, its promiscuous yoking of the comic with the tragic, lay at the heart of Rymer's objections to it. Jealousy and cuckoldry, after all, like the misalliance of age and youth,[1] were themes proper to comedy; and the triviality of the handkerchief plot epitomized for Rymer the generic disproportion that must result from transposing them into a tragic design. The words "monster" and "monstrous" punctuate his attempts to catalogue the oxymoronic mixtures of this "Bloody Farce," a play he thought would have been better entitled "the *Tragedy of the Handkerchief*."[2] Iago himself, as the inventor of this "burlesk" plot, was the very spirit of the play's monstrosity: "The *Ordinary* of *Newgate* never had like Monster to pass under his examination."[3] Much of the force of Rymer's invective stems from the way in which he was able to insinuate a direct connection between what he sensed as the generic monstrosity of the tragedy and the social and moral deformity he discovered in its

---

9. *The Comic Matrix of Shakespeare's Tragedies* (Princeton: Princeton Univ. Press, 1979), pp. 70–74. See also Cavell, p. 132.
1. The misalliance of youth and age in the play is treated by Janet Stavropoulos, "Love and Age in *Othello*," *Shakespeare Studies,* XIX (1987), 125–41.
2. Rymer, quoted in Vickers, pp. 54, 51. [See above, pp. 210 and 208.] Jonson seems to anticipate Rymer's mockery in the jealousy plot of *Volpone* (1606) when Corvino denounces his wife: "to seek and entertain a parley / With a known knave, before a multitude! You were an actor with your handkerchief" (2.3.38–40). In a paper exploring the relations between *Othello* and the myth of Hercules, "Othello *Furens*," delivered at the Folger Shakespeare Library on February 17, 1989, Robert S. Miola has suggested that the handkerchief is a version of the robe of Nessus; such ludicrous shrinkages are characteristic of comic jealousy plots—as, for example, in the transformation of Pinchwife's heroic sword to a penknife in Wycherley's *The Country Wife*. Certain objects become grotesquely enlarged to the jealous imagination or absurdly diminished in the eyes of the audience—it is on such disproportion that the comedy of jealousy depends.
3. Rymer, quoted in Vickers, p. 47. [See above, p. 207.]

action: the rhetorical energy that charges his use of "monster" and "monstrous" derives from their electric potency in the language of the play itself. It is clear, moreover, that for Rymer ideas of literary and biological kind were inseparable, so that the indecorum of the design was consequential upon the impropriety of choosing a hero whose racially defined inferiority must render him incapable of the lofty world of tragedy. "Never in the World had any Pagan Poet his Brains turn'd at this Monstrous rate," declared Rymer; and he went on to cite Iago's "Foul disproportion, thoughts unnatural" as a kind of motto for the play: "The Poet here is certainly in the right, and by consequence the foundation of the Play must be concluded to be Monstrous. . . ."[4]

Rymer's appropriation of Iago's language is scarcely coincidental. Indeed it is possible to feel an uncanny resemblance between the scornful excitement with which Rymer prosecutes the unsuspected deformities of Shakespeare's design and Iago's bitter pleasure in exposing the "civil monsters" lurking beneath the ordered surface of the Venetian state. It is as if the same odd ventriloquy which bespeaks the ensign's colonization of the hero's mind were at work in the critic. It may be heard again in Coleridge's objection to the play's racial theme: "it would be something *monstrous* to conceive this beautiful Venetian girl falling in love with a veritable negro. It would argue a *disproportionateness,* a want of balance in Desdemona."[5] Even G. K. Hunter, in what remains one of the best essays on race in *Othello*, echoes this revealing language when he insists that "we feel the *disproportion* and the difficulty of Othello's social life and of his marriage (as a social act)."[6] For all Hunter's disconcerting honesty about the play's way of implicating the audience in the prejudice it explores, there is a disturbance here that the nervous parenthesis, "as a social act," seems half to acknowledge. The qualification admits, without satisfactorily neutralizing, his echo of Iago—for whom, after all, concepts of the social (or the "natural") serve exactly as useful devices for tagging sexual / racial transgression.

"Foul disproportion, thoughts unnatural" [3.3.235] is only Iago's way of describing the feelings of strangeness and wonder in which Othello discerns the seeds of Desdemona's passion for him: "She swore, in faith 'twas strange, 'twas passing strange, / 'Twas pitiful, 'twas wondrous pitiful" [1.3.159–60]. Like *Romeo and Juliet,* the play knows from the beginning that such a sense of miraculous otherness, though it may be intensified by the transgression of social boundaries, is part of the ground of all sexual desire; what Iago enables the

---

4. Rymer, quoted in Vickers, pp. 37, 42.
5. T. M. Raysor, ed., *Shakespearean Criticism,* 2 vols. (London: J. M. Dent, 1960), Vol. I, 42, italics added. [See above, p. 231.]
6. "Othello and Colour Prejudice," p. 163, my italics. [See above, pp. 261–62.]

play to discover is that this is also the cause of desire's frantic instability. That is why the fountain from which Othello's current runs can become the very source out of which his jealousy flows.[7] Much of the play's power to disturb comes from its remorseless insistence upon the intimacy of jealousy and desire, its demonstration that jealousy is itself an extreme and corrupted (adulterate) form of sexual excitement—an incestuously self-begotten monster of appetite, born only to feed upon itself, a creature of disproportionate desire whose very existence constitutes its own (natural) punishment. The more Othello is made to feel his marriage is a violation of natural boundaries, the more estranged he and Desdemona become; the more estranged they become, the more he desires her. Only murder, it seems, with its violent rapture of possession, can break such a spiral; but it does so at the cost of seeming to demonstrate the truth of all that Iago has implied about the natural consequences of transgressive desire.

Iago's clinching demonstration of Desdemona's strangeness makes her a denizen of Lady Wouldbe's notorious metropolis of prostitution,[8] the city that Otway in *Venice Preserved* was to type "the whore of the Adriatic":[9] "In Venice they do let God see the pranks / They dare not show their husbands." It produces in Othello a terrible kind of arousal, which finds its expression in the pornographic emotional violence of the brothel scene—"I took you for that cunning whore of Venice / That married with Othello" [4.2.90–91]—where it is as if Othello were compelled to make real the fantasy that possessed him in the course of Iago's temptation: "I had been happy if the general camp, / Pioners and all, had tasted her sweet body" [3.3.344–45]. It is an arousal which his imagination can satisfy only in the complex fantasy of a revenge that will be at once an act of mimetic purgation (blood for blood, a blot for a blot), a symbolic reassertion of his sexual rights (the spotted sheets as a parodic sign of nuptial consummation), and an ocular demonstration of Desdemona's guilt (the blood-stain upon the white linen as the visible sign of hidden pollution): "Thy bed, lust-stained, shall with lust's blood be spotted" [5.1.36].[1] In this lurid metonymy for murder, Othello's

---

7. For an account of the social basis of these contradictions, see Stallybrass ["Patriarchal Territories: The Body Enclosed" in Susan Snyder, ed., *Othello: Critical Essays* (New York and London: Garland, 1998), pp. 251–74], pp. 265–67.
8. In Ben Jonson's *Volpone* (1606), Lady Wouldbe chats endlessly about (and embodies) the female promiscuity associated with the play's Venetian setting. [Editor's note]
9. For the opposite view of Venice, described by the traveler Thomas Coryat in *Coryat's Crudities* as "that most glorious, renowned and Virgin Citie of Venice," see Stallybrass, p. 265.
1. A curious sidelight is cast on nineteenth-century attempts to contain the scandal of the play's ending by the habit of having Othello finish off Desdemona with his dagger on "I would not have thee linger in thy pain"—a piece of stage business which must have heightened the sado-erotic suggestiveness of the scene (see Siemon, pp. 46–47). [See above, p. 300.]

mind locks onto the bed as the inevitable setting of the fatal end to which his whole being, as in some somnambulist nightmare, is now directed; and it is an ending that, through the long-deferred disclosure of the scene of sexual anxiety, can indeed seem to have been inscribed upon Othello's story from the very beginning.

In order fully to understand the potency of this theatrical image, it is necessary to see how it forms the nexus of a whole set of ideas about adultery upon which Othello's tragedy depends—culturally embedded notions of adulteration and pollution that are closely related to the ideas of disproportion and monstrosity exploited by Iago. The fact that they are linked by a web of association that operates at a largely subliminal level—or perhaps, more precisely, at the level of ideology—makes them especially difficult to disentangle and resistant to rational analysis,[2] and that is an essential aspect of the play's way of entrapping the audience in its own obsessions. It is above all for "disproportion"—a word for the radical kinds of indecorum that the play at once celebrates and abhors—that the bed, not only in Iago's mind but in that of the audience he so mesmerizes, comes to stand.

V

Contemplating the final spectacle of the play, G. M. Matthews produces an unwitting paradox: "All that Iago's poison has achieved is an object that 'poisons sight': a bed on which a black man and a white girl, although they are dead, are embracing. Human dignity, the play says, is indivisible."[3] But if what the bed displays is indeed such an icon of humanist transcendence, then this ending is nearer to those of romantic comedy—or to that of *Romeo and Juliet*—than most people's experience of it would suggest: why should such an assertion of human dignity "poison sight"? Part of the answer lies in the fact that Matthews, in his desire for humane reassurance, has falsified the body count. To be fair, it is quite usual to imagine two bodies stretched out side by side under a canopy—and this is how it is commonly played. But if Emilia's "lay me by my mistress' side" [5.2.243] is (as it surely must be) a dramatized stage direction, there should be three.[4] The tableau of death will then recall a familiar tomb arrangement in which the figure of a man lies accompanied by two women, his first and second wives; and read in this fashion, the bed

2. Kenneth Burke beautifully observes the power of inarticulate suggestion in the play: ". . . there is whispering. There is something vaguely feared and hated. In itself it is hard to locate, being woven into the very nature of 'consciousness'; but by the artifice of Iago it is made local. The tinge of malice vaguely diffused through the texture of events and relationships can here be condensed into a single principle, a devil, giving the audience as it were flesh to sink their claw-thoughts in." [See above, p. 247.]

3. "*Othello* and the Dignity of Man," p. 145.

4. Significantly, eighteenth-and nineteenth-century promptbooks reveal that Emilia's request was invariably denied.

can look like a mocking reminder of the very suspicions that Iago voiced about Othello and Emilia early in the play—a memorialization of adultery. It would be absurd to suggest that this is how Lodovico or anyone else on the stage consciously sees it; but, for reasons that I hope to make clear, I think the covert suggestion of something adulterous in this alliance of corpses, combined with the powerful imagery of erotic death surrounding it, helps to account for the peculiar intensity of Lodovico's sense of scandal. The scandal is exacerbated by the fact that one of the bodies is black.

Jealousy can work as it does in this tragedy partly because of its complex entanglement with the sense that Iago so carefully nurtures in Othello of his own marriage as an adulterous transgression—an improper mixture from which Desdemona's unnatural counterfeiting naturally follows. "[I]t is the dark essence of Iago's whole enterprise," writes Stephen Greenblatt, ". . . to play upon Othello's buried perception of his own sexual relations with Desdemona as adulterous."[5] Despite his teasing glance at the play's moral rhetoric of color ("dark essence"), Greenblatt is really concerned only with notions of specifically sexual transgression according to which " 'An adulterer is he who is too ardent a lover of his wife.' "[6] But this perception can be extended to another aspect of the relationship in which the ideas of adultery and disproportionate desire are specifically linked to the question of race.

In the seventeenth century adultery was conceived (as the history of the two words reminds us) to be quite literally a kind of *adulteration*—the pollution or corruption of the divinely ordained bond of marriage, and thus in the profoundest sense a violation of the natural order of things.[7] Its unnaturalness was traditionally expressed in the monstrous qualities attributed to its illicit offspring, the anomalous creatures stigmatized as bastards.[8] A bastard, as the moral deformity

5. p. 233.
6. Greenblatt, p. 248, quoting St. Jerome. Compare Tamyra's prevarication with her amorous husband (whom she is busy cuckolding with Bussy) in Chapman's *Bussy D'Ambois:* "your holy friar says / All couplings in the day that touch the bed / Adulterous are, even in the married" (3.1.91–93).
7. In addition to their usual technical sense, "adulterous" and "adulterate" came at about this time to carry the meaning "corrupted by base intermixture"; while by extension "adulterate" also came, like "bastard," to mean "spurious" and "counterfeit" (*OED*, adulterate, *ppl. a*, 2; adulterous, 3; bastard, *sb*. and *a*, 4. See also adulterate, *v*, 3; adulterine, 3). Thus Ford's Penthea, who imagines her forced marriage to Bassanes as a species of adultery, finds her blood "seasoned by the forfeit / Of noble shame with *mixtures of pollution*" (*The Broken Heart*, 4.2.149–50, italics added).
8. So, by one of those strange linguistic contradictions that expose cultural double-think, an illegitimate son could be at once "spurious" and "unnatural" and a "natural son." When the bastard, Spurio, in a play that performs innumerable variations on the theme of the counterfeit and the natural, declares that "Adultery is my nature" (*The Revenger's Tragedy*, 1.3.177), he is simultaneously quibbling on the idea of himself as a "natural son" and elaborating a vicious paradox, according to which—by virtue of his adulterate birth (*natura*)—he is naturally unnatural, essentially counterfeit, and purely adulterous. A very similar series of quibbling associations underlies the counterfeiting Edmund's paean to the tutelary of bastards in *King Lear:* "Thou, Nature, art my goddess" (1.2.1 ff.).

of characters like Spurio, Edmund, and Thersites and the physical freakishness of Volpone's illegitimate offspring equally suggest, is of his very nature a kind of monster—monstrous because he represents the offspring of an unnatural union, one that violates what are proposed as among the most essential of all boundaries.[9]

It is Iago's special triumph to expose Othello's color as the apparent sign of just such monstrous impropriety. He can do this partly by playing on the same fears of racial and religious otherness that had led medieval theologians to define marriage with Jews, Mahometans, or pagans as "interpretative adultery."[1] More generally, any mixture of racial "kinds" seems to have been popularly thought of as in some sense adulterous—a prejudice that survives in the use of such expressions as "bastard race" to denote the "unnatural" offspring of miscegenation.[2] More specifically, Iago is able to capitalize upon suggestions that cloud the exotic obscurity of Othello's origins in the world of Plinian[3] monsters, "the Anthropophagi, and men whose heads / Do grow beneath their shoulders" [1.3.143–44]; even the green-eyed monster that he conjures from beneath the general's "civil" veneer serves to mark Othello's resemblance to yet another Plinian race, the Horned Men (Gegetones or Cornuti).[4] In the Elizabethan popular imagination, of course, the association of African races with the monsters supposed to inhabit their continent made it easy for blackness to be imagined as a symptom of the monstrous[5]—not least because the color itself could be derived from an adulterous history. According to a widely circulated explanation for the existence of black peoples (available in both Leo Africanus and Hakluyt),

9. When Ford's Hippolita curses her betrayer, Soranzo, for what she regards as his adulterous marriage to Annabella, she envisages adultery's monstrous offspring as constituting her own punishment—"mayst thou live / To father bastards, may her womb bring forth / Monsters" (*'Tis Pity She's a Whore*, 4.1.99–101)—a curse that seems likely to be fulfilled when Soranzo discovers the existence of the "gallimaufry" (heterogeneous mixture) that is already "stuffed in [his bride's] corrupted bastard-bearing womb" (4.3.13–14).

1. *OED* adultery, 1b. It scarcely matters that Othello's contempt for the "circumcised dog" he killed in Aleppo shows that he sees himself as a Christian, since "Moor" was a virtual synonym for Muslim or pagan; and it is as a "pagan" that Brabantio identifies him [1.2.99].

2. In seventeenth-century English the word "bastard" was habitually applied to all products of generic mixture: thus mongrel dogs, mules, and leopards (supposedly half-lion and half-panther) were all, impartially, bastard creatures; and this is the sense that Perdita employs when she dismisses streaked gillyvors as "Nature's bastards" (*The Winter's Tale*, 4.4.83). In Jonson's *Volpone* the bastard nature of Volpone's "true . . . family" is redoubled by their having been "begot on . . . Gypsies, and Jews, and black-moors" (1.1.506–7). Jonson's location of this adulterate mingle-mangle in Venice may even suggest some general anxiety about the vulnerability of racial boundaries in a city so conspicuously on the European margin—one apparent also in *The Merchant of Venice*.

3. For Pliny, see "Textual Sources" in the bibliography, p. 389. [Editor's note]

4. John Block Friedman, *The Monstrous Races in Medieval Art and Thought* (Cambridge Mass.: Harvard Univ. Press, 1981), pp. 16–17. Calderwood notes the resonance of Othello's lodging at the Sagittary—or Centaur [1.3.115]—stressing the monster's ancient significance as a symbol of lust, barbarism, and (through the Centaurs' assault on Lapith women) the violation of kind (Calderwood, *The Properties of Othello*, pp. 22–25, 36).

5. See Newman, "Femininity and the monstrous in *Othello*," pp. 145–53; Elliot H. Tokson, *The Popular Image of the Black Man in English Drama, 1550–1688* (Boston: G. K. Hall, 1982), pp. 80–81; Friedman, pp. 101–2; and Calderwood, *The Properties of Othello*, p. 7.

blackness was originally visited upon the offspring of Noah's son Cham as a punishment for adulterate disobedience of his father.[6]

In such a context the elopement of Othello and Desdemona, in defiance of her father's wishes, might resemble a repetition of the ancestral crime, confirmation of the adulterous history written upon the Moor's face.[7] Thus if he sees Desdemona as the fair page defaced by the adulterate slander of whoredom, Othello feels this deface-ment, at a deeper and more painful level, to be a taint contracted from him: "Her name that was as fresh / As Dian's visage is now begrimed and black / As mine own face" [3.3.387–89]. Tragedy, in Chapman's metaphor, is always "black-fac'd"; but Othello's dark countenance is like an inscription of his tragic destiny for more rea-sons than the traditional metaphoric associations of blackness with evil and death. Iago's genius is to articulate the loosely assorted prej-udices and superstitions that make it so and to fashion from them the monster of racial animus and revulsion that devours everything of value in the play. Iago's trick is to make this piece of counterfeiting appear like a revelation, drawing into the light of day the hidden truths of his society. It is Iago who teaches Roderigo, Brabantio, and at last Othello himself to recognize in the union of Moor and Vene-tian an act of generic adulteration—something conceived, in Bra-bantio's words, "in spite of nature" [1.3.96]: "For nature so preposterously to err, / Being not deficient, blind, or lame of sense, / Sans witchcraft could not" [1.3.62–64]. Even more graphically, Iago locates their marriage in that zoo of adulterate couplings whose bastard issue (imaginatively at least) are the recurrent "monsters" of the play's imagery: "you'll have your daughter covered with a Barbary horse; you'll have your nephews neigh to you, you'll have coursers for cousins, and jennets for germans" [1.1.107–10]. Wickedly affect-ing to misunderstand Othello's anxiety about how Desdemona might

6. Flouting his father's taboo upon copulation in the Ark, Cham, in the hope of producing an heir to all the dominions of the earth, "used company with his wife . . . for the which wicked and detestable fact, as an example for contempt of Almightie God, and disobedi-ence of parents, God would a sonne should bee borne whose name was Chus, who not onely it selfe, but all his posteritie after him should bee so blacke and lothsome, that it might remaine a spectacle of disobedience to all the worlde. And of this blacke and cursed Chus came all these blacke Moores which are in Africa" (George Best, "Experiences and reasons of the Sphere . . . ," in Richard Hakluyt, *The Principal Navigations, Voyages, Traf-fiques & Discoveries of the English Nation*, 12 vols. (1598–1600; rpt. Glasgow: J. Mac-Lehose, 1903–5), Vol. VII, 264.

7. The association of blackness with adultery is also encouraged by a well-known passage in Jeremiah, where the indelible blackness of the Moor's skin is analogized to the ingrained (but hidden) vices of the Jews: "Can the blacke More change his skin? or the leopard his spottes. . . . I have sene thine adulteries, & thy neyings, y filthines of thy whoredome" (Jeremiah, 13:23–27, Geneva version). In the context of *Othello*, the passage's rhetorical emphasis on discovery is suggestive, as is the Geneva version's marginal note. "Thy cloke of hypocrasie shal be pulled of and thy shame sene." A second marginal note observes that the prophet "compareth idolaters to horses inflamed after mares," a comparison that may be echoed in Iago's obscene vision of Othello as "a barbary horse" [1.1.10]. I am grateful to my colleague Dr. Kenneth Larsen for drawing this passage to my attention.

betray her own faithful disposition ("And yet how nature erring from itself—"), Iago goes on to plant the same notion in his victim's mind:

> Ay, there's the point: as, to be bold with you,
> Not to affect many proposed matches
> Of her own clime, complexion, and degree,
> Whereto we see in all things *nature* tends,
> Foh! One may smell in such a will most rank,
> Foul *disproportion, thoughts unnatural.*
>   [3.3.230–35, Neill's italics]

If at one moment Iago can make infidelity appear as the inevitable expression of Desdemona's Venetian nature, as the denizen of an unnatural city of prostituted adulterers, at another he can make it seem as though it were actually Desdemona's marriage that constituted the adulterous lapse, from which a liaison with one of her own kind would amount to the exercise of "her better judgement" [238]— a penitent reversion to her proper nature. The contradictions, as is always the way with an emotion like jealousy, are not self-canceling but mutually reinforcing.

In this way the relentless pressure of Iago's insinuation appears to reveal a particularly heinous assault on the natural order of things. Not only in its obvious challenge to patriarchal authority and in the subversion of gender roles implicit in its assertion of female desire,[8] but in its flagrant transgression of the alleged boundaries of kind itself, the love of Desdemona and Othello can be presented as a radical assault on the whole system of differences from which the Jacobean world was constructed.[9] The shocking iconic power of the bed in the play has everything to do with its being the site of that assault.

In early modern culture the marriage bed had a peculiar topographic and symbolic significance. It was a space at once more private and more public than for us. More private because (with the exception of the study or cabinet) it was virtually the *only* place of privacy available to the denizens of sixteenth- and early seventeenth-century households;[1] more public because as the domain of the most crucial of domestic offices—perpetuation of the lineage—it was the site of important public rituals of birth, wedding, and death. In the

8. See Newman, passim; and Greenblatt, pp. 239–54.
9. Whether or not one accepts Foucault's notion of the sixteenth century as the site of a major cultural shift in which a "pre-classical *episteme*" based on the recognition of similarity was replaced by a "classical *episteme*" based on the recognition of difference, it seems clear that the definition of racial "difference" or otherness was an important adjunct to the development of national consciousness in the period of early colonial expansion. See the work by Cairns and Richards, Laurence, and Greenblatt (cited above, n. [4, p. 314]).
1. See Danielle Régnier-Bohler, "Imagining the Self" in [Philippe Ariès and Georges Duby, gen. eds., *A History of Private Life*, trans. Arthur Goldhammer, 3 vols. (Cambridge, Mass., and London: Harvard Univ. Press [Belknap Press], 1987)], Vol. 2 (*Revelations of The Medieval World*), 311–93, esp. pp. 327–30.

great houses of France, this double public / private function was even symbolized by the existence of two beds: an "official bed, majestic but unoccupied," located in the *chambre de parement,* and a private bed, screened from view in the more intimate domain of the bed-chamber proper.[2] Everywhere the same double role was acknowledged in the division of the bridal ritual between the public bringing to bed of bride and groom by a crowd of relatives and friends, and the private rite of consummation which ensued after the formal drawing of the bed curtains.[3] Part of the scandal of *Othello* arises from its structural reversal of this solemn division: the offstage elopement in Act 1 turning the public section of the bridal into a furtive and private thing; the parted curtains of Act 5 exposing the private scene of the bed to a shockingly public gaze. The scene exposed, moreover, is one that confirms with exaggerated horror the always ambiguous nature of that "peninsula of privacy"; "the bed heightened private pleasure. . . . But the bed could also be a symbol of guilt, a shadowy place [or a place of subterfuge], a scene of crime; the truth of what went on here could never be revealed."[4] The principal cause of these anxieties, and hence of the fiercely defended privacy of the marriage bed, lay in the fact that it was a place of licensed sexual and social metamorphosis, where the boundaries of self and other, of family allegiance and of gender, were miraculously abolished as man and wife became "one flesh."[5] Because it was a space that permitted a highly specialized naturalization of what would otherwise constitute a wholly "unnatural" collapsing of differences, it must itself be protected by taboos of the most intense character. In the cruel system of paradoxy created by this play's ideas of race and adultery, Othello as both stranger and husband can be *both* the violator of these taboos and the seeming victim of their violation—adulterer and cuckold—as he is both black and "fair," Christian general and erring barbarian, insider and outsider, the author of a "monstrous act" and Desdemona's "kind lord."[6] As the most intimate site of these contradictions, it was inevitable that the bed should become

2. See Dominique Barthélemy and Philippe Contamine, "The Use of Private Space," in Ariès and Duby, Vol. 2, 395–505, esp. p. 500.
3. See Lawrence Stone, *The Family, Sex and Marriage in England 1500–1800* (New York: Harper and Row, 1977), p. 334; and Georges Duby and Philippe Braunstein, "The Emergence of the Individual," in Ariès and Duby, Vol. 2, 507–630, esp. p. 589.
4. Régnier-Bohler, p. 329.
5. The archaic spells that form part of the convention of epithalamia and wedding masques testify to a continuing sense (albeit overlaid with a show of sophisticated playfulness) of the marriage bed as a dangerously liminal space in the marital rite of passage.
6. Othello is made up of such paradoxical mixtures—at once the governing representative of rational order and the embodiment of ungovernable passion, cruel and merciful, general and "enfettered" subordinate, "honourable murderer"—he is an entire anomaly. See Newman, p. 153: "Othello is both hero and outsider because he embodies not only the norms of male power and privilege . . . but also the threatening power of the alien: Othello is a monster in the Renaissance sense of the word, a deformed creature like the hermaphrodites and other strange spectacles which so fascinated the early modern period."

the imaginative center of the play—the focus of Iago's corrupt fantasy, of Othello's tormented speculation, and always of the audience's intensely voyeuristic compulsions.

At the beginning of the play, the monstrousness of Desdemona's passion is marked for Brabantio by its being fixed upon an object "naturally" unbearable to sight: "To fall in love with what she feared to look on! . . . Against all rules of nature" [1.3.98–101]. At the end she has become, for Lodovico, part of the "object [that] poisons sight." The bed now is the visible sign of *what has been improperly revealed* and must now be hidden from view again—the unnamed horror that Othello fatally glimpsed in the dark cave of Iago's imagination: "some monster in his thought / Too hideous to be shown" [3.3.110–11]; it is the token of everything that must not be seen and cannot be spoken ("Let me not name it to you, you chaste stars" [5.2.2], everything that the second nature of culture seeks to efface or disguise as "unnatural"—all that should be banished to outer (or consigned to inner) darkness; a figure for unlicensed desire itself. That banishment of what must not be contemplated is what is embodied in Lodovico's gesture of stern erasure. But, as Othello's quibble upon the Latin root of the word suggests, a *monster* is also what, by virtue of its very hideousness, demands to be *shown*. What makes the tragedy of *Othello* so shocking and painful is that it engages its audience in a conspiracy to lay naked the scene of forbidden desire, only to confirm that the penalty for such exposure is death and oblivion; in so doing, the play takes us into territory we recognize but would rather not see. It doesn't "oppose racism," but (much more disturbingly) illuminates the process by which such visceral superstitions were implanted in the very body of the culture that formed us. The object that "poisons sight" is nothing less than a mirror for the obscene desires and fears that *Othello* arouses in its audiences[7]—monsters that the play at once invents and naturalizes, declaring them unproper, even as it implies that they were always "naturally" there.

If the ending of this tragedy is unendurable, it is because it first tempts us with the redemptive vision of Desdemona's sacrificial self-abnegation and then insists, with all the power of its swelling rhetorical music, upon the hero's magnificence as he dismantles himself for death—only to capitulate to Iago's poisoned vision at the very moment when it has seemed poised to reaffirm the transcendent claims of their love—the claims of kind and kindness figured in the union between a black man and a white woman and the bed on which it was made.

7. For discussion of the "satisfaction" that the final scene grants an audience, see Calderwood, pp. 125–26.

PATRICIA PARKER

Othello and *Hamlet*: Dilation, Spying, and the "Secret Place" of Woman†

The lap or privity dilated or laide open . . .
> —Helkiah Crooke

Descried and set forth the secretes and privities of women . . .
> —Eucharius Roesslin

Some time ago, in an essay that argued for the convergence in *Othello* of narrative or rhetorical with the contemporary apparatus of judicial power, I began with one of the play's most controversial textual cruxes—the lines in act 3 whose "close dilations" Dr. Johnson tantalizingly suggested might be read as "close delations" ("secret and occult accusations") rather than simply as "dilations" in the current senses of either amplifications or delays.[1] I argued there that the reasons given by at least one modern editor of the play for excluding the resonance of "secret accusation" from the "close dilations" of the Folio text were indefensible. For they assumed the nonexistence of *dilation* (or its alternate *delation*) in the sense of "accusation" in Shakespeare's day, when even the most cursory search of early modern texts yields an embarrassing abundance of uses of the term in exactly this judicial sense, as well as instances of a paranomastic [i.e., punning] crossing of the two—delation and dilation, that which accuses and that which opens and amplifies.[2]

I want now to return to this subject anew, in order to consider the implications of reading both Shakespeare and the texts of early modern culture with an awareness of the historical resonance of their terms, not just for the purposes of local interpretation but as a way

---

† From *Representations* 44 (1993): 60–95. © 1993 by The Regents of the University of California. Reprinted with permission of the University of California Press. The author's quotations from *Othello* (and her emphases within them) have been retained, but bracketed references to this Norton Critical Edition. Most of the essay's discussion of *Hamlet* has been cut but with enough left (I hope) to tempt readers to examine the hidden and larger agendas of the original.

1. [See above, p. 217.] See *Othello* [3.3.126] and Patricia Parker, "Shakespeare and Rhetoric: 'Dilation' and 'Delation' in *Othello*," in Parker and Geoffrey Hartman, eds., *Shakespeare and the Question of Theory* (London, 1985), 54–74; with Arden editor M. R. Ridley's rejection of the "close dilations" of the Folio (and Second Quarto) and his use of the "close denotements" that appears only in the First Quarto, in his *Othello* (London, 1958), 99–100. Except where noted, *The Riverside Shakespeare*, ed. G. B. Evans et al. (Boston, 1974), is the modern text used here and italicization is mine.

2. See M. R. Ridley, ed., *Othello*, 99; and the *OED*'s citing of early modern English *delate* for "to accuse, bring a charge against . . . inform against" (including 1536 "dilatit of adultry"), Stow's 1598 "delators or informers" (s.v. *delator*), and (under *dilater*) Bishop Hall's 1640 "dilaters of errors, delators of your brethren."

of perceiving links between the plays and larger contemporary discursive networks. The two contexts I want to set beside *Othello* and
then, in diptych fashion, *Hamlet* are first the function of the delator
or informer as a secret accuser, associated both with spying and with
bringing something "hid" before the eye; and second, the language
of uncovering, dilating, and opening the "privy" place of woman, in
the quasi-pornographic discourse of anatomy and early modern
gynecology that seeks to bring a hidden or secret place to light.

I

Let us begin with the "close dilations" of the Temptation Scene.
It is here that Iago, the figure who will become "virtually an arche-
type of the informer" in this play,[3] introduces the hints and inferences that set Othello "on the rack," creating a sense of something
needing to be brought forth to "show":

> OTHELLO: Think, my lord? By heaven, thou echo'st me.
> As if there were some *monster* in thy thought
> *Too hideous to be shown.* Thou dost mean something.
> I heard thee say even now, thou lik'st not that,
> When Cassio left my wife. What didst not like?
> And when I told thee he was of my counsel
> In my whole course of wooing, thou criedst. 'Indeed!'
> And didst *contract and purse* thy brow together,
> As if thou then hadst *shut up* in thy brain
> Some horrible conceit. If thou dost love me,
> *Show* me thy thought.
>
> [3.3.109–19]

These central lines—forging their famously punning links between
monster and *show*, *hideous* and *hid*—lead to Othello's suspicion of
"close dilations, working from the heart" [126] and then to hunger
for information from one he assumes "sees and knows more, much
more, than he unfolds" [245].[4] Beyond their immediate resonance
in the Temptation Scene, the lines also forge links (through "contract
and purse . . . shut up . . . show") with the opening of the play or
theatrical "show," which begins with enigmatic reference to something not to be told ("Tush, never tell me!") and to a "purse" whose
mouth can be opened or shut [1.1.1–3].

In the semantic field of early modern English, the *close* of "close

---

3. Robert B. Heilman, *Magic in the Web* (Lexington, Ky., 1956), 63.
4. On these puns, see Michael Neill's "Unproper Beds: Race, Adultery, and the Hideous in
   Othello," *Shakespeare Quarterly* 40 (1989): 383–412. [See above, pp. 306–28.] Randle
   Cotgrave's *Dictionarie of the French and English Tongues* (London, 1611) gives for *monstre*
   "view, shew, or sight; the countenance, representation, or outward apparence of a thing."
   Both "contract, and purse" and "unfolds" (or "unfoulds") appear in the Folio and Quarto
   texts.

dilations" here means "secret" or "private"—the opposite of what is displayed or "shown"—as in Claudius's "we have *closely* sent for Hamlet" (3.1.29) in a context that clearly means "privily" or "secretly."[5] But it also manages to suggest the sense of something constricted or closed, a sense that echoes the scene in act 1 where Othello narrates his response to Desdemona's entreaty that he might "all [his] pilgrimage dilate" [1.3.152], opening to her "greedy ear" what had previously been known only in "parcels" or in part [148–54]. "Close dilations" convey the sense of partial opening and partial glimpses of something closed or hid, just as the resonances of "accusations" in Johnson's "occult" or "secret" sense surround Iago with hints of the informer who works behind doors.[6]

Dilation as "delation" also carried with it implications of a specifically *narrative* relation or report, just as dilation as *rhetorical* opening had to do with uncovering and bringing before the eye.[7] And *dilation* in the sense of "accusation" was a charge made "privilie" or "secretlie," a *delator* a "privie" or "*secret* accuser" or bearer of report.[8] The "close dilations" of the Folio's Temptation Scene, therefore, need not even be altered to the "close delations" of Johnson's emendation in order to convey an already overdetermined sense of "secret accusations," the activity of an informer carried out privately, without the knowledge of others, which comes in *Othello* only after the damage of accusations made in secret has been done. To look closely at the "close dilations" of this controversial text, then, is to discover the implications of *dilation* in the multiple senses of opening and informing, discovery and indictment, of bringing forth to "show"

5. See John Barret's *Alvearie or Quadruple Dictionarie* (London, 1573); and John Minsheu's *Ductor in Linguas* (1617) for *close* and *secret* as synonyms. See also *OED*, s.v.*close* A.I.4 ("concealed, occult, hidden, secret") for Tindale's 1526 version of Matthew 10.26 ("There is no thing so close, that shall not be openned").

6. "Dilate" for Othello's narrative opening and discovery in the scene before the Senate in act 1 appears in both Folio and Quarto texts. The other complex pervading Iago's "informing" is that of the *index* [2.1.253], a term that retains its compound Latin sense of forefinger, informer, and index to a book. See Minsheu, *Ductor* s.v. "index," "*ab indicando*, of showing"; and Barret, *Alvearie*, s.v. "index," "an accuser or appeacher: an utterer; a discloser of himself and other; the forefinger; the table of a book." *OED* comments on the links between "*index*|*indicate*" and "*indite*|*indict*" (*indicare*, "to give evidence against"), through "confusion of the L. verbs *indicare, indicere, indiclare*; thus in Tt., Florio has '*Indicare*, to shew, to declare, to utter; also to endite and accuse, as *Indicere*'; '*Indicere*, to intimate, denounce, manifest, declare . . . also to accuse, to appeach or detect.'" *Indite* as "write" is linked with *delatio* through Latin *deferre*.

7. For *delate* in this period as "narrate" or "report" (from *deferre*, "convey, deliver, report, indict, accuse"), see Ben Jonson's *Volpone* (2.6: "They may delate my slackness to my patron") and the *OED*'s "He . . . delated the matter to the Queen," under *delate*.

8. Apart from its English uses, see Richard Huloet's *Abecedarium* (London, 1552), which gives *dilatio* under "Accusation secretly made"; Barret, *Alvearie*, s.v. "delator" as "secret accuser" and "delatio" as "accusation or complaynt *secretly* made, a tale tolde *privily*"; Thomas Thomas's *Dictionarium Linguae Latinae et Anglicanae* (1587), under "delator," "secrete accuser . . . a tell tale"; "delatio" as "an accusation . . . secretlie made, a tale told privilie" as well as a "bill of complaint, or inditement"; "delateur" as "*privie* accuser" in Claude Desainlien's *Dictionary French and English* (1593) and in Cotgrave's *Dictionarie* as "such a one, as either in love unto Justice and the State, or in hope of reward or gaine, prosecutes offendors, or *publishes Concealements*."

something privy or "close"; and its range of meaning is a reminder of the inseparability of rhetorical and judicial in early modern discourse, of opening a "case" and bringing a "cause" to light.

II

That the "close dilations" of the scene in which Desdemona's accuser begins the secret work of his informing should summon the more ominous judicial sense of "information" is far from surprising in a play where reminders of the judicial loom so large, both in the domestic sphere and in the affairs of state—from the Moor's summons to answer the charge of "witchcraft" before the Venetian Senate in act 1 to his invocation of a justifying "cause" ("It is the cause, it is the cause . . .") as he prepares to be judge and executioner in the scene of Desdemona's death.[9] But in order to convey a fuller sense of the historical myopia of excluding an informer's "delations" from the resonances of the "close dilations" of the Folio text, we also need to set the language of this passage and its informing beside the contemporary context of delation, spying, and "privy" intelligence.

Here we encounter a wealth of contemporary reference to delators as "secret" or "privie" informers—those who inform *about* the secret and inform *in* secret—as part of what historians of the period describe as the "floating population" of informers and spies in the years before more full-scale development of the police and policing apparatus of the state.[1] G. R. Elton emphasizes the importance of "delations and informations" in the development of the means of "discovery" or bringing a hidden crime to light as early as Cromwell's regime.[2] Even more acutely in Elizabeth's reign, in the wake of the 1581 Act against Reconciliation with Rome and the papal bull *Regnans in excelsis* forbidding her subjects under pain of excommunication to obey "her orders, mandates and laws," the workings of Iago as accuser and informer have their counterpart in the multiplication of "delators" and spies encouraged by the need to ferret out recusants and harborers of secret treason to the queen.[3] In the context of this

9. See Winifred M. T. Nowottny, "Justice and Love in *Othello*," *University of Toronto Quarterly* 21 (1952): 330–44; and Katharine Eisaman Maus, "Proof and Consequences: Inwardness and Its Exposure in the English Renaissance," *Representations* 34 (1991): 29–52.

1. The phrase is from Alison Plowden, *Danger to Elizabeth: The Catholics Under Elizabeth I* (New York, 1973), 226.

2. See G. R. Elton, *Policy and Police* (Cambridge, 1972), chap. 8, on the "primitive police system" that depended on informing; and his "Informing for Profit: A Sidelight on Tudor Methods of Law-Enforcement," *Cambridge Historical Journal* 11 (1953): 149–67. Elton is less certain of its early central organization than Cromwell's biographer, Roger B. Merriman, in *Life and Letters of Thomas Cromwell*, 2 vols. (Oxford, 1902), e.g., 1:99, 360, which also stresses the importance of the development of espionage in the period.

3. See Lowell Gallagher, *Medusa's Gaze: Casuistry and Conscience in the Renaissance* (Stanford, Calif., 1991), 71, 295; Conyers Read, *Mr. Secretary Walsingham and the Policy of Queen Elizabeth*, 3 vols. (Oxford, 1925), e.g. 336; R. A. Haldane, *The Hidden World* (New

paranoid atmosphere of spying and being spied upon, one text from the decade before *Hamlet* and *Othello* reports on the omnipresence of "secret spies" who "do insinuate themselves into our company and familiarity" with such pretense of "zeal, sincerity, and friendship" that they are able both to "inform" and to "give intelligence" of the most "*secret* intents." Francis Walsingham—the secretary of state who so enlarged the Elizabethan network of intelligence—was described in his obituary notice as "a most diligent searcher of hidden *secrets.*"[4]

The business of detection and informing, of espial and bringing "privie secretes" before the eye, was part of the obsession in early modern England with things done "privilie" or in secret, in the confessional, the "secret chamber" of the heart, or the "closet" of a monarch.[5] And echoes of this network of informers, agents, and "intelligence" are everywhere in Shakespeare, from the "suborn'd informer" of sonnet 125 and the "poursuivant" of *Richard III* (part of what Elton calls the "primitive police system" of sixteenth-century England) to the "smiling pick-thanks and base newsmongers" (*I Henry IV* 3.2.25) who bear against Hal what Holinshed termed "informations that *privilie* charged him with . . . demeanor unseemelie for a prince" and the "tales and informations" gathered by Cromwell in *Henry VIII* (5.2.145). Especially resonant for *Othello* and the figure of "birdlime" applied to Iago [2.1.126] is the description of such "lynx-eyed" men as having the faculty of a "lime twig," able to "catch" anything that comes close.[6]

York, 1970); Alison Plowden's *The Elizabethan Secret Service* (New York, 1991), and John M. Archer, *Sovereignty and Intelligence: Spying and Court Culture in the English Renaissance* (Stanford, Calif., 1993), esp. chap. 2. The increase in informing for money inspired denunciations such as Bishop Hall's later one against "Delators, and informers" as "infamous and odious" (1649).

4. See respectively "Father Richard Holtby on Persecution in the North" (1593), in John Morris, ed., *The Troubles of Our Catholic Forefathers*, 3 vols. (London, 1877), 3:121; and Neville Williams, *Elizabeth I, Queen of England* (London, 1971), 261; with Lacey Baldwin Smith, *Treason in Tudor England: Politics and Paranoia* (Princeton, N.J., 1986).

5. For different manifestations of this preoccupation, see Patricia Fumerton, " 'Secret Arts': Elizabethan Miniatures and Sonnets," *Representations* 15 (Summer, 1986): 57–97; Elizabeth Hanson, "Torture and Truth in Renaissance England," *Representations* 34 (Spring, 1991): 53–84; Maus, "Proof and Consequences"; Christopher Pye, *The Regal Phantasm: Shakespeare and the Politics of Spectacle* (New York, 1990); Gallagher, *Medusa's Gaze*, 79, for Francis Bacon (himself a spy) on the "secret" and "insinuative" confessional, with Archer, *Sovereignty and Intelligence*, chap. 5; the related language of "discovery" in accounts of the New World and other "hidden" territories in Timothy J. Reiss. *The Discourse of Modernism* (Ithaca, N.Y., 1982), esp. 189–90; Patricia Parker, *Literary Fat Ladies: Rhetoric, Gender, Property* (New York, 1987), chap. 7; and Louis Montrose, "The Work of Gender in the Discourse of Discovery," *Representations* 33 (Winter, 1991): 1–41. Parts of this work call into question assumptions in Francis Barker's *The Tremulous Private Body* (London, 1984), as does, *avant la lettre,* Stephen Greenblatt's *Renaissance Self-Fashioning* (Chicago, 1980). On secrecy more generally, see Sissela Bok, *Secrets* (New York, 1982); and Frank Kermode, *The Genesis of Secrecy* (Cambridge, Mass., 1979).

6. See "A Yorkshire Recusant's Relation," in Morris, *Troubles,* 3:69; with Gallagher, *Medusa's Gaze*, 94–95; Geoffrey Bullough, *Narrative and Dramatic Sources of Shakespeare,* 8 vols. (London, 1973), 4:195. These are only a few of many Shakespearean instances, which

Things done in secret that depended on "intelligence" or report—crimes, like adultery and witchcraft, beyond the access of ocular proof[7]—are very much part of the atmosphere of espial and informing in the period before *Hamlet,* filled with attempts to ferret out an "occulted guilt" (3.2.80), and *Othello,* which introduces early on a bearer of reports who puts the Venetians in "false gaze" [1.3.19]. But the contemporary world of informing and "espials," of the "close" or secret both brought to light and judged, is also joined by an equally resonant context for both plays, one that involves a form of disclosure or espial concerned with the "secretes" of women and a female "close" or privy place. It is to this context that we now turn before returning to the language of these two plays.

III

> Like the letter, o, small and wondrous narrow . . .
> Too obscoene to look upon . . .
> —Helkiah Crooke

In order to link this sexualized and gendered context to the world of informing and spying out secrets, we need to consider once more the "close dilations" of the Temptation Scene, not simply as secret accusations but in their other sense as rhetorical *opening.* To *dilate* in early modern usage came with a sense of widening, stretching, or enlarging something "closed." Hence it meant both to "make large" and to speak "at large," expanding or discursively spreading out something originally smaller or more constricted.[8] In the rhetorical and narrative sense introduced into the play in Othello's reference to the request that he would *"all* [his] pilgrimage *dilate,"* the link with dilation made rhetoric itself a form of opening, illustrated by the figure of the open palm in contrast to logic's closed fist.[9] One of the most famous of early modern descriptions characterizes rhetorical dilation as an enlarging or unfolding through which the eye is

---

include "espials" (*I Henry VI,* 1.4.8) and informers (*Richard II,* 2.1.242) in the early histories, Parolles's informing in *All's Well That Ends Well* (4.3), "information" in *Measure for Measure* (e.g., 3.2.198), *King Lear* (4.2.92), *Coriolanus* (1.6.42). See also Jonathan Dollimore, "Transgression and Surveillance in *Measure for Measure,*" in Jonathan Dollimore and Alan Sinfield, eds., *Political Shakespeare: New Essays in Cultural Materialism* (Ithaca, N.Y., 1985), 72–87.

7. For witchcraft, see Maus, "Proof and Consequences," 38; and Karen Newman, *Fashioning Femininity and English Renaissance Drama* (Chicago, 1991), 73–93. On the general problem of evidence, see Barbara J. Shapiro, *Probability and Certainty in Seventeenth-Century England* (Princeton, N.J., 1983); and on slander and the problem of proof, Kenneth Gross, "Slander and Skepticism in *Othello,*" *English Literary History* 86 (1989): 819–52; with J. A. Sharpe, *Defamation and Sexual Slander in Early Modern England: The Church Courts of York,* Borthwick Papers no. 58 (York, Eng., 1980); W. S. Holdsworth, *A History of English Law,* 9 vols. (Boston, 1927), 3:409–11, 5:205–12.

8. See for example Thomas's *Dictionarium,* s.v. "dilato," "to stretch out in breadth, to extende or enlarge, to delaie"; Cotgrave, *Dictionarie,* "dilater," "to dilate, widen, inlarge, extend, stretch out, spread abroad, make broad."

9. See William G. Crane, *Wit and Rhetoric in the Renaissance* (New York, 1937).

enabled to see things previously "folded" or closed ("But if you *open up* those things which were included in a single word, there will appear flames pouring through houses and temples"). To *dilate,* then, was directly related to a *visual* sense of opening up to "show"— "like displaying some object for sale first of all through a lattice or inside a wrapping, and then unwrapping it and opening it out and displaying it *more fully to the gaze."* Descriptions of such rhetorical opening manage to suggest an eroticized, voyeuristic, or even prurient looking, not just a way to "spread abroad" something hidden or closed but a means through which "to open the bosom of nature and to *shew* her branches, to that end they may be *viewed and looked upon, discerned and known."*[1]

It is this dimension of *dilation* that enabled the easy movement between rhetorical and sexual opening, between the open palm of rhetoric and the open hand or palm taken (as in *Othello* or *The Winter's Tale*) as sign of the openness of a woman and her sexual appetite, a "frank" and "liberal" hand that argues a licentious or a "liberal heart" (*Othello,* [3.4.35–45]).[2] In Shakespeare, this link between opening a "matter" rhetorically "at large" and the sexual opening or enlarging of a woman is already familiar from the "Dark Lady" sonnets of a "large" and "spacious" female "will" (sonnet 135), a closed or "private" female place become the "wide world's *common* place" (137).[3] Concern that this secret or "privie" place might become instead a "common" place characterized in particular the anxieties of adultery, fear that a virgin, once opened, could not have her "opening" controlled. To open or *dilate* a virgin, the term used routinely in the period for such sexual opening, involved the threat of "enlargement" in every sense: the opening of a formerly closed and "privie" place which simultaneously opened up the possibility that a woman might be at large in a more threatening way—that, as Othello puts it, "we can call these delicate creatures ours, / And *not their appetites"* [3.3.271–72].

Close, then, in the "close dilations" of the Temptation Scene, carries the implication of "private" and "secret" in a sexual sense, a hidden place which only through opening could be displayed or "shown." And this sense of *close* as "secret" or "hid" in relation to the sexual "privitie" of woman informs the network of associations between this private female place and the language of spying, inform-

1. See respectively the discussion of "Abundance of Subject Matter" in Erasmus, *De copia* 2 (*ac totam oculis exponat*); and Henry Peacham, *The Garden of Eloquence* (1593; reprint ed., Gainesville, Fla., 1954), 123–24.

2. See *Riverside Shakespeare* note on *frank* (1223); *OED,* s.v. "frank" a2.2.b; and the play in *Love's Labor's Lost,* 3.1.120–21, on *enfranchise* and *Frances,* a name that appears in the form of *Frank* in John Marston's *The Dutch Courtesan* (1605) in relation to female sexual appetite.

3. On "private place" / "common place," see Parker, *Literary Fat Ladies,* 104 and 251, n. 12.

ing, or espial central to *Othello* and to *Hamlet,* including the scene
in a queen's "closet" to which a secret informer, or delator, comes
as spy. What I want to do before turning more directly to the plays,
therefore, is to consider the particular contemporary discourse that
combines both the dilating or opening of the "privitie" of woman and
the sense of bringing something hid before the inspection of the eye.
This is the gynecological discourse of a contemporary anatomy ded-
icated to the "ocular" discovery or exposing of a woman's "privity" or
"lap."

The language of the "close" or "secrete"—of a hidden "matter" or
"matrix" that might be dilated, opened, and displayed—pervades the
literature on the "privities" of woman in contrast to the exteriorized
sexual parts of man. Helkiah Crooke's "Of the Lap or Privities" ("in
Latine *pudendum muliebre,* that is, the womans modesty") treats, for
example, of "the outward privity or lap" of a woman as a "cleft" which
like a "doore" might be "opened" or "shut"—a sense of the "close"
or closeted behind a "doore" which pervades medical as well as popular references to this secret place. The orifice of the matrix or
womb—in ways highly suggestive when placed beside the familiar
Shakespearean euphemism for the female sexual orifice, the "O" or
"nothing" printed in early Shakespeare texts as a graphically smaller
"o"—is described in this same medical text as "like the letter, o, small
and wondrous narrow," yet capable of being *more open* according
to "the womans appetite."[4]

Crooke's and other discussions of this "privy" place repeatedly
treat of its capacity to dilate—first in the initial opening of a "closed"
virginity (where it is rare that "the Membranes are dilated with little
or no paine") and thereafter "in Copulation" and "in childbirth."
Renaldus Columbus—the anatomist who claimed, like another
Columbus, to have brought a previously hidden place to light—spoke
of the "mouth of the womb" or matrix as being *dilated with extreme
pleasure* in intercourse."[5] The sexual dilation of a virgin, or more
experienced woman, was thus in every sense an opening to

---

4. See Helkiah Crooke, *Microcosmographia: A Description of the Body of Man* (London,
1615), 232–34, 237.
5. See respectively Crooke, *Microcosmographia,* 236, for *dilation* as the routinely used term
for the sexual opening of a virgin; Audrey Eccles's *Obstetrics and Gynaecology in Tudor
and Stuart England* (Kent, Ohio, 1982), for passages on the "opening" of the cervix "in
Copulation and in childbirth"; Renaldus Columbus, *De re anatomica* (Venice, 1559), book
11, chap. 16, p. 445; and (beginning with the links between the two Columbuses) Thomas
Laqueur's *Making Sex: Body and Gender from the Greeks to Freud* (Cambridge, Mass.,
1990), 64ff. *Dilation* is of course still the term for the opening of the cervix in childbirth.
See also the sexual overtones of the repeated Shakespearean image of the chevril glove,
including its capacity for "stretching" linked with the ambivalent "capacity" of Anne Bullen
in *Henry VIII.* Stretching in order to "serve" in a sexual (including homoerotic) sense also
crosses with the "service" of artisan players in the highly sexualized language of class
difference in *A Midsummer Night's Dream* 5.1.78–81 ("Extremely stretch'd and conn'd
with cruel pain. / To do you service").

"increase," the enlarging of something "close" or closed whose opening was essential to fulfilling the command to increase and multiply. In ways resonant beside the "close dilations" of the Temptation Scene and its "contract and purse," the image used repeatedly in contemporary discussions of this "privie" female place was of something "dilated and shut together like a purse," a figure that appears in the work of physician Thomas Vicary ("open" or "shut together as a Purse mouth"), as in such popular texts as *De secretis mulierum* or "On the Secrets of Women."[6] The privity or "lap" itself was understood as something "folded" and hence needing to be unfolded in order to be available for "show"[7]—a sense of unfolding exploited not only in Othello's suspicion that his informer "sees and knows more, much more, than he *unfolds*" but in the obscene play on "lap" in *Hamlet,* as we shall see.

As with rhetorical dilation as an unwrapping or unfolding to the eye, the female "lap" or privity was thus something folded or closed as well as something secret or "close." Here, in the impulse of anatomical discourse to open up to "show," the links are even clearer between the language of the spy or informer exposing something secret to the eye and the discourses surrounding a woman's "secrete" place, not only brought to light but indicated and judged. In his discussion "Of the Lap or Privities," Crooke not only speaks of the little "o" which is "more open or more contracted" according to the "womans appetite"; he also provides an anatomical diagram of this secret place in which "the cleft of the lap or privity" is described as "dilated or laide open" to the gazer's view (220). The "dilating" of a woman figures therefore in these texts both sexually and visually, both as opening and as bringing a secret place before the eye.

This sense of "dilated" as visual opening is of course part of the ocular impulse of anatomy more generally—its preoccupation with what William Harvey called "ocular inspection," with what can or cannot be opened up to "shew," an impulse that has led recent commentators to align it with the specularity of theater. Like informing

---

6. See Thomas Vicary, *The Anatomie of the Bodie of Man* (1548; London, 1888), chap. 9, p. 77; Laqueur, *Making Sex,* 63–64; and *The Works of Aristotle the Famous Philosopher* (New York, 1974), 81 ("which may be *dilated and shut together like a purse*; for though in the act of *copulation* it is *big enough* to receive the glands of the yard, yet after conception it is so *close shut,* that it will not admit the point of a bodkin to enter; and yet again at the time of the woman's delivery it is opened so extraordinary"). The link between this "purse" and the mouth is exploited in the double meaning "delivered" of *Two Gentlemen of Verona* (1.3.137: "Open your purse, that the money and the matter may be both at once delivered"); see also the "purse / person" play in *2 Henry IV* (2.1.127) and in the homoerotic context of the Antonio / Bassanio relationship in *The Merchant of Venice,* 1.1.138.
7. See Huloet's *Abecedarium* ("*Lapped* . . . that which maye be lapped or folden"); and Minsheu, *Ductor,* who gives "lappe" as both "*Gremium*" and "to Lappe, or fould up." *Lapped* as "folded" is a common meaning in the period.

or espial, the vogue for anatomy in the early modern period involved a fascination with the ocular, with exposing what lay hid to the scrutiny of the gaze.[8] The impulse to open and expose as an epistemological hunger to "see and know" is in the case of the "privitie" of woman, however, a much more complicated impulse, a desire both to see and not to see, to display to the eye and to discourage or refrain from looking. Crooke himself both calls attention to the diagram displaying "the lap or privity dilated or laide open" to the view and warns that this place is *"too obscoene to look upon,"* a warning it shares with other descriptions of the "occult" or hidden parts of women. Beside the exposed anatomy of a man, its title page sets the more modestly opaque and closed body of a woman, covering her private parts.[9] Its text speaks particularly of the "o" or "fissure that admitteth the yard" as "a part thought too obscoene to look upon," adding that this is the reason, "sayth Pliny, that the carcasses of women do floate in the water with their faces downeward, contrary to mens which swimme upward; even Nature itself yeelding to modesty" (239)—a claim to which we will need to return in the case of the "o" of Ophelia and her more immodest drowning.

A sense of this secret female place as something too "obscene" for "show" recurs repeatedly in anatomical discourse. John Banister's *Historie of Man*—a text of anatomy published in 1578—claims "there is nothing so highe in the heavens above, nothing so low in the earth beneath, nothing so profound in the bowels of Arte, *nor any thing so hid in the secretes of nature,* as that good will dare not enterprise, *search, unclose or discover*" (Epistle Dedicatory). But when he comes in book 6 to speak, after the sexual "instrumentes" of man, of the corresponding parts of women, he writes: " * * * I am from the beginning persuaded, that, by liftyng up *the vayle of Natures secretes in womens Shapes,* I shall commit more indecencie agaynst the office of Decorum than yeld needefull instruction to the profite of the common sort * * * ." The marginal text records: "Why the partes of women are not here spoken of." The sense of a female "privity" too "obscoene" to be seen also lies behind the warnings

---

8. See *The Anatomical Lectures of William Harvey,* trans. Gweneth Whitteridge (Edinburgh, 1966), 4[lv]; with, among others, Laqueur, *Making Sex;* Luke Wilson, "William Harvey's Prelectiones; The Performance of the Body in the Renaissance Theater of Anatomy," *Representations* 17 (Winter, 1987): 69–95; Devon L. Hodges, *Renaissance Fictions of Anatomy* (Amherst, Mass., 1985), esp. chaps. 1 and 6.

9. For continental references, both medical and literary, to this "obscene" place, see, for example, Thomas Johnson, trans., *The Workes of that famous Chirurgeon Ambrose Parey* (London, 1637), 130; and Barthélemy Aneau's *Picta Poesis* (Lyons, 1552), 52, on the *obscoena lama* ("obscene bog") of the *cunnus,* in relation to an excessive female sexual appetite. On Crooke's title page and other such illustrations, see Newman, *Fashioning Femininity,* 2–5.

against and simultaneous stimulation of the gaze in anatomical treatises aware of bringing before the eye what otherwise would be
lapped, folded, secret, hid. Crooke warns in relation to the "obscoene
parts" of woman that caution must be exercised in describing and
hence displaying them vicariously to the eye: "We will first describe
the parts of generation belonging to men, and then proceede to those
of Women also; of which wee would advise no man to take further
knowledge then shall serve for his good instruction" (199). A kindred
sense of the pornographic dangers of opening and displaying "close"
and "secret" female parts sounds through Eucharius Roesslin's *The
Byrth of Mankinde* and its warning that some "wold have hadde this
booke forbidden" because it "described and set forth the secretes
and privities of women" in ways that allowed "every boy and knave"
to view them "openly."[1]

   Ambivalence, then, about opening up to "shew" this "secrete" part
produces what might be called the anatomical text's pornographic
doubleness, its simultaneous opening up and denying to the eye. In
this sense, exposures of a female "lap" or "private" are part of the
more general hunger in the period for pornographic or quasi-
pornographic display, not just in gynecological description or anatomical illustration but in the extraordinary growth of a "monster"
literature—the word itself (as in *Othello*) forging a link between
"showing" or "*demonstrating*" and the "monstrous" previously
unknown or hidden from vision.[2] Crooke's text both presents a
female "lap" or privity "dilated or laide open" to the eye and warns
its readers against the uses to which this dilation or unfolding might
be put—in a way not unlike the pandering and pornographic doubleness of Iago's simultaneous invitation to and prohibition of the
"ocular."[3] In a metaphor that already linked the opening of a woman
to the opening of a book, texts of anatomy that exposed such
"secretes" encountered the problem of *publishing* in the sense of
making "public," the double of the impulse to "display" (*displicare*,
"unfold") that in the instance of opening a woman up to "show"
risked turning a "private" into a "common" place.

---

1. See Eucharius Roesslin, *The Byrth of Mankinde, otherwise named the Woman's Booke*
   (1560), trans. Thomas Raynolde.
2. On the vogue for this literature, see among others Katharine Park and Lorraine J. Daston,
   "Unnatural Conceptions: The Study of Monsters in Sixteenth- and Seventeenth-Century
   France and England." *Past and Present* 92 (1981): 20–54; on *monster / monstrare*, see
   Ambroise Paré, *On Monsters and Marvels*, trans. Janis L. Pallister (Chicago, 1982), 196.
3. On *Othello* in relation to the rise of pornography in the period, see Lynda Boose, " 'Let it
   be hid': Renaissance Pornography, Iago, and Audience Response," in *Autour d'Othello*, ed.
   Richard Marienstras et al. (Paris, 1987).

IV

Tis an essence that's not seen . . .
—Othello

To return to the "close dilations" of *Othello* from the contemporary context of both judicial uncovering and the desire to see and not to see an "obscoene" and private female place is to become aware of the simultaneously sexual, judicial, and epistemological impulses of opening, dilating, or uncovering to the view that combine so powerfully in this play. It might indeed be said that *Othello* trains the domestic *political* activity of the delator or informer on the domestic *private* sphere of this "secrete" female place, in ways that involve not just the language of a crime to be uncovered but a simultaneously prurient and deeply ambivalent fascination with the "close" or privy locus of female sexuality, opened, "unfolded," brought forth to "show." The already cited passage of Iago's "close dilations" is resonant with the sense of something too "monstrous" or "hideous" to be shown, as with the sexual suggestiveness of the link with Cassio as one "acquainted" with Othello's wife [3.3.99]. And the partial glimpses that lead to the Moor's suspicion that his informer "sees and knows more, much more than he unfolds" [245] culminate in the demand for "ocular proof" [361] from an informer whose "report" and circumstantial evidence promise to lead him to a "door of *truth*" [3.3.409] linked with the privy "chamber" of a woman.

Within the almost unbearably protracted Temptation Scene, the "close dilations" that lead to this demand for "show" find their echo in a later passage whose terms are also both epistemological and sexual:

> IAGO: My lord, I would I might entreat your honor
> To *scan this thing no farther;* leave it to time.
> Although 'tis fit that Cassio have his place—
> For sure he fills it up with great ability.
>   [3.3.246–49]

Hidden within an informer's advice to "scan this thing no farther"— in lines whose "thing" appears to designate simply the matter under discussion (Desdemona's adultery)—is a "matter" that elsewhere in this scene is the "thing" or "common thing" [303–04] Emilia offers to her husband, the female privity or *res* that Iago vulgarly sexualizes when she intrudes to offer him what turns out to be the "trifle" of the handkerchief.[4] The advice against "scanning" this "thing," appearing to speak only to an epistemological hunger to "see" and "know," introduces into the lines that follow the double meanings of

4. See Erik S. Ryding, "Scanning This Thing Further: Iago's Ambiguous Advice," *Shakespeare Quarterly* 40 (1989): 195–96.

the "place" Cassio "fills up" with "great ability," a "place" whose sexual inference is joined by the threat to Othello's "occupation" through the obscener sense of "occupy."[5] "Scan this thing no farther" resonates with a *res* that is at once epistemological and sexual, as with a sense of scanning as the inspection of a matter or "thing" brought before the eye.[6]

Hunger to "know" as desire to "see" pervades the scene of Iago's partial or "close dilations" and Othello's "if thou dost love me, / *Show* me thy thought," in lines that link hunger to see what is hidden within Iago's mind to an increasingly obsessed fascination with what lies "hid" within Desdemona's "chamber."[7] *Show*, as in *Hamlet*, is a term that already reverberates with overtones of female sexuality—as in the pun on "shoe" and "shew" in *Two Gentlemen of Verona*, where the "shoe with the hole in it" is taken to represent the mother as the "worser sole" (2.3.14–18).[8] What is secret or unseen here, like the "dark and vicious place" of begetting in *Lear*, is the ambiguous "place" of all the double-meaning references to the "place" Cassio might occupy as Othello's "place-holder" or lieu-tenant.[9] At the same time, the almost tortuously condensed senses of "some *monster* in thy thought / Too *hideous* to be *shown*" register a double impulse like Crooke's presentation, "dilated and laide open" to the view, of something simultaneously "too obscene to look upon." "Hideous," as Michael Neill has brilliantly argued, is in this complex pun "virtually an Anglo-Saxon equivalent for the Latinate 'obscene,' " as that which according to a powerful though false etymology should be kept "offstage"—forging a link of sound between the *scaenum* or stage and the obscene as what should be hidden, unseen, not "shown."[1]

As has often been remarked, however, *Othello* provokes a constant, even lurid fascination with the offstage, hidden, or in this sense ob-scene. Much of its language, from the visually evocative rhetoric of Iago and Roderigo at its opening ("an old black ram . . .

5. The lines appear in both Folio and Quarto texts, as does this "common thing" and reference to Othello's "occupation." For *occupy*, see Parker, *Literary Fat Ladies*, 132; Christopher Marlowe's *The Massacre at Paris*, 4.5.4–9 ("till the ground which he himself should occupy"), in *Christopher Marlowe: The Complete Plays*, ed. J. B. Steane (Harmondsworth, Eng., 1969), 568–69, with the larger context of its citation in Peter Stallybrass, "Patriarchal Territories: The Body Enclosed," *Rewriting the Renaissance*, ed. Margaret W. Ferguson et al. (Chicago, 1986), 128.

6. My argument is meant both to intersect with and extend that of Stanley Cavell on the play, in, for example, his "Othello and the Stake of the Other," *Disowning Knowledge in Six Plays of Shakespeare* (Cambridge, 1987), 125–42.

7. On the homoerotic implications of this passage and the corresponding imagery of penetration through the ear, see Patricia Parker, "Fantasies of 'Race' and 'Gender': Africa, *Othello*, and Bringing to Light," in *Women, "Race," and Writing in the Early Modern Period*, ed. Margo Hendricks and Parker (London, 1993).

8. See Eric Partridge, *Shakespeare's Bawdy*, rev. ed. (New York, 1969), 121.

9. On *place / lieu-tenant*, see Michael Neill, "Changing Places in *Othello*," *Shakespeare Survey* 37 (1984): 124, 127–28; and Julia Genster, "Lieutenancy, Standing In, and *Othello*," *English Literary History* 57 (1990): 785–809.

1. See Neill, "Unproper Beds," 394. [See above, p. 314.]

tupping your white ewe") keeps attention centered on an unseen sexual coupling, or imagined coupling, that also involves the sexual opening of Desdemona as a virgin on her wedding night or, once Iago's inferences and "close dilations" begin, as a potentially already "open" and too "liberal" woman. The fact that this opening is happening offstage and hence is barred from more direct or ocular access prompts what mounts in the play both as a hunger for yet more narrative or report—the desire of now another "hungry ear" that an informer might "*all* [his narrative] *dilate*"—and as a desire that the hidden, "close," or secret be brought forth to "show." The audience of the play—and its critics—get caught up in its obsessive reference to this offstage, hidden scene, inaccessible to what Lacan called the eye's *invidia*. Obsession with what is available only in "close dilations" or partial glimpses—and the hunger to have dilated "at large" what has been glimpsed only in "parcels" or in part [1.3.153]—become in *Othello* the powerful dramatic counterpart of the obsessive scopophilia of jealousy, its obsession with glimpses possible only through a tantalizing *jalousie,* a link also forged in the language of rhetorical dilation as showing first through a "lattice" before opening more fully to the gaze.[2]

Desire in this play to bring the hidden forth to "show" emerges most clearly in the substitute fetish-object of the handkerchief— introduced first as the "thing" Emilia offers to show her husband after Othello's "show me thy thought" and his demand to "see" and "know." Through a pun on "matter" and female "matrix" that runs through *Hamlet* as through *Othello,* this "thing" is paired syntactically with something that is "the matter" ("*Des.* I will so. What's the matter? / *Oth.* That handkerchief . . ."; [5.2.47–49]). "Spotted" with strawberries [3.3.436], it is linked with Desdemona's sexuality, blood-stained wedding sheets, and hence with the "show" that signals a virgin's opening.[3] As a "thing" that *can* be "scanned" and "seen," it makes the invisible visible, standing, as "trifle," for a female "particular" otherwise out of the field of vision, forging links of sound with the open "hand" of Desdemona that argues something else too open and too "liberal." As the visible counterpart to the *rhetorical* uncovering of the lines on Cassio and Desdemona "naked in bed" [4.1.1–5]—narrative that appears to bring something offstage before the eye—it is associated with the exposure of secrets, standing in for "an essence that's not seen" [4.1.16] and figuring a magical ability "almost [to] read / The thoughts of people" [3.1.55–56]. As a form

2. *Celosia* as both "jealousy" and "a Lattice Window" appears in Richard Percivale's *A Dictionarie in Spanish and English* (London, 1599). See also Minsheu, *Ductor,* "lattises, *a latendo,* of hiding"; and Cotgrave, *Dictionarie,* "ialousie: f. lealousie, suspition, mistrust; also, a lattice window, or grate to looke through."

3. See Lynda Boose, "Othello's Handkerchief: 'The Recognizance and Pledge of Love,'" *English Literary Renaissance* 5 (1975): 360–74. [See above, pp. 262–75.]

of "show" that renders the private public, it appears to expose the "villainous secrets" for which Emilia is the "closet lock and key" [4.2.22] and thus to *publish* Desdemona's crime, offering a "thing" or "common thing" that makes this "privie" female place into a "common place," provoking Othello's "O thou *public commoner*" [4.2.74] as he delivers the judgment Iago's informing finally brings him to.

In the desire for "show" or "ocular proof" that begins with the "close dilations" of act 3, Iago plays both informer on a hidden crime, invoking all the language of judicial "proofs" [3.3.441] and pander to the simultaneously horrified and fascinated gaze. The partial glimpses offered by his informing lead toward the offstage "chamber" of Desdemona's sexuality and assumed offense. But the double impulse that in an anatomist like Crooke involves both the exposure of a "privity dilated or laide open" to the view and the sense that it is a place "too obscoene to look upon" also informs desire in *Othello* at once to see and to avert the eye. The sense of disgust conveyed in Othello's "she with Cassio hath the *act of shame* / A thousand times committed" [5.2.217–18] and the metaphorical displacements of his description of Iago as an "honest man" who "hates the slime / That sticks on filthy deeds" [151–52] resonate, as Edward Snow has argued, with disgust at the sexual act itself, with what Crooke terms "so obscoene a businesse" in a text that also describes the female orifice in particular as something "obscoene."[4]

We have already noted the ambivalence involved in the sexual as well as rhetorical opening or "enlargement" of a woman, as well as its relation to the anxieties of adultery, fear that a "closed" virgin, once "opened," might be enfranchised or "at large." In this sense the dilation or opening of a "privie" female place also involves something threatening to the privy or private as sole possession or private property, to closure and *en*closure at once. The sense that a woman can be either "closed" or dangerously "open" hovers in *Othello* around the association of Desdemona with the women of Venice in particular, simultaneously a "Virgin Citie" and the "wide world's common place," famous for its courtesans.[5] But it also underlies the exploitation in *Othello* of links between the two traditionally associated female orifices—closed or silent mouth and female "lap" or "privitie"—both suspect, and threatening, in their potential liberality. Desdemona's "parleying" early in act 2—in a scene filled with reference to the too "liberal" female tongue, mouth, and "lips," and to women's proverbial propensity to "disclose" secrets [2.1.155]—links her with the topos of the too open and unsecret female mouth (as will her

---

4. See Edward A. Snow, "Sexual Anxiety and the Male Order of Things in *Othello*," *English Literary Renaissance* 10 (1980): 384–413; and Stephen Greenblatt's reading in *Renaissance Self-Fashioning*, 232–54.
5. On Venice, see Ann Rosalind Jones, "Italians and Others: Venice and the Irish in Coryat's *Crudities* and *The White Devil*," *Renaissance Drama*, n.s. 18 (1987): 101–19.

resolution, later, to "talk Othello out of patience"), while the atten-
dant suggestion of sexual openness, her "parley to provocation"
[2.3.20] as Iago tellingly puts it, is a link made sotto voce in the
climaxing of this exchange with the hint of "strumpet" in "The Moor!
I know his trumpet" [2.1.176]. In relation to this threatening openness of "o" and mouth, Desemona is silenced as well as made more
passive-obedient in order simply to affirm her chastity as the play
proceeds, in contrast to the frankness of her speech at the beginning,
when, asking for an "ear" to her "unfolding" [1.3.242], she had
expressed desire for the "rites" of a marriage resulting from her own
will. The form of her death, then—in a striking departure from the
play's source—becomes the closing or stilling of her mouth, an act
that makes explicit the links between the two orifices throughout, a
symbolic "close" both to her speech and to the assumed crime of
sexual openness enacted on her wedding sheets.

The sense of closing—or attempting to close—what has been
"opened," in this linking of the "o" of a woman's "secrete" place with
the openness of her mouth, gathers force as the tragedy moves to its
own close, in the increasingly insistent references to the stopping of
women's mouths: in the desire to keep Bianca from railing "in the
streets" [4.1.158] and in Iago's command to Emilia to "speak *within
door*" and "charm" her tongue before she finally, too late, determines
to be "liberal" in her speech [5.2.225–28]. In relation to the stage
directing of Iago as the Moor's sole informer, the attempt to charm
or stop female tongues and other tongues as the play proceeds toward
its "bloody period" parallels this informer's need to prevent what is
called a further "unfolding" [5.1.21]. In this sense, the closing down
that takes over as the tragedy rushes toward its end involves a closing
off of further dilation or "increase," not just stopping mouths but
putting an end to Desdemona's threateningly open sexuality, along
with the nightmare of increase ("a thousand times committed")
glimpsed through the *jalousie* of Iago's informing. As a foreclosing
of "increase," the scene of her death (with all its images of symbolically regained virginity) echoes the desire for closure and perfection
already expressed in the scene of "parleying" in act 2—where Othello's yearning for death ("If it were now to die . . .") stands in striking
contrast to Desdemona's "The heavens forbid / But that our loves
and comforts should *increase* / Even as our days do *grow*" ([2.1.191–
93]).

The impulse to "see" and open up to "show"—driving obsession
with what is offstage and hidden from the eye—is countered corre-
spondingly as *Othello* moves to this close by the impulse to close off
or hide from sight. The play repeatedly eroticizes the offstage "chamber" linked with Desdemona's sexuality and hidden behind a "door"
before that chamber, and its bed, are finally uncovered to vision in

the play's last scene. But when what has been offstage, ob-scene, and hidden is finally brought forth to "show," it is only after this privy / ob-scene female place has been indicted. *"Enter Othello, [with a light,] and Desdemona in her bed"* is the stage direction in the Folio (supplemented by the "light" of the First Quarto) reproduced in most modern editions. But what is in this almost literal sense finally exposed or brought to light—the hidden place of Desdemona's sexuality and her "crime" [5.2.26]—is, almost as soon as it is shown, re-hidden and re-closed. The lines simultaneously bespeak desire to "put out the light, and then put out the light" [5.2.7], a sense that emerges in the gesture of repressing that extends to the whole of the spectacle the play has exposed, in the lines addressed by Lodovico to Iago, the simultaneous informer and pander responsible for this "show": "Look on the tragic loading [Q1: lodging] of this bed; / This is thy work. The object *poisons sight,* / Let it be *hid*" [5.2.368–70].

The final scene that leads to Desdemona's stifling in the "bed" she has "defil'd," one that invokes the satisfying of a "justice" ("The justice of it pleases"), begins with Othello's "It is the cause, it is the cause, my soul; / Let me not name it to you, you chaste stars," and then repeats. "It is the *cause* . . ." [5.2.1–3]. The judicial resonance of this repeated "cause" summons the judicial language so pervasive through the play, here invoked to authorize a husband as final judge and executioner of a too open or too "liberal" wife ("she must die, else she'll betray more men"; [5.2.6]). But the "cause" that cannot be named to these "chaste stars" also hides a language that has lurking within it the threateningly open "case" of an unchaste woman, through a complex interlingual pun linking *cause, case, chose,* and *thing,* the obscene, unnameable "case" of a woman whose opening provides the justifying "cause" of her death and the judicial proceeding of a husband against a female "chose" or "thing" that cannot be named to stars that figure the virginal coldness of a closed perfection.[6] Female "case" and legal "cause" are linked elsewhere in Shakespeare, before and after the staging of this scene.[7] But in this tragic context, what began as the opening of this case in the "close dilations" of Iago's informing here in the lines that move from "It is the cause" to "Put out the light" becomes, in every sense, a final closing

6. English *cause* descends from the same Latin *causa* as French *chose* or "matter" (a sense that *causa* has in Salic Law) and so easily crosses with the sexual meaning of *chose* or *thing* (as in the "bele chose" of Chaucer's Wife of Bath). In the legal sense it is "a matter before a court for decision" and hence often used for *case*. On the virginal / perfect here, see Janet Adelman, *Suffocating Mothers* (New York, 1992), chap. 3. Both "chaste starres" (or "Starres") and the repeated "cause" (Q1) and "Cause" (F) appear in Quarto and Folio texts here.

7. In Mistress Quickly's "my exion is ent'red and my case so openly known to the world" (*2 Henry IV,* 2.1.30–31) and in *Cymbeline* ("I will make / One of her women lawyer to me, for / I yet not understand the case myself"; 2.3.73–75).

of the case, an opening of the closed "chamber" of Desdemona's sexuality only to execute upon it the "foregone conclusion" of a predetermined justice. Othello's "It is the cause, it is the cause" summons the sense throughout the play of a monstrous parallel between a process of judgment, where the information laid by a secret accuser is enough to result in the death of the accused, and the suppressed, subliminal language of the sexual "cause" or "case," as something—secret, close, occult—always indited in advance.[8]

The tragedy that leads from Iago's tantalizingly partial or "close dilations" to Othello's demand for "ocular proof" ends with a gesture of repression and reclosing expressed not only by the desire that something that "poisons sight" be "hid" but by this informer's "Demand me nothing" [5.2.308], its verbal or rhetorical counterpart. The play that began with " 'Tush, never tell me" and with reference to the opening of a "purse" both opens up to "show" and then recloses, as if there were an underground link between the dilating or opening of a secret place to view and the theatrical "show" which, as in the root of "*thea*trical," depends on the sense of something viewed or "seen."[9] * * *

VIII

* * *

The contrasting sense of opacity—of what could not, even on stage, be brought to "show"—is also, finally, part of what Jean-Christophe Agnew and others have identified as the more general "crisis of representation" in the period, a crisis of which the public theater functioned paradoxically as revelatory instrument.[1] The obsessively staged desire to see or spy out secrets, or in the absence of the directly ocular, to extract a narrative that might provide a

---

8. On this "preposterous" structure of "foregone conclusion" [3.3.428], reversing effect and "cause," accusation and crime, see Joel B. Altman, " 'Preposterous Conclusions': Eros, *Enargeia,* and the Composition of *Othello,*" *Representations* 18 (Spring, 1987), 129–57; with Parker, *Literary Fat Ladies,* 67–69, 93, 112; and "Preposterous Events," *Shakespeare Quarterly* 43 (1992), 186–213.

9. See Joel Fineman on the links between Greek *epideiknunai* ("to show, display"), *deiknunai* ("to bring to light," "show forth," "represent," "portray," "point out"), and the "*thea*trical" as "the seen" in *Shakespeare's Perjured Eye* (Berkeley, 1986), 102–3; and Barbara Freedman, *Staging the Gaze* (Ithaca, N.Y., 1991), esp. 48, 70. Fineman's "The Sound of O in *Othello*: The Real of the Tragedy of Desire," *October* 45 (1988): 77–96, is similarly attentive to the etymological resonances of sound in this play, though its quasi-allegorical reading elides crucial gender and racial differences.

1. See Jean-Christophe Agnew, *Worlds Apart: The Market and the Theater in Anglo-American Thought, 1550–1750* (Cambridge, 1986), 97–98, on the "national, if not global, crisis of representation, one wherein traditional social signs and symbols had metamorphosed into detached and manipulable commodities," a crisis in which "professional theater offered itself, ironically, as the most credible instrument with which to visualize, so to speak, the lost transparency" of other acts.

vicarious substitute—not only in *Hamlet* and *Othello* but in plays contemporary with them—implicates both *show* and *tell*, eye and ear, in the broader sixteenth- and early seventeenth-century problem of testimony and report, the complexities of the relation between "ocular proof" and what in *Lear* is termed "auricular assurance" (1.2.92), a theatrical problem shared by the law courts and other contestatory sites of epistemological certainty and "evidence," of what might be reliably substituted for what could not be directly witnessed.[2]

IX

In the case of *Hamlet,* what emerges in its buried linkages involves not so much what is embodied in the characters of Gertrude and Ophelia as something in excess of embodiment,[3] the spilling of obsession with female "shew" into the obsession with secrets, spying, and "intelligence," producing what might be called (by analogy with kingship) the Two Bodies of woman in this play or, perhaps, the Queen's Two Bodies, given its staging late in the reign of a queen who emphasized her own tantalizing gender uncertainty—father and mother to her people, "frail" body of a woman and body of a king—as well as the controlled display but finally the opacity of her "closet," privy "chamber," and her "secretes."[4] What this intersection raises are the possibilities of what Joel Fineman elliptically suggested as the more political than psychologized reading of the proliferating eyes and ears of the famous Rainbow Portrait of this same queen, a portrait whose sexual inference is unmistakably invoked by the placing of an ear (another organ "lapped" or folded) over the locus of her "secrete" part.[5] What is important in eliciting from *Hamlet* or *Othello* their complex evocations of spying, informing, and exposing secrets in a context that also involves fascination with a hidden sexual "priv-

---

2. See Shapiro, *Probability and Certainty in Seventeenth-Century England,* on the problem of evidence across several fields in this period, including law; and on the complicating of the relation of eye and ear, Peter Stallybrass, "Reading the Body: *The Revenger's Tragedy* and the Jacobean Theater of Consumption," *Renaissance Drama,* n.s. 18 (1988): 121–48, with the discussion of *evidentia* in *Literary Fat Ladies,* 138–40. For another dramatic instance of obsession with the secret and the hid, see Michael Neill, " 'Hidden Malady': Death, Discovery, and Indistinction in *The Changeling," Renaissance Drama,* n.s. 22 (1991), 95–121.

3. See Jacqueline Rose, "Sexuality in the Reading of Shakespeare: *Hamlet* and *Measure for Measure,"* in John Drakakis, ed., *Alternative Shakespeares* (London, 1985), 95–118.

4. In addition to the instances in Fumerton and other works cited in note [5, p. 333] above, see the explication of the occult meanings of a royal "show" in "the hole matter opened" (as it is phrased in the almost simultaneously published text) of *The Quenes Maiesties Passage through the Citie of London . . . the Day Before her Coronation* (1559), ed. James M. Osborn (New Haven, 1960), 40.

5. See Joel Fineman, "Shakespeare's Ear," *Representations* 28 (Fall, 1989); with Christopher Pye's reading of the Rainbow Portrait in *The Regal Phantasm,* 68–73. For the "Lappe of the eare," see Huloet's *Abecedarium,* s.v. "Lappe."

ity" is the way the private in this sense crosses with the political in early modern England, linking the language of the plays and the discourses—anatomical, medical, theatrical, judicial—of the culture that forms the broader context for their demand to "see" and "know."

When Elizabeth delivered her famous pronouncement on the spectacle of monarchy—"We princes are set on stages in the sight and view of the world"—or when James warned his son that kings are placed on a stage "where all the beholders' eyes are attentively bent to look and pry into the least circumstances of their secretest drifts,"[6] both were addressing the circumstances of an England that included not only an increasingly elaborated secret service as the dispersed eyes and ears of state but also increasingly extended networks of mediation and representation, of go-betweens that simultaneously conveyed and enfolded messages and "secretes," as well as not infrequently interposing their own "will" between. It was also—in striking relation to both monarchs—an England that had frequent recourse to the language of a hidden "chamber," closeting, or secrets as a complexly deflected (or as in *Hamlet* "troping") cover for the simultaneously hidden and "open" secret of a homo-sexuality tied selectively to the visibility, culpability, and detection of other "monstrous" things.[7] This too, along with a homoerotics of the desire to "see" and "know," the self-consciously "theatrical" theater of Shakespeare—its "show" and "tell"—folds into its metaphorics of spying, of showing, and of opacity or withholding from vision.

Far, then, from perpetuating an earlier agenda of close reading that separated Shakespeare artificially from this history (and that, ironically, often resulted in an inability to read even the most fundamental verbal resonances of the plays) or abandoning careful reading altogether in reaction to that formal bracketing, we need to attend to the characteristic terms not only of the plays but of the culture contemporary with them. Striking examples of such simul-

6. See J. E. Neale, *Elizabeth I and Her Parliaments, 1584–1601,* 2 vols. (London, 1965) 2: 119; and *Basilikon Doron* (1609) in *The Political Works of James I,* ed. Charles H. McIlwain (Cambridge, Mass., 1918), 5; with Pye, *Regal Phantasm,* chap. 2, which starts from observations on theater and power in Stephen Greenblatt's "Invisible Bullets," originally published in Dollimore and Sinfield, eds., *Political Shakespeare,* 44.

7. I used a hyphenated "homo-sexuality" here to signal the crucial distinctions Alan Bray and others have drawn between early modern understandings and practices and post-nineteenth-century ones. See Alan Bray, *Homosexuality in Renaissance England* (London, 1982), also on *monster* as a sixteenth-century designation (13ff); Bray's "Homosexuality and the Signs of Male Friendship in Elizabethan England," *History Workshop Journal* 29 (Spring, 1990), 1–19; and on the "open secret" and the ambiguity of "lieu," Jonathan Goldberg's *Sodometries: Renaissance Texts, Modern Sexualities* (Stanford, Calif., 1992), esp. 48 and chap. 3. On the multiple contradictions involved in the simultaneous denunciation of sodomy among unforgivable "crimes" (James I. *Basilikon Doron*) and the practices of figures as prominent as Francis Bacon and the king himself, see Bruce R. Smith, *Homosexual Desire in Shakespeare's England* (Chicago, 1991), esp. 14, 26, 176. For the relation of *Othello* to this "monstrous" possibility, and its racial counterpart, in the union of Othello and Iago, see my essay in *Women, "Race," and Writing.*

taneously textual and contextual study have already been initiated, no longer attached to simply formalist or politically more conservative aims. My reading here starts in part from the premise that elements like the Dumb Show in *Hamlet* (or the "delations" of Claudius's scripted message to another king) operate in ways very different from the anachronistic assumptions of logical, psychological, or chronological plausibility on which so much critical energy has been spent,[8] but also from the conviction that the plays of Shakespeare—like other early modern texts—themselves offer us terms that if read historically would provide keys to the language of the culture they complexly demonstrate or hold up to "show."[9] To approach a culture as important to and yet distant from us as that now termed the "early modern" must be to take its own complexly developing language seriously. To read with care in this sense is not simply to add to the resources of cultural studies or cultural "poetics" those of a cultural semantics or philology, but to begin to explore the network of terms that shaped politics, institutions, and laws, as well as discourses of the body and all that we have subsequently come to think of as "literature."

MICHAEL D. BRISTOL

Charivari and the Comedy of Abjection in *Othello*†

If certain history plays can be read as rites of "uncrowning" then *Othello* might be read as a rite of "unmarrying." The specific organizing principle operative here is the social custom, common throughout early modern Europe, of charivari.[1] The abusive language, the noisy clamor under Brabantio's window, and the menace of violence in the opening scene of the play link the improvisations of Iago with the codes of a carnivalesque disturbance or charivari organized in protest over the marriage of the play's central characters. Charivari does not figure as an isolated episode here, however, nor has it been

8. On these assumptions as post-sixteenth-century historical productions, see among other recent work Margreta de Grazia's path-breaking *Shakespeare Verbatim* (Oxford, 1991).
9. I refer elliptically, of course, here to Raymond Williams's notion of "key words" from his *Keywords: A Vocabulary of Culture and Society* (rev. ed., London, 1983). Evelyn Fox Keller, in *Secrets of Life, Secrets of Death: Essays on Language, Gender, and Science* (New York, 1992), 56–72 (a discussion with obvious relevance to the present one), also begins from the importance of "key words" for any study of the intersection of gender and early modern science.
† From *Renaissance Drama*, new series, 21 (1990): 3–21. Reprinted with permission of Northwestern University Press. The author's quotations from *Othello* have been retained, but bracketed references are to this Norton Critical Edition.
1. See Neely, *Broken Nuptials*. On charivari, see Le Goff and Schmitt, Thompson, and Underdown 99–103.

completed when the initial onstage commotion ends.[2] Despite the sympathy that Othello and Desdemona seem intended to arouse in the audience, the play as a whole is organized around the abjection and violent punishment of its central figures.

Charivari was a practice of noisy festive abuse in which a community enacted its specific objection to inappropriate marriages and more generally exercised a widespread surveillance of sexuality. As Natalie Davis has pointed out ("Reasons of Misrule"), this "community" actually consists of young men, typically the unmarried ones, who represent a social principle of male solidarity that is in some respects deeply hostile to precisely that form of institutionally sanctioned sexuality whose standards they are empowered to oversee.[3]

As a violent burlesque of marriage, charivari represents the heterosexual couple in grotesquely parodic form. The bride, frequently depicted by a man dressed as a woman, will typically be represented as hyperfeminine. The groom, against whom the larger share of social animosity is often directed, is invariably represented as a type of clown or bumpkin. In addition, the staging of a charivari requires a master of ceremonies, a popular festive ringleader whose task is the unmaking of a transgressive marriage (Neill). Even in its standard form, a full-blown charivari would be a disturbing spectacle to witness. The charivari that forms the comical substructure of *Othello* is even more powerfully troubling, because here the role of the clownish bridegroom is conflated with a derisory and abusive image of "The Moor."

The following analysis sketches out an interpretation of *Othello* as a carnivalesque text.[4] Carnival is operative as something considerably more than a novel decor for the *mise-en-scène* or an alternative thematics for interpretation. The play's structure is interpreted schematically as a carnivalesque derangement of marriage as a social institution and as an illustration of the contradictory role of heterosexual desire within that institution. The grotesque character of this popular festive scenario is heightened by its deployment of the stereotypical figure of an African, parodically represented by an actor in blackface. Heterosexual desire is staged here as an absurdly mutual attraction between a beautiful woman and a funny monster.

At the time of the play's earliest performances, the supplementary character of Othello's blackness would be apparent in the white actor's use of blackface to represent the conventionalized form of "The Moor." In the initial context of its reception, it seems unlikely

2. Laroque; see also Nelson and Haines 5–7.
3. On the topic of "male solidarity" see Sedgwick.
4. Bakhtin, *Rabelais and His World* 145–96 and passim; see also his *Dialogic Imagination* 167–224 and Gaignebet.

that the play's appeal to invidious stereotypes would have troubled the conscience of anyone in the audience. Since what we now call racial prejudice did not fall outside prevailing social norms in Shakespeare's society, no one in the early audience would have felt sympathy for Othello simply on grounds that he was the victim of a racist society.[5] It is far more probable that "The Moor" would have been seen as comically monstrous. Under these conditions the aspects of charivari and of the comical abjection of the protagonists would have been clear to an audience for whom a racist sensibility was entirely normal (Newman).

At the end of the sixteenth century racism was not yet organized as a large-scale system of oppressive social and economic arrangements, but it certainly existed in the form of a distinctive and widely shared *affekt-complex*. Racism in this early, prototypical, form entails a specific physical repugnance for the skin color and other typical features of black Africans. This sensibility was not yet generalized into an abstract or pseudoscientific doctrine of racial inferiority, and for this reason it would have been relatively difficult to conceive of a principled objection to this "commonsensical" attitude. The physical aversion of the English toward the racial other was rationalized through an elaborate mythology, supported in part by scriptural authority and reinforced by a body of popular narrative (Jordan, Tokson). Within this context, the image of the racial other is immediately available as a way of encoding deformity or the monstrous.

For Shakespeare and for his audience the sensibilities of racial difference are for all practical purposes abstract and virtually disembodied, since the mythology of African racial inferiority is not yet a fully implemented social practice within the social landscape of early modern Europe. Even at this early stage, however, it has already occurred to some people that the racial other is providentially foreordained for the role of the slave, an idea that is fully achieved in the eighteenth- and nineteenth-century institution of plantation slavery and in such successor institutions as segregation and apartheid. The large-scale forms of institutional racism that continue to be a chronic and intractable problem in modern societies are, of course, already latent within the abstract racial mythologies of the sixteenth century, since these mythologies enter into the construction of the social and sexual imagery both of the dominant and of the popular culture. In more recent contexts of reception the farcical and carnivalesque potentiality of the play is usually not allowed to manifest itself openly. To foreground the elements of charivari and comic abjection would disclose in threatening and unacceptable ways the text's ominous relationship to the historical formation of

5. Hunter, "Elizabethans and Foreigners" and "Othello and Colour Prejudice." [For the latter, see above, pp. 248–62.] See also Jones and Orkin.

racism as a massive social fact in contemporary Europe, and in the
successor cultures of North and South America as well as in parts
of the African homeland itself. Against this background the text of
Othello has to be construed as a highly significant document in the
historical constitution both of racist sensibility and of racist political
ideology.

As a seriocomic or carnivalesque masquerade, the play makes visible the normative horizons against which sexual partners must be
selected and the latent social violence that marriage attempts to prevent, often unsuccessfully, from becoming manifest. To stage this
action as the carnivalesque thrashing of the play's central characters
is, of course, a risky choice for a director to make, since it can easily
transform the complex equilibrium of the play from tragedy to *opera
buffa*. Although the play is grouped with the tragedies in the First
Folio and has always been viewed as properly belonging to this genre,
commentators have recognized for a long time the precarious balance of this play at the very boundaries of farce.[6] *Othello* is a text
that evidently lends itself very well to parody, burlesque, and caricature, and this is due in part to the racial otherness of its protagonist
(Levine 14–20, Neill 391–93 [see above, pp. 311–12]).

The relationship of marriage is established through forms of collective representation, ceremonial and public enactments that articulate the private ethos of conjugal existence and mark out the
communal responsibilities of the couple to implement and sustain
socially approved "relations of reproduction." In the early modern
period the ceremonial forms of marriage are accompanied (and
opposed) by parodic doubling of the wedding feast in the forms of
charivari.[7] This parodic doubling is organized by a carnivalesque
wardrobe corresponding to a triad of dramatic agents—the clown
(who represents the bridegroom), the transvestite (who represents
the bride), and the "scourge of marriage," often assigned a suit of
black (who represents the community of unattached males or "young
men").[8] Iago of course is neither unattached nor young, but part of
his success with his various dupes is his ability to present himself as
"one of the boys." Iago's misogyny is expressed as the married man's
ressentiment against marriage, against wives in general, and against
his own wife in particular. But this *ressentiment* is only one form of
the more diffuse and pervasive misogyny typically expressed in the
charivari. And of course Iago's more sinister function is his ability to
encourage a kind of complicity within the audience. In a perfor-

6. Rymer 2: 27. [See above, p. 210.] See also Snyder 70–74.
7. See Alford; Belmont; Davis, "Charivari"; Grinberg; and Bristol.
8. For the importance of "youth groups" and of unmarried men see Davis, "The Reasons of
   Misrule."

mance he makes his perspective the perspective of the text and thus solicits from the audience a participatory endorsement of the action.

The three primary "characters" in charivari each has a normative function in the allocation of marriage partners and in the regulation of sexual behavior. These three figures parody the three persons of the wedding ceremony—bride, groom, and priest. The ensemble performs a travesty of the wedding ceremony itself. The ringleader or master of ceremonies may in some instances assist the partners in outwitting parental opposition, but this figure may also function as a nemesis of erotic desire itself and attempt to destroy the intended bond. In the actual practice of charivari, the married couple themselves are forced to submit to public ridicule and sometimes to violent punishment (Ingram, Muchembled). In its milder forms, a charivari allows the husband and wife to be represented by parodic doubles who are then symbolically thrashed by the ringleader and his followers.

This triad of social agents is common to many of Shakespeare's tragedies of erotic life, and it even appears in the comedies. Hamlet stages "The Murder of Gonzago" partly as a public rebuke to the unseemly marriage of Claudius and Gertrude (Davis, "Reasons of Misrule" 75). This is later escalated to a fantasy of the general abolition of the institution of monogamy, "I say we will have no moe marriage" (3.1.148). Hamlet's situation here expresses the powerful ambivalence of the unattached male toward marriage as the institutional format in which heterosexual desire and its satisfaction are legitimated. His objection to the aberrant and offensive union of mother and uncle is predicated on the idealization of marriage and in this case on the specific marriage of mother and father. This idealization is, however, accompanied by the fantasy of a general dissolution of the institution of monogamy back into a dispensation of erotic promiscuity and the free circulation of sexual partners. A similar agenda, motivated by a similar ambivalence, is pursued by Don John in *Much Ado about Nothing,* and by Iachimo in *Cymbeline.*

The argument I hope to sketch out here requires that readers or viewers of *Othello* efface their response to the existence of Othello, Desdemona, and Iago as individual subjects endowed with personalities and with some mode of autonomous interiorized life. The reason for such selective or willful ignorance of some of the most compelling features of this text is to make the determinate theatrical surfaces visible. To the extent that the surface coding of this play is openly manifested, the analysis presented here will do violence to the existence of the characters in depth. I believe that the withdrawal of empathy and of identification from the play's main characters is difficult, not least because the experience of individual subjectivity as we have come to know it *is* objectively operative in the text. It has been suggested, in fact, that the pathos of individual subjectivity was actually invented by Shakespeare, or that this experience appears for the first time in the history of Western representation in that great sociocultural laboratory known as Elizabethan drama (Belsey, Brecht).

Whether this view is accurate or not, however, there is the more immediate difficulty that we desire, as readers and viewers, to reflect on and to identify with the complex pathos of individual subjectivity as it is represented in Shakespeare's oeuvre. This is especially so, perhaps, for professional readers and viewers, who are likely to have strong interests in the experience of the speaking / writing subject and in the problematic of autonomy and expressive unity. The constellation of interests and goal-values most characteristic of the institutional processing of literary texts has given rise to an extremely rich critical discourse on the question of the subject; it is precisely the power and the vitality of this discourse that makes the withdrawal of empathy from the characters so difficult. But when we acknowledge the characters not only as Othello, Desdemona, and Iago, but also as components in a carnivalesque "wardrobe" that is inscribed within this text, then this wardrobe assigns them the roles of clown, transvestite, and "scourge of marriage" in a charivari.

The clown is a type of public figure who embodies the "right to be other," as M. M. Bakhtin would have it (*Dialogic Imagination* 158–67), since the clown always and everywhere rejects the categories made available in routine institutional life. The clown is therefore both criminal and monster, although such alien and malevolent aspects are more often than not disguised. Etymologically "clown" is related to "colonus"—a farmer or settler, someone not from Rome but from the agricultural hinterland. As a rustic or hayseed the clown's relationship to social reality is best expressed through such contemporary idioms as "He's out of it!," "He doesn't know where it's at!," or simply "Mars!" In the drama of the early modern period a clown is often by convention a kind of country bumpkin, but he is also a kind of "professional outsider" of extremely flexible social provenance. Bakhtin has stressed the emancipatory capacity of the clown function, arguing that the clown mask embodies the "right to be other" or *refus d'identité*. However, there is a pathos of clowning as well, and the clown mask may represent everything that is socially and sexually maladroit, credulous, easily victimized. And just as there is a certain satisfaction in observing an assertive clown get the better of his superiors, so is there also satisfaction in seeing an inept clown abused and stripped of his dignity. This abuse or "thrashing" of the doltish outsider provides the audience with a comedy of abjection, a social genre in which the experience of exclusion and impotence can be displaced onto an even more helpless caste within society.

To think of Othello as a kind of blackface clown is perhaps distasteful, even though the role must have been written not for a black actor, but with the idea of black makeup or a false-face of some kind. Othello is a Moor, but only in quotation marks, and his blackness is not even skin deep but rather a transitory and superficial theatrical integument. Othello's Moorish origins are the mark of his exclusion; as a cultural stranger he is, of course, "out of it" in the most compelling and literal sense. As a foreigner he is unable to grasp and to make effective use of other Venetian codes of social and sexual conduct. He is thus a grotesque embodiment of the bridegroom—an exotic, monstrous, and funny substitute who transgresses the norms associated with the idea of a husband.

To link Othello to the theatrical function of a clown is not necessarily to be committed to an interpretation of his character as a fool. Othello's folly, like Othello's nobility and personal grandeur, is a specific interpretation of the character's motivation and of his competence to actualize those motives. The argument here, however, is that the role of Othello is already formatted in terms of the abject-clown function and that any interpretation of the character's "nature" therefore has to be achieved within that format. The eloquence of Othello's language and the magnanimity of his character may in fact intensify the grotesque element. His poetic self-articulation is not so much the *expression* of a self-possessed subject but is instead a form of discursive indecorum that strains against the social meanings objectified in Othello's counter-festive *persona*. Stephen Greenblatt identifies the joke here as one of the "master plots of comedy," in which a beautiful young woman outwits an "old and outlandish" husband (234). Greenblatt reminds us here that Othello is functionally equivalent to the gull or butt of an abusive comic action, but he passes over the most salient feature of Othello's outlandishness, which is actualized in the blackface makeup essential to the depiction of this character. Greenblatt's discretion is no doubt a political judgment rather than an expression of a delicacy of taste. To present Othello in blackface, as opposed to presenting him just as a black man, would confront the audience with a comic spectacle of abjection rather than with the grand opera of misdirected passion. Such a comedy of abjection has not found much welcome in the history of the play's reception.

The original audience of this play in Jacobean England may have had relatively little inhibition in its expression of invidious racial sentiments, and so might have seen the derisory implications of the situation more easily. During the nineteenth century, when institutional racism was naturalized by recourse to a "scientific" discourse on racial difference, the problem of Othello's outlandishness and the unsympathetic laughter it might evoke was "solved" by making him a Caucasoid Moor, instead of a "veritable Negro" (Newman 144). Without such a fine discrimination, a performance of *Othello* would have been not so much tragic as simply unbearable, part farce and part lynch-mob. In the present social climate, when racism, though still very widespread, has been officially anathematized, the possibility of a blackface Othello would still be an embarrassment and a scandal, though presumably for a different set of reasons. Either way, the element of burlesque inscribed in this text is clearly too destabilizing to escape repression.

If Othello can be recognized as an abject clown in a charivari, then the scenario of such a charivari would require a transvestite to play the part of the wife. In the context of popular culture in the early modern period, female disguise and female impersonation were common to charivari and to a variety of other festive observances (Davis, "Women on Top"). This practice was, among other things, the expression of a widespread "fear" of women as both the embodiment of and the provocation to social transgression. Within the pervasive misogyny of the early modern period, women and their desires seemed to project the threat of a radical social undifferentiation (Woodbridge). The young men and boys who appeared in female dress at the time of Carnival seem to have been engaged in "putting women in their place" through an exaggerated pantomime of everything feminine. And yet this very practice required the emphatic foregrounding of the artifice required for any stable coding of gender difference. Was this festive transvestism legitimated by means of a general misrecognition of the social constitution of gender? Or did the participants understand at some level that the association of social badness with women was nothing more than a patriarchal social fiction that could only be sustained in and through continuous ritual affirmation?

Female impersonation is, of course, one of the distinctive and extremely salient features of Elizabethan and Jacobean dramaturgy, and yet surprisingly little is known of how this mode of representation actually worked (Rackin). The practice of using boy actors to play the parts of women derives from the more diffuse social practice of female impersonation in the popular festive milieu. Were the boy actors in Shakespeare's company engaging in a conventional form of ridicule of the feminine? Or were they engaged in a general parody of the artifice of gender coding itself? A transvestite presents the category of woman in quotation marks, and reveals that both "man" and "woman" are socially produced categories. In the drama of Shakespeare and his contemporaries, gender is at times an extremely mobile and shifting phenomenon without any solid anchor in sexual identity. To a considerable degree gender is a "flag of convenience" prompted by contingent social circumstances, and at times gender identity is negotiated with considerable grace and dexterity. The convention of the actor "boying" the woman's part is thus doubly parodic, a campy put-down of femininity and, at another level, a way to theorize the social misrecognition on which all gender allocations depend.

Desdemona's "femininity" is bracketed by the theatrical "boying" of his / her part. This renders her / his sexuality as a kind of sustained gestural equivocation, and this corresponds to the exaggerated and equivocal rhetorical aspect of Desdemona's self-presentation. As she puts it, "I saw Othello's visage in his mind" [1.3.250]; in other words, her initial attraction to him was not provoked by his physical appearance. The play thus stipulates that Desdemona herself accepts the social prohibition against miscegenation as the normative horizon within which she must act. On the face of it she cannot be physically attracted to Othello, and critics have usually celebrated this as the sign of her ability to transcend the limited horizons of her acculturation. These interpretations accept the premise of Othello as physically undesirable and therefore insinuate that Desdemona's faith is predicated on her blindness to the highly visible "monstrosity" of her "husband." In other words, her love is a misrecognition of her husband's manifestly undesirable qualities. Or is it a misrecognition of her own socially prohibited desire? Stanley Cavell interprets her lines as meaning that she saw his appearance in the way that he saw it, that she is able to enter into and to share Othello's self-acceptance and self-possession (129ff). In this view Desdemona is a kind of idealization of the social category of "wife," who can adopt the husband's own narrative fiction of self as her own imaginary object. Desdemona is thus both a fantasy of a sexually desirable woman and a fantasy of absolute sexual compliance. This figure of unconditional erotic submission is the obverse of the rebellious woman, or shrew, but, as the play shows us, this is also a socially prohibited *métier* for a woman. In fact, as Greenblatt has shown in his very influential essay, the idea that Desdemona might feel an ardent sexual desire for him makes Othello perceive Iago's insinuations of infidelity as plausible and even probable (237–52). The masculine imagination whose fantasy is projected in the figure of Desdemona cannot recognize itself as the object of another's desire.

Like all of Shakespeare's woman characters, Desdemona is an impossible sexual object, a female artifact created by a male imagination and objectified in a boy actor's body. This is, in its own way, just as artificial and as grotesque a theatrical manifestation as the blackface Othello who stands in for the category of the husband.

What is distinctive about Desdemona is the way she embodies the
category of an "ideal wife" in its full contradictoriness. She has been
described as chaste or even as still a virgin and also as sexually aggressive, even though very little unambiguous textual support for either
of these readings actually exists.[9] Her elopement, with a Moor no
less, signals more unequivocally than a properly arranged marriage
ever could that the biblical injunction to leave mother and father has
been fulfilled. It is probably even harder to accept the idea of Desdemona as part of a comedy of abjection than it is to accept Othello
in such a context. It is, however, only in such a theatrical context
that the hyperbolic and exacerbated misrecognition on which marriage is founded can be theorized.

At the level of surface representation then, the play enacts a marriage between two complementary symbols of the erotic grotesque.
This is a marriage between what is conventionally viewed as *ipso facto*
hideous and repellent with what is most beautiful and desirable. The
incongruity of this match is objectified in the theatrical hyper-
embodiment of the primary categories of man and woman or husband and wife. It is not known to what extent Elizabethan and
Jacobean theater practice deliberately foregrounded its own artifice.
However, the symbolic practice of grotesque hyper-embodiment was
well known in popular festive forms such as charivari. The theatrical
coding of gender in the early modern period is still contaminated by
the residue of these forms of social representation.

The marriage of grotesque opposites is no more a private affair or
erotic dyad than a real marriage. Marriage in the early modern
period, among many important social classes, was primarily a dynastic or economic alliance negotiated by a third party who represents
the complex of social sanctions in which the heterosexual couple is
inscribed.[1] The elopement of Desdemona and Othello, as well as
their reliance on Cassio as a broker or clandestine go-between,
already signals their intention deliberately to evade and thwart the
will of family interests. To the extent that readers or viewers are
conditioned by the normative horizons that interpret heterosexual
love as mutual sexual initiative and the transcendence of all social
obstacles, this elopement will be read as a romantic confirmation of
the spiritual and disinterested character of their love (Luhmann).
However, it can also be construed as a flagrant sexual and social
blunder. Private heterosexual felicity of the kind sought by Othello
and Desdemona attracts the evil eye of erotic nemesis.[2]

The figure of erotic nemesis and the necessary third party to this

9. Arguments for a chaste or virginal Desdemona are found in Nelson and Haines as well as
   in Janton. The idea of a sexually aggressive Desdemona is to be found in Greenblatt 237ff.
   and in Booth.
1. On the "triangular" character of erotic desire see Girard 1–52.
2. Dumouchel and Dupuy; see also Siebers.

union is Othello's faithful lieutenant, Iago. It is Iago's task to show both his captain and his audience just how defenseless the heterosexual couple is against the resources of sexual surveillance. The romantic lovers, represented here through a series of grotesque distortions, do not enjoy an erotic autonomy, though such erotic autonomy is a misrecognition of the socially inscribed character of "private" sexuality. His abusive and derisory characterizations of the couple, together with his debasement of their sexuality, are a type of social commentary on the nature of erotic romance. The notion of mutual and autonomous self-selection of partners is impugned as a kind of mutual delusion that can only appear under the sign of monstrosity. In other words, the romantic couple can only "know" that their union is based on mutual love *and on nothing else* when they have "transcended" or violated the social codes and prohibitions that determine the allocation of sexual partners.

Iago is a Bakhtinian "agelast," that is, one who does not laugh. He is, of course, very witty, but his aim is always to provoke a degrading laughter at the follies of others rather than to enjoy the social experience of laughter *with* others. He is a de-mythologizer whose function is to reduce all expressivity to the minimalism of the *quid pro quo*. The process represented here is the reduction of quality to quantity, a radical undifferentiation of persons predicated on a strictly mechanistic, universalized calculus of desire. Characters identified with this persona appear throughout Shakespeare's oeuvre, usually in the guise of a nemesis of hypocrisy and dissimulation. Hamlet's "I know not 'seems' " (1.2.76) and Don John's "it must not be denied but I am a plain-dealing villain" (*Much Ado about Nothing* 1.1.31) are important variants of a social / cognitive process that proclaims itself to be a critique of equivocation and the will to deception. It is ironic, of course, that these claims of honesty and plain dealing are so often made in the interests of malicious dissimulation. What appears to be consistent, however, in all the variants of this character-type, is the disavowal of erotic attachment and the contemptuous manipulation of the erotic imagination.

The supposedly "unmotivated" malice enacted by this figure is puzzling, I believe, only when read individualistically. Is Iago envious of the pleasure Othello enjoys with Desdemona, or is he jealous of Othello's supposed sexual enjoyment of Emilia? Of course, both of these ideas are purely conjectural hypotheses that have no apparent bearing on Iago's actions. In any case, Iago shows no sustained commitment to either of these ideas, as numerous commentators have pointed out. Nevertheless, there is an important clue to understanding Iago as a social agent in these transitory ruminations. Iago seems to understand that the complex of envy and jealousy is not an aberration within the socially distributed erotic economy, but is rather the fundamental precondition of desire itself. Erotic desire is not founded in a qualitative economy or in a rational market, but rather in a mimetic and histrionic dispensation that Iago projects as the envy-jealousy system (Agnew 6–7 et passim). In this system men are the social agents, and women the objects of exchange. Iago's actions are thus socially motivated by a diffuse and pervasive misogyny that slides between fantasies of the complete abjection of all women and fantasies of an exclusively masculine world.

Iago's success in achieving these fantasies is made manifest in the unbearably hideous tableau of the play's final scene. If the play as a whole is to be read as a ritual of unmarrying, then this ending is the monstrous equivalent of a sexual consummation. What makes the play unendurable would be the suspicion that this climax expresses all too accurately an element present in the structure of every marriage. This is an exemplary action in which the ideal of companionate marriage as a socially sanctioned erotic union is dissolved back into the chronic violence of the envy-jealousy system. Iago theorizes erotic desire—and thus marriage—primarily by a technique of emptying out Othello's character, so that nothing is left at the end except the pathetic theatrical integument, the madly deluded and murderous blackface clown. Desdemona, the perfect wife, remains perfectly submissive to the end. And Iago, with his theoretical or pedagogical tasks completed, accepts in silence his allocation to the function of sacrificial victim and is sent off to face unnamed "brave punishments."

Finita la commedia. What does it mean to accept the *mise-en-scène* of this play? And what does it mean to *know* that we wish it could be otherwise? To the extent that we want to see a man and a woman defying social conventions in order to fulfill mutual erotic initiatives, the play will appear as a thwarted comedy, and our response will be dominated by its pathos. But the play also shows us what such mutual erotic initiatives look like from the outside, as a comedy of abjection or charivari. The best commentators on this play have recognized the degree to which it prompts a desire to prevent the impending debacle and the sense in which it is itself a kind of theatrical punishment of the observers.[3] This helpless and agonized refusal of the *mise-en-scène* should suggest something about the corrosive effect on socially inscribed rituals of a radical or "cruel" theatricality.

The idea of theatrical cruelty is linked to the radical aesthetics of Antonin Artaud. However, the English term "cruelty" fails to capture an important inflection that runs through all of Artaud's discussion of theater. The concept is derived from words that mean "raw" or

3. In addition to Cavell and Greenblatt see, for example, Burke; Neely, "Women and Men in *Othello*"; Parker; Snow; and Stallybrass.

"unprocessed." In French "*cruaute*" expresses with even greater candor this relationship with "*le cru*" and its opposition to "*le cuit*." Cruelty here has the sense of something uncooked, or something prior to the process of a conventional social transformation or adoption into the category of the meaningful (Artaud 42 et passim). *Othello,* perhaps more than any other Shakespeare play, raises fundamental questions about the institutional position and the aesthetic character of Shakespearean dramaturgy. Is Shakespeare raw—or is he cooked? Is it possible that our present institutional protocol for interpreting his work is a way of "cooking" the "raw" material to make it more palatable, more fit for consumption?

The history of the reception of *Othello* is the history of attempts to articulate ideologically correct, that is, palatable, interpretations. By screening off the comedy of abjection it is possible to engage more affirmatively with the play's romantic *liebestod* [i.e., love-death]. Within these strategies, critics may find an abundance of meanings for the tragic dimension of the play. In this orientation the semantic fullness of the text is suggested as a kind of aesthetic compensation for the cruelty of its final scenes. Rosalie Colie, for example, summarizes her interpretation with an account of the play's edifying power.

> In criticizing the artificiality he at the same time exploits in his play, Shakespeare manages in *Othello* to reassess and to reanimate the moral system and the psychological truths at the core of the literary love-tradition, to reveal its problematics and to reaffirm in a fresh and momentous context the beauty of its impossible ideals. (167)[4]

The fullness of the play, of course, is what makes it possible for viewers and readers to participate, however unwillingly, in the charivari, or ritual victimization of the imaginary heterosexual couple represented here. Such consensual participation is morally disquieting in the way it appears to solicit at least passive consent to violence against women and against outsiders, but at least we are not howling with unsympathetic laughter at their suffering and humiliation.

Colie's description of the play's semantic fullness is based in part on her concept of "un-metaphoring"—that is, the literalization of a metaphorical relationship or conventional figuration. This is a moderate version of the notion of theatrical cruelty or the unmaking of convention that does not radically threaten existing social norms. In other words, the fate of Desdemona and Othello is a cautionary fable about what happens if a system of conventional figurations of desire

---

4. For other recuperative readings within quite different normative horizons see, for example, Newman; Barber and Wheeler 272–81; Heilman; Holland 197–216; and Kirsch 10–39.

is taken literally. But the more powerful "un-metaphoring" of this play is related not to its fullness as a tragedy, but to its emptiness as a comedy of abjection. The violent interposing of the charivari here would make visible the *political* choice between aestheticized ritual affirmation and a genuine refusal of the sexual *mise-en-scène* in which this text is inscribed.

Othello occupies a problematic situation at the boundary between ritually sanctioned reality and theatrically consensual fiction. Does the play simply depict an inverted ritual of courtship and marriage, or does its performance before an audience that accepts its status as a fiction also invite complicity in a social ritual of comic abjection, humiliation, and victimization? What does it mean, to borrow a usage from the French, to "assist" at a performance of this text? At a time when large-scale social consequences of racist sensibilities had not yet become visible, it may well have been easy to accept the formal codes of charivari as the expression of legitimate social norms. In later contexts of reception it is not so easy to accept *Othello* in the form of a derisory ritual of racial and sexual persecution, because the social experience of racial difference has become such a massive scandal.

The history of both the interpretation and the performance of *Othello* has been characterized by a search for consoling and anaesthetic explanations that would make its depictions of humiliation and suffering more tolerable. On the other hand, some observers, like Horace Howard Furness, have been absolutely inconsolable and have even refused to countenance the play.[5] The need for consolation is of course prompted by the sympathy and even the admiration readers and spectators feel for the heterosexual couple who occupy the center of the drama. The argument I have tried to develop here is not intended to suggest that the characters do not deserve our sympathy. Nevertheless, *Othello* is a text of racial *and* sexual persecution. If the suffering represented in this drama is to be made intelligible for us, then it may no longer be possible to beautify the text. It may be more valuable to allow its structures of abjection and violence to become visible.

Works Cited

Agnew, Jean-Christophe. *Worlds Apart: The Market and the Theater in Anglo-American Thought, 1550–1750.* Cambridge: Cambridge UP, 1986.

Alford, Violet. "Rough Music or Charivari." *Folklore* 70 (1959): 505–18.

5. Furness found the play horrible, and wished Shakespeare had never written it (2: 149, 156). See also Cavell 98ff.

Artaud, Antonin. *The Theater and Its Double*. Trans. Mary Caroline Richards. New York: Grove, 1958.

Bakhtin, M. M. *The Dialogic Imagination*. Trans. Caryl Emerson and Michael Holquist. Austin: U of Texas P, 1981.

———. *Rabelais and His World*. Trans. Hélène Iswolsky. Cambridge: MIT P, 1968.

Barber, C. L., and Richard P. Wheeler. *The Whole Journey: Shakespeare's Power of Development*. Berkeley: U of California P, 1986.

Belmont, Nicole. "Fonction de la dérision et symbolisme du bruit dans le charivari." Le Goff and Schmitt 15–21.

Belsey, Catherine. *The Subject of Tragedy: Identity and Difference in Renaissance Drama*. London: Methuen, 1985.

Booth, Stephen. "The Best *Othello* I Ever Saw." *Shakespeare Quarterly* 40 (1989): 332–36.

Brecht, Bertolt. *The Messingkauf Dialogues*. Trans. John Willett. London: Methuen, 1965.

Bristol, Michael D. "Wedding Feast and Charivari." In his *Carnival and Theater: Plebian Culture and the Structure of Authority in Renaissance England*. New York: Methuen, 1985. 162–78.

Burke, Kenneth. "*Othello*: An Essay to Illustrate a Method." *Hudson Review* 4 (1951): 165–203.

Cavell, Stanley. *Disowning Knowledge in Six Plays of Shakespeare*. Cambridge: Cambridge UP, 1987.

Colie, Rosalie. *Shakespeare's Living Art*. Princeton: Princeton UP, 1974.

Davis, Natalie Zemon. "Charivari, honneur et communauté à Lyon et à Genève au XVIIᵉ siècle." Le Goff and Schmitt 207–20.

———. "The Reasons of Misrule: Youth Groups and Charivaris in Sixteenth-Century France." *Past and Present* 50 (1971): 49–75.

———. "Women on Top: Symbolic Sexual Inversion and Political Disorder in Early Modern Europe." *The Reversible World: Symbolic Inversion in Art and Society*. Ed. Barbara A. Babcock. Ithaca: Cornell UP, 1978. 147–90.

Dumouchel, Paul, and Jean-Pierre Dupuy. *L'Enfer des choses: René Girard et la logique de l'économie*. Paris: Seuil, 1979.

Furness, Horace Howard. *Letters*. Ed. Horace Howard Furness. 2 vols. Boston: Houghton, 1922.

Girard, René. *Deceit, Desire, and the Novel: Self and Other in Literary Structure*. Trans. Yvonne Freccero. Baltimore: Johns Hopkins UP, 1965.

Greenblatt, Stephen. *Renaissance Self-Fashioning: From More to Shakespeare*. Chicago: U of Chicago P, 1980.

Grinberg, Martine. "Charivaris au Moyen Age et à la Renaissance. Condamnation des remariages ou rites d'inversion du temps?" Le Goff and Schmitt 141–47.

Heilman, Robert. *Magic in the Web: Action and Language in* Othello. Lexington: U of Kentucky P, 1956.

Holland, Norman. *The Shakespearean Imagination: A Critical Introduction*. Bloomington: U of Indiana P, 1964.

Hunter, G. K. "Elizabethans and Foreigners." *Shakespeare Survey* 17 (1964): 37–52.

———. "Othello and Colour Prejudice." *Proceedings of the British Academy* 53 (1967): 139–63.

Ingram, Martin. "Le charivari dans l'Angleterre du XVIᵉ et du XVIIᵉ siècle. Aperçu historique." Le Goff and Schmitt 251–64.

Janton, Pierre. "Othello's Weak Function." *Cahiers Elisabéthains* 34 (1988): 79–82.

Jones, Eldred D. *Othello's Countrymen: The African in English Renaissance Drama*. Oxford: Oxford UP, 1965.

Jordan, Winthrop D. *White over Black: American Attitudes toward the Negro, 1550–1812*. Chapel Hill: U of North Carolina P, 1968.

Kirsch, Arthur C. *Shakespeare and the Experience of Love*. Cambridge: Cambridge UP, 1981.

Laroque, François. "An Archaeology of the Dramatic Text: *Othello* and Popular Traditions." *Cahiers Elisabéthains* 32 (1987): 13–35.

Le Goff, Jacques, and Jean-Claude Schmitt, eds. *Le charivari: Actes de la table ronde organisée à Paris (25–27 avril 1977) par l'Ecole des Hautes Etudes en Sciences Sociales et le Centre National de la Recherche Scientifique*. Paris: Mouton, 1977.

Levine, Lawrence W. *Highbrow / Lowbrow: The Emergence of Cultural Hierarchy in America*. Cambridge: Harvard UP, 1988.

Luhmann, Niklas. *Love as Passion: The Codification of Intimacy*. Trans. Jeremy Gaines and Doris L. Jones. Cambridge: Harvard UP, 1986.

Muchembled, Robert. "Des conduites de bruit au spectacle des processions. Mutations mentales et déclin des fêtes populaires dans le Nord de la France (XV–XVI siècle)." Le Goff and Schmitt 229–36.

Neely, Carol Thomas. *Broken Nuptials in Shakespeare's Plays*. New Haven: Yale UP, 1985.

———. "Women and Men in *Othello*: 'What should such a fool / Do with so good a Woman?' " *The Woman's Part: Feminist Criticism of Shakespeare*. Ed. Carolyn Ruth Swift Lenz, Gayle Greene, and Carol Thomas Neely. Urbana: U of Illinois P, 1980. 211–39.

Neill, Michael. "Unproper Beds: Race, Adultery, and the Hideous in *Othello*." *Shakespeare Quarterly* 40 (1989): 383–412.

Nelson, T. G. A., and Charles Haines. "Othello's Unconsummated Marriage." *Essays in Criticism* 33 (1983): 1–18.

Newman, Karen. " 'And wash the Ethiop white': Femininity and the Monstrous in *Othello*." *Shakespeare Reproduced: The Text in His-*

tory and Ideology. Ed. Jean E. Howard and Marion F. O'Connor. New York: Methuen, 1987. 143–62.

Orkin, Martin. "Othello and the 'Plain Face' of Racism." *Shakespeare Quarterly* 38 (1987): 166–88.

Parker, Patricia. "Shakespeare and Rhetoric: 'Dilation' and 'Delation' in *Othello*." *Shakespeare and the Question of Theory*. Ed. Patricia Parker and Geoffrey Hartman. London: Methuen, 1985. 54–74.

Rackin, Phyllis. "Androgyny, Mimesis, and the Marriage of the Boy Heroine on the English Renaissance Stage." *PMLA* 102 (1987): 29–41.

Rey-Flaud, Henri. *Le charivari: Les rituels fondamentaux de la sexualité*. Paris: Payot, 1985.

Rymer, Thomas. *A Short View of Tragedy. Shakespeare: The Critical Heritage*. Ed. Brian Vickers. 6 vols. London: Routledge, 1974–81. 2: 25–59.

Sedgwick, Eve Kosofsky. *Between Men: English Literature and Male Homosocial Desire*. New York: Columbia UP, 1985.

Shakespeare, William. *The Riverside Shakespeare*. Gnl. ed. G. Blakemore Evans. Boston: Houghton, 1974.

Siebers, Tobin. *The Mirror of Medusa*. Berkeley: U of California P, 1983.

Snow, Edward A. "Sexual Anxiety and the Male Order of Things in *Othello*." *English Literary Renaissance* 10 (1980): 384–412.

Snyder, Susan. *The Comic Matrix of Shakespeare's Tragedies*. Princeton: Princeton UP, 1979.

Stallybrass, Peter. "Patriarchal Territories: The Body Enclosed." *Rewriting the Renaissance: The Discourses of Sexual Difference in Early Modern Europe*. Ed. Margaret W. Ferguson, Maureen Quilligan, and Nancy J. Vickers. Chicago: U of Chicago P, 1986. 123–42.

Thompson, E. P. "Rough Music; Le Charivari Anglais." *Annales: Economies, sociétés, civilizations* 27 (1972): 285–312.

Tokson, Elliot H. *The Popular Image of the Black Man in English Drama, 1550–1688*. Boston: Hall, 1982.

Underdown, David. *Revel, Riot, and Rebellion: Popular Politics and Culture in England, 1603–1660*. Oxford: Clarendon, 1985.

Woodbridge, Linda. *Women and the English Renaissance: Literature and the Nature of Womankind, 1540–1620*. Urbana: U of Illinois P, 1984.

EDWARD PECHTER

"Too Much Violence": Murdering Wives in *Othello*†

> These stage directions make one think rather of the murder of
> Nancy by Bill Sikes [in Charles Dickens's *Oliver Twist*], than of
> Othello and Desdemona. Even now there is too much violence.
> Why should Desdemona spring out of bed, to be brutally thrust
> back into it? . . . "Tradition" was right in confining Desdemona to
> her couch: Mr. Fechter is wrong in hazarding the ludicrous effects
> of the opposite course.
>
> Sir Theodore Martin

It is a truth universally acknowledged that, of all the acts of violence
against women represented on the English Renaissance stage with
such generous abundance and peculiar gusto, Othello's murder of
Desdemona, followed quickly by Iago's murder of Emilia, is the most
appalling. Once we proceed beyond this proposition, however, universal agreement is out of the question, and even a rough consensus
may be too much to expect. We cannot be sure what these enactments of violence did to or for their audiences, or what their audiences did with them, why they continue to fascinate us four
centuries later, or whether any substantial connection exists between
Renaissance interests in such enactments and our own. In specu-
lating about these matters, I take my lead from Sir Theodore Martin's
reaction to Charles Fechter's mid-nineteenth-century prompt book.
"Even now," Martin says, "there is too much violence" (quoted in
Sprague, 214). The introductory phrase serves as a reminder that the
normative theatrical practice in Martin's time was to downplay, if
not eliminate, Desdemona's resistance at the end; but more striking
than its frame of reference, "even now" echoes the effectively originating act of violence in *Othello*, Iago's appalling image (and enactment) of an assault—not only on Brabantio's daughter but on
Brabantio himself: "Even now, now, very now, an old black ram / Is
tupping your white ewe."[1] The echo is presumably unintentional, but
the comment as a whole pulsates with an anger that renders the issue

---

† Adapted and reprinted with permission from *"Othello" and Interpretive Traditions* (Iowa
City: University of Iowa Press, 1999) and from *Women, Violence and English Renaissance
Literature,* ed. Linda Woodbridge and Sharon Beehler (Tempe: Arizona Center for Medieval and Renaissance Studies, 2003).
1. [1.1.85–86]. All *Othello* quotations are taken from Honigmann's Arden 3 edition and will
henceforth be interpolated parenthetically; bracketed references are to this Norton Critical
Edition. The idea that Iago's words assault Brabantio himself is reinforced by the pun on
"ewe / you"; see Neill, "Changing Places," 122. The similar pun in Webster's *White Devil*
(1.2.239–41), a play saturated with *Othello* echoes, has been called "obvious" (Luckyj,
21). Iago twice echoes his own violent phrase, first to describe the Turkish invasion
[1.1.148], subsequently to describe the sudden and inexplicable rage of Cassio and Montano: "friends all, but now, even now, / In quarter and in terms like bride and groom"
[2.3.169–70].

of conscious control highly problematic. When he made the comment, Martin had been married for ten years to Helena Faucit, one of the premier Desdemonas of the nineteenth-century stage, so his overheated reaction may be taken to reflect a personal investment; but the stage and critical history of *Othello* indicates that the scene of Desdemona's and then Emilia's murder has deeply disturbed audiences across a range of personal and historical experience. From this angle, Martin's peculiar response is also a typical one. Reacting with too much violence to the problem of too much violence, he reproduces a kind of turmoil that extends back in a more or less unbroken line of reception to the earliest evidence we have for this play's effect, Henry Jackson's description of an Oxford audience in 1610, "moved . . . to tears" by "the celebrated Desdemona" who, though dead, "entreated the pity of the spectators by her very countenance" (quoted in Evans, 1978). If in this respect Martin may be said to embody tradition, tradition is also the substance of his appeal, as the appropriate and even perhaps remedial response to the problem. " 'Tradition,' " he says, "was right." Martin, I argue, was wrong. Tradition, the nightmare of history registered in the weight of previous theatrical and critical response to *Othello*, does not solve the problem of too much violence: it reproduces and thus perpetuates it.

In his essay "The Women's Voices in *Othello*," Eamon Grennan calls the Willow Song scene (4.3) "one of the most dramatically compelling scenes in Shakespeare."

> To account for the perfection of the sequence one could point to its intimacy, the quotidian familiarity of its action, its unhurried simplicity, its willingness to be ordinary. One might also refer to the atmosphere of private freedom within this protected feminine enclosure[, an] interlude suggesting peace and freedom, within the clamorous procession of violent acts and urgent voices. (277)

Grennan emphasizes the felt difference of the scene as an interlude closed off from the aggressive anxiety of the male-dominated action on either side. Kenneth Burke understood the scene in much the same way, as characterizing the affective economy of Shakespearean tragic practice in general: "*Act IV:* 'The Pity of It.' Indeed, might we not, even as a rule, call this station of a Shakespearean tragedy the 'pity' act? There can be flashes of pity wherever opportunity offers, but might the fourth act be the one that seeks to say pity-pity-pity repeatedly?" (174). Burke gives many examples—Cordelia's reunion with Lear, Ophelia's death, Mariana at the grange—working out of similar material: a quiet lull in the action, women's voices and vulnerabilities, songs, pathos.

In distinguishing between women and men, or between the conventional tragic effects of pity and fear, both Grennan and Burke seem inevitably to consign Emilia and Desdemona to a secondary or dependent status. Hence for Burke,

> when Desdemona says to Othello, who has just struck her, "I have not deserved this," she almost literally repeats the Aristotelian formula for pity (that we pity those who suffer unjustly). . . . Desdemona's "willow" song is particularly sad because, in her preparations for Othello's return . . . there are strong forebodings (making her rather like a victim going willingly towards sacrifice). She seems doubly frail, in both her body and her perfect forgiveness—an impression that the audience will retain to the end, so that the drama attains maximum poignancy when Othello, hugely, throttles her . . . [F]rom this point of view . . . the "pity act" might serve to "soften up" the audience so that they would be more thoroughly affected by the butchery still to come. (174, 178)

In this version, *Othello* functions as a purgative ritual in which Desdemona, though she performs an important role, is nonetheless subordinated to the decidedly more compelling energies embodied in the male protagonist's actions.

To a remarkable degree, current critical response continues to operate within a similar affective economy: the violence perpetrated on the female body, in *Othello* and elsewhere on the Renaissance stage, is understood as instrumental, serving personal or cultural needs that are defined in terms of male interests; it either redeems or reinforces the patriarchal order.[2] This continuity may reflect the depth of interpretive tradition. The subordination of female presence is strikingly evident throughout the play's long stage history. The Willow Song—"what most moves us . . . the brief, beautiful pause in

2. For Leonard Tennenhouse, "it is ultimately Shakespeare himself who deprives Desdemona of her capacity to speak" or to "exercise patriarchal authority. These political features are returned to the male by way of Othello's vengeance, which operates, then, much as a theater of punishment," produced by "Shakespeare's collaboration with Iago" (125–26). According to Mitchell Greenberg, "Patriarchal ideology, an ideology that finally the tragedy espouses," serves to drive the action in which Othello sacrifices Desdemona: "Venice, Venetian society, can no more tolerate this extravagant, sexual, uneconomical other than can Brabantio. In order to save itself, Venice (England) must rid itself of what it most fears in itself. But before it can afford to do away with its excessive barbarian, it uses him to destroy that other threat to Patriarchy, the willful independent female, whose act of sexual and political 'freethinking' shook the foundations of society" (31). Susanne Collier focuses on the stabbed or nearly stabbed heroines of *Cymbeline* and *Philaster*, who are said to illustrate the "attempt to eradicate female powers, both physically and politically" (42). For Sara Eaton, the aestheticized bodies of the Lady (*Second Maiden's Tragedy*) and Hermione (*Winter's Tale*) are framed as monuments to deprive them of their capacity to arouse sexual or epistemological anxiety. Celia Daileader also focuses on the Lady and on Webster's Duchess, whose dead bodies, though, she sees as invested with religious feelings of miraculous sacrifice. In the most recent and most richly sustained study of this subject, Karen Bamford ranges through a wide variety of Jacobean plays, identifying three scenarios in which stage rapes performed the "cultural work" of "managing patriarchal anxieties" (24).

the center of action" (Grennan, 277)—is absent in the First Quarto. Perhaps it was added in revision or, more likely, cut when the company lost the boy's voice required to bring it off.[3] The scene as a whole has been consistently eliminated or reduced in performance. Helena Faucit, remarking that she "never saw this scene acted but once, and that was in Dresden," lamented "how sad it is that the exigencies of our stage require the omission of the exquisite scene . . . so important for the development of [Desdemona's] character, and affording such fine opportunities for the highest powers of pathos in the actress!" (73). Faucit was speaking about the "theatrical exigencies" of a later stage—chiefly the extensive script-cutting required to accommodate the elaborate and time-consuming scenic spectacles of nineteenth-century production. Since the scene was not needed for the plot, it must have been a prime candidate for elimination.

But more is involved than the material demands of Victorian *mise-en-scène*. The scene was cut from the eighteenth-century stage as well, going back at least to Addison's time. According to Francis Gentleman writing in the *Dramatic Censor* (1770), "If Desdemona was to chaunt the lamentable ditty, and speak all that Shakespeare has allotted for her in this scene, an audience . . . would not know whether to laugh or cry, and Aemilia's quibbling dissertation on cuckold-making, is contemptible to the last degree" (quoted in Carlisle, 181). Gentleman takes us beyond strictly theatrical exigencies to more broadly cultural determinants. Like Ophelia's songs, which were similarly censured at the time, the Willow Song scene was felt to diminish the dignity of tragedy with domestic female babble, thereby disrupting or contaminating at once the norms of genre and gender. Too much womanly presence interferes with the appropriate effects, generating laughter instead of tears, pathos instead of fear, chronicles of small beer instead of the history-making of politics and war; it demands restriction ("guardage" [1.2.70]), if not elimination.

How do we explain this felt need? Writing about the exclusions from the First Folio to the Shakespeare canon over the centuries based on the changeable criteria of what "sounded right," Stephen Orgel remarks that the early "texts may, of course, be unauthentic, but they may also be evidence that Shakespeare had a greater range of styles than we care for" ("The Authentic Shakespeare," 3).[4] Diana Henderson expands on the point: "During the nineteenth century,

---

3. See Honigmann's discussions (*Dramatist's Manipulation of Audience Response*, 346–48, and *The Texts of "Othello*," 39–40).
4. Elsewhere Orgel marshals evidence to conclude that Renaissance plays are not "generically pure," offering their audiences rather "a very fluid set of possibilities" ("Shakespeare Imagines a Theater," 46; see also "Shakespeare and the Kinds of Drama"). The *locus classicus* of this view remains Johnson's *Preface to Shakespeare*, where it is offered with mixed feelings—at once the transcendence and transgression of generic norms.

the heyday of gendered ideology of separate public and private spheres, the generic tag *domestic tragedy* developed as a way of acknowledging these classically improper or 'impertinent' plays" (174). Renaissance audiences seemed to think of genres less as fixed and rigorously distinct categories than as a set of generative possibilities; and (if we credit Thomas Laqueur et al.) they may have thought of gender and sexual difference in a similarly fluid way. When at the end of *Othello* Lodovico exhorts us, with Iago and the others on stage, to "look on the tragic loading of this bed" [5.2.368], he points to the bodies of Othello, Desdemona, and Emilia. That the women share space with the protagonist, not just as adjuncts but as presences who have earned their own place in the story, presumably did not jar on the sensibilities of the original spectators (hence Jackson's absorption in Desdemona at the end), as it did on the nineteenth-century interpreters, theatrical and critical, who labored diligently to erase them from the final picture (Siemon).

The restoration (and even highlighting) in our time of the Willow Song scene, and of a female presence generally in *Othello,* is an extraordinary accomplishment. Whether or not it constitutes a recovery of Shakespearean intentions, it does seem to have opened up more interesting literary and theatrical possibilities than the ones transmitted to us by the interpretive tradition. About Emilia, whom I shall turn to first, this seems specially true. But tradition is not always obedient to the reformative will. It is shaped often by the kind of irreversible and recalcitrantly material accidents I have mentioned—an adolescent boy actor's voice cracking in the ring, an author's or somebody else's second thoughts, changing theatrical technologies; and by others I will get to: the Victorian star system, for instance. And then there are still others that are unmentionable because, like Althusserian ideology,[5] they cannot be externalized into perception. Some objects poison sight. Even the visible ones are not necessarily changeable as a consequence of critical understanding. The immovable mass of inertia accounts for a lot in history— theatrical, critical, and otherwise—and in *Othello,* where inertia is named Iago, the potentially emancipatory and clarifying efforts of innovation are brutally frustrated. From this perspective, we might be skeptical about the new forms of prominence given to the women in *Othello:* are they truly discontinuous with the old forms of erasure? Perhaps current attentiveness to the women's voices in the play is, even now, just a subtle way of silencing them yet again.

"Alas! she has no speech" [2.1.108], says Desdemona, dismissing Iago's nasty complaints about Emilia's noisiness. Desdemona seems

5. According to the sociologist Louis Althusser, ideology is inside us, forming beliefs, assumptions, and values that we cannot examine with objective critical detachment.

right until the middle of the play. Emilia has no existence apart from her instrumentality to the plot. She passes the handkerchief to Iago, but does not know what she is doing: "what he will / Heaven knows, not I, / I nothing, but to please his fantasy" [3.3.299–301]. We need a verb here. Whatever we supply—"do, know, am"—seems less consequential than the absence itself. Emilia fills a place in the plot, but the play does not encourage any deeper interest on our part.

In the context of these expectations, her sudden eruption into prominence is remarkable. Bradley in 1904 saw this pattern of emerging prominence:

> [T]owards few do our feelings change so much within the course of a play. Till close to the end she frequently sets one's teeth on edge; and at the end one is ready to worship her. . . . From the moment of her appearance after the murder to the moment of her death she is transfigured; . . . who has not felt in the last scene how her glorious carelessness of her own life, and her outbursts against Othello . . . lift the overwhelming weight of calamity that oppresses us, and bring us an extraordinary lightening of the heart? (*Shakespearean Tragedy*, 196–98)

Bradley must have been reading his way out of the theatrical tradition; Victorian productions drastically cut her part (they probably recognized and wished to avoid the risk of an upstaged protagonist). But Bradley, though he could not have known it, was also reading his way into future performances, both theatrical and critical, through to our own time. On the twentieth-century stage, Emilia's enraged refusal to be silent—"like a bellow from the mouth of Melpomene herself," in Herbert Farjeon's description of Edith Evans; "I don't believe Mrs Siddons could touch her"—can "come to dominate the play."[6]

For all her bellowing, though, Emilia's change takes place quietly under the diversely inflected reiterations of "my husband" [143–52]. The play does not specify what is going through her mind, evidently trusting us to endow Emilia with something like our own thoughts, reviewing her actions and their contribution to the catastrophe. Whatever she comes to realize, Emilia commits herself to resistance:

---

6. Quoted in Hankey, 321, who gives three other instances of Emilia's domination in twentieth-century productions; and compare Siemon's "domestic 'virago' double" (45 [see above, p. 298]). Bradley seems to have anticipated subsequent critical as well as theatrical interest in Emilia. His claim that Emilia is "the only person who utters for us the violent common emotions which we feel, together with those more tragic emotions which she does not comprehend" (197) has been frequently reiterated: Emilia is "the mouthpiece of all the feelings in us which are simply angry with Othello, but this judgement of him is not meant to keep its prominence for long" (Empson, 227); Emilia "protects, rather than endangers, the tragic engrossment" (Burke, 185); Emilia's "fearless and ferocious condemnation [is] calculated both to vent and to dispose of our feelings of moral outrage" (McAlindon, 144).

OTH: Peace, you were best!
EMI: Thou has not half the power to do me harm
        As I have to be hurt. O gull, O dolt,
        As ignorant as dirt! Thou hast done a deed

                    [*He threatens her with his sword*].

        —I care not for thy sword, I'll make thee known
        Though I lost twenty lives. [165–70]

This is thrilling, both reckless bravado and heroic self-affirmation in
the Stoic mode, asserting that "she can endure more than he can
inflict (*harm* = hurt)" (Honigmann, *Othello,* 318). But Emilia may
be claiming a power less grand and assertively masculine than self-
sufficiency. For one thing, Shakespeare (and other Renaissance writers) treat Stoic claims with skepticism;[7] for another, "harm" does not
quite equal "hurt." The difference, unelaborated but arresting, points
to an order of sensibility separate from Othello's murderous rage. To
this rage she is totally vulnerable, and it would be self-deluding to
assert otherwise. But if he can indeed harm her, he cannot hurt her,
because the hurt derives from Desdemona's death. The power she
claims then takes the form of the affectionate loyalty she feels for
her mistress, which is hers quite independently of the consequences
(almost inevitably lethal, to be sure) of expressing it.

    This may be more than we, hearing her speech, can know at this
point. It is certainly more than Emilia knows; she still hasn't figured
out the narrative facts, let alone their meaning. Even as she begins
to intuit the truth—"I think upon't, I think I smell't, O villainy!"
[5.2.196]—her indignant exclamations give way to quiet reflection,
as though the quality of her voice has caught up with the inaudible
mental processes that have been propelling her forward: "Good gentlemen, let me have leave to speak. / 'Tis proper I obey him—but
not now. / Perchance, Iago, I will ne'er go home" [200–02]. The
thoughtfulness here is directly opposite to the mindlessness—"I
nothing, but to please his fantasy"—at the beginning. Absorbed then
into the conventional narrative of wifely obedience, she now seeks
to do something Othello himself (and Cassio) could not, find a position of her own outside the space defined by Iago's malignant
norms—in her case, literally outside Iago's home. Even now she
accepts the conventional story as "proper"; she understands her
greater loyalty to Desdemona and to the truth as transcending but
not undermining the law. Her deference, requesting the "gentlemen"

---

7. Brutus is the substantial instance in Shakespeare. Honigmann (*Othello,* 318) cites a very
   close analogue to Emilia's speech from *Henry VIII,* 3.2.387 ff., but the speaker is Wolsey.
   "To suffer, as to do, / Our strength is equal" (*Paradise Lost,* 2.199–200) is another good
   analogue, which, according to Merritt Hughes's note, echoes Mucius Scaevola thrusting
   his hand into the fire; but the speaker is Belial.

to let her speak, echoes Desdemona at the beginning, submitting to the senate's authority. The extraordinarily intimate direct address, "Perchance, Iago, I shall ne'er go home," managed only once earlier in the play [4.2.117], makes clear that she is still inside his home. (The effect is like Othello's heartbreaking "uncle" to Gratiano four lines later and at 252: at last he is part of the family [Honigmann, *Shakespeare: Seven Tragedies*, 94].) Emilia is not sure what she is doing or where she is going; she makes it up as she goes along, feeling her way into a new selfhood, or into selfhood at last. Modern audiences may see her on the path to Nora's exciting exit from Torvold's home at the end of *A Doll's House*; but if we don't know where Nora is going, it is even less clear where Emilia can go, given the limited possibilities for women in the Renaissance. Before we can consider such possibilities, she is abruptly dispatched—as by Frank Finlay, Olivier's Iago, with "a brisk and business-like stab in the back" (Tynan, 19).

Desdemona's is another voyage. Unlike Emilia, Desdemona begins with a powerful voice, trumpeting her love for Othello to the world with a self-declared "downright violence" [1.3.247], too much violence for some tastes; but she seems to dwindle away during the course of the play, and "Nobody. I myself" [5.2.127] in her final speech seems to constitute an act of self-erasure, an accession to nullity. This quality—or absence of qualities—made her of little interest to eighteenth-century interpreters: "a part of 'unvarying gentleness' " with " 'no shining qualifications,' " according to Gentleman, Desdemona "is sufficiently characterized by terms like 'fond' and 'simple' " (Carlisle, 240, 241). Coleridge's sustained reflection on Desdemona's characterlessness said much the same thing, but made a virtue of defect. For him, recessiveness was precisely the source of her power as a profoundly moving object of desire.

> "Most women have no character at all", said Pope, and meant it for satire. Shakespeare, who knew man and woman much better, saw that it, in fact, was the perfection of woman to be characterless. Everyone wishes a Desdemona or Ophelia for a wife—creatures who, though they may not always understand you, do always feel you, and feel with you. (Foakes, 185 [see above, p. 233])

Coleridge's description established the terms for nineteenth-century response. Hazlitt, who brought a different set of critical and political concerns to Shakespeare, nonetheless says of Desdemona that "her whole character consists in having no will of her own, no prompter but her obedience" (205 [see above, p. 229]). Anna Jameson acknowledges a "transient energy, arising from the power of affection," but insists that the "prevailing tone to the character" is "gentleness verging on passiveness—gentleness, which not only cannot resent—but cannot resist" (175). Bradley at the end of this line recognized that Desdemona changes during the course of the action, beginning with "the active assertion of her own soul and will" and "showing a strange freedom and energy, and leading to a most unusual boldness of action" (165–66). But like Coleridge and Hazlitt, Bradley understood the later absence of will as Desdemona's essential quality ("Desdemona is helplessly passive. She can do nothing whatever. She cannot retaliate even in speech; no, not even in silent feeling" [145]), and this condition inspired his own deeply affectionate response: "the 'eternal womanly' in its most lovely and adorable form, simple and innocent as a child" (164) and full of "heavenly sweetness and self-surrender" (165). [See above, pp. 236 and 242–43.]

Such dissent as there was in the nineteenth century came mostly from the theater. The Booth edition (1881) records Ellen Terry's remark that although "my appearance was right" for Desdemona (that is, "a poor wraith of a thing"), "it took strength to act this weakness and passiveness of Desdemona's. I soon found that like Cordelia, she has plenty of character" (quoted in Siemon, 44 [see above, p. 297]). Later on, Terry complained that "no character in Shakespeare . . . has suffered from so much misconception," as "a ninny, a pathetic figure"; in fact, Desdemona "is strong, not weak" (128–29). Helena Faucit in 1885 reflected similarly on Desdemona's appeal for her as a young woman growing up early in the century: "I did not know in those days that Desdemona is usually considered a merely amiable, simple, yielding creature, and that she is generally so represented on the stage. This is the last idea that would have entered my mind" (246). Both Faucit and Terry could build on a performance tradition dating back to the late eighteenth century (Hankey, 52–53), when "the awesome, majestic" Sarah Siddons "surprised" and "amazed" audiences "at the transition from her erstwhile tragic majesty to sweet tenderness. The part even seemed to change her physically, 'absolutely [lowering] the figure of the lovely being which had been so towering in Euphrasia, or terrific in Lady Macbeth' " (Rosenberg, 51). But Siddons's performance did not establish either a norm or an ideal for the part on the nineteenth-century stage. For Elizabeth Inchbald, writing at the beginning of the century, " 'her face can never express artless innocence, such as the true representative of the part requires: her features are too bold, her person too important for the gentle Desdemona.' " As Carlisle wryly comments, "too much tragic majesty remained" (241). At the beginning of the next century (1911), William Winter made much the same complaint, describing Siddons's performance as "greatly overweighting a part the predominant and essential characteristic of which is gentleness" (250). Unlike Inchbald, who could well have seen Siddons's performance, Winter was working only with hearsay; but his very willingness to trust report testifies to the established stability of the nineteenth-century consensus.

One way to measure the power of this consensus is to focus on Desdemona's resistance in the murder scene. Othello's "Down, strumpet!" and "Nay, if you strive—" [5.2.80, 82] are textually embedded stage directions that call unambiguously for Desdemona's physical struggle. George Swan understood as much in his advice to Garrick: "he was convinced [that] Desdemona should so effectually resist Othello's efforts to smother her that he would be forced to use the dagger after all. Swan interpreted the text to imply that Desdemona twice struggles from Othello's grasp." But Swan's advice was hypothetical, probably not deriving from theatrical practice and almost certainly not leading to it.[8] In a similar way, a strongly resistant Desdemona on the nineteenth-century stage remained only an un- or under-represented possibility. Though his acting edition called for fierce struggle, "Fechter's performances apparently did not enact" them fully if at all (Siemon, 43 [see above, p. 295]), for reasons already suggested by Martin's evocation of Nancy and Bill Sikes.

Or consider the case of Fanny Kemble. Playing the role for the first time in 1848, she determined to " 'make a desperate fight of it . . . for I feel horribly at the idea of being murdered in my bed. The Desdemonas that I have seen, on the English stage, have always appeared to me to acquiesce with wonderful equanimity in their assassination. On the Italian stage they run for their lives.' " But she was thwarted on the one hand by an apparently edited script (" 'Shakespeare's text,' " she worried, " 'gives no hint of any such attempt' ") and on the other by the material realities of costume and taste: "against that possibility was the 'bedgown' she was wearing" (Sprague, 213; Carlisle, 259). When Kemble revisits the question in 1884, however, she

> berates Salvini for failure to follow the stage tradition and the manifest "intention of Shakespeare" . . . for a passive Desdemona . . . : "The terrified woman cowers down upon her pillow like a poor frightened child. Indeed, the whole scene loses its most pitiful elements by allowing Desdemona to confront

8. Swan played Othello at the Theatre Royal, Dublin, in 1742, but it "is not clear whether his notes reflect the business that he himself had used or whether they were the result of his ruminations after his retirement from the stage." In either event, "The typical stage Desdemona in the eighteenth century probably did not put up the vigorous struggle Swan imagined for her. Nor did she in the nineteenth century." George Skillan's advice much later, in the French's Acting Edition, that anyone of Desdemona's " 'quality and strong spirit' naturally reacts with abhorrence to the sudden threat of violent death and fights for self-preservation," was also probably relegated to the realm of unrealized potential. For this material, see Carlisle, 258–61.

Othello standing, instead of uttering the piteous pleadings for
mercy in the helpless prostration of her half recumbent position." (quoted in Siemon, 43 [see above, p. 296])

Kemble's change of mind probably had something to do with the
weight of contemporary opinion against making a fight of it. Siemon
quotes an "outraged response" in mid-century "to Brooke's Desdemona [Sarah Anderton] having 'struggled in almost an erect position'
as 'out of character' " (43 [see above, p. 296]). It probably had something to do as well with the sheer power of the normative tradition—
the "unalloyed delight," as Charlotte Vandenhoff's 1851 performance was described, "to see her sad, fearful, yet gentle as a bruised
dove bend meekly to the implacable jealousy of the swart Othello,
and receive her death, while kissing the hand which gives it" (quoted
in Carlisle, 244). Sustained exposure to this sort of thing—reiterated
assertions that "tradition was right" (to recall Martin's words at the
top of this essay—must have been very difficult to resist.

This is not to say that resistant Desdemonas did not appear: Gus-
tavus Brooke's and Salvini's (as well as the other Italians'), as we
have seen; Madge Kendal opposite Ira Aldridge; Faucit and Terry as
well. But these possibilities too were under-represented. Faucit "fell
as a victim to the star system," which required that a leading actor,
"whether woman or man, had to shine as the dominant light in a
play, not merely contribute to the effect of chiaroscuro." As a consequence, "she rarely acted the role during her touring days, the
longer and much the finer part of her career." As for Terry, though
"she gave a memorable interpretation, spirited as well as pathetic,"
her "theatrical fortunes were bound up with" Irving, and when he
abandoned Othello after 1881, Terry's "Desdemona was lost to the
stage from that time. [Hence] the two actresses who should have
been most identified with the role actually performed it for relatively
brief periods" (Carlisle, 249–50). Like the dramatic character, the
role on the pre-twentieth-century stage is saturated with the pathos
of defeated potentiality.

Maggie Smith, who performed opposite Laurence Olivier in the
premier production of our time, suggests how far we have come from
the nineteenth-century theatrical tradition. Smith, of course, is not
"a poor wraith of a thing," like Ellen Terry; her body type did not
predispose her to representing a bruised dove, and she played Desdemona out of her own strength.

The milksop Desdemona has been banished from this stage and
a girl of real personality and substance comes into her own.
Fighting back, not soppily "hurt", but damned angry, she makes
the conjugal battle less one-sided and so more interesting and
certainly more exciting. When these two throw the book at each

other bodies come hurtling after it; and what a relief it is not to see two high-bred ninnies bleating reproachfully at each other from opposite sides of the stage but actually striking each other to the floor in the grandeur of their agony. (Tynan, 16)

But in modern criticism, as distinct from theatrical interpretation, the image of Desdemona's self-surrendering sweetness has managed to sustain itself. Burke's willing victim, "doubly frail, in both her body and her perfect forgiveness," can sound surprisingly soppy, like residual angel-in-the-house sentiment. Burke's locus, to be sure, is ritual enactments rather than gender norms or marital relations. Whether or not every man wants a woman like Desdemona, as Coleridge claimed, every sacrificial plot does, and "the willow song casts her perfectly in the role of one preparing meekly for sacrifice" (Burke, 184).

This relocation of affect portends a more radical change in recent criticism: a withdrawal or even reversal of the veneration in earlier response. Jane Adamson is struck by "Desdemona's strange passivity in the face of the violence that assails her" (236). Where nineteenth-century audiences delighted in Desdemona's prostrate speechlessness, for Adamson "her peculiar passivity" is "most disturbing" (220): "what we find hardest to bear" in the murder scene is Desdemona's "terrible silence. . . . She has no strength or will to resist it or even to cry out for help" (257). More recent criticism, motivated by an augmented methodological and ideological self-consciousness, has nonetheless experienced a similar discomfort.[9] Ania Loomba recalls that "as undergraduates at Miranda House, Delhi[,] . . . who were 'dissatisfied' with Desdemona's silence in the face of her husband's brutality, we were told that we did not 'understand' her because we had never been 'in love.' " Loomba acknowledges Desdemona's self-assertiveness early in the play, but laments that "she then betrays it by her submissiveness. Discussions with my own students located such a betrayal as the source of our own uneasiness" (39).

Whether celebrating or deploring it, critical traditions have been remarkably consistent for two centuries in describing Desdemona as silent, submissive, and in a sense even complicit in her own murder. It is therefore worth noticing on what an unsubstantial foundation this massive interpretive edifice has been constructed. Despite Adamson's "terrible silence" and Loomba's "silence in the face of her husband's brutality," Desdemona vigorously protests her innocence in the murder scene [5.2.59–62, 67–69] and, finally desperate, looks

---

9. Adamson, working in an attenuated Leavis tradition, claimed no systematic grounding for her response, though such claims were being made, particularly in America, where, according to one relatively unsympathetic description that appeared in the same year as *"Othello" as Tragedy*, "many of today's younger critics find it hard to write 'innocence' without writing 'life-denying' in front of it. [They] often see [Desdemona's] innocence as a neurotic defense mechanism, or even at one extreme a 'life-destroying' characteristic, the epitome of 'the sexual unreality the race longs for' " (W. D. Adamson, 179).

for any expedient to protect herself against Othello's murderous assault: "O, banish me, my lord, but kill me not!. . . . Kill me tomorrow, let me live tonight! . . . But half an hour! . . . But while I say one prayer! . . . O Lord! Lord! Lord!" [79–85]. This is not merely speech; it seems to be the powerfully sustained eloquence Henry Jackson heard in 1610 ("she pleaded her case very effectively throughout"). As Anthony Dawson argues, "Jackson's account . . . puts into question the reading of the victimized, subjected Desdemona that some recent critics have seen as central to the cultural work the play is said to have performed" (35). Along with the embedded stage directions, "Down strumpet!" and "Nay, if you strive," Desdemona's words, cut away by nineteenth-century script doctors, have been by strong twentieth-century interpreters simply erased.

Such extraordinary reconstructions of the murder scene cannot have been created out of nothing; but if we look backward over the action of the play it is hard to find the evidence of acquiescent self-surrender on which they would be based. Perhaps the earliest relevant episode shows Desdemona, just before the Temptation Scene, acceding to Othello's request to cease soliciting for Cassio and "to leave me but a little to myself": "Shall I deny you? No, farewell, my lord" [3.3.86]. But this is hardly a defeated submission. Othello has apparently already informed Desdemona that he intends to reinstate Cassio [3.3.44 ff], and he promises as much here again: "I will deny thee nothing" [83]. Moreover, Desdemona's exit speech, "Be as your fancies teach you? / Whate'er you be, I am obedient" [88–89], makes obedience sound like self-affirmation, almost bravado. If we hear an echo of Emilia's "I nothing, but to please his fantasy," this probably registers as contrast. Unlike Emilia, Desdemona manifests a distinct and even freely critical identity, implying perhaps that Othello is caught up in silly obligations of military protocol ("your fancies"), while she at least is holding up her end of the bargain. Indeed, commentators are sometimes irritated by her needling here, although Othello's "Excellent wretch!" just after confirms the context of affectionate delight within which he has understood the exchange.

With the first signs of Othello's madness, Desdemona maintains this tone, meeting his insistence head on with her own ("The handkerchief!" "I pray, talk me of Cassio" [3.4.91] and resistance ("I'faith, you are to blame" [94]. Her first instinctive reaction to the slap is a protest, "I have not deserved this" [4.1.235]. After the appalling "rose-lipped cherubin" speech, when Othello accuses her of being a "strumpet," she is again angrily assertive in denying the charge: "By heaven, you do me wrong" [4.2.82]. This is not "peculiar" or "strange passivity in the face of violence"—it is not passivity at all; and in the context of the Renaissance theatrical practice, audiences of *Othello* would have much more likely been impressed by Desdemona's self-assertion than by her passivity.[1] Even at the end of the bordello scene, although by now almost fully traumatized ("Do not talk to me, Emilia; / I cannot speak, nor answers have I none / But what should go by water" [104–06]), Desdemona generates an impressively sarcastic anger: " 'Tis meet I should be used so, very meet. / How have I behaved that he might stick / The small'st opinion on my greatest misuse?" [109–111]. These lines are delivered on an empty stage, Desdemona's only soliloquy; the play seems to be going out of its way to emphasize resistance in the face of inexplicable hostility—which is just what Henry Jackson heard.

That this resistance seems to diminish in the course of the dramatic action is certainly true, but the question is what we make of its diminution. About her request to Emilia, "Lay on my bed my wedding sheets . . . And call my husband hither" [4.2.10 7–08], Neill says that "Desdemona shrouds herself here in a narrative of eroticized self-immolation as self-consciously as Othello in his final speech will dress himself in the narrative of heroic self conquest," pointing to "the fashion, increasingly popular amongst aristocratic women in the early seventeenth century, for having one's corpse wound in the sheets from the marriage night" (*Issues of Death*, 165). But Desdemona is not acting with coherently self-conscious purposivity, and in its immediate context her request may seem to be a hopeful gesture, designed to "win my lord again" [4.2.151], presumably by reminding him of what she remembers about the shared delight in their original union.

By the Willow Song scene, she has abandoned protest (at least temporarily) for acquiescence. "We must not now displease him," she tells Emilia [4.3.17], acceding to Othello's request for Emilia's dismissal. The accession may have the effect of facilitating the murder, but what is her intention? One place to look for an answer is in the long and tortuous speech, addressed to Emilia or herself or both, with which Desdemona first reflects on the meaning of Othello's transformation:

> Something sure of state
> Either from Venice, or some unhatched practice
> Made demonstrable here in Cyprus to him,
> Hath puddled his clear spirit, and in such cases
> Men's natures wrangle with inferior things

---

1. The Renaissance stage at this time was rich in examples of the performance of passivity, faithful wives who were astoundingly acquiescent to bizarre husbandly assaults on the model of the protagonist of *Patient Grissil*, a joint venture by Dekker, Haughton, and Chettle produced in 1600, which was evidently quite popular and generated a series of spinoffs and imitations. The passivity of Annabel in *The Fair Mad of Bristow* and of Luce in *The London Prodigal*, both in the King's Men's repertoire at the same time as *Othello*, is especially worth noting (see Pechter; Knutson, 115–18; and Woodbridge's discussions of the "Patient Grissill figure," 125–26, 198–99, 211–17, and 358).

> Though great ones are their object. 'Tis even so,
> For let our finger ache and it indues
> Our other healthful members even to that sense
> Of pain. Nay, we must think men are not gods
> Nor of them look for such observancy
> As fits the bridal.
>
>   [3.4.137–47]

Desdemona begins with an attempt to account for Othello's inexplicable harshness as a displacement of political irritation ("something sure of state"). In effect, she buys into a distinction between the male public sphere and the female domestic sphere ("inferior things"), thereby abandoning her earlier desire to share the totality of Othello's life. This distinction between male and female nature is almost immediately negotiated with a sense of shared bodily existence: "our finger" is not a peculiarly female possession. But then bodily existence seems to have become gendered female, as in the next lines "we" is clearly limited to women in contrast to the men as "them." In acknowledging the inevitable abatement of love from "the bridal," Desdemona picks up on Emilia's speech just a minute or two earlier, " 'Tis not a year or two . . . / They belch us" [3.4.100–03.] She lacks Emilia's disgusted abhorrence, but moves toward the origin of such beliefs in Iago's voice. As Othello himself had succumbed to a generalizing misogyny, "that we can call such delicate creatures ours," so Desdemona begins apparently to settle into a generalizing misandry—us and them. She echoes his acquiescence in necessity (" 'Tis destiny unshunnable," "Nay, we must think"), both of them echoing Iago at the very beginning ("Why there's no remedy. 'Tis the curse of service"). Who can blame her? She has more of a cause, and after all, the wine she drinks *is* made of grapes. Maybe Auden was right to think Iago was right: "given a few more years . . . and she might well, one feels, have taken a lover" (269).

    This entire process is abruptly reversed, however, in the extremely awkward and complicated set of reconsiderations at the end of Desdemona's speech:

>   Beshrew me much, Emilia,
> I was, unhandsome warrior as I am,
> Arraigning his unkindness with my soul,
> But now I find I had suborned the witness
> And he's indicted falsely.
>
>   [147–51]

Turning on the earlier self who was arraigning Othello's unkindness, she tries to recapture the feelings of their reunion on Cyprus, when Othello had addressed her as "my fair warrior." Her status as an "unhandsome warrior," though, seems still to occupy the present ("as I am"), and it is difficult to sort out the putatively real Desdemona at the end of the speech from a variety of superseded voices earlier on. Can "my soul" be totally re-created into a new "I" that now suborns its own earlier position? The attempt at a willful self-reconstruction may be qualified by a passive resonance in "find"; from this position, the different beliefs at the end of the passage are not so much affirmed as observed in a way that renders them problematically abstract, maybe even dissociated.

It is possible to understand this speech as "a nervous *refusal* to acknowledge—even to herself—that Othello could possibly be jealous or suspicious" (Adamson, 225; Adamson's emphasis). Desdemona is then pathologically self-deluding, deliberately disconnecting herself from the truth of her situation in a way that abandons self-protection. If "Nobody. I myself" constitutes self-cancellation, then this speech seems to be the place from which she embarks on the course that reaches that termination. But is Desdemona refusing the truth of what Othello has become or affirming the reality of what he was when she saw his visage in his mind, and further affirming the value of her continuing response? "Unkindness may do much, / And his unkindness may defeat my life / But never taint my love" [4.2.161–63]. Like Emilia at the end, Desdemona asserts her own power here. Othello's unkindness may defeat her life, but it is her choice to love him. Julia Genster is one of several recent commentators who hear in Desdemona's "last words," asking to be commended to her kind lord, "not an act of submission but a challenge" (804–05).[2] From this perspective Othello was right (though he had the wrong word for it) to say "That we can call these delicate creatures ours / And not their appetites"—sensing in Desdemona a powerful energy that he would never fully own, that was Desdemona's own self.

In the beginning of the Willow Song scene, responding to Emilia's "Would you had never seen him!" Desdemona once again reaffirms her choice: "So would not I; my love doth so approve him / That even his stubbornness, his checks, his frowns /—Prithee unpin me—have grace and favour" [17–21]. In the way "my love" is represented as acting independently of and in contradiction to the self-preserving "I," Desdemona strikes a note of passivity and self-

---

2. According to Wine, " 'My kind lord' is the Othello whose 'visage' she saw 'in his mind'; her 'Nobody' could be only the 'false', stereotypical Moor as Othello is now. The effect of these words is to remind Othello of what he knew when he addressed the Senate" (34). Calderwood pursues a similar line: "She announces in effect that her acceptance of his authority has derived not from his institutional status as her husband, not from his masculine capacity to do her harm, but from consent freely given, from nothing more forceful than the 'downright violence' of her own love as she declared it before the Senate" (36).

exposure that may seem to verge on masochism. But the song that
follows, for all its plaintive pathos, moves into a stronger and more
assertive tonality. According to Joel Fineman,

> The central, we can say the most Shakespearean, fact about this
> 'Willow song' is that it is *not* by Shakespeare, and would have
> been recognized as such, i.e., as non-Shakespearean, by the
> original audience of the play. What is called Desdemona's 'Wil-
> low song' is, in fact, a traditional ballad, reproduced in miscel-
> lanies, that appears to have captured Shakespeare's aural
> imagination. (94; Fineman's emphasis)

But the even more important fact is that ballads in the play are part
of the anonymous tradition by which Iago acquires power over people's souls, as in his transformation of Cassio at the end of act 2. If
he performs his cultural work "close to the unstable ground of consciousness itself" (Neill, "Unproper Beds," 395 [see above, p. 315]),
this is precisely the place from which Desdemona's discourse is generated in the scene. Like Brabantio at the beginning ("Have you not
read . . . / Of some such thing?"), she is traumatized to the point
where anything comes out of her mouth that has found a place in
her mind ("Mine eyes do itch, / Doth that bode weeping? . . . I have
heard it said so" [58–60]), including especially the song: "That song
tonight / Will not go from my mind" [30–31].

In this context, the remarkable thing is that the song does not take
possession of Desdemona's soul; she takes possession of the song.
She substitutes a female singer, and her affection for "Barbary" is
clearly a displacement of her affection for Othello. The play goes out
of its way to emphasize her transformative power by calling attention
to her mistake: "Let nobody blame him, his scorn I approve—/
[*Speaks.*] Nay, that's not next" [52–53]. The words pick up on her
own claim at the beginning of the scene, "My love doth so approve
him," now establishing "I" and "my love," problematically disconnected earlier, as an absolute identity. Revising herself, she also
revises tradition. The "right" line in the versions that survive is "her
scorns I do prove."[3] The original audiences would not have focused
on the details, but might well have sensed the fundamental difference between the tradition, which emphasized the passive suffering
of unrequited love, and Desdemona's version, which proclaims even
in the midst of such grief a continuing affirmation of her own power
to love. "O, you are well tuned now: but I'll set down / The pegs that
make this music, as honest / As I am" [2.1.97–99]. Honest Iago keeps

---

3. Honigmann reproduces from Furness (277) the version derived from Percy's *Reliques*
(1765), cautioning that we "should not assume, however, that Percy's version gives the
ballad verbatim as Shakespeare found it" (*Othello*, 339–40).

his promise for everyone in the play, with the partial exception of Emilia. But Desdemona sings her own song.

When Alan Sinfield declares that "Desdemona has no character of her own" (54), his uncanny echo of Coleridge's claim that "Desdemona has no character at all" is striking evidence for the continuity over the centuries with which we have been replacing Desdemona's voice with silence and transforming her presence into absence. The nineteenth century doted on its own created emptiness, and now we deplore it; but the tenacity with which the basic structure has sustained itself is remarkable—and perplexing. The adorably prostrate Desdemona served the nineteenth century in ways that look either silly to us now (Lillian Gish tied to the railroad tracks) or pornographic. The objectionably prostrate Desdemona of contemporary opinion must also be serving important cultural needs, but it is difficult to be sure what they are. Robert Brustein once said that "the passive, virtuous, all-suffering Desdemona is a part . . . difficult to cast in an age of women's liberation" (quoted in Wine, 67); but current criticism has generally cooperated in maintaining the construction of Desdemona as instrumental and subordinate to male designs larger than any that might be claimed for her own. Some substantial basis exists for this construction. It seems accurate to say that "Desdemona only invokes the right to owe duty to her husband and not her own autonomy"; even the strongest theatrical Desdemonas have represented the character as fundamentally unwilling and almost unable to imagine selfhood in terms of an exclusively self-enclosed or self-contained space.[4] But to conclude from this that Desdemona

---

4. Compare Maggie Smith's reaction to the slap: it "is not the usual collapse into sobs; it is one of deep shame and embarrassment, for Othello's sake as well as her own. She is outraged, but tries out of loyalty not to show it. . . . 'I have not deserved this' is not an appeal for sympathy, but a protest quietly and firmly lodged by an extremely spunky girl" (Tynan, 10). The sentiment described here is similar to Faucit's, explaining why Desdemona struggles against the murderous Othello: " 'I felt for *him* as well as myself, and therefore I threw into my remonstrances all the power of passionate appeal I could command. . . . I thought of all his after-suffering, when he should come to know how he had mistaken me! The agony for him which filled my heart, as well as the mortal agony of death which I felt in imagination, made my cries and struggles no doubt very vehement and very real' " (quoted in Carlisle, 260).

In both these passages, Desdemona's feeling for herself is represented as inextricably bound up with her feeling for Othello. It may be, though, that the performance is being thought through in terms of theatrical dynamics as much as of character. Faucit's Brabantio said that her strength "restored the balance of the play by giving [Desdemona's] character its due weight in the action," and Faucit reports that Macready liked her strength: "I added intensity to the last act by 'being so difficult to kill' " (quoted in Carlisle, 249). This sounds like Tynan's point about Maggie Smith and the greater theatrical interest and excitement in a "less one-sided" struggle.

By contrast, Fanny Kemble's emphasis on Othello's "inefficient clumsiness . . . his half smothering, his half stabbing her," as proving "how tortured he must have been" (quoted in Carlisle, 259), tries to draw attention away from Desdemona and over to the protagonist's internal struggle—the consistent endeavor of the nineteenth-century stage, and closer to the self-erasing false consciousness that contemporary criticism tends to find in the play.

therefore does not serve the interests of "our critique of the silencing of women in literature and in the classroom" (Loomba, 40) moves into much more speculative territory. It assumes—unnecessarily if not wrongly—that Desdemona's affectionate generosity necessarily constitutes an acquiescence in her own victimization, and perhaps even contributes to the continuing disempowerment of at least some members of the audience.

Henry Jackson's response—not only moved to tears by the pathos of Desdemona's situation, but impressed with the power of her performed selfhood—is an intriguing exception to subsequent interpretation. There is no reason to believe that Jackson was a protofeminist, but as Paul Yachnin points out (26–31), his rhetorical training seems to have predisposed him to an appreciative response to theatrical performance independent of his own particular opinions. Yachnin argues that Renaissance theater negotiated a "powerless" position for itself—meeting the audience in a space outside the normalizing structures of real belief and action (1–24). This is not the space within which most current interpretation wishes to engage with Renaissance drama. We're interested in role models; maybe we have to be.[5] However we explain it, the fact of Desdemona, subdued to the very quality of Othello rather than committed to her own autonomy, is simply an intolerable prospect, not to be endured. It so violates fundamental convictions about the world that it has been rendered invisible. We see instead the passivity and prostration inflicted on us by a perverse interpretive tradition, thereby reinforcing this tradition in a way that, like Desdemona herself as we fabricate her, seems to cooperate with the forces that defeat desire. O, the pity of it.

Works Cited

Adamson, W. D. "Unpinned or Undone? Desdemona's Critics and the Problem of Sexual Innocence." *Shakespeare Studies* 13 (1980): 169–86.

Adamson, Jane. *"Othello" as Tragedy: Some Problems of Judgment and Feeling.* Cambridge: Cambridge University Press, 1980.

5. Role models do not work well with tragedy, where no prudent course of action is available and where every path leads to catastrophe; but current critics are just doing what Coleridge was doing, and Rymer, and (more generally) Sidney and Heywood and other apologists for poetry around the time *Othello* was written: claiming some influential connection between the actions performed on the stage and the beliefs of the spectators. Connections always exist between fictional plots and ideological agendas, though we tend to sound foolish when we make them. Empson says that "you ought to be able to appreciate in literature beliefs you don't agree with," but immediately adds that "when these rather subtle points are broadened into a confident dogma they lead I think to bad criticism" (242).

Auden, W. H. "The Joker in the Pack." In *The Dyer's Hand and Other Essays*. New York: Random House, 1948, 246–72.

Bamford, Karen. *Sexual Violence on the Jacobean Stage*. London: Macmillan, 2000.

Bradley, A. C. *Shakespearean Tragedy: Lectures on "Hamlet," "Othello," "King Lear," "Macbeth."* London: Macmillan, 1904. Rpt. 1964.

Burke, Kenneth. "*Othello*: An Essay to Illustrate a Method." *Hudson Review* 4 (1951): 165–203.

Calderwood, James. *The Properties of "Othello."* Amherst: University of Massachusetts Press, 1989.

Carlisle, Carol Jones. *Shakespeare from the Greenroom: Actors' Criticisms of Four Major Tragedies*. Chapel Hill: University of North Carolina Press, 1969.

Collier, Susanne. "Cutting to the Heart of the Matter: Stabbing the Woman in *Philaster* and *Cymbeline*." In Kendall, *Shakespearean Power and Punishment*, 39–58.

Daileader, Celia R. "(Off) Staging the Sacred." In *Eroticism on the Renaissance Stage: Transcendence, Desire, and the Limits of the Visible*. Cambridge Studies in Renaissance Literature and Culture 30. Cambridge: Cambridge University Press, 1998, 79–106.

Dawson, Anthony B. "Performance and Participation: Desdemona, Foucault, and the Actor's Body." In James C. Bulman, ed. *Shakespeare, Theory, and Performance*. London and New York: Routledge, 1996, 29–45.

Eaton, Sara. " 'Content with art'?: Seeing the Emblematic Woman in *The Second Maiden's Tragedy* and *The Winter's Tale*." In Kendall, *Shakespearean Power and Punishment*, 59–86.

Empson, William. "Honest in *Othello*." In *The Structure of Complex Words*. London: Chatto and Windus, 1951, 218–49.

Evans, G. B., et al., ed. *The Riverside Shakespeare*. Boston: Houghton Mifflin, 1997.

Faucit, Helena. *On Some of Shakespeare's Female Characters*. Edinburgh: Blackwoods, 1885. Rpt. New York: AMS Press, 1970.

Fineman, Joel. "The Sound of *O* in *Othello*: The Real of the Tragedy of Desire." *October* 45 (1988): 77–96.

Foakes, R. A., ed. *Coleridge's Criticism of Shakespeare: A Selection*. London: Athlone Press, 1989.

Furness, Horace Howard, ed. *A New Variorum Edition of Othello*. 7th ed. Philadelphia: Lippincott, 1886.

Genster, Julia. "Lieutenancy, Standing In, and *Othello*." *English Literary History* 57 (1990): 785–809.

Greenberg, Mitchell. "Shakespeare's *Othello* and the 'Problem' of Anxiety." In *Canonical States, Canonical Stages: Oedipus, Other-*

ing, and Seventeenth-Century Drama. Minneapolis and London: University of Minnesota Press, 1994, 1–32.

Grennan, Eamon. "The Women's Voices in *Othello*: Speech, Song, Silence." *Shakespeare Quarterly* 38 (1987): 275–92.

Hankey, Julie. *Othello*. Plays in Performance Series. Bristol: Bristol Classical Press, 1987.

Hazlitt, William. *Characters of Shakespear's Plays*. In P. P. Howe, ed. *The Complete Works of William Hazlitt*. London and Toronto: J. M. Dent, 1930, 165–361.

Henderson, Diana E. "The Theater and Domestic Culture." In John D. Cox and David Scott Kastan, ed. *A New History of Early English Drama*. New York: Columbia University Press, 1997, 173–94.

Honigmann, E. A. J. *Shakespeare: Seven Tragedies: The Dramatist's Manipulation of Audience Response*. London: Macmillan, 1976.

———. *The Texts of "Othello" and Shakespearian Revision*. London and New York: Routledge, 1996.

———, ed. *Othello*. Walton-on-Thames: Thomas Nelson, 1997.

Hughes, Merritt Y., ed. *John Milton: Complete Poems and Major Prose*. New York: Odyssey, 1957.

Jameson, Anna B. *Characteristics of Women—Moral, Poetical, and Historical*. 1832. Rpt. *Shakespeare's Heroines*. London: George Bell & Sons, 1905.

Kendall, Gillian Murray, ed. *Shakespearean Power and Punishment: A Volume of Essays*. Newark, Del.: University of Delaware Press; London: Associated University Presses, 1998.

Knutson, Roslyn Lander. *The Repertory of Shakespeare's Company, 1594–1613*. Fayetteville: University of Arkansas Press, 1991.

Laqueur, Thomas. *Making Sex: Body and Gender from the Greeks to Freud*. Cambridge, Mass.: Harvard University Press, 1990.

Loomba, Ania. *Gender, Race, Renaissance Drama*. Manchester: Manchester University Press, 1989.

Luckyj, Christina, ed. *The White Devil*. London: A. & C. Black, Ltd., 1996.

McAlindon, T. *Shakespeare's Tragic Cosmos*. Cambridge: Cambridge University Press, 1991.

Neill, Michael. "Changing Places in *Othello*." In *Shakespeare Survey* 37. Cambridge: Cambridge University Press, 1984, 115–31.

———. *Issues of Death: Mortality and Identity in English Renaissance Tragedy*. Oxford: Clarendon Press, 1997.

———. "Unproper Beds: Race, Adultery, and the Hideous in *Othello*." *Shakespeare Quarterly* 40 (1989): 383–412.

Orgel, Stephen. "The Authentic Shakespeare." *Representations* 21 (1988): 1–25.

———. "Shakespeare and the Kinds of Drama." *Critical Inquiry* 6 (1979): 107–23.

————. "Shakespeare Imagines a Theater." In Kenneth Muir, Jay L. Halio, and D. J. Palmer, ed. *Shakespeare, Man of the Theater: Proceedings of the Second Congress of the International Shakespeare Association, 1981.* East Brunswick, N.J., London, and Mississauga: Associated University Presses, 1983, 34–46.

Pechter, Edward. "*Patient Grissil* and the Trials of Marriage." *Elizabethan Theatre 14* (1996): 83–108.

Rosenberg, Marvin. *The Masks of Othello: The Search for the Identity of Othello, Iago, and Desdemona by Three Centuries of Actors and Critics.* Berkeley: University of California Press, 1961.

Siemon, James R. " 'Nay, that's not next': *Othello*, V.ii in Performance, 1760–1900." *Shakespeare Quarterly* 37 (1986): 38–51.

Sinfield, Alan. *Faultlines: Cultural Materialism and the Politics of Dissident Reading.* Berkeley: University of California Press, 1992.

Sprague, Arthur Colby. *Shakespeare and the Actors: The Stage Business in His Plays (1660–1905).* Cambridge, Mass.: Harvard University Press, 1948.

Tennenhouse, Leonard. *Power on Display: The Politics of Shakespeare's Genres.* New York and London: Methuen, 1986.

Terry, Ellen. *Four Lectures on Shakespeare.* Ed. with an intro. Christopher St. John. London: Martin Hopkinson Ltd., 1932.

Tynan, Kenneth, ed. *"Othello": The National Theatre Production.* New York: Stein and Day, 1967.

Wine, Martin L. *Othello.* Text and Performance. London: Macmillan, 1984.

Winter, William. *Shakespeare on the Stage.* New York: Moffat, Yard and Co., 1911. Rpt. New York: Benjamin Blom, 1969.

Woodbridge, Linda. *Women and the English Renaissance: Literature and the Nature of Womankind, 1540–1620.* Urbana and Chicago: University of Illinois Press, 1984.

Yachnin, Paul. *Stage-Wrights: Shakespeare, Jonson, Middleton, and the Making of Theatrical Value.* Philadelphia: University of Pennsylvania Press, 1997.

Selected Bibliography

Given the magnitude and diversity of commentary on *Othello,* a single list of publications would be daunting and unwieldy, so I have divided the information below into fourteen compact lists and / or brief discussions, generally following the sequence of material printed earlier in this book. The first three sections supplement the discussion and bibliography introducing "Sources and Contexts": Textual Sources; Contextual Sources—Race; and Contextual Sources—Women, Marriage, Domesticity. The next seven, keyed to "Criticism," provide information about the earlier authors up to and including Bradley, the texts from which their discussions are excerpted, and the critical contexts within which they produced their claims about *Othello.* The next three offer tips to readers who want to increase their understanding of *Othello's* interpretive afterlife; subjects here include theater history, movies and videos / DVDs, and recent spinoffs and offshoots. A final section refers readers to other books currently available whose purposes overlap in one respect or another with this Norton Critical Edition.

1. TEXTUAL SOURCES

The Cinthio tale reprinted in this edition is taken from John Edward Taylor's 1855 translation, as reprinted on the same pages with the Italian by Furness (376–89) and, more recently, reprinted in facsimile. Ross (263–75) and Dean (255–64) include excerpts from Cinthio in their own translation. Geoffrey Bullough publishes his translation of the whole tale, along with excerpts from Cinthio's introduction (239–52). Bullough's translation is reprinted in Honigmann (369–87), where it is accompanied by a long list of verbal parallels. Bullough also includes excerpts from a "possible source" in a story of jealousy and uxoricide in Geoffrey Fenton's 1567 translation of Bandello's *Tragicall Discourses* (253–62) and a "probable source" for details of the dispute between the Turks and the Venetians for control of Cyprus in Richard Knolles's 1603 *Generall Historie of the Turkes* (262–65). In addition, Bullough analyzes the Shakespeare's various alterations to Cinthio and discusses (apart from Fenton and Knolles) a variety of other texts, from which he provides no excerpts, but which probably contributed to the process leading to the composition of the play: John Leo Africanus's *Geographical History of Africa* (translated by John Pory in 1600), as a source of much information and opinion, including distinctions between North Saharan and sub-Saharan places and persons; Gaspar Contareno's *Commonwealth and Government of Venice* (translated by Lewis Lewkenor in 1599), for an admiring account of the Venetian social and political order; and Pliny's *Natural History* (translated by Philomen Holland in 1601), for many of the exotic details associated with Othello's background and speech.

Bullough, Geoffrey. "*Othello*." In *Narrative and Dramatic Sources of Shakespeare*. Vol. 7, *Major Tragedies*. London and New York: Routledge and Columbia, 1975, 193–265.

Burton, Jonathan. " 'A Most Wily Bird': Leo Africanus, *Othello* and the Trafficking in Difference." In Ania Loomba and Martin Orkin, ed. *Post-Colonial Shakespeares*. London and New York: Routledge, 1998, 43–63.

Contareno, Gaspar. *The Commonwealth and Government of Venice*. Trans. Lewis Lewkenor. London: 1599. Rpt. New York: Da Capo Press, 1969.

Dean, Leonard F. *A Casebook on "Othello."* New York: Thomas Crowell, 1961.

Furness, Horace Howard. *A New Variorum Edition of Othello*. 7th ed. Philadelphia: Lippincott, 1886.

Honigmann, E. A. J., ed. *Othello*. Walton-on-Thames: Thomas Nelson and Sons, Ltd., 1997.

Leo Africanus. *The History and Description of Africa: and of the Notable Things Therein Contained / Written by al-Hassan ibn Mohammed al-Wezaz, al-Fasi, a Moor, Baptized as Giovanni Leone, but Better Known as Leo Africanus: Done into English in the Year 1600 by John Pory*. Ed. Robert Brown. London: Hakluyt Society, 1896.

Pliny, the Elder. *Pliny's Natural History; A Selection from Philemon Holland's Translation*. Ed. J. Newsome. Oxford: Clarendon Press, 1964.

Ross, Lawrence J., ed. *The Tragedy of Othello, The Moor of Venice*. Indianapolis and New York: Bobbs-Merrill, 1974.

Taylor, John Edward. *The Moor of Venice: Cinthio's Tale and Shakspere's Tragedy*. London: Chapman and Hall, 1855. Rpt. New York: AMS Press, 1972.

Zhiri, Oumelbanine. "Leo Africanus's Description of Africa." In Ivo Kamps and Jyotsna G. Singh, ed. *Travel Knowledge: European "Discoveries" in the Early Modern Period*. New York: Palgrave, 2001, 258–66.

2. CONTEXTUAL SOURCES—RACE

Racial issues have greatly interested recent critics. The following items should give readers a representative sampling of current opinion and critical belief, including particular studies of *Othello,* general reflections about the relevance of racial categories to Renaissance texts, and claims about the political responsibility of critics for engaging with such topics.

Bartels, Emily C. "Making More of the Moor: Aaron, Othello, and Renaissance Refashionings of Race." *Shakespeare Quarterly* 41 (1990): 433–54.

Callaghan, Dympna. " 'Othello Was a White Man': Properties of Race on Shakespeare's Stage." In Terence Hawkes, ed. *Alternative Shakespeares, Volume 2.* London and New York: Routledge, 1996, 192–215.

Chedgzoy, Ruth. "Blackness Yields to Beauty: Desirability and Difference in Early Modern Culture." In Gordon McMullan, ed. *Renaissance Configurations: Voices, Bodies, Spaces, 1580–1690.* Basingstoke: Macmillan; New York: St. Martin's Press, 1998, 108–28.

Erickson, Peter. "Images of White Identity in *Othello.*" In Philip C. Kolin, ed. *"Othello": New Critical Essays.* New York and London: Routledge, 2002, 133–45.

Freinkel, Lisa. *"The Merchant of Venice:* 'Modern' Anti-Semitism and the Veil of Allegory." In Jean E. Howard and Scott Cutler Shershow, ed. *Marxist Shakespeares.* London and New York: Routledge, 2000, 122–41.

Hall, Kim F. " 'These Bastard Signs of Fair': Literary Whiteness in Shakespeare's Sonnets." In Loomba and Orkin, *Post-Colonial Shakespeares,* 64–83.

———. *Things of Darkness: Economies of Race and Gender in Early Modern England.* Ithaca: Cornell University Press, 1995.

Hendricks, Margo, ed. "Forum: Race and the Study of Shakespeare." *Shakespeare Studies 26.* Cranbury, N.J. London and Mississauga, Ontario: Associated University Presses, 1998, 19–79.

———, and Patricia Parker, ed. *Women, "Race," and Writing in the Early Modern Period.* London and New York: Routledge, 1994.

Loomba, Ania. " 'Delicious traffick': Alterity and Exchange on Early Modern Stages." *Shakespeare Survey 52.* Cambridge: Cambridge University Press, 1999, 201–14.

———. " 'Local-Manufacture Made-in-India Othello Fellows': Issues of Race, Hybridity and Location in Post-Colonial Shakespeares." In Loomba and Orkin, *Post-Colonial Shakespeares,* 143–63.

———, and Martin Orkin, ed. *Post-Colonial Shakespeares.* London and New York: Routledge, 1998.

Neill, Michael. " 'His Master's Ass': Slavery, Service, and Subordination in *Othello*." In Thomas Clayton, Susan Brock, and Vicente Forés, ed. *Shakespeare and the Mediterranean: The Selected Proceedings of the International Shakespeare Association World Congress, Valencia, 2001.* Newark, Delaware, and London: University of Delaware Press and Associated University Presses, 2004, 215–29.

———. " 'Mulattos', 'Blacks,' and 'Indian Moors': *Othello* and Early Modern Constructions of Human Difference." *Shakespeare Quarterly* 49 (1998): 361–74.

de Reuck, Jenny. "Blackface and Madonna: Race and Gender as Conditions of Reception in Recovering *Othello*." In R. S. White, Charles Edelman, and Christopher Wortham, ed. *Shakespeare: Readers, Audiences, Players.* Nedlands: University of Western Australia Press, 1998, 220–32.

Suzman, Janet. "South Africa in *Othello*." In Jonathan Bate, Jill L. Levenson, and Dieter Mehl, ed. *Shakespeare and the Twentieth Century: The Selected Proceedings of the International Shakespeare Association World Congress, Los Angeles, 1996.* Newark: University of Delaware Press; London: Associated University Presses, 1998, 23–40.

Vaughan, Virginia Mason. "Race Mattered: *Othello* in Late Eighteenth-Century England." *Shakespeare Survey 51.* Cambridge: Cambridge University Press, 1998, 57–66.

3. CONTEXTUAL SOURCES—WOMEN, MARRIAGE, DOMESTICITY

Like race, these topics are at the center of a great deal of current critical interest and have engaged earlier critics as well. The first list below includes examples of Renaissance domestic drama and of critical commentary on this material as well as on literary representations of the domestic in the Renaissance more generally. The second list emphasizes interests in social history. (The distinction is not hard and fast and allows for a lot of overlap.)

Adams, Henry Hitch. *English Domestic or Homiletic Tragedy, 1575–1642: Being an Account of the Development of the Tragedy of the Common Man Showing Its Great Dependence on Religious Morality, Illustrated with Striking Examples of the Interposition of Providence for the Amendment of Men's Manners.* 1943. Rpt. New York: Benjamin Blom, 1965.

Belsey, Catherine. *Shakespeare and the Loss of Eden: The Construction of Family Values in Early Modern Culture.* London: Macmillan, 1999.

Callaghan, Dympna. "Looking Well to Linens: Women and Cultural Production in *Othello* and Shakespeare's England." In Jean E. Howard and Scott Cutler Shershow, ed. *Marxist Shakespeares.* London and New York: Routledge, 2000, 53–81.

Cannon, Charles Dale, ed. *A Warning for Fair Women* (1599). The Hague: Mouton, 1975.

Clark, Andrew. *Domestic Drama: A Survey of the Origins, Antecedents, and Nature of the Domestic Play in England*. 2 vols. Salzburg Studies in English Literature. Jacobean Drama Studies 49. Salzburg, 1975.

Comensoli, Viviana. *"Household Business": Domestic Plays of Early Modern England*. Toronto: University of Toronto Press, 1996.

Dubrow, Heather. *Shakespeare and Domestic Loss: Forms of Deprivation, Mourning, and Recuperation*. Cambridge Studies in Renaissance Literature and Culture 32. Cambridge: Cambridge University Press, 1999.

Lieblein, Leanore. "The Context of Murder in English Domestic Plays, 1590–1610." *SEL* 23 (1983): 181–96.

Morgan, Arthur Eustace. *English Domestic Drama*. Folcraft, Pa.: Folcraft Press, 1912.

Sturgess, Keith, ed. *Three Elizabethan Domestic Tragedies: Arden of Faversham, A Yorkshire Tragedy, A Woman Killed with Kindness*. Harmondsworth: Penguin, 1969.

Symonds, John Addington. "Domestic Drama." In *Shakspere's Predecessors in the English Drama*. London: Smith, Elder, & Co., 1884, 412–84.

Wilkins, George. *The Miseries of Enforced Marriage*. 1607. Ed. Glenn H. Blayney. Oxford: Malone Society Reprints, 1964.

Ezell, Margaret J. M. *The Patriarch's Wife: Literary Evidence and the History of the Family*. Chapel Hill: University of North Carolina Press, 1987.

Goody, Jack. *The Development of the Family and Marriage in Europe*. Cambridge: Cambridge University Press, 1983.

Hull, Suzanne W. *Chaste, Silent and Obedient: English Books for Women 1475–1640*. San Marino: Huntington Library, 1982.

Orlin, Lena Cowen. *Private Matters and Public Culture in Post-Reformation England*. Ithaca: Cornell University Press, 1994.

Powell, Chilton Lathan. *English Domestic Relations, 1487–1653: A Study of Matrimony and Family Life in Theory and Practice*. New York: Columbia University Press, 1917.

Wright, Louis B. *Middle-Class Culture in Elizabethan England*. Chapel Hill: University of North Carolina Press, 1935.

Ziegler, Georgiana. " 'My Lady's Chamber': Female Space, Female Chastity in Shakespeare." *Textual Practice* 4 (1990): 73–90.

4. RYMER

A lawyer, critic, and occasional poet and playwright, Rymer achieved some eminence during his lifetime (he was chosen to be the royal archivist at the end of his career), but is known today almost exclusively for his 1693 attack on *Othello*, excerpted above. The text is taken from the unique early quarto edition (London, 1693), *A Short View of Tragedy, Its Original, Excellency and Corruption. With Some Reflections on Shakespeare and Other Practitioners for the Stage*. A facsimile edition was published by the Scolar Press in 1970. The authoritative modern edition is available in *The Critical Works of Thomas Rymer,* edited with an introduction and notes by Curt A. Zimansky (New Haven: Yale University Press, 1956).

5. GILDON

Gildon was a prolific editor, essayist, critic, and occasionally poet and dramatist. The first two passages are taken from the first edition (London, 1694) of his *Miscellaneous Letters and Essays on Several Subjects: Philosophical, Moral, Historical, Critical, Amorous, &c. in Prose and Verse*. The full title for his response to Rymer is "Some Reflections on Mr. Rymer's *Short View of Tragedy* and an Attempt at a Vindication of Shakespeare, in an Essay Directed to John Dryden Esq." The third excerpt is from the extensive *Remarks on the Plays of Shakespeare* in Gildon's edition of *The Works of Mr. William Shakespear,* vol. 7, claimed as an appendage in 1710 to Nicholas Rowe's 1709 edition of Shakespeare's plays. Though the claim was spurious, the *Remarks* are by "a very long way the most extended account of the plays to have appeared by that date," an "inaugurating moment" in the history of Shakespeare criticism (Holland, 1.xxvii). No modern edition of Gildon exists, but a facsimile edition of the *Miscellaneous Letters* in conjunction with Dennis's *Impartial Critick* is available with a preface by Arthur Freeman (New York and London: Garland, 1973); and Pickering and Chatto issued a facsimile of vol. 7 of the Rowe edition (London, 1999), from which Holland's introduction is quoted just above.

6. JOHNSON

Journalist, literary critic and biographer, lexicographer, poet, playwright, fiction writer, moralist, conversationalist, Johnson was so smart and influential that in the days of the period-course curriculum, "The Age of Johnson" was commonly offered by English Departments throughout North America. The excerpts from the preface to his edition of Shakespeare—a foundational document in the history of Shakespeare criticism that manages to be entertaining and shrewdly intelligent at the same time—are taken from *The Plays of Shakespeare. Accurately Printed from the Text of Samuel Johnson, George Steevens, and Isaac Reed. With the Preface of Dr. Johnson, and a Copious Glossary* (Edinburgh, 1832). Johnson's notes to *Othello* are quoted from vol. 19 of the twenty-one-vol. edition of *The*

*Plays of William Shakespeare, with the Corrections and Illustrations
of Various Commentators, to Which Are Added Notes by Samuel Johnson and George Steevens* (London, 1813). The authoritative modern
edition of these texts may be found in vols. 7 and 8 of the Yale edition
of *The Works of Samuel Johnson, Johnson on Shakespeare,* edited by
Arthur Sherbo with an introduction by Bertrand H. Bronson (New
Haven and London: Yale University Press, 1968). Bronson's subsequent *Selections from Johnson on Shakespeare,* edited with Jean M.
O'Meara (New Haven and London: Yale University Press, 1986),
reprints some of Johnson's extensive quotations from earlier editors
not included in the 1968 edition.

7. LAMB

Lamb's occasional *Essays,* written under the pseudonym Elia, were
very popular throughout the nineteenth century and still make enjoy-
able reading. The *Tales from Shakespeare,* written with his sister
Mary and published in 1807, significantly shaped the ideas and
images by which Victorian children (and adults) came to appreciate
Shakespeare. Lamb was on friendly terms with many of the poets
and critics of his time, including Coleridge, Wordsworth, Hazlitt,
Leigh Hunt, and Robert Southey, among whom existed a regular
traffic of ideas and sentiments. Lamb's claim for Shakespeare's superiority as a literary rather than theatrical experience was frequently
echoed (both about *Othello* and Shakespeare in general) by subsequent critics, including Coleridge and Bradley in excerpts above.

The Lamb essay excerpted above was originally published in 1811
in the *Reflector* under "Theatralia No. 1. On Garrick, and Acting,
and the Plays of Shakespeare, Considered with Reference to Their
Fitness for Stage Representation." The text is taken from Lamb's
*Complete Works in Prose and Verse: From the Original Editions, with
the Cancelled Passages Restored, and Many Pieces Now First Collected,* edited and prefaced by R. H. Shepherd, two vols. (New York:
Hoventon, 1874), 1:253–65. The authoritative modern edition may
be found in *The Works of Charles and Mary Lamb,* edited by Edward
Verrall Lucas, seven vols. (London: Methuen, 1903–05), 1:97–111.

8. HAZLITT

In his remarkably productive career, Hazlitt produced journalism,
theatrical reviews, paintings, a biography of Napoleon, essays and
books of literary criticism and history, moral philosophy, psychological and epistemological theory, and what would now be called cultural and political critique. His specific observations about
Shakespeare have long been appreciated for their acute intelligence,

but his refusal to compartmentalize (for Hazlitt, the imagination was not a specialized poetic faculty but the motor of all human behavior) has tended until recently to obscure the systematic coherence and power of his Shakespearean commentary.

The first passage included above is put together from original periodical publications: "On Mr. Kean's Iago" and "On Mr. Kean's Iago (Concluded)," *The Examiner* (July 24 and August 7, 1814), 478–79 and 505–07. Discussion specific to Kean's performance is generally deleted, following the pattern Hazlitt suggested when assimilating this material into the *Othello* chapter of *The Characters of Shakespear's Plays* (1817). The third excerpt above is taken from this chapter up to the point where Hazlitt turns to the Iago material that occupies him for the rest of his discussion. My text is taken from an 1869 publication edited with minor revisions by William Carew Hazlitt (the author's grandson), which also included the *Lectures on the Literature of the Age of Elizabeth,* as reissued in London by George Bell and Sons in 1901 (Bohn's Standard Library edition).

The authoritative modern edition of *The Complete Works of William Hazlitt* is edited by P. P. Howe, twenty-one vols. (London: Dent, 1930–34). *The Characters* may be found in 4.165–361. The *Examiner* pieces may be found in 5.211–21, as Hazlitt reprinted them in 1818 in *A View of the English Stage*—that is, without the note about "the rankness and gross impropriety of the personal connection" between Othello and Desdemona. (Howe published the note separately and discusses some of the debate it generated in 20.401–02.) For a generous sampling presented with great intelligence and sympathy, see R. S. White's edition, *Hazlitt's Criticism of Shakespeare: A Selection* (Studies in British Literature 18; Lewiston, Queenston, and Lampeter: Edwin Mellen, 1996).

9. COLERIDGE

Coleridge was a polymath of titanic intellectual energy. Though his philosophical, theological, and political writings no longer excite general interest, his innovative poetry arguably remains a presence (the conversation poems opened doors for Wordsworth into territory we continue to explore), and his criticism still a vital force. His central ideas—the distinction between poetic and scientific language, the imagination as reconciler of opposites, the organic unity of poetic texts—served generations of critics until very recently and retain substantial authority. Most important, in working out his ideas about the special unity of poetic language, he developed the interpretive strategies of "practical criticism" (he invented the phrase as well as the practice), which sustain the study of literature even now in high school and college classrooms.

Shakespeare was always Coleridge's primary exhibit of literary value, though given the scattered and occasional nature of his Shakespearean commentary, it is hard to represent anything like the full and coherent scope of his thought. Only a small portion of Coleridge's Shakespearean commentary was published by the author; the rest derives from lecture notes transcribed by his auditors or written by Coleridge himself in manuscripts, from transcripts of his conversation (*Table Talk*), and from material edited (and sometimes augmented if not constructed) after Coleridge's death by his son-in-law and nephew, Henry Nelson Coleridge, and published as Coleridge's *Literary Remains*. All the passages included here are quoted from Ashe's edition except for the first Desdemona passage, which is quoted (including the final translation of the Latin phrase) from p. 111 of the 1989 *Selection* Foakes produced from his authoritative *Lectures on Literature 1808–1819*. Four of the excerpts are not based on Coleridge's 1819 lecture notes: the first Iago passage is taken from Coleridge's *Lear* lecture given a week after the *Othello;* the third Othello passage is from *Table Talk* for December 29, 1822; the first Desdemona passage is taken from notes for an 1813 lecture comparing *Othello* and *The Winter's Tale;* the second Desdemona passage is taken from *Table Talk* for September 27, 1830. The last three sentences of the first Othello passage and the whole of the last passage were published (by Ashe and more recent editors) in conjunction with the 1819 lecture, but derive from *The Literary Remains*. Foakes does not include these passages, and earlier modern editions by Raysor and Hawkes acknowledge doubts about their authenticity. They are included here partly because, as Hawkes says of one of them, "it represents the spirit of Coleridge's own analysis, and makes a good point which is tacitly in the body of the original manuscript" (176); in addition, the passages were accepted as authentic for a century after Coleridge's death and continue to be represented as part of the Coleridgean legacy even now and even among scholars who may know better.

Ashe, T., ed. *Lectures and Notes on Shakspere and Other English Poets by Samuel Taylor Coleridge*. 1883. Rpt. London: George Bell and Sons, 1897.

Foakes, R. A., ed. *Coleridge's Criticism of Shakespeare: A Selection*. London: Athlone, 1989.

———. *Samuel Taylor Coleridge: Lectures on Literature 1808–1819*. 2 vols. London and Princeton: Routledge and Princeton University Press, 1987. *The Collected Works of Samuel Taylor Coleridge,* vol. 5.

Hawkes, Terence, ed. *Coleridge's Writings on Shakespeare*. New York: G. P. Putnam's Sons, 1959.

Raysor, Thomas Middleton, ed. *Coleridge: Shakespearean Criticism*. 2nd ed.; 2 vols. London: Dent, 1960.

10. BRADLEY

The son of an Evangelical minister, Bradley was educated at Oxford University, where he encountered some of the leading figures of Victorian intellectual life. He taught philosophy at Oxford, moved into literature at the universities of Liverpool and Glasgow, and finally returned to Oxford as Professor of Poetry from 1901 to 1906. First published in 1904, *Shakespearean Tragedy* is technically a twentieth-century production, but as Bradley acknowledges in the preface, the book is "based on a selection from materials used in teaching" dating from his early career, and it resonates with ideas and critical assumptions derived from nineteenth-century thought. Despite its adherence to apparently old-fashioned ideas—a tendency to focus on the protagonist's inner life independently of the action, much derided in early twentieth-century modernist reactions to Victorianism; an idealist commitment to transcendence strongly repudiated by currently dominant materialist and historicist criticism—the book has sustained an enormous popularity through to our own time. The current edition displays John Everett Millais's drowning Ophelia on its cover—to suggest either (misleadingly) that the book centers on protofeminist concerns or (more persuasively) that it continues to interest readers despite its own distance from prevailing critical norms

Readers interested in finding out more about Bradley's life and work might start with Cooke and then branch out to the relatively sympathetic account in Hunter and the relatively unsympathetic one in Hawkes. Bradley develops the methodological and theoretical assumptions behind the discussions in *Shakespearean Tragedy* in the essays collected in his *Oxford Lectures on Poetry* (1909; rpt. Bloomington: Indiana University Press, 1961)—of which the three listed below are the most immediately relevant.

Bradley, A. C. "Hegel's Theory of Tragedy." In *Oxford Lectures*, 69–95.
———. "Poetry for Poetry's Sake." In *Oxford Lectures*, 3–34.
———. "Shakespeare's Theatre and Audience." In *Oxford Lectures*, 361–93.
Cooke, Katharine. *A. C. Bradley and His Influence in Twentieth-Century Shakespearean Criticism*. Oxford: Clarendon, 1972.
Hawkes, Terence. "A Sea Shell." In *That Shakespeherian Rag: Essays on a Critical Process*. London and New York: Methuen, 1986, 27–50.
Hunter, G. K. "A. C. Bradley's *Shakespearean Tragedy*." In *Dramatic*

Identities and Cultural Tradition: Studies in Shakespeare and His Contemporaries. Liverpool: Liverpool University Press, 1978, 270–85.

11. PERFORMANCE (*OTHELLO* ON STAGE)

Othello has excited theatrical audiences since the beginning, and this popularity shows no sign of abating. The history of the play's theatrical interpretation in many ways reflects (or is reflected by) the values and beliefs represented in literary interpretation; but theatrical performance has its own more or less autonomous interests, and while many of the commentaries excerpted in this book take account of performance, the subject really deserves a book to itself. The items listed below should introduce readers to the rich and fascinating traditions of *Othello*'s stage history.

Carlisle, Carol Jones. "Actors Criticisms of *Othello*." In *Shakespeare from the Greenroom: Actors' Criticisms of Four Major Tragedies.* Chapel Hill: University of North Carolina Press, 1969, 172–263.

Ford, John R. " 'Words and Performances': Roderigo and the Mixed Dramaturgy of Race and Gender in *Othello*." In Philip C. Kolin, ed. *"Othello": New Critical Essays.* New York and London: Routledge, 2002, 147–67.

Hankey, Julie. *Othello.* Plays in Performance Series. Bristol: Bristol Classical Press, 1987.

Kaul, Mythili. "Background: Black or Tawny? Stage Representations of Othello from 1604 to the Present." In Mythili Kaul, ed. *"Othello": New Essays by Black Writers.* Washington D.C.: Howard University Press, 1997, 1–22.

Matteo, Gino J. *Shakespeare's "Othello": The Study and the Stage, 1604–1904.* Salzburg Studies in English Literature. Salzburg: Institut für Englische Sprache und Literatur, 1974.

Odell, George C. D. *Shakespeare from Betterton to Irving.* Vol. 2. New York: Scribner's 1920.

Potter, Lois. *Othello.* Shakespeare in Performance. Manchester: Manchester University Press, 2002.

Rosenberg, Marvin. *The Masks of Othello: The Search for the Identity of Othello, Iago, and Desdemona by Three Centuries of Actors and Critics.* Berkeley, Los Angeles, and London: University of California Press, 1961.

Spencer, Hazelton. *Shakespeare Improved: The Restoration Versions in Quarto and on the Stage.* Cambridge: Harvard University Press, 1927.

Sprague, Arthur Colby. *Shakespeare and the Actors: The Stage Business in His Plays (1660–1905).* Cambridge: Harvard University Press, 1948.

————. *Shakespearian Players and Performances*. Cambridge: Harvard University Press, 1953

Stanislavski, Constantin. *Stanislavski Produces "Othello."* Trans. Helen Nowak. New York: Theatre Arts Books, 1963.

Vaughan, Virginia Mason. "Representations." In *"Othello": A Contextual History*. Cambridge: Cambridge University Press, 1995, 93–232.

12. PERFORMANCE (MOVIES AND VIDEOS / DVDS)

The movies changed everything, rendering performances of *Othello* accessible to a much broader audience than could afford (or were comfortable with) going to see plays. Digital technology changed things further, allowing still more of us to watch taped performances of *Othello* on the TV at home or in the classroom, where they have installed themselves as an immeasurably valuable resource. Cinematic and video / DVD versions of *Othello* have proliferated amazingly. Consult pp. 208–27 of Kenneth S. Rothwell and Annabelle Henkin Melzer's *Shakespeare on Screen: An International Filmography and Videography* (New York: Neal-Schuman, 1990) for a comprehensive list of *Othello*s produced up to about 1989. For more recent information, run a search for *Othello* on that indispensable web resource, The Internet Movie Database (www.imdb.com), and you will find at least thirty-four items (probably more by the time this sentence is read and acted on).

Here are six notable *Othello* performances from the last fifty years currently available as videos (some as DVDs), each with its own web address for more detailed information:

Orson **Welles** directs himself as Othello in a movie released in 1952 <http://us.imdb.com/Title?0045251>.

Stuart Burge directs a film version of John Dexter's 1964 London production, featuring Laurence **Oliver,** 1965 <http://us.imdb.com/Title ?0059555>.

Jonathan **Miller** directs Anthony Hopkins and Bob Hoskins in a version made for the BBC, 1981 <http://us.imdb.com/Title?0082861>.

Janet **Suzman** directs John Kani's Othello in a taped version of a production staged in Johannesburg, 1987 <http://www.films.com/Films _Home/item.cfm?s=1&bin=3030>.

Trevor **Nunn** directs Willard White and Ian McKellen in a taped-for-TV version of his 1989 Royal Shakespeare Company production <http://www.films.com/Films_Home/Item.cfm?s=1&bin=6008>.

Oliver **Parker** directs Laurence Fishburne and Kenneth Branagh in a movie released in 1995 <http://us.imdb.com/Title?0114057>.

Only a small fraction of what's available, these *Othello*s have attracted the most extensive response (the boldface names above reappear in the list of critical discussions printed a little further down).

Seeing plays and movies are different experiences, seeing taped performances on TV different yet again. In terms of critical interest, however, these phenomenological or textual distinctions are often blurred; even the short list above mixes movies, taped or cinematic versions of plays, and made-for-TV productions. More slippage occurs in the list below. Though most of the items there are included for their critical commentary on one or more of the six performances listed above, I have also thrown in discussions of two particularly interesting recent European productions—one directed by George Tabori for the Akademie Theater in Vienna (Carlson) and one by Peter Zadek for the Deutsches Schauspielhaus in Hamburg (Engle); an English production featuring David Harewood and Simon Russell Beale at the National Theatre (Liston), directed by Sam Mendes; and an American production, the much-discussed "photo-negative" version directed by Jude Kelly for the Lansburgh Theater in Washington, D.C., 1997, featuring Patrick Stewart as a white Othello playing with and against an almost entirely black cast (discussed by Iyengar, Johnson-Haddad in "The Shakespeare Theater," and others as indicated in the titles below).

The flip side of this slippage is an over-rigid distinction between the items listed below and the ones included in "Performance (*Othello* on Stage)," above. I included items above when they ranged widely over theatrical history, but this range did not prevent Vaughan (for example) from sustained commentary on Welles and Nunn, or Potter (for another) from engaging with the Suzman and Kelly productions. One further omission deserves emphasis. The black performer Paul Robeson played Othello in two productions, one in London in 1930, the other in New York in 1943, and these performances (along sometimes with those of Ira Aldridge, another black actor, who performed the part in Europe in the nineteenth century) have received a great deal of attention of late—in Vaughan and Potter again (the latter makes Robeson the pivotal figure in her book), as well as among other critics listed below whose focus (as their titles suggest) is on racial issues

Boose, Lynda E. "Grossly Gaping Viewers and Jonathan Miller's *Othello*." In Boose and Richard Burt, ed. *Shakespeare, the Movie: Popularizing the Plays on Film, TV, and Video*. London and New York: Routledge, 1997, 186–97.

Buchanan, Judith. "Virgin and Ape, Venetian and Infidel: Labelings of Otherness in Oliver Parker's *Othello*." In Mark Thornton Burnett and Ramona Wray, ed. *Shakespeare, Film and Fin de Siècle*. New York: St. Martin's, 2000, 179–202.

Buhler, Stephen M. "Three Versions of *Othello*." In *Shakespeare in the Cinema: Ocular Proof*. Albany: State University of New York Press, 2001, 11–32. [Parker]

Bulman, J. C., and H. R. Coursen. *Shakespeare on Television: An Anthology of Essays and Reviews*. Hanover and London: University Press of New England, 1988. [Miller]

Carlson, Marvin. "*Othello* in Vienna, 1991." *Shakespeare Quarterly* 44 (1993): 228–30.

Cartmell, Deborah. *Interpreting Shakespeare on Screen*. New York: Palgrave 2000. [Welles]

Coursen, Herbert R. "More Iago Than Moor." In *Shakespeare in Space: Recent Shakespeare Productions on Screen*. Studies in Shakespeare 14. New York: Peter Lang, 2002, 22–24. [Parker]

Davies, Anthony. "Filming *Othello*." In Davies and Stanley Wells, ed. *Shakespeare and the Moving Image: The Plays on Film and Television*. Cambridge: Cambridge University Press, 196–210. [Welles]

———. "Orson Welles's *Othello*." In *Filming Shakespeare's Plays: The Adaptations of Laurence Olivier, Orson Welles, Peter Brook and Akira Kurosawa*. Cambridge: Cambridge University Press, 1988, 100–18.

Dorval, Patricia. "Shakespeare on Screen: Threshold Aesthetics in Oliver Parker's *Othello*." *Early Modern Literary Studies* 6.1 (May 2000): 1.1–15 <http://purl.oclc.org/emls/06-1/dorvothe.htm>.

Engle, Ron. "Audience, Style, and Language in the Shakespeare of Peter Zadek." In Dennis Kennedy, ed. *Foreign Shakespeare: Contemporary Performance*. Cambridge: Cambridge University Press, 1993, 93–105.

Hodgdon, Barbara. "Race-ing *Othello*, Re-engendering White-out." In Lynda E. Boose and Richard Burt, ed. *Shakespeare, the Movie: Popularizing the Plays on Film, TV, and Video*. London and New York: Routledge, 1997, 23–44. [Oliver]

Howlett, Kathy M. "The Voyeuristic Pleasures of Perversion: Orson Welles's *Othello*." In *Framing Shakespeare on Film*. Athens: Ohio University Press, 2000, 52–91.

Iyengar, Sujata. "White Faces, Blackface: The Production of 'Race' in *Othello*." In Philip C. Kolin, ed. *"Othello": New Critical Essays*. New York and London: Routledge, 2002, 103–31. [Oliver and Nunn; also Stewart and the two Robesons]

Jacobs, Alfred. "Orson Welles's *Othello*: Shakespeare Meets Film Noir." In Jonathan Bate, Jill L. Levenson, and Dieter Mehl, ed. *Shakespeare and the Twentieth Century: The Selected Proceedings of the International Shakespeare Association World Congress, Los Angeles, 1996*. Newark: University of Delaware Press; London: Associated University Presses, 1998, 113–24.

Johnson-Haddad, Miranda. "Patrick Stewart on Playing Othello." *Shakespeare Bulletin* 16 (1998): 11–12.

————. "The Shakespeare Theatre *Othello*." *Shakespeare Bulletin* 16 (1998): 9–11.

Jorgens, Jack J. "Orson Welles's *Othello*." In *Shakespeare on Film*. Bloomington and London: Indiana University Press, 1972, 175–90.

————. "Stuart Burge and John Dexter's *Othello*." In *Shakespeare on Film*. Bloomington and London: Indiana University Press, 1972, 191–217.

Kauffmann, Stanley. "Shrinking Shakespeare." *New Republic* 214 (February 12, 1996): 30–31. [Parker]

Liston, William T. *"Othello." Shakespeare Bulletin* 16 (1998): 23–24.

MacLiammoir, Micháel. *Put Money in Thy Purse: The Filming of Orson Welles' "Othello."* London: Eyre Methuen, 1976.

Mason, Pamela. "Orson Welles and Filmed Shakespeare." In Russell Jackson, ed. *The Cambridge Companion to Shakespeare on Film*. Cambridge: Cambridge University Press, 183–98.

Miller, Jonathan. *Subsequent Performances*. London: Faber, 1986.

Rafferty, Terence. "Fidelity and Infidelity." *New Yorker* 71 (December 18, 1995): 124–27. [Parker]

Rothwell, Kenneth. *A History of Shakespeare on Screen: A Century of Film and Television*. Cambridge: Cambridge University Press, 1999. [Welles, Olivier, and Parker]

Suzman, Janet. "South Africa in *Othello*." In Jonathan Bate, Jill L. Levenson, and Dieter Mehl, ed. *Shakespeare and the Twentieth Century: The Selected Proceedings of the International Shakespeare Association World Congress, Los Angeles, 1996*. Newark: University of Delaware Press; London: Associated University Presses, 1998, 23–40.

Swander, Homer. "Musings on the Stewart / Kelly *Othello*." *Shakespeare Bulletin* 16 (1998): 13.

Tatspause, Patricia. "The Tragedies of Love on Film." In Russell Jackson, ed. *The Cambridge Companion to Shakespeare on Film*. Cambridge: Cambridge University Press, 135–59. [Welles, Olivier, and Parker]

Tynan, Kenneth, ed. *"Othello": The National Theatre Production*. New York: Stein and Day, 1967. [Olivier]

Willis, Susan. *The BBC Shakespeare Plays: Making the Televised Canon*. Chapel Hill & London: University of North Carolina Press, 1991. [Miller]

Wine, Martin L. *"Othello": Text and Performance*. London: Macmillan, 1984. [Miller and Olivier]

13. SPINOFFS

About ten years after *Othello* was first produced, John Webster (amusingly represented as the creepy street urchin hanging morbidly around the theater in John Madden's film *Shakespeare in Love*

[1998]) wrote a play called *The Duchess of Malfi*, in which the protagonist, strangled apparently to death, revives, only to be strangled
again. The similarities with Desdemona's death cannot be coincidental, especially since Webster's *Duchess* is filled with so many
Shakespearean echoes, from both *Othello* and other plays. The
Duchess's double death is one of the earliest examples of an *Othello*
spinoff: material from Shakespeare's play is developed and absorbed
into a new imaginative construct that derives power from proximity
to the Shakespearean original. This process occurs repeatedly from
Webster's time to our own, when it seems to be intensifying and
proliferating.

The concept of spinoff (or sometimes offshoot) leaves up in the
air whether audiences need or ought to know they are hearing echoes
of a Shakespearean original. Without endorsing ignorance, we
should acknowledge that knowledge—too much, the wrong kind, or
inappropriately applied—can have undesirable consequences. An
audience watching *The Duchess of Malfi* with *Othello* on the brain
might have difficulty engaging with Webster's very different kind of
dramatic power. This problem is even clearer with more recent spinoffs. If when watching Geoffrey Sax's *Othello*—the made-for-British-
TV movie I mention in the first paragraph of the preface to this
book—you focus intensely on its many transformations of
Shakespeare, you'll be too detached or distracted to enter into the
thrilling representations of race and sex and power relations as they
play out in the film's contemporary London setting. Sometimes *Othello* spinoffs seem to want not only to mute their *Othello* echoes, but
to eradicate them altogether. Consider the other cinematic version
I mention in the preface, Tim Blake Nelson's *O*. What's in a name?
Sax's title will most likely suggest a Shakespearean connection even
to spectators who had never read or seen *Othello* or anything else
Shakespeare wrote. But by changing the name of his film to *O* (*Othello* was the movie's working title prior to its eventual release), Nelson (or the producers or distributors or some other amorphously
anonymous Hollywood agency) effectively guaranteed an audience
for most of whom no Shakespearean connection existed. (In this
respect, *O* resembles the movie and TV spinoffs of *Othello* fascinat-
ingly described by Tony Howard and Marguerite Rippy in the essays
cited below.) And yet who would deny *O* status as an authentic *Othello* spinoff, propelled (no matter how tenuous the connection or
invisible its presence to the audience) by the titanic energies of the
Shakespearean original?

The *Othello* spinoffs listed below are not a representative sampling, merely a group of items (and some commentaries about them)
that I find particularly interesting. All are current works with one
exception, Aphra Behn's *Oroonoko* (1688), a prose romance about a

royal slave with sexual charisma, who murders his wife, is tortured, and commits suicide in a bloody climax. Highly popular in its day Behn's work was itself spun off in Thomas Southerne's dramatic adaptation (1695) through which it had a strong impact on the anti-slavery debates sustained through the eighteenth century. *Oroonoko* largely disappeared from view for two centuries, but was rediscovered in our time when racial concerns coincided with feminist interests (Behn was effectively the first professional woman writer) to generate an extraordinary amount of critical attention. In this sense, *Oroonoko* is not really an exception to the contemporary content of the items listed below.

Salman Rushdie's prominence in this list derives from the extent to which his books keep coming back to *Othello,* beginning at least as early as Saladin Chamcha's literal enactment in *The Satanic Verses* of Othello's metaphor in 3.3.182 (he turns into a goat), and developing in a variety of ways there and in later novels. Salih's and Phillips's works are undeservedly less well known than Rushdie's. Salih's *Season of Migration to the North* plays with ironic intelligence against the sentimentalized charisma with which some later versions of Shakespeare's protagonist have been endowed. "I am no Othello," says the murderously seductive Mustafa Sa'eed at the book's center. "Othello was a lie" (95). Against this romanticized mendacity, the breathtaking evocations of Sudanese village life may offer some compensatory truth. Phillips's *The Nature of Blood* is a quiet and reflective book, juxtaposing Jewish and African diasporic narratives from current to Renaissance times. Unemphatic, almost laconic in its refusal to comment on (let alone connect) its disparate material, Phillips's book is nonetheless as impressive as the more flamboyant and dramatic fictions of Rushdie and Salih.

The Vogel and Sears plays (both conveniently accessible in the Fischlin-Fortier anthology) along with Ann-Marie MacDonald's amusing *jeu d'esprit* testify to the continuing power of *Othello*'s women—their stories, points of view, sensibilities—to excite and reinforce feminist interest. Sears goes beyond the other two by centering the action on an invented black woman, Billie, whom the (never-seen-on-stage) Desdemona character displaces in the Othello character's affections. In this context, Murray Carlin's play is in all respects the odd man out. Focusing on a Caribbean outsider rehearsing *Othello* with a privileged South African women with whom he is having an affair, *Not Now, Sweet Desdemona* puts the Othello character, for all his sense of besieged masculinity, into the driver's seat. In its gender relations and political aspirations (including a comically unillusioned but emphatically happy ending, as the couple decide, of all things, to get married), Carlin evokes the 1960s—a time rapidly coming to seem as remote as the high Victorian age. This may explain why *Not Now, Sweet Desdemona* has long been out of print and the author has disappeared into oblivion (or at least I haven't been able to find out anything about him).

Behn, Aphra. *Oroonoko.* Ed. Joanna Lipking. New York and London: W. W. Norton, 1997.

Carlin, Murray. *Not Now, Sweet Desdemona: A Duologue for Black and White within the Realm of Shakespeare's "Othello."* Nairobi, Lusaka, and Addis Ababa: Oxford University Press, 1969.

Cartelli, Thomas. "Enslaving the Moor: *Othello, Oroonoko,* and the Recuperation of Intractability." In *Repositioning Shakespeare: National Formations, Postcolonial Appropriations.* London and New York: Routledge, 1999, 123–46.

————. " 'Like Othello': Tayeb Salih's *Season of Migration* and Post-colonial Self-Fashioning." In *Repositioning Shakespeare: National Formations, Postcolonial Appropriations.* London and New York: Routledge, 1999. 147–68.

Ferguson, Margaret. "Transmuting Othello: Aphra Behn's *Oroonoko.*" In Marianne Novy, ed. *Cross-Cultural Performances: Differences in Women's Revisions of Shakespeare.* Urbana: University of Illinois Press, 1993, 15–49.

Fischlin, Daniel, and Mark Fortier, ed. *Adaptations of Shakespeare: A Critical Anthology of Plays from the Seventeenth Century to the Present.* New York and London: Routledge, 2000.

Hopkins, Lisa. "Review of Sax's *Othello.*" *Early Modern Literary Studies* 8.1 (2002): 11.1–4 <http://www.shu.ac.uk/emls/08-1/othelrev.htm>.

Howard, Tony. "Shakespeare's Cinematic Offshoots." In Russell Jackson, ed. *The Cambridge Companion to Shakespeare on Film.* Cambridge: Cambridge University Press, 293–313.

MacDonald, Ann-Marie. *Good-night Desdemona (Good-morning Juliet).* Toronto: Coach House Press, 1990.

Mitchell, Elvis. "The Moor Shoots Hoops" (review of O). *New York Times* (August 31, 2001). <http://www.nytimes.com/2001/08/31/movies/31OTHE.html?ex=1004776881&ei=1&en=a9860aa261e3318b>.

Nelson, Tim Blake, dir. O. 2001. <http://us.imdb.com/Title?0184791>.

Owens, W. R., and Lizabeth Goodman, ed. *Shakespeare, Aphra Behn and the Canon.* London and New York: Routledge, 1996.

Phillips, Caryl. *The Nature of Blood.* New York: Knopf, 1997.

Rippy, Marguerite Hailey. "All Our *Othello*s: Black Monsters and White Masks on the American Screen." In Courtney Lehmann and Lisa S. Starks, ed. *Spectacular Shakespeare: Critical Theory and Popular Cinema.* Madison and Teaneck: Fairleigh Dickinson University Press, 2001, 25–46.

Rushdie, Salman. *Fury.* Toronto: Random House, 2001.

————. *The Moor's Last Sigh.* Toronto: Random House, 1995.

————. *The Satanic Verses*. New York: Viking, 1988.

Salih, Tayeb. *Season of Migration to the North*. 1969. Trans. Denys Johnson-Davies. Rpt. Oxford: Heinemann, 1991.

Sax, Geoffrey, dir. *Othello*. 2001. <http://us.imdb.com/Title? 0275577>.

Sears, Djanet. *Harlem Duet*. Scirocco Drama Series. Toronto: J. Gordon Shillingford, 1997.

Singh, Jyotsna. "Othello's Identity, Postcolonial Theory, and Contemporary African Rewritings of *Othello*." In Margo Hendricks and Patricia Parker, ed. *Women, "Race," and Writing in the Early Modern Period*. New York and London: Routledge, 1994, 287–299.

Vogel, Paula. *Desdemona: A Play about a Handkerchief*. New York: Dramatists Play Service, 1994.

14. BIBLIOGRAPHIES, COLLECTIONS OF CRITICISM, STUDY GUIDES

The following books, all currently available, share one or the other of the two main purposes of this Norton Critical Edition—either representing the critical tradition or explaining the historical context. The play, of course, exists in many editions, some of which are listed under "Works Cited" for "A Note on the Text" (pp. xvi–xvii).

Dean, Leonard F., ed. *A Casebook on "Othello."* New York: Crowell, 1961.

Hall, Joan Lord. *"Othello": A Guide to the Play*. Greenwood Guides to Shakespeare. Westport, Connecticut, and London: Greenwood Press, 1999.

Hadfield, Andrew. *A Routledge Literary Sourcebook on William Shakespeare's "Othello."* New York and London: Routledge, 2003.

Mikesell, Margaret Lael, and Virginia Mason Vaughan, ed. *"Othello": An Annotated Bibliography*. New York: Garland, 1990.

Nostbakken, Faith. *Understanding "Othello": A Student Casebook to Issues, Sources, and Historical Documents*. Westport, Connecticut, and London: Greenwood Press, 2000.

Potter, Nicholas, ed. *William Shakespeare: "Othello."* Columbia Critical Guides. New York: Columbia University Press, 2000.

Scott, Mark W., ed. *Othello*. In *Shakespearean Criticism: Excerpts from the Criticism of William Shakespeare's Plays and Poetry, from the First Published Appraisals to Current Evaluations*. Vol. 4. Detroit: Gale, 1987, 362–608.

Snyder, Susan, ed. *"Othello": Critical Essays*. New York: Garland, 1988.

Wain, John, ed. *Shakespeare's "Othello": A Casebook*. Rev. ed. Basingstoke and London: Macmillan, 1994.